Wisdom of Communities

Wisdom of Communities

Volume 2
Finding a Community

Published by
The Fellowship for Intentional Community
Rutledge, Missouri

The Fellowship for Intentional Community, Rutledge, MO 63563

ISBN: 978-0-9995885-1-2
Printed by CreateSpace.

Cover design: Megan Cranford, www.megancranforddesign.com

Layout design: Marty Klaif

Project managers: Chris Roth, Christopher Kindig

FINDING A COMMUNITY
(Wisdom of Communities, Volume 2)

CONTENTS

II. SEEKING AND VISITING COMMUNITY: TIPS AND RESOURCES

III. COMMUNITY EXPLORATIONS: STORIES AND REFLECTIONS

Introduction

Like the majority of attempts to start an intentional community (it's estimated that 90 percent fail), many personal searches for intentional community fizzle out due to lack of adequate information, guidance, or exposure to fellow travelers' stories.

In both cases, ignorance of the wide array of options possible, and of the breadth of resources and support available through the Fellowship for Intentional Community and allied groups, undoubtedly contributes to the "failure" rate.

This volume on "Finding a Community" and the previous volume in this series, on "Starting a Community," address the need for one-stop collections of stories to help founders and seekers. They are meant to complement the *Communities Directory* (available in print and online: ic.org/directory), COMMUNITIES magazine, a quarterly publication focused on Life in Cooperative Culture, and educational resources available through Community Bookstore (ic.org/bookstore).

These books should broaden anyone's outlook on what is possible and how to pursue their dreams of community. Within each section we hear from a range of voices spanning a great diversity of perspectives and experiences. In this volume, we start with stories about the wide range of intentional community types that one might choose to explore—from income-sharing groups, gift-economy communities, service-oriented groups, and activist communities to groups sharing privately-owned land, cohousing projects, senior-oriented communities, shared living within households, and neighborhood-wide initiatives. We then hear about tips and resources for seeking and visiting communities, followed by an extensive collection of personal stories and reflections resulting from authors' community explorations, offered in order of original publication date.

Most articles are drawn from the past decade of COMMUNITIES magazine, with one excerpted from the *Communities Directory* and a few from older issues of COMMUNITIES that were also excerpted in *Best of COMMUNITIES*, Volume II. Every issue of COMMUNITIES contains further treatments of these same themes, so we hope that you'll not only learn from these past stories, but also keep up with new ones by subscribing to the magazine (ic.org/subscribe).

Thanks for making use of these resources, and good luck on your community journey!

Chris Roth
Editor, COMMUNITIES
April 2018

I

INTENTIONAL COMMUNITY TYPES:

A SAMPLING

Tracking the Communities Movement:
70 YEARS OF HISTORY AND THE MODERN FIC

By Sky Blue and Betsy Morris

Since 1987 The Fellowship for Intentional Community (FIC; ic.org) has been a primary resource for documentation, support, and networking among secular and religiously based intentional communities. While several associations and networks exist for some of the specific types of intentional community (which include communes, housing cooperatives, student cooperatives, ecovillages, and cohousing), FIC has the largest reach and history. New experiments in shared living continue to pop up, under new names, such as coliving or cohouseholding.

FIC began as the Fellowship of Intentional Communities, formed in 1948/49 as a mutual aid network among 20 communities mostly in the eastern US. Pacifism, simple living, equality, and agrarian self-sufficiency on land held in common were common values. A majority were religiously affiliated, but not in mainstream traditions. Secular influences included Robert Owen, the Rochdale Pioneers, Bolton Hall, writings of Henry George, and Ralph Borsodi's *Flight from the City*, which spoke of the value of returning to agrarian lifestyles and attracted educated professionals and artisans.

One of the early FIC's founders was Arthur Morgan, later president of Antioch College. Morgan, among other things is credited with conceiving of the land trust (based on the principles of Henry George). In 1937, Morgan cofounded Celo Community, Inc., a land trust community of 40 homesteaders in rural North Carolina that continues to govern itself by consensus. Celo residents also started a private "organic school" based on child-centered education methods, developed by Mildred Loomis, an influential educator, and later cofounder of the Heathcote community in Freehold, Maryland. Morgan's children continue his legacy through several intentional communities and the nonprofit Community Solutions, Inc. (www.communitysolution.org). Celo and Heathcote still operate and are among the oldest ICs in the *Communities Directory.* Although FIC's members and ICs in general remain predominantly European American, several other of the founding communities started by Quakers were among the first places in the United States where whites and blacks could choose to live as equals. Early founders also helped create the first Black community land trust (CLT) in the US.[1]

Pre-FIC communitarians had already split with other US cooperativists who favored urban programs with government financing to build housing cooperatives and publicly managed housing projects for the poor and working class. By 1961, another split by members primarily seeking expression of their religious way of life left FIC in a near dormant state for many years. The rapid increase in ICs from the 1960s, '70s, and '80s prompted another round of outreach and organizing. Leadership transferred to another generation of younger, mostly rural communitarians.

The change in name to Fellowship for Intentional Community in 1987 was subtle but important. Rather than an informal mutual aid association, the new Fellowship for Intentional Community restructured its gover-

---

1. Antioch College was a pioneer in educating both women and African Americans. Robert and Marjorie Swann—an Antioch graduate and a Quaker, respectively—were students of Morgan and classmates of Coretta Scott King. They helped King relatives create the first large-scale land trust/farmer's cooperative with African American farmers (the Federation of Southern Cooperatives), as well as the National Community Land Trust Network and important land trust initiatives in Massachusetts. In 1972, Bob Swann with Ralph Borsodi also founded the E.F. Schumacher Society and the local currency movement.

5

nance and administration, incorporated as a 501(c)(3) nonprofit governed by a board of directors, and developed ongoing projects managed by staff, most of whom live in intentional communities around the country. The board expanded its mission to promoting the principles of intentional community to the larger world. Its activities include publishing COMMUNITIES magazine (starting in 1992, when it revived then-20-year-old magazine after a very brief hiatus) and the *Communities Directory*, in print since 1994 and online since 2004 (ic.org/directory).

Definitions

The mission statement of the FIC is *to support and promote the development of intentional communities and the evolution of cooperative culture.*

FIC defines cooperative culture as encompassing both ICs and a broad array of other practices, found in other organizations and in movements. It offers the following definition.

Cooperative Culture: *The sum of attitudes, customs, and beliefs among people that are characterized by sharing, empathy, self-responsibility, understanding and celebration of differences, peaceful conflict resolution, high regard for connection and relationship, interdependence, and care for how things are done as much as what gets done.*

Examples of movements and organizations that current FIC leadership sees as representing cooperative culture include worker cooperatives (usworker.coop) and other kinds of cooperative business (www.ncba.coop), Transition Towns (transitionus.org), permaculture networks (www.permaculture.org), time banks (www.timebanks.org), community gardens (www.communitygarden.org), car sharing (carsharing.org), and the wide range of groups represented by the New Economy Coalition (www.neweconomy.net) and the US Solidarity Economy Network (www.ussen.org).

The FIC's definition of *community* is not meant to contradict or replace other definitions of community. It is simply the definition the organization uses to help give context to its definition of *intentional community*.

Community: *A group of people who identify with each other. The association could be based on any combination of geography, history, language, religion, vision, purpose, philosophy, or common social, economic, or political interests.*

The FIC's definition of intentional community is meant to be as broadly encompassing as possible while clearly delineating a specific set of groups:

Intentional Community: *A group of people who live together or share common facilities and who regularly associate with each other on the basis of explicit common values.*

No one owns the term intentional community. Anyone who wants to identify as an intentional community is free to do so, and some groups that the FIC would identify as intentional communities do not choose to use that label. FIC communities, board, and staff have personal and business ties with many other secular IC networks, as well as research groups such as the Communal Studies Association (www.communalstudies.org), Cohousing Research Network (www.cohousingresearchnetwork.org), and Commonomics USA (www.commonomicsusa.org).

An intentional community can be thought of as a set of social and economic relationships, the physical (as opposed to online, or virtual) place or places where these relationships intersect and are carried out, and the explicit common values that provide the basis for members to decide how these relationships and places are organized.

In more illustrative terms, conjure up an image of an extended family compound or a traditional village and you will have an idea of what many people are attempting to emulate or replicate. In our modern world, and especially in urban centers, life is necessarily more complicated than in a traditional village, but, in rural or urban settings, the aim is to have an integrated, interconnected, interdependent life with others that provides both social and economic benefit, as well as providing a place to live out other values, such as sustainability, social justice, or spiritual/religious tenets.

> **An intentional community can be thought of as a set of social and economic relationships, the physical place where these relationships intersect, and explicit common values.**

The *Directory*

There are 1442 public listings in 65 countries in the online *Communities Directory* as of July 2017, including ICs in various phases of development (forming, reforming, established, or disbanded).

Listing in the *Communities Directory* is voluntary, by answering a lengthy online questionnaire. FIC does reserve the right to request more information or edits and, if necessary, exclude listings that appear to:

• Advocate violence;
• Restrict the ability of their members to leave or to contact people outside the community;
• Substantively misrepresent themselves in their listing.

6

In 1990, the first published Directory reported: "More than 8,000 people, including over 2,000 children, live in 186 of the more established North American intentional communities and extended family groups listing in the first edition of the Directory of Intentional Communities (1990). Of course, these 186 communities represent just a small fraction of the North American communities movement.

"Over 700 more intentional communities in FIC address files have declined to provide public listings for the Directory. There are thousands more residing in traditional monastic enclaves or service groups, tens of thousands living in Hutterite colonies, and millions of indigenous Americans living communally. So the information in this Directory describes just a small portion of the cooperative lifestyles practiced in North America."

As of July 2017, of the 1442 public listings, 747 were "established" (at least four adults living together on a site for at least two years), and 79% of the Directory's "established" listings are in North America (US, Canada, Mexico). The 544 established communities in the US identify themselves with the following community types (multiple responses are frequent):

Established Communities in US by Selected Types		
Total Respondents	544	100.00%
Communes (income sharing)	87	15.99%
Ecovillages (focus on sustainability)	139	25.55%
Cohousing (private homes with common facilities)	214	39.34%
Shared House/Cohousehold/Coliving	170	31.25%
Student Coops	40	7.35%
Transition Town	2	0.36%
Religious/Spiritual	13	2.39%
School/Educational/Experience	3	0.55%
Other (including economic enterprises)	77	14.15%

These numbers need further clarifying. These are voluntary categories not legal structures or screened in any way. Newer communities are frequently small and aspirational, and use models of existing communities as a touchstone for future development. A few entries are multi-site networks or include multiple neighborhoods. Also, many communities identify with multiple types. And, as mentioned before, many communities (including many religious/spiritual communities with their own pre-existing networks, most indigenous groups, and groups which wish to remain more private) choose not to list themselves at all.

Community Types and Organizing Principles

Housing Cooperatives and Student Co-op Houses: The Cooperatives movement began in 17th century England and France as a concerted resistance to the loss of cultural and economic resources under rapid industrialization fueled by capitalism. Housing cooperatives, built and financed by unions and socialist/communist parties for their members, were a source of urban housing, endorsed by federal policies through the 1980s. Federal policies and programs encouraged and helped finance thousands of cooperatives, both in business and housing, from the 1930s to the 1980s.

The Rochdale Principles of Cooperation (established in England in 1844 and with minor additions; see en.wikipedia.org/wiki/Rochdale_Principles) remain as values espoused by the National Association of Housing Cooperatives established in 1958 and the North American Students of Cooperation founded in 1960s. Both groups offer some combination of training, communications, financing, and political lobbying for members along with annual conferences open to the public. They are:
- Open, voluntary membership *without discrimination to those who wish to join.*
- Democratic governance; one member–one vote.
- Economic participation of members (shared or limited return on equity).
- Surplus belongs to members.
- Education of members and public in cooperative principles.
- Cooperation among cooperatives.
- Concern for the community (in which they are located).

Communes: ICs that identify as communes typically involve higher levels of economic involvement, social engagement, accountability, and participation. Historically, religion combined with ethnic ties and/or political ideologies brought people into communal living groups, each with their own internal economies. The Hutterites and Bruderhof were communal income-sharing societies present in the 1940s founding of FIC. The Federation of Egalitarian Communities (FEC), whose purpose is similar to the original FIC, was founded in December 1976 for secular purposes. The organization was originally inspired by the networks of mutual support observed among Israeli kibbutzim by Kat Kinkade, cofounder of Twin Oaks, East Wind, and Acorn Communities.

Cooperation amongst FEC communities ranges from loans and labor exchange to sharing community-building skills and shared outreach. FEC also administers PEACH (www.thefec.org/about/projects/peach), a cooperatively financed "self-insurance" health care fund, which also acts as a revolving loan fund. The FEC currently has six full member groups and 11 other allied Communities in Dialogue. (See www.thefec.org.)

Each member community of the FEC agrees to these commitments:
• Holds its land, labor, income, and other resources in common.
• Assumes responsibility for the needs of its members, receiving the products of their labor and distributing these and all other goods equally, or according to need.
• Practices nonviolence.
• Uses a form of decision making in which members have an equal opportunity to participate, either through consensus, direct vote, or right of appeal or overrule.
• Actively works to establish the equality of all people and does not permit discrimination on the basis of race, class, creed, ethnic origin, age, sex, sexual orientation, or gender identity.
• Acts to conserve natural resources for present and future generations while striving to continually improve ecological awareness and practice.
• Creates processes for group communication and participation and provides an environment which supports people's development.

> # Historically, religion combined with ethnic ties and/or political ideologies brought people into communal living groups, each with their own internal economies.

Cohousing: The term cohousing was coined by architects Katherine McCamant and Charles Durrett in their highly influential book, *Cohousing: A Contemporary Model for Housing Ourselves*, published in 1987. The term and the first edition were based on a type of intentional community that had become widespread in Denmark by the 1980s (and that has continued to grow and evolve). For many years, the Cohousing Association of the US and cohousing communities identified with these six characteristics of cohousing McCamant and Durett summarized from their extensive study of Danish cohousing:
• Participatory Design Process
• Neighborhood Design balancing privacy and spaces for spontaneous socializing
• Extensive Common Facilities
• Resident Management
• Non-Hierarchical Leadership
• Independent Incomes

The Cohousing Association of the US website (cohousing.org) currently characterizes cohousing communities by:

Relationships
• Neighbors commit to being part of a community for everyone's mutual benefit.
• Cohousing cultivates a culture of sharing and caring.
• Design features and neighborhood size (typically 20-40 homes) promote frequent interaction and close relationships.

Balancing Privacy and Community
• Cohousing neighborhoods are designed for privacy as well as community.
• Residents balance privacy and community by choosing their own level of engagement.

Participation
• Decision making is participatory and often based on consensus.
• Self-management empowers residents, builds community, and saves money.

Shared Values
• Cohousing communities support residents in actualizing shared values.
• Cohousing communities typically adopt green approaches to living.

Ecovillages: The Global Ecovillage Network (GEN) emerged through American and European communitarian environmentalists, in response to the Club of Rome's *Limits to Growth* Report. The definition that first became widely used was Robert Gilman's: "a human scale, full-featured settlement, in which human activities are harmlessly integrated into the natural world, in a way that is supportive of healthy human development, and can be continued into the indefinite future."

Today, the Global Ecovillage Network "embraces a holistic approach to sustainability encompassing the Social, Cultural, Ecological and Economic dimensions of human existence." "Ecovillages are communities in which people feel supported by and responsible to those around them. They provide a deep sense of belonging to a group. They are small enough that everyone feels safe, empowered, seen and heard. People are then able to participate in making decisions that affect their own lives and that of the community on a transparent basis."

(See ecovillage.org/en/article/dimensions-sustainability.)

One-hundred-fifty-nine ICs in the Directory identify GEN and 46 identify the Ecovillage Network of the Americas as networks with which they affiliate.

Religious Communities: Thirty-seven Directory entries define themselves as primarily religious or spiritual organizations—while many others reported religious affiliations as a group or among their members, and only 228 checked the box for "Not a particularly religious or spiritual community." Many communities are unaffiliated with any particular tradition, or consider themselves religiously ecumenical while still having a dominant spiritual practice, such as the Zen Center or the Maharishi University Fellowship in Iowa (transcendental meditators). Christian and Jewish communes or student coops may be listed in both of their categories, or just one. Other ICs, however, are clearly associated by religious affiliation, such as the Catholic Order of Benedictine Fathers, the Catholic Worker House network, Camphill communities (associated with Rudolf Steiner), and the Twelve Tribes.

Implications

The ICs that we know are not isolated utopias, romantic idylls, or scientific experiments. They consist of living, breathing people who know what the world has to offer, and are doing their best to bring their desires for peace, sociability, cooperative autonomy, economic justice, and environmental responsibility to life pro-actively. These values are ones many people around the world share, but cannot realize alone or within institutions dominated by people seeking profit or power above concern for people and the planet. Intentional communities are broadly characterized by an emphasis on

- **Cooperative/participatory democracy**
- **Cooperative economics**
- **Gender equality**
- **Satisfying interpersonal relationships and conflict resolution**
- **Living well while decreasing waste and increasing renewable resource consumption and waste**

The *Communities Directory* provides multiple snapshots into a parallel world, where people are dreaming and then becoming empowered agents, able to take collective and personal actions in creating and then sustaining a nexus of institutions, relationships, and activities made real by their choice to continue participating in them over time.

Most forming groups and young ICs fail, and many established communities grow, decline, and learn by trial and error on their own what works and does not. Nevertheless, we observe convergences, groups learning from experience and observation of other ICs to find core values and practices that work best over time. ICs may start as unique to their own time and place, but become examples for managing and incorporating key features, such as shared governance, use of consensus, or shared ownership of land.

Secular ICs can become quite sophisticated and multidimensional over time, within the context of transparent vision and purpose and consent-based governance. The communities are not simply engineering solutions; they function because of the willingness of members to put collective attention and creativity to sustaining and supporting high quality communication and personal relationships—foundational to any material or technological success they reach.

The articulation of cooperative culture—*in practice*—is one of the contributions of ICs to

a world seemingly dominated by competitive global capitalism and exploitive relationships of people and planet. IC pioneers have also written and trained thousands, offering a unique depth of experience gained in practices of team-building, trust-building, and getting the work done cooperatively. A number of communitarians have gone professional and influenced the larger field of organizational development. One example is the GroupWorks Card Deck (groupworksdeck.org), instigated by a former member of Twin Oaks and Acorn, and promoted widely in the National Coalition for Dialog and Deliberation. Fifty people contributed to the final product, which is available as a free download. Another example

> The articulation of cooperative culture— *in practice*—is one of the contributions of ICs to a world seemingly dominated by competitive global capitalism and exploitive relationships of people and planet.

is the Network For a New Culture (www.nfnc.org) which offers workshops in human awareness and intimacy, but specifically designed to help people live more cooperatively with each other in everyday circumstances.

We invite researchers to look more deeply at ICs, beyond the typical one-off case study. FIC would be happy to collaborate with efforts to do high quality independent research to test the findings presented here that can be shared within the communities movement and with the rest of the world. ✦

Sky Blue is Executive Director of the Fellowship for Intentional Community. Betsy Morris, Ph.D. is co-organizer of Cohousing California. This article is adapted and updated from a paper first presented at the mini-conference "Re-embedding the Social: New Modes of Production, Critical Consumption and Alternative Lifestyles" hosted by the Society for the Advancement of Socio-Economics, June 24-26, 2016 at the University of California, Berkeley.

REFERENCES AND RESOURCES

FIC Identity Statement: docs.google.com/document/d/1mVMJmpEDh4xN6LSKC76ww53mS4JsyWrcC404EET5LHo/edit?usp=sharing.

Curl, John. 2008. *For All the People: Uncovering the hidden history of cooperation, cooperative movements, and communalism in America*: library.uniteddiversity.coop/Cooperatives/For_All_The_People-History_of_Cooperation_in_America.pdf.

Miller, Timothy (1998). *The Quest for Utopia in Twentieth-century America: 1900-1960*. Syracuse University Press. ISBN 0-8156-2775-0.

Christian, Diana Leafe, 2003, *Creating a Life Together: Practical Tools to Grow Ecovillages and Intentional Communities*, New Society Publishers; New Edition, ISBN 0-86571-471-1, foreword by Patch Adams.

Christian, Diana Leafe, 2007, *Finding Community: How to Join an Ecovillage or Intentional Community*, New Society Publishers, ISBN 0-86571-578-5.

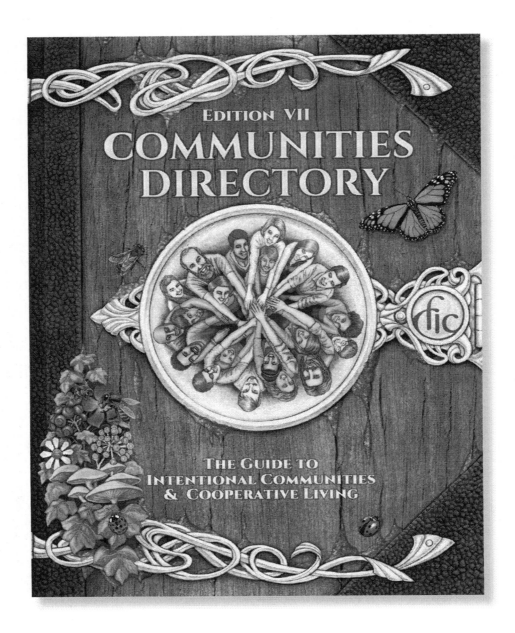

Communities Directory book!

In addition to profiling more than 1,000 communities, this new book includes full-page maps showing where communities are located, charts that compare communities by more than 30 qualities, and an easy index to find communities interested in specific pursuits. Also included are articles on how to start or join a community, the basics of group dynamics and decision-making, and countless additional resources and links to help your community thrive!

Order your book today: www.ic.org/New-Directory

Balancing Act:
How Much Are You Willing to Share?

By Janel Healy

I think it's safe to say that you are an idealistic person. As a supporter of COM-MUNITIES, you've probably thought long and hard about how to live a life that's more just—and just better—and it looks like you've come to the conclusion that living communally may be the answer.

But how "communal" do you have to get before you're truly living according to the ideals of Right Livelihood?

Ask this question to someone who's living in an income-sharing community, and the answer may sound a bit extreme. At neighboring egalitarian communities Twin Oaks and Acorn, located in rural central Virginia, all the "big stuff" is cooperatively owned—from houses and cars to bank accounts and businesses. For some of these communes' members, environmental concerns are motivation enough to share almost everything. Valerie, who's been living at Twin Oaks for two decades, believes, "Anyone who wanted to be living according to Right Livelihood would share cars. It's much less of a footprint on the earth." For others, such as Tom from Twin Oaks, it's all about the worker-owned businesses. "Income sharing *itself* is right livelihood," he asserts. "We don't have an ownership class, so we're not working hard to make others rich. Here, workers are managers—not just tools for producing capital."

When it comes to supporting good causes, income sharing is a testament to "power in numbers." If your economic unit is two people, your chief concern may be keeping your "unit" afloat financially. You may not have much leeway in terms of choosing a job that fits in with your values, nor time to volunteer or money to donate. But when your economic unit is say, 25 people (Acorn's current population), the group has more resources, time, and skills to put towards endeavors its members believe in. And when your economic unit is nearly 100...well, take it from Twin Oaks—you can pool your resources so efficiently as to live on about $5,000 per person per year. Those who are sick, elderly, or otherwise unable to fully pull their weight can be supported by the dozens of members who can, and the group has even more freedom to decide how to invest its money, time, and resources positively.

However, even though income sharing can be a successful way to band together to provide a secure and moral livelihood for a group, it's not easy. In fact, as a relatively new member, I must say that adjusting to life at Twin Oaks is still an ongoing challenge. It's been difficult getting used to having little financial autonomy. I feel frustrated that public possessions at Twin Oaks can get trashed easily—people tend to forget about the personal responsibility that comes with collective ownership. And I can't help but feel uneasy that folks who aren't working as efficiently as they could be are getting the same amount of "labor credits" as those who are.

I also sometimes find myself wondering what more I could be doing for the world. Am I living as closely to the notion of Right Livelihood at Twin Oaks as I could be? How far out does one have to reach in order to be living responsibly?

After speaking with several members of both Acorn and Twin Oaks in preparation for this article, though, I've come to realize that living in an income-sharing community as well as living by the guidelines of Right Livelihood are delicate balancing acts. There's no manual specifying how to embody Right Livelihood in every situation, nor is there a manual on how to thrive within the challenging environment of an income-sharing community (although Twin Oaks *does* have a 200-page book of community policies). I'm starting to understand that it's all about perspective, and about finding satisfaction, not guilt, in challenging yourself to do the best you can do. And living in an

Tom, who runs Twin Oaks' organic cut flowers business, tending to seedlings that will eventually become gorgeous flowers to sell at local farmers' markets.

intentional community—especially in an income-sharing community, where collectivism can allow for a greater expression of values—provides the challenge to raise the bar in terms of responsible living.

For instance, because Acorn is a consensus-based community with biweekly meetings, its culture of discussing all group decisions face to face encourages members to think deeply about the choices they make. According to River, who's been a Virginia communard for the past 25 years, this is especially true with purchases. "Modern society is based on impulse buying," he explains. "If I were living on my own, I might go to the grocery store and pick up ramen noodles for dinner without thinking much about it." But when you're sharing your meals with a group, he says, you have to talk to each other about what kind of food to purchase and eat. "It forces you to question these things. There's a discussion about, 'What's the best way to do this, not just for personal health but also for the earth?'"

At Twin Oaks, you don't have to think very hard at all about using less fuel or electricity to have a lighter impact on the land. It's just a part of everyday life because of the community's culture of home and car sharing. "The way we live and share everything is more ecological, but it's easy for us to make those choices," Valerie says. "Mainstream society is not set up to make those choices. Often there are other priorities."

But does Twin Oaks adequately challenge its members to do service outside of the intentional communities movement? In a classic case of poor perspective, I've recently felt discouraged at the thought that Twin Oaks doesn't. I thought that the community's lack of emphasis on serving those in need was keeping me from emphasizing it in my own life. However, in talking to Ira, who moved to Twin Oaks in 1985 and then became a founding member of Acorn in 1993, I realized it's my own fault that I haven't been contributing to good causes outside of the communities movement since I've lived at Twin Oaks.

Ira and Andros of Acorn Community watering and working with the community's roselle plants (to be used eventually for tea leaves).

Janel Healy

A culture of discussing all group decisions face to face encourages members to think deeply about the choices they make.

All I have to do is go out and do it.

"When I lived at Twin Oaks, I'd take different crews of people to local farms to harvest peaches and other stuff the community didn't grow," Ira told me. "I didn't do it for labor credits, at least at first. I'm just into supporting local farmers, so that they can support their families. This makes it more likely that they will continue farming using organic principles."

Because Ira has energy and people organizational skills, she was able to tap the vast pool of skills and labor available to her at Twin Oaks when she wanted to start a project or embark on a service mission. If she had been living outside of community, it could have been much harder for her to rally people together to volunteer their time and money to support a cause. "It's all about having enough energy to work on projects because it's the right thing to do and not necessarily because it'll make money or fulfill your labor quota," Ira imparts. "Anywhere you live, living according to the ideals of Right Livelihood takes a lot of energy. It might take even more energy outside of community."

Now, Ira is constantly able to tap into her enthusiasm for changing the world through local agriculture thanks to Acorn's heirloom seed business, Southern Exposure Seed Exchange (SESE). Acorn, with sheer good luck on its side, had the option of purchasing SESE at a time when the community was looking for an ethical, organic agriculture-related business to sustain itself. "We realized that good seed is the foundation of sustainable agriculture," says Ira, "and so SESE was like putting on a pair of shoes that was just right."

Down the road at Twin Oaks, the major community businesses are Twin Oaks Tofu and Twin Oaks Hammocks. For some Oakers, producing hammocks—leisure products made with synthetic rope—doesn't quite match up with their idea of Right Livelihood. However, as Acorn's Andros observes, "Hammocks sustained Twin Oaks long enough for the community to be able to survive. Twin Oaks has since reinvested that money into ventures that are arguably more righteous."

Sarah Rice

Author hauling clean laundry from Twin Oaks' main laundry facility back to her building: "Even the way we do laundry here at the Twin Oaks Community is an example of Right Livelihood (in an ecological sense). We have only three washing machines for almost 100 people, and whenever it's sunny, a lot of us hang clothes out to dry instead of using a power-intensive dryer."

Income-sharing communities can be challenging places to live, but they provide an immense array of opportunities for doing good.

Andros, who's been living at Acorn for the past three and a half years, has a point. The hammock business, although not necessarily "sustainability"-focused, allowed Twin Oaks to simply exist. As Twin Oaks' first business, it gave a community of resource sharing and egalitarianism a chance to put down roots. Now, Twin Oaks has a variety of businesses that focus on sustainability through supporting local and/or organic agriculture—the community grows organic seeds for SESE and other seed companies; buys local, organic, and non-GMO soybeans for its tofu; and grows and sells organic cut flowers at nearby farmers' markets.

Plus, as Ira pointed out, it's important for an income-sharing community to have many different jobs that are suited to various people and skills. "The hammock business is useful for Twin Oaks because almost anyone can learn [hammock-making] quickly and can use it to contribute to the group," she explains. "Making healthy vegan tofu seems more ethical to a lot of Oakers, but the work isn't suited to as many people. It's important to have a culture where a large amount of people can contribute through a wide range of jobs."

Talk about a lesson in perspective.

Another Right Livelihood issue with which my fellow communards grapple is how much to allow our community businesses to grow. To Ira, the ability to have enough money to purchase local and/or organic food to supplement what Acorn can grow is extremely important. She remembers that she thought she'd "died and gone to heaven" the day Acorn, thanks to SESE, could finally afford to purchase organic coffee. "Right livelihood entails living a life that isn't all fancy but does allow you to buy the things you think are right," says Ira. "We grow some of our own things, but we also want to buy food from organic and sustainable sources." Twin Oaks' Tom might agree. "Right livelihood is not just what you do to make money—it's what you do with the money," he told me.

On the other hand, Pam, manager of the prolific Twin Oaks garden for the past 15 years, is dubious of the idea of using money to vote for change. She'd rather her community simply be the change by becoming even more self-sufficient. "Do we want to focus on how much to earn and what to spend it on, or do we want to reduce our dependence on the cash economy?," she ponders. "The latter is my preference."

From Pam's perspective, how can anyone—or any community—really know that what they're buying is coming from an ethical source? A business could sell a product that it claims to be organic, but if the business has, say, a hierarchical power structure and poor working conditions, there isn't an intention of Right Livelihood behind the product. In this global economy, as Andros put it, there could be "an element of exploitation and unsustainability" in every financial transaction.

But should our communities stop buying things altogether? It doesn't seem realistic (nor good for morale)—not when so many people deeply enjoy or have even come to feel they need some of the comforts of modern life. The answer must therefore lie somewhere between dependence and complete independence when it comes to the cash economy. It's just another balancing act.

Although diverse opinions and perspectives of members can be stressful to those living in community—especially to those living in tightly knit income-sharing communities—it may actually be that this diversity keeps a community centered. Personally, I'm learning to take in many perspectives in order to have a balanced diet of food for thought. As River recommends, "Holding conflicting ideas in your head at once seems to be the best way to be flexible." I'm learning to embrace both the frustrating and the positive—income-sharing communities can be challenging places to live, but they provide an immense array of opportunities for doing good. Acknowledging how my community could do better in terms of Right Livelihood is necessary for "raising the bar" for the group and for myself, but it's also important to appreciate the ways in which my community does allow me to live according to my values.

Living in an income-sharing community is not the only way to lead a life according to the ideals of Right Livelihood, of course. Worker-owned cooperatives often share the ideals of Right Livelihood that Twin Oaks and Acorn hold so dear, as do other intentional communities that don't pool their earnings. "A lot of different communities and co-ops are part of the solution to a more equitable world," Ira explains. "It's not just one size fits all!" But for some people, income sharing is the perfect values match. "Most communities choose to do certain things together, but the more you do as a group, the more powerful it is," says River. "The ability to share resources creates something bigger than myself. I think that's a common human desire—to come together with other people to create something bigger."

When I think about the long term, I'm not yet sure where my life will fall along the spectrum of Right Livelihood lifestyles. I want to challenge myself to live as morally as possible, and although income-sharing communities are one great way to do that, I know there are other options. But for now, I'm appreciating the wonderfully just nature of sharing. I'm grateful to be living in a place where egalitarianism discourages the greed that seems to be plaguing much of the world. Tom puts it best: "For the few to have much, the many must have little. But at Twin Oaks, everyone *has*." If that's not Right Livelihood, I don't know what is.

For more information about secular income-sharing communities, visit the Federation of Egalitarian Communities online at www.thefec.org. 🐝

Janel Healy, a California native, has been living at the Twin Oaks Community in Louisa, Virginia for the past year. An avid sculptor of words, Janel has most recently written for Survive and Thrive TV, Positive Impact Magazine, *and the previous issue of* COMMUNITIES. *Janel also spends her time making tofu, caring for chickens, and marketing for the 2011 Twin Oaks Communities Conference. One of her goals is to spread knowledge about the intentional communities movement to people across the country.*

More Perspectives from Acorn

I have lived at Acorn for only seven months, but it feels right to me to live communally. I feel good about sharing cars and farming equipment. If we were living separately in mainstream society, we would be using 25 cars, 25 washing machines, 25 toasters, 25 blenders; the list goes on and on. Now we share five cars, two washing machines, one toaster, one blender, etc. In my old apartment building in New Jersey, there was no recycling program. Acorn has a compost pile and recycles everything that can possibly be recycled. Surplus clothes go to Goodwill and surplus vegetables go to a local food bank. It makes me feel good to hang the laundry outside to dry, that our main residence only has one air conditioner (to store the seeds for our business), and that I haven't driven a car in seven months. I love growing and eating our own fruit and vegetables, knowing that they were not touched by pesticides and that they were handpicked by myself or people I know.

I don't miss my $60,000 a year job. Ultimately, it is not about money. To me, it's about living right.

I finally found a place to live where I feel good about myself and the impact I have on the earth. Before I started living at Acorn, I felt lonely, angry, scared, and unappreciated. Now I feel support, friendship, love, and appreciation. Life is not perfect, but it sure feels a hellofalot better.

—**Jacqueline Langeveld**
Acorn Community

I've been in community for most of the past eight years, and I've been at Acorn for most of the past two years. Since coming to community, I've been grateful for the chance to live close to the earth and in relative harmony with it, tending gardens, drying herbs, etc., and for the chance to live with people who understand my desire to do these things. I don't feel I make sacrifices for sustainability; I feel I've escaped the mainstream pressure to consume. I've never wanted my own car, my own house, my own computer, or the most fashionable clothes. In community, that doesn't make me weird. However, some people at Acorn might miss those things, the same way I sometimes wish I could build up more of a fund for travel or for something like retirement.

At Acorn, and in large part thanks to SESE, we don't just try to reduce our own ecological footprint; we also contribute to the sustainability endeavors of many others. We sell seed to gardeners and small farmers. We answer customers' questions about gardening, host seed swaps, and give workshops. We cooperate with other similar seed companies. Together, we help keep heirloom varieties alive. I send out donations of seeds to school gardens, community gardens, and the like. When we plant too much of something for ourselves, I pack up the extra for the local food bank. The same goes for when we plant, say, melons according to how much seed we need, but can't eat all the fruit. When students at nearby colleges move out and throw away huge amounts of perfectly good stuff, I ask myself how we can organize better salvage operations, responding to authorities' concerns, and perhaps giving what we can't use to charity. All in all, I am so glad I don't have to sell my time to earn a salary. The work I do here is not for money, but for the benefit of the community, society, the earth, and my own growth.

Though Acorn and Twin Oaks are egalitarian communities, we couldn't claim to be perfectly fair, or to be perfectly sustainable, or to have worked out all our differences. One of the difficulties with adjusting to life in an income-sharing community can be the level of trust our fellow communards expect of us. I sometimes get frustrated trying to reduce the amounts of food, electricity, and work time that we waste. Yet in the larger scheme of things, I trust that Acorners will continue to do the work that ensures that our basic needs will be met. I trust that if one of us gets very ill, that person will be taken care of. I trust that we will continue to listen to one another when making hard decisions.

—**Irena Hollowell**
Acorn Community

November, 1963. In the middle of the Pentagon's grey corridors, the inner courtyard is a green haven for civilians and military on their lunch break. On a crisp fall day, an attractive young matron waves to her navel lieutenant husband. It is 12:15 pm, and Kay has nothing on her mind except the small picnic basket she has brought. Along with the rest of the United States, she is oblivious to preparations in a Dallas office building, perhaps on a nearby grassy knoll, which at this moment remain suspended in time, subject to intervention and choice, if we only knew.

If we only knew then what we know now...

Plunked down in the middle of the 20th century, reverted to his childhood body, but his memory intact, Joshua Leyden takes a run at revising his own life, and changing a future that needs some tinkering.

"Held me every step of the way. A great read, challenging ideas, fascinating and seductive." – David Kahn, Harvard Faculty.

Consider two trains heading in opposite directions, but stopped in a station. While the trains wait, it is possible to change between them. Transferring passengers would then head down their own timelines, reviewing past images incrementally. So it is with memories. So it is with dreams.

"Wonderful, touching characters, reworking our fate." – Hazel Henderson, Economist.

...and the most outrageous, yet logical path for time travel ever.

Each night, the sun went down, Nora to bed, and Josh prowled around her soul, searching for a key to unlock their mystery. While Nora slept beyond a narrow wall, Josh fought the need to break on through to the other side – replaying every mistake he'd ever made in either life. Rising, hitting the brandy, writing in a notebook lest the typewriter wake the girl. He couldn't even feel sorry for himself when he knew Nora had it far worse.

It's about time: A love story, both provocative and playful...

Paul Freundlich, Founder of Green America and Dance New England; for a decade an Editor of "Communities"; filmmaker, essayist and activist has created a journey that transcends time and reworks reality. **Available from Amazon**.com **[search: Paul Freundlich]**

Participatory Budgeting in an Income-Sharing Community

By Adder Oaks

Sharing income among a hundred people is a formidable challenge. At Twin Oaks Community, the combination of income-sharing and egalitarianism forms the core of community identity. About 90 adult members and over a dozen children live together on our rural farm in Virginia that is Twin Oaks. All of the money we make we share, not by dividing it up evenly, but rather by using our collective resources to meet the individual needs of all members. It is the combination of sharing our resources and having a fair say in how those resources are used that brings community cohesion and a shared direction. But it is a logistical headache and often a political nightmare to work out how exactly to allocate these shared resources. A couple years into my membership at Twin Oaks, I joined the economic planning team just in time for a revamp of our community budgeting process. The decades-old process was ailing, suffering from a lack of participation and impact of individual voters. Many members felt that their vote did not make a difference. After several years of trial and error, twists and turns, arguments and animosity, pizza parties and free cookies, we are finally settling on something that works well.

Twin Oaks has a long history of Participatory Budgeting, a democratic process in which community members directly decide how to spend part of a public budget.[1] For us, the public budget includes both money from our businesses and the non-business work we expect our members to do. Twin Oaks values its internal labor as much as it values its money. Not only is our labor keeping the community businesses such as hammock crafting and tofu production afloat, but it serves invaluably in our domestic lives. The time that members spend cooking dinner, harvesting wood for heat, growing food, teaching children, and scheduling doctor visits are all considered to be contributions to the community just as is our income-producing work. All work is compensated with "labor credits" which are self-reported and are required to meet the work quota of 42 hours per week (on average). Each year we take a look at both the income we have available and the number of hours we collectively expect to work and make a plan about where that money will go and where we'll spend our time. With a net annual income of about $700,000 and nearly 200,000 hours of labor, this is no small task.

For years the community used a process dubbed the Trade-Off Game. Unless one is a budgeting nerd like myself, this process is less fun than the name suggests. Each participating member, which was anyone interested, would be given a list of different managerial areas and the resources available (money and hours). Playing the "game" meant coming up with a balanced money budget and a balanced labor budget. One might assign $12,000 to building maintenance, $65,000 to food, $500 to recreation, 450 hours to cooking community meals, 8000 hours to the vegetable garden, 2000 hours to building maintenance, and so on. As long as the total money and hours matched those available, the player's game was valid. Everyone's games would be averaged together to produce the final budget.

Having each person set up a balanced budget is arduous and we would never get the participation, let alone a sensible budget, if we insisted that each person make such a detailed analysis. So we seeded the game with a planner take, a sensible budget offered by a small group made up of the economic planning team, the labor manager, and the current members of our rotating board of directors, along with one or two members at large. Everyone would then tweak the planner take, boosting or cutting the budgets as they saw fit, making sure to cut a dollar from one area for each dollar added to another. Caps were instituted as a precaution to avoid coming out with a budget that is too wonky to fit the community, requiring that no player could vote to cut or raise an area by more than 20 percent.

Inevitably, the final budget would come quite close to the planner take each year, leaving players scratching their heads as to how their participation mattered. Even worse, dishonest play was implicitly encouraged. I might want the food budget dropped by 10 percent, but I can bet someone else will vote to raise it. So what do I do? Vote to cut it by 20 percent to balance them out. In fact, I might cut a large area that I actually like if I know others will vote to raise it. That will leave me with lots of money to distribute among the small areas I support. The Trade-Off Game quickly became an exercise in strategic play, rather than a process for determining the actual desires of the community. Was this what egalitarian income-sharing was supposed to look like?

When I joined the economic planning team in 2013, revamping the game was an idea already brewing. We had seen a record low in participation with a mere 11 members playing (out of over 90

adult members) and the team had already put out surveys trying to figure out why exactly people did not seem invested in determining where our shared resources go. Enough members had expressed willingness to try a new process that we felt we had to look seriously into what other strategies we might use.

This was an exciting introduction to the team. I had studied mathematics in college but had no real training in economics or budgeting. I was also still relatively new to Twin Oaks, just starting to feel at home enough that it made sense for me to be one of the people guiding the community through this budgeting process. I was still learning the ins and outs of our finances while simultaneously brainstorming for a way to do things that would be truly democratic. I was part of the team working to more fully actualize the ideals of my home. We hoped that we could come up with a system that would get people to participate, enjoy it, understand more fully our community needs, and share our resources in a way that truly reflected communal desires. Voting systems might not be the thing that gets most people's hearts racing, but I felt inspired by the possibility of meeting such a democratic ideal.

Our solution came to us in a system that had

Skylar and Nina dress up for our annual Beltane festival.

already been introduced to Twin Oaks: Fair Share Voting (FSV).[2] FSV is a powerful voting system that is ideal for allocating shared resources, yet it is woefully unheard of. It is a ranked voting system, much like the Instant Runoff Voting that gained some attention during the 2016 presidential election season. Third-party candidates support ranked voting systems because they allow voters to put their true preference at the top of the list without running the risk of wasting their vote. If that candidate is not a finalist, then the ballot will be considered a vote for their second favorite option, and so on down the line.

Fair Share Voting works the same way, but is used when trying to allocate a certain quantity of resources to some set of proposed projects, each with its own proposed budget, whether large or small. Each person ranks their choices, but each ballot is represented by an equal share of resources. If 10 people are using FSV to allocate $10,000, then each ballot is essentially allocating $1000. A player who ranks a small project as their top vote will spend less of their initial voting power, measured in dollars, than someone who ranks at the top a bigger project, even when those two projects both get high rankings from other voters. And the more people that vote for an area, the less is spent by each person, since the cost required to fund a project is shared among the ballots that ranked it high enough. But if a voter's top-ranked choice is not supported by others, then the tally will consider the next item on their ballot without them having wasted a vote on a loser. And even if they voted for a winner, their ballot can still fund items further down in ranking as long as there are still dollars left on the ballot. Majority support does not mean only majority funding. Most of the money goes to the areas the majority supported, but a large minority may use its share to fund other projects.

Twin Oaks has used Fair Share Voting to vote on one-time project allocations in the past, but adapting FSV for ongoing budgets was a different beast altogether. So many of our programs would not make sense if their budgets happened to be voted way up one year and way down the next year. Take the dairy program, for example. We have so many cows, so many calves born over the course of the year, and expect a certain amount of milk from them. If the program gets cut one year in both our labor and money contribution, what will we do? Sell a bunch of the cows? Let the lactating cows go? What if it gets funded back to its usual amount the following year? Do we then buy ourselves a new herd? We needed a way to give the membership direct influence on these ongoing budgets while respecting the fact that they are ongoing and long-term. We decided that we, those administering the budgeting process, would set absolute minimums on all the community budgets. That way people would still rank all of the areas at the levels they wished them to be funded, but even an area that no one ranked would still get the minimum funding required to maintain the infrastructure of the community. Armed with this clever implementation of FSV, we were ready to reinvigorate community involvement in budgeting.

Of course, increasing participation is not as simple as saying "Hey! Check out this new voting system! It's so cool, you won't believe it!" Few members think about our budgets on a day-to-day basis, let alone the details of our budgeting process. For the first time in my life, I found myself employed in something of a PR campaign. I was making signs and posters, writing papers for our discussion board, and talking up this new process as much as I could. Many members were skeptical of such a shift, so I did what I could to assuage their fears (and did not completely succeed with some). Even more members, however, remained apathetic. Whether they played or not, they argued, the most important needs of Twin Oaks would be

"I just don't care," I heard way too many times. "Whatever people decide will be fine."

prioritized. We're not going to let our buildings fall apart or see ourselves starve because too few people put a vote in for those areas. "I just don't care," I heard way too many times. "Whatever people decide will be fine."

The fact is, people do care. Spend a day on the farm listening to people and you will hear comments about our budgets all over the place. "I can't believe we spend so much money to put

Photo courtesy of Adder Oaks

Adder, Puck, Anni, Megan, Kami at a budgeting summit.
Sunya Margulies

berries and nuts in our granola." "Why can't I claim labor credits for the time it takes me to drive to the doctor?" "Damn, I'm glad we decided to buy those new solar panels." Our annual budgeting process might not be on the mind of those making such utterances, but they are talking about the resource allocation determined by just that process.

The solution to getting people to turn up for this new voting game was simple: pizza. We turned the game into a series of pizza parties. Members would show up and we would have the electronic ballots pulled up on community computers and personal laptops. People would cast their vote while eating pizza, and we would be there to answer any questions about how to interface with the ballot and how the votes would be tallied. This strategy worked remark-

the community won't fall apart, but are we really ready to operate with a food budget cut in half? We're going to be eating a lot of rice and beans." As much as we tried to educate all the players, it was hard for them to really see the impact of their voting choices. Many ballots used up their shares in the top few areas, leaving several areas severely bloated and many more unrealistically meager. The members also felt fatigued by the game, having to rank every single area. We have well over a hundred areas to budget for, ranging from food to bike maintenance to local relations. The budgeting team ended up taking the results and editing them heavily. We came up with a balanced budget that worked well enough, and when we shared it with the community no one balked. But the democratic ideal we were aiming for was missed by a long shot.

Our next several economic planning meetings felt pretty depressing. We had spent a good half of a year getting ourselves and the community amped up about a new revolutionary voting process that would change everything. And then it failed. We seriously considered scrapping FSV altogether and returning to the Trade-Off Game. We knew that the latter would never really provide the egalitarian input we strove for, but it was within the comfort zone of the community. Would they support yet another revamp?

Thankfully, our disappointment in our first attempt to use Fair Share Voting subsided. Rather than scrap it, we decided to tackle the problem of ongoing budgets from a different angle, while still preserving FSV. Rather than using voting to build each budget from scratch or an absolute minimum each year, we would propose budgets that reflect the status quo and use FSV to adjust them. If providing status quo services leaves us with extra cash or hours, we would vote on which areas to bump up. We could also use the adjustment when status quo would leave us lacking cash or hours, which might happen if our businesses do not do as well as previous years, baseline costs such as energy

Is pizza really a stronger motivator than our shared economy?

ably well. (Disturbingly well, I might think. Is pizza really a stronger motivator than our shared economy?) Those of us on the econ team were quite happy with ourselves, content with a job well done. That is, until we tallied the results.

It turns out that our implementation of FSV was setting ourselves up for disaster, a disaster which manifested. We were not realistic about setting minimum budgets. We looked at the results of some areas and said to ourselves "Sure,

or insurance go up, or the working population of the community is expected to be low. FSV works much the same in this case, except that it is used to vote for cuts; areas that one would most be willing to see reduced are ranked at the top. Each player's fair share is made up of "negative dollars," and everyone is required to rank enough areas to ensure that the necessary cuts will be made.

The past three years, we have used this method of budgeting, which we call The Adjustment Game. We meet and set status quo budgets, decide whether we need add games or cut games, come up with a list of areas that could be supplemented or reduced, and present those areas to the community to vote on. We have continued at times to use pizza, cookies, and coffee to motivate people to play. But the game is becoming more routine now. We do not have to re-explain every bit and contrast it against the old system. The new system is the standard now. And it's doing what we

Janel and Steve talk at our annual Anniversary celebration.

Photo courtesy of Adder Oaks

Keenan and Christian prepare for a wasp battle.

Photo courtesy of Adder Oaks

hoped for: it provides real opportunity for the membership to directly influence budgets in a fair way, is an easy enough ballot to understand that everyone can play, and creates community buy-in for our collective budgets.

However, I hesitate as I write such optimistic words, knowing that this will be read by the members of my community. The fact is, not everyone feels empowered by our budgeting process. Each year when new budgets are set, there are always some who denounce the results. It is tempting for me to wave off these concerns, chalking them up to the grumps who didn't get their way. The long-term members who spent years doing it the old way just don't want to adjust. The new area manager is simply annoyed that the other members are not excited about their project. Another member has personal animosity toward another and is using this opportunity to play out social drama.

But I have to take their concerns seriously. As much as we try to democratize the process, the fact is that those administering the game do have considerable sway. We have to ask ourselves questions such as, "How exactly do we determine what budgets represent the status quo?" "Which areas do we consider up for adjustments in years where we have to cut?" "Are we really making the game easy and accessible to all?" These are important questions that require close examination. We will continue to examine them and continue to tweak the game in years to come.

While each budgeting cycle brings in some grumbling, the nature of that grumbling is beginning to shift. It used to be complaints that the process did not make sense, that one's vote did not count, that it was either too confusing or too simple to be useful. Now I hear complaining about the votes themselves. Some are shocked that we voted to bump up personal spending allowance over low-cost community services, such as shared musical instruments for community performances. Others retort that allowance has been too low for too long, and the music is just a pet project for some. Another chimes in that our food budget should take precedence over either concern if we really want to have a healthy and varied diet. This is what we want. Our budgets may be controversial, but they are engaging. The apathy is past. Our economic planning does matter and people know it. We might just be getting closer to that democratic ideal. ☙

Adder Oaks has been a member of Twin Oaks Community in Louisa, Virginia for six years. Sharing his life and income with a hundred others, he works as an economic planner, tutor, and parent. Adder is co-host of the podcast Commune Dads.

1. Definition from the Participatory Budgeting Project, www.participatorybudgeting.org.
2. For a detailed description of Fair Share Voting, please visit: bit.ly/2InE3xw.

Grace and Claire.

Photo courtesy of Adder Oaks

Stephay, Lindsey, Adder, Anni, Megan, Kami at a budgeting summit.

Sunya Margulies

Sabrina and Nina repaint the original farmhouse.

Photo courtesy of Adder Oaks

Communal Studies Association

Encouraging the study of
Intentional Community since 1975

Our Mission: * Provide a **forum** for the discussion of Intentional Community
* Help **preserve** America's Communal Sites
* To **communicate** the ssuccessful ideas and lessons learned from
Intentional Communities

We hold an **Annual Conference** each fall at an historic
communal site. We encourage all to come and
participate, learn and contribute to the discussion.

We also publish a **journal** and a **newsletter**, both
issued twice-yearly.

Special registration and **membership rates** are available
for community members.

For more information or to join us, visit our website
www.communalstudies.org

Fifty Years of Utopian Intentioneering
AT TWIN OAKS COMMUNITY

By A. Allen Butcher

Twin Oaks was begun as an "experimental community" in central Virginia in 1967. After the community's first five years Kat Kinkade, one of the cofounders, published a book about Twin Oaks titled *A Walden Two Experiment*, in which she wrote on the first page that "we are trying to make a new and better society." (Kinkade, p. 1) Fifty years on it is time to evaluate the Twin Oaks experiment.

As a former member of both Twin Oaks and East Wind, and a lifelong communal researcher, I've identified several primary lessons learned from Twin Oaks' history. In this article, I'll describe three:
• Theories notwithstanding, the optimum population of such communities is so far about 100 adults.
• A labor-credit system makes it possible to create a society that does not use money internally.
• In an egalitarian time-based economy, domestic labor or "women's work" can be valued equally with all other labor or "men's work" including income-generating labor.

(For a much longer treatment of the subject, including additional lessons learned about ease of communal life, clashes between ideology and practicality, and failures of communal childcare, see the "Fifty Years" blog post at www.Intentioneers.net.)

100-Member Limit (as of 2017)

While B. F. Skinner, whose novel *Walden Two* provided the inspiration for Twin Oaks, populated his fictional Walden Two community with 1,000 pliable members, the practical population limit for the self-willed people comprising egalitarian societies is set by the experience of Twin Oaks (TO) and East Wind (EW), currently at under 100 adults each. At whatever population level, Twin Oaks will continue to represent the standard for secular, egalitarian communal societies in America.

Kat Kinkade wrote in her 1972 book about Twin Oaks that 1,000 members was "our theoretical goal." This was one of the design parameters that she and the other East Wind cofounders took with them to Missouri, although in the initial EW bylaws the theoretical goal was reduced to 750 members, since the *Walden Two* idea of 1,000 did not seem to be practical. In 2010 EW reset its "membership ceiling" at 73, less than a tenth of the original goal, while the community's 2016 population level slightly exceeded that. (Kinkade, p. 42; EW Legispol 2011, section 11.52)

Neither Twin Oaks nor East Wind seems to want to grow larger, probably because of the concern for the communication and other quality-of-life problems resulting from an ever-growing population, however slow that growth may be. In 2017 Twin Oaks is looking to purchase more contiguous land, although probably to create another communal group upon it rather than to expand its current mem-

Twin Oaks 50th Anniversary banner and performers.

McCune Porter

bership. If this land is acquired and a new income-sharing community is founded upon it, that will increase the number of satellite communities of Twin Oaks in Louisa County to six, with Acorn being the largest at around 30 or 40 members.

While one may tend to think that the communal labor system, governance processes, social contract, and other aspects of these communities should be able to accommodate much larger numbers of people, TO and EW, at least, seem to have reached a practical limit. The growth of Twin Oaks is now essentially delegated to its newest satellite communities, most of them founded in the same county of Louisa, while East Wind has yet to create any communal satellites in its Ozark County.

There is much to be said about the numbers game for identifying ideal population levels for different types of intentional communities. Among primitive clans and tribes the anthropologist Robin Dunbar says that 150 people is the average human's cognitive social limit, according to his plotting of "overall group size against the

Many hands make light work while raising trusses on a new residence.

Photo courtesy of www.twinoaks.org

neocortical development of the brain." Meanwhile, the paleo-anthropologist Richard Leakey writes that the number 25 is the typical limit for the clan, and 500 for the minimum size of a breeding population, constituting the "dialectical tribe" with which the individual identifies. (Leakey & Lewin, pp. 111, 113-4; Ryan & Jethá, p. 171)

Among the various forms of contemporary intentional communities: the religious Hutterites split when they reach 150; most cohousing groups have 40 to 70 adults; and some Israeli kibbutzim had over 1,000 members before they gave up communalism and became collective communities on government land trusts. The kibbutzim estimated that a population of about 350 people is needed in order to maintain a complete age-range from youngest to oldest over the generations.

A Revolutionary Invention: Labor-Credit Systems Can Replace Money

There had long been the ideal, since at least the early 19th century in England, of creating an economic system which would reward workers with the full value of their labor, rather than the capitalist model of business owners taking as much from labor as they can get. Ronald Garnett explains in his 1972 book, *Cooperation and the Owenite Socialist Communities in Britain: 1825-45*, that "The basis of communitarian thought was equality—economic rather than political—in that the labourer had a right to the full value of the product of [his or her] labour." Much of the development of this theory was due to the excesses of poverty and debasement resulting from the dispossessed and deprived underclass during the beginning of the Industrial Revolution in first England, then France, Germany, and later in America and elsewhere. To create economic justice, it was believed, a society or a culture had to do away with the use of money internally and substitute something else. However, finding something which would substantially serve the ideal took about 140 years. (Garnett, p. 26)

From the mid 1820s to the early 1830s the idea of a time-based currency, so named in the present author's School of Intentioneering, was developed in England, with the principle designer or intentioneer being the Welsh industrialist Robert Owen (1771-1858), who had earlier been influenced by Gerard Winstanley's 1652 book, *The Law of Freedom*, and by the Quaker, John Beller's 1695 book, *Proposals for Raising a College of Industry of All Useful Trades and Husbandry*, which was a call for a form of publicly-supported education program designed as an intentional community. Beller's educational-community idea has occurred to many others through time as well, from the ancient Greek philosopher and mathematician Pythagoras, to the New England Transcendentalists at Brook Farm, to Findhorn University in Scotland. (Rexroth, pp. 151-2)

Robert Owen's and others' ideas about time-based economies resulted in giving workers a form of paper scrip stating the amount of time the worker had contributed, which were then redeemed in a community store for goods and services, essentially comprising an alternative exchange system to that of the official currency. The "labour theory of value" was explained by Owen as goods being "exchanged on the equitable principles of labour, for equal value of labour through the medium of Labour Notes." The labor exchanges served to bring the trade unions into the cooperative movement. (Garnett, pp. 139, 141)

Intermediary exchange associations were set up to facilitate the circulation of both labor notes and monetary currencies, yet the whole system imploded by 1834 as there was no standard equivalencies for converting "labor notes" into British currency, which resulted in the destruction of many cooperative societies including the first co-op stores, labor exchanges, trades syndicalism, and the movement for the eight-hour workday. (Garnett, pp. 140, 142)

Robert Owen brought the labor notes idea to America with his communal experiment at New Harmony. However, every attempt to use forms of labor notes in intentional communities through the 19th century in America (as in Britain), such as at New Harmony in Indiana (1825-27), and at Kaweah (1885-92) and Altruria (1894-5) both in California, resulted in the labor notes system being the first thing to be abandoned as the communities began to fail.

By Donald Pitzer's count, there were a total of 29 Owenite communities: 19 in the US, one in Canada, and nine in England, Scotland, Ireland, and Wales. They developed preschools and "communal" childcare systems, and at various times and to different degrees, experimented with communalism. At 12 years Modern Times was the longest lived. (Pitzer, pp. 122-3)

Not until Kat Kinkade developed the vacation-credit labor system at Twin Oaks Community in the summer of 1967 would a successful communal labor-credit system be invented. Edward Bellamy had included a time-based "credit card" system in his *Looking Backward* utopian fiction (1888), and from this B. F. Skinner got the idea that a community could use ledger accounts for managing individual labor contributions with no form of exchange of anything like coins or paper bills. In *Walden Two* Skinner wrote, "Bellamy suggested the principle in *Looking Backward*." (Skinner, p. 46)

June 16, 1967 is the day Twin Oaks members moved onto the land.

Photos courtesy of www.twinoaks.org

Garden activity: plants carted post-harvest to compost pile.

Hammocks has been one of TO's main collective businesses since the early 1970s.

Fall harvest from the organic vegetable gardens.

Outdoor meal: at picnic tables outside Zhankoye (main dining hall).

Changing the tilt of the solar panels on TO's off-the-grid residence— done four times a year to get maximum sunlight exposure to the panels.

Bellamy, Skinner, and others have also suggested rewarding labor differently for different types of work in communal society. Walden House (in Washington, DC), Twin Oaks, and East Wind all experimented with "variable-credits" for 10 years from 1966 until about 1976, rewarding some work done with more labor-credits than other work, until members decided to value all labor equally. It is an important lesson to keep in mind that variable compensation for labor is an aspect of monetary economics, while being both impractical and anathema to time-based economics.

Building upon Skinner's idea of ledger accounts, Kat Kinkade's brilliant innovation, called by the present author the "vacation-credit labor system," set a weekly work quota that all members agree to meet, with vacation time earned by working over-quota. This time-based economy, called at Twin Oaks simply the "labor-credit system," became, as Twin Oaks member Mala stated to a reporter, "the glue that keeps this community together." (Mala, quoted in Rems)

It is phenomenal how the thing that was usually given up first when communal groups failed, their time-based economy, became the most important thing that now makes them successful! Kat Kinkade essentially created the first complete alternative economic system to that of monetary economics, and sadly, very few people outside of the egalitarian communities movement know anything about it. It would seem that such an achievement would be worthy of much pride and promotion, yet most people think nothing of it. Reporters and academicians come and go and rarely ever understand the significance of Twin Oaks' vacation-credit labor system.

Extending equality in America from the political system to the economic system was the whole point of Bellamy's *Looking Backward,* which was immensely influential around the end of the 19th century. Today the labor-credit system is essentially the portal to a parallel reality existing within global monetary economics, enabling the very thing that has eluded social reformers since the early Industrial Revolution—a truly egalitarian economic system.

Feminism Is ALIVE When All Labor Is Valued Equally

Along with the idea that workers ought to receive the full value of their labor is the sentiment that all labor that directly benefits the whole community or society ought to be valued equally. The feminist ideal of domestic work or "women's work" being valued equally with income-generating work and all other work typically performed by men is served via the vacation-credit labor system. This is another fantastic achievement and characteristic of Twin Oaks and other egalitarian communities providing an important lesson. While feminists and others have looked for ways for women to earn money for housework as a way to create economic equality, only non-monetary, time-based economies, including labor exchanges as well as quota and anti-quota labor systems, value "reproductive work" the same as all other labor.

While people generally discount the idea that in a labor-credit economy a doctor is rewarded the same for their work as someone cleaning a barn, there have been doctors who have been members of Twin Oaks, East Wind, Ganas, and other egalitarian communities. Clearly, for many people the benefits of egalitarian economics are seen as being more important than differential compensation for labor. For this "Feminism is ALIVE" communal lesson the egalitarian ideal of valuing domestic and income work equally is a major success for Twin Oaks and its associated groups comprising the Federation of Egalitarian Communities.

Kat Kinkade wrote a letter to anthropologist Jon Wagner saying about Twin Oaks that "absolute sexual equality is fundamental to our idea of equality, and equality is fundamental to our approach to changing society. There is no platform of our ideology that is more central." (Kinkade, quoted in Goldenberg, p. 258)

In her chapter titled "Feminism at Twin Oaks" in the 1993 book *Women in Spiritual and Communitarian Societies in the United States*, Zena Goldenberg quotes Jon Wagner stating an endorsement of Twin Oaks' egalitarian culture in his comment that Twin Oaks "may be among the most non-sexist social systems in human history." (Wagner, quoted by Goldenberg in Chmielewski, Kern, & Klee-Hartzell, p. 258; Wagner, pp. 37-8)

The Future: A Growing Network

Now arising in Louisa County, Virginia is the dynamic of an interdependent, growing number of communal groups around Twin Oaks. The idea of a network of communal and collective groups in local proximity in America as a force for social change has been a goal since at least the publishing of the 1884 book by Laurence Gronlund titled *The Cooperative Commonwealth*. Whether this is called today "radical decentralism," "deep democracy," "democratic confederalism," "communal municipalism," a "regional commonwealth," or something else, this is a fascinating story now developing, with challenges to be identified, lessons to be debated, and glorious revelations yet to be realized and celebrated! 🖉

Portions of this article were previously published by the author in the 2016 book, The Intentioneers' Bible: Interwoven Stories of the Parallel Cultures of Plenty and Scarcity, *currently available only as an ebook on Amazon.com. The* Intentioneer's Bible *tracks several themes including time-based economies, equality of the genders, and communal childcare through the prehistory and history of Western Civilization. A. Allen Butcher is a former member of East Wind and Twin Oaks communities, currently living collectively in Denver, Colorado.. Contact the author at 4thWorld@consultant.org, and see www.Intentioneers.net.*

A calf is fed as part of the Dairy Program. Female calves become milk cows, male calves become beef.

A member prepares dinner at our main kitchen-dining building (Zhankoye).

Photos courtesy of www.twinoaks.org

REFERENCES

Butcher, A. Allen. (2016). *The intentioneer's bible: Interwoven stories of the parallel cultures of plenty and scarcity.* Self-published at Amazon.com.

Goldenberg, Zena. (1993). The power of feminism at Twin Oaks Community. In W. Chmielewski, L. Kern, & M. Klee-Hartzell (Eds.), *Women in spiritual and communitarian societies in the United States.* Syracuse, NY: Syracuse University Press.

Garnett, Ronald George. (1972). *Co-operation and the Owenite socialist communities in Britain, 1825-1845.* Manchester, England: Manchester University Press.

Kinkade, Kathleen. (1972). *A Walden Two experiment: The first five years of Twin Oaks Community* (2nd Ed.). Louisa, VA: Twin Oaks Community, Inc.

Kinkade, Kat. (1994). *Is it utopia yet? An insider's view of Twin Oaks Community in its 26th year.* Louisa, VA: Twin Oaks Community, Inc.

Leakey, Richard, & Lewin, Roger. (1978). *People of the lake: Mankind and its beginnings.* New York: Avon.

Pitzer, Donald E. (Ed.). (1997). *America's communal utopias.* Chapel Hill, NC: Univ. of North Carolina Press.

Rems, Emily. (2003 winter). "Ecovillage people." *BUST* magazine. www.thefec.org/about/media/bust-magazine-article-ecovillage-people

Ryan, C. & Jethá, C. (2010). *Sex at dawn: How we mate, why we stray, and what it means for modern relationships.* New York: Harper Collins Publishers.

Rexroth, Kenneth. (1974). *Communalism: From its origins to the twentieth century.* New York: Seabury Press.

Skinner, B. F. (2005). *Walden Two.* New York: McMillan. (Original work published 1948)

Wagner, Jon. (1982). *Sex roles in contemporary American communes.* Bloomington, IN: Indiana University Press.

COME CREATE COMMUNITY WITH US!

EcoVillage in formation in the mountains of Anton, Panama

THIS IS OUR PALETTE

HTTP://8THLIFEPANAMA.ORG
@8thLifeAstoria

In 2003, "La Cité Écologique" was founded, in Colebrook New Hampshire, on 315 acres of beautiful land surrounded by forest and mountains. Our ecovillage gives priority to education, optimal living to its members, a cooperative culture with resilience in its development and social entrepreneurship. So far, we have built one single family building, two large community residences, where people live in a kind of condo arrangement, and one community building (all powered by solar). We are expanding new building projects, to give a home to growing families and/or new members. We've created businesses, non-profits, a nonprofit school, and an organic farm, that helps better serve ours, and the local community. Visitors are welcome to our annual Open House in June, and Harvest Celebration in September. Guided tours, and internship programs are also available from May through October.

Contact: Leonie Brien (603) 331-1669
www.citeecologiquenh.org

La Cité Écologique
of New Hampshire
An Ecovillage since 2003

Servant Leadership in Cooperative Business:
STIRRING IT UP AT EAST WIND NUT BUTTERS

By Sumner Nichols

*E*ast Wind Community is a founding member of the Federation of Egalitarian Communities (FEC) in the hills of the Ozarks. East Wind Nut Butters, founded in 1981, is equally owned and operated by the members of East Wind Community and is currently its dominant source of income. East Wind Nut Butters produces peanut, almond, cashew, and sesame seed butters. East Wind Community is composed of 73 members who live on over 1000 acres of beautifully forested land.

Here I am again, sitting at a desk dazed by a big bright monitor. Scrutinizing spreadsheets. Writing emails. Staring at the weather. How did I allow this to happen? I came to East Wind to get away from all this, didn't I? That is what I thought I wanted, at least. Of course, everything besides the familiar humming of a computer and the ringing of phones is different.

After graduating from the honors business school at Indiana University in 2012 I didn't have many plans. While my friends sought higher education and high paying jobs I had little interest in either. Disillusioned with the state of the world and the society I grew up in I came to desire an alternative to what I was observing on a daily basis. Three years and some Google searches later my discovery of IC.org led me to schedule visitor periods at East Wind and Twin Oaks.

In March of 2015 I made the two-day bus journey towards southern Missouri to make my intrepid first visit to a fully income-sharing community. A month before, my year stint as a secretary for a small family business ended when I decided to pursue this incredibly different path. That tiny amount of time spent in the office workforce of America proved to be invaluable in the role I was soon to fill.

Nearly immediately I fell in love with East Wind. The land, the people, the sense of opportunity and promise. After visiting East Wind and Twin Oaks for "official" visitor periods and checking a number of places in between I knew that East Wind was where I wanted to be.

I lived and labored at East Wind for about seven months as a "working guest on the waiting list." Essentially this meant that because the membership of East Wind was at its legislated full capacity of 73 people I had to wait to become a member. Benefits such as having a room, receiving a $150 dividend each month and full medical coverage did not apply to me. However, I also was not beholden to the rules concerning working for East Wind's dominant business: East Wind Nut Butters. All members who wish to receive their monthly dividend must work a set number of hours (the "Industrial Quotient" or simply "IQ") each week. This number is determined by the General Management Team of the business and ranges from zero to eight. I was not required and in fact was discouraged from working IQ hours during my time as a working guest.

For a young man looking to learn about food production and homesteading this could not have been a better arrangement. East Wind's weekly labor quota is 35 hours. These hours can manifest from gardening, cow milking, building maintenance, cooking, cleaning, working in the business ("IQ" hours), and a plethora of other things that community values as useful labor. Without the burden of having to work in the business (I worked just three factory shifts in the first seven months I lived at East Wind) I was free to pursue passions known and unknown. Gardening, woodworking, cow milking, cart building and maintenance, and food processing consumed both my mind and body. I could not get enough and learned more practical skills than I had in my 24 years prior.

This time was precious. Finding friends. Bonding with an amazing new partner. Coming into my own as an adult. Easing into the idea of East Wind being home. My existence was relatively carefree and I was grateful to have found such a special place. Not being a member meant that no serious responsibilities fell upon my shoulders.

Often, while sitting at this desk in front of this ridiculous screen, I am reminded of my college days. Listening to Ratatat, Beethoven, anything nonlyrical really and reading, studying, analyzing. Except this is an actual challenge. This is the real world. Decisions with consequences. Responsibility and accountability to oneself and others. No grades, just results and outcomes. I am a manager.

Photos courtesy of Sumner Nichols

I am an entrepreneur. These are the roles I play at East Wind. A business with three million dollars in sales a year can't exist long without a group of people taking on particular niches and holding such positions to maintain stability and continuity.

An active sales manager and a vision of where the business was heading were desperately needed when I first began working in the office for Nut Butters. Everything else was already in place. Delicious and nutritious nut butters made fresh in daily batches. A production team composed of experienced and talented individuals working together to manufacture tried and true, simple and wholesome, one- and two-ingredient products. A meticulously managed warehouse full of almond, cashew, peanut, and sesame seed butter. An established regional brand with an impeccable food safety record.

East Wind Nut Butters was doing everything right in terms of producing high quality staple foods, but its major failing was in being sluggishly responsive to an increasingly competitive health food market. In 1981, when the business was founded, all-natural and organic peanut butter was a true novelty. Look at your grocery store shelf today and you'll see that today's market is saturated with more nut butter brands and varieties than ever before. All-natural, organic, claims of "Superfood!," etc. abound. It's easy for a small brand that relies on word of mouth and that barely advertises to get lost in all the marketing noise.

One of the first decisions I made after being elected as the General Manager and Sales Manager of Nut Butters was to change our label vendor. Going with a smaller, more local printer reduced costs significantly and also made changing the labels less of a hassle. East Wind has always relied on the quality of their products and word of mouth to maintain business. I liked that the advertising budget was incredibly minimal. I don't like the idea of "selling" someone on something they don't need. However, marketing nutritious staple foods to the general public is sufficiently palatable to my ethical standards. Making clear on our labels why East Wind Nut Butters is different than the other brands was a top priority. "Single Ingredient: 100% US grown Valencia peanuts." This phrase would have meant very little to me two years ago. Until recently I was unaware of the fact that most peanuts are imported from China and India and that there are many different varieties of peanuts. The nice thing about US-grown Valencia peanuts is that when you roast and mill them they make a nice, thick, nutrient-dense peanut butter. With Chinese peanuts there is a need to add things like palm oil, hydrogenated oil, excess salt, and sugar to make the peanut butter something a person might actually find tasty, though still not something a health-conscious person would want to put in their body.

Making slight changes to our labels is a relatively small decision in the grand scheme of things. What about expanding business?

A larger facility and new products? Radically changing the business model? These are all considerations that any entrepreneur thinks about. When to scale up. When to drop products and when to introduce new ones. All of these big-

Leaders here are servants, and servants are leaders. I am one of many and in this I find comfort.

ger decisions have a context. Context is of the upmost importance for *any* business. I am one of 73 equal owners in this business. I am not a Silicon Valley cowboy with angel investors and a dream. Keeping a level head close to the Earth is my top asset. Any big project needs to be thoroughly thought out in the full context of East Wind. More than that, it needs to be effectively communicated if it is ever to become a reality.

If you want to make a major organizational change and have this change be effective you need to communicate clearly to those who will be affected. Such an effort cannot be a top-down, out-of-the-blue affair. Constantly eliciting feedback and figuring out the priorities of a community of 73 people takes a lot of time and energy. Communication attempted by an individual to an entire community can be difficult and it is in this realm that I still have much to learn. Patience and planning are prerequisite to any ambitious endeavor in this setting.

East Wind meetings can be boring by their very nature. No one intends them to be, of course. They require a lot of deliberation, and involve long spans of waiting to speak. The standard meeting, in which we rotate through single speakers talking and everyone else listening, is not the most efficient way of discussing a multi-faceted idea. Redundancy and tangential lines of thought quickly dampen any sense of momentum. On occasion, I am reminded of how I felt during Occupy Bloomington circles.

Typically, less than a third of the community is in attendance for community meetings. All meetings must be proposed by a member of the community and 10 percent of all members must sign the proposal to get the meeting scheduled. At some points in the year there will be no meetings "on the stack" and weeks go by without having an "official" community meeting. At other points there is a lengthy list of issues—policies on how common spaces are used, an idea to repurpose a defunct building, policies on pets—and very consistent weekly meetings. Many meetings see less than a third of the community participate. Not everyone cares to spend an afternoon talking about things that may not affect their lives much.

The most contentious issues and votes are the

most well-attended. Budget meetings and membership votes pique plenty of people's interest, but even for these I've learned to expect no more than half of the community to be in attendance. The format of the meeting, the weather on the day of the meeting, and the location of the meeting have a significant impact on how many people attend and how productive the meeting is. The meeting format at East Wind that has become commonplace is by no means set in stone and those with the energy and the will find more creative ways of percolating their ideas through the collective East Wind conscience. Exploring this art can be vexing. I have come to believe that the commune setting is the ultimate teacher due to its all-encompassing scope. How can humans live with each other? What type of society are we shaping? How are we to live?

Such considerations are rarely given much time or energy in the majority of the corporate world. Really simple ideas like growth and monetary profit dominate. By ignoring the living Earth and the interests of others it becomes possible to make decisions that are close-to-optimal through that limited lens. It's easy when you look at numbers on a spreadsheet and all you have to do is maximize profit. Clearcut rainforest and cheap palm oil, abused workers and cheap imports—if you don't see these things and don't think about these things then it is easy to go about your day in a society that rewards you for your "success." The ability to deny is a strong evolutionary trait. It exists within all of us. It can allow us to make sense of this world. It can allow us to make sense of this world in the worst ways. Feeding into these habits is a culture founded upon endless growth and destruction; a culture of convenience and consumption; a technoutopia of iPhone cults and pick-your-own realities created by a web of social media platforms.

Forgive my digression. Where I came from, what I was born *into* reminds me of what I wish to avoid passing down to succeeding generations. My motivation is in building something; build-

ing upon an inheritance that many lay claim to. We stand on the shoulders of giants. My contribution to this legacy, whether footnote or volume, remains to be seen. The manner in which I manage East Wind Nut Butters defines me, both externally and internally, whether I like it or not. Respect for a job well done is accepted awkwardly. Scorn for a mistake, typically self-inflicted, is not taken lightly. The trap of thinking that my work in the business is, in isolation, my most important role in community is an easy one to fall into.

The delusions of grandeur that consume my ego at times are not always useful. A solid block of manual labor working in the garden or a grounded conversation with a fellow communard soon alleviates the problem. For this relief I am grateful. Ambition that is constantly checked is potently transformative. This has been my experience at East Wind. Leaders here are servants, and servants are leaders. I am one of many and in this I find comfort. We live to serve. It sounds religious or like a corporate tagline, but the sentiment is sound. Serving each other. Serving your landbase and watershed. Serving the living systems that allow for your existence.

What is it to lead in community? It is subtle. It is pronounced. It is the patience and foresight to wait for the right time and let energies flow organically. Generally, people want to help and people want to make things happen. For the biggest projects it is a matter of anticipating the roadblocks and the bottlenecks and eliminating or reducing them to maintain high participation and morale. My two years at East Wind have been sufficient to accumulate a small amount of wisdom on the matter. Two more will bring a greater grasp. Everything in due time.

As I sit here at this desk listening to Washed Out and finishing up an email by click clacking on the keyboard I take a break to stare out the window and ponder possible futures. I have never experienced such optimism and passion for life. Total engagement. This weird and wonderful place, this income-sharing commune has provided the environment, the proper context, for my potential to become kinetic. Where am I? Where is East Wind? Where shall we head? 🐦

Sumner is a 26-year-old white male attempting to live a moral life in an age of decline. He desires to create and build. Gardening, cow milking, maintaining East Wind's fleet of hand carts, and dishwashing are some of his favorite labors. In his downtime he plays various card and board games or spends time with his lovely boyfriend. On nice sunny afternoons you will find him and his friends along East Wind's mile of Lick Creek. Recently, he has become enthralled with birding and taking pictures of our avian friends. By the time this article is published you should be able to see some of his bird pictures, amongst many others, on the eastwind.org website.

Living Out a Gift Economy in Community with Others

By Tina Dunn (with input from others in the Jesus Christian community)

Love is the most powerful force we can possibly harness. Unlike food, clothes, and other material things, no one can steal or control the love you personally choose to give. That is one thing that makes love so powerful. Love only requires personal choice at the individual level first, it costs nothing to practice, and the more you give it away, the more you get back.

Our community (the Jesus Christian community in Sydney, Australia) is based on a philosophy of doing everything that we do for Love, the kind of radical love that Jesus taught. This has led us to live out a Gift Economy based on the following motto: "Work For Love Not For Money."

We found that when our motive and purpose is to promote and grow in Love, we live in harmony with God and the rest of Creation. Doing this, we have discovered our needs being met, and the means to keep building a better world have been provided without having to dedicate our time to work we do not believe in or to producing things for the sole purpose of making money.

Here are some practical tips and experiences that have made living out a Gift Economy possible for our community:

Simplicity

For the Gift Economy to work for us, we first had to learn to live on less, instead of focusing on getting more. This has been quite liberating. It starts with a willingness to live on the bare minimum: food and clothing, and it grows into managing all of our resources responsibly.

Living in this way can be fairly humbling and it does have its challenges. When you have money in your hand you tend to think, "I can buy what I want, when I want it." Having little or no money forces you to be more creative, resourceful, and patient. In the consumer societies in which most of us have grown up, we are accustomed to acquiring whatever we want instantly, sometimes going into debt if we don't immediately have the cash to get it. But when we have to wait for things to come, we discover what it is we really need and what we can live without.

One of the discoveries we have made by seeking to live simply has been the abundance of resources already available as discarded "waste" in many developed nations. In fact, most of our food and clothes, and a lot of other needs, have been met through things that we have found thrown out! We have been able to furnish and kit out entire houses and vehicles with a wide variety of items we have found thrown away over the years. Surprisingly, we often experience an overabundance of material goods, including luxury food items discarded by supermarkets. As a bonus, we regularly find enough to share freely with others as well. As a result, we always have enough.

Because we don't want to contribute to the ever-growing pile of unnecessary material goods in the world, we seek first to use what is already freely available. And this has eased much of the pressure that communities normally feel to generate steady incomes to acquire resources. This issue of simplicity has been one of the first key factors in living out a successful Gift Economy model.

Sharing

Sharing is practically synonymous with community. All communities must share their resources (time, energy, money, possessions, etc.) in some way. In our community we share *all* of our income and resources. No one calls anything their own. This attitude dramatically reduces disagreements related to material things, because we are all in it together. If times are tough, they are tough for all of us, and if things are going well, they go well for everyone. Deep mutual trust is built when we have this level of material equality, and as a result it is rare to have disputes over finances or belongings in our community.

One of the reasons we have been successful with this level of sharing has been making clear our requirements for membership. Like the primitive Christians, when someone joins our community, they quit their secular job (if they had one) and sell all their possessions. The proceeds are distributed to the poor, and if necessary, used for various needs within the community itself.

This initial and individual leap of faith sets the tone for how we manage our resources as a community. It takes faith to put your life in the hands of an unseen force, but we can testify from personal experience that there is nothing

Living simply and sharing what we have with each other.

An example from a project we did to get people thinking about their relationship to money.

to fear, and that God is faithful and true to His promises. Our brothers and sisters who share the journey with us help us along the way, and there is always enough for everyone.

I think most "trouble" comes when people have seen, or start to see, the *community* as their means of support. Communities fail when their members forget that the community should always be seen as a platform for better practicing Love. It's about taking personal responsibility and seeking to help others to do the same. Whatever we do should flow from personal conviction and not just because "the group" says so. Being vigilant about weeding out personal and corporate greed in any decision-making is highly important.

What is needed for a successful community based on a Gift Economy are people who are willing to work in harmony with each other and who seek to use the resources lovingly provided as an expression of love, rather than trying to devise ways to exploit them for personal gain. Once we do that, we find harmony; life stops being a struggle for survival and becomes an expression of genuine liberty and prosperity.

We were created as free beings with personal autonomy; we need to practice that independence of spirit in conjunction with the realization that we have an intrinsic interdependence with the world, with others around us, and with the Creator of it all. Changing our motivation (from "what can I get" to "what can I give") and then finding (or creating!) a community of like-spirited individuals who share our vision is a helpful expression of this.

Sharing, therefore, is another key factor in living out a Gift Economy as a community.

Working for Love

The Gift Economy functions on giving and receiving freely, rather than buying and selling, or demanding and taking. Living out a Gift Economy means continually looking for ways to give. We strive to give from ALL our resources available: money, possessions, energy, and time. "Working for Love, Not Money" is the natural conclusion to this type of giving. We give our energy and time to others without demanding anything back for it.

This new way of "doing business" is not something any of us came up with on our own. We discovered it in the teachings of Jesus. He said that we cannot work for both God and money at the same time, and that it is impossible to serve one without cheating the other. He said that God feeds the birds and clothes the flowers and will do the same for us if we seek to build God's kingdom first. These truths are fundamental to our Gift Economy.

Working for Love is not unique to our community. It is practiced in different ways by other communities, religious and otherwise, and there are even examples of it in society at large. For example, plenty of people in our society are willing to volunteer time and service to causes that they are interested in, whether it be Amnesty International, a political party, a soup kitchen, or walking their elderly neighbor's dog. This desire to give is intrinsic to all of us. I think committed communities like ours differ from others in that we have decided to make Love and sharing the basis on which we live our entire lives. For us, working for love is our full-time job—and we see so much genuine need for Love in the world that we are never going to run out of work to do!

While we believe in doing everything for Love and without expecting anything in return, we are not entirely removed from the economic system (yet!) and we still use money (see section below on "Accepting Gifts"). We see greed ("the love of money") as being the root cause of evil in our world.

So our emphasis is on not doing anything *for the purpose* of making money or gaining material wealth. In this way, we seek to combat corruption in ourselves and to, hopefully, give testimony that another way of doing things is possible—here and now.

A lot of people tend to view this kind of lifestyle as being unproductive, and only for those who don't want to work (or who can't work). Society has been led to believe that unless there is a financial/material exchange then the goods or services have no value. Taking even just one example of a demanding job that isn't materially rewarded—raising children—we know that such a teaching is false. There are so many jobs that don't get done—even when people are paid to do them—that we happily do for free simply because we believe they have value in and of themselves.

It is a challenge to personal pride knowing that many people do not value the concept of working for love, yet I know for myself that the sense of purpose I have in my life, and the fact that I am living in accord with my conscience, is more than recompense for what others may think of what I am doing. Obviously, part of getting the job done requires confronting the prejudices of society, loved ones, peers, etc. That can be too tall an order for some people, but it is essential if we are to do the work that needs to be done in making real, lasting improvements to the world around us.

Virtually any genuinely productive and positive work that is normally done for money can be done even better for love. We can create, build, fix, and improve almost anything for love. In fact, when love is our motivation (rather

> # Communities fail when their members forget that the community should always be seen as a platform for better practicing Love.

Modern-day gleaning.

Sharing of ourselves brings greater satisfaction than a paycheck.

A really simple way to show love to a stranger.

Photos courtesy of Jesus Christians

than money), we can concentrate on the best jobs that have the best chances of producing the best results we want to see in the world.

For our community, a lot of our work is, like this article, looking for ways to show and inspire others with how this Gift Economy works. We produce and distribute literature, music, and videos which do just that. We also get involved in a wide range of different projects aimed at reinforcing the concept of working for love and not money. We experiment with offering free work to people, making a point of not accepting payment for the work that we do. We have spent time in developing countries helping local populations with the issues that were important to them. We have been involved in initiatives started by others such as Buy Nothing Day, promoting freeganism, holding free markets—and everything in between, from campaigning for refugee rights to staging money-burning demonstrations, donating kidneys to strangers, and walking 2000km across the Nullarbor desert in Australia without taking any food or a change of clothes. All of these have helped to emphasise that this Gift Economy works here and now in the real world.

Working for love demonstrates that the traditional economic model is not necessary when our focus is on helping others, and it is fundamental to the Gift Economy.

Accepting Gifts

The Gift Economy is founded on giving, but it inevitably leads to receiving as well. Jesus said, "Give, and it will be given to you: good measure, pressed down, shaken together, and running over will be put into your bosom. For with the same measure that you use, it will be measured back to you." Other religious leaders have called it "sowing and reaping" or simply "giving and receiving."

A practical way of encouraging a Gift Economy is to work on a "no-conditions donation basis." Many people already use this model online, where they offer their music, books, and other digital content in exchange for a donation of any amount or for free, left at the discretion of the person wanting the product or service. We have simply extended this concept into the tangible world by offering our physical goods and services on a donation basis. Because we are working for love, we are willing to give our products, time, and energy for free. If we receive nothing in exchange for what we give we are happy to have given for free, and if we happen to receive a donation, it's a bonus! So, in effect, there is no way that we can actually lose out on the deal!

We accept donations for the books and DVDs that we produce, and because people value the material, we usually receive enough to cover the cost of printing and more. For people who want to purchase our material in bulk, we usually ask them to simply cover the cost of printing or production. This means that our goods and services are very accessible and so it has made it easier for people to share more of our materials with others.

Having said that, we are seeking to move more and more towards developing total independence from cash. We especially value gifts already purchased or that incorporate useful recycled unwanted goods, because these usually represent more time, effort, and care on behalf of the giver.

Accepting gifts is an important ingredient to living out a Gift Economy, but we cannot rely on such gifts. If we do, we can easily be tempted to start worrying about what kind of gifts we receive as a result of our giving, which will hamper our efforts in working purely for love. Ultimately, our faith needs to be in something bigger than ourselves and our strategies for acquiring resources.

Living by Faith

We recognize that a Gift Economy works because, ultimately, that is how God operates. We have freely received from God and so we can freely give. And it is this element of faith that has made the Gift Economy sustainable for us as a community, because we do not always receive as a direct result of our giving. We trust that provision will come when we need it and from ANY source that God chooses to use.

Our community has occasionally experienced what we would regard as "miraculous" provisions. For example, we have had many experiences of having a specific need met about the same time that the need arises, without the giver knowing about the need. We have done numerous experiments of living without money and seen that we have never lacked what we needed.

This invariably gives us renewed faith that God is aware of our situation, and that he won't let us down when HE thinks we really need something. Most of our needs are not met immediately, and sometimes, when we think we need something, there is more to be gained by learning to live without it. But God has also provided for us much more abundantly than we have asked, not just materially but also in rich spiritual experiences that we would not exchange for any amount of money!

We are conscious that not all communities share our Christian convictions. But we encourage all communities that wish to explore a Gift Economy to have faith in Love. Believe that Love is the highest power that exists in the universe, and believe that if our lives are dedicated to serving Love faithfully, then all our needs (material, emotional, and spiritual) will be met.

Moving Forward

We believe that motives play a fundamental role in the kind of society or community that we are presently a part of, and the one that we want to be a part of in the future. If the motives are skewed, the results are going to be skewed. Personal commitment to values that go beyond a materialistic vision of life is essential. We believe that being willing to go without so that others will have enough, sharing what we have with others, trusting that our lives have value, and that God/Love is the means AND the end, are revolutionary ideas that have the power to transform the world in which we live, should we put them into practice.

Many people sense deep down that the way the system is currently structured is not what life is or should be about. Something instinctively tells us all that there must be an alternative. Hearing about the Gift Economy has inspired many to make significant changes in their lives. They don't always choose the same lifestyle as we do, but we have been able to make connections with people who are trying to make sharing and selflessness a bigger priority in their lives, and who are taking steps to disengage from materialism. All of that represents success in our eyes.

As the rest of the world continues at full speed towards a more materialistic and digital model, we continue seeking ways to deepen our understanding and practice of the Gift Economy. Many countries are seeking a "cashless society" where all monetary transactions are digitally recorded and greater restrictions on commerce are put in place. But we are choosing to move towards practicing a "moneyless" model where we don't interact with the monetary system in any way, digital or otherwise. This is, for us, the natural progression to this concept of working for God/Love.

However, we are not the forerunners in this area! A few trailblazers out there have already been living without money for many years! These include Suelo in the US, Mark Boyle in the UK, and Peace Pilgrim, who walked for peace in the US for over 20 years before her death. These are a few examples of a wider movement of people who are moving towards a different economic model than that presented by our current world system.

The great thing about this model is that, in agreement with what Jesus said, this works even with as few as two or three people, so it can get started almost anywhere and any place, and without any infrastructure or set-up costs. Putting love into practice can be done even when you have nothing materially. It just requires faith to believe it and, most importantly, to act on it. 🖎

This article was a collaboration by a few brothers and sisters (including Tina Dunn, primary author) in the Jesus Christian community, who have been living the principles of a gift economy for a few decades. They can usually be found distributing books and DVDs on the streets of Australia, rain, hail, or shine, or cooking a fabulous feast of freshly-found food in their mobile home. They can be contacted at fold@idl.net.au.

The Gift Economy of Standing Rock

By Murphy Robinson

Wood smoke chugging out of winter lodging tents on a -20 degree Fahrenheit morning.

In only a few months, a small encampment of a few Lakota people dedicated to protecting the Missouri River from the Dakota Access Pipeline (DAPL) became the center of international attention, swelled to house up to 14,000 people at its peak in early December 2016, and was supported entirely by volunteers and countless donations of both money and goods.

Many people from around the US and beyond traveled to North Dakota to support this fight for indigenous sovereignty, treaty rights, and environmental justice. Residents of the resistance camps existed within a capitalism-free zone, where nothing was for sale and everything from delicious meals to winter camping gear to expert medical care was available for free.

I first visited Standing Rock in early November 2016, and returned to spend five weeks in late December and January volunteering as a white ally to the indigenous "Water Protectors." I spent my days splitting firewood, cooking meals, installing woodstoves, doing small carpentry projects, shoveling snow, sharpening chainsaws, doing dishes, and—on one rare occasion—livestreaming footage of police violence from the frontlines. During both visits I lived at Oceti Sakowin Camp, the largest of the three Water Protector camps and the location closest to the front lines of the fight against the pipeline. Oceti Sakowin is made up of many smaller camps organized by tribal group and other themes, and I quickly found a home at Two Spirit Nation, a community of two-spirit, queer, and transgender Water Protectors from many different indigenous nations, as well as their non-indigenous allies.

Most of my observations here will center on the deep winter weeks at Oceti Sakowin Camp, when nighttime temperatures regularly hit -25 degrees Fahrenheit, daytime temperatures sometimes failed to creep above zero, and cold winds whipped the open plain. The gift economies of direct action camps and festivals are easier to fathom in warm months, but during this period we all depended on the gift economy for our daily survival in a very real way. It's notable that as of my departure in late January, not one person had died at the camps—compare this to large urban centers in cold states that see regular deaths from hypothermia among the houseless population under similar conditions.

Lin Migiziikwe Gokee-Rindal, an Anishinaabe Water Protector, was impressed with the collaborative culture at the camps. She reflects that she was "touched and inspired by the ways in which the people showed up for each other and how people in close proximity quickly became family. In harsh conditions and under extreme circumstances, a culture of mutual aid and a framework of traditional Lakota values...led to a thriving and close-knit community."

What did this gift economy provide for us?

•**Housing.** The winterized camp consisted of many army tents, wall tents, tipis, yurts, and a few tiny houses and RVs. Nearly all were heated with woodstoves, sometimes supplemented with small propane heaters. Most people slept on cots padded with several sleeping pads. You had to know someone at camp to get housing easily, but in an emergency you could spend one night in the warming tent maintained 24 hours a day near the Medic station. Arctic sleeping bags and endless piles of blankets were readily available for free if you hadn't been able to bring your own. Residents in each structure took turns stoking the woodstove throughout the night.

• **Food.** Some camps had their own kitchens that would cook two or three meals a day, but there were also several public kitchens in the camp that would feed anyone who walked in their doors looking for food. All the kitchens were staffed entirely by volunteers and stocked with donated ingredients. Meat is a staple of the Lakota diet, and I ate many meals of deer, buffalo, and elk meat donated by local hunters and ranchers. Sometimes we'd get a chance to eat Indian Frybread Tacos and other local specialties. At Two Spirit Nation, we had two sizable tents full of canned goods, granola bars, butter and cheese, pasta and crackers, tea and hot cocoa, meat and fish, and endless boxes of winter squash and root vegetables. Much of it was from organic farmers from Maine to Oregon, who had donated their extra crops to support the cause. Even in late January we still had enough food to feed our 15-person camp for another few months...or at least until the first real thaw, when all the frozen meat and produce would go bad.

• **Water.** When it never gets above freezing, liquid water becomes a commodity. A heated water truck would make the rounds of camp most days, and small groups with access to a car would fill up five-gallon jugs offsite. The trick was keeping them unfrozen, so we usually kept them in the living spaces, which we heated around the clock with woodstoves. Melted snow was used only for dishwater, since persistent rumors circulated about harmful chemicals being sprayed in the atmosphere over our camps (as of this writing, there is no reliable scientific evidence to support this).

• **Sanitation.** Oceti Sakowin Camp boasted two composting toilet tents. Each large army tent contained 15 stalls, with two attendants supervising them 24 hours a day. The attendants kept the tent heated with a woodstove, and changed the compost bags when the bucket in a stall got close to being full of sawdust, toilet paper, and human waste. One side of each tent was reserved for "Moon Stalls" where tampons, pads, and baby wipes were always available in each stall. The toilet system was one of the most organized parts of the camp, although exactly where our compost was going to go after it left camp in those nice biodegradable bags remained somewhat mysterious.

• **Security and Fire Response.** An indigenous security team equipped with two-way radios monitored the two gates of camp 24 hours a day, and did patrols around camp. A second Women's Security team was formed in response to several assaults at the camp, and maintained a safe housing space for women and two-spirit people. Three or four times during my stay, we woke in the middle of the night to people yelling "FIRE!" and rushed to the scene of a blazing tipi or shack, probably set afire by poor woodstove management. While these fires were too far along for our small fire extinguishers to make a difference, there was usually a person in full firefighter gear present who could probably have rescued anyone stuck inside. While the victims of these fires generally lost everything, they could easily get a new set of winter clothes and a new arctic sleeping bag from the donations available in camp.

• **Medical Care.** The Medic Wellness Area boasted winterized yurts and tipis for doctors and street medics, herbalists, bodyworkers and acupuncturists, midwives, and mental health workers. All these services were available at no charge. A licensed doctor was usually on duty in the medical yurt, and there were free-for-the-taking stations for herbal tea, fire cider, basic medical supplies, hygiene items, and condoms. At the time when I departed, three healthy babies had been delivered at camp, and the medics had handled countless front-line injuries from rubber bullets, chemical weapons, concussion grenades, and water cannons.

• **Fuel and Firewood.** Firewood was consistently the most sought-after commodity in camp. Somehow regular deliveries of whole logs consistently showed up, and each camp would send a few people with a chainsaw and truck or sled to get wood for the day. The general rule was to cut enough wood for your camp, and then cut some more and leave it for people who didn't have a chainsaw. We all split the wood back at camp, and took turns stocking all the heated structures for the day. Every Saturday a propane truck arrived and filled our empty canisters with fuel for cooking and heating. I suspect these deliveries were paid for out of larger donation funds administered by Oceti Sakowin Camp or the Standing Rock Sioux Tribe.

• **Winter Gear.** Endless bags of donated clothing and bedding arrived at Standing Rock during October, November, and December. Much of it was unsuitable for arctic conditions, but there was enough high-quality gear to outfit the winter crew of Water Protectors (about 600 people) several times over. Anyone could visit the donation tents at any time and take anything they wanted.

• **Tools.** Each smaller camp had an assortment of tools, and there was also a large construction building that would loan out any power tool you could think of as long as you left your ID with them as collateral. They provided everything from electric drills to ladders to chainsaws to a sewing machine. They also had 2x4s, particle board, and screws that you could ask for, and they'd give you what you needed if you could show them a sensible construction plan and materials list.

• **Spiritual Leadership and Ceremony.** There were a few heated gathering spaces of different sizes that hosted everything from daily prayer circles to a huge Christmas Eve dinner with traditional singing and drumming. There were also several sweat lodges that any indigenous spiritual leader could use for the traditional Lakota Inipi ceremony of prayer, healing, and purification.

• **Use Your Imagination...** The abundance of physical donations led to a lot of things being creatively repurposed. My buddy and I cut up donated sweatshirts to make crocheted rugs for the living spaces, and unraveled donated sweaters to produce yarn to knit extra-warm wool underwear. I pulled from the scrap pile outside the construction building to build shelves in our living space, and countless donated blankets were used to seal out the draught in winterized tipis. Whatever you needed, there was probably a way to make it with the tools and materials available at camp.

The gift economy at Standing Rock manifested itself according to the principles of indigenous

Highway sign.

In the warmer months, the Art Tent printed banners and signs for all to use at the actions.

Murphy and Molly installing a woodstove in a tipi.

Murphy and Molly built shelves for storage in winter tents.

culture. The Lakota people name generosity and compassion as two of their core values, and I saw those values in action every day. Much of the system depended on each group taking just enough for their own short-term needs, and leaving the rest for others. At home my instinct is to stockpile what I need for my own survival (two years' supply of dry firewood, etc.), but that sort of strategy has its roots in the questionable idea that individual survival is possible without collective survival. In the capitalist economy of mainstream culture, it's common for one household to thrive while an adjacent one is struggling to meet its basic needs. Houseless people freeze to death huddled next to spacious and luxuriously heated buildings inhabited by more "successful" folks.

In contrast, at Standing Rock we defined success as our collective survival. Therefore we took just the firewood that we needed, checked on the elders every day, brought food and coffee from our kitchen to the compost toilet attendants, and helped anyone who asked us for assistance. This culture of abundance seemed logical and easy in a situation where our needs for survival were simple and a steady flow of money and donated goods was pouring in all the time. I couldn't help but wonder what it would take to create a steady-state gift economy, which could exist without these flows from the outside capitalist world.

When I finally left Standing Rock my friend and I stopped at a co-op food store in Minneapolis to obtain some much-dreamed-of fresh vegetables to munch on. It was such a shock to be asked to pay for food again. It made me wonder what it would take for our larger society to turn its ship around and set a course for a more generous and compassionate form of economy. It seems that these values arise in us spontaneously when a natural disaster hits and we are suddenly in a survival situation, such as Hurricane Katrina in New Orleans or Hurricane Sandy in New York City. The rest of the time, our whole economy depends on a me-first, get-ahead value system based on competition and survival of the fittest (or, in a rigged system like ours, the most privileged). When luxuries and conveniences become symbols of status, we tend to become self-serving.

When people become passionate enough about collective survival, luxuries and conveniences lose their appeal. How can we help each other prioritize our collective well-being? How can we encourage ourselves to expand our definition of "the collective" to include the Lakota concept of "all my relations": the four-leggeds, the winged ones, the stone people, the star people? When we listen to the prayers of indigenous people and orient our values in this ancient way, the path to a truly sustainable gift economy can unfold before us. ❧

For further reading on pre-colonization economic history and gift economy theory, see The Indigenous People's History of the United States by Roxanne Dunbar-Ortiz and Sacred Economics by Charles Eisenstein.

Murphy Robinson is a wilderness guide, hunting instructor, and founder of Mountainsong Expeditions in Vermont. She lives in a Tiny House on a community organic farm in the mountains. You can contact her through her website, www.mountainsongexpeditions.com.

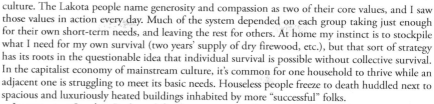

Dawn over the Native Nations flags on Flag Road.

Dawn over Oceti Sakowin camp in January.

Photos courtesy of Murphy Robinson

A World of Possibility:
Communities & Global Transformation

ILLUSTRATIONS: ETHAN HUGHES

"when we dream alone it is just a dream, when we dream together it becomes reality" ~ unknown

By Ethan Hughes and Sarah Wilcox-Hughes

This article is based on a simple premise: What befalls one of us befalls all of us. Can we sit on our cob benches enjoying the beautiful views out our strawbale cabin windows if the world all around us is crumbling? What befalls industrial society befalls intentional communities, cohouses, spiritual centers, and ecovillages. Most of us communitarians are still highly dependent on mainstream society to meet our food, clothing, housing, communication, entertainment, and transportation needs.

In this time of needed change, does the communities movement have the capacity to transform the global economic- military-industrial complex? We are suggesting that the answer is yes, if the movement chooses to become socially and politically involved at a new level.

To ground this article in reality we will offer examples of two communities that demonstrate what a few passionate individuals can accomplish on a local and global level: the Ark of Lanza del Vasto, a 60-year-old community movement in France based on Gandhian nonviolence, and the Possibility Alliance, a one-year-old community in Missouri. We will also give a glimpse as to what society could look like if the communities movement, as a whole, joined in the ruckus! Let us begin this journey in France.

*A small body of determined spirits
fired by an unquenchable faith in their mission
can alter the course of history.*

~MAHATMA GANDHI

I believe in the essential unity of all that lives. Therefore, I believe that if one being rises, the whole world rises with that being, and if one being falls, the whole world falls to that extent.
~MAHATMA GANDHI

The Ark

In 2004, we found ourselves at La Borie Noble, a community of the Ark, a movement founded by Lanza del Vasto in 1948. Several things struck us as unique and radical in contrast to the dozens of communities we had lived in or visited in the United States and Canada.

First of all, the community was far more physically sustainable and land-based than any community we had ever seen. La Borie grew three tons of wheat on site by horse power and made their clothing, pottery, furniture, and tools on site without the use of fossil fuel or electricity. There was no refrigeration; candles provided illumination; and the group had its own dairy, bakery, and hand-powered printing press.

The second thing that struck us was that far more political activism was happening at the Ark than we had ever seen before. One Ark member, Jean-Batiste, was facing 10 years in prison and a 200,000 euro fine for scything GMO crops with Jose Bové, the radical French farmer who "deconstructs" McDonald's whenever he has the opportunity. Their activism reached the front pages of major European newspapers and tens of thousands have rallied behind them. In our 15 months there, we were to re-evaluate what was possible for a single community to achieve.

During the Israel and Lebanon war in 2006, the Ark hosted over 40 Palestinian and Israeli youth for a 10-day reconciliation initiative. The war, the history, the tension, and the conflict were right in front of us, at a time when most Westerners kept a safe and passive distance from the issue, viewing it from the other side of a television, radio, or computer, or not at all. What if

PHOTOS COURTESY OF THE POSSIBILITY ALLIANCE

the communities movement started to open its doors to those from war zones? What if we sat with inner city gangs, soldiers, and prisoners at our dinner table? With this level of interaction, the passive would become active. The "others" would become our friends as they did at the Ark during those 10 days.

The Ark also created a national organization in France to oppose nuclear power and weapons. What if every community headed up an internationally active organization? In 2007, they organized an international peace gathering in India on the 60th anniversary of Gandhi's death. Hundreds of groups from around the world came together to share strategies and to network.

Go and act according to the conclusions you've yourself drawn, and don't waste any more time thinking whether it's difficult or not, ACT.

~VINOBA BHAVE

That is only what is currently happening at the Ark. Over the years they have blocked the expansion of military bases on the Larzac Plateau (which involved over 100,000 people, making it one of the largest acts of nonviolent civil disobedience in French history) and they nonviolently overtook two nuclear power plants. They worked to end the practice of torture during the Algerian war and to end nuclear testing in the South Pacific. The Ark actually perceived (and still perceives, to a large degree) its communities and their self-sufficient cooperative lifestyles not as ends in themselves, but rather as training grounds for Gandhian-style nonviolent peace forces that would change the political shape of France and Europe, leading their movements away from war and oppression toward peace, justice, and equality.

What we need is more people who specialize in the impossible.

~ THEODORE ROETHKE

The Possibility Alliance

In April 2007, we returned to the US by bike, boat, and train to create a community in northeast Missouri with a spirit similar to that which we had experienced in France at the Ark.

(Ironically, since our visit there, internal politics have split La Borie Noble into smaller groups, with the minority, which had been holding the land-based, simplicity aspect of the project, leaving to start a new community. This fracture deepens our own commitment to keep both political activism and simplicity linked, and to do the inner work to transform internal politics into an opportunity for growth and insight).

A small body of determined spirits fired by an unquenchable faith in their mission can alter the course of history.
~MAHATMA GANDHI

ABOVE: The rebuilt 400-year-old hamlet at the Ark of Lanza del Vasto, a 60-year-old community movement based on Gandhian nonviolence in La Borie Noble, France. The tower hosts the bell of mindfulness which rings throughout the day, inviting you into the present moment.

Our community and sanctuary have yet to be named, but we call the overarching organization the Possibility Alliance. Our community has three permanent on-site members plus our infant daughter, Etta Iris. However, we want to include our families and friends who have supported our efforts and made this experiment possible through love, encouragement, networking, financial contributions, and labor.

When you come to the edge of all that you know, you must believe in one of two things— there will be earth upon which to stand, or you will be given wings.

~ UNKNOWN

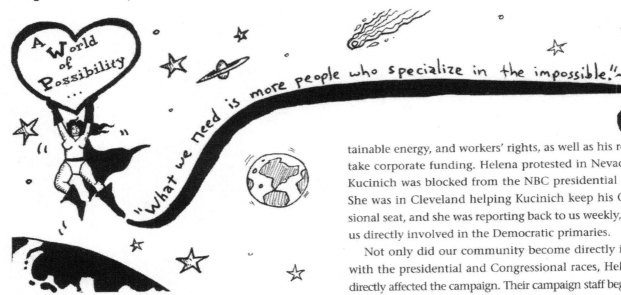

The mission statement of the Possibility Alliance is to work toward the upliftment of all beings, and awaken to our true nature, which we believe is love. See the sidebar on opposite page for The Possibility Alliance's five guiding principles.

Whatever you can do, or dream you can,
begin it. Boldness has genius, power,
and magic in it.

~GOETHE

As we share some of what our experiment has accomplished in one year with three adult members, please keep in mind that our project is bike-powered (car- and petroleum-free), human-to-human communication (computer-free), high on life (substance-free), candle-lit (electricity-free), and is day by day coming closer to the goal of 100% local food (where the small amount we do not produce will come from within 200 miles of the sanctuary). We have already hosted over 200 visitors and have offered several weeklong educational courses to both college and high school students. We supply this background in order to show what is possible with a very small group that is mostly unplugged from the industrial paradigm.

With love even the rocks shall open.

~HAZART INAYAT KAHN

During the first year of the project one of our members, Helena, spent two months volunteering with the Dennis Kucinich campaign for the presidency and for Congress. Our project supports his vision for a Department of Peace, sus-

tainable energy, and workers' rights, as well as his refusal to take corporate funding. Helena protested in Nevada when Kucinich was blocked from the NBC presidential debates. She was in Cleveland helping Kucinich keep his Congressional seat, and she was reporting back to us weekly, keeping us directly involved in the Democratic primaries.

Not only did our community become directly involved with the presidential and Congressional races, Helena also directly affected the campaign. Their campaign staff began using the train for transport instead of flying, taking public buses instead of renting cars, and eating more local and organic foods. These ripples began with Helena's commitment to remain faithful to her lifestyle choices, and her willingness to invite others in to participate with her.

In our own state of Missouri, we have played a key role in starting a community bicycle co-op in our neighboring college town, Kirksville. We have also joined CAPE (Citizens Against Polluting the Environment), which led us to the Missouri Statehouse on a campaign to support local farmers' rights and to oppose the construction of CAFOs (Concentrated Animal Feeding Operations). We participated in Truman State University's symposiums for Peace Week and Earth Week, as well as a climate change sit-in. We led a bike awareness program at the public middle schools in the area. We served at Outreach Mission, a group providing free services

ABOVE: The Strawbale pick-up. (The local farmer was surprised and delighted to have his first bicycling client.) Lots of big trucks beeped and waved on the highway! (Missouri)

38

ABOVE: *Putting up hay into the barn in Missouri (which turned into a hay wrestling match shortly after this photo was taken).*

to the homeless, battered women, and victims of house fires. We joined and worked with FFLPP (Friends for La Plata Preservation), a group which restored the La Plata Amtrak Station and is working to create a cultural center in town. We participate monthly in Critical Mass, a bike ride that occurs in cities and towns around the world the last Friday of every month to promote bicycle rights and ecological awareness. On the local level, we helped a neighbor rebuild his house that burned down, hosted an Amish School on the land, moved an elderly woman to her new home, weeded a neighbor's garden, and continue doing other simple acts that build community.

Our activism also takes place on the land. All three members are war-tax resisters. We choose to live under the poverty line and not contribute finances to the industrial-military-economic complex. We open our doors to anyone at no cost. All are fed and sheltered here with nothing asked in return. All that we do off site, on behalf of the project, is volunteered free of charge. For example, Helena declined a paid position with the Kucinich campaign but chose to work as a volunteer.

We accept donations, but only when they are freely given from a place of gratitude. We believe it is a political act to remove ourselves from the free market (money) economy and to transform it into a gift economy. We give away 20% of all our donations to other projects and people we believe in within the local, state, national, and international arenas. We choose not to be a nonprofit organization and currently have no legal title defining us. This frees up an incredible amount of time and

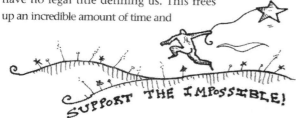

SUPPORT THE IMPOSSIBLE!

EAT POSSIBILITY FOR BREAKFAST!!

The Possibility Alliance Mission Statement

The mission statement of the Possibility Alliance is to work toward the upliftment of all beings, and awaken to our true nature, which we believe is love. The five guiding principles that ground our mission are:

1. Simplicity: continually shrinking our ecological footprint and our needs—this includes striving to provide for our own food, clothing, and shelter through our own labor, and trading for or buying what we cannot yet provide for ourselves, as locally and mindfully produced as we can find

2. Service: outward service on the local, state, national, and international levels, helping individuals, organizations, ecological habitats, societies, and all life-forms in need

3. Nonviolent social and political activism: engagement in the world on behalf of peace, ecological sanity, and justice, even at the risk of imprisonment, physical harm, and suffering in general

4. Inner work: cleansing fear, hatred, impatience, judgment, and greed in ourselves through open communication, meditation, yoga, NVC (nonviolent communication), prayer, laughter, present moment awareness, etc.

5. Celebration: applying the above four principles in a spirit of joy and refusing to be motivated by guilt

Each member of the community spends a minimum of one month per year out in the world participating in social and political change. Each person chooses what s/he is passionate about on the local, state, national, or international level.

avoids weeks of paperwork. Through many generous donations, we recently paid off the 80-acre sanctuary (thanks, friends!).

The above is an incomplete list. Now imagine if all communities and ecovillages made outward activism and service as common as consensus meetings, potlucks, and skinny dipping. There are over 10,000 communities, cohousing groups, ecovillages, spiritual centers, radical farms, and squats in the world—many listed and many under the radar. If the average membership per community is 10, then all of the sudden there is a very large group that could be mobilized for political and social activism. We would guess that the following numbers are conservative estimates. If each community sent its members out in the world for one month doing service and/or activism of the individual's choice, that would be 100,000 people contributing 3,000,000 days a year toward social and political transformation.

Nonviolence is violated by holding on to what the world needs.
~MAHATMA GANDHI

A vision without a task is a dream. A task without a vision is drudgery. But a vision with a task can change the world.
~BLACK ELK

Can we find alternatives to staying within the walls of our communities as the food riots increase, the bombs keep falling, commodity prices soar, the prisons fill, the poverty gap rises, and ecosystems continue to be destroyed?

Our answer at the Possibility Alliance is "YES." We are aware that thousands of individuals from within communities are doing amazing work in the world. What we are proposing is a unified shift in the communities movement where all members would spend some time going out into the world to serve. In order to facilitate such service work, communities could support one another through trainings, skill sharing, financing, and networking. We are not suggesting forcing anyone to do anything, rather offering this idea as an invitation to action.

Can we afford to partially hide in our communities and ecovillages? Is the human world in desperate need? Is life as we know it—all life on this planet—at risk? Do the poor, sick, and disabled have a place at our table? How can members of mainstream society, many of whom are poor and marginalized, believe that the communities movement is a viable option if they are not included and supported?

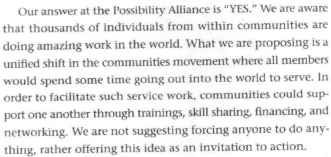

Whoever saves one life, it is as if s/he saved the entire world.
~ TALMUD

The Haul of Justice

There is a final element to our experiment that we would like to share. The Possibility Alliance serves as the umbrella to and headquarters for an international bicycling service group known as the Haul of Justice. Over 500 people have dressed up as their own self-created superheroes, such as Compashman, Huggernaut, Dr. Dharma, The Golden Rule, and Queen Bee.

They have collectively bicycled over 12,000 miles in 23 states, England, Ireland, British Colombia, Thailand, and Mexico, providing over 50,000 hours of community service. The group has also responded to national emergencies such as Hurricane Katrina, sending 40 superheroes to Mississippi and Louisiana—some staying for up to three months in the disaster zone. All of these superheroes are volunteers, and the organization has no official status.

What if every community and ecovillage became the home base for and supported one service organization? This could mobilize millions more people in the communities movement. We are only three and we are doing it. What can an ecovillage of 20 or 40 do?

LEFT: Thirteen of the 56 superheroes who participated on the 2003 Arizona ride (more than the Avengers, Justice League, or the Fantastic Four!).

Gamble everything for love if you're a true human being.

~RUMI

Perhaps this article sounds like a challenge. We write it as a rallying cry to go deeper. The last surge of radicalism in the communities movement was in the early 1970s—the back-to-the-land movement influenced by people like Helen and Scott Nearing. Back then it was radical for professors to become homesteaders. It is not anymore. We believe we need to unify the communities movement and build stronger bridges to mainstream society.

We need direct contact with the disaster areas, inner cities, and war zones. Education, tours, magazines, and websites are useful, but should we be taking greater risks? Do we have the courage to eat with the poor, go to jail, visit the public schools, respond to emergencies, and use our privileges to serve the struggling billions of the world and aide the threatened habitats and species worldwide?

the great and mysterious life force in the universe, the power that sends light from 93 million miles away to grow flowers in the cracks of streets and that launches 50-ton humpback whales out of the sea into the sky. Call it what you like—Great Spirit, Love, the Tao, Buddha Nature, God, Goddess, the unmanifested—it does not matter. This incredible force is real. Tapping into even a tiny bit of this power has allowed us to achieve what we have so far. Trusting in life makes it easier to reduce our cravings for things and set aside some of our personal needs. We find that with so little, we are thriving and laughing often!

Statistically, the probability of any one of us being here is so small that you'd think the mere fact of existing would keep us all in a contented state of dazzlement and surprise.

~LEWIS THOMAS

ABOVE: Oh-Boy and Grateful Green stop to pick blueberries on the Maine Superhero ride.

You say you can't create something original? Don't worry about it. Make a cup of clay so your brother and sister can drink.

~RUMI

We are a tiny one-year-old community, an experiment to see what opening ourselves to love and practicing nonviolence can do. We are imperfect. On many days we are filled with doubt, and fall short of our visions for ourselves and the world. Other days, we are frightened by our light and terrified about living the truth in our hearts. Our experiment, in the end, is not about us. It is about becoming vessels of something bigger—

It is a giant leap, we believe, for most of us to live in community after being raised in a nuclear family in a socially isolating society. We celebrate all that has been done by the communities movement and all that is being done. The question remains...can we do more? Not motivated by guilt or anger, but motivated by love and inspiration? Can we do more while keeping

In dreams and in love there are no impossibilities.

~JANOS ARNAY

our inner peace and balance, enjoying this life and this beautiful world? We at the Possibility Alliance spend plenty of time making music, laughing, singing, weeping, climbing trees, romping about the woods, hooting, playing games, juggling,

DUCKBILLED PLATYPUS + LOCALLY MADE PROPELLER HAT + JAR OF HOMEMADE KIM-CHEE + SLAM POET = WORLD WIDE SPONTANEOUS AWAKENING

☆ TRY YOUR OWN EQUATION OF POSSIBILITY!!!
A PUBLIC SERVICE ANNOUNCEMENT.

face painting, lying in the grass, and dancing. Without all these things, what we are helping to create would be missing the foundation of love and joy upon which we base our work. We believe there is a great opportunity in this moment, a chance for all of us to support one another and live our wildest dreams. ✽

The superhero service bike ride will be crossing Missouri September 15 to October 15, 2008, starting at the Possibility Alliance's sanctuary. If you are interested in joining, please call the superhero hotline at 660-332-4094, or write us at the Possibility Alliance, 28408 Frontier Lane, La Plata, MO 63549.

The Possibility Alliance is interested in creating a network that links communities and ecovillages who are planning or involved in acts of social and political engagement. If you would like to be connected to such a network, please contact us.

Grinnell College students make their first butter during a weeklong local foods course at the Possibility Alliance.

Sarah and Ethan give flying lessons to the youngest Possibility Alliance member, Etta Iris, by the old cedar tree, Missouri.

Ethan Hughes likes to dress up in costumes, draw cartoons, and is willing to do anything for his own and society's transformation. (He even dressed up as a giant penguin and jumped into a frozen lake.) He enjoys bicycles, beets, and reptile watching. He has been bitten by a moray eel, chased by a hippo, and clubbed at the WTO in Seattle. He has also rehabilitated orangutans (it's time) and climbed the world's highest active volcano.

Sarah Wilcox-Hughes loves growing food and flowers, singing opera in rubber boots, and laughing at very high pitches. She enjoys making her own clothes, breastfeeding, and experimenting with goat cheese recipes. She has played fiddle in an Irish Jig Band, biked across Ireland dressed as a superhero, and swum with whale sharks.

Our thanks to Victoria Albright, Sarah's mom and a superhero in her own right, who converted the original handwritten manuscript of this article into digital form, contributed suggestions, and used her email account to help it see the light of day in Communities.

"great souls and how they should be. Become one yourself."
"waste no more time talking about"
~Marcus Aurelius

POCSHN co-organizers.

POCSHN conference 2015.

POCSHN co-organizers.

Photos courtesy of Deseree Fontenot

Moving Beyond Diversity Towards Collective Liberation: Weaving the Communities Movement into Intersectional Justice Struggles

By Deseree Fontenot

Struggles for equitable land-use and affordable housing have intensified across the country at an unprecedented rate in recent years. Decades of extractive urban renewal policies[1] and the entry of predatory financial institutions[2] into real estate markets have resulted in waves of displacement, gentrification, and housing insecurity for low income communities and communities of color in urban, suburban, and rural areas.

How can the Communities Movement address the suburbanization of poverty, the gentrifying face of the urban inner city, and the stark economic challenges of rural and agrarian communities? With a historical lack of racial, socioeconomic, and cultural diversity in the dominant narrative of intentional communities, what interventions might be necessary to make this movement more impactful in a time of great social and ecological crises? How could an entire discourse about collective placemaking and modeling ecologically sustainable lifeways be strengthened by a grounded racial and economic justice analysis and practice? What would it take to build a more accountable and expansive Communities Movement that is grounded in deeply intersectional justice work? How might we proliferate radically inclusive models of community, land stewardship, and governance that transform our relationships to land, place, home, and each other?

These are some of the questions that the People of Color Sustainable Housing Network[3] (POCSHN) has been tackling in our organizing work over the last three years in the San Francisco Bay Area. POCSHN is a resource network for self-identified people of color (POC) interested in building intentional, healthy, collective, and affordable housing communities in the Bay Area and beyond. The network was established in response to extreme increases in housing costs, rapid gentrification, and the lack of racial and socioeconomic diversity in the predominant intentional community, cooperative, and cohousing movements around the country. Our central vision is to create an entire ecosystem of cooperatively-controlled POC-centered communities that are ecologically, emotionally, spiritually, and culturally regenerative spaces.

POCSHN was founded in February of 2015 by long-time Bay Area residents, Tavi Baker and Lailan Huen. It started as a Meetup Group—

hosting events, trainings, and field visits to cohousing, cooperative, and farm sites that were primarily led or owned by people of color. Since our first day-long POC Sustainable Housing Convening in August of 2015, we have brought together groups and individuals passionate about collective land acquisition, cooperative living, and co-ownership models. Our efforts also include educational workshops at local and national convenings (including a keynote address at the 2016 West Coast Communities Conference), community study groups, and strategic partnerships with vision-aligned organizations including the Sustainable Economies Law Center[4] (SELC) and our fiscal sponsor, the Northern California Land Trust[5] (NCLT).

POCSHN has grown to become an intergenerational project with six core organizers (mostly volunteer-based) and a 1,200-person broader member base. Our time doing this work has made it abundantly clear that people are hungry for cooperative solutions to the housing crisis and want to be a part of shaping them.

Our efforts are POC-centered (though not exclusive) because our aims are to support communities on the front lines of racialized violence in the work of creating and reclaiming spaces that honor our historical legacies of survival, resistance, and ancestral placemaking practices. Many people have come to our network with horror stories about navigating white-dominated collective houses, cooperatives, communities, and other institutions—stories of unexamined power dynamics, tokenism, and problematic expectations rooted in a lack of ongoing personal and collective engagement with issues of race, class, and other types of identity formation that shape our lives.

It is important to acknowledge that building meaningful alliances across difference is hard work and is a particularly intimate task to come home to in community. However it is the deepest work we must do in order to enable a politics of solidarity to blossom into action. The work of cultivating skills in nonviolent communication, community governance, and effective responses to conflict must go hand-in-hand with the work of examining and transforming our relationships to wealth, land, and power. POCSHN is committed to building a narrative around community co-ownership that interweaves these frameworks—with the hope of co-creating and sustaining cooperative living and co-ownership projects that are rooted in grassroots efforts to bring about more sustainable ways of relating to people and the planet.

Over the last three-plus years of organizing, we have encountered and incepted a number of visionary strategies that we believe are worth replicating and supporting within the Communities Movement. Here are three key strategies we recommend engaging to deepen your community's work on issues of race, class, and privilege:

1. Study Up!

There are many resources out there that unravel histories of settler colonial violence, labor extraction, discriminatory urban planning, radical land-based resistance movements, cooperative and community land trust history, and more! At the end of this article is a list of resources to check out on issues of displacement, national movements, and land histories. Use these resources as jumping-off points for conversation within your community. Folks should also engage the breadth of work out there on anti-oppression praxis, including the Catalyst Project[6] and Showing Up For Racial Justice[7]. Collective study and discussion is one way we can build shared understandings of the complex past and present that we are all accountable to and more holistic visions of the futures we seek to create.

2. Engage in Redistributive Politics

The radical redistribution of wealth, land, and power is key to creating the world we want to live in. There are community projects doing this work at various scales and it's worth looking at one community trend here. POCSHN has been in contact with a few different long-time rural and semi-rural intentional community projects that have engaged in the work of redistributing some of their land to people-of-color-led collectives. While I don't have permission to mention them directly in this article, I believe that this could be one way of approaching questions of diversity for groups who may have started off as a fairly homogenous bunch who now wish to expand their membership, rather than the usual "add and stir" inclusion model where a few folks who carry marginalized identities are admitted. Let's instead work towards models that put forth a greater shift in governance and representation.

3. Support Radical Financing Models

With the cost of land and housing skyrocketing in many areas around the country, it is more important than ever that we invest in financing models that build community-wide assets and long-term permanently affordable spaces that are out of the grips of the speculative market and into the hands of the people. A couple really awesome efforts we would like to share: The Sogorea Te' Land Trust established the Shuumi Land Tax[8] for non-Indigenous people who live in traditional Chochenyo and Karkin Ohlone territory to make a voluntary annual financial contribution to their critical community work of bringing land back into Indigenous stewardship. Secondly, Liberating 23rd Ave Community Building[9], a long-time, low-rent community building in East Oakland, ran a successful crowdfunding campaign to help collectively purchase their multi-use building.

What's Next for POCSHN?

POCSHN is launching two exciting initiatives in the coming year: The

East Bay Permanent Real Estate Cooperative (EBPREC) and the Community Co-Ownership Initiative[10].

In partnership with the Sustainable Economies Law Center, we formed the East Bay Permanent Real Estate Cooperative, an umbrella project that is a California cooperative corporation that can raise capital through multiple small investments, keep land permanently affordable, and provide a limited equity appreciation model for residents. For more information about this exciting initiative, visit the EBPREC website, www.ebprec.org.

The Community Co-Ownership Initiative is a partnership between the Northern California Land Trust and POCSHN, along with other members of the Bay Area CLT Consortium[11] (BACCLT) to diversify and expand access to shared ownership and resident-controlled housing through leadership training, development of new financing tools, and technical support. The partnership leverages the technical expertise and stewardship knowledge of NCLT with the broad reach and engagement of POCSHN's diverse grassroots membership. As POCSHN's fiscal sponsor, we are partnering with NCLT to build joint organizational capacity, cultivate prospective and existing cooperative resident groups, and establish new sites for permanently affordable housing across the Bay Area.

If you are interested in helping to grow, connect with, and support the work of POC Sustainable Housing Network, please visit our website at www.pochousingnetwork.com.

Resources to Explore on Land Justice:
Urban, Rural, and Suburban Issues

Land Justice: Reimagining Land, Food and the Commons in the United States: foodfirst.org/land-justice-re-imagining-land-food-and-the-commons

Revolutionary Urban Spaces: Study Group Reading List: docs.google.com/document/d/1lXTqmEO28UeqWoQrckv8IdmPl8QyQtVzDvLiPQrbevs/edit?usp=sharing

Right to the City Alliance: righttothecity.org

Urban Displacement Project: www.urbandisplacement.org

Sogorea Te' Land Trust: sogoreate-landtrust.com

Suburbanization of Poverty: "The Changing Geography of US Poverty": www.brookings.edu/testimonies/the-changing-geography-of-us-poverty

"Housing Challenges in Rural America Persistent, on the Rise": nlihc.org/article/housing-challenges-rural-communities-persistent-rise

Down on the Farm: Wall Street: America's New Farmer: www.oaklandinstitute.org/sites/oaklandinstitute.org/files/OI_Report_Down_on_the_Farm.pdf

Movement Generation: Justice & Ecology Project: movementgeneration.org

Arc of Justice (film): www.arcofjusticefilm.com—documentary about New Communities, Inc., the first community land trust in the US that was created by black farmers in the face of land loss and discrimination. ✍

Deseree Fontenot is a co-organizer of the People of Color Sustainable Housing Network (www.pochousingnetwork.com). She is a farmer, scholar, and activist based in Oakland, California. Deseree holds an interdisciplinary Masters of Arts in Social Transformation from Pacific School of Religion where she focused on ecology, African-diasporic spiritual traditions, and geographic histories of food and land-based movements. She is passionate about transforming relationships to food, land, and place by addressing land access, tenure, and pathways to community co-ownership.

---

1. www.overgaardtonnesen.dk/TEKSTERNE/09-Weber-Extracting-Value-from-the-City.pdf
2. www.antievictionmap.com/wallstreet
3. www.pochousingnetwork.com
4. www.theselc.org
5. nclt.org

6. collectiveliberation.org
7. www.showingupforracialjustice.org
8. sogoreate-landtrust.com/shuumi-land-tax
9. www.youcaring.com/thetenantsandthecommunity-773671
10. www.pochousingnetwork.com/projects
11. www.bacclt.org

Active Communities:
Why working towards improving our world should be a defining part of any intentional community

By Michael Kenny

Living justly and in harmony with the planet has been a key component of many intentional communities. Many who are attracted to the intentional community lifestyle have themselves been social, community, or environmental activists. Yet we often fail to define intentional communities as vehicles for social change outside of the context of the personal lifestyle changes of members living in our communities. Intentional communities themselves possess great potential in providing the resources needed for an individual or group to give back to the wider community, be it through social enterprise, activism, or volunteerism. An intentional community can facilitate greater social and environmental change by providing space for meetings, offices, and storage for local nonprofits and activist organizations, acting as a local hub for environmentalists and social justice activists, and having on-site residents and visitors available as activists and volunteers. Intentional communities can even act as green business incubators, housing social enterprises or worker cooperatives.

When a group of us formed the Toronto Ecovillage Project back in 2004, having a strong social justice aspect for our group and our future community was essential to us, though it was never defined or explicit. When our group re-formed in 2009, I and the other activists involved decided that we needed to be explicit about the kind of community we were trying to create. We sought to define our vision through the creation of a new term, in order to avoid confusion with other established concepts of intentional communities. The term we came up with was **Active Community**.

An active community can be defined as the following:

1. Sustainability. An active community is designed to be environmentally, financially, and socially sustainable.

2. Active. Members of the community are active within the community, and the greater neighbourhood, municipality, and region where the community resides. They are active in making the world a better place, be it through activism, volunteerism, advocacy, politics, social enterprise, or through environmentally and socially sustainable living. Such communities also provide resources or assist those engaged in being active, whether it is activism, social enterprise, or the like. Such communities are active at making a better world.

3. Community. The community is designed to maximize a sense of community and encourage socialization. Community members should have a proven history or desire for involvement, and continued involvement is either encouraged or required. Opportunities for socialization are maximized through on-site facilities and community planning of events.

4. An active community is **not limited by its size**. An active community can be as small as a house, or as large as a neighbourhood, town, or city. The work of Jane Jacobs, who believed that you require higher population density to provide a vibrant community life, has inspired our vision. Many proponents of ecovillages and cohousing argue a case for smaller-scale communities. We, however, believe community can occur at any scale.

5. Encourage healthy living. Food, fitness, and safety are required for healthy living. Urban agriculture, community supported agriculture, and farmers' markets can provide affordable, healthy, and locally grown food options. A communal kitchen with optional meal plans should be an option offered. All food should be organic if feasible, with vegetarian and vegan meal options. Physical fitness should be encouraged through the creation of on-site fitness facilities and proximity to parks and recreation trails. Sites chosen should be free or cleaned of any potential contamination, and all building materials and cleaners used in the building should be free of chemicals. The community should adopt a chemical-free living policy based on the precautionary principle, restricting the use of chemicals and smoking within the community.

Many existing intentional communities could fit this description, whether or not they describe their community as having an activist focus. The growth of the intentional communities movement in the past two decades has created numerous new communities. For an activist such as myself, it is important to make the distinction that the community I am to be a part of actively commit to making the world outside the immediate community a better place. As new communities are formed in the future, I hope more communities will commit to activism, social enterprise, and similar endeavours, and that those communities will be distinct by defining themselves as active communities. ❧

Michael Kenny is Executive Director of Regenesis (www.theregenesisproject.com) and Co-Coordinator of the Toronto Ecovillage Project and Toronto Social Justice Centre.

An Inspiring Journey in Ecovillages

By Nébesna Fortin

I was born in an ecovillage in Canada, La Cité Écologique, where I got the chance to be involved as much as possible in all aspects of the community. Starting at the high school level, we were invited to participate in one or many businesses that interested us. We could enroll in internships and practical hands-on learning classes in all areas: cooking, accounting, sewing, gardening, and others. We were invited to manage and do all the planning of great projects like the preparation of a meal for all members each week, creating a theater play by getting younger kids involved, and so on.

One of our projects was to take care of three greenhouses. Yes, it was a big challenge, and yes, at one time, all the plants burnt in the sun and were flooded the week after! Now, I can imagine how confident and patient the adults were, who sacrificed the production of three greenhouses, the plants, and all this growing space, for the only result of giving us a formidable learning experience. When my class graduated, we went to Europe. Having some friends living in France, we visited the area and decided to visit some other ecovillages such as Damanhur in Italy and Sieben Linden in Germany. At that time I discovered myself and my aspiration of creating more bridges between existing ecovillages, but it was still pretty blurry and just a dream.

At 18 years old, I was given the opportunity of becoming the kitchen manager for our ecovillage. I was happy to have this great chance, and once more, I admired the devotion and acceptance of the adults who let me have my experiences and take assurance in this managing position, while always being there to support me. This was one unique and precious opportunity to really get involved in my ecovillage. Later that year, we created a partnership with an intentional community in California, Ananda Village. This project also had businesses and a school and we did an exchange program with them. It was an eye-opening opportunity, getting to talk with young adults who had a similar childhood. We connected quickly, becoming best friends. We were sharing so many experiences, re-

flections, and dreams. It make me realise there was a bunch of like-minded people wishing for and working toward a better society. As the years passed by, I was called to change jobs and eventually was involved in public relations. It then became clearer that I wanted to create links between ecovillages in order to better support each other. I also wished to see more youth involved in the development of ecological and community-based projects.

It's been five years now since I started coordinating the internship program and the touristic aspect of La Cité. Through those years I have been able to visit many other communities and ecovillages. In the fall of 2012, with a group of high school kids, I traveled to inspiring communities such as The Farm, Sirius, and Earthaven in the US. Then an important step of my journey started in 2013 with a meeting in Schweibenalp (Switzerland) were I was introduced to NextGEN. This great group within the Global Ecovillage Network is working to connect the next generation to the ecovillage movement. It was so energising to meet with those active young adults coming from all over the globe. It made me feel part of an important worldwide family. I joined NextGEN NA core team, and later that year, traveled to Twin Oaks and Acorn for an FIC meeting. At the end of that same year the Ecovillage Network of Canada annual general meeting convened at Whole Village in Ontario. All was getting clearer: we needed more people informed about what those communities are experiencing. The lessons learned in all those micro-societies could be beneficial to so many more people wanting to be involved in this transformative movement.

My aspiration of getting more and more involved in sharing the ecovillage lifestyle with youth brought me to become involved with Gaia Education. As a NextGEN representative I wish to create learning opportunities for youth to explore their full potential and co-create community in their day-to-day environment. The Ecovillage Design Education (EDE) course offered by Gaia Education seems to me one of the best ways of making this happen. Once more I was brought to Europe, and this time to the oldest ecovillage, Findhorn, to participate in the EDE training. Wow! Being there was so energising! I could

Photos courtesy of Nébesna Fortin

feel the support; the work invested in the creation of something new, something big.

During my stay, I came across people from so many great initiatives: there was the New Story Summit just getting finished, then the Circle Project core-team meeting and the different EDE participants who were starting their communities and networks. There was a girl from a Native tribe who was studying to become a lawyer in order to protect and support the transition for her community. There were also mayors and delegates from villages and towns wishing to engage in the creation of sustainable politics for their municipalities. It confirmed for me that the time for change has come—that if all of us realize how many people are out there, moving toward a more sustainable lifestyle, we will no longer feel alone.

Having visited over 16 communities across Europe and the Americas, I can think of some divergences and preferences, but most of all, I can see the common thread of people working to create a better world. Indeed, I have a natural preference for La Cité Écologique ecovillage, since it is my home, but the beauty lies in diversity. I strongly believe there is not one unique perfect formula for sustainability, but a million. A million perfect ways of doing it right, of living in the respect of all living beings, of honoring uniqueness within all of us.

Back at La Cité, with a group of friends and the support of all our community, we set up a learning center and in July 2015 we offered the first Canadian EDE. Now I can say that the first step in this incredible journey is done. It is the starting point of the next one. It is the beginning of sharing what is going on in the ecovillage movement and getting new people involved in the creation of new community-based ecological initiatives.

I can't wait to meet more great people, living their dreams, building together the world they wish to pass on to the next generation. May our paths meet, may your journey be safe, sprinkled with joy, laughter, and love. 🍃

Nébesna Fortin works for the CAP Eco-Community Learning Center (www.cape-cocommunautaire.org), lives at La Cité Écologique (www.citeecologique.org/index2), and is the NextGEN North America representative for Canada (www.nextgenna.org).

Therapeutic Community: A Century at Gould Farm

By Steven K. Smith

Gould Farm.

It was a warm August morning at Gould Farm's Roadside Store and it promised to be a hot, busy day. Though it was only mid-morning, beads of sweat were forming on my brow and my cooking apron sported half-dried blots of pancake mix. This morning I was assisting a client (or "guest" in Gould Farm parlance) I'll call Jeff as he made an omelet. Both Jeff and I were hoping, after weeks of practice, that this day Jeff would make his public debut on the grill.

Diagnosed with a major mental illness, Jeff had come to the Farm several months before. He had not started in the stressful environment of Roadside, but rather began developing basic work skills by raking leaves, tending a greenhouse, making maple syrup, or participating in one of dozens of opportunities Gould Farm made available.

Like most guests, Jeff was likely referred to the Farm by a psychiatrist. While at the Farm Jeff, like all guests, had contact with one of several social workers who lived on the Farm, learned about medications from the Farm's registered nurse, and saw one of two psychiatrists who regularly visited the Farm. But his contacts were not limited to professional and administrative staff. Jeff would have worked with individuals his own age, perhaps a volunteer with Brethren Volunteer Service, or from another volunteer agency, with no professional training in mental health. He may have worked with a recent college graduate interested in organic farming, which Gould Farm practices. Gould Farm guests benefit from both those who are clinically aware

Photos courtesy of Steven K. Smith

Roadside Store.

of their problems and those who relate to guests as peers.

Work and social skills were often lost to those, like Jeff, stricken with mental illness in young adulthood. Re-learning or learning those skills for the first time was and is the essential gift the Farm imparts extraordinarily well to its guests. The Farm's Roadside Store was the next-to-final step within the Gould Farm agenda, before one considered moving on to the Farm's more independent, Boston-area programs.

A guest's first Roadside job was usually washing dishes or waiting tables; then later, for some, working the cash register—or possibly working the grill. Making anything, but particularly an omelet, on a small grill in a quick-paced environment, is a precarious enough balancing act, especially when cheese, sprouts, and other ingredients are added. What ingredients are added first? Last? For anyone, but especially for those with major thought disorders, producing an item to be consumed and purchased

---

Re-learning or learning work and social skills for the first time is the essential gift the Farm imparts to its guests.

---

could be overwhelming. Many customers in August came from among the thousands of tourists from Boston, New York, and elsewhere, who fled the cities for the Berkshires to enjoy Tanglewood, Jacob's Pillow, and other venues for the arts and culture. A Hollywood actress was said to frequent Roadside. At times (although this was far from the case) it felt like the store was catering to all the tourists at the same time!

The store is located on Rt. 23 a few miles outside the village of Monterey, and about two miles from the Farm's central hub. While a 2004 issue of *Bon Appetit* had cited Roadside as having one of the best breakfasts in the country, its reputation was already well established in the region. Thus, there was not only a reputation to maintain but also, within the Gould Farm enterprise, a mission to accomplish—assisting primarily young adults to cope with persistent mental illness.

Gould Farm acquired the Roadside Store in 1976, but the Farm itself had a much longer history. One of the nation's oldest, if not the oldest, psychiatric rehabilitation facilities, it was founded by William and Agnes Gould and several of their close family members in 1913. Informed by a Christianity that was neither sectarian nor doctrinaire, yet steeped in the Sermon on the Mount, the Goulds had finally realized their dream, attempted about seven times earlier in as many sites, to establish a haven for those suffering in mind and circumstance. First, inner city children arrived on the Farm, followed by others with different and at times more severe situational or addiction-related conditions. The 1950s ushered in the advent of psychotropic medications

Gould Farm.

that allowed a seriously impaired population to meet the minimum requirements of work and community, skills that they may not have had without these medications. (I thank Anna Melinda Duhon's 2003 Harvard Bachelor's thesis for this insight.)

To its credit, the Farm decades later did not forget inner-city kids when it invited African American youngsters from the Atlanta area to live at the Farm for a number of weeks during the turbulence caused by the Atlanta Child Murders (1979-1981). Further back, the Farm had helped Vietnamese refugees in the 1970s and, back even earlier, German Jewish and other refugees during the 1930s and 1940s. Most recently, the Farm hosted a family that lost a loved-one in Iraq. Indeed, the Farm has a distin- guished history responding to world crises while helping those at the Farm.

For almost 100 years Gould Farm's relative "success" addressing the needs of its guests, like Jeff, has been due, I believe, to avoiding a monolithic approach toward treatment while embracing meaningful work and social engagement in a community setting. As a former Executive Director put it almost 30 years ago:

> The mode of our life together is "working with," "playing with," "celebrating with," "eating with," "sharing with," "suffering with"—all of the things that hap- pen when a number of people live in close proximity. We do not see ourselves as therapists, but we consider our life together as "therapeutic" in the deepest sense of the word—tending toward healing and new and independent life. We do not have work-therapy, but we work; we do not have occupational therapy, but we make things and learn skills; we do not have music therapy, but we sing and play instruments... We do not have therapies as compartmentalized activities, but—by intention at least—the whole life of the community encapsulates what is meant by the term therapy.[1]

The therapeutic power of intentional community (or any environment with strong social ties) is that it attacks a major byproduct of mental illness: social isolation.

Before I continue with the story of Jeff and the omelet, I need to back up and add a couple historical and personal notes. About a year before working with Jeff I had returned to Gould Farm as a full-time staff while studying law part-time in Springfield, Massachusetts, about 60 miles east. I had grown up at the Farm in the `70s and `80s when my father was its Executive Director and my mother, the Farm's psychiatric nurse; both left in the early 1990s. I returned there thinking I knew the

place intimately. The Berkshire Hills were as exquisitely beautiful as I remem- bered them decades past. About 500 of the Farm's roughly 650 acres were still wooded and wild, with the remains of old stone walls running through the woods, disappearing then reemerging like the veins in the weathered hand of a New England farmer. One could still lose oneself in the seclusion of the woods, yet with a short walk in any direction find a familiar landmark.

The roughly 100 acres of cleared land still hosted the Farm program; its nucleus was still the 200-year-old behemoth of a colonial house (with additions added through the years), called Main House,

1. Smith, Kent D. "Gould Farm: Rehabilitation Through Intentional Community." Paper presented at the International Association of Psycho-Social Rehabilitation. May 29, 1981.

2. Infield, Henrik F. 1955. *The American Intentional Communities: Study on the Sociology of Cooperation.* Glen Gardner, New Jersey: Glen Gardner Community Press. Pg. 79.

Main entrance leading into Gould Farm.

which housed the administrative offices and kitchen and in which people still ate and square danced together. Clustered around Main House were the maple syrup house, the dozen or so cabins tucked in the woods, and a sauna. Indeed little physically had changed. Programmatically there were some differences. Community lifestyle changes, however, were happening in front of me.

How a community like the Farm adapts to outer cultural and societal change is a phenomenon that fascinates me and one I try to understand. How, I would ask myself, does a community pass on traditions and which traditions does it choose to pass on, and why? How was the Farm allowing cultural and societal changes to affect its program? Whatever the answers, the Farm seemed to be carefully synthesizing the old and the new or, with sensitivity, replacing old ways with new ways. I came to believe these changes were not jeopardizing the Farm's therapeutic model.

For example, the standard five-days-a-week evening, family-style meal I remembered was now down to a couple days a

week, the rest being buffet style. This change in itself may not have been programmatically significant, but communal meals were significant in maintaining a family-like atmosphere in which people felt welcomed and were missed if not at the table. Sociologist Henrik F. Infield noted the importance of communal dining at Gould Farm in the 1950s: "All (Gould Farm) activities are essentially optional, including work as well as attendance at regular Sunday morning services...*The only regularity that, for obvious reasons, must be insisted upon is attendance at meals.* [Emphasis added.] These are all taken in common, with the exception of breakfast which some of those who live in the cottages may arrange to have at home. The seating of the guests is not left to chance, but is planned with some care, especially in cases that need attention."[2] Infield likely saw that the consistency of the family-style meals distinguished the Farm from "any mental hospital or sanatorium."

We did not lose our communal soul by changing from primarily family-style to buffet-style meals. We were still eating together and guests and staff still found fellowship at meals.

Did perceptions of efficiency and convenience lead to implementing more buffets? Did buffets threaten semblances of family cohesion and order often found around the dinner table? More buffets may have brought benefits that I did not appreciate. Personally, I missed more family-oriented meals, but realized there might have been demands on the community that required this and other changes. I also began to realize, from actually living in community, the obvious: that a community cannot be, and does not remain, static. New ideas are often implemented, perhaps discarded, and sometimes reincorporated in more meaningful ways.

The appearance of outside consultants is also a somewhat new phenomenon at the Farm. Perhaps changes in Executive Director tenancy (now more trained in fields other than theology) has allowed this trend to emerge. My sense is that these developments are not in themselves problematic. Indeed, an outside perspective is often needed and sought. But such perspectives bring challenges. The Farm witnessed the removal of after-dinner desserts based on one consultant's perceptions that the Farm's kitchen staff was overstretched. What this consultant might not have predicted was that shorter meals, as I and some others thought, may have meant people spending less time together in an important community function. Despite some mild protest, community members desired this change, noting the health benefits of having fewer sweets. Desserts were eliminated from evening meals, yet today, without desserts, community members do in fact still socialize around the dining room tables long after meals formally end.

Wider staff participation, beyond the Executive Director, in administrative decision-making has been more pronounced recently than in the past. This, I believe, is a healthy trend, a moving away from what some may have considered a more vertical or hierarchical

Main House.

model. Where once the Executive Director, with the Board's backing, made policy decisions, new ideas are now often circulated between committees. Differing views are reconciled in committee then, after further vetting, given back to the Executive Director. But "horizontal hierarchy" poses its own challenges; groups, rather than an individual, may then speak for an institution and be as prone to inflexibility as their "vertical" counterpart.[3] Gould Farm, like many organizations, has tried different styles of leadership depending on the challenges confronting the Farm at any given time. What has worked or been thought to have worked in the past may not be appropriate for the present.

Another challenge Gould Farm now faces is the loss of an elder population. The last remaining elder died in March 2010, at age 99; she had come to the Farm in 1930. Executive Directors in the past had often drawn from an elder's wisdom that, until about 20 years ago, was as rich and diverse in background as the Farm's general population. The term "elder," when I was a child at the Farm, was typically reserved only for those who arrived at the Farm before about 1940. I am thinking, fondly, of two women who came to the Farm before Will Gould's death in 1925. Both died on the Farm in 1985. (Their children and grandchildren now sit on the Gould Farm Board.) The Farm's present elder population arrived at the Farm in the late 1970s or mid 1980s, a still notable tenancy; most had little contact with the early Gould Farm pioneers.

The diminishing of this population may deprive a community of guidance through difficult times; without them, new leaders lack an important source of organizational history. Elders remind us that what we think is new has actually been tried before; at the same time, elders sometimes look backward instead of forward. Nevertheless, they often encourage leaders and others to take new routes toward organizational goals consistent with a community's mission. Their passing may also jeopardize multi-generational dimensions of community. Gould Farm, I believe, understands the implications of fewer elders and is responding accordingly.

Another challenge for any community is handling staff expectations of the meaning of "community." What Gould Farm *is*—or what some think the Farm *was*—varies beyond its 1992 Statement of Mission which, in part, reads:

Steeped in the tradition of social service and spiritual fellowship envisioned by

---

3. See Browning, Don S. "Religion and Civil Society in James Luther Adams, Abraham Kuyper, and Catholic Social Teachings. *Criterion.* Spring/Summer 2010.

4. Sacks, Oliver. "The Lost Virtues of the Asylum." *New York Review of Books.* Vol. 56, No. 14. September 24, 2009.

Various barns on the Farm property.

its founder, and reaching out in an ever changing world to those suffering in mind and spirit, Gould Farm's mission is to help the people who come here find the inner strengths and outer resources needed to meet the challenges that life imposes. The Farm seeks to provide a family-like community within which all members can find respite and draw strength while respecting the individuality and dignity of all.

For some staff, the Farm is the embodiment of a long-sought ideal of community, while for others, illusions of "community" are shattered when the Farm fails certain of their communal or therapeutic expectations. Such expectations sometimes, though infrequently, lead toward personal discontent and dissent leading to departures. Cycles of enthusiasm and disillusionment concurrently repeat within any community, something familiar to those acquainted with community dynamics. (It is during times of change that elders may be especially important in maintaining and interpreting an organization's mission.)

Any institution that revels in past glories or accomplishments while ignoring current realities fast becomes obsolete. Gould Farm does not so revel, but remains rooted in its past. We are not without our own challenges but we are addressing these challenges. We rightfully cheer, with a healthy sense of pride, that we are the oldest therapeutic community in the United States, but this means little if we are not creative in our endeavors or if we fail to maintain what so many observers and community members notice as our signature, communal value: kindness.

Both the academic and therapeutic worlds and the popular press have recognized Gould Farm's approach toward treating those with persistent mental illness. *Bon Appetit* has acknowledged our pancakes at Roadside and Dr. Oliver Sacks has noted our therapeutic programs in the *New York Review of Books*.[4] In 2005 Former Gould Farm Nurse Nancy Smith and current Gould Farm Director John Otenasek helped launch Crossing Creeks, a therapeutic community in Rockingham County, Virginia, inspired by the Gould Farm model. Although that project was short-lived, Harrisonburg-based Mennonite visionary and activist Ron Copeland helped a nonprofit acquire Crossing Creeks and, under a different name, it is still used for a similar purposes. Former Gould Farm Treasurer Virgil Stucker has initiated successful programs inspired by Gould Farm in Virginia, Michigan, and, more recently, CooperRiis, in North Carolina.

The late Gould Farm Director and Harvard Divinity School professor, James Luther Adams, noted this about Gould Farm: "[A] community of this sort cannot grow in wisdom and stature without taking inventory from time to time... In the Gould Farm of the future there will be, as in the past, new treasures as well as old. Indeed, without new treasures, the old ones are themselves likely to disappear... Gould Farm cherishes its past, but it also moves venturingly into the burgeoning present." This balancing and synthesis of the past and present remain challenges for Gould Farm.

So, what finally happened with Jeff and the omelet? The heat of that August day did not disappoint. As noted earlier, we had spent the prior weeks in "training," during which time Jeff and I had broken down the omelet making process into small steps. Now it all came together and Jeff later that day did make breakfast, without assistance, for a satisfied customer. In so doing Jeff, despite his illness, was able to function in a highly stressful environment and was able to take the skills he learned at Gould Farm with him to the Farm's Boston program. Community, committed staff, expectation of work in increasingly demanding settings, and plenty of support all made this possible, and make this possible every day at Gould Farm. ❧

Steven K. Smith is an Investigator at the Winchester Office of the Public Defender, Winchester, Virginia. He serves on the Gould Farm Board of Directors and is a member of the Winchester chapter of the National Alliance on Mental Illness. He has written for the Mennonite Quarterly Review *and* Latin American Perspectives. *The views in this article do not reflect those held by the Gould Farm administration or the Farm's Board of Directors. He may be reached at stevenks2003@yahoo.com.*

He thanks Larry Abrams and Catherine McKee Mendelsohn for comments on prior drafts of this article. He also thanks Professors Calvin Wall Redekop and Charles A. Miller for their friendship and conversation around this and related topics.

Camphill:
Working with Special People

By Diedra Heitzman and Jan Martin Bang

Collecting the eggs.

Many issues cry out for solutions in the world today: devastating agricultural practices and food distribution systems that fail to provide for much of the earth's population while wasting usable food; water shortages and pollution; and the end of many ecosystems in their current form. Water, like oil, may well be the cause for wars within this generation. Old forms of leadership, governance, and organization fail, and there are huge disparities of resources, financial and otherwise, in country after country. Civil discourse gives way to anger and hatred. Is mental illness on the rise? What is mental health in a time of increasing stress and insecurity?

Relating to these realities can create a profound sense of distress. Yet real work toward solutions and with nature can restore balance, purpose, and hope. Currently many of us want to understand how to integrate the increasing number of people with autism and so-called mentally challenging and handicapping conditions, and to inspire social forms that encourage dignity and self-advocacy for vulnerable citizens. Can facing these challenges bring solutions in other aspects of life as well? Can we find sustenance and answers in wisdom about the role of human beings in the cosmos? Can intentional communities work to increase mental health while addressing the issues that create the stress—and through that work can we all become healthier in body, soul, and spirit?

Camphill communities embody realistic and practical ways to address many of these issues. Their work is based on Rudolf Steiner's insights on agriculture, economy, ecology, human health, social forms, education, the arts, and spiritual practice—which continue to inspire many "daughter" movements, including Camphill. Worldwide, the Camphill Movement is present in over 20 countries. It has been in North America for 50 years, with 11 full member communities, two affiliates, and related communities developed by former Camphill residents.

Camphill communities integrate examples of healthy living. Community members learn by experiencing internal processes and struggling to realize ideals—efforts which often strengthen each individual. Acting to make life better surely has a positive impact on mental health, counteracting especially depression and despair. And the work of Camphill is now attracting interest because of its particular pertinence to evolving global social and environmental challenges.

The first Camphill was created in the 1940s by Austrian refugees from Nazism who were inspired by the Spiritual Science of Anthroposophy developed by Rudolf Steiner. They met in Vienna in the 1930s, brought together by Dr. Karl König. They fled Vienna after the Nazi annexation of Austria and met up in Scotland just before World War II broke out. There, in what became Camphill Schools, they began working with children with mental handicaps, and joined by others, eventually created intentional communities where adults with mental handicaps were welcomed.

Camphill's main realm of service is to vulnerable populations, particularly children, youth, and adults who have been diagnosed with so-called developmental disabilities and other similar diagnoses. However, Camphill communities work to integrate those with and without labels in a communitarian structure which serves both the communities and the larger world. Camphill communities incorporate ecovillage lifestyles, biodynamic farms, and training programs; they are nonprofits with entrepreneurial aspects as well as income, resource, and task sharing.

Camphill life is challenging socially, full of intensive work, and not for everyone. It demands a high degree of idealism and willingness to put what society labels as valuable on the shelf and to extend value to everyday tasks. Brushing someone else's teeth may be as important as performing a play, harvesting squash more important than shopping.

Yet in Camphill something amazing can happen: people with so-called handicaps turn out to be helpful socially as teachers and guides. Those who come to the communities expecting to serve do that, but also learn they are being given unexpected gifts. When this occurs, and the narrow definitions fall away to reveal each person for the whole person he or she is, something almost indefinable happens: interest, respect, and love emerge. These qualities can contribute to an experience of gratitude—a step toward well-being. The next step is discovering that helping each other—and being helped by others—builds an integrated healthy society. Relating to shared tasks and to the natural world develops inner and outer strength.

There are many expressions of Camphill, as well as ongoing evolution in each community. Some typify small village life, including agriculture. These include Camphill Special Schools, Camphill Soltane, and Camphill Kimberton, all in Pennsylvania, Camphill Triform and Camphill Copake in New York,

Midsummer celebration.

All photos by Jan Martin Bang

Heartbeet Lifesharing in Vermont, Camphill Village Minnesota, and Camphill Nottawasaga and the Ita Wegman Fellowship in Canada.

These communities include work on biodynamic farms and gardens, often combined with food processing such as cheese making, herb drying, and preserve making. The surplus products are often sold, sometimes through community supported agriculture (CSA) projects. Many communities offer baking, weaving, candle making, and woodworking. Herb growing may be combined with a medical practice and concomitant massage, art, and music therapies. Some communities have a shop or a café open to the public and arrange cultural events serving the local area.

Camphill Copake is home to Turtle Tree Seeds, growing, collecting, and distributing biodynamic seeds nationwide. Several communities offer training in therapies, while Camphill Ghent will offer elder care within an innovative cohousing village and

Camphill: Glimpses of Community Life

By Wanda Root

CSA pickup place at Kimberton.

agricultural context. Camphill Special Schools has developed college credits for its seminar in Curative Education, with a B.A. completion program in partnership with Prescott College in Arizona.

The Sophia Project serves homeless and indigent families in a distressed section of Oakland, California. Other urban/suburban centers include Camphill California, Sophia Creek in Ontario, Cascadia Society in North Vancouver, British Columbia, and the Hudson Project in Hudson, New York.

Through the presence of the Camphill communities and Waldorf Schools, surrounding regions have seen growth in various areas: local organic and biodynamic food production and distribution, anthroposophical training opportunities, sustainable business practices, interest in mission-related investing, anthroposophically-extended medical practices and therapies, and the arts. ❧

Diedra Heitzman has been a member of Camphill Village Kimberton Hills since 1983. She loves her life in Camphill: she is able to accompany so many fascinating people on life journeys, has learned about things she never expected to learn, has seen first-hand the power of community and the fruits of anthroposophy, and has seemingly endless opportunities to express ideas and learn more.

Jan Martin Bang, born in Norway, grew up in England and lived for 16 years as a kibbutz member in Israel before joining Camphill Solborg in Norway. He is now a close neighbour of Solborg and writes about community and the environment. He has written a book on Permaculture Ecovillage Design published by Floris Books in 2005, called Ecovillages—a practical guide to sustainable communities. *A second book,* Growing Eco Communities—practical ways to create sustainability, *was published by Floris Books in 2007.* Sakhnin—a portrait of an environmental peace project in Israel *and* The Hidden Seed—the story of the Camphill Bible Evening *were both published in 2009. He has just edited* A Portrait of Camphill, *published to coincide with the 70th anniversary of Camphill.*

There is a wooded, quiet valley in rural upstate New York. There are some old red barns, cows graze in the outlying meadows, and a brook runs through the valley. A peace-drenched, seemingly forgotten place, it is the home of Camphill Village.

Come, choose a path, walk down it and enter this landscape. Come, take a tour. Your guide greets you with an ear-reaching grin, an energetic and prolonged handshake, and bubbling vivacity. She seems proud that you have come to see her village. The way she talks, you might think she owned the place. And, as much as anyone else, she does.

Along the way, you pass a tall, determined, rather elegant man intently guiding a profoundly handicapped woman down the country road. Suddenly, he drops her hand, spins around three times, bends down, picks up a leaf and crumples it between his fingers. He sniffs it, gingerly, then goes back to fetch his charge and proceeds with renewed determination. You meet many people on the way to work, and they check your progress repeatedly.

"Who are you?"

"Nice day!"

"You happy?"

"It's my birthday tomorrow."

There is openness, friendliness, and warmth.

You meet a baker along the road, aproned and capped in white, carrying a bright blue bucket of fresh loaves. Someone else approaches, but only continues on slowly, buried in solitude. An officious looking gentleman passes. He nods rather curtly, checks his timepiece, and moves right along with his briefcase under his arm. An inspector? No, he is the village courier, delivering internal mail and messages.

Do you hear that loud "Ya-a-Hoo-o-!" echoing down in the valley? The farmers are bringing in the cows from pasture. One farmer wears an unusual three-cornered hat—his t-shirt—wrapped around his head. The other has a broad, contagious grin. If you follow their footsteps, you would come to Sunny Valley barn where you could watch them hand-milk their cows.

Here come the gardeners; their wheelbarrows overflowing

Greenhouse at Copake.

All photos by Jan Martin Bang

Camphill household in Norway.

with spinach and onions. One stops, picks up a basket of vegetables, and carries it into the house. He wipes his muddy boots, hastily, and proceeds through the boot room inside. Would you like to go inside too?

You wander into the living-dining room. There is a round wooden table set for 12 with a vase of fresh flowers in the center on a handwoven cloth. The windowsills are filled with plants

and crystals. Original artwork adorns the walls. Your guide pops into the kitchen.

If you had really taken a tour of the village, your guide would have made sure you had also seen the wood shop, the bakery, the weaving shop, the healing plant workshop, and the gardens. You would have been reminded to stop at the gift shop on your way out of the village. ❦

Wanda Root spent the '70s in Camphill communities in Scotland and has lived and worked in Camphill Village Copake, New York for the past 30 years. She took special delight in her years of homemaking and the enriching human relationships developed through life-sharing. She loves literature and poetry, travel and pilgrimage, and is especially interested in exploring and cultivating the social art. She has recently co-edited Seeds for Social Renewal, the Camphill Village Conferences. *Her piece is a much shortened version of an article she originally wrote for* Village Life: The Camphill Communities *which was published in 1986/87 for the 25th Anniversary of Camphill in North America.*

Camphill:
The Way of My Brother

By Bill Prensky

My brother Jonathan arrived on October 5, 1956, plunking himself down in New Rochelle, New York, in the midst of our family.

Jon's birth was surrounded by a lot of confusion. There were tests, conferences, talking with doctors. We were told that Jon was a Down's syndrome baby, somehow different from the rest of us. This confusion didn't end with the diagnosis. A lot of questions remained to be answered: Was he truly? How severely? I was in the fifth grade, and these questions intruded into my life.

By the time he was two, it was clear that Jon was different. He had stayed a "baby" brother far longer than the brothers of my friends. He needed things done for him much longer. He didn't learn to walk well. He didn't speak so well. People wanted to know "what was wrong with him."

Jon taught me to see others in a clearer light. He was my barometer. Jon evoked a reaction from everyone. Nobody was immune. And these reactions revealed each person's character. He was slow to develop, and behind his age group physically, verbally, and in independence. Even at five and six he had to be pushed in his stroller, and couldn't express himself in a manner which was recognized as "normal." No one escaped reacting to him, even if only for a fleeting moment. And in that reaction each person's psyche was revealed, and nothing afterward could change the truth of that vision.

I began to decide certain things based on those reactions: I wouldn't shop at certain stores, because the owners' reactions to Jon were not kind or understanding. I judged the adults around me in the manner in which they related to Jon.

There were those who just accepted him and loved him simply. Jon's grandmother was one. A Russian Jewish immigrant, she had no notion of Down's syndrome. She just loved him and took care of him, as she did the rest of her grandchildren. Our brother Sam, the youngest of the family, accepted him. As Sam quickly outraced Jon and surpassed him in physical and mental development, he quickly shifted gears and became the protector and older brother.

Still, Jon was an outcast. The society in which he found himself had no place for him. His behavior was disquieting, his abilities too limited for him to find a comfortable place in state school or in special education classes.

And then a small article appeared in a local paper. Word was passed from parent to parent. A lecture was going to be given on disabled children and on Camphill Special School, this "place" in Pennsylvania where everything was different. It

Flowforms at Copake.

Jam making at Camphill Le Beale in France.

Jam for sale at Camphill Le Beale in France.

Harvesting vegetables at Camphill Kopisty in the Czech Republic.

All photos by Jan Martin Bang

grabbed the attention of a number of parents who had been searching. They went to listen, and sat spellbound. Interviews were set up. Carlo Pietzner sat in a motel room and interviewed, not the parents, but the children. He had long and meaningful conversations with Jon and a number of other special children. A decision was made. They would go to Camphill.

Jon left home and went to Camphill Special School. There he began a life quite different from what would have been possible for him at home. Living in a house among a number of houses around the village, with other villagers, with house parents, children, and farm animals, he entered a world that slowly began to work with him to evoke that special Camphill magic: to help him find all that he could express, manifest, develop.

Jon grew up. He went from Beaver Run to Camphill Village, Copake, New York, with a couple of detours in between. ❧

Bill Prensky is a businessman living in New York.

●●●

These three articles are shortened and edited extracts taken from the book A Portrait of Camphill, *published in 2010 to coincide with the 70th anniversary of the Camphill Movement. North American distributors are Steinerbooks: www.steinerbooks.org. Find out more about Camphill: www.camphill.org.*

Diversity at Camphill Soltane

By James Damon, Tai Shinohara, and Bethany Walton

That this article has three authors, rather than one, is of no small note. Indeed, we climbed a minor mountain in this collaborative effort. We all have varying heritages, viewpoints, and writing styles, so instead of cobbling our opinions into one definitive definition of diversity, we each chose to explore different ways in which diversity manifests itself in our community.

The Camphill Soltane Community

Camphill Soltane is one of over 100 communities within the larger Camphill movement stretching across the world. Camphill communities were developed as places that would uphold the inherent dignity and value of those people who are marginalized by society. While this could refer to many populations, most Camphill communities have primarily served those with developmental or intellectual disabilities.

Camphill Soltane, located outside of Philadelphia, is a transitional and residential community which helps young adults with special needs ("students") discover who they are and find their place in the world. The college-like atmosphere of the Learning For Life program works to foster a joy of learning, along with teaching important life and pre-vocational skills. Soltane also includes a small population of older people with special needs who work as "residents" in a range of on- and off-site workshops. Students and residents with disabilities share their lives with live-in supporters ("coworkers"), who make at least a year-long commitment to living at Soltane—although some have been here for many years. Many coworkers are AmeriCorps members. Hired faculty from the surrounding area lead some of the classes and work areas. Together, students, residents, coworkers and their families, and staff members make up the Camphill Soltane community—90+ people in all.

Diversity of Abilities

In a community, simply having a collection of hobbies, races, or backgrounds is not enough. In order for diversity to really exist and be sustained, it has to be truly supported and differences have to be both honored and respected. Soltane places priority on fostering the growth of everyone who lives here, and people receive real opportunities to grow and achieve what they want out of life.

Here at Soltane this can be particularly challenging because our community members have a wide range of abilities. For their entire lives, our students and residents have been labeled as "retarded," "special needs," or "disabled"—all definitions of what they are not ("normal"). This has pushed them to the margins of society. Yet their uniqueness is the very definition of diversity.

This is what makes Camphill Soltane and what we are trying to achieve here

Author Bethany Walton working with student Ted H. in the raised bed vegetable garden.

Photos by Catherine Dodge Smith

so important. Within our community we try to look positively at what our students and residents can do, find out what they want, and then support them in the achievement of that goal. For example, one student, Jeff, absolutely loves to work outside or in any place that will get him a little dirty. While raking leaves or washing a window he'll loudly exclaim to anyone around him, "Gettin' down and dirty!" and simultaneously smudge a little dirt on his jeans. It is because of conversations with Jeff and also simply recognizing what he likes to do that Soltane was able to find him jobs in both a local garden/arboretum and a recycling center. Together with his job coaches, Jeff gets the chance to learn important life and work-related skills while doing something that he enjoys. Rather than fitting him into jobs someone else might want him to do, we've found ways to allow Jeff to express his unique identity through his work.

If an atmosphere of respect is present and already cemented within the community, then individual uniqueness will naturally begin to appear and flourish. In this way the community as a whole gives its members the confidence to share who they are. If this precedent is not set, then at least for our students and residents, Soltane would be no different from the rest of society.

However, it is important to note that the diversity of abilities that we have here at Soltane has limits. The community has recognized that there are some people we cannot adequately support, those with dual diagnoses (developmental disabilities along with mental health issues) or severe mental disorders, for example. Thus, recognizing the limits to the kind of diversity that a community can achieve is just as important as being accepting of it.

Lastly, while we encourage our students and residents (and community members in general) to voice concerns and goals related not only to their own lives, but to the community as a whole, not everyone can really articulate or grasp what it means for a community to grow and progress into the future. This is, in a way, a challenge of our own diversity. What Soltane has done well is to foster a feeling of trust that those in charge of Soltane's future will have the best interests of the community and its individual members in mind.

Socioeconomic Diversity

When Soltane was founded in 1988, the first individuals with special needs who joined the community were financed entirely through private pay. Fundraising made up what was needed to run the community above and beyond this tuition. The founding coworkers of Camphill Soltane realized that a private pay set-up would exclude some individuals with disabilities who might wish to join the community, but whose families could not afford that expense. Thus, one of Soltane's earliest fundraising campaigns was to establish an endowment whose purpose would be to make financial aid in the form of scholarships available to individuals based on need; in addition, one donor bequeathed money specifically set aside for scholarships for minority applicants. Then, about two years ago, Soltane began working within the public funding environment so that individuals with special needs who could access money from their state's public welfare system might be able to use those funds at Soltane.

Student Courtney B. and author James Damon making handmade instruments in the woodworking studio.

Today, 55 percent of students and residents are funded entirely by private pay, 23 percent receive scholarship assistance from Soltane, and 28 percent use public funding; some people rely on a combination of these methods to fund their residential or work placements at Soltane. One economically disadvantaged individual is fully funded by a private donor who was inspired by Soltane's approach to inclusive community living many years ago. Together, all of these efforts have given us a more socioeconomically diverse body of students and residents.

Our work is cut out for us here: recent cuts to public funding threaten the financial stability of some families with a member who is disabled, and the value of our endowment shifts with the stock market. But despite the unstable funding environment, the commitment to socioeconomic diversity in our student and resident body remains strong.

Author Tai Shinohara works with student Lenny L. in the Learning for Life program.

Interpersonal Diversity

Another aspect of diversity at Soltane is interpersonal diversity. When actively

---

Diversity is important only insofar as we recognize meaningful differences as ways in which we learn from, and are inspired by, each other.

---

supported in the community, this leads to opportunities for individual members to express and develop their passions, which in turn creates opportunities for a more enjoyable and full life for other members.

A second-year coworker, Krisztina Kajtar, grew up in France and later moved with her family to Hungary. As a young adult, she had a formative experience with a musical troupe in Hungary, where she gained skills in choreography, set creation/design, group dynamics, and performance. This year at Soltane, Krisztina is offering a musical class which incorporates much of her artistic experience. She is thrilled to see the students and residents having so much fun with music and dance. During a recent moment of rare concentration and focus on the part of all of the musical players, Krisztina experienced an "aha!" moment as she saw how the students and residents were empowered by the opportunity to work together in new ways to create a body of work to share with others. "I am finally doing something that makes sense to me and to the world," Krisztina says.

Recognizing Diversity in Community

If we encourage and support diversity, then its development and growth within the community will be healthy and will act as a strengthening element.

We need to recognize that diversity is really just another slice of the pie, and by focusing too much on our differences we negate our similarities and potentially our ability to work well together. If we really wanted to focus on differences we could look at toenails and hairlines, but that would surely get in the way of our overall goal to grow together into being more autonomous individuals with a gift to share with the world. The real point is that diversity is important only insofar as the community recognizes and encourages meaningful differences as ways in which we learn from, and are inspired by, each other. ❧

All three authors are AmeriCorps members and first-year coworkers at Camphill Soltane. James Damon is from Philadelphia and enjoys running and volunteering. Taichi Shinohara is from outside of Boston; he is particularly interested in not only specific types of therapies such as Eurythmy or Cognitive Therapy but also how to make community and relationships a therapeutic force. Bethany Walton is from Schuylerville, New York and is passionate about being involved in community work with marginalized populations. You can contact the authors at jdamon, tshinohara, or bwalton@camphillsoltane.org.

COMMUNITY LIVING
as Social Activism in Camphill

By Kam Bellamy

In my younger days I fancied myself to be quite the social activist. I traveled to Washington DC to see the Clothesline Project and march against violence against women. In New York I spoke out at a Take Back the Night rally and walked topless through the streets of the City shouting, "Wherever we go, however we dress, no means no and yes means yes!" to show that even half-dressed, I had rights to my body. I visited the Greenham Common Women's Peace Camp in England—an inspiring group whose work to this day influences my approach to life and to activism. I marched in protests opposing the World Bank, and in general was up for any "good fight" that came my way.

At a certain age, I became tired of fighting. Fresh out of college I took a job at an anti-hunger organization. I loved my job, but the weight of being "anti-hunger" in my work life, while fighting the military-industrial complex and violence against women in my free time, became more than I could stomach. I decided I wanted to work for something. As someone who was trying to create a more peaceful world, I realized I needed to stop fighting—to stop thinking about what I didn't want in the world, and to start creating what I did want.

While studying Race and Gender Studies in college I read Riane Eisler's book *The Chalice and the Blade*, in which she talks about "gylanic" societies—social systems based on the equality of women and men. I loved her book, and she articulated a lot of what I already knew in my heart: that societies did not need to be based on a culture of domination, and that humans could build (and in some situations already had built) cultures based on a model of partnership. I wanted to be part of such a culture, and express my activist self by modeling with others that a partnership-based society could exist. *The Oxford English Dictionary* defines activism as "the policy or action of using vigorous campaigning to bring about political or social change." Did I need to "vigorously campaign" or "protest" in order to bring about political or social change? Did I need to "fight" for nonviolence to create a culture of respect? I hoped not.

In 1994 while backpacking through England, I walked into a beautiful, seemingly idyllic valley in a remote area of North Yorkshire and came upon a Camphill community called Botton Village. In Botton Village, people of all abilities lived side by side, each contributing what they could to the community, and in turn having their needs met by the community. Individuals living in Camphill work out of anthroposophy, and believe that "in a community of human beings working together, the well-being of the community will be the greater, the less the individual claims for him/herself the proceeds of the work s/he has done." We turn the proceeds of our work over to our fellow-workers, and in turn our needs are satisfied by the work done by others.

Three years after first walking in to Botton Village, I returned to stay, initially thinking I would live there for one to three years, to learn about and experience community life. Though I have moved from community to community, 20 years on I am still living in Camphill. (There are more than 120 Camphill communities throughout the world—most in Europe and the US and Canada, but some also in Southern Africa, India, Russia, and Vietnam.)

To me, community living is the highest form of social activism. Sharing resources, sharing burdens, expanding the concept of family beyond those who are related by blood: these are revolutionary concepts—not to be taken lightly. We can fight against certain political figures or certain economic, military, environmental, or human rights issues. But until we can find an alter-

At Triform Camphill Community (Hudson, NY) individuals of all abilities make lasting friendships built around trust and respect

Ben Kulo

Autumn at Camphill Special School means a bustling life where students live and study at this residential Waldorf school community.

native to the culture of domination, we will not succeed in addressing any of these things. Community living, to me, offers a real alternative to this culture.

Being a member of a Camphill community means making a commitment to ensuring that the needs of all your fellow community members are met. It also means establishing trust with others in your community that they will work to meet your needs. In Audre Lorde's 1979 address titled "The Master's Tools Will Never Dismantle the Master's House," she states that when we "learn how to take our differences and make them strengths" then true equality can be achieved. This is what we strive to do in Camphill. Valuing the wholeness at the core of each individual, we focus on what each individual brings to our community, whether it be a warm smile and a cheeky sense of humor, an ability to grow vegetables, or a keen knack for accounting—every individual's contribution is valued. When we know that others are dependent upon each of us to give to the best of our ability, a strong work ethic is cultivated.

Choosing to live in community made the personal political in my life in a very real way. Excusing myself from participating in the culture of domination allowed the very living of my life to be an expression of activism.

I love that in Camphill communities people of all abilities are given voice. People with "special needs" live side-by-side with people "without" special needs, and work together, celebrate together, and by and large self-govern, practicing consensus decision-making.

Today, CMS (the Centers for Medicaid and Medicare Services) is pushing to remove people with special needs from intentional community settings. Such settings, they say, are "isolating" and "restrictive." For me, as a person labeled "non-disabled," I can only say that community living offered a freedom from the isolation many experience in the modern world—the isolation of needing to be dependent solely on one's own resources for survival, and the isolation of not knowing who would care if I had what I needed or not. Community living also gave me freedom—I was not restricted to doing only the work that could produce money for the survival of my family. I was allowed and encouraged to do work that was meaningful, whether it was caring for my daughter, cooking lunch, working in the vegetable garden, or managing the accounts for the community. My work, and the work of all in the community, regardless of "capability," was meaningful and valued.

Going forward, we must be careful that this tightening of regulations does not have the effect of restricting the freedom of and consequently isolating people with disabilities in the name of inclusion. All of us, regardless of ability, need to be able to express our ideals and lead full, active, and whole lives by choosing to live in community. To restrict those who have been labeled "disabled" from so doing is unconscionable.

I may need to return to "vigorous campaigning." 🦆

Kam Bellamy is a longtime Camphill coworker and currently serves as the Executive Director at Camphill Hudson.

In Camphill communities individuals of all abilities live and work together to create community. Annie and Kaye are part of Camphill Hudson and share an apartment in downtown Hudson, NY.

Thomas de Leon

Artistic expression and an active lifestyle are important in Camphill communities, seen here at Triform in Hudson, NY.

Ben Kulo

Ben Kulo

Drama and performances are commonplace in the communities, this production was recently held at Camphill Hudson and centered around Camphill's agricultural roots.

A feeling of stewardship has always been a strong principle in Camphill communities.

Ben Kulo

The candle workshop at Camphill Village Copake (Copake, NY) creates a wide variety of 100% beeswax candles for use by the community and for sale to the public through retail stores and catalogs.

INNISFREE VILLAGE:
Lifesharing in a Service Community

By Nancy Chappell

I have lived and worked at Innisfree Village for most of the last 24 years. I raised my son here. I have enjoyed a lifestyle of sharing, learning, caring, and laughing with people from around the world as well as with people with Intellectual Disabilities. We all have things we need and gifts we can give.

I can cook a meal for 20 with little effort and give some decent haircuts. I am not very good at measuring carefully and cutting things in a straight line. That's where my friend Willy comes in. He can be very exact and very literal. He challenges me to think in other ways or at least to consider the world from various people's viewpoints. I can practice a foreign language here, get help with my computer, or car, or bicycle. Hugs are free here and given quite freely.

This is a full, rich life that is not for everyone, but could be for many of you. We have quite a few similarities to egalitarian communities: we share resources, grow many of our own vegetables, have a pool of vehicles for our use whether "work"-related or for personal time. We are free to go in and out of each other's homes. We get fresh bread and granola delivered to our house twice a week. We have movie night, birthday parties, dances, and potlucks. There is always someone to be with. Finding alone time is possible but requires a bit more effort.

Some of the ways we are different from egalitarian communities: we have a Board of Directors, an Executive Director, and are bound by the License granted to us by the Department of Social Services for the State of Virginia. The population with Intellectual Disabilities, whom we call Coworkers, pays tuition to live here. Or more precisely their families do. In a more perfect world (and perhaps in more socialist-type democracies) this would be free to all who need it and a birthright of being a citizen. Unfortunately, we don't live in that world here in the US (yet?).

Innisfree Village is a Lifesharing community with adults with Intellectual Disabilities. We are a Service community in that we serve adults with disabilities. We were established in 1971 by some parents of young people with disabilities wanting a place for their children to grow and thrive in a community of respect and beauty.

Our mission includes:

1. Being a model therapeutic environment with people with intellectual disabilities, emphasizing empowerment, interdependence, and mutual respect of all community members.

2. Evolving with the changing needs of the individuals with intellectual disabilities within the Village community and beyond.

3. Valuing work and fostering creativity through artistic crafts, stewardship of the land, and daily community life.

4. Promoting efforts in the stewardship of our land to acknowledge the reciprocal relationship between our human health and our natural environment.

5. Encouraging the integration of community members into the larger society through participation in cultural, educational, recreational, religious, and volunteer programs.

6. Relying for its financial resources upon family support, the spirit of volunteerism, and private funding.

7. Supporting and encouraging the talents and individuality of community members from diverse educational, national, ethnic, and social backgrounds

We are a community of about 75 people, 60 of whom live here. It is a dynamic community, as people do come in and out on a regular basis. The 40 Coworkers make up the foundation of our community. Philip, Bee, and Marny all arrived here in the 1970s. Kevin, Sian, Corinne, and the two Brookes arrived in the past five years. We all arrive from various places and bring differing problems, needs, and gifts. The more dynamic part of our community is the Residential Caregiver Volunteers who come from around the world to serve for at least one year within our community. At the moment, we have Volunteers from 20 to 68 years of age who have come from Germany, Maine, England, California, Alabama, Zambia, Michigan, Spain, New York City, and Japan.

We have 10 houses spread out on our 550 acres. Each house has one to six Coworkers living there, with one to three Volunteers who live together. This is what Lifesharing means. Our day starts with breakfast in our homes and we need to "get to work" by 9. One of my favorite times of the day is between 8:45 and 9 a.m. when everyone is heading out and walking to work. I lovingly refer to this as our morning rush hour.

We have seven main workstations where we might work. The Farm is where we collect and wash eggs from our 300 or so chickens. We consume this within the village and usually have enough to sell to some local restaurants and health food stores. We also have about a dozen mamma sheep. We are just learning how to shear the sheep, then clean, card, and spin the wool into a workable product.

We have two gardens; one is the Vegetable Garden, which grows veggies on about five acres of land. We have a CSA about six months a year, that is mostly for our use, with a few select customers outside of the community. We also have an Herb Garden which grows herbs and flowers. We sell flower bouquets in a local grocery store and once or twice a year will provide flowers for weddings. Our herbs also yield fresh (in season) or dried (out of season) basil, oregano, sage, dill, parsley. We make a variety of teas that get put into tea bags and also we make an assortment of soaps.

Our weavery and woodshop have both been up and running since the early '70s. We are especially known for our beautiful cutting boards, placemats, and scarves. We sell to some local craft stores as well as various artisan fairs.

Our bakery produces about 50 loaves of bread twice a week, for our own consumption. In addition, we make granola that is enjoyed by the Village and sold in some local stores, including Whole Foods. The making of our communal lunches is one of our workstations. All 70 of us join together for a delicious vegetarian lunch four days a week. We have some excellent—and possessive—garlic peelers and cheese graters, so we probably eat more than our share of garlic and cheese at our lunches, thanks to Heyward and Katie.

Is it paradise, you ask? Some days yes and some days no. As in most communities, we have to deal with difficult personalities. There are people in community that we may not like but need to find a way to live with. Because we are looking for the best in our Coworkers and try to work with people's strengths, that can also help in dealing with the Volunteers and Staff who live or work here. Our Coworkers can have challenging behaviors above and beyond what the general population has to deal with. Fortunately, having a large property means that people are free to move about and take long walks when frustration or anger is our motivator.

Folks with seizure disorders need a vigilance that most of us do not require. At Innisfree Village, we work long hours and may have little time for ourselves. It is necessary to be flexible, have patience, and enjoy a healthy sense of humor.

New Volunteers are joining and leaving our community every few months. This keeps a dynamism but is exhausting, as we are continually offering thorough training for the life and the guidelines here, as well as constantly saying goodbye.

Coworkers might come to the end of their lives here and that can be difficult, powerful, and sad. Can we keep someone here or do we need to find another end-of-life situation for them? The most we can do is to consider each situation on its own and join with their families for the best option.

On a lighter note, a colleague just piped in with these "hardest aspects of our community": working 24/7, allergies, Virginia summers, cohabiting with spiders and snakes. I can say that this challenges me regularly. I just walked home to put away some of our eggs and meat in my fridge, to find a black snake wiggling on my kitchen floor. Not fun for me. For many people, especially for those not used to our climate and life in the country, these are the biggest challenges.

One needs to **want** to live with people differently-abled in a rural environment and to be willing and able to share of themselves in a community that is big and sometimes messy, but where smiles and hugs are plentiful too.

There are many opportunities to experience life in a Service Community, whether one commits for one year or 24 years. The benefits of Lifesharing are limitless. We welcome visitors and more importantly, Community Members. ❧

Located in Crozet, Virginia, in the foothills of the Blue Ridge Mountains, Innisfree Village welcomes visitors and new Community Members (see www.innisfreevillage.org). Nancy Chappell is Innisfree Village's Associate Director.

Photos courtesy of Nancy Chappell

66

CREATING THE IDEAL INTENTIONAL COMMUNITY
(OR REVITALIZING AN EXISTING ONE)

I, Sahmat, grew up in intentional communities and have lived in 10 of them. I have been so dedicated to Community with both humans and Nature that I've been called "The Community Guy". The communities I grew up in shared a fairly strong "sense of community". I call this deep and sustained sense of community "Common-unity" because it's a state of unity we share in common, with the unique individuality of each human and each species still honored. It's this state of Common-unity that I've found most valuable in life and to me it's the main reason for living in an intentional community. When a group is deep in Common-unity together, there's a shared sense of love, joy, and peace that tops any other group experience.

However, I've found that in all the communities I've lived in, the sense of community is not nearly as deep and sustained as it could be. It's precisely this lack of Common-unity that is the root cause of the catastrophic global suffering of racism, wars, child abuse, abuse of women, environmental and species destruction, etc. So the ultimate goal is ending global suffering through "Global Common-unity": the spreading of Common-unity throughout the world by forming a global network of Common-unity-dedicated Communities.

So I've spent my life learning how to create Common-unity-dedicated communities that share true Common-unity: a deeper and more sustained sense of community. There are two keys to starting a Common-unity community (or moving an existing community into deeper Common-unity):

1. The first key to Common-unity is for everyone to be "Common-unity-dedicated" as their top common priority. This doesn't seem to be the case in any existing community, which results in focus and energies being bled off into other priorities. So maintenance of Common-unity doesn't get enough time and energy.

2. The second key to Common-unity is to learn "Common-unity Skills", skills that must be practiced to maintain Common-unity: Speaking from the Heart, Empathetic Listening, Emptying of Ego-attachments, Conflict Resolution, Consensus, Heart Wound Healing, Cooperative Housing, and Cooperative Economics. Modern culture does not teach us these skills.

We at the Alliance for Global Community have developed free workshops that train you in these Common-unity Skills. The workshops contain the Sharing Circle process developed by M. Scott Peck, a Nature connection exercise developed by John Seed and Joanna Macy, healing exercises developed by Byron Katie and Richard Moss, and exercises in creating Cooperative Housing and Cooperative Economics. We've tested various versions of these Common-unity Skill Building workshops over the past 25 years, and we've found them to be quite effective in teaching Common-unity skills that can help maintain Common-unity. If you'd like to start a Common-unity-dedicated community, or if you'd like to bring more Common-unity into an existing community (perhaps through a Common-unity sub-community or "pod"), you need to learn or improve these Common-unity skills as soon as possible.

To find out how to sign up for a free public Common-unity Skills workshop or schedule a free workshop for an existing group or community, please go to my website thecommunityguy.org There you can also find out how to get a free copy of the book "Skill Building for Global Common-unity". You can contact Sahmat directly at info@thecommunityguy.org or at 434-305-4770.

COMMON-UNITY WITH HUMANITY AND NATURE

THE GESUNDHEIT! INSTITUTE:
A 45 Year-Old Communal Hospital Experiment

By Patch Adams

I entered medical school in 1967 to use medicine as a vehicle for social change. I immediately saw that hospitals were expensive, hierarchical, frantic, unhappy places easily causing burnout to all levels of staff. I saw nothing "healthy" about a hospital setting. There were high levels of racism and sexism where the rich "elite" were treated so much better than the disadvantaged poor. I decided to spend my four years in a medical school studying hospitals with the idea upon graduation to create a hospital that addresses all the problems of care delivery, not as the answer, but to show that answers to these problems are possible. Two years into medical school, in 1969 I went to visit the Twin Oaks community. After having wonderful words with Kat Kincade and others, I realized I was a communal person—part of the great tribe called human.

When I graduated in 1971 no one gave us a hospital, so I decided to form a commune that was a hospital open for 24 hours a day, seven days a week for all manner of medical problems from birth to death. For 12 years we did this experiment, mostly with 20 adults and our children (three were physicians) in a large six-bedroom house. In the peak years we had 500-1000 people in our home with from five to 50 guests a night. We did not distinguish the patient from the "non-patient." Instead, our focus was to try to have a relationship with everyone who came. If one came "as a patient," our ideal was to have a three- or four-hour-long initial interview (instead of the 7.8-minute one we were taught) and to visit their home. By 1980 we had gathered enough resources together to purchase 321 acres in West Virginia (the least served state for healthcare).

Everything was given freely. We didn't feel like a charity since our focus wasn't on helping the "poor." We simply didn't want people to think they owed us something in return. We wanted them to be excited to belong to something called community, a nest of care.

In this same flavor, we never heard anyone praise insurance companies. They are, after all, one-quarter to one-third of the cost of care created by the practice of medicine. So, we never had anything to do with them. One can never know before a treatment what the effect of that treatment would be, so we need the right to make a mistake, so we are the only hospital in the United States that refuses to carry malpractice insurance.

In medical school, we never had a single lecture on health and so had to discover how to spark interest and give examples of exercise, diet, love, and spirit. For example, we would host all-night dance parties, and yoga sessions during the day, as examples of exercise. For dieting, we kept extensive gardens and learned to feed lots of people. We showered everyone we met with love and affection; my longest hug was 12 hours! To encourage spiritual growth, we allowed all practices to show themselves, and generally feel that spiritual means love in action.

At this time the only complementary medicine that was legal in our state was chiropractic medicine, so we welcomed it. Then, we broke the law by welcoming acupuncture, homeopathy, naturopathy, and so many more—even some that others may think are profoundly strange.

We were all so well known for our integration of human and play that others began calling us "the Zanies"! For me, it was so thrilling and enchanting to be alive every day for those 12 years.

Since those early days I have been constantly, relentlessly raising the funds to build a hospital. This ideal hospital will be a technologically modern hospital that will show a happy, funny, loving, cooperative, creative, and thoughtful atmosphere. A hospital that will run at only 10 percent of typical operating costs.

In those early years, we never asked for money. And so, we ran with little support for those 12 years. In fact, our staff had to work outside jobs—imagine having to pay to

In March of 2002, we took 22 clowns from six different continents and 10 tons of aid to Afghanistan for five weeks. This is outside of a pediatrics hospital in Kabul.

Here we are working in our community site in West Virginia, summer 1990.

In August of 2003, 20 clowns visited Argentina, Colombia, Uruguay, Chile, and Easter Island, with two to three engagements per day for three weeks. We cut a basketball in half and painted it red for the photo!

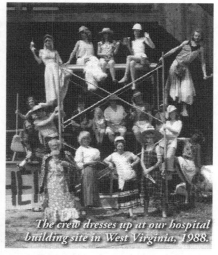

The crew dresses up at our hospital building site in West Virginia, 1988.

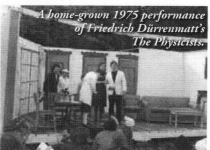

A home-grown 1975 performance of Friedrich Dürrenmatt's The Physicists.

practice medicine! And yet, no staff left in the first nine years. I believe this is because the playful, deep, friendly practice of care is such an enchanting experience that it is worth paying to do. No one was making a sacrifice to be there. Love, play, and care are so seductive of appreciation.

All these years later, I'm still raising money for our dream hospital—even though a majority of financial promises have fallen through, and we may have asked over 1400 foundations for a grant. With all the setbacks, we still look to the successes that have sustained our effort.

We are a political project. And, as a political project, we realized that our style had become so intense, we would soon run the risk of burning out many people. It was then that I realized that to continue our project, we have to build a communal ecovillage to protect this dream of a hospital. It became clear that every staff person must have a room for their own and the other projects that hold their interest (like the arts). The way we had been was no model to show possibility—we had to actually have a hospital, albeit our style of hospital. We had refused publicity up to this point. We realized that if we were to raise the millions of dollars we need to build and endow our hospital, we would have to bring in publicity. In order to raise this money, I would become some sort of a celebrity. So, we closed our doors in 1983 and held a press event. Shortly after we closed the hospital, I was invited to lecture and perform all over the world. We tightened up the communal home for six to eight people for the next 15 years—waiting for that chance to build our fantasy.

By 1985 I was feeling such an emptiness from not being able to do direct care that I started our clown trips to foreign countries. This was a second wonderful exploration of communal living because the clown trips were a totally random collection of people. People have ranged in age from three to 88, from over 50 countries, and many come with no prior experience. We started in the Soviet Union and we have gone there usually with 35-40 people for two weeks. Our Russia trip is now in its 31st year! Using the same six qualities—happy, funny, loving, cooperative, creative, and thoughtful—complete strangers become a coordinated team of beautiful clowns. Over 150 trips have happened since the initial outing, involving over 6000 people; maybe only five or six did not work out.

Photos courtesy of Patch Adams

Of course, the big trick was that all were going to human suffering with love and fun, which extracted these six qualities out of whoever came. The trips have been universally enchanting. Twenty-three years ago

We've taken clowns into war zones, refugee camps, and horrible disasters all over the world.

we were touring some orphanages in such an unhappy state that we were overjoyed when we met our astonishing friend Maria. Maria began work that has continued all these years with over 600 orphans, exceeding our wildest dreams.

In these years we've taken clowns into war zones, many refugee camps, and horrible disasters all over the world. Eleven years ago we were touring the Peruvian Amazon with a group of clowns when we came upon an unsettling number of children (ages three to five) that have been afflicted with gonorrhea. Our shock has emboldened us to return there every year since then and help out in any way we can. Now we team up with 100 clowns from all over the world for a two-week extravaganza filled with humanitarian projects and clowning for all. We will return this August! For this past year we have also maintained a year-long presence in the area with four women who moved there to see what can happy: a doctor, a psychologist, and two musicians. A similar project was started in Nepal eight years ago by our dear partners, Ginevra and Italo.

In 1999, Hollywood released a film about my life called *Patch Adams*. I agreed to do this foolish thing because they promised to help us build our hospital. The film made hundreds of millions of dollars—but we made no money from the film. We are here to end capitalism after all. However, the film did make my speaker fees go way up, and so another kind of communal project developed where I could give a talk, and with volunteers we could build a clinic or school in a poor country. The fees also made it possible to build three beautiful buildings on our West Virginia property in preparation for the big buildings we want for the hospital. In the last few years, through three bequests and some sweetly eccentric people, we have

received such donations that as I write we are putting the roof on our first big building.

In 1987, at a conference of the International Cybernetics Association, I met a radical group of artists and activists who put the conference on, and I instantly felt a connection. The next five years we got closer and they changed their name to the School for Designing a Society (designingasociety.net). We invited them to do the school in the summer on our land in West Virginia because it was like the missing piece for our project. We are here to teach and show social change. So right was this union, that we decided that the first big building we would build will be a school building. We had agreed from the beginning that our medical and clowning work would be free, and our educational work would be how we would raise our funds. By educational work, I mean lectures, speeches, workshops, and classes. Here was an in-house way to raise funds and to teach nonviolent revolution. What may be interesting to communal societies is that we have combined our communities, but kept the styles for each community as they are. The School has also created clown trips that have clowning in the morning, and education in the afternoon and evening. They have annual trips in Ecuador and Costa Rica. They have also returned recently from a clowning event in Mexico.

So yes! We have failed to build the hospital that I began in 1971, and was sure it would be funded in four years. Imagine my glee when I realized that the delay has been a great gift! The design of the hospital is a lot more intelligent now than we ever dreamed at the beginning. For

In Peru, clowns perform a sex-education skit, with Patch as a spermie.

Following a series of hurricanes in Cuba, clowns partner with the National Children's Theater group, "La Colmenita" to bring cheer to the disaster area.

Clowns from 15 different countries parade in Belen, Iquitos, Peru.

Participants in annual "Laughing Body" seminar enjoy the mud pit.

Patch's wedding, the community's first, in 1975. The theme of the wedding was Louis the XIV, with all dresses and garments made in the community.

Every year since 1985, 40 clowns travel to Russia for two weeks and take a picture at this location.

Our annual Commune Christmas Picture, taken in 1978 in Charles Town, West Virginia.

example, environmental consciousness and desire have really progressed these 45 years. So we will have 120 staff, all living together in our communal ecovillage. This will eliminate 85 percent of the village's ecological footprint. Permaculture and other ideas have leapt into our concept. With our global outreach and fame we are connected all over the world in our project, and those of other countries. It is thrilling! Clowns are now going into hospitals in over 130 countries, and in Argentina laws have been passed to require pediatric departments in every hospital to hire clowns. I lecture 300 days out of the year, and have done so for over 30 years in 81 counties, spreading seeds of a love revolution of enlivening community and a call to end capitalism. I have corresponded with letters to 130 countries so it feels like a global family—each with their own special directions of care.

I have never been discouraged; in fact the pursuit has given me a vigorous life. The smartest thing I ever did was be communal. This was the sweetest gift to myself. The hospital, the clown trips, the lectures and correspondences have made me feel that the earth is my commune, and all of us are truly brothers and sisters. Let's get to work!

Our funding must be right around the corner!

In Peace, Patch ❧

Patch Adams, M.D., founder of the Gesundheit! Institute, is a doctor, clown, activist for peace, justice, and care for all people, and lifelong reader of COMMUNITIES *magazine (since its birth in 1972). See www. patchadams.org.*

Coming of Age in Service Community

By Jen and Hilary Bayer

We're Jen and Hil, 17-year-old twin girls born and raised at Magic, a service learning community where today about 20 people share three adjacent houses a few blocks from Stanford University in Palo Alto, California. Magic community is the keystone project of a public service organization also called Magic, which owns the properties we occupy. The mission of both Magics is to demonstrate how people can more successfully address individual, social, and environmental ills by using science to know and do good.

Magicians serve at several levels. A half dozen residents who've lived here from five to more than 40 years are "fellows." They receive room, board, and other basics on terms similar to those offered by the Peace Corps and some monastic communities. Fellows serve residents here for shorter stays by modeling how to use valuescience to be healthier, to be more cooperative, and to care better for Earth. They lead other residents and volunteers from outside Magic in serving neighbors by closing streets to eliminate short-cutting, planting street and park trees, organizing picnics and block parties, lobbying local government to repair streets,

and similar actions. Magicians also serve a larger surrounding community with programs that range from salvaging farmers' market surplus for a social services agency that feeds the hungry, to planting and caring for trees and other native species on local open space lands, to life coaching, to teaching hatha yoga and swimming.

Researching and teaching valuescience—scientific methods and principles applied to questions of value—underpin and are central to Magic's service. Fellows teach people from around the nation and the world at Stanford, at Magic, and in educational, business, service organization, and governmental settings in the US and abroad. They also publish in scientific journals with international circulation, and in the popular press.

In more than 40 years since Magic was founded, the San Francisco Peninsula where we live has gone from being birthplace of the Grateful Dead and the Whole Earth Catalog, and home to Ken Kesey and the Merry Pranksters, to birthplace of Facebook, Google, and Apple, and home to thousands of people who've joined the one percent by creating these and other technology enterprises. Magic has flourished through these sweeping changes by demonstrating how a valuescience approach to health, cooperation, and stewardship can be means to further individual and common good.

Growing up at Magic has been mostly fun, sometimes confusing. As the two of us transition to adulthood we're understanding better benefits we've enjoyed here and challenges we've faced and may continue to face if we decide to stay here or base our lives on ideas we've learned here. We hope this writing will be useful to young people growing up in residential service communities, to parents raising children in such communities, and to anyone thinking about creating or joining a community of this kind.

When we were small children we took it all for granted: that we had more than one mom and one dad, that all of them were single, that we walked or biked everywhere, that we were outside exploring nature most of each day, that we were able to have fun without TV, junk food, new clothes, Santa Claus, Easter Bunny, or Tooth Fairy, and that we were able to be good people without god. We saw science as how everybody learned. We thought Saturdays were for planting and caring for native trees, shrubs, grasses, and forbs in parks and open space, that Sundays were for salvaging surplus food from farmers'

Hil hanging laundry, her regular chore at three.

Oak Habitat Stewardship - 100 volunteers headed out to plant native California oaks on openspace land.

Hil (left) and Jen (right) at six at San Gregorio State Beach on their first ride to the beach, 26 miles each way over a 2,000 foot ridge.

Photos courtesy of Jen and Hilary Bayer

Jen peeling carrots with dinner cook at three.

Hil vacuuming, age three.

Jen, age six, and Robin putting cattle excluder on young tree.

Hil and Jen cutting cordwood, age eight.

market for the food bank, and that when adults talked it was about how people can use evidence and reason for common good. Someone was always around to help us, teach us, or play with us.

Then we went to kindergarten at our local elementary school, because parents wanted to cultivate solidarity with neighbors by supporting public schools, and because they wanted us to be with age peers. It was our first taste of being different. We met nice kids and had good times, but we'd been taught from before we can remember to question everything, even what parents told us, and we were in trouble from the start when we did that at school. To PTA moms, "Why do you sell junk food to raise money?" To teachers, "Why do you let boys monopolize playground equipment? Why do we watch movies in 'physical education'?" To classmates, "Why do you believe in god and Santa Claus? Why do you leave other kids out? Why do you throw clothing on the ground?" Everybody treated us as if we were weird. We had a hard time imagining that so much we learned at home was wrong, and an equally hard time concluding that everyone at school was crazy.

When we started in school we needed to eat before everyone else and go to bed early. Interacting with adults over supper and afterwards had been a big part of our social lives and we missed it. During first grade parents let us stay up in the evenings, sleep in, and go to school at 10:30, so that we entered without disruption as kids returned from recess. We were late so often that the district attorney threatened to put us in foster care and send Mom to jail. When she offered Mom a "no contest" plea with a $100 fine and a year's probation, Mom said, "I'll consider it." One of us piped up, "Mom, we were late more than a hundred days. That's 50 cents a time. Take it!" The DA looked surprised, maybe less because a seven-year-old did the math, than because she told Mom what to do in that setting.

Recoiling from this encounter with "the system," parents enrolled us in a charter school that sends a teacher to Magic once a month to assess our learning. We settled back into life at home and started taking a more active role in the household and with Magic projects. We felt good assisting new residents as they learned about living in community, and in transitioning from being mostly cared for and supervised to doing more useful work.

One thing we really enjoyed was dragging adult residents to run and swim with us, and leading them on bike rides up and over the Santa Cruz Mountains to the ocean. We loved it when they called us personal trainers and told friends about us. Watching them shed pounds and become stronger and more enduring, we understood better why Magic fellows took so much satisfaction in helping people become healthier, and why prior residents so often came back and expressed appreciation for healthful living habits they formed while here.

By the time we were old enough to go to middle school we were supervising fieldwork crews on nearby open space where a half million people hike each year. Being young, and female on top of that, we had some "interesting" interactions with volunteers. Though many quickly realized that we were strong and knowledgeable, some ignored our instruction. We learned a lot explaining to men two, three, or four times our age and twice our size why the tree they planted was likely to die unless they dug it out and replanted it.

Magic fellows have been pioneers in drawing attention to and working to arrest decline of California's native oak populations. They've led tens of thousands of volunteers in establishing thousands of native oaks. The oaks project is a great example of how Magic promotes health, cooperation, and stewardship based upon valuescience. Volunteers, many of whom have little experience with manual labor, dirty their hands, get tired and sore, and gain new appreciation for this kind of work and for those around the world who do it day in and out. School kids, retirees, clerks, venture capitalists, engineers, lawyers, and more come together and give. All of us feel good working together without any compensation except satisfaction generated by caring for the environment we share.

When fellows explain that species we plant can live for centuries, and that only if we and people everywhere re-examine and change our ideas about value—about what we want and how to get it—will they be able to do so, volunteers have incentive to reflect. One former resident, a mechanical engineer, started volunteering on the oaks project and is now Apple's arborist. At the company's new campus he's overseeing the largest urban planting west of the Mississippi since Golden Gate Park in San Francisco more than a hundred years ago. A

Jen and Hil with Farmers' Market food salvage volunteers and portion of a day's donations.

Hil explaining valuescience to Magic visitors, age 16.

Jen presenting dinner, age 16.

Jen with watering crew, age 16.

Jen and Hil receiving donated surplus oranges from FarmerBob.

middle school volunteer later became Mayor of Palo Alto and described in his inaugural address how he and his family transformed their relationship with nature as a result of his planting with Magic.

Since we were 13 each of us has prepared supper one night each week for about two dozen residents and guests. We've a set of guidelines evolved over the years so that we eat in a way that reflects concern for diners' health, for other people's work and wants, and for Earth. We aim to be efficient in our use of labor and other resources as we procure and prepare food, and maintain kitchen, dining areas, equipment, and furnishings. We've become closer with several residents by inviting them to be sous-chefs to us in preparation for taking a cook night themselves.

As we've grown older we've become more able to participate fully in community social life and to interact with residents and the larger Magic service community more purpose-fully. One resident taught us to knit and included us in a knitting circle. Another taught us computer programming. Others help us learn to sew, to paint and draw, to play music, to dance, to repair bicycles, and to maintain buildings and furnishings. In all of these activi-ties we've developed a better sense of how people beyond a single family can live together and learn to feel and express more love for each other and for those beyond our doors.

Ever since our experience in public school we've been aware that we were different. From the time we were nine until we were 16 a Magic board member took us and one of the moms to a family camp near Lake Tahoe. Being there was like school all over again. People frowned when they heard we lived in community. As we grew older we felt less and less comfortable with prying questions about family and home life. We sometimes wished we were "normal" even though when we went on overnight trips with the other kids we were glad to be who we were.

In the past year or so we've come to see growing up at Magic in a different light. We've paid more attention to valuescience, to how every part of our lives to date has been based on it, and to how we've gained and lost as a result.

We've heard thousands of conversations at Magic about valuescience and "ecological analysis." For many years these seemed self-evident (e.g., Why drive when we can walk or bike?), or too abstract for our young brains (e.g., How might "saving lives" today adversely affect those who may live tomorrow?). Recently as we're increasingly asked, "Where do you want to go to college?," "What do you want to be when you grow up?," we've been think-ing more about what we want to ask of and offer to others, and looking at valuescience in a new way. Having been taught to question, we're wondering how much of it to keep and how much to shed.

Jen guiding volunteers watering, age 16.

Jen and Hil, age 16, fellows, and residents gather for resident birthday celebration over evening meal on porch of Magic residence.

We first learned to describe valuescience in simple terms before we went to school. We understood in some primitive way that we had ideas about what we wanted, that we based these on predictions about how we were going to feel when we got it, and that we were sometimes mistaken. Eating too much pizza, getting sunburned, and playing in poison oak remain vivid reminders that what we think we want can be very different from what we really want.

From before we can remember we learned to think of science less as a set of facts or theories than as a way of life. We saw that by introspection and observation we were able to discern repeating pattern and use it to make predictions more successful than we were able to make by other means. We understood that this was a way to have meaningful choice, to get more of what we want and want more of what we get.

Only recently have we come to see more clearly how this has to do with public service. Effective service is a combination of good intention and competent action. Valuescience underpins both.

Though many of us have been conditioned to think that people who know better what we want and how to get it will ever more rapaciously plunder Earth and exploit those around us in pursuit of wealth and fame, we have growing scientific basis to reject this. More than 50 years ago Abraham Maslow discovered that loving and caring for others and ultimately transcending our sense of separate self are key to living and dying well. Researchers today are gathering mounting evidence for these conclusions. They've shown, for example, that we may derive more satisfaction by giving than by keeping for ourselves or receiving. And they've affirmed Maslow's findings that people who work for common good are more satisfied and feel a greater sense of meaning and purpose.

Sound analysis also is essential to serve. Tube wells in Bangladesh are illustrative. With unanimous support of government, diverse NGOs, and expert consultants, Bangladeshis sank millions of tube wells to tap drinking water from a shallow aquifer and end reliance upon surface waters teeming with disease-causing microbes. Only later did public health workers realize that the aquifer was contaminated with arsenic, resulting in tens of millions of people being permanently damaged in what the World Health Organization terms "the largest mass poisoning in human history." Countless other schemes to "help" others have similarly, albeit usually less spectacularly failed.

Only to the extent that we've evidence and reason sufficient to support predictions about outcomes of our service efforts can we anticipate that we will achieve intended results. We find this humbling, and it's the biggest lesson we're taking from valuescience practice to date. Even as we engage in putative service through Magic, we wonder how well we're predicting consequences. Will trees we plant die young as a result of how humans are altering climate? Will volunteers think that planting a tree makes jetting around sustainable? Will salvaging food and feeding the hungry contribute to perpetuating a system where some lack necessities while others wallow in luxury? Will teaching valuescience be one more example of idealism forever short of real?

If we do embrace a valuescience-based existence with all its questions, how will we interact with those who prefer simple answers? Will we be shunned for eating, dressing, grooming, traveling, sheltering, relating, parenting, religing, communicating, and more in ways we think compatible with scientific understanding of our own and other humans' place in the universe? Will we be able to create sangha, community of shared practice, with others who find merit in valuescience? Will we be able to evolve how we serve in a manner that we think has integrity and that others deem worthy of support? What lessons learned coming of age in a valuescience service learning community shall we carry forward, and which shall we shed? ✍

Effective service is a combination of good intention and competent action. Valuescience underpins both.

Jen and Hilary Bayer live at Magic, an intentional community owned and operated by a public service organization located in Palo Alto, California, founded in the early 1970s on the premise that individual health and awareness, social peace and fairness, and environmental protection are tightly connected, and that ecology is a framework for addressing all of these issues. Magicians see themselves as cognitive activists, aiming "to bring about social change by evolving the framework we use to think about the world and our place in it, often by reframing debates or redefining terms."

Hil and Jen loading salvaged peaches, nectarines, and leeks for transport to food bank.

Jen and Hil after piano recital in dresses they made, age 15.

ACTIVISM AND SERVICE AT BLACK BULGA COMMUNITY: Inspiring, Nurturing, Challenging, and Not All Hard Work

By Geoff Evans

Our small rural land-sharing community, Black Bulga, comprises 13 people and is located in the forested, healthy, and clean headwaters of the Karuah River in the Hunter Valley in Australia, near the city of Newcastle, which is about 100 miles north of Sydney. We have been forming together as a community for seven years and have owned our land for five years.

We formed as an explicitly "service" or "activist" community having gotten to know each other mainly through social change activist networks. We are very fortunate. We enjoy a healthy environment in a country where there is relatively little violence or war. Being aware of our special luck, we were determined when we formed our community that our purpose was not to retreat from the world. Rather our purpose is to create a community that will sustain us, and inspire us to engage with the wider world to help make it a better place for our generation and those that follow.

Our shared commitment to activism gives Black Bulga a distinct purpose, and our commitment to service and activism is written into the vision and values sections of our bylaws: "Our vision is to act as custodians of the rural land upon which we live, working together to create a sustainable and just future in our immediate community and in the wider world." The values written into our bylaws include commitments to use our collective resourcefulness and creativity to care for the land, and for each other, our neighborhood, region, and the planet. While we subscribe to no particular ideology, our politics is informed by ecological libertarian socialist values. We pay attention to how we can support each other to sustain our activism in the spirit of these values.

Our members' activist work spans multiple roles and locations, including as frontline defenders joining local residents blockading proposed gasfields in the nearby town of Gloucester and elsewhere; as managers of social change organizations; as activist trainers, community organizers, and facilitators; as mentors and elders to a wide community of activists in multiple fields and in different places and age groups; as educators and researchers in a wide range of academic and activist programs including in family wellbeing and sustainability; in international community development and medical aid work; as practitioners in community arts and sustainable food growing; and as parents and allies to fellow parents. Our collective and individual activism inspires us, exhausts us, nurtures us—and challenges us.

The youngest and oldest Black Bulga community members (and friends) marching for climate action in Sydney in November 2015.

We have found that our social change activism builds local community and connects us with our neighbors as well as the wider world. In fact, we did not need to go far to find opportunity to put our individual and shared passions for social change into practice. In our local valley, our service work gets literally "down amongst the weeds." We are

and other residents from the length of the Karuah River catchment together to learn about and fight the proposal. We formed the Karuah River Protection Alliance and together we spoke out strongly through local and national media, to government officials, and directly to the company. Following our extensive lobbying the proposal was dropped, and by winning the campaign, we helped secure the future of the valley for nature-based tourism and sustainable food growing.

Before the campaign we were known rather disparagingly as "The Commune," but through the campaign our neighbors got to appreciate the campaigning skills of the "new kids to the block," while we admired their skills and capacity to organize locally. The campaign sped up the process of us being accepted as part of the community. We now share farming knowledge, host our neighbors' horses and cattle on our land, regularly have meals together, and celebrate family events such as children's birthdays, Spring

Balancing social change work with building a strong community poses many challenges.

proud to have been instrumental in forming a local Landcare network to protect our river catchment from weed infestations. In Australia, this Landcare movement has been a powerful social movement that has brought farmers and environmentalists together at grassroots and national levels, with government funding support. As Landcarers we've worked and sweated in hot sun and along riverbanks with our neighbors, removing weeds and creating space for local native plants to regenerate. John Mac, the Black Bulga member who leads this work, reports the benefits:

"This service work builds local community networks to collectively protect our local environment. We have in our valley, between us, hundreds of years of land management knowledge. We share stories of about what is effective and efficient land management, and what doesn't work and is a waste of time and effort. We also share lots of cakes and cups of coffee."

We have among our members some very experienced activists who have spent decades campaigning around mining, environmental protection, and human rights, working with mine–affected communities locally and globally. When a gold mine was proposed upriver in upper reaches of the Karuah River in 2011, soon after we had bought our land, the mine-owners may not have realized who they were taking on. The whole catchment community saw the mine as a threat, with the risk of sediment pollution and, potentially, cyanide contamination jeopardizing local farming and tourism industries and the rural lifestyle and amenity.

We were quick to act, and with our neighbors, we used the extensive networks throughout the valley to bring farmers, eco-tourism business operators, oyster farmers,

and Autumn (Fall) Equinox, and New Year's Eve.

While our valley is mining-free, thousands of residents and farmers in neighboring valleys across the Hunter Valley are fighting the devastating impacts of vast open-cut (open-pit) coal mines and the threat of gasfields with severe impacts on their environments and health. The Hunter is one of the world's largest coal-exporting regions, with hundreds of millions of tons of coal exported from the port of Newcastle annually to North and East Asia. The region is also the home of coal-fired power stations that have historically been the major source of Australia's electricity. Together these industries make the Hunter region one of the world's climate change hot-spots. Many times our members have joined frontline action against coal and climate change including blockading gasfields in the nearby town of Gloucester with local residents, and other peaceful blockades and lock-ons at coal mines and coal export terminals in Newcastle and elsewhere.

Balancing externally-oriented social change work with building a strong and viable intentional community poses many challenges. Our service and activist work takes our focus away from building our relatively new community and from working on our land. This challenge is compounded by the fact that actually living and working on our land is very difficult as it is quite remote and there are few jobs in the local area. We have had to find ways to transition from careers in large cities to work that we can do from the land or in nearby towns. Jemma, who manages a small international development organization as well as co-parenting three children under eight years old recently moved from Sydney to Newcastle, as part of her family's strategy to be closer to the land and spend more time at Black Bulga, highlights the tension:

"To make Black Bulga grow and thrive in the long-term, it needs people there, planting through the seasons, working together, creating a hub. But it is a tricky tension to manage—how to be on the land while still being an active part of social change campaigns. At the moment, we are all in the transition to spending more time at Black Bulga. We have monthly community meetings, regular all-in working bees, and big social gatherings. There is a real network of friends and family—many of whom work in social change—who have a genuine connection to Black Bulga, who visit regularly, talk politics, get their hands dirty, dream and replenish. I love that the Black Bulga community is bigger than just the group of unit holders."

The heavy demands and occasional heady excitement that comes from activist work—which in some cases allows us to travel the world, be in the national media spotlight, and confront powerful political and corporate interests—makes a stark contrast to the work of building community and caring for food crops, stock, and buildings. John, who is often away supporting local coal and gas campaigns around Australia and globally, reflects that "It is too easy for me to live in my head but Black Bulga helps to keep me grounded. The place has a wildness that replenishes the soul."

Another member, James, who develops education programs for activists, also grapples with the challenge of balancing his external community and Black Bulga community focus: "I try to meet my own and my intentional community's needs by being at Black Bulga as much as possible and when here, I get stuck into a hands-on project such as building work, and joining in the cooking and sharing of great food, and reading and playing with the children. Black Bulga helps me keep the relentless demands of work in its box. It's not easy, but my fellow community members help me meet this challenge."

As individuals, and as a community, we are still in transition when it comes to combining our activism with a rural farm-based lifestyle. We are trying to work part-time rather than full-time. We use internet, Skype, and email technologies as much as possible so we can work from the land. Our aim to make Black Bulga an arts and ecology education center is part of our community's purpose but, like living on the land permanently, we recognize that this vision is long-term and is happening in small steps. Dan, who recently held a successful solo exhibition of paintings inspired by the vast and ever-changing Black Bulga skies, comments:

"The arts and ecology project is part of a lifelong journey of the community. We are giving effect to the vision by organizing arts and ecology events and activities on the land, even though we don't yet have a building specifically for this purpose. Our community celebrates the equinox and solstice with gatherings that involve rituals that range from reverent to ridiculous. We have raced down the river on inflatable rafts, built clay pizza ovens and cooked seasonal feasts to eat under the stars, made beautiful lanterns and ugly effigies of 'baddies' to set alight, woven baskets from weeds, and healed a gully with plantings. Already many friends and community come here to draw, paint, and take photos; some have learnt blacksmithing; others have come to write, take nature walks, go bird-watching, and more."

The community consciously works on integrating the service elements of our lives with the personal and community care elements of our lives in an intentional community. Deb, who works in family studies and relationship research programs at the region's university and across Australia, as well as with academics and family relationship professionals and activists in India, Southeast Asia, and the US, identifies the need for balance here: "At Black Bulga we work hard at supporting each other to pay good attention to both our work and personal lives. The demands of managing complex decisions about the future of the community requires care and a strong commitment to listen to and support each other. We look out for each other. This work on building

positive relationships helps us be whole, well-balanced people at Black Bulga and in our family, professional, and activist lives as well."

Prue, mother of two-year old Blake, is a campaigner supporting communities trying to stop fracking for gas in various parts of the state. She is often away from home: "Activism work can be hard on the family. Luckily I have a very supportive partner, but the activist life requires a strong and constant focus on our own well-being individually and collectively, particularly on our work as parents. All members of the Black Bulga community are great support and allies to us as parents, and to Blake as a young toddler."

As individuals and as a community we at Black Bulga know that service and activist work is incredibly important, rewarding, and challenging lifelong work. Our community is a vital support foundation for us being able to go out into the wider world as effective change agents. As many of our friends are also activists, we recognize they have the same challenges balancing service and personal lives as we do. We encourage them to get "out of the city and into the bush" and to use Black Bulga as a place to enjoy nature, and to swim, walk, and play together with family and friends. Reconnecting with the rhythms of nature—and enjoying collectively-grown and cooked food, fireside conversation under starry skies, and being woken by the sounds of the dawn chorus of birds—helps us see that service and activist lives are not all hard work. ❧

Geoff Evans is a wannabe farmer. He keeps the Black Bulga dream alive through activism on mining, climate change, and community development, and working with the community to build a small house and grow an organic garlic crop each year on the land.

Black Bulga hosting a celebration dinner for the Community Organising Fellowship in our big strawbale shed in July 2015.

Photos courtesy of Geoff Evans

Urban Kibbutzim: A Growing Movement

By Anton Marks

The first kibbutz was established over 100 years ago, and over the following century, a network of almost 300 full income-sharing agricultural communes was established all over Israel. The plan was based on anarchist principles, whereby this federation of communities would coalesce into a whole cooperative society, without centralized government or borders.

Fast forward to the year 2017. The rural kibbutz communities are in retreat, there's a strong central government and, albeit for very different reasons, the country has no clear borders.

However, there are those who have picked up the mantle of taking responsibility for shaping the society, young people who are establishing hundreds of urban communes that, both individually and as movements, are effecting change in the inner cities—communes of educators who are working against violence, racism, homophobia, and poverty.

I am a member of Kibbutz Mishol, one of the many intentional communities that have been established over the past 20 years. We are 130 people, all living under one roof, making decisions together, bringing our children up together, sharing all of our income, 10 cars, our living spaces, and a handful of dogs, cats, and chinchillas.

Our kibbutz is in the city; in fact, we are situated in one of the most deprived neighbourhoods in the country—and it's a choice. We've made this choice to work together with our partners in the local municipality, and together with our partners who live in this city, to shape the wider community for the benefit of all of its citizens—Jews, Arabs, those from the former Soviet Union, from Ethiopia, asylum seekers, religious, secular, left, and right.

We have established a nonprofit organization through which we run all of our educational projects. For example, we run a local public elementary school, non-formal education in after-school centres, a youth movement, a coexistence project, and educational tours to Poland. In addition, we have teams of people working together taking responsibility over the inner functioning of our community—looking after our cars, our building, our children, our finances, our learning, our relationships, and our culture.

It's a healthy tension in our lives: to what extent are we focused on the internal—living together and improving our relationships, creating a community that makes decisions by consensus, challenging societal norms when it comes to gender roles, understanding the different needs and different abilities of our members—and to what extent on the external—our interactions and impact on the surrounding society? Do we exist for ourselves, as a lifestyle choice, or is our aim to use community as a vehicle for changing the world around us?

The kibbutz-building enterprise started as a way of addressing the needs of a developing society and a developing economy—agriculture, creating towns and villages, defending the borders, building a public health system, a nationwide union, newspapers, etc. Today the needs of the country can be found in the inner cities, draining the social swamps of society, rather than the physical mosquito-infested swamps of the early 20th century backwaters of the Ottoman Empire.

Photos courtesy of haaretz.co.il

These urban communes, largely situated in the geographical and economic peripheries of Israel, springing up like mushrooms after the rain, are a model of how an alternative society can be built within the existing capitalist society—not as isolated independent communities, but as a network of communities which together offer an example of how society can be structured in a more just and equitable way. ❧

Anton Marks has been active on the international communal scene for many years; he is a board member of the ICSA (International Communal Studies Association) and has attended three of their international conferences. He has also been general secretary of the Intentional Communities Desk (formerly known as the International Communes Desk) and was editor of their magazine C.A.L.L. for 15 years.

It's Not Just the Curtain: Crossing the Class Divide at the Bloomington Catholic Worker

By Laura Lasuertmer

The curtain that divides the hallway between guest room and members' bedrooms.

Our short hallway is divided in the middle by a curtain that hangs from ceiling to floor. In front of the curtain is a door to our guest room and the full bathroom. Behind the curtain are the doors to our bedroom and our kids' room.

Peggy lives in the guest room. She is a thin woman in her mid-50s, with long, curly hair that she dyes red to cover the gray. Her energy level is enviable, and as she sweeps the living room she recounts how a man at the overnight shelter took her aside to ask, "What kind of speed are you on?"

"I don't do that," she says to me, "I've just always had this energy. I like to work. I like to volunteer. Otherwise I just sit around feeling anxious." So she swept the kitchen too and even under the rug by the front door where we leave our shoes.

Peggy had been staying at the shelter but due to a disagreement with a staff member, she decided to leave. She moved in with us a week ago, which means she is halfway through her "two-week trial." Next Thursday, we'll meet with her to ask how her time here has been. If all is going well, we'll invite her to stay for two months, renewable up to a year.

Each family at the Bloomington Catholic Worker lives with people experiencing homelessness. These "guests" stay in our guest rooms, cook in our kitchens, shower in our bathrooms, and join us for meals throughout the week. Even as we live closely with these people, trying to form a bridge across class divides, we do not aim to live in intentional community with them. We make distinctions and create boundaries between the members of our community and the guests of our community. These distinctions, like the curtain dividing our hallway, can be problematic sometimes. They can inhibit our ability to form deep relationships with guests, and they mirror the class divide that already exists between us. Still, they are what allow us to share our homes with people year after year, to care for folks we might otherwise never meet. For example...

One Friday, a few months after Peggy moved in, I answered a knock on the front door.

"Can I speak with the owner?" asked a man in a gray t-shirt and baggy jeans. Big, round glasses sat on his squat nose and a brown ring of hair smiled behind his otherwise bald head. It was Michael. He'd been my client while I was working at the day shelter a year ago.

"The community owns the houses," I replied. "But you can speak with me. What's up, Michael?"

"I haven't slept in three days. I've got 56 more days on parole and every time I put my head down to sleep, the cops wake me up and tell me to move. I get in trouble just once and I'm back in prison." I was surprised how coherent his speech was. At the shelter, I'd most often seen him struggling to stand up straight, his words coming out thick and dry.

"Our guest beds are full," I told him. It was a warm mid-October day. The leaves had already started to fall. The sky was a blue so deep it seemed infinite. "But I can sling up the hammock in the back yard if you want to take a nap."

"Please," he said. We walked around the house to the backyard. A picnic table sat in front of two tall black locust trees. My young kids, Alice and Leo, came out to join us and busied themselves with the soccer ball.

"Have you heard of Team Takeover?" Michael asked as I wrapped a black strap around a tree. "They're a gang, a street gang. See my thumb?" He pointed to a thin, deep cut on his thumb joint. "RP did that. Said he'd take my pinky off if I don't give him $300 on the 3rd when I get my disability check."

"That's insane," I said as I hooked the hammock into the straps.

"Can I sleep here tonight?" Michael asked.

"I'm not sure. We don't usually let people camp out. But let me run inside and talk to David about it."

Would you let Michael stay the night in your backyard? Our community intentionally invites these situations and questions. We want people to show up at our houses while we are eating dinner, having a meeting, playing outside with our kids—maybe not every day, but definitely sometimes. We want our lives to be interrupted by the needs of others.

Michael's situation was compelling: he needed a safe place to sleep. It helped that I knew him and that he was clearly sober. I ran the idea past David, who agreed, and went back outside. I found Michael already asleep. He passed the afternoon that way. It was early evening when I saw him swing his legs over the side and sit up.

"You can stay tonight," I said, taking a seat at the picnic table. "Should I set up the tent?"

"Naw. That hammock was great," he said. "Thanks. I haven't slept like that in weeks."

"I'm glad," I said. "Is it alright if I run through the rules we have for guests?"

"That's cool."

"Our big rule is that this is safe and sober housing."

"That's fine," Michael said. "I've been sober since I got out of prison a month ago, and I am done—done!"

"Great," I said. "Because we won't let you stay if you're using. And are you legally allowed to be around children?"

"Yeah," he said. "You want my D.O.C. number? You can look up my record. I don't have no sex crimes, nothing like that."

"Sure. I'll check it online. So the other main rule is that guests have to be out of the house, or I guess the backyard in your case, from nine to five."

"That's no problem. I just need a place to sleep."

"We'll take it a night at a time. And we'll have interviews on Wednesday afternoon. Peggy just found an apartment and is moving out on Monday."

"Can I get an interview?" Michael said.

"For sure," I said.

Later that night, I looked up Michael's criminal record. There were a few theft charges along with some misdemeanors for public intoxication and trespassing, similar to the records of many people who stay with us. I got him a sleeping bag and a pillow. He went to bed at eight and was still sleeping when I went out at seven-thirty the next morning, drops of rain starting to fall.

"Michael! It's raining! Grab your backpack and come inside for breakfast."

"I slept the whole night," he said sitting up. "I didn't wake up once. Can I come back tonight?"

"Sure," I said. "Come back any time after five."

That night the temperature dropped to the 40s. I wondered if we should let Michael sleep on the couch. David was hesitant. He didn't know Michael and thought we should wait until we formally interviewed him with other community members. Our guest room was already full, David reminded me. Michael said he would be fine outside, so we gave him extra blankets and said goodnight.

Michael stayed with us a few more nights. On the day of the interview, he called to say he didn't need the bed. He felt safer being away from Bloomington, so he was going to camp out with a buddy in the next town over.

What is ideal when it comes to offering hospitality? Should we never turn away a person in need?

"If you're sure," I said, "but call us if you need anything."

"I will," he said.

And he does. We check in with each other every few weeks, so I know that he'll be off parole in 20 days. In a month, thanks to a permanent supportive housing program, he'll be moving into an apartment.

What is ideal when it comes to offering hospitality? Should we never turn away a person in need? We've learned that thinking we can help everyone is not realistic and not

BCW weekly potluck with community members and guests. Mark, a guest, enjoys a meal with Alice and Tressa.

Sarah Lynn Gershon, a BCW member, always smiles when she does dishes after potluck.

Photos courtesy of Laura Lasuertmer

healthy. To be able to provide comfortable, peaceful places to live, we say no to some people in need. We say "no" to people with untreated mental illness, "no" to people actively using drugs or alcohol. We say "no" to people who are sex offenders. We say "no" because we recognize that we must also be hospitable to our children and ourselves, creating safe environments that further our well-being. We're walking the middle road, and finding that even with these

of respite and healing—so we do not require our guests to believe anything we believe or to participate in our communal activities, except for eating dinner with us on Thursday nights. They do not attend our business meetings. They do not contribute to our common bank account. They are not required to cook community meals or attend daily morning prayer. We also ask our guests to be out of the houses from nine to five daily, so that families have a break from sharing their space. We do invite our guests to eat and pray with us, if they are so inclined, but it is up to them. Some guests leave early every day and arrive back late in the evening. Other guests eat dinner with us every night, use the kitchen, read books to our kids, and take to sweeping the floors. Community members, on the other hand, contribute half of their income to the common account, participate in consensus-based decision making, practice confession and reconciliation, go on retreat together, attend morning prayer together, and share childcare duties.

> **Our guests connect us with the urgent and harsh reality of poverty. They keep us aware of struggle and injustice in our community, showing us where to take action. We rely on our guests to help us grow and to keep us grounded in gratitude.**

These distinctions between guests and members mean that we have to work hard to make our guests feel welcome and to get to know them well. They move into a well-established community with a middle class culture, and that can exaggerate the feeling of being an outsider. In between caring for our children, working, and participating in community life, it can be hard for us to take time to be with our guests. When our family lives dominate, what we offer to guests is simply a safe place to live. When we are more intentional about spending time with our guests, our hospitality builds genuine, reciprocal friendships that endure even after a guest has moved out.

restrictions, our guest beds are full. I've learned that we do what we can. A hammock outside on a cold night is not much to offer someone, but it's better than sleeping in an alley or under a bush.

Guests come to us because they need a place to stay, not because they are eager to participate in the shared life of our community. While our community is religious, we are not an evangelical mission. We want to offer our guests a place

This way of living doesn't eliminate class divisions, but it brings us closer to one another. Peggy and Michael, and all our guests, are an integral part of the Bloomington Catholic Worker. They connect us with the urgent and harsh reality of poverty. They keep us aware of struggle and injustice in our community, showing us where to take action. They remind us why we don't aspire to build big houses and live in the suburbs. They ask us to share space and resources, reminding us that while we despise destitution we do desire to live, like them, with less. We rely on our guests to help us grow and to keep us grounded in gratitude. 🐚

Laura Lasuertmer is a member of the Bloomington Catholic Worker (BCW) community in Bloomington, Indiana. She enjoys writing collaboratively with people living in jail and on the streets.

A former guest, Gustavo, created this mosaic for the entryway to Little Way House.

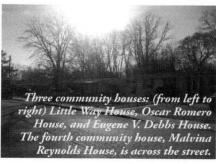

Three community houses: (from left to right) Little Way House, Oscar Romero House, and Eugene V. Debbs House. The fourth community house, Malvina Reynolds House, is across the street.

The kids in the community put on a show while the parents gather at another house for a roundtable discussion.

can we shorten this

Opportunity Village Eugene
Pioneering New Solutions for the (Formerly) Homeless

By Alex Daniell

Opportunity Village Eugene is Eugene, Oregon's newest intentional community. In less than three months, in late summer and fall of 2013, for less than $60,000, it went from an empty public works parking lot to a village housing 30 people. There have been many players, major and minor, male and female, straight and gay; organizers, volunteers, and villagers themselves. It is a self-governing village, with oversight and veto power over Village Council decisions by the board of the nonprofit organization Opportunity Village Eugene, which is chaired by Dan Bryant, minister of the First Congregational Church downtown.

Opportunity Village (www.opportunityvillageeugene.org) is governed by the Village Manual and its Village Agreements (www.opportunityvillageeugene.org/p/community-agreement.html). The Village Manual is an improved version of similar documents written by the residents of other homeless camps, like Dignity Village and Right to Dream Two in Portland, Oregon. It is authored by Andy Heben, who is also the urban designer of Opportunity Village.

Nine Conestoga Huts, insulated vinyl-sheathed shelters made from a combination of reused and new materials, were built in the village by Community Supported Shelters (communitysupportedshelters.org). I have designed, and built with the help of many others, all 18 of the solid-walled buildings in the village, including dwellings, a bath house, a kitchen, a front office, and also an outdoor grill. Like the Village Manual, the Backyard Bungalows (hebenaj.wix.com/backyardbungalows) we've built are improved versions of the dwellings erected by residents of other homeless villages. They are modular designs, composed of panels that are constructed in the shop and assembled on site in big work parties.

In July I submitted four of these prototypes, all under 100 square feet, with interchangeable wall and roof systems, to the city of Eugene and the state of Oregon for pre-approval to house the homeless. All four were accepted without any alterations. I now have nearly a dozen prototypes that have passed inspection by the city.

Ted Drummond, a longtime leader in the First Christian Church's annual house-building Mission to Mexico, erected a heated 30-foot yurt for the villagers just days before the early-December snows came. Andy, Ted, and I are partners in the micro-housing business I founded in 2012, called Backyard Bungalows. Our mission is to build Affordable Villages, after the model of Opportunity Village.

When the city of Eugene broke up the Occupy camp in December of 2011, they promised to give the homeless another piece of land. Dan Bryant, a minister who wears a leather jacket and drives a motorcycle, Jean Stacey, a fiery

Our last "Big Build." We've had five so far, all on the last Saturday of the month.

lesbian advocate for the homeless, and Andy Heben, a young urban designer who wrote his thesis on homeless camps around the country which he visited, went around touting the idea of Opportunity Village.

I was working at the time with Erik de Buhr, finishing up one of my Bungalow designs for Jerry and Janet Russell, who have given endlessly to the communities movement in this region. We were also working on the Conestoga Hut, a design that Erik and his partner Fay Carter created in a moment of need at the Occupy camp. At the December 2012 open forum Eugene city council meeting, on the heels of an enraged speech by Jean Stacey, who was camped out with SLEEPS near a Conestoga Hut we had set up earlier in the day, I made a proposal to the city council. I proposed that the Conestoga Hut be permitted as a vehicle in the St. Vincent de Paul car camper program, where homeless people can sleep in their cars in business and church parking lots. Though the city attorney had said that this ordinance would take two months to expand, the council did so in three days. That night they also approved the site for Opportunity Village.

In the following days the Conestoga Hut got a lot of press and Erik and I had a divergence of opinion. While Erik and Fay wanted to start their own nonprofit professional organization independent of Opportunity Village, called Community Supported Shelters, with the hopes of becoming the village's main housing provider and building Opportunity Village almost entirely out of Conestoga Huts, I wanted to work with Opportunity Village, and to build a village of two dozen micro-houses each of which looked unique—in the process creating a prototype for an affordable village. So I went to an Opportunity Village steering committee meeting.

At this first meeting the group was ecstatic. On the heels of a solid year of pleading with the city to provide the piece of land that they had promised, they were talking of the great popularity they would have, of the micro-businesses they would incubate, of the Academy they would set up. Playing devil's advocate, I mentioned that they had no villagers, no approved structures other than the Conestoga Hut, and no site plan. I proposed that they set up a core group of villagers, and begin orienting them in the philosophy, agreements, and rules of the Village Manual, so that a village culture would be in place before the village itself opened.

Brent Was, father at the Church of the Resurrection, took the lead in this process, and Andy and Ann and several volunteers dove into the paperwork. We began the application and intake process almost immediately. A particular focus was placed on vetting couples and single women, so that there would be a strong female presence in the village. This has proved invaluable, as women have come to dominate both the governance and administrative responsibilities of the village.

At this point I began working with Andy Heben. In addition to producing sketch-ups for my prototypes, working on the site plan, and hammering out the operating agreement with the city, Andy worked tirelessly writing and rewriting the Village Manual, based on the ongoing input of many well-meaning contributors, myself included. It is a brilliant document. I made dozens of copies, and handed them out to everyone. It is a brief, clear set of agreements and rules villagers must understand and agree to before joining the village. Based on simple majority and occasionally two-thirds majority vote at the village meetings, it uses simple clear language that can be interpreted but cannot be corrupted by the board or by the villagers. We read it out loud line by line during our biweekly orientations, with open discussion.

Of particular importance was the village site plan. Despite the difficulties it

Ron and Kathy—married in the village.

Kathy, Rhonda, and Fredricka in the village kitchen.

entailed, Andy avoided orienting the Bungalows and Conestogas in a grid, instead orchestrating them in a series of graceful circular courtyards that maximize a feeling of openness on the small site. By orienting four distinct roof systems thoughtfully, and placing the generous used doors and windows optimally for both light and privacy, we created a village that appears to have grown organically. Each Bungalow is trimmed, painted, and finished individually by its owner. There are distinctly masculine and feminine structures. The most popular prototypes seem to be the Lean To, the Club House, and Dianne's Love Shack, with its purple cornice and black gargoyles.

It's long after supper. I sit with Craig and Randy in the yurt. The flickering light and steady hiss of the pellet stove fill the large, dim space. Chairs and fold-up tables, a coffee pot, and donated food in plastic bags are neatly arranged along the walls. The newest villager, Mandy, drifts by and says hi. Terry comes in and sets up her laptop.

Craig is a quiet, confident hippie, with a bandana over his forehead. He is a father, and a natural leader in the village. "How come no one's in here?," he asks.

"Because it's not below 34 degrees," Randy replies, "so no one thought that they'd be allowed to sleep in here tonight."

The village is full of rules, but they are good rules. The villagers seem to need them. People do file unwarranted complaints, but it's not something the board worries about. It takes time for the villagers to settle in and learn a different way than the Eugene Mission, where a lot of applicants come from. Actually, Craig and I agree, things are going really well. Ernie and Katie and Jones and Matt all have jobs, and two other people just found work too.

"How much more time," I ask Craig "do you have on the Village Council?"

"Two weeks." He smiles serenely.

So far only one person has finished out their three-month term. The only man on the five-person Council, Craig has spoken of stepping down, but the Council has pleaded for him to stay, saying that they need his masculine presence. Craig presented with me at the Central Lutheran Church adult education program recently, answering questions for a half-hour. The Lutherans have donated thousands of dollars worth of materials and thousands of work hours in the shop. They, and Dan Hill of Arbor South, who donated $15,000 worth of materials, were the backbone that allowed us to build Opportunity Village.

"Some people on the board think that it's ridiculous that so few Council members finish out their terms."

"What's ridiculous about that?" Craig asks. "It's not like anyone is getting kicked out of the village. It's a clear sign of the health of the democratic process."

With the stress of a continual influx of new people—living in tents during at least part of their probationary period—and the rest of the village living in unheated Bungalows and Conestogas, Village Councilors have to be steady. When someone is not, they get voted off. No hard feelings.

"The women are much more involved in the administration and governance tasks, and the men are more involved in construction—roofing and finishing the Bungalows. Most of the cooking has been implemented by the women, with much of the infrastructure work being done by their men."

"Why does the Village Council need a male presence? In order to feel credible in the eyes of the male villagers?"

"Probably."

Andy, Joline, and I, along with a half dozen villagers, sit before the warm flames of the fireplace at Papa's Pizza Parlor, eating taco pizza and drinking dark beer at a fundraiser for the village. Every villager needs to come up with $30 a month towards utilities. There is no drinking within 500 feet of the gate but we are farther away than that.

To my left is Anton, a working cobbler, who has repaired two pairs of my shoes and refuses to be paid. He is Greek, so I don't push it. His wife, Fredricka Maximillia Sanchez, a tall beautiful woman, talks of her four daughters, and the honorable lives they lead. Hal, across the table, is a computer programmer. Louis sits to my right, a crafter of wooden inlaid jewelry, who is designing a micro-business that can employ villagers doing piecework. Carl and Dianne have finished out their Bungalows with architectural details and color schemes that we can use as models for regular paying clients. Mark Hubble is one of the original founders of the village.

Ron and Katherine Griffith, who were married at the village, speak of their gender roles:

"It's a reverse relationship," Katherine says, in her North Carolina accent, "and it always has been, ever since Ron tore his ACL. I work, and he does the cooking and cleaning. I don't care if I never wash another dish in my life."

In the last village meeting, in the interests of keeping peace in the community, Richard James and Louis volunteered to wash all the unwashed dishes.

"They make sure we get stuff done," Ron says.

All the villagers are required to do eight to 10 hours a week staffing the front desk, cooking, cleaning, doing paperwork, and/or roofing, insulating, and finishing the Bungalows. Katherine does more than her share, on and off the Village Council.

"I do the electronics, and home improvements. A lot of times when the women try to do the heavier physical labor the men step in and say: 'Let me do that.' I don't care; I let them. Break your back. I don't feel threatened by it. I don't have to do that stuff. If someone wants to do the hard work let them do it."

Mark Hubble, who was the public figure of homelessness at the presentation Dan and he and I gave to the American Institute of Architects, who was the lead speaker at the opening of Opportunity Village, who has been the subject of several articles, and who resigned from the Village Council, shakes his head.

"When we started out it was just a dozen of us, and I liked to take care of my girls. Now everything is different. It's an intentional community."

"I don't think this is an intentional community " Hal chimes in. Hal was voted off the Village Council.

"If this were an intentional community, it would be more intentional about who it let in. Someone else here is footing the bill. We're bringing in outside labor, rather than doing the work ourselves. This is a transitional homeless camp, nothing more."

Craig disagrees: "This is still an intentional community. It's just a different intention. The intention is shelter. What comes through is something very much like the intention of food—the cycle of sowing and growing and harvesting and feasting. This act of building, of cultivating shelter for ourselves and others, builds community like you wouldn't believe. Even those who participate in only part of the cycle still go away with a greater sense of community. The builders of this village are sowing the seeds for another village. The villagers themselves will be the mentors, the seeds for the creation of the next community."

On December 9th, one year after my first presentation at the open forum city council meeting, I spoke again before the mayor and city councilors of Eugene. The homeless of Whoville, a big tent camp jammed in beside the overpass next to the courthouse, threatened with being disbanded in the snow, spoke first. Then Jean Stacey made another impassioned plea. I offered a solution. I spoke of the Conestoga Huts I advocated for last year, now permitted and sheltering 20 people. I spoke of the Backyard Bunglows in Opportunity Village, permitted and housing 20 people. All had come at no cost to the city, state, or federal government. Then I said that we could easily build a second Opportunity Village. The next day an anonymous donor gave $25,000 to Opportunity Village, restricted for the purposes of building a second Opportunity Village, as a challenge grant for $25,000 more. Someone also gave another $12,000 to finish this first village. So far we have spent around $70,000 on Opportunity Village.

The first legal urban camping site in Eugene is about to open across the street from us, run by Erik de Buhr and Community Supported Shelters. Ted and I are visiting Erik and a helper, when Mark Hubble comes up as the welcome party, offering blankets and food for the first residents. He has applied for the job of one of the five property managers who get Conestogas at the 15-person site, which is fenced, monitored, and secure. Mark is the seed of a new village.

Hal says it's time to go home, and leaves. I go to get another beer. When I get back they are playing stupid human tricks. One game, called "Mad Dog," involves holding a plastic ruler with an open box of Tic Tacs taped to either end, clamped in your mouth. You shake your head up and down, and whoever spills the most Tic Tacs wins. Another involves stacking as many Ding Dongs as you can on your forehead.

(continued on p. 77)

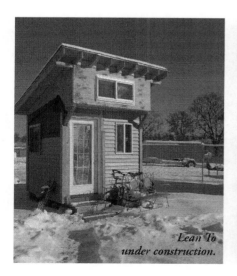

Lean To under construction.

Village Circle at Opportunity Village. Graceful circular courtyards like this one maximize a feeling of openness on the site.

OPPORTUNITY VILLAGE EUGENE: PIONEERING NEW SOLUTIONS FOR THE (FORMERLY) HOMELESS

(continued from p. 61)

First Joline, with five, and then Louis, with six, are in the lead. Then Andy steps up. First he tries the trick while sitting, but we call foul. Then he arranges all the Ding Dongs on the table first, so they will best fit, and then mashes them down on his forehead, to howls of protest. But he wins in the end, by bending the rules.

In a way Opportunity Village itself is bending the rules. But this is because the rules need to be bent. We have to make sure that we adhere to the intention, and not the letter of the law. The city and the neighborhoods do not want shanty-towns. They decrease property values and increase disease. But a nice clean orderly village with rules and sound governance? At $2,500 a person in direct set-up costs? Well, that's hard to beat. The big concern is governance. And that is a big concern. An Opportunity Village board member needs to be at every village meeting. A half dozen people have been kicked out so far by the villagers, with good cause. This is a good thing.

I vetted the first people. Some, I thought, were never going to make it. But it's amazing to see the spirit with which people lift themselves up. The truth is, if you give a homeless person a home then they're no longer homeless. This is the opportunity of Opportunity Village. ❧

Alex Daniell is a designer and builder of small residential structures. He has owned and redesigned six houses, and built several more. He has visited over 30 intentional communities, and lived for two years at the Walnut Street Co-op in Eugene. He consults as a financial advisor and belongs to the Wordos, a science fiction and fantasy writers group.

HOMELESSNESS AND TINY HOUSES:
Two Worlds Intersect to Foster Community

By Kerri Fivecoat-Campbell

Life is a funny thing. Take mine, for example. One day I'm helping my mom plan a memorial service for my brother, Steve, who died homeless in an alley in Fargo, North Dakota. Seemingly in a flash, my husband and I come very close to losing our own home during the Great Recession. The very next instant, I'm evaluating how our decision to move to a tiny home in the woods intersects with my experience writing my brother's story and how I might use my experience with the homeless and tiny homes to help build tiny house communities.

Tiny homes are all of the rage, starring in reality television and frequent news stories. Millennials, caught in an economy that continues to undercut the middle class and socked with five-figure school loans, love them. Generation Xers and young Baby Boomers such as ourselves, who were caught in layoffs during the recession and are still paying off debt we incurred to live, love tiny homes. Older Baby Boomers who are downsizing are all interested in how tiny house living can save them money and help them simplify their lives.

How does that add up to advocacy for the homeless? As the tiny house movement—a moniker given by the media that stuck—has grown, advocacy organizations across the country are trying to figure out how to build tiny house communities to help the homeless. Some have been successful and some are still struggling.

My Own Journey

It was a cold, gray day in late January 2001 when I began what would be a few hours' search to try to find my brother who had been missing since late 1999. A Vietnam veteran, Steve had left the home he shared with our parents nearly two decades before. His mind and soul were lost those years he had spent in the war and for reasons we couldn't understand, he went searching. Steve always remained in contact with us, though, especially taking care to call our mom and even send her a little money when he came off drinking binges to work.

That was until December 1999 when he didn't call Mom on her birthday or at Christmas. We had no way to reach him and so we had to wait. By December 2000 when he still didn't make contact with anyone in the family, we all knew something was terribly wrong. When I began making those calls in January 2001, I thought finding him would be harder, but one call to the Social Security Administration confirmed our worst fears.

Once my grief had subsided to a manageable level, I vowed to our mother I would try to find out what went wrong. Why, when we thought he had access to the best medical care through the Veteran's Administration, Steve couldn't be helped. My research involved poring through over 300 pages of accessible VA medical records and even speaking with a doctor who had once treated my brother.

The reasons Steve wasn't helped are many and complex, but the ending was not. Steve had died of a combination of hypothermia and alcohol poisoning. The result of my exhaustive research, the book, *No Immediate Threat: The Story of an American Veteran*, although cathartic for my grief, did little to provide an answer to America's homeless problem, except for noting the obvious: The homeless need homes, no matter what types of problems and addictions that they may suffer.

Two years after my book was published, my mother died and mired me in new grief for the last surviving member of the nucleus of the home in which I had grown up. My husband Dale and I decided to move to our 480 square foot lake home with the hopes of building a larger home within the year. We sold our home in Kansas City, Kansas and I left my volunteer work with the homeless behind to heal my heart in the woods.

Photos courtesy of Mark Solomon

Little did we know that the largest economic downturn to hit the world was just around the corner. The Great Recession claimed about 80 percent of my freelance writing business and resulted in an 18-month layoff for my husband from his new job. As I worked tirelessly to rebrand my business to fit changing reader habits and technology and my husband went to work for minimum wage, we began using credit cards to survive.

One day before a planned meeting with a real estate agent to see if we could unload our tiny house and property for at least what we owed, Dale was called back to his job. We escaped homelessness literally by a day.

During that time, I realized we had stumbled into a movement of people who were choosing to move to smaller homes. When I realized this movement lacked a community of people to discuss the lifestyle, I founded livinglargeinourlittlehouse.com. The site provides a global virtual community forum in the tiny house movement of people who help each other navigate the nuances of a downsized life. As time went on, I began hearing more about tiny house communities that were helping the homeless.

The Tiny House Movement and Advocacy

One of the earliest and possibly one of the most publicized tiny house communities to assist the homeless to spring up has been Occupy Madison, a Wisconsin-based nonprofit. In November 2014, they opened three homes on private property and have aspirations, as soon as more funds are raised, to build more.

Operation Northern Comfort and A Tiny Home for Good, two nonprofit organizations that help the homeless in Syracuse, New York, built two tiny homes on a vacant lot on the south side of the city this past spring. The organizations partnered and found the volunteers to do the work, while the lot was owned by the city.

In one of the most recent tiny house community stories, Veterans Community Project, a nonprofit founded by veterans in my hometown of Kansas City, have finished one 240 square foot home on what they hope will one day be a 50-house community called Veterans Village.

Chris Stout, a veteran and president of Veterans Community Project, said in a press release, "We identified too many veterans suffering from PTSD and addictions who were going untreated and not doing well in traditional shelters. We decided as vets that we had to do something to help."

Of course, this project tugged at my heart. What if Steve had such a community to go to during his life? Things might have been different for him.

Two Books Intersect

When I began writing my current book, *Living Large in Our Little House: Thriving in 480 Square Feet With Six Dogs, a Husband and One Remote—Plus More Stories of How You Can Too*, the book's focus was to write about the people who have chosen to live a tiny house life. But I could not ignore in my research and mention in my book the nonprofits that are taking what seemingly is a hipster movement of tiny house development and turning it into a vehicle to help the homeless.

I've reached out to a couple of programs that I plan to meet with in the next few months, including the Veterans Community Project, to see how I, as one of the voices for the tiny house movement, can help these efforts. It's as if the only two books I've ever written, subjects that weren't seemingly connected at all, have now come together.

I believe those of us who have chosen a life in the tiny house movement and who have come together as a global community can help those who have no homes become a part of it. It would be wonderful if the millions of people who enjoy the tiny house television shows, internet pages, and books all come together to help in this effort. ❦

Kerri Fivecoat-Campbell is a freelance writer and author living her dream in a 480 square foot cabin in the woods with her husband, Dale, and their five recycled (rescued) dogs. Kerri's latest book is Living Large in Our Little House: Thriving in 480 Square Feet With Six Dogs, a Husband and One Remote—Plus More Stories of How You Can Too.

In 2003, "La Cité Écologique" was founded, in Colebrook New Hampshire, on 315 acres of beautiful land surrounded by forest and mountains. Our ecovillage gives priority to education, optimal living to its members, a cooperative culture with resilience in its development and social entrepreneurship. So far, we have built one single family building, two large community residences, where people live in a kind of condo arrangement, and one community building (all powered by solar). We are expanding new building projects, to give a home to growing families and/or new members. We've created businesses, non-profits, a nonprofit school, and an organic farm, that helps better serve ours, and the local community. Visitors are welcome to our annual Open House in June, and Harvest Celebration in September. Guided tours, and internship programs are also available from May through October.

Contact: Leonie Brien (603) 331-1669
www.citeecologiquenh.org

MIKE & HEIDI — SUNNY — BUCK & ANNIE

"Who's in charge?" If we had not needed to answer that question repeatedly for Sonoma County officials, it might have been possible NOT to reproduce the Straight World's hierarchy, although Morningstar Ranch's hierarchy was very fluid compared to straight society's. Subgroups did form, such as "the wino camp" down by the front gate that we all were so grateful for, since previously they had been screaming and carrying on beside Lou Gottlieb's cabin. The yogis remained around the barn, the good-time more transient types in the Upper House, and the heavy kitchen staff and organizers in the Lower. But the outside forces required an imposed structure instead of just waiting for one to grow itself naturally, as it did at Wheeler's Ranch down the road. At Wheeler's, a "Group Head" finally emerged that evolved beyond just having Bill Wheeler play cop whenever necessary. Brother Bill, by the way, poured himself heart and soul and inheritance into the community, and grew more in spirit and nobility than anyone throughout those years. I thank him for all he did from the bottom of my heart—and the same for Lou.

Admittedly, Lou finally tired of the "Who's in Charge" role after having been fined 30 or more times (totaling over $14,000) and finally jailed for not obeying

This article reflects the author's experiences at two Open Land communities, Morningstar Ranch and Wheeler's Ranch, starting in 1966 (see www.diggers.org/home_free.htm for a 25-chapter history, "Home Free Home"). The following is excerpted from a paper presented at the "West of Eden: Communes and Utopia in Northern California" conference, hosted by the Department of Geography and the Institute of International Studies at UC Berkeley, March 25, 2006, and now appearing in the author's new book, A Planetary Sojourn (Calm Unity Press, San Francisco, CA, 2008).

the injunction forbidding anyone but himself to live at Morningstar. He tried to place his imported guru from India at the ranch "to chant the Bhagavad-Gita in impeccable Sanskrit and elevate the vibes." However Chiranjiva, Shiva Incarnate, or "Father" as he was addressed by his devotees, preferred the pleasures of city living. "I did not come all the way from

India to shit in the woods!" he told us. "I could do that in my village!" He described our hippie rural life as "divine infantilism" and set up an urban headquarters in San Francisco.

Lou's search for someone "higher than he was" to surrender to, as he put it, conjures something that Sociology calls "dominance ranking." I have noticed

LOU ROSS Joe Penny Lucy Santiago Robbie Susan Mary Charlie Victoria KATY DOG Fluid Floyd
WALLY man Cindy Asan Sis

Thanksgiving, 1967. Photo was taken at Morningstar Ranch's request by the Sonoma County Sheriff's Department.

COURTESY OF SONOMA COUNTY SHERIFF'S DEPT.

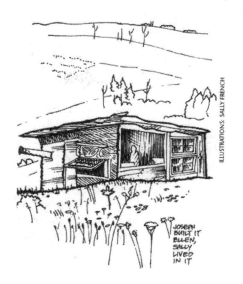

Politics on Open Land

By Ramón Sender Barayón

that humans, along with other animals, tend to rank each other within social groups by using various sensory stimuli that include odor, pheromones, aura, height, carriage, sunny personality, and perhaps that vague term "charisma." In Lou's case, he ranked high as a consummate combination of professorial jokester and knife-sharp intellect that had survived a PhD at UC Berkeley.

Actually, charisma is not really all that vague. Anyone who has ever been in Bill Clinton's presence would agree he's in the high charisma percentiles, while our current White House resident barely moves the shakti-meter's needle. I would suggest that there's an innate human tendency, when entering a gathering, for one's senses to sweep the crowd and immediately create a rough hierarchy of "who's doing what to whom," a dominance ranking that continues to adjust as you sort people out. First impressions are a rough take from the amygdala, a tiny organ in the center of the brain that triggers the "fight or flight" reflex. Your impressions then are refined further by feedback mechanisms from various slower sensory inputs. "Oh! That's a stick—not a snake! I don't have to scream and run!"

I think human relationships tend to fall into archetypical structures depending

D.D. Lou Morningstar.

on the size of the group, the same way crystals do: four-sided, six or eight, or the classical twelve surrounding the Alpha, as described in the New Testament. Just how many human roles are there anyway? The boss, the consigliere or legal eagle, the padre or shaman, the jester, the bodyguard or bouncer, the Judas, the hit man. That's seven so far. Then there's the Romeo, the sleaze-bag, the schlmiel and the schlmozzle, the wino, the hanger-on, the warrior, the thief, and the victim. Sixteen total, although I'm sure there are more. For our sisters, many of those mentioned have their female counterparts, and we also have of course the wife, the vamp, the fallen woman along the lines of Mary Magdalene, the brusque no-nonsense organizer, and the "other woman." I'm sure we could think up many more, but at least these suffice to demonstrate the complexity of human interrelations, and at Morningstar they all thrived. Lou added more categories to the general list: the Basket Cases, the Impossibles, the Super-Rappers, the Bush Rabbits (who scattered into the bushes when the cops arrived).

• • •

We all are tribals in our DNA. When we express our innate nature, tribe creates the village model embedded in our genes. Cities are "stacked" villages, some functional, some not. It takes a village to fulfill our humanity, even if that "village" is a semi-abstract corporate body or a dysfunctional community around a common interest, such as UC Berkeley.

I believe that each of us is here on earth to accomplish our own innate purpose, and I think that a low-demand communal lifestyle can help us discover what it is. Morningstar's open-door and anarchistic lifestyle allowed new arrivals an opportunity to see themselves and their aspirations reflected back in the

MIKE'S "ATTIC" HOUSE

Politics on Open Land

clear mirror it provided. Ultimately it seemed that Morningstar functioned as some sort of healing center, which perhaps could be ascribed to the fact, as we learned some years later (1971), that the ranch had been dedicated and named for The Virgin Mary even before Lou bought the place. That might account for the visions of the Divine Mother that were reported by various folks during the '60s. It seemed that many people discovered what innate task had brought them

Morning Star Faith

Thy Open Land Church

Thy 4 Missions of Planetary Purity
Open Earth, Open Air, Open Fire, Open Water

1. **Open Earth:** The opening of lands as sanctuaries for the One, naked, nameless and homeless. The purification of the land by replenishment of the soil, invisible land use, and Voluntary Primitivism. Welcoming the Divine Nature in our children.

2. **Open Air:** The opening of all communications channels, open airings, airwaves. The purification of the air by planting graves and gardens. The Divine Wind of the Spirit speaks in the treetops. Listen!

3. **Open Fire:** Opening of all energies to all. No exclusive ownership of gas, electricity, coal, wood, money. The purification of life forces in the fire of worship. The open hearth. The opening of our bodies and hearts to the open solar fire.

4. **Open Water:** Open seas, oceans, rivers, streams and hot springs. We are water brothers with all life. Open emotions – express your feelings. The purification of water. Stop pollution.

From the Morningstar Manifesto.

planetside to accomplish, and this perhaps was the most healing aspect of Open Community.

Of course there were also Open Land failures. One guy seemed to come on the land at Wheeler's Ranch just to O.D. under the cross on the hill. Another guy, Oak Grove Ronald, was a kind of minor Charles Manson type who wanted to form a cult that would include a man and a woman from each sign of the zodiac. He used LSD to magnetize people into his orbit, and in 1972 made a power play to take over the ranch. One of the very few community meetings was held and an elder spokesperson elected to offer Ron a deal: the community would trade him and his people their schoolbus in return for the buildings they had constructed and their immediate departure. If they didn't leave, he could not guarantee their safety. Ron and his followers left shortly thereafter, to the immense relief of everyone.

The event served to demonstrate to everyone that they had the ability to self-govern and unite when necessary to accomplish a necessary task. I think it was a turning point in the Wheeler Ranch folks' feeling that they could succeed, and I do believe that Wheeler's would have evolved into a self-sustaining, viable village if the county had not destroyed the community. By then Morningstar's dwellings had been bulldozed at least three times, with Lou charged not only for the labor incurred but also fined almost $15,000 on 30 or so separate contempt-of-court citations for not ordering hippies off the land.

The early '70s were depressing times, but when Jerry Brown became Governor of California, he at least was able to get Cabin Class structures added to the building code, which allowed each county to vote

whether or not to accept so-called "below-code" buildings that did not include indoor plumbing, electrical wiring in the walls, or a concrete pad insulating the inhabitants from the sweet touch of Mother Gaia.

Meanwhile, the county's threats forced us to organize into a corporation, and Bill's attorney recommended a church structure. He asked me to set down the belief system that I thought we had evolved, and with the help of others I wrote the Morningstar Faith articles. The attorney decided on the name Ahimsa Church, and part of its tenets expressed our need NOT to live on a concrete pad and NOT to use flush toilets. Bare earth floors and a post-hole digger with a roll of toilet paper on one handle were just fine, and squatting turned out to be a great hemorrhoids cure!

When people ask me what is necessary to start a rural open land commune, I reply, "First buy a cow, or preferably two. The cows will call the meetings twice a day because if you want fresh milk, you have to go to milking. That way no one

(continued on p. 76)

After the bulldozers.

PUBLISHER'S NOTE
(continued from p. 8)

lined). Because it involved a question of organizational values, I told him I couldn't make the call on my own and that FIC's Board of Directors would have to chew it over.

Still, I encouraged him to bring the idea forward and not shy away just because it was challenging (that's the Board's job after all). Over the years, we've learned that there's a strong relationship between our readership and the people who shop at natural food stores. In that regard, Whole Foods is a great fit. Yet we also believe there is a strong small-is-beautiful sentiment among our readership—

Trying to run a meeting?
FIC has some tools you need—
the best books around on
consensus facilitation.
store.ic.org

people who will greet a Whole Foods ad with the same enthusiasm as opening a container of leftover egg salad that's been left in the sun for three days. So it's not obvious which way to go.

In June, at the FIC's organizational meetings in New Mexico, I diligently brought this issue up for Board consideration. Just as with John and me, the Board struggled as well. While we're always looking for additional advertising revenue, our main concern was the values match between Whole Foods and our readership. Though no match is perfect, was this one good enough?

Ultimately, we decided to ask for reader input. We invite you to visit communities.ic.org, click on the hyperlink for the Whole Foods poll, and give us your opinion. We'll conduct this poll through the end of the year and let you know what you tell us. If nothing else, we'll find out a bit more about who our readers are, as well something about who you think FIC is. And that's always a good idea. ❀

POLITICS ON OPEN LAND
(continued from p. 56)

THE "YACHT CLUB"   SALLY FRENCH

can say, 'Hey, who d'you think you are calling a meeting, head honcho or sumthin'?' Cows have no guru aspirations. And while you're at it, you might as well evoke the ancient Vedic tradition and worship them. They're very sweet and benign goddesses."

All our experiments in dissolving traditional societal assumptions have been useful, even if only to discover certain innate truths about the human animal. And according to Erich Fromm, "[Isolation of the individual] brings on a sense of separation from others and from himself, a lack of joy and, finally, an indifference to life itself—his own life and that of others." Open Land community melts that lack. Open land opens hearts. ❀

Ramón Sender Barayón has lived in various intentional communities, including the Bruderhof (1950s) and its exact opposites, Morningstar and Wheeler's ranches (1960s-'70s). His books include the online history of both sixties communes (badabamama.com/HomeFree.html) and published titles: a Spanish Civil War family memoir (A Death In Zamora, 2003), collected essays and articles (A Planetary Sojourn, 2008), Being of the Sun co-authored with Alicia Bay Laurel (Harper & Row, 1973), The Morningstar Scrapbook (1976), and the novel Zero Weather (Family Publishing, 1980).

Nobody Likes Bosses

By Molly Shea

The law. In my anti-authoritarian household, the law isn't always held with the utmost regard. There's good reason for that. Here in what we now call the United States, our laws enforce racist standards and we put black communities in prison at alarmingly high rates. Women are prevented from making choices about their own bodies and their own safety. Cops are allowed to murder innocent (often brown) people. It is legal to pay folks with developmental disabilities below minimum wage. Queers and trans folks are often confronted with hate and violence. Migrants from other countries are deemed "illegal" and forced into detention centers. The list of unjust laws created and upheld by society could go on and on. Luckily, throughout history and today as well, brave folks have taken action to intentionally break, rewrite, and create alternatives to unjust laws.

If it's not obvious, I encourage you to do the same. If I believed in a higher power, I'd thank it for putting the fight for justice inside so many kind souls. With everything inside of me, I sincerely thank those who have fought for justice and who fight for it now.

While collective action is needed to create large-scale, systemic change, intentional communities like mine can become the seedbed for exploring and exemplifying the world we envision. The challenges of the "real world" impact us and forms of oppression come in through the back door, but we also have room to create systems that promote equity. As an intentional community, we've chosen to create our own laws, our own agreements, and our own cultural norms that help bend us towards a fair and liberated shared experience. While that sounds easy—to decide your own rules together and then choose to collectively enforce them—it's proven to be complicated and not always straightforward.

Here in our Columbus, Ohio-based community, the Midden, we're a group of folks with good intentions who care about each other and the world. While that's a solid foundation, it doesn't mean we always have the tools, time, and energy to really show up for each other. For a long time, our household chose to systematically build a culture of empathetic communication. We agreed on a check-in system, where every member was

"required" to check in (have some one-on-one time where both folks got to chat and share what's going on with them and how things have been together) with every other member of our household. Sometimes, we did this well and it served us. Sometimes, we upheld this agreement, but it didn't really serve us. More often, we didn't create the time to connect with folks in that way.

Having an agreement like that, and watching it go by the wayside, can actually be more hurtful than simply never checking in. We tried to rework it a few times, tried to recommit, but right now, we've just stopped. For now, that's how we've chosen to enforce it: by letting it go. It's a bit more organic now; we regularly share with each other before we get down to business at our house meetings, and as a small household, we often have a sense of what's going on with folks. Ideally, we even know how and choose to support each other.

In our community, part of our budget is set aside to help cover health and wellness needs of individuals. Folks can use it to pay for a doctor's visit, for vitamins, for travel expenses to a support group, or whatever else folks need to take care of themselves. When we first set this up, we had an approval process. Folks would say what the expense was, and we'd all agree or disagree to help pay for it. Part of the intention was to get our wellness out of the dark hole of shame and into our collective consciousness that would allow us to support each other through our ailments. What actually happened, though, was a lot different. Folks felt judged for what they needed and felt like we were putting each other on trial for the very personal choices we make about how to tend to ourselves. After a lot of hurt feelings and additional shame, we decided to alter, or amend, that agreement. We didn't ditch the whole thing, and we chose to keep our wellness fund. Now, folks use it however they see fit. There is no approval process. If you have a wellness expense, you can have the house help you cover it. We have lost some of the intention to know what's going on with each other, but not all of it. We still see it as an expense if we want and i think we are more comfortable talking and sharing about our physical and mental health. While in many ways, this was a small change to our agreement, it has had substantial impacts in our community.

We've had a long-standing divide in our labor—the ways folks contribute to our shared home. We contribute in a variety of ways; much of that (like emotionally or energetically participating in each other's lives) can't possibly be calculated, and for the most part we've chosen not to. We've tried a variety of ways to account for the tasks that keep our home running—tending a garden, fixing the roof, walking the dog, cleaning the counter, etc. We've dug into those systems and have plenty of history and lessons to share, but more recently we've found ourselves focused in on how we pay our bills.

> **Without cultural change, our good intentions and our laws don't take us that far.**

Bills in an intentional community that rejects capitalist principles?! Yes, of course. We have to pay off our house and pay our utilities, but we also choose to help cover shared food, tools, supplies, and other odds and ends. The question is, how do we do that in a way that a) covers our bills and b) creates equity amongst ourselves? We've had a variety of systems and agreements to help us achieve that. Most of our norms have helped us reach those goals in some ways, and failed in others. In our attempts to hold ourselves accountable, we've remade and we've significantly reworked our agreements. Right now, we're trying out an income percentage contribution system. It's working, but not perfectly. And to be frank, the hard part is how it *feels*. How it feels to folks to pay in at a certain rate, how it feels to have some people pay more or less than you, to cover expenses you wouldn't personally choose, to not be able to decide you'd rather cut back that month to save up for whatevertheheck. How it feels to have a set of agreements, of laws, that tells you what to do with *your money*. In all of our agreements, that's been the hard part.

Nobody likes bosses. Even when you are the boss. Even when you decide to get rid of bosses and share the rulemaking together. We don't like being told we're doing it wrong, that we're not doing what we agreed to, that we are prioritizing ourselves individually over our shared, collective selves. Actually, I think we just don't like being told what to do. Even worse than bosses? Laws. Once we put them in place, we have to choose how and if we are going to enforce them. And if we're not going to enforce them, do they even exist? But without them, can we coexist and even thrive? While I'm still a firm believer in a need for rules, norms, agreements...*laws*...the lesson I keep learning is that those things don't create cultural change. We create cultural change, and without that, our good intentions and our laws don't take us that far. There is some magical balance out there, an equilibrium between the law and the culture. Here at the Midden, we're striving to find it. We'll keep striving, but if we come up with the solution, we'll be sure to let ya'll know. 🐝

Molly Shea is a member of the Midden, in Columbus, Ohio. She's also a cooperative owner of Pattycake Bakery, teaches self-defense, works with the Beehive Collective, is an anti-sexual assault advocate, and is part of a radical cheerleading squad. Occasional reflections on her life can be read on her blog, www.moreadventuroustoday.blogspot.com.

COMMUNITY
ECONOMICS

BY
TREE BRESSEN

When Community Land
Is Privately Owned

*There tends to be
an attitude in the
movement that
common ownership
is inherently superior.
I might even agree
with that attitude.
However, in contrast
to the orthodoxy, i've
also visited places
where private
ownership, either
temporary or even
long-term, seemed to
be working out okay.*

*I became curious:
What factors make
such a situation
go well rather
than badly?*

When most of us think of intentional community, we think of a place where some or all of the land or property is owned in common. There tends to be an attitude in the movement that common ownership is inherently superior. I might even agree with that attitude. However, in contrast to the orthodoxy, i've also visited places where private ownership, either tempory or even long-term, seemed to be working out okay. I became curious: What factors make such a situation go well rather than badly?

First, let's consider the obvious challenges. Property ownership on the part of some members conveys immediate material privilege. It also tends to influence psychological and interpersonal dynamics considerably. In our socially unjust society, ownership is a form of rank or power-over. Owners get to accrue equity in property, while renters' money just disappears into the void. However, in spite of all that, i still think that if held consciously, and with requisite willingness and skill to have healthy conversations about it, private ownership does not necessarily have to break the sense of community in a place.

When eight of us started Walnut Street Co-op in 2000, we faced a fairly common situation: We all wanted to live in community, but only one person had enough money to buy a house in our town. He went ahead with it, and we all moved in. The goal all along was to transfer ownership to the group. However, again like many groups, we didn't get around to it for a while. In fact, frankly, we might never have gotten around to it if the owner hadn't decided firmly, after several years, that he wanted out. In the fall of 2002, one night at our weekly meeting, he announced that if we didn't buy the property from him by spring he was going to put it on the market. Whew! While we felt shocked and upset, i have to say that it also lit a fire under our butts. A core group formed, and by dint of much hard work, successfully met the deadline. (For part of the story of how we did it, see "Our Community Revolving Loan Fund" in COMMUNITIES #128, Fall 2005.)

However, what's worth noticing here is that even in the years before the group assumed ownership, the place already felt like a community. I believe that most sightseers could have sat in on nine out of ten meetings without being able to tell that one person owned the

Walnut Street Co-op in Eugene, Oregon: The original building was purchased by one person and converted to co-op ownership three years later.

In a unique model on Salt Spring Island, British Columbia, EcoReality Co-Op owns the land and all structures, but members "vest" in individual structures from which they can produce income.

house. We all shared in cooking and chores. We all attended meetings. When the house needed work or when someone was having a hard time, we each did our best to help out, according to individual skills and availability. When a room came open, we all interviewed and selected new housemates by consensus.

The owner laid down the law on one or two things at the beginning, like insisting that no illegal substances be brought onto the property (a guideline that the group later kept, by the way, after the transition to co-op ownership). And that was about it. Aside from that, he held his role lightly, with grace i might even say. So that when we did finally pass from individual into group ownership, the shift was relatively smooth, and changed almost nothing about our day-to-day lives together. The main difference was that the newly formed core group now had extra responsibilities: planning for long-term maintenance, drawing up annual budgets, and making payments to the lenders in our community revolving loan fund. The former owner moved on to other community ventures.

Based on that experience, my visits to other communities, and conversations with other people in the communities movement, i offer the following list of recommendations to help guide owners and tenants who may find themselves in the situation of attempting to form a community while occupying privately owned land. These recommendations are offered in addition to all the other important elements that any forming community benefits from having, like strong friendships and a good

vibe among everyone living there, and a sense of larger purpose beyond the welfare of individual members.

What helps landowners and tenants attempting community living on privately owned land:

• **Owner being clear and up front about what decisions are up to the group versus what decisions the owner is ultimately maintaining control over.** For example, capital improvement decisions might be up to the owner, while lifestyle choices (e.g., whether the kitchen is vegetarian, or what time do quiet hours start) might be up to the full group to decide. The more clear these agreements are, the better; thus, writing them down helps. The more decisions can be made by everyone, the more likely you are to actually have a community rather than a "feudal lord and serfs" situation; so probably the default should be that decisions are made by all unless there is a strong reason to do otherwise. The owner can still be included as one of the decision-making members, and protecting the owner's interests is a concern that any member can bring up if it's relevant to a particular proposal.

• **Clarity of agreements.** For example, having a signed lease, or, if work trade is expected, then specifying how many hours and what's included. Again, writing down the basics is useful, both

In Oakland, California, Mariposa Grove's original three buildings, purchased by Hank Obermayer in 1999, were converted to community land trust condominium ownership nine years later.

JAN STEINMAN

The goats were free. Jan and Carol used fuel (and ferry fare) to pick them up, built facilities for them, fed them, and cared for them. Now they are being transferred to community ownership at EcoReality Co-op. What is a fair price?

Even in the years before the group assumed ownership, the place already felt like a community.

because it forces you to get clear and for referring back to later.

• **Which hat when?** There will be times when the owner is speaking as the owner, and wants to be heard that way. However, unless everyone stays pretty conscious, there will be times when the owner is attempting to put out their preferences as one group member, but instead is interpreted by others as dictating by fiat. Many unhappy misunderstandings can be averted by a commitment on all sides to be as clear as possible about which hat the owner is wearing when. If anyone isn't sure in a particular case, they should ask.

• **Transparency.** Openness builds trust. I recommend the owner be entirely open about their title to the land, mortgage payments, and other arrange-

ments, including having open accounting books for the shared property that any community member can examine whenever they want. Potential members should also be realistic with the owner about what they are likely to be able to put into the pot.

• **Simultaneous move-in.** Walnut Street Co-op was blessed in that, because we actually started as a group, everyone initially moved in around the same time. We all talked over who wanted which bedroom, and common spaces were furnished collectively. We were spared the

situation of moving into someone's established territory.

• **Common spaces controlled by all.** Whose books occupy the shelves of the library? Whose art hangs on the walls? In order for a place to feel like their home, other community members besides the owners will need to have equal influence over furnishings, and ability to have their cherished personal possessions in common space.

• **Owner not being too attached about too many things.** Ooo, this is a tough one, isn't it? It's hard for people to change their personalities, so it's up to owners to be self-aware about this and for other residents to screen for it before choosing to join. I suggest that owners who are more laid back are more likely to succeed in co-creating a happy community around them.

• **Members who are personally reasonably emotionally secure.** We're not demanding perfection here, but the less secure the other residents are, the more likely they are to project concerns and upsets onto innocent owners.

• **Attention, if needed, on other power factors besides ownership** (for example, gender, race, class background, popularity, political alliances, and so on). Being willing to look at the many power dynamics at play reduces inappropriate

Have you ever visited a community where the property is supposedly heading toward group ownership, but has been owned by one person for more than a decade?

Mike Nickerson, author of Life, Money, and Illusion, *discusses local economics in a workshop in an EcoReality Co-op conference space that is community-owned, but the profits from which go to two community members who funded its purchase.*

targeting of ownership privilege. In a hierarchical society, we all have situations where we are one-up and situations where we are one-down. It's unfair to expect only the owner to face up to their own one-upness.

• **Trust.** This item was added to the list courtesy of Hank Obermayer, former owner at Mariposa Grove in California. He describes it this way: "Trust that what the owner says is what they mean, both intellectually, and as what they will truly work toward. That has to do with incoming members trusting the owner's maturity, ability, and openness. It can also include the owner's trust of others who are involved in making community decisions that the owner is liable for."

• **Owner letting go of, um, greed, or a desire to achieve mainstream profit margins.** I hear the wail of community owners: "Oh sure, i'd be happy to have group ownership, i just want to be compensated for all the years of work i've put

in on the land," or "As long as others buy in for equal portions," or, worse yet, "As long as others buy in for the amount of money the land is worth now," when the owner bought it years ago when the market was a lot lower. If you can find members who are willing to do that, fine. But otherwise, your attachment to profit is likely to keep you from ever having the community you supposedly want.

At Walnut Street, the founding group fortunately had a conversation about how much the property would be sold for later. While that did not prevent tensions from arising during the final negotiations, it certainly helped provide guidance and made it easier to arrive at agreement. In the end, the group paid an amount that provided significant profit to the owner, while still being significantly under market value at the time of resale.

• **A transition plan to arrive at group**

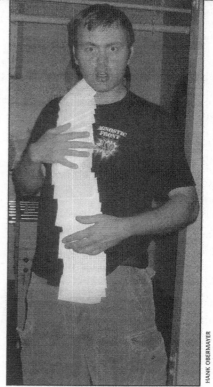

Mariposa Grove community member with his To-Do list after a community-wide brainstorming meeting.

Common Problems with Private Ownership of "Community" Land

By Jan Steinman

- The people with the most effort to contribute generally are young and have little or no money.

- Past labor is generally not valued at all, or assumed by the owner to have been completely compensated for by free rent or meals.

- Property prices rise faster than tenants' ability to raise money, or even to perform work-trade.

- Banks won't touch mortgages on commonly-held property—at least not at home-mortgage rates. (Business loan rates are considerably higher.) This means the owner must become the banker as well—yet another position of hidden power.

- Unless the parties are essentially equal in net worth, power imbalances will remain in any share-based system. Even in cooperatives that have equal votes or consensus, there is hidden power imbalance if the equity distribution is vastly unequal, which can eventually cause resentment unless great care is taken.

- The day-to-day grind of running the place tends to put equity sharing on the back burner. I know of three sites where the owners have expressed an interest in sharing equity for some years, yet none of them actually have done so. I don't doubt their intentions, but this is an example of "hidden power," in that people of privilege rarely view themselves as such. The "status quo" is good enough for the owner, and the serfs don't want to rock the boat by pestering the owner about following up on the owner's previously expressed intentions. ❁

Jan Steinman is cofounder of Eco-Reality, a forming ecovillage in the Southern Gulf Islands of British Columbia, Canada (www.ecoreality.org).

Group ownership issues arise not just with real estate, but with buildings, temporary structures, vehicles, farm equipment, and even crops. This greenhouse was owned by two community members who moved it to EcoReality Co-op. Now it will be transferred to communal ownership in exchange for co-op shares—fair price to be determined.

JAN STEINMAN

ownership. Have you ever visited a community where the property is supposedly heading toward group ownership, but has been owned by one person for more than a decade? There are plenty around. If you really want other people to make a place their home, it'll be more likely to happen if you and they work out a realistic plan for joint legal ownership. Read the relevant chapters of Diana Leafe Christian's book *Creating a Life Together* for more information on legal options for incorporation and property ownership. And speaking of that excellent book, check out "When You Already Own the Property," on page 23 of the same title, for further perspective on the themes raised here. ❁

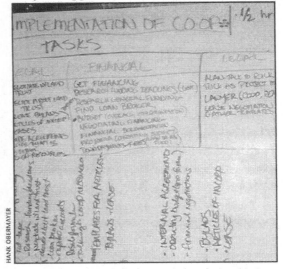

HANK OBERMAYER

Detail of the tasks and timelines whiteboard when Mariposa Grove first thought it was going to become a limited equity housing co-op. The group spent an entire retreat discussing legal ownership structure issues. Says Hank Obermayer: "It's not what we ended up doing, but we went fairly far down that path before changing directions."

Tree Bressen works as a freelance facilitator and teacher of consensus, facilitation, and group skills for intentional communities and a wide variety of other organizations, centered in the Cascadia bioregion. See www.treegroup.info. After living in intentional communities for most of her adult life, she presently lives in an informal collective household where the property is owned by one resident. (Tree also deliberately uses a lower-case "i" in writing as an expression of egalitarian values.)

Class-Harmony Community

By A. Allen Butcher

In my search for community I have looked to communal societies, community land trusts, cohousing, and others to find a form of intentional community that would be accessible to working class families without many assets other than an abiding commitment to cooperative living. I emphasize "families" because surprisingly to me, I have learned that the communities which practice sharing to the greatest degree are the least welcoming of children.

Raising a child in community had always been my dream. I had dropped out of college to join a rural commune called East Wind, only to be kicked out after eight years of work and commitment for having a child without getting permission from the community. Today East Wind Community continues to restrict its child population to about one child for every 10 adults, which is not a problem for them because they can always attract more young adults, many of whom, however, eventually want to have children, which often then as in my experience results in their having to leave their home.

I knew that many monastic societies were childless because of the inheritance issue, which is that children in communal societies often want a share of community assets when they come of age so they can leave the community into which they were born. Also, parents want to leave their children an inheritance other than the community itself. Unfortunately, other community members often do not want the drain on communal resources that children represent. It is my belief that this is ultimately why the dominant culture is a private-property system and is not and never will be communal.

Still committed to the lifestyle, I joined another communal society, Twin Oaks Community, which attempted for about two decades to maintain a communal childcare tradition, in which parents give decision-making power over their children to the group. This was a wonderful experience for my child and me, yet sometime after we left Twin Oaks, their communal childcare program ended. Today, both of these communal groups use a collective childcare system where the parents are primarily responsible for their children, while the communities may refuse some or all support for the children. In this way communal groups push out people with children, or else give up communalism in favor of the sharing of private property in collective intentional community. These social dynamics also occurred in the communal groups of the Catholic Worker movement, and in the secular Israeli kibbutz movement before they changed from communal to a cohousing-like format; while the Hutterites and Bruderhof focus upon socialization methods for keeping their children in their communities, which the secular groups normally will not do.

I wrote a book which among other things discusses children in all of these communal traditions, titled *The Intentioneer's Bible*, and with that documentation I think it is time for communal societies to read the writing on the wall and admit that communal society and children do not mix well. As far as I know I'm the only person putting that truth about communal society into print.

I left the Federation of Egalitarian Communities with my child about the time that the cohousing movement was taking off in America, and I think that movement is much more appropriate for people with children,

except that it is expensive to buy into cohousing, which makes that type of community beyond the means of the working class. If a working class family is lucky they may be able to rent a cohousing unit, yet purchasing is usually not an option for the working class, so their time renting in cohousing is usually limited.

I spent a decade working for the cohousing movement yet never joined one because that community model is not accessible to working class people. Through hard work I eventually acquired a four-unit apartment building with the idea of creating some kind of child-friendly, low-income community, yet the rents are what support me now and I cannot give that up until I have some other kind of income.

I do have renters with children, and I keep my rents under the market rate, so in a sense I have created a small, child-friendly, working-class-friendly community (considering the local rental market). Yet what kind of community is this where I am the owner and everyone rents from me? This is far from the classless, egalitarian communal society I know and love. When I have to state my occupation I now write "Landlord," which is a particular breed of capitalist. However enlightened I may be, I am still a capitalist landlord. How could I call what I've created a "community"?

The realization finally came to me that I had gravitated toward a model of intentional community that is quite common, yet that most of us have not acknowledged. In fact, when I first came to this city I lived in such a "community," where the owner lived in the house while renting to myself and others. This and similar communities have been in the FIC Directory for decades.

It seems that a lot of people naturally fall into doing this kind of community, as I did. I wanted community, I could afford to purchase property, and that is how it happened. Yet what kind of community is this? Fairly recently the terms "coliving" and "cohouseholding" have appeared in the FIC Directory and this magazine; some of these instances must refer to this model of owner/renter community, yet those names do not clearly state that they are comprised of an owner with renters. The term "class-harmony community," however, does clearly state the nature of the community as being comprised of two or more economic classes, with at least one capitalist-owner and more than one worker-renter.

Things get complicated in the communities movement when considering property ownership. Take for example Ganas Community. In the FIC Directory they list 80 members in eight different residences, with 10 of the members comprising the communal ownership core-group, while 70 others rent from them as in a collective community, sharing the core-group's commonly-owned property. The Directory chart does not explain that; one has to read their listing and extrapolate a little to understand it. Ganas states that a subgroup owns the property, and that subgroup is communal. So Ganas is both communal and collective, or a form of what I call an "economically diverse" intentional community, a category which includes community land trusts, while in this case Ganas is also a class-harmony community

I realized that this really is a common form of intentional community after reading the recent article in COMMUNITIES (issue #176) by Sky Blue

> ## This model is the best opportunity for working class people with children to live in community.

103

and Betsy Morris titled, "Tracking the Communities Movement: 70 Years of History and the Modern FIC." The authors include a category in their analysis of the 2016 FIC Directory listings which they call "Shared House/Cohousehold/Coliving," yet the authors do not explain this category as they do the other forms ("coliving" could mean anything!), reporting only that this type of community accounts for 31 percent of the Directory listings. Only cohousing had a larger showing, at 39 percent.

Before the newest FIC Directory was printed, I transcribed much of the 2010 Directory into a database and ran a statistical analysis. I omitted listings stating that they had only one or two members, while Sky and Betsy went further in omitting listings with fewer than four members, assuming that forming communities will be counted in the future when or if they grow in membership.

Betsy and Sky counted 544 established US communities with "at least four adults living together on a site for at least two years," while my preliminary count totaled 738 American intentional communities in the 2016 FIC Directory with one or more members, regardless of longevity. Among these 738 communities, 154 groups or 21 percent indicated that their land is owned by an individual or a subgroup of members, while 41 groups or 27 percent of that number are forming groups, according to my criteria of fewer than three adults, not Betsy's and Sky's criteria of fewer than four adults. (154 groups with land owned by individuals – 41 with fewer than three members = 113 groups) Divide 113 groups by 738 total listings and the quotient is 15 percent. The class-harmony communities of one owner or a subgroup of property owners plus renters comprises 15 percent of American intentional communities with three or more members in the 2016 FIC Directory.

Although most of us are unaware of the full extent of the class-harmony communitarian category, a few have started working with this subset of intentional communities. Jennifer Ladd published an article in COMMUNITIES issue #159 (Summer 2013) titled, "Yes, Wealthy People Want to Live in Community in Sustainable Ways Too! Fourteen suggestions from those who are trying it." The author uses the term "cross-class projects" for this type of community, calling the landlords "primary funders."

Jennifer Ladd created a nonprofit organization called "Class Action," and for a few years has been networking people having money and/or real estate who want to build intentional community. Jennifer writes in her COMMUNITIES article, "Many people with wealth are looking for ways to leverage their resources for good—to help heal the environment and to support the emergence of a new culture based on cooperation and collaboration." You may not have noticed that article, yet Jennifer's work is an indication of great potential for expansion of the communities movement. In my view, this is the best potential opportunity for working class people with children to be able to live in community!

Consider two indicators of the possibilities for growth of the class-harmony community model. First is part of Arthur Morgan's legacy, the original founder of the Fellowship of Intentional Communities (the FIC's former name) in the late 1940s at The Vale in Ohio. In *The Intentioneer's Bible* I wrote the story of Celo Community, founded in 1936, which is an example of financial support for communitarianism by a wealthy conservative.

A significant source of support and of members for the forming of Celo came from the Quaker social service organization called the American Friends Service Committee (AFSC), and other anti-war pacifists. The irony is that the financing for the 1,250 acre land purchase came from a wealthy Chicago industrialist. William Regnery believed in the ideal expressed in earlier times of the "Roman citizen-soldier" and of the "Jeffersonian landed yeomanry" as the foundation of a democratic republic. George Hicks in his Ph.D. thesis titled, *Ideology and Change in an American Utopian Community*, wrote about William Regnery that he was, "a conservative businessman, a mild anti-Semite, a staunch opponent of President Roosevelt and the New Deal,...[yet he held] a nostalgic belief that people who lived in rural villages and earned their living by subsistence farming constituted the virtuous and self-reliant bedrock of republican government."

This is an example of the convergence of opposing political-economic theories and ideals in the communitarian movement. William Regnery met Arthur Morgan and asked him, as Timothy Miller writes, "to suggest a project of substantial social value that he might underwrite." It probably did not take Morgan long to come up with the idea of bankrolling a communitarian settlement. And the form it was to take was the School of Living's design of homesteads leased from an association that owned the land. Because of this land tenure design, and the longevity of Celo Community, Celo is now considered to be the first successful community land trust. The initial Celo board of directors included Arthur Morgan, William Regnery, and Clarence Pickett, the executive secretary of the AFSC. (Timothy Miller, *The Quest for Utopia in 20th Century America, Vol. 1*, 1998, pp. 156-7, 231 n.100, quoted in *The Intentioneer's Bible*, Amazon.com)

Second, for corroboration of Jennifer's statement above about "many people with wealth...," see the 2010 edition of the book *Philanthrocapitalism* by Matthew Bishop and Michael Green. The authors present Ted Turner, the founder of the CNN cable news channel, who gave $1 billion of his personal wealth to the United Nations in 1997, calling upon others of the super rich elite who are "awash in money" to "give the money away that you have no idea what you're going to do with." About a decade later Bill Gates of Microsoft, Oprah Winfrey of daytime talk-show fame, Warren Buffett a.k.a. the "Wizard of Omaha," and many others provide what Bishop and Green call "the most dramatic evidence so far of a movement—philanthrocapitalism—that has grown hand in hand with the rise in the number of very rich people on the planet." (Bishop & Green, p. 5)

In his 2014 book , *Unstoppable: The Emerging Left-Right Alliance to Dismantle the Corporate State*, Ralph Nader writes that Warren Buffett and Bill Gates were "the first among the 114 billionaires

Patio socializing at Dry Gulch Community, the author's class-harmony community in Denver, Colorado.

Photos courtesy of Allen Butcher

who signed a pledge to give away at least half their wealth to 'good causes.' When you look at their website [givingpledge.org], you'll see that just on this list are possibilities that would take us beyond tilting at windmills." (Nader, p. 181)

Jennifer Ladd in her article quotes Diana Leafe Christian in her 2003 book, *Creating a Life Together*, where she writes about creating community "When You Already Own the Property," that "if you cannot or don't want to release full control but still want to live in close proximity with others, please do so and enjoy it—but don't advertise it as 'community'!" (Christian, p. 24) For a long time I felt this way as well. No longer.

There you have it. Some people do not consider this type of community, what I am calling class-harmony community, to be a bona fide, legitimate form of intentional community, even though as much as 15 percent of all the listings in the 2016 FIC Directory with three or more members are class-harmony communities. This is the kind of misunderstanding and divergent opinion that proliferates in part because of vague terminology that engenders confusion about what is really involved.

Class-harmony community is a very old story. Consider one of the most famous historical class-harmony communities, New Lanark. This was a Scottish milltown acquired by Robert Owen through marriage in the early 1800s, which he turned into a form of philanthrocapitalism. He did far more than anyone else at the time to turn his factory into a socially-responsible manufacturing firm, providing social services for his 1,400 mill workers, mostly women and children, including among other things reducing hours of work, improving housing, giving every family a garden plot, and creating the first early-learning, developmental childcare facility. All of Owen's later intentional community attempts failed, including the famous New Harmony community in Indiana, although today we know how to create successful secular communal societies through the use of time-based economics. Another historical example of capitalists creating community is Jean-Baptiste-Andre Godin's "Social Palace" in France existing most of the last half of the 19th century.

What happened to that early communitarian class-harmony movement? True, Owen went too far with trying to transition his communities from collective community to communalism while knowing very little about it, losing much of his wealth in the process. Yet what really killed it was the advocacy of Karl Marx and Friedrich Engels for class-conflict through their ideas of communist "scientific socialism." They referred to Owen's and Godin's work as "utopian socialist," denigrating and sneering at the "optimum little republics" which Owen, Godin, Fourier, Saint Simon, and others created or inspired.

In a sense, the contemporary class-harmony community movement counters all forms of class-conflict-inspired communism. The two are surely not the same thing, and if a class-harmony community movement is to emerge, it will likely be necessary to easily and repeatedly respond to charges that coliving and the rest is communist. That is actually the main reason that I suggest the name "class-harmony community," as this name anticipates a coming storm of disrespectful, intolerant red baiting, by emphasizing peace and harmony between the socioeconomic classes of the wealthy, or at least the propertied class, and the un-propertied working class.

Economic and political inequalities among people have led to social conflicts all through the history of civilization, yet at the same time through much of our history we have seen people give up their wealth to live in cooperation. This was advocated and practiced by the pre-Christian stoics and others, and continued through the entire history of Catholic monasticism and other forms of religious community, renewed in our time with what is now called "New Monasticism."

Knowing now that communal society is inherently biased against children, we can add communalism to the list of cultural factors that limit the number of children that people want to have, along with urbanization and increased educational and career opportunities for women. This is another feather in the cap of communalism. Along with the reduction of resource usage through sharing commonly-owned property, communal societies also serve to reduce human overpopulation of the planet. This leaves collective and economically diverse forms of community like cohousing, community land trusts, and class-harmony communities to create child-friendly intentional community. ❧

A. Allen Butcher is a former member of East Wind and Twin Oaks communities, currently living collectively in Denver, Colorado. Portions of this article were previously published by the author in the 2016 book, The Intentioneer's Bible: Interwoven Stories of the Parallel Cultures of Plenty and Scarcity, *currently available only as an Amazon ebook, and other portions are from a forthcoming book,* Intentioneers and Illuminati: Interweaving the Parallel Cultures of Plenty and Scarcity via Myth, Allegory, Reason, and Mysticism. *Contact the author at 4thWorld@consultant.org, and see www.Intentioneers.net.*

Socializing outside the finished shop and guest room.

Shop and guest room construction at Dry Gulch Community.

Temporary housing at Dry Gulch Community.

Finding a Community

At the Bruderhof, we believe that sharing our lives and finances in community is the answer to all that is wrong with society today. We're not perfect people, but we're willing to venture everything to build a life where there are no rich or poor; where everyone is cared for, everyone belongs, and everyone can contribute.

Want to learn more of our story, and find your place in it? Visit **bruderhof.com** to schedule your visit today.

COHOUSING LIFE BY CHARLENE DICALOGERO

Cohousing for Non-Cohousers

It's been my hope to be able to live in a cohousing community since the early '90s, when I first heard about the concept while living in a three bedroom colonial on half an acre in small-town western Pennsylvania. After many relocations, life changes, and meetings, I finally moved into my one bedroom condo in Camelot Cohousing in a small town not far from Boston two months ago. There are also over 20 other households now living in our brand new community, many of whom participated in the arduous development process, which took about six years from first formal meeting to move-in. While it's clear to me that most members of Camelot put in extensive time and energy to make our community a reality, I have also been aware that some of the same neighbors were dubious about the merits of making a life in cohousing versus living in a more typical single-family home or condo. I took the opportunity to interview three neighbors about how they came to their decision and how they are finding the experience so far.

A Practical Choice

John, 38, is the father of two young children, and, like many in Camelot, works in the high tech industry in eastern Massachusetts. He grew up in different places, with significant time in South Carolina and in suburban communities. As his wife Kim reports, he retains that southern friendliness, and I felt immediately comfortable settling into the kitchen table as he set the baby monitor and dug into a bowl of bean soup. He and Kim were acquainted with several people in the founding group, from whom they first heard about the project.

"Given a brief description of the idea of cohousing, I wouldn't have said, oh, that's for me," John related. Years before, he'd known a friend who had lived in a cooperative household in Cambridge. Although in many ways, including financially, it seemed like a great situation, he was aware of a tension in the atmosphere, and the housemates' frequent attempts to get away from it. "There was not a lot of personal space, and it seemed like people had to subscribe to a set of beliefs," he explained.

Some members were initially dubious about the merits of making a life in cohousing versus living in a more typical single-family home or condo.

Juli and Chris coming to say "Hi".

Kids look on while games are played in the common house.

Chris and Nolan drawing on the walkway.

The memory of that air of constant discord or discomfort led John and Kim to approach the Camelot group with caution as well as interest. Knowing several people a bit to begin with and having some common interests was a plus for John, as was the design emphasis on distinct public and private spaces. "I don't think Kim and I would consider ourselves extroverts. That could be a common misconception that you have to be." Reading one of the key cohousing books was also helpful for him: "I'm not a big financial risk taker. Being able to see examples of what others had done was important for me to understand it. Things seemed to work very well."

While some of the group was interested in the "green" angle of cohousing, John was more attracted by the pragmatic personal benefits of sharing lawnmowers and common facilities. "Using less stuff is a practical and logical conclusion, not political, for me," he says, alluding to the savings of buying a moderately sized three-bedroom instead of the ubiquitous minimansion on two acres, and using the almost 6000 square foot Common House for bigger parties, energetic children's play, accommodating overnight guests, and exercise, among other activities.

The Big Test

Once John and Kim understood the basic nuts and bolts of

the concept and this project, they agreed on a strategy for when to make their commitment, financially and emotionally. "We wanted to see the group have a serious disagreement and how they got through it."

The conflict they'd been waiting for came just before the papers to buy land were signed. It was a process-oriented disagreement about when to use a blocking red card in consensus decision making. "There were really impassioned arguments on both sides," he recalled, yet the group worked through it. He observed that the people who most cared about the issue got together outside of meetings and resolved it. Camelot as a community passed their "test" by being able to come to an agreement about rule creation, something John felt was particularly difficult because it brings out individuals' personal values and beliefs about what is right and wrong. He thought it perhaps even more challenging than committing to signing on the dotted line with the group's LLC for a multi-million dollar loan. "When emotions are high, that's the real test of consensus," he concluded. He and Kim also agreed that how people treated each other post-conflict was very important.

Twenty-Somethings in Cohousing

I next spoke to a neighbor and good friend (via member-

Lula plays it safe while riding dad's shoulders; Maggie tags along.

ship on the same committee for years) who lives a few houses away from me on the pedestrian path. Karen, 29, and her new husband Sean have been involved with the group almost since the beginning, in 2003. In fact, they had started dating in college, and were not yet engaged when Karen was in grad school earning a degree in research chemistry in another state and Sean started attending Camelot meetings.

While many members have described cohousing as "the fun of college without the papers or bad food," I wondered how a person in her twenties would come to consider the idea of committing time and significant money to cohousing. She pointed out, "I was already spending time with these particular people on shared hobbies." The original idea for Camelot came out of the group of friends wanting to live near each other so they could spend less time driving and more time having fun. "So I thought, if following other people's cohousing blueprint makes it easier, that's great." She added, "I liked the idea of cohousing but I can't imagine if this hadn't worked out, joining another cohousing group. It's the sort of thing I'd have done when I was older."

The Common House was a major carrot motivating her as well. "If the Common House we designed wasn't part of the deal I don't think I would have been so keen on it. That's what got me excited enough to work on it. I wouldn't go to all the trouble just to build houses next to each other." Among the various amenities Karen has started to take advantage of, the sewing room rates highly, and is where she'd have been if I hadn't knocked on her door to corral her for this interview.

For the Kids (and even very private adults)

Jeff is the neighbor I know the least in this group. Their household has three generations: he and his wife are in their thirties, with Ginny very visible as the head of the Maintenance and Pool Committees; I am frequently greeted by their two children, Chris and Julianna, as they scooter, bike, or race past; and Ginny's mom Jan is a nurse and has given me advice and support for my 91-year-old father's health problems. Camelot

did a lot of its organizing via email and Google calendars, and these continue to be major communication channels in the community, but Jeff is one of the infrequent posters and was less often at meetings. I do remember discovering his sense of humor when we went through the uniquely difficult process of selecting a name for our street. I was partial to his "We-named-this-road-by-consensus Road" suggestion, but alas, the sign to accommodate it would probably fall outside any town's size regulation.

He offered to be interviewed as he watered the newly seeded garden area across which our two houses face each other. True to my sense of him when he's spoken or written to the group, Jeff is very family-oriented in his response to my question, "why did you choose to live in cohousing?" "Ginny and I went back and forth. First she was gung ho and I was hesitant, and then we'd switch. A number of us had talked about making our own neighborhood. The main driving force for me was a safe environment for the kids."

He noted that in 2003 they were living in "a great little town" in western Massachusetts, close to where he grew up, but it wasn't near friends and family. However, he got laid off from his university job, and both the job and rental markets (they had rental properties) were drying up. Given those changes, they decided it was time to move on. However, they weren't sure if this was where they wanted to be or the people they wanted to be with. They were the first household to go through a formal process of joining as Observers, then graduating to Associate status with some input into decisions, before finally putting down five percent of the estimated cost of what became their three-bedroom home to become full Equity members. This process was designed for the pre-built phase, to help the new members get information about the group and the project and give everyone time to get acquainted and see if there's a match, before serious money becomes involved on the new household's part.

Jeff seemed pretty satisfied with how Camelot is working for his kids. Chris broke his elbow badly while playing a few weeks ago, and had to have surgery. "I was touched by all the neighbors who offered to help in various ways, like taking care of my daughter while we were staying at the hospital."

The other big concern for Jeff was that the group might "force him to participate." He'd read about communities where people wore red hats when they wanted to signal that they were not interested in socializing—a prospect that didn't interest him at all. But people seem to have gotten the message without the need for special headgear (so far), and he reported having sufficient privacy in his home. And Jeff is also clear that when he's outside on the path or elsewhere in the community, he can expect to

Outside the common house.

"Don't join cohousing if you need to win arguments."

he's been spending out and about in the community. "I've been to almost every meal," he realized, which in our community means eating in the Great Room with other neighbors two to three times a week.

Advice for Non-Cohousers Considering Cohousing

Collective wisdom is something I believe in more and more as I accumulate experiences with different groups, including my new neighbors. I asked each of them for their advice for similarly reluctant or unsure potential cohousers. Here are some pearls I was thrown by my three—dare I say "former non-cohousers, now happily cohoused"—neighbors:

"Knowing the people in community is as important if not more important than the physical structures. The idea is to have some sort of connection with your neighbors." *(John)*

"It's not that different from living in a condo complex, but you *do* know everyone by name, and we make sure you will." *(Karen)*

"Don't judge a book by its cover. No matter what you've heard or read, you can best tell by experiencing it to see if it could work for you. Once I was able to start walking into my house as it was being built, and participate in setting up structures for post-move-in, it definitely made it more real for me." *(Jeff)*

"We're not around very much. Even when you're not here, it's here for you. I don't feel like I need to be here for things like common meals all the time. It's worth it for the moments you get." *(Karen)*

"I think each cohousing group probably has its own feel. [Judge each group on its own merits.]" *(John)*

"Don't join cohousing if you need to win arguments." *(Karen)*

And this is after only five months, at most, of cohousing life—think how smart we'll be after five years or five decades! ❀

be interrupted (which our group calls "being cohoused," when someone stops you on your way to somewhere and suddenly it's an hour later and you can't remember what you were going out for to begin with).

He does, however, like to cook, including for common meals, and is good at it, I can objectively report. He even emailed the group to announce that he was making and jarring up salsa in three flavors, if anyone wanted some.

Welcome to the Honeymoon!

All the neighbors I interviewed seemed happy with how things are going at the two- to five-month point. John, whose household was one of the first three to take up residency, considered significant the point in February when they started having people over as more folks moved in. The second milestone was passed when, as more households with children arrived, son Joe, five, could just go outside and play with other kids. The two parents realized they didn't have to think twice about Joe grabbing his scooter and shooting out the door, because the houses are away from the roads and they already knew all the people living a short walk (or scoot) away.

Karen reported that the first several months have been good, but the first week was miserable. She'd been so busy working on marketing the project to prospective neighbors that she hadn't prepared for the "we're finally moving in!" She had also worried she and Sean wouldn't have enough room in their two-bedroom plus townhouse for all their belongings. Happily, she found that "all this stuff about being able to live in a smaller house in cohousing works out—at least it did for us, having gotten a house with a basement!"

Jeff said sometimes it's still a shock to realize he's actually living in Camelot. He was pleasantly surprised at how much time

Charlene DiCalogero lives in Camelot Cohousing in Berlin, Massachusetts, where she is the Chair of the Membership, Marketing, and Fun Team when she's not at her grants administration job in Cambridge or performing as a singer-songwriter. If you're interested in living in Camelot or the "super green" Mosaic Commons Cohousing community right next door, please contact her at charlene@camelotcohousing.com.

COMMUNITY AND HEALTH:
Immigrant Senior Cohousing in the Netherlands

By Dorit Fromm and Els de Jong

All photos courtesy of Anand Joti

Top image: Two apartments per floor were made available to Santosa group members, who also share a meeting room. The service provider, Laurens, is located on the ground floor of the seniors-only building. Above: The group members of Santosa on an excursion to view other cohousing projects during the development of their community.
Opposite page left: The common house at Anand Joti, located on the ground floor, left, is available to be rented out. Apartments are located above.
Middle: The future residents of Anand Joti participated in the development process.
Right: Andre Bhola received training in checking blood pressure and blood sugar levels and he staffs the clinic at Anand Joti once a week.

When cohousing was initially transplanted to the US from Europe (starting with a community built near the state capitol in Sacramento in 1991), Californians commented that of course the model worked in Europe—its countries didn't have diversity issues like California. In cohousing, residents own private homes, and share common spaces which they manage and maintain together. Now, 18 years later, it's clear that the concept works in the US, with over 100 current cohousing communities—and that what binds them together are not homogeneous residents but a shared interest in creating community and the willingness to work through challenges.

Still, cohousing communities in the US are not particularly diverse. People sharing similar viewpoints do often seem to feel most comfortable with each other; and unlike their European counterparts, American communities usually develop without the help of nonprofits or welcoming municipalities, so they are limited to offering mostly market-rate housing.

For those reasons—and counter to American assessments of homogeneity—a much wider diversity of residents lives in cohousing in a country like the Netherlands than in the US.

Amsterdam, the capital of the Netherlands, holds a rich mix of cultures with more than a third of residents first or second generation immigrants. In their traditions, many generations typically live under one roof. But the same cannot be said for the Dutch, at least since the 1950s. Most modern Dutch housing units are apartments for the nuclear family, with little room for extended families.

As for Dutch service flats which provide assisted living for seniors, they have never been freely chosen by ethnic immigrants. Living in this kind of an institution forces them to adapt to Dutch culture and food to a much greater extent than they were used to previously. Quite the opposite has shown to be their inclination. As they age, these elders have less interest in integration and a preference for reminiscing back to their roots—talking about their youth and speaking their mother tongue. Their children, therefore, feel a sense of shame in having their aging parents cared for by others and in an institution.

The dilemma of living alone when needing more support and supervision, especially in an environment where the language, beliefs, and religion are not one's own, led to the idea of cohousing projects designed specifically for aging immigrants. Rental cohousing, developed by nonprofit organizations, presented a viable alternative to standard senior housing: elders can live together and support each other. In this way they often live for a longer period of time without professional care.

Surinamese Cohousing

Anand Joti means "peace and light" in Hindustani. As we sit in the little outdoor patio next to Andre and Betty Bhola's apartment door, overlooking the quiet, well-kept common garden, it seems to us a fitting description for this ethnic senior cohousing community. Andre Bhola is the project's spokesman.

He successfully bridges the three worlds of Surinam, the Netherlands, and Hindu culture, as does this development that he helped to instigate.

The residents of this 24-unit housing development originally came from Surinam in South America. This ethnically diverse former colony of Dutch Guinea became independent in 1975, and many Surinamese immigrated at that time to the Netherlands. In Amsterdam, Anand Joti (founded in the late 1980s) helps Hindustani Surinamese, who make up about 10 percent of the city's population. The foundation, mostly run by volunteers, has developed housing, day care, and other services, and has a special focus on health

As they age, these elders have less interest in integration, and a preference for reminiscing back to their roots and speaking their mother tongue.

education. For example, they've developed dramas and sketches in Hindustani around the subjects of obesity, heart disease, poverty, and other elder issues. The foundation helped to create Anand Joti cohousing, which opened in 1997.

Healthy Day-to-Day Life

At the once-a-week afternoon tea gathering for residents in the common space, Indian music plays as residents sip and talk. Traditionally, a pot of the dark Indian tea (chai), is spiced with cardamom, cinnamon, and cloves and mixed with milk and a number of heaping teaspoons of sugar. For the residents at Anand Joti, sugar is one of the ingredients best left out.

South Asians are estimated to have five times the risk level as Europeans for diabetes. Aside from genetic predisposition, eating unhealthy foods, not exercising, and stress greatly increase the chances of becoming diabetic and having complications, such as cardiovascular illnesses.

About half the residents of Anand Joti have diabetes, and the weekly activities organized in the common house include exercise classes geared to interest the seniors. There's a yoga class three times a week, and a Bollywood dance class, taught by volunteers. Residents stroll to the common house for classes and a handful also buddy-up for more Nordic exercises, like walking.

A small health office—a mini-clinic—is in the common house. By its door, a prominent display offers literature on diabetes and other health issues. André received training in checking blood pressure and blood sugar levels and he staffs the clinic once a week, explaining how to use the medicine provided by health practitioners.

The common house is used every day, contributing to a strong sense of community, as well as social and mental health. Twice a week residents meet for tea or coffee, Wednesday nights feature Hindi singing, Thursdays a reading group, and on Friday nights residents play cards and discuss Hindu history. A highlight, once a month, is watching Bollywood movies together.

Other common activities include resident participation in management, governance, and maintenance, including

The pedestrian-oriented neighborhood, with nearby school and family housing, creates an important counterpoint to the seniors-only cohousing Anand Joti.

At Anand Joti, Andre engaged the group in discussing difficult issues, such as social problems, disease and health, and conflict among residents.

taking care of the garden and cleaning the common house. The residents observe Hindu festivals, and celebrate the New Year and Christmas. They get together for an excursion twice a year, and have taken courses on managing together as a community. A Hindustani organization gives courses on aging, with an emphasis on managing income.

Residents also lend a helping hand to each other, for example shopping for each other. When someone falls ill, residents help them out by taking them to the doctor and cooking for them.

The community has encountered some economic difficulties in recent years. As the residents age, they need more help and services but their elderly pension is limited. Also, rents are rising, as is the extra fee for use of the common facilities that each household pays.

Development

For those coming from a foreign country who may not speak the language, navigating the process of development becomes extremely difficult. At Anand Joti, Andre acted as the liaison between the nascent group and the many organi-zations whose cooperation and funding pushed the project forward. An intermediary who speaks the language and understands the culture has the trust of the forming group, and can help them articulate their needs and desires. Whether it's somone in the group working for a cultural organization, or someone knowledgeable about the development process working with a motivated potential resident, at least one person is needed who can communicate the requirements and constraints of the development process.

An ideal time to bring in the theme of health is when the group is forming. The culture of caring about health and the group's needs requires nurturing and development along with the physical form. At Anand Joti, Andre engaged the group in discussing difficult issues, such as social problems, disease and health, conflict among residents, and other issues that are not typically discussed. For senior collaborative living, it is very important that the group think about the care they want to give to each other, and so make their limits clear. Residents cannot take the place of nursing support but they can provide social support, subtle monitoring (to the extent that they know who is up and about daily), and some short-term help when a resident is not seriously ill.

Santosa

Unlike Anand Joti, where residents moved into a tailor-made building, Santosa is an example of a "speckled" co-housing community, where Javanese (Indonesian) Surinamese households are "speckled" throughout a non-cohousing apartment building. Nico van den Dool, a cohousing consultant, contacted the nonprofit housing owner, Laurens, about the renovation of their large 235-unit senior complex, located in Rotterdam. With one wing of their phased upgrade completed, they discovered that about 10 percent of the displaced residents were not returning, freeing up apartments.

These service flats, located in a suburb, offered a number of advantages. Aside from a relatively quiet neighborhood, the seniors-only building amenities include a restaurant, a hairdresser, pedicure, laundry, billiards room, library, and several guestrooms. An organization providing professional home care services has an office in the building and can provide needed care.

Working with a local organization, the Spirit Foundation for Surinamese, Nico began forming a group in 1999. Members at first expressed reluctance to move out of their downtown neighborhood, but the expense and difficulty of finding appropriate housing persuaded them to look elsewhere. Thanks to the fact that they can live among other people of similar origin and ethnicity, these Surinam seniors were willing to take the bold step of moving to this apartment building in a "white" neighborhood. They saw the nearby shopping center and proximity to transit as strong advantages.

The group members all live in two-room apartments, grouped two to a floor, and they share a group common room for meetings. Typically, speckled cohousing groups have an "agreement of cooperation" set up with the owner. When a suitable apartment becomes available the owner informs the group. The group has created a preferred profile describing their group and the type of people they feel would comfortably fit in. They contact people on their waiting list, and then prepare a proposal with their preferred person. When the group doesn't have a candidate, the owner rents the apartment in the typical way. For Santosa, which began with less than 10 households, the model has allowed the group to grow. The number of group members is contractually limited to 18 by the owner.

Social Interchange and Care in Santosa

Ethnic minority elders, in general, are comfortable with being socially connected to each other. They often meet and talk. When someone has the flu, a neighbor brings a bowl of soup. The people in the cohousing project look after each other, and call in a doctor for another member when necessary. They care about each other, but they can't do nursing tasks. Living in a senior cohousing group can in some way extend the time that a person lives independently, but if someone really needs nursing, professional home care is necessary. In this type of collaborative housing, seniors of the same ethnic minority live near each other, allowing the provision of culturally adapted professional care.

Usually, the members meet together twice a week in the community room. A volunteer from the group's cultural organization, who also assisted with the start of the project, joins them in the community room to talk, to make coffee and tea, and to answer questions or give a helping hand when needed. Besides this set meeting, the group members see one another informally daily. They meet each other in their shared common room but also in their own apartments, or after dinner in the lobby. Some of the comments from residents:

"We know each other very well. Like family. If we cook a meal, we say 'come over and have dinner with me' just like a family."

"We see each other every day. And if we miss someone, we make a phone call."

"I can't see very well anymore, so it is difficult for me to go out to shop or the market. But I still can go to this communal room and meet other people."

The Santosa members are older than the typical residents of the building; the youngest member is in her 60s, the oldest over 85. The cultural organization acts as the intermediary between them and the Dutch health care system. When someone becomes ill, often other group members contact Spirit Foundation, and they in turn call the sick person, find out what's wrong, and contact appropriate care. A doctor, dentist, or other professional then pays a visit.

Several of the Santosa residents receive professional home care. When the caregivers see a problem, they also make contact with the cultural organization, which contacts not only the seniors, but also their adult children. The children will be informed, for example, that their mother, having ignored her diet, is now not doing well. This is especially helpful when the children are not living nearby.

Minority Seniors Increasing

The number of seniors belonging to an ethnic minority in Holland will be increasing in the coming years and will rise almost 700 percent by 2050. In that year, one out of six non-western immigrants will be over 65 years old. So far, at least five ethnic groups have cohousing developments in Holland. Aside from Anand Joti, there are other senior cohousing developments for Hindustanis, and also for Chinese, Moroccans, Turks and other ethnic groups.

As far as the speckled variety, they "number at least 10" according to Peter Bakker of the FGW (Federation Gemeenschappelijk Wonen), the Dutch umbrella organization for cohousing.[1] A relatively new model, it also works for native Dutch elders, who grapple with similar needs of affordable, timely, and supportive housing.

The US will also see a rise in seniors who are immigrants, many of them minorities. As American seniors become more diverse, housing and care aimed at specific cultures will be in demand. The social and health benefits make this a useful model to explore. ❋

Dorit Fromm is an architect who writes, researches, and consults on innovative communities, design, and aging. Her articles have appeared in Urban Land, AARP Journal, ArcCa, *and other publications, and she is the author of* Collaborative Communities: Cohousing, Central Living and Other New Forms of Housing.

Els de Jong is a Dutch freelance social researcher specializing in housing studies. She is interested in innovative housing projects with the aim of improving apartment living. See www.wono.nl.

[1]An ongoing discussion within FGW: should the speckled model be called cohousing? The question arises because of the ease of joining and leaving, and also because different community models that we would group under the term cohousing *(centraal wonen)*—for example, senior cohousing—also have different names in Dutch.

Future Anand Joti residents participated in the development process.

Aging in Community

By Raines Cohen

Oswald Skene

I feel blessed to be part of a parallel evolution in the field of aging, a newly emerging phenomenon we in the movement call **"Aging In Community"** (not to be confused with the important but relatively mundane "Aging In Place" that we build on). New community-based people-powered institutions and models for cooperation are giving us the opportunity to overcome the multi-billion-dollar aging-industrial complex trying to put us into prefabricated generic slots in nursing homes. We need to help each other to get past the well-intentioned efforts of our own families to "take care of us" in ways that strip us of autonomy.

A new perspective is that we can gain control of our lives, and even elements of choice in our deaths, and earn independence through interdependence, as my wife Betsy Morris, a longtime community researcher, has written. People are dealing with complex systems necessary for their own sense of well-being. Empowerment comes from peoples' discovery that in sharing information and ideas, access to a greater whole becomes integral to one's personal success. Passionate groups of users—amateurs and professionals interacting freely in structured settings—became a community of stakeholders with the power to reshape the system itself, first through voluntary exchanges among themselves, and then by translating social connections and trust into economic and political clout.

A Movement of Many Pieces

Aging in Community is a ragtag movement of ordinary people banding together and stepping forward to fill in gaps of the patchwork of care with overlapping efforts, regional and national, "multiple centers of initiative," people just like you who are, just in the past decade:

• Building "village model" support structures that can help us stay in our homes, connecting to neighbors rather than isolating ourselves as we age.

• Creating new cohousing neighborhoods and ecovillages specifically designed to provide homes that we can live out the rest of our lives in, transforming our collective impacts on the earth for the benefit of generations yet to come.

• Forming Elders' Guilds and studying Sage-ing, collaborative courses, Second Journey workshops, and study groups for conscious aging, where we together re-imagine old age and embody the wisdom to help heal the future.

• Becoming Earth Elders dedicated to creating a just, sacred, and sustainable future.

A few people are exploring new areas of development in the movement, including:

• Supporting developers creating ElderFire communities, ElderShire neighborhoods, and "GreenHouse" nursing homes.

• Sharing strategies to remake our cities and towns into Aging-Friendly Communities that will meet our aging populations' needs.

• Supporting each other with Senior Networks that keep people connected and engaged across distances through computer communications.

The term "Aging In Community" appears to have been coined early this century by participants in Second Journey's workshops on Spirit, Service, and Community. I credit White House Conference on Aging member Janice Blanchard from Colorado as the one who has done the most to popularize the term, forging a foothold with talks at American Society on Aging national conferences and throughout the "industry of aging." It's going to take a lot of us working together in this regard to help the movement see that we're all working on the same essential core, despite differences in scope, scale, and methods.

We're still in the early stages of finding each other, and as a self-help citizen-organized movement, we're in the decommodifying business, so you can't (yet) just look up your local Aging In Community center and say "I'd like one of those villages by next week in green, please." A few national organizations support matchmaking and group development for some types of community efforts, but at the moment, if you want one of these groups to meet your needs, the odds are that you'll have to step up and make it happen. Fortunately, there's a lot of help available.

Curious? Join me, if you will, on a brief journey through some of these innovative efforts and what makes them so essential to our little revolution in aging.

Cohousing

In Denmark in the early 1970s, families looking for deeper connections with neighbors and support for raising kids together pioneered a new form of neighborhood, one combining private homes with a large shared area. A common house included shared kitchen and dining area that they could use together a few times a week, while they still had the independence of their own kitchens in their own homes. Cars were pushed to the edge, with design for walkability. Folks could share in childcare, but weren't forced to do everything together. This "yes, and" principle of adding choices turned out to provide a high quality of life without adding much cost to basic homeownership.

If you want one of these groups to meet your needs, you may have to step up and make it happen. Fortunately, there's a lot of help available.

People live in smaller, greener homes, living richer lives for less.

We call this **cohousing**. In more than 100 neighborhoods across the country, it offers condominiums with community, developed by the residents. In these "intentional neighborhoods" that start green and get greener, you know your neighbors and build the shared experience that makes it easy to trust and share. These are projects that cities will approve and banks will finance (even when the economy is stalled everywhere else), because the future residents are part of the process, investing and sharing an interest in the success of the project; they've got "skin in the game."

Senior Cohousing

It turned out that these same cohousing neighborhood design principles had a lot to offer aging Boomers, including:

• Shared guest rooms to accommodate visiting family members or shared long-term care providers, living independently rather than in your own house so you don't get into that whole servant/master dynamic.

• Shared meals to keep people talking to one another and aware of significant events in each others' lives

• Community connections that keep people active, because they know they'll hear from their nice but nosy neighbor if they don't get dressed and get the paper by noon.

Senior cohousing, recently imported to the US by Charles Durrett (decades after he brought over the original intergenerational form with his architect/author wife, Kathryn McCamant), is just getting off the ground here, with a handful of communities established in California, Virginia, and Colorado, and a couple dozen more in the development process. The Cohousing Association of the United States (Coho/US) is helping these bold pioneers challenging bureaucrats, land-use regulations, and their own fears that can keep them from realizing their visions.

(continued on p. 77)

Definition of an Elder

An Elder is a person who is still growing, still a learner, still with potential, and whose life continues to have within it promise for, and connection to the future.

An elder is still in pursuit of happiness, joy, and pleasure, and her or his birthright to these remains intact.

Moreover, an elder is a person who deserves respect and honor and whose work it is to synthesize wisdom from long life experience and formulate this into a legacy for future generations.

—Barry Barkan, Elders' Guild

Elders' Guild

Our Vision is a world in which powerful and conscious elders join together in common purpose to bring healing, joy, and connection to our lives, our families, our communities, and our world.

Our Mission is to create the communities where we re-imagine our old age, look after one another, and embody the wisdom that will enable us to help heal the future.

www.eldersguild.org

(a project of the Live Oak Institute, Berkeley, CA; regular meetings take place twice a month in Berkeley)

AGING IN COMMUNITY

(continued from p. 45)

Part of what is driving this movement, according to Durrett, is the tendency of Boomers to reinvent society's institutions as they engage them. "What is more audacious than 25 seniors deciding that they should build their own neighborhood?," Durrett asks. "What is more audacious than 25 seniors deciding, 'hell, they don't know how to do it, we're gonna figure out out how to do it.' All these seniors should stay in their houses, not just be told to be happy in assisted care. This generation understands that the Stepford country is not where it's at."

The Danish national aging curriculum, which he is adapting for domestic consumption, helps people band together in "study groups" to talk about all the taboo topics of aging that are important to discuss before crises arise:

- health
- death
- finances
- co-care agreements
- spirituality

Through work together mapping these strange new (and old) territories, cohousers are able to efficiently partner with professional developers and co-create neighborhoods that will be able to better meet their needs, increasing the odds that they can remain in their homes over time without either becoming a burden to their neighbors or facing unreasonable obligations of unlimited support.

Village Networks

Starting with Boston's Beacon Hill Village in 2001, this model is now spreading around the world.

These are member-based neighborhood networks that help people stay in their homes as they age, by making where they live into **aging-friendly communities**, overlaying services and community.

In the "Beacon Hill Village Model," people (typically 50+) in a particular area band together to form a nonprofit organization providing "concierge services," one-stop shopping for transportation, home-care, house maintenance, medical, and care-management services.

Typical membership fees are $500 to $1000 per person or household per year, with mature villages offering reduced-fee subsidized memberships for people who can't afford the full fees.

Memberships include basic transportation for shopping and excursions, and regular social events, but additional trips and other services are usually offered on a fee-for-service basis, with membership discounts. They publish newsletters, host parties, and help people get to know each other better and form "affinity groups" with shared interests.

Network operators screen service providers, using their leveraged group-buying power to get quality service with member discounts. ❧

For more information about all of these models, see www.agingincommunity.com/models.

Sections of this article are excerpted from Raines' Cohen's chapter in the book Audacious Aging: Eldership as a Revolutionary Endeavor *(Elite Books, 2009).*

Raines Cohen is a Northern California Regional Organizer with Cohousing California, a regional umbrella group fostering the creation of green intentional neighborhoods (ecovillages) throughout the state. He has spent a quarter century launching grassroots nonprofit organizations and helping them manage their growth. He served two terms on the Cohousing Association of the United States national board and currently is a Fellowship for Intentional Community board member. He is a Certified Green Building Professional and Certified Senior Cohousing Facilitator, helping people create new choices for retirement, and a member of the National Aging In Place Council and founding member of The Elders Guild.

Green Houses:
Providing Humane Care for Elders

By Deborah Altus

Resident of an Asbury Park Green House on the patio where she grows roses.

The term "greenhouse" normally brings up images of a building for growing plants. In the caregiving field, however, the word has taken on a completely different meaning. The new meaning of greenhouse does not focus on plants or buildings but, instead, describes a model of caring for older people in small, resident-centered group homes. Why the term greenhouse? The Green House model is designed to provide the optimal environment for the health and well-being of elders in the same way that greenhouses are built to provide the optimal conditions for plants to thrive.

The founder of the Green House model, Dr. William Thom-

as, refers to these homes as intentional communities. Thomas is a key player in what is known as the "culture-change" movement in long-term care. His work focuses not simply on designing humane living environments for elders but on changing the way society views aging—earning him a spot on the *Wall Street Journal's* list of the 12 most influential Americans shaping aging in the 21st century.

In the 1990s, Thomas, a geriatric physician and professor at the University of Maryland, developed the Eden Alternative, an approach that brings person-centered schedules, children, plants, and animals into nursing facilities to humanize the institutional environment. One of Thomas' goals is to alleviate what he sees as the "three plagues" of long-term care institutions: loneliness, helplessness, and boredom.

With the Green House model, Thomas has proposed a radical shift from the medical focus of traditional nursing facilities. To Thomas, the medical model of long-term care is flawed because it views aging as a disease. In contrast, the Green House model views aging as a natural part of the life course. In this model, older people are looked up to as wise elders rather than treated as sick patients. They live in small (six to 10 bed) family-style homes rather than hospital-like institutions. Their schedules are person-centered rather than staff-centered. And their needs are addressed from a holistic (bio-psycho-social-spiritual) perspective rather than a medical one.

In Green Houses, the direct service providers, who are typically Certified Nursing Assistants (CNAs), are called Shahbazim, a Persian word meaning "royal falcon." Thomas chose this word because he feels strongly that caregivers should be honored and respected. He refers to the Shahbazim as "the midwives of a new elderhood." The role of the Shahbazim is much broader than that of traditional CNAs. They cook, clean, do laundry, and provide personal care, much as a family member would do. This is part of the Green House plan: to create a family-style environment that feels like home rather than an institution.

The nursing station, often the hub of activity and power in a nursing facility, is deliberately kept small in the Green House

A Songaian Perspective on Long-Term Care

Songaia Cohousing Community, in Bothell, Washington, looked into the Green House model as they explored ways to ensure that members could age in place at Songaia. Member Craig Ragland went to an all-day Green House workshop and came away inspired that people were trying to establish a greater sense of community in long-term care settings. However, he realized that this model "was not tuned to an intentional community setting" and would not work well for them. He found the Green House model too closely tied to the medical model to fit with his community's goals and also felt that the private space provided by a group home environment was inadequate. Ragland is interested in creating what he calls a "community model," where the community, itself, helps to manage the care of older members, or provides onsite housing for caregivers. In addition, he sees the need for suites, similar to studio apartments, where older residents would have sufficient private space to socialize with friends and family and be able to prepare snacks or the occasional meal. These suites would be optimized to meet the needs of elders. When an older member moved into a suite, his/her home would be available for occupancy by younger people—thereby keeping the average age of the community at a healthy level.

—Deborah Altus

Exterior of one of the Green Houses at Asbury Park retirement community in Newton, Kansas.

Photos courtesy of Deborah Altus

model and located at the periphery. This is done to normalize the environment and to encourage staff to interact with the elders. The Shahbazim oversee the day-to-day operations of the home, while nurses act in a consulting role but are responsible for clinical outcomes. Green Houses are often built in clusters so that homes can share nurses, which helps to keep costs down.

Each elder has a private room and bath which opens onto a central living area called the hearth room—the focal point of activity in a Green House. The hearth room is situated next to an open kitchen where elders and Shahbazim can interact during the daily routines of cooking, cleaning, and other activities.

Residents are able to furnish their rooms with their own belongings. "I have my nice furniture and my pretties in here," says a 75-year-old Green House resident. She describes the Green House as "like home" and says that the other residents are "like a family." She notes that she is "very satisfied" with living in the Green House and says that it "makes us feel like we aren't being thrown away." She particularly likes the fact that she can determine her own schedule, as she prefers to stay up late to watch television and sleep late in the morning. She loves to tend the roses in the Green House garden and sit on the front porch with other residents when the weather is pleasant.

Tom Williams, the CEO of Asbury Park in Newton, Kansas, has overseen the construction of four Green Houses on the campus of his continuing care retirement community. Williams, who has been in charge of much bigger projects throughout his career, says that building the Green Houses is the most gratifying thing he's done. "We are making a place where people can spend the last years of their life with dignity," says Williams. "We grow up in households that are nurturing, protective, and caring, and this is what we get in a Green House."

When asked if he sees a change in the residents' demeanor after they move into a Green House, Williams responds with one word: "joy." He notes that a couple of residents who arrived in wheelchairs started getting up and using walkers as a result of the more nurturing, stimulating environment of the Green House. He also points out that the Shahbazim like being part of a team and appreciate the chance to develop family-like relationships with the elders.

One staff member, age 54, who works as a Shahbaz, says that the thing she likes the most about the Green Houses is that they "give back home to people who have had everything else taken from them." She loves having the time for one-on-one interaction with residents, something she didn't have when she worked in a traditional nursing facility. "We have time to give better care here," she says. "You aren't on a tight time schedule and you can give holistic care—care for physical and mental needs."

Another Shahbaz notes that staff become so close to the residents that some even call on their days off to see how the elders are doing. "They are like family to us," she says. When one of the residents died, "it was like when my Grandma passed." She notes that the Green House residents are much calmer than those in the nursing facility—even the residents with dementia. She also says that the family members of the residents love the Green Houses. "They are comfortable here. They come in more than they did in the main building. They have a place to sit and socialize with the residents and staff."

This is not to say that Green Houses are without their problems. Williams is the first to admit that any new approach will have kinks to work out. Dealing with zoning, building codes, and licensing can be challenging for Green House adopters because local and state officials are often unfamiliar with this type of housing. The cost of care is not cheap and is similar to that of a traditional nursing facility. Green Houses may accept some residents on Medicaid, but Williams points out that it would be difficult to break even with all Medicaid patients. Nurses and CNAs who have worked in traditional nursing facilities may find it challenging to adjust to their new roles. And administrators may find this new path hard to navigate without established programs to emulate. "We've had to learn as we go," says Williams, "but the rewards have been worth it."

The use of the term "intentional community" by Green House founder Thomas may seem like a bit of a stretch to those involved in the Fellowship for Intentional Community. The Green Houses are run by paid staff members. Some residents, such as residents with dementia, may not intentionally choose to live there. Residents aren't involved in decisions about who shares their home, who works there, or how their money is spent. Yet, unlike many nursing facilities, the residents can personalize their schedules. They live in a home-like environment rather than a large institution. Their caregivers act more like family members (e.g., they cook, clean, do laundry, provide personal care, and offer activities) than nursing assistants. They have their own bedrooms with their own furniture and they eat family-style meals. Even if "intentional community" may not be the appropriate descriptor, the Green House model appears to be an important step toward humanizing the care of frail elders.

Author note: Portions of this article were taken from an article written by Deborah Altus for the Fall 2009 issue of Speaking of Kansas, *entitled "Green Houses Bring Culture Change in Long-Term Care to Kansas" (pp. 3-4).* ❧

Deborah Altus is a professor at Washburn University in Topeka, Kansas. She conducted sabbatical research on the Green House model in Spring 2009. Deborah is a member of the Editorial Review Board for the FIC, former president of the Communal Studies Association, and a board member of the International Communal Studies Association.

> *The hearth room is situated next to an open kitchen where elders and Shahbazim can interact during the daily routines of cooking, cleaning, and other activities.*

Shared Living— When Home Is a Community

By Carol Pimentel

All photos courtesy of Carol Pimentel

Casa Caballeros.

Why would anyone voluntarily give up having a place of her own? "I could never do it," say my more traditional friends, shaking their heads in wonder. "I could never handle other people in my home. I can't even take house guests for more than three days! I need to have my own space."

Having one's own house (and washer, dryer, garden, lawn mower, stuff) may be the American Dream, but some of us have a different dream: a dream of learning to live more cooperatively with others and sharing resources rather than each needing to have our own. And as it happens, the skills it takes to live closely with others and low on the food chain are extremely useful when the economic systems of the larger culture hit the skids.

I've lived in shared households all my adult life. Shared living has always been my chosen lifestyle, both for the companionship and the sharing of resources. When other young women were dreaming of becoming brides, my dream was to find my tribe. I was part of several start-up groups exploring intentional community, but none of them got off the ground. However, at age 35, I joined with three other women to buy a large house on an acre of land in San Luis Obispo, California as an experiment in community living on a small scale.

None of us could have afforded to buy property alone, and none of us wanted to dedicate our lives to earning enough to do so. We reasoned that if we shared living expenses we could all be free from the rat race. We called the place Caballeros House, and buying it jointly was a splendid decision. There was lots of turnover in the household as people's lives changed, but for 20 years there was always a houseful of folks living and growing together.

Communication

Conflict was inevitable, and we had to learn how to manage it. One day a few months after we had moved in, Maxine came home to find a new piece of wall art mounted at the end of the hall. "Who put that there?" she demanded. "I did," replied Elizabeth mildly, "I think the colorful herb and flowers in the poster look nice there." "Well I don't like it," grumbled Maxine, slamming her door. Elizabeth's feelings were hurt, and we all tiptoed around on eggshells for a day or two. Finally we called a house meeting to discuss what had happened and how we would handle such things in the future. The real issue was not the poster, of course, but territoriality. Max was sensitive to changes being made without consulting her, and Liz wanted the freedom to experiment without new additions being shot down. We came up with a simple policy that we called "Try it for a week." Anyone could bring anything into the house on a trial basis and the others would wait a week to pass final judgment. As it turned out, we discovered that an immediate negative reaction frequently dissipated after living with the change for a while. "Try it for a week" saved us innumerable arguments and much unpleasantness, and we often laughed remembering the stir caused by that inoffensive poster.

Living with others presents challenges. Relationship dynamics can get prickly and fantasies that the household will meet extended family needs or that everyone will pitch in equally may not pan out. Mutual adjustment is necessary. It takes a couple of months for a new resident to get into the flow of the household, and there's a lingering emptiness when a much-loved person departs. It's all part of the ebb and flow.

Communication is the key to making it work. Every new resident at Casa Caballeros had a long interview, in which we shared our values of recycling, composting, and conserving energy and resources, to determine whether s/he would be a good match for the household. We talked about mutual respect and the importance of communicating with one another about needs and irritations so that we could mutually adjust to prevent chronic complaints or resentments. There was no structure or expectation of how much we would interact; that was allowed to develop organically. Sometimes we shared meals, late night schmoozing, or celebrations. Always we respected one another's privacy.

Alternative economy

Eventually I married one of my housemates. When two of the original owners chose to move on, Don and I purchased their interests and Casa Caballeros entered a new phase as a shared home. Don was a remarkable artist/builder who transformed the yard with small outbuildings and tree plantings. Living in the outbuildings allowed us to include more people in the main house. The rental income covered most of our expenses, so we rode out the financial downturn of the '80s without blinking an eye.

Valuing frugality, we all lived well on the cast-off treasures of others. We seldom paid retail price for anything, since with patience anything could be found at swap meets or garage sales, everything from boots to vacuum cleaners to table saws to glittering sequined gowns.

Every Sunday at 6 a.m.—no kidding, *every* Sunday—Don was up and off, flashlight in hand, to what we called the "Church of the Holy Swap," the weekly swap meet, to inspect the offerings of the day, coming home a few hours later to display his bounty. He had a great eye and the skills to repair and upgrade virtually anything. I remember when he brought home a plastic grocery bag of dirty looking sticks of wood and some rusty springs, which he assembled into a lovely Mission style rocker. Friends would

An outbuilding at Casa Caballeros.

Valuing frugality, we all lived well on the cast-off treasures of others. We seldom paid retail price for anything, since with patience anything could be found at swap meets or garage sales.

place orders with Don, and sure enough, within a few weeks he could usually come up with the item.

Don was not alone in his dedication to reuse and recycling; we all held these values, and others in the household learned to be "bottom feeders" too. Sometimes we'd toodle around construction sites scavenging building materials. Those materials went into tidy resource piles to be used as needed for building projects on the property.

When the local university let out for the summer, we invited friends to join us with their trucks for the annual dumpster dive day. Armed with rubber gloves and dressed in garbage clothes and throwaway shoes, we went from dorm to dorm and behind student apartment buildings on a mission to rescue usable items students had predictably tossed into the trash. We loaded up on enough unopened sundries like dish soap, shampoo, and cleaning supplies to last for months. We scored so much—clothing, appliances, office supplies, furniture, and even jewelry—that we couldn't use it all. Some items we sold second-hand for cash, but we'd donate much of it at the end of the day. Sometimes we'd take a few kids with us. It was a fun adventure for them to be allowed to get dirty and find so many cool things for free. We'd talk about the extravagant waste they'd seen and how they felt about donating to the homeless shelter. It was a great learning experience.

When a household is made up of people with a variety of skills, everyone is enriched. Physical skills, interpersonal skills, and creativity are all valuable contributions. Don was indisputably the swap meet king, our procurer of goods for very little cost. Allen was the consummate host and chef extraordinaire, often spontaneously firing up the grill and inviting anyone who was home to participate. I was the nurturer, communicator, and mediator, attending to relationships and dynamics in the group and willing to confront problems when they arose. Terry brought music. Kari was a gardener. Elizabeth, our elder, was the "ground." While the rest of us were busy with work, activities, and multi-tasking, her days were filled with reading, caring for the chickens, and deadheading the flowers. Her deep centeredness and quiet spirit permeated the atmosphere and brought peace to us all, while our activity enlivened her. Everyone pitching in with chores meant less burden on any one individual.

Beyond ourselves

In anticipation of Y2K, several friends joined us to expand our gardens so we could all share the organic produce, fruits, and nuts. We developed the yard into a food forest, with a flock of chickens for fresh eggs. The security of knowing we were in it together prevented many a sleepless night, and though the crisis never happened, we all loved gardening together and sharing the bounty. And with so many of us involved, whatever tool we needed someone was bound to have.

Taking community and resource sharing beyond our own household, we formed an informal group with several couples and singles that we called The Barn Raisers. Anyone who had a big project could put out a call and those who were free would descend *en masse* and work miracles. Together we cleaned and painted houses, installed cabinets, cleared yards (lots of this!), and once we even installed a huge metal bridge over a creek. Our workdays always

Casa Caballeros' Memory Wall.

included wonderful meals and socializing together, sometimes into the wee hours. I wonder how much money we collectively saved over the years by helping each other in these ways?

We made the house and property available for any number of community events and groups. There were weddings, ceremonies, Cub Scout campouts, bonfires, meditation groups, workshop retreats, and big potlucks. A Mardi Gras float was built in the yard one year.

All good things come to an end

The community at Caballeros house lasted from 1985 through 2006, when sea changes in our lives dictated that Don and I sell the house and go our separate ways. We invited anyone who felt connected to the place to a huge "house closing" party to honor the many years of community sharing. About 150 people came to share stories, look at the photo wall, write in a memory book, hug, laugh, wipe away tears, and say farewell to an era. Three young people who had spent time with us as children were part of the celebration. One drove up with her daughter from Los Angeles, one drove down from college in Davis, and one flew in from Brussels, Belgium. All of them said they wouldn't think of missing the event, Caballeros had been such an important part of their early lives, showing them an al-

ternative way to live.

Not everyone has the temperament to share a house with other non-related adults, with all the comings and goings and the juggling of personalities and emotions involved. But for those who choose this lifestyle there is great wealth to be found in the realms of personal growth, shared resources, spontaneous celebration, and financial freedom even in economic downturns. Now, that's MY kind of "social security!" ❋

Carol Pimentel was Mistress of Caballeros House in San Luis Obispo, California for over 20 years. She now resides with a housemate in Asheville, North Carolina, where she has a relaxed private practice as a counselor and organizing consultant. She is also Facilitator of Community Life at the Jubilee! Community. Wherever she finds herself, building community is Carol's form of activism and her art in the world. She loves to share her experience and offers consulting, problem solving, and coaching to others living in or contemplating shared housing. Carol may be contacted at carolpim14@gmail.com.

Householding: Communal Living on a Small Scale

By Elizabeth Barrette

Householding involves the practice of intentional community in a single house with a group of people not all related to each other. Similar terms include "sharehousing," "shared house," "sharehouse," and "group house." Householding offers most of the same advantages of companionship and economy as other forms of intentional community, but on a smaller scale that some people find more accessible. For many people, a shared house is their first experience with communal living—and in times of economic hardship, the frugality may cause people to try it who might not otherwise consider it.

Shared Houses

Householding is related to other types of intentional community. It is most closely connected to urban housing cooperatives, student co-ops, and cohousing. These models tend to feature concise living arrangements, often under a single roof.

A key feature of householding is the house itself. Shared houses typically evolve from large buildings such as farmhouses or Victorian mansions. They have multiple bathrooms and bedrooms, and generous common rooms and kitchens. It's possible, though more challenging, to share a smaller building. The number of bathrooms may prove more of a limiting factor than bedrooms in household population. Our house, Fieldhaven, is a large farmhouse with three current residents; it also hosts many events for our local like-minded community. Ravan Asteris, who also contributed input to this article, lives in a household of four adults over 40 (plus the landlord downstairs), five cats, and one dog in an 1890s Victorian house.

Shared houses may be short-term or long-term establishments. Those started by college students rarely last more than a year or few. During my college days I was a frequent guest, sometimes overnight, at one called Illinois Street House. Shared houses started by more settled adults can last for decades. Some even become famous in certain subcultures. For a while, I had friends at Lytheria in Milwaukee, Wisconsin: a modest mansion with individual bedrooms and large common rooms, and a waiting list for would-be residents. The Bhigg House in Winnipeg, Canada houses an assortment of musicians and other creative people; this household has collectively been invited to science fiction conventions as Guest of Honor.[1]

Forming a Household

A household forms when several people decide to live together. This can come about in various ways. All benefit from careful planning and communication beforehand. Economic hardships, however, may force unplanned moves or leave friends in need of emergency housing. Don't overlook these opportunities—it may be awkward, but helping each other through hard times is what community is all about.

The first approach to householding involves inviting people to move in with you.[2] This works well for a single person or couple with a large house, or at least a spare room; if your budget is tight, renters can help. It also benefits seniors, who often own a house but wish for more company. Pass the word among friends and family that you seek housemates. Check newspapers and bulletin boards in your area to find people who need living space. One trick for attracting housemates is to undercut the going rate for housing; another is to let people pay rent with barter instead of cash, especially if you aren't desperately broke. Ideally, seek people whose needs and interests mesh well with yours.

Stay alert for housing emergencies, a common dilemma in times of foreclosure and layoffs. Among the best ways to create a strong household is to provide living space for a friend who needs it on short notice. Start by offering temporary lodging, such as two to four weeks; use that time to test your compatibility. If you make a good fit, formalize a longer-term arrangement. If it doesn't work out, at least the emergency is taken care of and your friend has time to search for another place.

Economic hardships may force unplanned moves. Don't overlook these opportunities—helping each other through hard times is what community is all about.

The second approach to householding involves moving into someone else's place. This is easiest for a single person with minimal baggage, but may work for more people or possessions. First, use social networking (in person and/or online) to find opportunities. Perhaps some of your friends have a spare room they would like to rent out. Maybe someone has moved out early from a shared house and you could take over their lease.

If you can't find space with anyone you know, broaden your search. Local newspapers and bulletin boards may mention communal living opportunities. Check nearby colleges, because students frequently band together for housing and sometimes leave early. Finally, browse intentional community directories for shared houses or co-ops open to new members.[3]

The third approach to householding involves gathering a group of people who then rent or buy a place together. College students often do this, as one year's friends become next year's housemates. Experienced householders do it too. This way you can choose a building that meets your needs; you know how many bedrooms and bathrooms you need, and what other facilities or parameters are important. You also enter the household as equals; nobody has to move into somebody else's space or let someone into theirs.

On the downside, it can prove difficult to find a place that everyone likes. You may have to prioritize needs over desires, and that requires careful negotiation and honesty. Some towns have laws against unrelated people living together; even where it's legal, some landlords disapprove. These complications come up less often in college towns where students commonly rent houses together, or in cities or neighborhoods with old-fashioned "walkable" construction where duplex or triplex houses are common and amenities nearby.

Money Matters

In order to succeed, shared living requires a careful discussion of money, preferably at the beginning. Members must be absolutely clear about who contributes what, and when, and how. Ideally, one or more "anchor" members should have reliable income and credit, allowing the household the option of including others with different contributions.

Many groups choose to establish a household account, filled by rent or other arrangements, for paying common expenses such as utility bills and grocery shopping. This makes the bookkeeping easier; the household account can be managed by the person with the most financial or mathematical skill, and available for anyone to review upon request. Ravan Asteris adds, "In general, it is a good idea to start out with everyone making deposits, and then paying bills and buying common supplies out of the central account. This helps figure out what your real household expenses are. It's also good to overestimate the amount needed. Anything that isn't used in one month can be shunted to the savings, for months when the utilities spike or there are unexpected expenses (what do you mean, the neighbor kids broke a window?)." [4]

> *Remember that under a single roof, you can't just walk away from conflicts—they come back to bite you later.*

Some expenses tend to increase substantially as more people join a household. These include water, electricity, and phone bills. Your budget needs to account for this. The house phone may not increase much if everyone has their own cell phone, though.

Some expenses tend to stay the same, or increase only a little, as the household grows. These include heating/cooling, garbage, internet connection, and cable/satellite TV. Unless you choose to add more services, or add a lot of people, standard family packages usually cover these.

You can find many ways to save money by living together.[5] It is more economical to eat together than for everyone to buy their own food; budget more for communal groceries and take advantage of bulk pricing. Gather for activities, and you only have to light one or two rooms, not the whole house. Recycling, composting, and vermiculture reduce the need for garbage service. Share newspaper, magazine, and other subscriptions. Walking and biking save wear on the household car(s). Finally, brainstorm money-saving ideas with your housemates.

Talking Points

Like other types of intentional community, a shared house benefits from fluent communication skills. Talk with your potential housemates before moving in together and discuss important points. It helps to have at least one person with facilitation and/or mediation experience.[6] Some households set formal meetings; others communicate more casually. Figure out what works for your group.

Practice verbal self-defense and avoid hostile language.[7] If you're new to householding, your job includes learning from more experienced members. If you've shared living space before, your job includes teaching communal skills to newcomers. Remember that under a single roof, you can't just walk away from conflicts—they come back to bite you later. Therefore, don't let disputes simmer until they boil over. Deal with them at once, gently if possible and firmly if necessary.

Explore the parameters for potential housemates. Do you want a like-minded group or a diverse group? Does it include employed, unemployed, self-employed, or part-time workers? Is the household open to children, college students, middle-aged adults, and/or seniors? Can you have pets and livestock, owned individually or collectively? What are people's dietary and other needs? What is the policy regarding tobacco, alcohol, and other substances? There are many ways to assemble a community, so read about some previous examples.[8]

Agree on a decision-making process for the household. Most groups prefer participatory options such as democratic, egalitarian, or consensus methods. If one person owns the house, however, that can lead to a more autocratic situation, which may or may not work for you.

Define what constitutes personal vs. public space. Which rooms are common rooms? What equipment is shared and what is private? What are the rules for using common space and equipment? How do housemates give each other necessary privacy? What balance between companionship and privacy do people want?

Discuss the distribution of chores and other responsibilities. Who does the cooking, cleaning, repairs, and other upkeep? Who has special skills or limitations? Express thanks for tasks completed; everyone enjoys being appreciated. Also compare "mess quotient," one of the commonest reasons for domestic friction that people rarely consider. How messy or tidy should public spaces be? What about individual bedrooms or other private places? Generally, divide chores based on ability and interest, so that nobody has to do things that they hate, that they do poorly, or that aggravate their health issues. Two types of task should be shared by all: those that everyone dislikes, and those that everyone enjoys.

Compare people's wake/sleep schedules and work/home schedules. Discuss your tastes in music, conversation, and other aspects of noise level. Do you want to establish specific quiet times or revel times? Could you use the physical layout of the house to separate noisy activities from peaceful ones? Here at Fieldhaven, we've found that having people on different sleep schedules poses no serious problems—as long as the day sleeper is upstairs, not downstairs near the door that makes a racket every time it opens or closes.

Explore your thoughts regarding guests. Can housemates bring home anyone they want, at any time? Do guests need to be known to other housemates? Are visits to be planned or spontaneous? May guests spend the night in a housemate's room, or in common space such as a couch? Households that frequently host overnight guests may want to invest in a futon or hide-a-bed sofa. Fieldhaven has two, a full-size couch and a loveseat, because we have several out-of-state friends who need crash space when visiting.

Finally, consider the issue of trust. Ravan Asteris explains, "If A hands B $20 to go to the store and get XXX, will they actually get it or return the money? If C falls off a ladder, will D call 911, and not just leave the house? You can be friends with people, but not trust them enough to live with them. Everyone has their faults and foibles, but if those faults are in the trustworthiness area, and are outside the bounds of what can be coped with by the rest of the household, the household will break down very quickly and/or expel the person that they can't trust. This doesn't mean that they have to be always honest, always perfect accountants, always 'clean,' or whatever, but they have to keep the trust of the household." [9]

Homemaking

Although economic and other practical reasons may cause people to share a dwelling, it takes more to create a thriving and cohesive household. For that you need homemaking skills, the knowledge and practices that merge individuals into a group. Pay attention to the group dynamics, nurture the collective identity, and generally encourage housemates to cooperate on projects. Create customs and traditions that define your household as a social unit.

Food provides comfort as well as nourishment. If possible, prepare meals collectively and eat together. [10] Team up for canning or freezing fruits and vegetables for later use. Take advantage of crock pots and other methods that fill the house with delicious smells for hours before a meal. Share recipes by creating a cookbook of household favorites. Exchange the news from each other's successes and challenges of the day over supper.

Spend leisure time together. Find out who enjoys the same crafts or hobbies, and who would like to learn new ones from someone else. Encourage "lapwork" activities such as sewing, knitting, or woodcarving that people can do while conversing. Share board, card, roleplaying, or physical games once or twice a month. [11] Movie nights are popular. Also consider music nights if your housemates sing or play instruments.

Finally, name your household. While not obligatory, a name helps make it real and memorable. It also gives you an easy way to talk about your shared house and your collective housemates. You might choose a name inspired by the house or yard, location, favorite literature, mythology, or other characteristics. It should sound interesting and welcoming. Above all, it should capture the spirit of the place and the people who call it home.

This is your dream. Give it roots—and then give it wings. ✳

Elizabeth Barrette writes nonfiction, fiction, and poetry in the fields of alternative spirituality, speculative fiction, and gender studies. She supports the growth of community in diverse forms and is active in local organizations. Her favorite activities include gardening for wildlife and public speaking at Pagan events and science fiction conventions. Visit her blog at gaiatribe.geekuniversalis.com.

1. "Minicon 30 Fan Guests of Honor: BHIGG HOUSE" by Steve Glennon, reference taken 3/25/09.
www.mnstf.org/minicon/minicon30/bhigg-house.html
2. "How to Find a Housemate or Roommate" by Pondripples, eHow, reference taken 3/26/09.
www.ehow.com/how_4730509_housemate-roomate.html
3. *Communities Directory, 2007: A Comprehensive Guide to Intentional Communities and Cooperative Living* by Fellowship for Intentional Community. Fellowship for Intentional Community, 2007.
4. "Money Talks" by Ravan Asteris, LiveJournal Community Householding, 2/26/09.
community.livejournal.com/householding/1328.html
5. "Household Budget Tips" by Always Frugal, 2004-2009.
www.alwaysfrugal.com/
6. "Tree Bressen's Group Facilitation Site" by Tree Bressen, 2008-2009.
treegroup.info/
7. *The Gentle Art of Verbal Self-Defense* (Revised Edition) by Suzette Haden Elgin. Fall River Press, 2009.
8. *Shared Visions, Shared Lives: Communal Living Around the Globe* by Bill Metcalf. Findhorn Press, 1996.
9. "Essentials: Trust" by Ravan Asteris, LiveJournal Community Householding, 2/22/09.
community.livejournal.com/householding/772.html
10. *Cooking Time Is Family Time: Cooking Together, Eating Together, and Spending Time Together* by Lynn Fredericks. William Morrow & Co., 1999.
11. "Team Builders, Ice Breakers, Songs, Name Games and Other Fun Games" by Resident Assistant, 1998-2008.
http://www.residentassistant.com/games/

> *Although economic and other practical reasons may cause people to share a dwelling, it takes more to create a thriving and cohesive household.*

GREEN AND RESILIENT NEIGHBORHOODS:
Portland, Oregon and Beyond

By Jan Spencer

Early going for greening the neighborhood: Jan Spencer's permaculture back yard.

In late September, I had the much anticipated opportunity to visit several ecovillages in Portland, Oregon. Always on the short lists of greenest cities in the country, Portland is located where the Willamette River meets the Columbia. Ten thousand years ago, this location was periodically submerged under 400 feet of water, thanks to the glacial Missoula Floods.

These days, people are flooding into Portland and I was on my way to stay the night at Columbia Ecovillage and next day, visit Cully Grove Garden Community and Kailash Ecovillage. I was to discover ecovillages come in all sorts of flavors.

Columbia Ecovillage: Planting the Seeds

A friend connected me with a fellow at Columbia. Denny and his wife Anne had lived at Columbia Ecovillage (CEV) from the beginning, about eight years. As it turned out, Denny was a highly informative and enjoyable host. Our interests were the same—how to green our homes, but also, reach further into the neighborhood and community. We had a great time.

Arriving at CEV, and veering right past a sign advising "Watch for Children," I entered a mostly shaded parking lot. It was surrounded on all sides by 1970s-era two-story apartment buildings that contain 37 condominiums. There is ample and thoughtful landscaping, much of it edible, a number of large trees, a covered and secure bike shed with dozens of bikes and trailers inside. I saw an extensive recycling area, and chipped wood paths that connected the parking area with attractive two-story buildings where residents live.

This all looked well cared for. The first residents I talked with in the parking lot were friendly and pointed me to where Denny lived. Stepping past a kid's trike on the chip path under a chestnut tree and up the stairway, I came to Denny and Anne's comfortably arranged three-bedroom apartment. Within minutes, I had made friends with Denny, Anne, and their two resident cats; we were soon back out the door to see Columbia Ecovillage.

Columbia occupies almost four acres in an older neighborhood. It has a condominium ownership model. The founders bought an old farm house behind the apartment complex in 2004 and were later able to buy the apartment complex with the intention of creating a cohousing community. They took on the liability of a sizable upfront investment. Once the word was out about the new project, it did not take long to attract interested persons to buy in.

Eight years later, Columbia looks to be thriving. Denny showed me around. The place has many attributes common to cohousing such as shared laundry, arts and crafts space, kid space, and common house. We ran into several other members out near the entrance. A comment was, "It takes 15 minutes to walk across the parking lot." Not because it's such a big parking lot; rather, you always run into people you need to talk with.

The outback open space was maybe half the land area of CEV, which included extensive bamboo plantings and huge black walnut trees. The veggie gardens were personal plots and the cooperative fig grove featured seven different kinds of figs. The chickens looked happy. A cluster of multi-thousand-gallon rainwater storage tanks clearly showed the group was serious about water storage.

A number of well maintained older outbuildings date back to the farm days. One they call the speak-easy, where members and friends gather to play music, make noise, and have fun. The most distant ecovillage boundary provided views of neighboring properties. I saw gardens and creative-looking outbuildings on the large lots where others seemed to have similar ideas to Columbia. Denny affirmed that many of the neighbors were on good terms with CEV.

Residents of Columbia confer in the parking lot.

Cooperative living can mean shared tools, such as these at Columbia.

Entrance to Columbia Ecovillage welcomes with free library, landscaping, and bench.

Participation is a core value at Columbia. There are frequent shared meals, informal get-togethers, work parties, and committees. Members are required to participate at least nine hours a month in community projects, while some people take on many extra tasks as their time and interests allow. There are pod work groups for chickens, rainwater system, book-keeping, yoga, public relations, maintenance, special events, hosting visitors, managing the Common Hall, and more.

Columbia is governed as a self-managed condominium. Work and decision making take place in four self-organizing domains: administration, facilities/maintenance, land use, and social life.

Overall, Columbia looked great. Most of the members I met were Baby Boomers. Their collective values were all good; protect nature, conserve resources, respect each other, egalitarian management, and balance group needs with self.

Denny was a wonderful host to show and tell about the ecovillage. He also knew a great deal about what was happening in the nearby neighborhood. That was next on the agenda.

We passed by front yard gardens here and there on the leafy streets of Cully Neighborhood. We visited a half acre property that included an eco-minded preschool, a Gypsy-looking tiny house, and quarter acre flower farm. Denny kept up a running commentary of anecdotal greening-the-neighborhood stories the whole time.

I was already impressed with everything when we came upon a cluster of five homes with both practical and amusing features. There were front yard gardens, a co-op house that hosted community happenings, a Bathtub Museum, vernacular public art, and a streetside reclamation spot for neighbors to repatriate small items

stolen by a four-footed cat burglar.

I asked Denny if Columbia Ecovillage may have had a hand in greening the neighborhood. Modest as he was, he told me the neighborhood already had a history of eco-friendly culture that predates Columbia, but he also said Columbia has certainly had some positive influence and adds significantly to that culture.

Our 42nd Avenue: Greening the Neighborhood

Like my suburban property in Eugene, an ecovillage such as Columbia is great but, again, the scale needs to go far beyond several dozen exceptional households in a neighborhood with thousands that are not so forward-thinking.

Denny told me about a small nonprofit, Our 42nd Avenue, helping to green the neighborhood. I was about to see a small but very significant tool, and projects it is facilitating, with enormous potential for transforming economy and culture.

42nd Avenue in Cully Neighborhood, just south of Killingsworth, is ground zero for small-scale eco-minded economic renewal. It's a several-block commercial area, four or five blocks from CEV, with several empty or underused commercial buildings, although the zone already can boast of several vibrant stores and cafes.

In their own words, "Our 42nd Avenue is economic development by the community, for the community, a collection of residents, business owners, local employees, commercial property owners, community institutions and others."

From their website, their vision: "42nd Avenue will be a welcoming, safe, walkable and eco-friendly commercial district that nurtures a diverse population with affordable goods and services. The district will be distinct for its vibrancy, with attractive storefronts, an interesting streetscape, and destinations where people can gather and meet their everyday needs. The environment will foster stronger connections amongst community members and stimulate local economic development and employment opportunities."

Economics is the dominant force that has shaped empires, started wars, fabricated culture, determined haves and have-nots all through history; from the Phoenicians, to Marxism, to the Chicago School, right up to the present. Just about all the escalating social, political, environmental misadventures of our time are a product of global market capitalism. From my perspective, creating green, uplifted, and healthy alternatives to market capitalism is the most urgent task of our time. What would a society look like where the economic system's task was to serve the public good rather than monetize, exploit, and degrade it? Our 42nd Avenue is the choreographer of a set of modest actions—a model that could be upsized as much as people involved want to take it.

Denny took me to the last farmers' market of the season in the midst of the 42nd Avenue redevelopment zone. There were farmers and craftspeople from the nearby neighborhood. A person from Our 42nd Avenue was tabling to explain the group's work. I saw lots of mixing and mingling, buying and selling. The market was eco-friendly, festive, a coming together at the neighborhood scale.

I met several of the farmers, had a beer, and chatted with a lot of people.

Afterwards, Denny showed me some of the small farms in the nearby neighborhood and they were beautiful. People were building businesses with specialty crops and value-added food-related activities. One property was owned by supportive neighbors, another made available by a community-minded church.

One fellow at the market had a startup across the street, incubated by Our 42nd Avenue. His budding new business, still very small, is an urban farm and garden store, to sell products and provide services to both home gardeners and larger urban farms. Perfect!

Up the street was a sizable empty commercial space. Our 42nd Avenue was in discussions with the property owners, local businesses, and interested community members to make creative new use of that space that would be true to the ideals of Our 42nd Avenue and the neighborhood.

This brief exposure to a small urban area caused me to imagine. I had seen small but important elements of a more green and local economy. Certainly this part of the neighborhood is not going off the mainstream grid, but if there is to be a greening of the neighborhood culture and economy that moves in a mindful direction, this could be what it might look like in the early going. Everything that I saw can grow, inspire nearby commercial zones to do likewise, form clusters, and expand much more widely into the community.

My Communal Backstory: Texas, Arkansas, Israel, and more

My own awareness of ecovillages and intentional communities started 45 years ago in north central Texas, of all places. Whitehawk was an intentional community north of Denton, Texas, where I went to college. Several friends lived there, out north of town past the shuttered and bunkered Nike missile base.

In the mid '70s, it was off the grid; the 12 or 15 homes were all earth-sheltered ferrocement burrowed into the south-facing slopes of the prairie landscape. Most had exposed glass walls facing the south. Except for the windmills, the place looked a bit like a moon base.

About the same time in the late '70s, I became involved with a back-to-the-land community in the Arkansas Ozarks named Sassafras. We were off the grid and three miles from a paved road. Steep Cave Mountain Road up to our place blew out more than one radiator.

Our neighbor's kids would nail dead birds on the gate we had to open to cross his property to access ours. We grew a considerable amount of our own food in this gorgeous and rugged Ozark valley that ranged in elevation from 1200 feet above sea level down at Beech Creek to over 2300 feet at the cliff above, only a quarter mile away. You could drink the water in the creek. You could get lost in the caves on the property.

A favorite pastime was working things out with each other. We were all OK. We had community projects, frequent sweat lodges, workdays, and an outdoor kitchen, complete with resident rattlesnake under the woodbox. The place was on the commune circuit with many visitors in the summer. The community's unique coming-to-an-end is a favorite counterculture story in the northwest Arkansas Ozarks.

In the mid '80s, I spent a month as a volunteer on a nonreligious kibbutz in Israel. My final few miles of travel arriving to the kibbutz was in an armored personnel carrier. The place was near Nazareth and was home to about 500 people.

On a rocky hilltop, Kfar Hahoresh was a planned community with a large central recreation space surrounded by nice landscaping, residential and service buildings, all very modern. Kids grew up together, not with their parents. Most of the older ones couldn't wait to leave. There was a primary school and basic health care on site.

Almost everyone worked at the kibbutz. An important community business was a large automated kosher bread factory. When I had a choice of jobs, I always went to the avocado orchards down in the valley.

A majority of the residents were from eastern Europe, emigrating in the mid 1930s when Fascism was on the rise. There were few if any private cars. I can appreciate the site design, social and economic aspects far more now than when I was there, 35 years ago.

I spent two early springtime weeks on a foggy, chilly, and rocky hilltop in south Italy with a group of radical pacifist Catholics. They were into extreme voluntary simplicity. It was cold, no electricity, no machines. Core to their beliefs was that any involvement with the mainstream economy was complicity in damage that economy did to people and planet.

The common denominator of all these places was some kind of disaffection for the mainstream culture and economy and what it did to people and the environment. These visits and the passage of time give me more of an appreciation for the ideals of living more green, modestly, and cooperatively.

Back to the Present: Cully Grove Garden Community

After leaving Columbia Ecovillage, I shifted only a quarter mile, still in Cully Neighborhood, to another ecovillage called Cully Grove. While Columbia and Kailash, which we will have a look at shortly, made use of existing built infrastructure, Cully Grove is an infill project on an undeveloped two acres.

Instead of a conventional subdivision of 16 detached homes, the plan for Cully Grove was to build relatively modest eco-friendly homes, to preserve open space with heritage trees, and design for social interaction and cooperation among the residents. The results are beautiful.

There is a shared garden area, shared bike shed, community house, and shared workshop

Cully Grove combines residential density with open space, saving heritage oak trees.

Farmers' market on 42nd Avenue brings the Cully Neighborhood together.

Front yard gardens build community in the neighborhood.

Photos courtesy of Jan Spencer

space. Interestingly, if you don't have a car, you don't pay for parking. The homes are insulated above code, and appliances are more energy-efficient than they have to be.

Which brings us to cost. These are full-size, 1500-square-foot homes and nicely appointed. Cully Grove is a more upscale project than Columbia, and even more so compared to Kailash.

borhood. It was like the Wild West for drug dealing with occasional shootouts in the parking lot. Many of the 32 one-bedroom apartments were not fit to live in. That all changed with the new sheriff and deputy.

Today, Kailash (KEV) strikes me as a grand slam home run of socially and ecologically thoughtful urban renewal. Perhaps the most impressive features of Kailash are how the down-and-out infra-structure has been repaired and repurposed; also the long list of social and outdoor amenities for the 60 or so residents; and finally, how living at KEV is accessible to people of modest means.

A lot has been accomplished since 2007. Kailash is surrounded on three sides by newer two-story apartments. To the east, one finds brick, '40s-era suburban-bungalow-type houses on sloping streets with many trees. It's a nice-looking neighborhood.

Amidst many social and outdoor amenities, living at Kailash is still accessible to people of modest means.

KEV is a great example of the benefits of open space as a function of residential density. In land use planning, greater residential density can also translate into more open space. About half of Kailash is residential and parking; the other half is garden, orchard, and open space.

Cully Grove is a beautiful place and quite possibly, some homeowners could afford more than this. It makes me wonder: how do people with both money and concerns about eco and social footprints reconcile the two?

Kailash Ecovillage: A Grand Slam

I left Cully Grove and drove five miles south to Kailash Ecovillage with a high level of anticipation. I already knew a good deal about Kailash thanks to its very informative website and was not disappointed.

Ole and Maitri Ersson bought a run-down apartment complex in SE Portland in 2007 with a loan from a progressive local bank. At the time, the complex was notorious in the neigh-

Early on, 16 parking places and several smaller concrete areas were depaved and turned into garden, a great example of reclaiming automobile space in favor of productive use. In 2010, the acre next door, covered with blackberry jungle, was purchased to complete the current two-acre size of KEV.

The outdoor part of Kailash includes 46 individual garden plots and shared garden projects. There are 53 fruit trees, a small vineyard, blueberries, cane fruit, and a large bamboo patch that screens the perimeter, making for a nice green enclosure. There is also a cooperative tool shed and small intimate contemplative area with a wet weather brook, hammock, and sitting area. Also outside is a large compost area and shared covered bike area. There is a greenhouse and space for small individual and creative outdoor projects. The KEV website has extensive documentation of all these features.

The apartment building has seen upgrades since its Wild West days. In addition to the one-bedroom apartments are many amenities such as an 1100-square-foot community room, community kitchen for events, games collection, big screen TV with surround sound, internet station, and more. Kailash has hosted meetings from outside the ecovillage along with in-house parties, discussions, and gatherings.

Kailash Ecovillage transforms two acres with depaving, gardens, and many creative projects.

Place making in Cully Neighborhood adds flavor, personality, and identity.

There is also a laundry room and the mail room has member bios at each mail box so people can become better acquainted. This may sound like an infomercial but it serves to show the detail of planning for making life at Kailash a positive experience for all involved.

Participation is essential for keeping all this going. There are teams to take care of the bike area, library, compost and recycling, fruit trees, garden, and indoor amenities. A car share project is in the works. Members are asked to commit a minimum amount of time to the community.

KEV also reaches out to the wider neighborhood. There are several garden plots used by people in the neighborhood. Wood chips delivered are made available to anyone in the neighborhood. There is a community bulletin board down by the street. Kailash actively networks with other ecovillage and cooperative living groups in Portland.

Kailash has a ham radio for disaster use while several members are active in the neighborhood association and city emergency response program. The scale of Kailash gives it the capacity to reach out like this in so many different ways.

Members' rent is similar to the surrounding neighborhood. That means people of average means can afford this very unusual ecovillage lifestyle. I can see residents here as students in a sort of school for ecological and cooperative lifestyles where they can experience alternatives to mainstream economy and culture. The "graduates" are likely to apply their "degrees" at KEV to positive effect in the wider world.

A grand slam. That's a good way to describe Kailash Ecovillage. I honestly could not imagine a more complete repurposing of a two-acre patch of urban infrastructure and space. You can find much more detail and photos at the Kailash website, www.kailashecovillage.org.

Re-Greening Humanity: Multiple Centers of Initiative

The three ecovillages I visited all have a keen interest in reducing their members' ecological footprints while building social cohesion. They all make use of existing urban land use opportunities. Each one started with an ambitious idea that resonated enough that others wanted to be involved.

There has never been a time in human history where reducing our eco footprints and building social cohesion have been more important. These qualities are vital requisites of perhaps modern humanity's greatest adventure, fitting into the natural world.

One can find allies, assets, and opportunities for this historic adventure just about anywhere. All over the country, a growing number of people are not only concluding the current mainstream economy and culture are not appropriate, but they are taking initiative to pioneer alternatives.

Initiative comes in many forms, such as changes to one's own home and property as in Cully Neighborhood. One property making mindful changes often leads to a nearby neighbor or two or three doing something similar, like the five front yard garden cluster near the Bathtub Art Museum.

> These three ecovillages all have a keen interest in reducing their members' ecological footprints while building social cohesion.

Cully's emerging clusters, ecovillages, neighborhood farms, and Our 42nd Avenue support each other and all help move these ideas further into the neighborhood and beyond. And they have company.

Progress is a single front yard garden in Beaumont, Texas, the only one locals have ever seen, that starts to cause a buzz in the neighborhood. Elsewhere, someone might buy the property next door, taking the fences down, and that sets off a chain reaction and a few years later, all the back yard fences are gone and a shared identity emerges between a dozen houses. That's what happened at N Street Coop in Davis, California.

A group of neighbors might start to coalesce because of a shared geographic characteristic like Enright Ridge in Cincinnati. East Blair in Eugene, Oregon is a legal nonprofit that owns 11 residential properties, and they are managed in a mindful way that benefits the members, the environment, and the neighborhood.

> # A growing number of properties in the neighborhood are trading grass for garden, creating edible landscapes, catching rainwater, depaving, building with natural materials, and more.

These and other examples of organic transition towards economic and cultural transformation are the previews of a more green and peaceful future.

River Road Neighborhood: Permaculture and Paradigm Shift

River Road Neighborhood, three miles northwest of downtown Eugene, Oregon has a small but significant and growing identity as a place with an appreciable number of people interested in permaculture and paradigm shift. There have been dozens of permaculture site tours over the past 10 years to show and tell the growing number of properties in the neighborhood that are trading grass for garden, creating edible landscapes, catching rainwater, depaving, building with natural materials, making use of passive solar design, and constructing small accessory dwellings.

River Road hosted the 2015 Northwest Permaculture Convergence at the neighborhood recreation center, in the middle of this suburban neighborhood. Many of the event coordinator positions were taken by residents in the neighborhood. The neighborhood association played a big part in putting on the convergence. Part of the event was free and open to the community. Over 700 people from the neighborhood, Eugene, and beyond attended the event.

We have had other permaculture events, classes, and work parties. A 65-tree filbert grove on public property along the Willamette River has been restored in cooperation with the city. Several like-minded property owners have taken down back yard fences. A small but growing number of people are buying properties in the neighborhood because they know there is a small but growing momentum for creating a more green and resilient neighborhood.

A new opportunity has presented itself that can be an important catalyst for greening our neighborhood. The city of Eugene is putting a

substantial amount of staff time and resources into a high profile neighborhood visioning process that is intended to help guide our neighborhood into the future. The entire series of meetings, discussions, and input will take over a year. Public participation is an essential part of the effort, with the city sending out lots of mail to neighborhood residents explaining the importance of the visioning process and urging them to participate.

To insure alternative perspectives in the neighborhood are part of the process, the River Road Green and Resilient Caucus has formed. The Caucus asserts the mainstream economic system and the consumer culture it has created are the cause of a wide range of well documented social and environmental problems such as climate change; social, economic, and political disequity; damage to public health; resource issues; and much more.

Further, the Caucus states that to plan a future for the neighborhood based on the same land use, transportation, and development assumptions and policies that have already caused so much damage to public health and the environment is continuing to live in a highly flawed past, not a vision for a green and resilient future. Three members of the Caucus are also board members of the neighborhood association, while overall, the neighborhood association board is sympathetic.

The first public meeting attracted well over 300 people sitting at round tables in discussion groups of eight to 10 people. The Caucus contributed an impressive display of posters, photos, and explanations along a wall, describing suburban permaculture, front yard gardens, green neighborhoods, and ecological approaches to economy and culture.

Over 50 posters about green and resilient living were given away while dozens of people browsed the display. Many discussion groups included permaculture-minded neighbors who added green and resilient content to the conversations and written comments.

The Caucus is also writing a "Green Paper" that will inform the visioning process with more detail about greening the neighborhood; it will go out to the neighborhood and become part of the public record. We are using this rare opportunity of public process to put green, resilient, and permaculture ideas out to the wider community.

There are tens of thousands of neighborhoods all over the country with green and resilient potential. They all have assets, allies, and opportunities already there to work with. They just need to be called on. Small projects can inspire larger projects which can lead to clusters. Clusters can grow into ecovillages, eco-neighborhoods, and eco-communities. The more, the sooner, the better. ❧

Jan Spencer lives in Eugene, Oregon. He has traveled for over five years out of the country, all over Europe, east, central, and south Africa, New Zealand, Israel, and Central America. Jan has been transforming his quarter-acre suburban property for 17 years. His interests are a fusion of permaculture, urban land use, economics, neighborhoods, and social uplift. Jan has been on the board of his neighborhood association for over 10 years. He has made presentations on the East and West Coasts and in between, written blogs for Mother Earth News, *and is available to present to colleges and conferences both in person and via internet. His website is www.suburbanpermaculture.org; contact him at janrspencer@gmail.com.*

Neighbors discuss green and resilient ideas at big neighborhood visioning event.

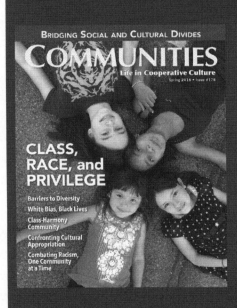
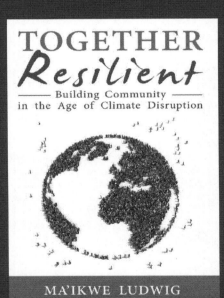
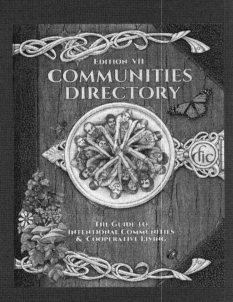

II

SEEKING AND VISITING COMMUNITY:

TIPS AND RESOURCES

Publisher's Note BY SKY BLUE

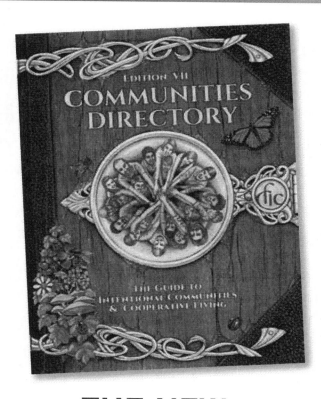

THE NEW
COMMUNITIES DIRECTORY:
A Star Chart for Seekers and Founders

If you've ever participated in forming a community, or talked with people who have, you probably have some idea of what's involved. And if you have some idea of what's involved, you've probably asked yourself, why would anyone in their right mind want to do such a thing? It's like starting a family or having a child. You really have no idea what you're in for, and that's probably a good thing because you might not do it otherwise.

The reasons for starting a community are not dissimilar from those for starting a family or having a child: Desires for intimacy, to be bonded to other humans, to be part of the unfolding story of humanity, to contribute to and have hopes for the future, to feel like your life matters, to be intimately involved and watch in fascination the growth of another being, or, simply, because it's something you just need to do. But it's intensely hard work, and it doesn't always work out the way you thought it would.

The sense of intimacy, satisfaction, and meaning that living in community provides, being part of a village or a tribe, is something that is clearly lacking in most of mainstream society. Most of the blueprints for building community have been discarded. There are pockets around the world where traditional cultures and village life remain intact, but in most places it needs to be recreated, and in many places we're already several generations removed from the experience. Part of the work of the Fellowship for Intentional Community is documenting this recreation, and this issue of COMMUNITIES is focused on this endeavor.

But you don't have to help start a community to be part of this, and indeed there are plenty of reasons not to join the ranks of the pioneers. One in particular is that there are lots of communities already in existence and almost every one of them needs help. It's not a good idea to move to a community expecting it to change to suit you, but it's inevitable that the more you invest yourself in a community, while also accepting the community for the unique being that it is, the more you will come to suit each other.

Work is underway to produce the 7th printed edition of the *Communities Directory*. Preliminary work for this has been focused online. Over the last few months we've been working hard to have all communities in the online Directory update their listings, and we're going to start requiring that groups update or verify their listings at least once per year. We've also been tweaking the new listings questionnaire to try to make sure communities are providing the most useful information possible. We ran a highly successful crowdfunding campaign to finance the new Directory, raising almost $12,000 from over 170 donors, through online and offline channels. It was gratifying and humbling to see importance of this work reflected in this outpouring of support.

The Directory is an important road map to finding those places where the blueprints are being recreated. It serves not only those looking to join a community, but also those potential pioneers who can learn from the trailblazers before them. The Directory becomes a star chart, in which communities are the points of light guiding us to new hope. It also helps define the movement and lets each community know that it's not working in isolation.

The Directory is the keystone in the support we offer for the development and promotion of intentional communities. The bridge to cooperative living also includes COMMUNITIES magazine, as well as our *Best of* COMMUNITIES series, which pulls together the most helpful articles on the most important topics in building community. The Community Bookstore isn't just any online store; it includes only titles related to intentional community and cooperative culture. Ic.org's classifieds are another way we help people find community, and events we host or cosponsor are also essential aspects of the work we do to make sure you have the resources you need to get where you want to go.

This is our mission, to offer lifelines to those out there immersed in the challenges of recreating society. We couldn't do it without your support. ✒

Sky Blue (sky@ic.org) is Executive Director of the Fellowship for Intentional Community.

In 2003, "La Cité Écologique" was founded, in Colebrook New Hampshire, on 315 acres of beautiful land surrounded by forest and mountains. Our ecovillage gives priority to education, optimal living to its members, a cooperative culture with resilience in its development and social entrepreneurship. So far, we have built one single family building, two large community residences, where people live in a kind of condo arrangement, and one community building (all powered by solar). We are expanding new building projects, to give a home to growing families and/or new members. We've created businesses, non-profits, a nonprofit school, and an organic farm, that helps better serve ours, and the local community. Visitors are welcome to our annual Open House in June, and Harvest Celebration in September. Guided tours, and internship programs are also available from May through October.

Contact: Leonie Brien (603) 331-1669
www.citeecologiquenh.org

La Cité Écologique
of New Hampshire
An Ecovillage since 2003

Notes from the Editor BY CHRIS ROTH

The Quest for Community

My search for an intentional community began as a thought exercise during high school. I pored over pages of COMMUNITIES in my school library, including some of its "Directory" issues, and eventually ordered a booklet from the Federation of Egalitarian Communities, whose member groups seemed most aligned with my values. I then set all that aside to follow the beaten path to traditional undergraduate education, as most of my classmates were doing, but made a sharp turn after two years to enroll in a traveling environmental education community to finish out college. (My interest in intentional community had been restimulated by a couple visits to a monastery during early college breaks, followed a few years later by my first Directory-sourced visit, to a very idealistic, albeit sparsely populated indigenous-inspired intentional community in northern Wisconsin.)

After graduation, I resolved to enroll in the school of real life rather than further formal education, and relocated to a Native American reservation, where I was reminded daily of the stark contrast between native ways and the "settler" ways that had pushed those native ways onto isolated reservations, and in some cases (but fortunately not in this one) extinguished them entirely. Here in northern Arizona, much of the traditional culture and set of worldviews was still intact, and even more than that, the sense of community (innate and inherent, not "intentional") was palpable and even assumed. It was with regret that I recognized after a year and a half that I couldn't fully remake myself as a native member of this tribe, and that my own path was calling me elsewhere.

Within a year of rejoining "white" society—a year in which I never felt at ease with the culture shock of returning to more mainstream America—I found myself at my first long-term intentional community, a rural educational center holding more in common with my former Native American home than with the suburban East Coast town in which I'd grown up. I'd gone there for the education (in organic gardening), but quickly discovered that the community aspect had just as much, or more, to teach me—both when it worked well, and when it was dramatically dysfunctional.

After a couple of years, with another "Directory" issue of COMMUNITIES in hand, I set out to find the "perfect" intentional community. (I still thought in terms of perfection and the "ideal community," because I hadn't yet recognized that finding or creating community is largely about the journey, rather than simply the destination, and that community itself is a process, not a static state or utopian end goal.)

The Directory led me once again to member groups of the Federation of Egalitarian Communities, in which I ended up spending most of the next two years, interspersed with other community visits. Ties of affinity to people, culture, and land then drew me back to the Pacific Northwest—but the dysfunction in my former Oregon community hadn't disappeared. After some particularly disillusioning experiences (instead of working together, my "community" eventually headed to court with suits and countersuits), I decided that intentional community was too difficult and intense for me. For a while, I found I was more comfortable working on small organic family farms, where the focus was clearly on one farmer's goals rather than on everyone's sometimes-clashing needs, desires, and agendas. But after a few years of helping out on others' farms, I longed for more robust and empowered community in which we'd all be co-creators.

At one point I even drew up a description of my ideal community, having decided that I needed to start it myself. My "forming community" listing almost appeared in a print version of the *Communities Directory*—but I withdrew it before press date, as I recognized the many advantages of becoming part of an already-initiated project, if at all possible, rather than starting a new one. My personality seemed better suited to joining with others to help a struggling group survive and thrive, rather than creating a struggling group from scratch. I also found that I was more happy and fulfilled in situations where there were obvious challenges that I could help address—where I knew I was making a difference—rather than where all systems were already established and a comfortable status quo prevailed.

I joined my current intentional community almost two decades ago, and over the ensuing years it's undergone many changes, as have I—both internally and in my roles in the community. I even spent a year away, exploring intentional community in a different part of the country, when I felt both I and my home community had fallen into ruts (fortunately, we both extracted ourselves). My sense of community now extends far beyond the bounds of my home community: my ties to others in town and elsewhere (many of them ex-community-mates) are just as strong as any I have to my current community-mates; my far-flung family of birth is also an essential part of my community; and the even larger number of people in the communities movement—especially those who choose to read and/or contribute to this magazine—are also important parts of my extended community.

As someone who benefited early on from COMMUNITIES and then the FIC, I've felt gratified to be able to give back over the years. Whether hand-drawing the maps in the 1990-91 *Communities Directory* when living at Sandhill Farm (with the snow-covered northern Missouri roads impassable at times that winter, this was a way to travel virtually), or contributing articles to the magazine in the 2000s, or editing the magazine for the last eight years, I've felt happy to be doing something to aid others in finding or creating community in their own lives. Sometimes small seeds (like those we in the FIC have the opportunity to plant through this magazine, the Directory, and other offerings) can grow into beautiful gardens, orchards, savannas, and forests. We hope this issue of COMMUNITIES will plant more of those seeds.

A final note: No magazine issue can be a comprehensive resource on our intentionally broad topics. Additional resources that will complement this issue include *Best of* COMMUNITIES Volumes I and II, numerous past articles posted on ic.org, other sources cited by various authors in this issue, and of course the new *Communities Directory.*

Chris Roth (editor@ic.org) edits COMMUNITIES.

A Useful Tool for Founders and Seekers: SPECTRUMS

By Ma'ikwe Ludwig

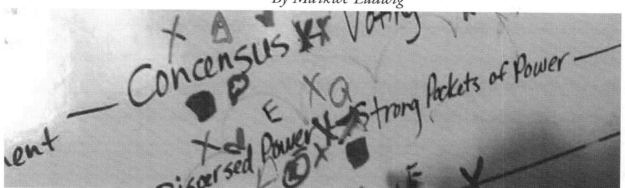

Ma'ikwe Ludwig

I'm a little obsessed with spectrums. The world is pretty much one big grey area as near as I can tell. Anyone who has ever spent any time with me as a facilitator or a facilitation teacher knows that spectrums are one of my go-to tools.

In workshops I teach about starting an Intentional Community as well as finding a community home, I use this particular set of spectrums (see worksheets). These are things that every community lands on somewhere, either deliberately or by default.

Here's how I suggest people use them.

For Founders

It is very important that you get clear about what things are essential to you in your community vision and what things you don't really care about. I recommend going through these spectrums and marking on each one the perfect spot in your mind of how your community will be set up. (I do this with an X or some other simple symbol.) Then I would also mark (perhaps using a highlighter marker or brackets) your range of tolerance. In other words, you might have a preference, but for most of these you also will likely have some flexibility about how close to the ideal it needs to be in order for you to feel excited about all the work of creating a community.

As an example, you might ideally want to be very rural, but could live with being in a small town. So in that case, you'd mark an X all the way over on the far side above rural, and then place a bracket or highlighter mark from the rural side to, say, one-third of the way across the spectrum.

You may find that you have no opinion or preference for some of them. That's great! That means that your vision has some flexibility and will allow other people's preferences to come into play. However, it is very important to be as honest as you can be about your answers. If you really want to live in a community that is income-sharing or has a strong spiritual orientation, it is fine to place an X and then have no brackets at all. This will help people who are considering joining you know exactly what they are joining.

Many founders make the mistake of thinking that they can answer all these questions after they have five or six or 10 people they really like who have decided to join. The pitfall in waiting to get clear about that is that you run the risk of not having enough alignment among that group and wasting a lot of everyone's time.

Get clear about your must-haves, articulate those clearly, and recruit from that place. Then drag this spectrum worksheet out and let folks know that the group is welcome to answer the rest of those questions or just let yourselves default to something. Doing this well will create a much stronger, aligned, and clear core group to build from.

For People Seeking a Community

I recommend following the same procedure as above for seekers: mark on each of these spectrums your ideal and your range of tolerance. Then step back and do a little soul searching. You may have a preference, but how strong is it? Which ones of these are your make or break criteria? The same advice about honesty applies here. Be as real with yourself about these answers as you can be.

Hint: If each of your answers is just an X or has a very narrow range to it, you are likely to be very disappointed when you get out there and start searching. One of the first lessons of community is to be able to articulate your preferences and then widen back into flexibility for the sake of being able to connect and work with others. Filling this worksheet out is a first chance at seeing just how flexible or rigid you currently are. Having a strong preference on four to six of these is probably healthy and will help your search be productive.

Seekers should take this with them when they visit places. I'd recommend sitting down with someone who has been in the community you are visiting for a while (at least three years if the group is established) and asking them for their realistic take on their community and how well it matches your preferences. This can be an invaluable guide for sorting out the communities that might really work well for you.

Once you've narrowed your search in this more logical way, I'd recommend setting this aside and considering communities from a more intuitive or felt place. Regardless of what the spectrums say, which one feels right or the most like home? Is there a community that didn't quite match your answers, but your attention keeps getting drawn back to it? Can you flex and grow into that community? Is there something the spectrums didn't cover that you have found through your process really is more important than these criteria?

By the same token, if a place looks great on paper but feels wrong, trust your gut. Preferences can (and very likely will) change, but a good intuitive hit is almost always worth listening to.

Choosing an intentional community home is really all about being intentional. And generally, that will be a healthy mix of logic and love, criteria and intuition. Let me know if these spectrums help you on your journey! ❧

Ma'ikwe Ludwig lives at Dancing Rabbit Ecovillage, where she serves as the Executive Director of the ecovillage's nonprofit. She teaches workshops on group process, sustainability, and starting intentional communities. Her latest project is the Materialized Empathy project, a model policy development organization dedicated to economic and ecological justice, including helping reduce legal barriers to sustainable community formation. She can be reached at maikwe.ludwig@gmail.com.

Spectrums for Individuals within Groups

The following are common scales that describe basic approaches to life. In a healthy group, there are people spread out throughout these scales. All traits have a valuable aspect to them and all have pitfalls. Ideally, the membership of an organization takes into account these sorts of things when trying to find a good roles for someone to play, e.g., quick decision-making is valuable in a work-party leader, but not so much for budget team members, where you want more measured thinking; good facilitators see meetings as being both for decisions and connection; if everyone has a strong sense of aesthetics, you need great alignment or you're in trouble.
Suggested uses: Perspective. Create an exercise to get to know each other better.
Use to reduce judgment.

Interprets Negatively ←	→ Interprets Positively
Slow to Decide ←	→ Quick to Decide
Slow to Change ←	→ Quick to Change
Fact-Based ←	→ Non-Rational-Based
Meetings Are to Decide ←	→ Meetings Are to Connect
Manifest by Actions ←	→ Manifest by Intention
Follower ←	→ Leader
Planner ←	→ Doer
Holds a Grudge ←	→ Lets Things Go
Works on Stuff Privately ←	→ Enrolls Others in Process
Sticks to First Take ←	→ Changes Mind Easily
Gives Mostly Work ←	→ Gives Mostly Thinking
Strong Aesthetic Sense ←	→ Not Strong on Aesthetics
Prefers Noisy Bustle ←	→ Prefers Solitude
Comfortable in Groups ←	→ Nervous in Groups

Copyright 2007/2013 Sol Space Consulting www.maikwe.net maikwe.ludwig@gmail.com

---

Spectrums for Intentional Communities

ICs come in lots of flavors. Every group falls somewhere on these spectrums, which affect the feel, culture, and experience of being in the group (though be aware that the answers to these can change over time, and changes are not necessarily about how healthy or vibrant the group is). Misalignment in any one of these spectrums makes it a tough fit.

Income Sharing ←		Tithing		→ Independent Finances	
High Resource Sharing ←				→ Low Resource Sharing	
No Cost to Join ←				→ High Cost to Join	
Spiritually ← Same	Spiritually ← Diverse	Supports → Spiritual Practice	Tolerates → Spirituality	Secular →	Intolerant of Spirituality
Rural ←				→ Urban	
Mission Driven ←				→ Member Quality of Life Driven	
Inwardly Focused ←				→ Outwardly Focused	
Family Size ←				→ Village Size	
Low Technology Use ←				→ High Technology Use	
Mainstream Appeal ←				→ Radical Appeal	
Deep Alignment ←	Consensus ←	Voting →	Small Decision Group →	Sole Leader	
Flat Power ←	Dispersed Power →	Strong Pockets of Power →		Very Lopsided	
Strong Group Role ← in Conflict Resolution				→ Group Hands Off with Conflict Resolution	
Rules-based ←				→ Relationally-based	
"Moving Toward" ← Energy				→ "Resisting" Energy	

Copyright 2007/2011 Sol Space Consulting www.maikwe.net 660-883-5506

Community Search
RESOURCES

By McCune Porter

*E*ditor's Note: *The Fellowship for Intentional Community receives many inquiries, especially via our web contact form (www.ic.org/contact-fic), from people interested in intentional community living. Working from our Virginia office (located at Twin Oaks Community), longtime FIC staffer McCune Porter answers most of these inquiries, and when appropriate also forwards them to others within the organization who may be able to help.*

Here's a standard email McCune sends out to community seekers, containing some of the most helpful resources we know about.

• • •

Greetings,

We offer the following tools to help search for intentional communities that meet particular criteria:

1) ONLINE DIRECTORY

Search www.ic.org/directory for communities that meet any requirements you may have. Contact the communities individually on the list you generate to start correspondence with each community on the list. To contact an individual community, use the contact information at the upper right of that community's listing.

Communities by type: Ecovillages, Cohousing, Communes, Co-ops, Christian
www.ic.org/directory/community-types

Communities by geographic list
www.ic.org/directory/intentional-communities-by-country

Directory Advanced Search
www.ic.org/directory/search

Search using maps
www.ic.org/directory/map

The Search Our Site box at the top right of every page on our site might also prove useful if none of the other online Directory search tools seems to help locate what you're seeking.

2) ONLINE BULLETIN BOARD PLUS CLASSIFIED ADS

Post your interests in our classified ads section, which is read by thousands of people. Many free post categories are available as well as paid listings.

www.ic.org/community-classifieds

3) IN PRINT

Our print resources may be helpful, particularly the *Communities Directory*, COMMUNITIES magazine, and the book *Finding Community: How to Join an Ecovillage or Intentional Community.*

Shop here for the *Directory*, COMMUNITIES magazine, and other titles:
www.ic.org/community-bookstore

4) NETWORKING EVENTS

Attend one or more regional or national intentional community events. These are typically the best way to meet people already living in intentional community and/or who have visited one or more intentional communities.

www.ic.org/intentional-community-events

5) VISIT/TOUR LOCAL COMMUNITIES

A visit to or tour of intentional communities near your place of residence can be very useful. (Always pre-arrange such visits—never show up without an appointment to visit or tour.)

6) FORUMS

There are community-related discussion forums on some third party sites, for example:

www.reddit.com/r/intentionalcommunity
intentionalcommunity.tribe.net
www.facebook.com/groups/636532239809454

Sincerely,
McCune
FIC Staff

Additional Editor's Note: McCune also manages our magazine subscription list, assembles FIC's weekly eNews (subscribe via left-hand column at ic.org), and keeps a general eye out for things needing attention. With a reputation for being exceptionally dependable, detail-oriented, and dedicated, he has provided essential "glue" and consistency over many years within an ever-evolving organization. His humility would also prevent him from writing anything like the above, so this paragraph is partly a stealth attempt to give him at least a little recognition. Thanks McCune!

CREATING THE IDEAL INTENTIONAL COMMUNITY
(OR REVITALIZING AN EXISTING ONE)

I, Sahmat, grew up in intentional communities and have lived in 10 of them. I have been so dedicated to Community with both humans and Nature that I've been called "The Community Guy". The communities I grew up in shared a fairly strong "sense of community". I call this deep and sustained sense of community "Common-unity" because it's a state of unity we share in common, with the unique individuality of each human and each species still honored. It's this state of Common-unity that I've found most valuable in life and to me it's the main reason for living in an intentional community. When a group is deep in Common-unity together, there's a shared sense of love, joy, and peace that tops any other group experience.

However, I've found that in all the communities I've lived in, the sense of community is not nearly as deep and sustained as it could be. It's precisely this lack of Common-unity that is the root cause of the catastrophic global suffering of racism, wars, child abuse, abuse of women, environmental and species destruction, etc. So the ultimate goal is ending global suffering through "Global Common-unity": the spreading of Common-unity throughout the world by forming a global network of Common-unity-dedicated Communities.

So I've spent my life learning how to create Common-unity-dedicated communities that share true Common-unity: a deeper and more sustained sense of community. There are two keys to starting a Common-unity community (or moving an existing community into deeper Common-unity):

1. The first key to Common-unity is for everyone to be "Common-unity-dedicated" as their top common priority. This doesn't seem to be the case in any existing community, which results in focus and energies being bled off into other priorities. So maintenance of Common-unity doesn't get enough time and energy.

2. The second key to Common-unity is to learn "Common-unity Skills", skills that must be practiced to maintain Common-unity: Speaking from the Heart, Empathetic Listening, Emptying of Ego-attachments, Conflict Resolution, Consensus, Heart Wound Healing, Cooperative Housing, and Cooperative Economics. Modern culture does not teach us these skills.

We at the Alliance for Global Community have developed free workshops that train you in these Common-unity Skills. The workshops contain the Sharing Circle process developed by M. Scott Peck, a Nature connection exercise developed by John Seed and Joanna Macy, healing exercises developed by Byron Katie and Richard Moss, and exercises in creating Cooperative Housing and Cooperative Economics. We've tested various versions of these Common-unity Skill Building workshops over the past 25 years, and we've found them to be quite effective in teaching Common-unity skills that can help maintain Common-unity. If you'd like to start a Common-unity-dedicated community, or if you'd like to bring more Common-unity into an existing community (perhaps through a Common-unity sub-community or "pod"), you need to learn or improve these Common-unity skills as soon as possible.

To find out how to sign up for a free public Common-unity Skills workshop or schedule a free workshop for an existing group or community, please go to my website thecommunityguy.org There you can also find out how to get a free copy of the book "Skill Building for Global Common-unity". You can contact Sahmat directly at info@thecommunityguy.org or at 434-305-4770.

COMMON-UNITY WITH HUMANITY AND NATURE

Red Carpets and Slammed Doors
Visiting Communities

By Geoph Kozeny

Hoping to visit a community? The good news is that most communities welcome visitors, and a majority of those are open to new members. The bad news? Because so many community seekers want to visit, many communities at some point experience visitor overload and feel burned out from the seemingly never-ending flow of strangers. The best news: if you're considerate and persistent, the odds are good that you'll be able to arrange a visit and have a great experience.

An essential element of planning a satisfying visit is getting really clear about exactly what you want from a community. In other words, what is the purpose of your visit? You'll save considerable time and effort if you can learn to intuit how well any given community's reality will match the picture you've envisioned. There's definitely an art to this prescreening process, as it's based solely on information from written materials, letters, phone calls, emails, and perhaps a website—nothing physical that you can actually see, touch, smell, or taste.

While you're exploring communities from a distance, it also pays to sort through, point by point, all the different characteristics you think you want. Ask yourself: which attributes are mandatory, which are strong preferences, and which are nice but not necessary? This Directory is probably the best resource you'll find to aid in wrapping your mind around the possibilities. Carefully study each group's entry in the cross-reference chart and its written description in the listings section. With practice you can learn to use that information to spot potential incompatibilities in visions, values, and social norms. And please, don't assume that the community welcomes visitors just because they're listed in this book. Be sure to check out the "Visitors Accepted" column in the charts. Even under stress, many overloaded communities will agree to host more visitors, usually due to a sense of mission or obligation, but beware: often it is only the visitor coordinators and a few others who are enthusiastic about the idea. Some community members, typically acting from instinct rather than clarity, will go about their daily lives while keeping a low profile and acting distant in a weary, mostly subconscious attempt to minimize interactions with the newest batch of "tourists"—which might turn out to be you. Try not to take it personally.

Introductions and First Impressions

Usually the best line of first contact is through a friend who knows the community and is willing to give you a personal referral. If you don't have a friend with direct connections, friends-of-friends can prove just as effective. Use your network of friends and acquaintances creatively. Let it be known that you're interested in visiting certain communities, and ask your friends if they—or anyone they know—has a connection to those groups. If through correspondence, or especially through a visit, you make a connection with a member of one community, ask that person if they can recommend an especially good contact at the other communities you hope to visit. If your feelers yield a connection, be sure to open your introductory letter or phone call by saying "So-and-so over at Community X referred me to you." On the other hand, avoid giving the impression that you're a name-dropper, or that you're trying to do an end-run around their official channels. Alienating the community's designated visitor coordinator is far from being the optimal way to start a visit.

If no leads materialize, there's still a reasonably good chance of making a fruitful connection through self-introduction. Avoid sending an email or letter that poses a long list of questions about the community, but provides little or no information about who you are and what you're seeking. Although there's a wide range of styles that can work well in a letter of inquiry, a good general formula is to give approximately equal emphasis to: (1) describing what you're looking for, how you heard about them, and why they interest you; (2) telling about your history, skills, and special needs; and (3) posing questions about their community and their visiting protocols.

Your letter should be short, to the point, and engaging—if you send a long letter, you run the risk of overwhelming them right off the bat, or of having your letter shunted to the needs-to-be-answered-but-requires-a-lot-of-time-and-energy-to-deal-with pile. Such letters, unfortunately, only occasionally make it back to the top of the priority pile. Usually a one-page letter (or the equivalent in email) is best, and two pages should be the absolute maximum—anything longer than that reduces your chances of getting a prompt response. If you want to be remembered, enclose a photo, artwork, doodles, an interesting article, or something else eye-catching to make your letter stand out in the crowd (but please—no confetti, glitter, or other mess-making surprises). And, if you are sending a paper letter, be sure to include a self-addressed stamped envelope (SASE).

You may also want to consider first visiting one or more groups located in your region. Even if they are not likely candidates for where you'll finally want to settle, you can hone your visitor skills. The fact that they're relatively easy to get to means you can get some visiting experience under your belt without a large investment of your time or resources. It can be pretty devastating to use up all your precious vacation traveling cross-continent to visit your dream community, only to discover that it's not at all what you had in mind (which is fairly common, by the way). Instead, go through the steps face-to-face with real people, and get comfortable doing the interviews, the work, and the socializing.

Following Up

The sad truth is that many groups don't respond to correspondence in a timely fashion, in spite of good intentions. The reality is that living in community can be very demanding—there's always so much to be done—and answering a stack of correspondence doesn't usually rank as high on the chore list as milking the cows, supervising the kids, taking out the recycling, or building the new community center.

If your letter or email has received no response after two to four weeks, try a follow up. If you still receive no response a brief phone call is probably in order. Try to pick a time when folks are likely to be around and not otherwise busy. Often early evenings, or right before or after a meal, are good times to call. If you reach an answering machine, identify yourself, leave your number, and ask them to call you back at their convenience. Suggest times when you're most reachable, and explain that when they do get through, you'll be happy to hang up and call them right back on your dime.

When you reach a live person, first introduce yourself—mentioning your referral if you have one—and explain that you're interested in visiting. Be sure to note that you've already sent a letter. Ask whoever answers if he or she is a good person to talk with about visiting and

arrangements, and verify that this is a good time to talk. If the time's not right, make a date to call back at a better time. If they suggest you talk with someone else, note the new name, and ask for suggestions about how and when to reach the identified contact person. When you do finally connect with your contact person, be sure to verify upfront all the details related to visiting (see sidebar on p. 18).

If you wrote and got no response, it's usually far better to call first rather than show up unannounced. However, if they have no phone listing in the Directory, if their line's always busy, or if their published number has been disconnected and the community has no listing in Directory Assistance, then an exploratory "Hello" might be in order. If you've tried well in advance to reach a community but received no reply, it may work to "drop by" for a few minutes to introduce yourself—but be sensitive to their energy levels. Be prepared to find accommodations elsewhere, and arrange to come back when it's convenient for them. A 10- or 15-minute visit may be all that's appropriate if you catch them in the middle of something—but if your timing's good, you might get the deluxe two-hour tour right on the spot, plus get invited to dinner. Be flexible. Drop-in visitors can be especially awkward for groups that are far off the beaten path, but in most cases you can locate a park or a campground within commuting distance.

If they remember your letter, they'll know you made a bona fide effort to set up a visit and that they were the ones to drop the ball by not responding—so make your letter memorable.

> Always remember: the community you want to visit is also somebody's home.

Fitting In

Always remember: the community you want to visit is also somebody's home, so plan on using the same standards you would use if visiting a hometown friend or relatives you see only occasionally. Often it's helpful to figure out why they're open to visitors in the first place. They may be: seeking new members, needing help with the work, wanting the stimulation of meeting new people, and/or spreading their vision (e.g., egalitarianism, ecovillages) or religion (including the promotion of "community").

What will they gain from your stay? There are infinite ways to plug in and make yourself useful. Pitch in with everyday chores such as gardening, farm work, construction projects, bulk mailings, cooking, cleaning, dishes, or childcare. You may gain "Much Appreciated Guest" status if you have special skills to offer: layout or graphic design (newsletters), computer skills, meeting facilitation, storytelling, music, or massage. One fellow I met is a chiropractor who plies his trade for free at each community he visits. A woman therapist offers private and group counseling sessions to community members. Another fellow built a solar oven at each community he visited. Alternative building technologies, permaculture, and composting toilet expertise are all skills generally in high demand. Often, however, the most appreciated contribution is your willingness to pitch in to help with whatever boring chore needs doing at the moment.

Some groups are not organized in a way that lets them take advantage of visitor labor, and your desire to pitch in can actually become more of a headache for them than a help. Use your intuition in such situations. Make suggestions, but be open—offer, but don't push too hard. If they aren't able to involve you in the work and don't have much time to spend with you, be prepared to entertain yourself: bring books, tapes, musical instruments, etc.

Some groups use a buddy system for orienting visitors, pairing each visitor with a community member who can serve as a guide and a liaison. Having an identified support person to turn to is often helpful. If the community you are visiting doesn't use such a system, you might look around for someone willing to fill that role. It's important to be clear about your underlying motives so that both your expectations and the community's are realistic. Are you seeking a community to join, or gathering ideas about how groups deal with various issues so you can start your own? Perhaps you are just curious about shared living options and open to being inspired. Perhaps you're looking for a love affair or relationship. That may, in fact, be a possibility, but usually you'll alienate community members who sense you're on the prowl for romance rather than looking for community. What you're most likely to get in those situations is the hot seat, the cold shoulder, an invitation to leave, or some unpleasant combination of the three.

Sometimes awkward situations will come up, and it can take fairly sophisticated interpersonal skills to set things straight with your hosts. After all, many people have been conditioned to be stoic, and your hosts may be reluctant to say anything "impolite" about something you're doing that's bothering them. In those cases it's up to you to initiate the process of exploring any concerns or annoyances that they're sitting on, and it's much better to get those things out in the open early in your visit, before unexpressed resentments fester. Gracefully facing awkward issues head-on will give you the option to work on them and to develop a rapport with your hosts. Ignoring the tension will usually feed the sense of alienation or mistrust, and prompt your hosts to close up a bit more with every interaction. It's a warm and wonderful feeling to be included by the group and to experience a sense of "being in community" during your first visit, but don't count on it. Deep connections often take time, and sometimes come only after mutual trust and friendship have been solidly established.

Beyond First Impressions
"Being human" implies that we all bring along some baggage from our conditioning, and that we are seldom capable of living up to our own high standards. The discrep-

ancy between our visions of an ideal world and the reality of our daily lives is probably the most common catalyst underlying the creation of new intentional communities As a result, what we say we're going to do, both as individuals and as communities, is usually a lot more grandiose than what we actually accomplish. Keeping that perspective in mind while visiting communities can help keep your expectations in line with probabilities, and may ultimately help you avoid setting yourself up for a lot of unnecessary disappointment.

Visiting communities is much like dating—people have a tendency to put their best foot forward and try to hide what they consider to be weaknesses. It's helpful to fine-tune your eyes and ears to pick up pieces of the hidden story, and to sensitize yourself to what kinds of conversations and interactions will give you an accurate sense of the underlying day-to-day realities.

Remember, undesirable habits are easily obscured when members are on their best behavior. If you visit at least a handful of communities, you can compare and contrast their strengths and weaknesses. There's no better way than visiting to learn what to look for and where to find it.

To dig deeper, learn how to ask friendly but penetrating questions. After you've gotten to know a new group well enough to get more personal, try posing such open-ended queries as:

- What are some of the things you like best about living here? The least?
- What's the most difficult issue your community has had to deal with in the last year, or in the last five years?
- How many members have left in the past year or two, and why did they leave?
- How has the community changed over the years? What changes would you like to see in the future?
- What are some of the big challenges your community is facing now?
- How has living here contributed to your personal growth and happiness?

If the community members perceive you as being sincere, interested, and open-minded, most will be willing to engage with you in a thoughtful dialogue. However, if they sense that you've already made up your mind about what's right—and are likely to pass judgment on them—not much information will be forthcoming.

Avoid stereotypes of how you think communities should be. If you assume they will have any particular standard or feature you associate with "communities"—things like art facilities, organic gardens, health food, homeschooling, sexual openness—you're asking for disappointment. Many will have at least a few of those features, but few will have them all. Being outspoken or opinionated about the "shoulds" is an easy way to wear out your welcome fast—or to not get invited in the first place, if it shows up during the introductory phase. If something you value highly seems to be missing, ask them about it. Would they be open to it in the future? Would there be room and support for you to introduce it? Present your concern as, "Is it likely the group would be open to this?" rather than, "I couldn't live here unless."

While probing for deeper understanding, be sensitive to members' needs for privacy and quiet time, and to what kind of energy you're putting out. If you make a good personal connection, chances are good that they'll be happy to offer you hospitality. Otherwise, hosting you tends to become a chore for them, or worse, an annoyance.

What's Really Important?
Having talked to thousands of community seekers over several decades, I am convinced that most of us do not truly know what would make us happy, nor do we see how habits we've developed over the decades stand in the way of our accomplishing the things we say we want. It's only after we've tried something a time or two that we really understand how important, or not, that thing is to our happiness. For example, I've witnessed dozens of back-to-the-land dreamers who moved to the country to do gardening, raise livestock, chop wood, and carry water—only to discover that those things are hard work that cause calluses, sunburns, mosquito bites, sore backs, and are subject to the harsh unpredictabilities of nature. Many of those dreamers adapt to the reality and subsequently thrive in that environment, but nearly as many decide to move back to a more urban, less physically demanding lifestyle.

Real-life experience can be similarly eye-opening for folks with visions of a community based on the idea of

Living in intentional community is a lot of hard work, but it's a noble undertaking that offers great rewards for those with enough vision and perseverance to stick with it.

cooperative businesses, and consensus decision making. Living that way can certainly be inspiring and fulfilling, but because most of us have grown up in a society that emphasizes individualism and competition, we are often surprised by how challenging and frustrating the cooperative life can be. Often we fail to see how our attitudes and actions are contributing to the problems rather than generating solutions.

One problem stems from the fact that we conduct mostly mental research and don't get nearly enough hands-on experience. The best way to learn about yourself, and about the communities themselves, is to visit. In that context you can experiment with balancing work involvement with social involvement, and experience how easy (or not!) it is for you to adapt to a new culture.

Love at First Sight?
Investigating communities that are based on the idea of

creating a better life can be very refreshing. However, be warned: there is a tendency to fall in love with the first group visited. It usually pays to check out a few more anyway. Your first impression may be based on the excitement of discovering the many ways the group's vision matches your own, but be sure that you also look for the differences. For a good match, both you and the community need to be able to tolerate each other's rough edges. There may have been some common interactions that you missed. Did you get to see the group go through a meeting process? Did you watch them deal with a challenging issue? People's rough edges are most likely to show up when they're under heavy stress, so unless you saw them under pressure, you'll probably leave with an incomplete picture of how well they fare when dealing with interpersonal tensions.

If you do witness them working on a conflict, try to hear both sides and watch to see if they approach differences with an open mind. If you develop closeness with folks in one subgroup, you will most likely see and hear an incomplete picture of the issues and norms in question. Seek out members holding an opposing point of view, and see if you can understand their side of the issue. It's also possible that a few influential members are away, and the vibe at the community may be very different when they're home—more supportive if it's a primary nurturer/diplomat who's absent, or more strained if it's the chief skeptic/troublemaker who's gone. Additionally, there may be other visitors present whose issues or energy affect the dynamics.

You can learn a lot from other visitors, and from folks living in other communities. Both groups have a perspective that's somewhat detached from the hubbub of the everyday reality, and it's quite possible that they've witnessed the group under stress. Ex-members are also a great source of perspective on what tensions might be lurking below the surface, and how deep they're submerged.

It's usually a good idea to let your first impressions percolate before deciding to make a commitment to join a community. After a first visit, spend some time away from the group to see how well your initial impression holds up when you're no longer being influenced by their energy and enthusiasm. It's especially interesting and informative to listen to yourself handle questions about the community posed by your pre-community friends and acquaintances.

A Never-Ending Quest
No two communities are identical and, in fact, no community is the same today as it was five years ago—nor will

it be the same five years hence. Visions change, priorities change, the cast of characters change, people get older, the weather gets colder. This ever-evolving nature makes the search for a community to join both interesting and challenging. What you experience during a first visit is unlikely to remain static, yet you must decide based on that initial impression. And you must be prepared to adapt to the shifts in values and priorities that will inevitably come with the passage of time.

With that in mind, pay careful attention to the ideas and interactions that feel best to you, noting whether it's the philosophy, the lifestyle, the place, or the people that touch you at the deepest level. If you feel yourself drawn most energetically to a group whose stated philosophy isn't very well aligned with your own, it will probably not work out for you to be there for the long haul. However, if they're open to it, consider spending more time with them in order to explore what makes it work for you on the energetic level. Similarly, for a community with ideals matching yours but a shortage of group chemistry, try spending enough time with them to learn about what's either lacking or overdone—what's getting in the way of the synergy?

Sorting through all the complexities can be overwhelming, and the best thing you can do to gain perspective and solace is to connect with others who can relate to what you're going through. If you know of friends who are also on a community quest, consider creating a support group to share experiences, insights, and leads. Scan the ads in the alternative press and on the bulletin boards of nearby co-ops and health food stores, looking for announcements of support groups and networking opportunities. Check out the Intentional Communities Web site, www.ic.org, and follow the links from there. Or participate in one of the FIC's community conferences, a veritable cornucopia of seekers, networkers, and communitarians coming together to share information on the hows, whys, and wheres of shared living. It's a special opportunity to learn a lot in a few days about a number of communities from a wealth of experienced communitarians, all in an atmosphere of community.

Living in intentional community is a lot of hard work, but it's a noble undertaking that offers great rewards for those with enough vision and perseverance to stick with it. The first step in that process is finding a group compatible with your vision of a better world, and the rest of the work—for the rest of your life—will require an open mind, creativity, flexibility, commitment, integrity, common sense, and a lot of heart. Daunting? Yes, but worth it.

Get Things Clear Up Front

- Confirm that the community allows visitors, and that you'll be welcome to visit.
- Do they have particular times when visitors are welcome, regular visitor days, or a visitor program? Plan to be flexible to accommodate their scheduling needs.
- Do they have written Visitors' Guidelines that they could send to you? Do they have policies or agreements about smoking, drugs, alcohol, diet, kids, pets, nudity, celibacy, quiet hours, etc., that you need to know about in advance? Usually it's best to leave pets at home.
- Do they have any literature about themselves that you can read in the meantime? Brochures? Copies of articles written about them? A website?
- Are there any costs involved (visitor fees, utilities, food)?
- Verify length of stay, and any work that will be expected of you. If no work is expected, ask if you'll be able to help them with their work projects. (This is one of the best ways to get to know individual members as well as to learn about the community's daily life.)
- Confirm what you will need to bring: bedding, towels, shampoo, rain gear, work clothes and gloves, special foods, etc. Inform them of any unusual needs you may have (diet, allergies, medications). To the extent possible, plan to cover for yourself so that meeting your special needs doesn't become a burden on the community.
- Let them know if you can provide your own accommodation, such as a tent, RV, or a van to sleep in. Sometimes, if they're feeling overwhelmed with visitors, being self-sufficient in that way will increase your chances of getting invited.
- If you are traveling by public transportation and need to be picked up, try to arrange a convenient time and place of arrival. If a special trip is required to pick you up, reimburse the community for their travel costs.
- Even if a community requires no visitor fees, offer to pitch in a few bucks for food and utility costs. Especially when visiting small communities, I like to bring a special treat for the members—a bag of fruit, almonds, gourmet coffee, ice cream (or non-dairy desserts for the vegans).
- If you need to alter your dates or cancel the visit, please inform the community immediately. They may have turned away other visitors in order to make room for you.

BY JULIE PENNINGTON

Visiting Communities: Tips for Guests and Hosts

On the second night of my visit to an intentional community, I lay shivering in my soggy tent making plans for revenge. It was the second day of thunderstorms, and my precious few still-dry clothes were piled inside my sleeping bag for preservation. The water supply had been out at the campsite where I was sleeping for my entire stay, and the rain dripping through my tent roof was no substitute for a real shower. All I wanted in the whole world was running water and a roof. This was not at all what I thought my long-

awaited community visit would be like. My damp skin, dirty feet, and angry attitude came together to transform me from the smiling guest I had been at arrival to the bitter pouting one I'd become.

In the months preceding the visit I wrote letters, emailed, and spoke on the phone with my future hosts. Because of time restraints on my part, I could not stay for the regular guest period, and the community worked with my requests and allowed me to come outside of the normal visitor program. I was grateful

and asked the necessary questions to ensure that all my ducks were in a row for the visit to go over smoothly. I brought as gifts homemade jam and blankets that I had crocheted myself, and wrote checks to more than cover my expenses. When I arrived I took care to respect the members' busy lives and thanked them for every conversation and meal. I wanted to do my part to be a "good guest," one whom community members would be glad to have as a new member. I was so intent on my role as a guest that I acted nervous and awkward and walked on eggshells to not disrupt their normal routines.

By day three of my damp and soggy predicament, still wearing my moldy dress and tangled hair, I was pretty sure I'd get no invitation to shower in someone's home or sleep on someone's floor. I knew that I had to stop walking on eggshells around these people and take responsibility for my own needs. I mentioned to leaders in the community, my host, and any other sympathetic ear that I was sleeping in the lightning with no water. But complaining that your neck hurts doesn't always get you a full-body massage. A few community members lamented my situation but did not offer any assistance, and I began to resent their clean clothes and well-rested spirits. I was feeling sorry for myself, and I was getting grouchier with each falling raindrop.

Why didn't I insist on what I needed? Advocate for myself more directly? I felt indebted to the group for their flexibility and assumed that I would have been pushing it to ask for anything more than the joy of their company and a place for my tent. This was when I threw my good-visitor hat into the plastic bag with the rest of my soaked belongings and became angry. I felt that if the community really wanted me to be there, they

should take responsibility to pick up on my needs.

I spent the rest of my visit bitter and pouty.

Whether you live in a co-op, an ecovillage, an income-sharing commune, or any other type of intentional community, the best way to gain new members is through hosting visitors. It's an essential tool for furthering the communities movement and spreading the good word

Keep your objectives in mind and don't hesitate to ask for what you need.

about community living, but it nevertheless is a task. I have come to believe that a good visiting experience is a two-way street. Both visitor and host must make commitments to one another for a short period, and there are things that each can do to make the time pleasant and productive.

As a guest, you can certainly take steps to get the most out of your experience. Set aside enough time for your stay to really get a feel for the community you are considering joining. Write a letter

beforehand introducing yourself. Learn as much about the community as possible before the visit. Come prepared with questions and a good idea of what you're looking for. A piece of advice I've clung to during my visits to communities is "asking to ask." Remember that the community is not a tourist spot, but a home (and sometimes a workplace) to its members. Before ambushing residents with questions over their morning granola, it is a good idea to ease into conversation about the community by saying something like, "May I ask you a question?" By doing so, you give the member an opportunity to decline if she is busy or not in the mood to act as community spokesperson. Take the time to read other articles about how to visit communities (such as Geoph Kozeny's "Red Carpets and Slammed Doors" in the 2000 edition of the *Communities Directory*) or just ask experienced members for tips before you plan your trip.

Properly hosting a guest in a community takes a little more time and energy than simply showing the visitor where to eat and sleep. So what can we do as hosts to make the visitor's experience a good one? A structured visitor program sends the message to potential members that the community is well organized and cares about its guests.

A community should first decide what its position on visitors will be. What times visitors will be welcome, how long a visit can be, how many visitors you can host at a time, whether you can accommodate children, whether you can—or want to—accommodate pets, etc. Will there be one person or a team devoted to guests? What responsibility does the average member have to interact with the guest and tend to her or his needs?

It's a good idea for your group to draft a general letter about what to expect as a visitor in your community. Also, you might want to photocopy or reference an article about how to visit communities and send it to visitors ahead of time. A visitor liaison person or visitor team should be available to the visitors before their arrival to answer any questions and should inform other members of upcoming visits. Once the guests have arrived, the liaison person can make them feel welcome by introducing them to other community members. Suggest which members they can ask about various aspects of the community. Point out which members are in charge of labor, food, and finances, and which are long-time, experienced members, as compared to relatively newer members. Every community member has a special perspective on their community life, and visitors can make most efficient use of their time if they know whom to ask which kinds of questions. If you choose to do this, though, remember to ask the members' permission first for their various areas of expertise.

I've mentioned some steps you can take as a visitor before arriving at a community. But, as my soggy tale illustrates, good preparation may not grant you good-visitor status for your actual stay. What I learned from my visits this summer was the simple virtue of honesty. I was thrilled to be at the community I had dreamed about visiting for years, but my assumption that community members could read my mind put a damper on the trip. I am sure that members would have been eager to help had they only known what I needed.

Visitor periods are generally too short to learn every detail of community life, so it is to your advantage to make the most of your time spent there. If you consider the tips above before your trip, you'll be off to a good start. When you

> ### I am sure that members would have been eager to help had they only known what I needed.

arrive, keep your objectives in mind and don't hesitate to ask for what you need. An attitude like I had could prevent you from getting what you came to experience. Keeping a journal of your stay is a great tool to help when you return home and consider membership in that particular community. You are there to gather information and check out the vibe of the group and the land. Keep your contact information of particularly helpful members, since more questions will probably arise after you leave and reflect on the experience. Remember your criteria for the community you'd like to join. Your visit may be exciting, and the members may be friendly and interesting, but no amount of warm personalities will make an omnivore comfortable in a vegan community or a lover of city amenities comfortable at a rural, off-grid ecovillage.

Since this summer, I've dried off, grown up, and learned a lot about what it means to be a good visitor and a good host. Visiting communities (and hosting visitors at your own community) can yield some terrific experiences and fascinating new friends. If you pay attention to these and other tips and don't forget to bring a good attitude, you just may find the "utopia" you've been looking for!

Julie Pennington, co-editor of this issue, can be found on the front porch of House of Commons Co-op in Austin, Texas, preaching the power of community and eating Tofutti Cuties in bulk. julieepennington@hotmail.com.

SUSAN PATRICE

Wisdom begins with recognizing we are not alone...

www.exemplars.world – a resource for finding community

Exemplars salutes **"Communities"** Magazine for presenting a mix of intentional, usually non-traditional constructions that range from tested success to humbling failures, continuums between the poles of hierarchy and democracy; open and closed relationships; unbridled freedom of expression and respect for privacy; collective will and individual expression – and for recognizing community in many places.

Exemplars.world is a portal to help us understand and organize; a searchable, on-line library of the possible. There is a narrative that ties it all together, and for each organization or community, there is a brief description and a link to their web page. To add Exemplars, or comment, contact pfreundlich@comast.net

EXAMPLE:
DANCE
NEW ENGLAND

Starting Point: 1980. Cohort of cooperatively-run, community dances in New England. **Organizing Strategy:** By bringing people from the different dances together, raise the level of engagement to greater than the sum of the parts; costs kept low by reliance on volunteer energy; inclusion of provocative dance forms like Contact Improvisation to deepen community experience. **Tools:** Summer camp, year-round events, Community Directory. **Outcomes:** In 2017, the community pooled resources,, and purchased a 417 acre camp for events consistent with its values. **Primary Resource:** http://dne.org. Dance New England offers a social nexus for the thousands who have attended its events. Kids are born and integrated into a next generation of lively participants, The structure requires organizing and hard work, and rewards with frequent pleasures., The decision-making is consensual, women at least equal in leadership, and the mode of participation, collaborative.

BY JULIE PENNINGTON

Planning a Community Visit

ROD RYLANDER

ROD RYLANDER

People visit intentional communities because they're curious about community living, or to get ideas about land, work systems, or meeting facilitation for example, or to take workshops on community-related topics such as conflict resolution, permaculture, or meditation. However, the majority of people visiting communities do so because they're seeking one to join themselves. If you consider all that you could learn from visiting a community, it's possible to fulfill more than one purpose during your stay.

You may already have a sense of community living and may already know of several communities you'd like to investigate. Ask yourself what intrigues you about communities and what in particular you like about the communities you've heard of. What questions do you have about community living in general? Write your questions and concerns down and use them as a starting point to find out more.

The *Communities Directory* is probably the most useful resource for the initial criteria-gathering stage of the process. Flip through the *Directory's* cross-reference chart and become familiar with some of the points you'll want to consider in your search: location, purpose, population, decision-making style, shared or independent income, diet, substance use, and so on. Also check out the "Communities Seeking Members" ads in the back of *Communities* magazine.

Make a list of personal priorities. Are you looking for an ecovillage, a back-to-the-land-style rural group, an income-sharing commune, a cohousing neighborhood, or an urban co-op? Are spirituality, diet and health lifestyle, relationship style, or gender orientation most important to you? What kind of financial investment could you make to a group? As you ask these and other questions, consider your current lifestyle. What are the aspects of your life that give you happiness and fulfillment? What are the aspects you would most like to change? Be realistic and try to recognize those things that you don't want to live

without or those things you most want to give up. In my own case, for example,

The more you know about what you're looking for, the easier it will be to plan your trip.

what I love about my life at my co-op in Austin is the opportunity to abstain from eating animal products, enjoy local live

music several nights a week, and the warm climate. This helped me set parameters for my search, such as geographic regions with a warm climate, proximity to a major city's cultural life, and places with a vegan-friendly diet. I'm uncomfortable with my dependence on cars, so I might keep my eyes open for a community with a car co-op or one small enough to bike around.

The more you know about what you're looking for, the easier it will be to plan your trip. This is also a great place to start a communities journal, like Sue Stone did. *(See "Excerpt from a Community Seeker's Journal," pg. 29.)* Write down all of your priorities now. It will be useful to reflect on them later (and after visiting many communities, some of them might change).

Now that you have an idea of your search criteria, it's time to start finding some communities that might suit you well. You'll find links to individual community listings on the websites of the Fellowship for Intentional Community (FIC), publishers of this magazine *(ic.org);* Ecovillage Network of the Americas *(ena@gaia.org);* and the Cohousing Association of the U.S. *(cohousing.org).*

If you cannot find a website for a particular kind of community, don't assume that such a community doesn't exist or isn't worth visiting (maybe they just don't have a website). Again, use the cross-reference chart, the map, and the index in the *Communities Directory* to hone your options. If you have time, attend a communities conference such as an FIC regional gathering, Twin Oaks' annual communities gathering over Labor Day weekend, The Farm's new conference in May, or a Northwest Intentional Communities Association gathering, to meet community representatives and find out more. Mention to acquaintances in the communities movement that you are planning a visit and see what they have to offer. Ask if your friends know anyone at the communities that interest you. Gather information and make a list of pros and cons of each of those top several communities that seem to most closely match your needs. Then ask members of these communities if the facts you have are still accurate. Keep in mind that

communities are made up of individuals. When the membership changes in small communities, it is likely that at least some aspects of the group also change. Make sure that the groups you are considering visiting are open to hosting guests.

Begin contacting communities several months before you'd like to visit. Many groups have set times that they are open or closed to visitors, so keep your travel dates flexible. Don't assume that they will be able to fit your schedule (although if they are, remember to acknowledge their accommodation). Also consider how much time you can afford to take off work for your trip and how much time you will need to accomplish your goals at each community. While planning my own long communities tour, I felt that I needed at least five days at each place, and this estimate worked well for me. I was searching for a community to join, but if you have different reasons for visiting communities, you might want more or less time than this.

It is a good idea to visit at least two communities on any given trip. It will help your perspective and make the most efficient use of your travel time. If you find one or two communities that you definitely want to visit, open up the *Communities Directory* to the maps section and draw a line between the two places and see which other communities may be roughly near the route. Even if you had no interest in some of these groups during your original research, consider them again. Every group of people living intentionally together has something to teach the community seeker. You might want to use communities along your route as rest stops in which to reflect on the previous community visit and prepare for the next. A spiritual retreat community with hot springs among cozy cabins would make for a great rest stop!

When contacting communities to request a visit, follow the community's suggestions described in their *Directory* listing or on their website. In your letter or email message introduce yourself and tell the group how you heard about them and why you are interested in visiting; for example, that you're considering

potential membership or in just learning more about community. Ask about their visitor policy. If you know someone at

Ask if it is a convenient time to ask about the community.

the community or even a friend-of-a-friend, mention this connection. Tell briefly about your experience, skills, or interests, and any special needs you may

have. Provide contact information for someone to get back to you, and, if it's a snail-mailed letter, include a self-addressed stamped envelope. By enclosing a photo of yourself, a sketch, or something else that will make your letter unique and memorable, you are more likely to ensure a prompt response. Remember that some communities may get many requests to host visitors, or answer their correspondence infrequently, so don't be frustrated if you don't get an answer right away—one reason you should allow ample time to plan before your visit. If you don't receive a response from the group in two to three

its home to strangers if it had nothing to gain. What can you do, then, to make your stay a mutually beneficial experience? Find out why this group is open to visitors in the first place. They may be looking for new members, but they might also need help with work, want to spread their philosophy, gain income from guest fees, or simply enjoy the motivation of having new people to spend time with. *(See "Guess Who's Coming to Dinner?," pg. 43.)*

Many communities need help with work. You might offer to do those mundane tasks that make community members groan (think washing dishes). Also bring old clothes and your work gloves, in case they need help hauling brush, stacking firewood, or other outdoor jobs. It's a nice gesture to bring a gift if you can, but be sensitive to the culture of the community when choosing what to bring (don't present

Don't pretend that the community is exactly what you are looking for if it isn't.

home-brew to a substance-free community, for example). Try to bring either something functional from their wish list or a nice treat everyone can enjoy. Offer any special skills or talents you have. If you are a musician, offer to play a concert; if you're an artist, offer to create a piece for them or decorate a wall. Be creative.

Let's assume that you and your host have been in contact several times, you've made specific arrangements, and you're ready to be on your way. The time you spend traveling there, by bus, shared vehicle, or plane, is perfect for pulling out your community-visiting journal. Write what you know and like or dislike about what you've heard of the community, any questions you want to remember to ask its members, and your expectations.

When you arrive at the community, you will likely get a tour and be shown a

weeks, try another approach. If you've emailed, you might just send another email. If you've sent a letter, a phone call might be a better way to catch someone. Be considerate of the group and if you must call, try to do so in early evening rather than late at bedtime or first thing in the morning when members may be busy getting ready for work.

When you make contact with your potential hosts, they may or may not tell you everything you need to know about your visit. Many groups will send a letter describing what to expect on your visit and what you should plan to bring with you. If the group is not forthcoming with these tips, make sure and ask plenty of questions. What special items should

you pack? What might the weather be like at that time of year? Will you need bug spray, a rain poncho, a flashlight? Be sure to find out where you will be staying and if you should bring a tent or sleeping bag. Are children and pets welcome with visitors? Will your diet be accommodated? What is the best way to get to the community? Can you provide your own transportation? What are the parking rules? What is an appropriate amount of money to cover your expenses? Who should you direct further questions to? Will this person be your host when you arrive?

While hosting visitors is often enjoyable for the community, it can also be a lot of work. The group would not open room, dorm space, or campground in which to set up your temporary home away from home. You should know who your main liaison in the community is, as that person can fill you in on mealtimes, community happenings, and any labor assignments they may have planned for you. If you don't have labor assignments, take the initiative to jump in and help wherever you see a need. The group may not have work and activities planned for your entire stay, so use this time to relax, get a feel for the community, talk to members, and reflect on your surroundings. It is a good idea to set aside time for journaling while you are there. Write about what you do, see, and feel. There is a lot to remember about the community you visit, so record facts for review later. Because food and diet are especially important to me, writing down what each community served at dinner helped me to recall memories and how I felt during each stay.

Talk to a variety of members, and remember the golden rule of "asking to ask." Before dumping a mass of questions on someone, ask if it is a convenient time to ask about the community. Don't be offended if the honest answer is "No." What for you is a vacation spot is really someone's home, and members have responsibilities and lives of their own that they will have to address. If you meet someone you are particularly interested in speaking with but they're too busy to talk, you might ask when a better time might be. Helping a community member to garden, wash dishes, or perform other tasks can also be a great time to chat about the community, if the member is comfortable doing so.

In addition to the questions you have already thought of, you can ask how a particular member came to be a part of the community, what she likes and dislikes about it, and how she feels they have addressed their vision as a group. Asking different members what they feel the community's priorities are will give you a good perspective on the group's diversity and their overall adherence to goals. You can also ask what different members find challenging in the community, or what they'd most like to improve or change.

After you return home, consider sending a thank you note. It makes community members feel good, helps reward them for the sometimes arduous task of hosting visitors, and may help them remember you kindly if you decide to return to learn more.

The most important thing to remember during your stay, however, is to be honest with yourself and with the group. It is easy to become enchanted with many aspects of community life, but you should remember what you are looking for and objectively evaluate how the particular group and setting mesh with your personal vision. Definitely put your best foot forward and be gracious, but don't pretend that the community is exactly what you are looking for if it isn't. Neither seekers nor communities benefit from gaining new members who aren't a good fit. If you don't find your dream home during the visit, you probably wouldn't be happy there as a member. Hopefully, though, the community you visit may turn out to be exactly what you have been looking for. Either way, plan it out and make the most of your opportunity to be part of the magic of community. Good luck!

Julie Pennington, co-editor of this issue, and veteran community visitor, lives at a co-op community in Austin, Texas.

Author Julie Pennington.

The Art and Ethics of Visitor Programs

By Blake Cothron

All around the world we're now witnessing an exciting upsurge of interest in intentional communities and alternative living arrangements. This is very promising news for any of us who are proponents of a more conscious, equitable, regenerative, and sane world. Major challenges face the intentional communities movement and any similar projects. The challenge I'd like to highlight now is the integration of new members and volunteers in a holistic, ethical, and meaningful way. We must ask, *what are we in our individual situations doing to provide an ethical, hospitable, meaningful, and fair introductory experience for newcomers in our community?*

How often have we in community witnessed the following scenario: an enthusiastic and good-natured new person is invited into your community who has useful skills, heart, and potential to contribute much to your community, but soon experiences internal challenges, becomes disheartened, and then departs? I've watched this drama unfold too many times (and been the disillusioned new person myself). As facilitators and creators of intentional communities we need to deeply consider why there is such a high turnover rate of potential new members and communitarians. We can start by first exploring a few crucial questions: why do people enthusiastically decide to explore membership in intentional community in the first place? Why do they often leave so soon? How can a visitor program better meet the holistic needs of new people and warmly integrate them into the community?

People choose to pursue intentional community life for many different reasons. Some are looking for a way out of the "rat race," and a simpler, more natural and holistic life. Others choose cooperative living to engage in educational or humanitarian work. Some wish to pursue their spiritual path while living with other seekers and practitioners of their faith. I think most can agree, however, that we basically all choose intentional community for very similar foundational reasons: we want deeper

connections with other people and the Earth, more meaning in what we do, and to live a healthier, simpler, and more regenerative lifestyle. Personally, I chose to first explore community living in 2006 because I believed there had to be a much better way to live than I was experiencing in my struggling and crowded hometown. I craved a more integrated existence, simplicity, deeper relationships, involvement in organic agriculture, and living more in tune with nature.

I think it's important to remember how we all felt when we were first new to community. How did you feel? Were you excited, amazed, maybe a bit bewildered? Were you very open-hearted and generous, or were you quiet and reserved? I was a bit of all of those and also painfully idealistic and naïve. It's important for us to remember that joining a community is usually an enormous step out of the status quo and our privacy-addicted mindsets; it can be a culture shock. We can easily forget what it's like for a new person to join the group and how much of a dramatic internal shift they often must make to function cooperatively.

Sometimes we just *expect* them to understand what is to us common knowledge: why recycling is important, the virtues of not having a television, or the real dangers of GMO's, for example. We sometimes *expect* new people to *accept* our community lifestyles outright, with little to no time for adjustment. It's important to remember that anyone who is exploring intentional community is in the rare two percent or so of the population and deserves recognition and patience for that fact alone.

We must be real here and recognize that welcoming new people into our communities and farms is no simple task. It takes *much* time and effort to host someone properly, and even more consciousness and energy to create an integrated and holistic experience for them. And of course there are always some people who try, and then find out that community living is just not for them, or who are simply not good matches for the community. Yet the way we go about hosting someone will dramatically affect their experience and the likelihood of any future involvement in our community. What is often overlooked out of perceived practicality is the loving human touch and interaction, as well as practical arrangements like good housing and trying to match compatible people to your project, which makes all the difference.

Many times I traveled to a community as a prospective member or intern and experienced myself and others being treated like the means to a goal, and later on I also caught myself

intimate, meaningful communication and sharing into a newcomer's stay is therefore vital. Imagine a new person being warmly welcomed over chai and relaxed casual conversation, instead of practical details and "breaking them in" with immediate work projects or orientations. How does the first option feel over the second?

We need to make sure we extend respect and warmth while fostering personal communication with new people. Too often I've seen rural communities operating like little boot camps with new people treated impersonally like "new recruits." The focus is on productivity,

> # Too often I've seen rural communities operating like little boot camps with new people treated impersonally like "new recruits."

embarrassingly on the other end as well. It's all too easy to view new people, whether interns, apprentices, or prospective members, as energetic, free labor for all of our needy projects, and to treat them in that one-dimensional way. From experiences I had facilitating WWOOF volunteers in a farm community, I realized I had to become more sensitive to the fact that every person is a multi-dimensional being with different needs, desires, proclivities, fears, skills, dreams, and maturity level, and that interacting with them sensitively and respectfully is essential. We need to honor each person's journey and complex needs while treating them in a holistic way.

The first step, before we even *begin* to offer live-in programs in our communities, is to discern *why* we wish to begin a visitor program and how to best meet the needs of the visitors. Are we wanting to temporarily host someone simply to lend us a hand and teach them a skill, such as natural building, or are we offering an opportunity to explore potential membership? These two scenarios necessitate different strategies and arrangements. Depending on the purpose of the visit, we then can make arrangements to meet their basic needs and organize for their guidance from a community member or team.

Beyond this physical, basic level, I am advocating for the creation of a nurturing environment for interacting with a new person based on their multi-dimensional existence, so that they feel sustenance on many levels and both they and the community can better get their needs met. Let's explore some of the factors involved and how this holistic approach can be manifested.

In most successful community endeavors I will attest that effective communication is the foundation, and in general most deep, fulfilling relationships are based on open communication. So it's important to remember that people come to community generally seeking a more meaningful, fulfilling, and connected reality. The modern world is depressingly impersonal, as more computers, machines, and isolation prevent genuine human interaction and communication, even on a basic level. Integrating

labor, and accomplishing goals, often for the benefit of a desired image or material aim. Personal development, reflection, spirituality, and emotional/artistic expression are curtailed in favor of pushing onward "the glorious mission." This is not a sustainable approach. We need to examine our community situations and *very honestly ask ourselves*, "are we collectively facilitating a sustainable, meaningful, and holistic experience for ourselves as well as newcomers?" Likewise we need to ask, "are our advertisements and outreach material accurate, up-to-date, or even *true*?"

Here's a story to dramatically illustrate this point: several years ago I found online a listing for a dynamic-sounding intentional community, complete with a dedicated group of conscious permaculture pioneers and an incredible organic mini-farm educational center overflowing with abundance and diversity. I was excited and scheduled my visit as an intern. As I pulled into the property backed dramatically by thousands of acres of steep, wild, dark, misty mountains; I was in awe of the beautiful setting. There indeed was an impressive diversity and abundance of fruit orchards and gardens...but what I quickly noticed an absence of was a *community*. The center was operated entirely by one man and his wife.

"Well," I figured, "this place is so amazing maybe it will still work out somehow." That evening I was shown my choices of housing. One was a dark, creaky, musty hundred-year old barn outfitted as a sort of dormitory, with lightbulbs hanging from the ceiling and raggedy old blankets and mattresses strewn about. The other option was a small, 8'x 8' unheated shack with gaps between the uninsulated wall boards just big enough to let the freezing March wind and snow blow inside during my first night. The "simple, organic diet" they offered consisted of nearly-spoilt dumpstered food, and the consensus decision making was made between the man and his wife. As *educational* as this center was, I left after about three days, feeling relieved to be gone yet disappointed and somewhat scattered.

It was not the cooperative and holistic community it was advertised as, and now I was very inconvenienced and hundreds of miles away from home and had to abruptly make new plans. The lesson for me was to not be naïve about trusting that a website is entirely accurate and honest, and to openly ask *a lot* of pertinent questions before making a move to a community. The online description of this community was 10 years old and obviously needed a lot of revision. Portraying our projects or community as something they are not is simply not ethical. Likewise, it's not ethical or useful to offer new people substandard housing and food or inhumane work and living arrangements, yet it's all too common.

The act of integrating new people into our communities is a delicate, sacred responsibility.

Now ask yourself, how would you feel being asked to eat and live in what is being offered to *your* interns or visitors? The fact that an arrangement is "livable" (sometimes survivable is more accurate) does not make it sustainable or humane. We need to extend our own human needs and desires to newcomers in community, who are vulnerable people as well. Let's be as generous as we can. Create living arrangements which are nice and inviting and foster a sense of privacy, safety, and nurturing. These things go a long way in helping a new person feel welcomed, appreciated, and respected, which will likely lead them to consider staying on longer.

As well as meeting basic physical needs, it's just as important to make an effort to meet the emotional and mental needs of a person. This is why I advocate scheduling a special time, perhaps once a week, to hold a "checking-in" session and ask them how their experience is going. How have they been feeling? What do they like best? What has been challenging? How has their image of the community changed so far? What is inspiring them? What would they change if they could? This could be done in a comfortable private room, over dinner, or in a nice natural setting. Try to facilitate it as a warm, personal exchange, not like a formal interview or going down a list of questions. And, unless necessary to do otherwise, keep their answers private or at least not completely public.

This small, simple exchange, I believe, can make a dramatic impact on a new person's feelings of connection and being cared for, as well as facilitate more internal clarity about their own experience. This will help not only them, but the community also, to have more clarity about how the visit is going and to help balance out any issues and potential problems early on.

Many times, new people will leave a community for very simple and often avoidable reasons. Lack of a private room, lack of vegan diet options, etc. can all be deal-breakers. Many times this can be avoided by clear communication and agreements beforehand. However, I'd say a majority of people leave community because of *lack of integration into the group*. Communities can become very close-knit or even form cliques that can be difficult or nearly impossible to penetrate, with new people often treated like outsiders. This can be avoided by inviting new folks to community events, meals, and outings. Allow them to introduce themselves in front of everyone and share a bit about themselves. Host an open mic or talent show and encourage them to express their artistic sides. Have fun! If they express interest, facilitate a small personal project for them; perhaps painting the kitchen or planting a fruit tree. This will help them feel a sense of contribution and meaning—innate human needs.

The act of integrating new people into our communities is a delicate, sacred responsibility. We want new people to feel positive about joining our communities. Both parties are taking a risk. They are trusting us to facilitate a good experience for them; to keep them safe and nurtured, and to offer them what we have advertised. We want them in turn to have a positive, dynamic, and educational experience, and contribute to and potentially join our community. We all want to get our needs met by the whole event.

I admit, I'm still an idealist. I do not mean to offend those who offer well-meaning, but still deficient visitor programs. I believe that integrating even one (or more) of these suggestions into your visitor program will dramatically improve the experience of your visitors and lead to better outcomes for everyone involved. In summary, I'd like to highlight these important points:

Be Honest: Make sure any outreach material is accurate, honest, and up-to-date. Be *very clear, honest, and descriptive* about the housing situation, food quality, daily schedule, spirituality or religious focus, privacy, fees, local climate, mission of the community, alcohol/tobacco use, and the communities' basic expectations of visitors. Ambiguity leads to problems, disappointments, and chaos.

Be Fair: Make sure your situation is nurturing and balanced for a *multi-dimensional person*. Share decent housing that is clean, heatable, at least somewhat private, and that feels cozy and safe. If all you have available is sub-par, make that very clear, and post pictures of it. Create their schedule to be livable and not arduous. Allow at least *one full day* per week of off-time for rest and reflection, ideally with no expectations of their attending anything. If you are to charge something, take into account all the labor they will be doing.

Connect: Welcome new people warmly and stay in close communication with them throughout their stay. Get to know them and engage the new person in events and outings. Have a friendly, personal, and private meeting time with them at least once during their stay to check in and connect. Be sensitive to their needs, varying moods, and desires. People usually join community because they want more connection, meaning, and deeper relationships.

Create space for new people to express themselves and contribute: If they show an interest in a personal project or contribution, try to help them to do it. Keep it small and realistic. Share opportunities for art, music, dance, and recreation.

Be Real: Be open about (at least some of) the challenges and issues facing the community. Be open and real about the mission, focus, and mood of the community, and expect openness from them as well. Learn from each other and be accepting of their enthusiasm and a fresh, new perspective on your community. ❧

Editor's Note: We invite responses from communitarians to the questions and concerns Blake presents in this article. We'd like to present a diversity of perspectives on the issues raised, and you can help with that. Please let us know what you think.

Blake Cothron is an artist, writer, organic agriculturist, and holistic life teacher, currently founding the Vedic Living Farm project in Kentucky. He practices Ayurvedic medicine, Goddess worship, and Ashtanga Yoga, and can be reached at healandserve@ gmail.com.

III

COMMUNITY EXPLORATIONS:

STORIES AND REFLECTIONS

Sue Stone and Geoff Stone.

Excerpts from a Community Seeker's Journal

BY SUE STONE

From 1994 through 1998, Sue and Geoff Stone, who had lived in Ozark, Arkansas for 14 years, visited dozens of communities looking for one to join. Here are excerpts from Sue's journal, with her personal observations and insights of the sometimes inspiring, sometimes arduous, community-seeking process.

December, 1994, Missouri.

On Winter Solstice weekend in December Geoff and I visited a small community on 75 acres in Missouri I'll call

Warm Springs. We felt comfortable there soon after we arrived. The couple who'd invited us, Sam and Debra (not their real names) seemed genuinely interested in us and our ideas and experiences. It was easy to talk with them and we seemed to have a lot in common.

When we first arrived, I was surprised to see just an ordinary little house. We had tea with Sam and their two boys, who were making pumpkin pies in a toaster oven. The boys took us on a tour. It was pretty land, but there wasn't much there in terms of physical infrastructure: a shed for outdoor cooking, a teepee, a sweat lodge, a children's fort. The home-schooled boys were impressive: mature, knowledgeable, serious.

Saturday I helped Debra fix up the teepee and Geoff helped Sam prepare the sweat lodge. Debra took me on a short hike to a spring. She told me about the women's group that meets there, and showed me the women's altar. She told me about how they had lived in a teepee when the boys were small.

Saturday night was what community is about

for me. Other people arrived, including another couple, Roger and Sarah, and their son, and two men from St. Louis. We had a potluck dinner, talked, and played drums. Geoff and I talked a lot with Roger, who actually owns the land. He had lived at Ananda Village in Cali-

The bathroom was a choice between an indoor toilet which didn't flush or a long walk to a cold outhouse.

fornia, and told us about that community. He was excited to learn about Geoff's greenhouse, and I got the feeling that we would really be an asset to their community, if we chose to go there.

The solstice ceremony was held around a fire. We lit candles and spoke of our feelings about the past fall and the coming of the winter and the new year. We went into the teepee and talked and played drums. That night Geoff and I slept in our tent, at least tried to, as it was really too cold to sleep well. The moon was full, and we were beside the creek and I could hear it all night.

The weekend was hard in a lot of ways. The bathroom situation was a problem, a choice between an indoor toilet which didn't flush or a long walk to a cold outhouse. I was tired from not getting enough sleep, and felt grubby and uncomfortable and cold much of the time. And there was also the unknown: What is going to happen next, and when, and what will it be like?

A new guest came the next day for the sweat lodge ceremony to be held that afternoon. I liked hanging around inside near the stove that morning, talking and drinking coffee. One visitor was a musician, a drummer; another was a young man from Syria. The third was a storyteller, very interesting and personable. They were all so nice—friendly, warm, interested in us and seemingly glad to have us there.

KIMCHI RYLANDER

I kept crying at the ceremonies. It all felt so right to me. I felt awkward and uncomfortable and apprehensive, and yet like it was where I wanted and needed to be. Even though Geoff and I couldn't stay for the entire sweat lodge ceremony, I loved it and I felt wonderful afterwards, and I felt so loved and appreciated. They thanked us for being there!

What I really appreciated about these people was their dedication and commitment to the land. Sam wants to respect the land as the Native Americans do, and do the celebrations and ceremonies to honor it and work with it. Sarah worked with Starhawk and does rituals with women's groups. The group also wants to have a garden and passive solar houses. And they have already worked hard to build good relationships with the local community.

They'd like to buy more land adjacent to their property. I could see us being part of that, and helping to buy that land. The problems I could see with this community are that there doesn't seem to be much opportunity for getting jobs outside, and the land is pretty isolated. Also, it would be a small community. They are only two hours from St. Louis, so that is a resource for people and a market for products or services. What I liked best about it was the people, the Earth ceremonies, and their dedication to the land. It seemed like a definite possibility.

January, 1995, Arkansas.

A few weeks later we visited Thomas (not his real name), who plans to start a community on his small parcel of land in the crystal-mining area of Arkansas outside of Hot Springs. We were there to take his workshop on ferro-cement construction and attend his birthday party.

His land is really pretty, and has a nice, year-round stream. I found Thomas a kind, interesting, and talented guy. I enjoyed walking in the hills, learning to do ferro-cement work, and talking with him and his friends. The party was another taste of how I imagine community would be: good music, really interesting conversation, and especially drumming by candlelight. I felt so good after that weekend, energized yet relaxed.

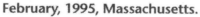

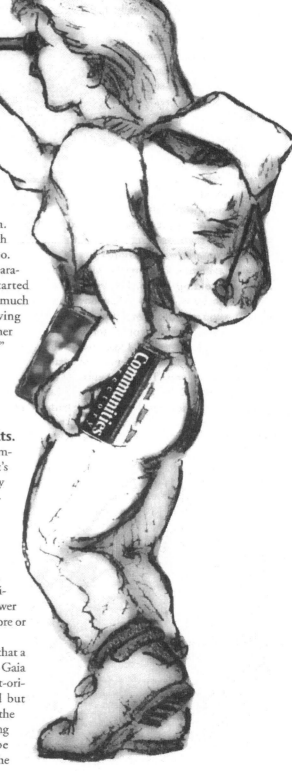

I kept crying at the ceremonies. It all felt so right to me.

Yet, Thomas doesn't have much land, so his future community would be small, and there aren't many good sites for passive solar construction, or even for a garden really. He has had a lot of experience with communities, though. Geoff likes him and works well with him, and I certainly like him, too. Also it would be really easy, comparatively, to get started there, certainly much easier than moving somewhere farther away. But "easy" is not what the community search is about. It's about what we want, whatever that is!

February, 1995, Massachusetts.

First day. We're here at Sirius Community in Massachusetts, and it's beautiful! The main community building is made with all this hand-hewn natural wood. The guest area is like a sort of rustic cabin, but really comfortable. Separate rooms lead off a hallway sitting area, with a wood stove and a place to fix tea. Best of all: three showers, several toilets and a bathtub! We've had a shower and a rest and I feel normal again, more or less.

We have pretty much concluded that a nearby community we just visited, Gaia (not their real name), is too activist-oriented for us. They love their land but otherwise seem so focused on saving the world that organizing and maintaining their own community seem to be neglected. And I really didn't sense the central focus.

I expect Sirius to be different. It is much more physically comfortable, of course, but it is 16 years old, so they've had more time to get it together. Anyway, it is nice to be here, finally. I expect I'll want to join and already I'm trying to figure out how it could be done. I guess I should just "be here now" for the present.

Second day, morning. Dinner last night felt like my concept of what community is all about: people sitting around a table after a meal, talking and sharing, then working together to clean up afterwards. Dinner began with everyone standing silently in a circle holding hands. Everything here starts that way. We saw a slide show about Sirius and introduced ourselves, met some members, and had an orientation.

I slept really well and feel pretty good today. I still think I'd prefer my own bathroom, but I guess I might eventually get used to this down-the-hall set-up. Other members besides the guests use the bathrooms here, and there is no gender designation, so

you might be washing up or showering or using the toilet next to someone of the opposite sex. Of course, the toilets and showers have doors, and usually there isn't anyone else there, but it still seems strange.

In some ways Sirius doesn't fit my concept of a community, as most of its members don't live here. It seems more like a church. You pay dues to belong and donate eight hours of work a week. You might rent living space here, or get it somewhere nearby. You have to earn your own living somehow. There are shared meals, but you have to subscribe to them, and take your turn supplying and cooking a meal. You can pay $25 a month for a share of garden

"Easy" is not what the community search is about. It's about what we want, whatever that is!

produce, and $20 to use community bulk foods. It's not like the sort of community where everyone lives together. But they are, nevertheless, working toward goals which are similar to ours.

Second day, afternoon. So far I feel really good here. Right now I'd love to stay forever. After breakfast we had a tour. Breakfast (and meals in general) are in the farmhouse, the original building here. There's a kitchen and a living/dining room with a wood stove, a few chairs and couches, and three long tables, with windows looking out over the garden. It's cozy and

neat, though well-used. Also, there is a library and a bulletin board. People hang out there before and after meals. Before meals and before going off to work projects everyone stands and holds hands in silence for a few minutes, to "realize oneness." There's a short blessing before meals, sometimes announcements, and the menu. After meals, they discuss what work needs to be done.

After the tour we spent two hours in a meeting where we were told how Sirius operates. I got the feeling that the only way to get here would be to move to the area and find some way to live, and meanwhile spend months or years working through the membership process. I was told later that "exploring members" can rent space here, assuming it's available and that you have enough income. Anyway, it's not as hard as I thought it would be. The people are so nice—warm, friendly, helpful. I'm sure there are problems at times, but they all seem happy and relaxed. I haven't noticed anyone rushing around or looking stressed.

Again at lunch it was relaxed and congenial, lots of interesting conversation. People just pitch in and help clean up, and it seems to go quickly and smoothly. After lunch, I helped with a mailing at the farmhouse, and Geoff helped with firewood. I went for a walk on the trail through the woods.

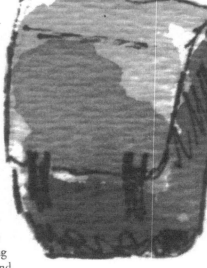

Every place I've been so far I can imagine myself living, so I guess I can't be sure my feelings at this point are a reliable gauge. After one day, how can I really have enough information? This is really the first operational community I've experienced. I just keep thinking how good it would be to live here. But there are disadvantages; for example, housing costs seem double those in Arkansas, and there aren't many jobs close by. It would be a half-hour commute to get to work, most likely. And part of the reason for community living is to get away from that stuff! There's a possibility of a job here in the community, perhaps, or a business operating out of the community eventually. So it might work out, if we really wanted to be here.

Third day, evening. Geoff and I spent the time before dinner discussing pros and cons and possibilities. We just go around and around and back and forth. I am already tired of the uncertainty, but I guess it will go on anyway!

Last night one of the founding members, Bruce, gave a talk on the role of community in the modern world. He said there is typically a breakdown of the forms and structures in society, then a period of chaos. Then comes a time of creation of a multitude of possibilities for new forms and structures, after which there is suddenly a "quantum leap" to a new form, a new level. He talked about how it is easier to grow and evolve and expand one's consciousness in a supportive and energized environment such as Sirius. He talked about how living outside is oppressive and can tend to hold one down and prevent this expansion, unless the person is very strong and evolved. This struck such a chord with me—that is exactly how living in Ozark feels to me!

After breakfast I had a massage with a woman who lives here, and it felt so good! Then I joined in for part of the circle dancing, in the new octagonal meeting hall. I kept looking around the room, at the people, the beautiful building, the

woods outside, thinking, "I'm really here! I'm dancing at Sirius!"

There was a meditation before lunch. There was one yesterday, too, a half-hour "meditation for planetary healing." At lunch there were several visitors, as today was Open House, and the dining area was really crowded. Everyone managed to get fed and find a seat and there were several shifts for the dish-washing and cleanup. After lunch we had a closing meeting, where everyone, including the leaders from the guest department, shared their thoughts and feelings about the weekend. I said I was impressed by the care everyone seems to take with everything—people, buildings, dishes, etc.—and that it feels very good being here.

It really does. I'm sitting here by this fire, curled up in a chair, feeling right at home. An occasional person walks through, and I can hear people moving around upstairs. It's peaceful, comfortable, safe and secure; no need to lock doors or worry about other people. Everyone is a friend. It's hard for me being in this situation, feeling like I need to be in a place like this. But our

search is about what Geoff and I both want, not just about what I want. If it were just me I'd try to find a way to be here at Sirius, but it's not just me. It could be another four years before Geoff is ready to do this. I hope it doesn't take that long! I wish we could just stay here.

I know I can't know enough in two days to be sure this would be the right place. I may visit others that are as good, or better. But I've spent 14 years of my life in Ozark and I'm tired of it! While there have been good times and I've grown and learned a lot, some-

Dinner last night felt like my concept of what community is all about.

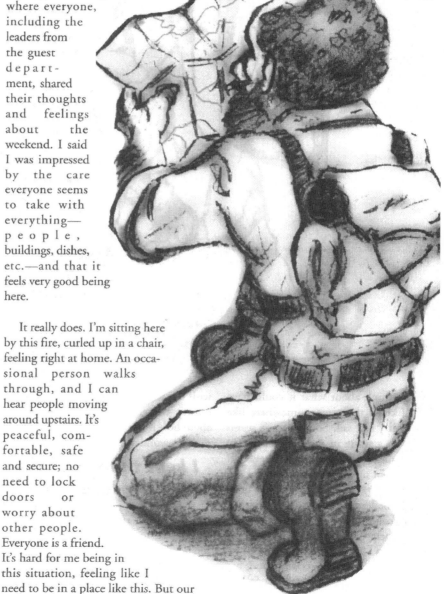

JACOB STEVENS

times I think about what it could have been like all this time, somewhere like this, and I feel sad. Sometimes it seems like such a waste of time to not live in community, and how much do I have left? I don't want to waste any more time.

Fourth day, morning. Geoff has gone with the building crew to do some logging. He'll be coming back early to help fix lunch and I'll help with that. I decided to stay here and go for a walk, then take it easy.

Last night's dinner was very good, but there wasn't much conversation for us. The members sat together, and we were

with the interns. It was comfortable and homey there, though. I was thinking about how it would be if we joined a community, wondering how long it would be

I kept thinking, "I'm really here! I'm dancing at Sirius!"

before we really had friends and felt included. It seems easy for me to feel left out and not part of things. I know people enjoy being with friends and carrying on their relationships, and it's not the same

when new people are there, so I understood the situation. But I expect it might be hard at first in a community, like moving anywhere.

It's probably been good being here the extra days. On the weekend the guest department people were here for us, and there were four of them and six of us, so they'd be around at meals, etc., to talk to us and answer questions. Now people are going about their normal business, and there aren't many of them. Most work outside, and only a few work here, so it's pretty deserted and quiet. If the building crew were working today on the conference center there would be lots of noise next door, but they are out logging. We have to find our own ways of being, which is more real.

I love this place, and I long to be part of something like this. Being here, though, would probably involve working outside the community, at least for several years. I have been feeling that I'd prefer a place where more people actually lived and worked in the community. That may happen here eventually. There is talk of building more member housing, community businesses, a larger greenhouse, and expanded guest housing. Right now, though, it would be more like moving to a new town in the ordinary way. You'd have to find a job, locate housing, and so forth. But you'd live here, or near here, and participate in the activities, work and meals and food sharing. It would be a good life, a large improvement on Ozark. But I'm not sure it is what we were picturing when we came up with this idea to live in community. We'll see, I guess, when we visit East Wind, what it's like to live in a community where people live and work all the time.

They talk here sometimes about how you can "create community" anywhere you live, and that community is not necessarily living with other people. Someone also said it's not so important what is accomplished in a physical sense in community but how it's done—the relationships and growth and learning of people. It's respect for your tools and your surroundings. It's your own growth and learning, peace of mind and spiritual focus that is important. It's the journey that matters, not the destination.

Fourth day, afternoon. I ended up making most of lunch, mixed together a

few batches of leftover beans, made some cornbread, and found some apples. Geoff made some salad with the apples, raisins, and sunflower seeds when he got back. Another member was there, fortunately, to find a recipe and give suggestions. It gave me another taste of what community life would be like. Geoff went back to help with the logging again. I guess he is doing my four hours of work for today. Most of what is going on today

Sometimes it seems like such a waste of time to not live in community, and how much do I have left?

is with the apprentices and a couple of members only. It seems like most of the work on the building and in the garden gets done by apprentices, as the members usually work only eight hours a week. I have decided to spend my last afternoon taking it easy, reading and writing. Hauling brush might be more fun, but this is my last day of vacation—might as well re-create!

New members, a family from the West Coast, live near us in this building, The father does carpentry, so he can earn a living anywhere. They have two young children and have been here five months. They probably aren't going to stay. They have decided they want a community where people mainly live together, that being the main focus and purpose, rather than as it is at Sirius, with the focus on the ecovillage, gardening, and conference center. This place doesn't suit them. Too much energy goes into the various projects, they said, rather than into real community living. In a way, I agree. It all seems quite scattered here. It's a nice place, but where is the community? I do understand the idea that "community" takes different forms, and this is a community in many ways, somewhat like a church is, but more so, because of the gardening and meal-sharing. But I think Geoff and I are looking for more than this in terms of people living together. Though we also want the gardening and sustainable living parts, too. Maybe we just won't find exactly what we want. Maybe we will have to create it ourselves ultimately, somehow. I'm sorry what I'm seeking isn't here. But I guess it's still a possibility. It'll be awhile before we are ready, and Sirius is still evolving.

Sue and Geoff Stone eventually found their community home in Earthaven Ecovillage in North Carolina, which they joined in 1999. Sue has been active on the membership and airspinning (minutes and decisions) committees, and Geoff on the finance committee.

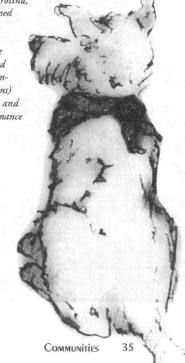

The author on day three of a desert solo vision quest, part of his apprenticeship program at Lost Valley Educational Center in Oregon.

THE
Dilettante's
JOURNEY

~ PART I ~

**How do you pick a community to join if
you're interested in . . . EVERYTHING?**

I yanked up my 5,000th root of the day. This one loosened and slid out of the dirt without a fight. I stood up and stretched my back. The sun was hotter than hell, and I knew there'd be a headache later, no matter how much water I drank. I was out of shape for this kind of work.

I saw Farmer, one of my hosts at Earthaven, balancing on a beam of his barn's new roof. I could tell from two hundred yards that he was smiling at me, checking in. I lifted both arms and released a "Wahoo!" I was blistered, burning up, and out in the field alone, but I was having a blast. I could hear some lively music coming from the boom box and tried to guess who it might be. Phish, maybe? I wondered briefly if they always listened to jam bands around here.

So this was Earthaven. I'd heard of this ecovillage for years and followed some of its progress with interest. Finally I was here, and better yet, I'd discovered the Gateway project.

Gateway Field was new at Earthaven. After the morning tour, Clark, the tour guide, had told me he suspected I would enjoy working with this particular gang. Earthaven had always seemed to have everything going for it—courses, businesses, at least two serious quarterly publications, and the whole place was off-grid—but it never had a farm. And for me, no community without one would ever do. Now I was clearing roots from several acres of freshly cleared topsoil, a forest just two weeks earlier, which lay between a sparkling stream on one side and a brand new barn-in-progress on the other.

I came in for a break and Farmer, 31, gave me a quick tour of his and his 21-year-old partner Brian's state-of-the-art tool shop, complete with every construction tool they would ever need. Oh, and did I mention the shop was solar-powered? Oh, and did I tell you it was inside a former U-Haul truck? Oh, and did I say the truck runs on biodiesel? I marveled at their super-rig and wondered how the hell these young home-builders afforded it.

Farmer pointed to the perfect spans of timber they were using for the barn's frame and said he'd negotiated them for free from a local lumber operation, which would otherwise burn, dump, or chip these "mill ends" as waste. He explained

that he and Brian had raised the money to buy and equip the truck from building homes for other Earthaven members, and raised most of the Gateway project money from multiple friendly loans from community members, with no collateral. "For ten years I've wanted to clear some acres and start a farm," he said, smiling. "This is my dream."

He mentioned that the band I'd heard earlier was not Phish, but Widespread Panic. Then he added, "But we don't just listen to jam bands around here." We got back to work—Brian and Farmer bickering on the roof, another visitor-helper and I standing below, hoisting up metal roofing and laughing at them.

I have told myself and others, like a mantra, that I aim to someday live in intentional community. I have read books and articles, watched documentaries, and traveled around the country to learn more about them. My values continue to evolve away from those of unsustainable cities and toward those of most intentional communities. I have enrolled in courses and even taken jobs that I hoped might lead me into the bosom of intentional community. But here I am, eight years later, still hanging out in Los Angeles.

My mother looked at me once and said matter-of-factly, "You're a dilettante." I was stung, and went straight to the dictionary to confirm that she was indeed calling me an indolent, decadent, grape-eating faux-aristocrat. She explained that she had simply observed me as something of a dabbler, a sampler of life. While the dictionary does offer some of the more scathing definitions I feared, I have come to understand what she meant. As you'll see, the way I conducted my search for community only proves her point.

> *I have told myself and others, like a mantra, that I aim to someday live in intentional community.*

Lost Valley

The Dilettante got his feet wet at Lost Valley Educational Center in Dexter, Oregon, in the summer of 1998. I'd learned about the apprenticeship program by way of an encounter with their lovely quarterly, Talking Leaves. I knew nothing of intentional communities and couldn't even imagine the physical environs of such a place, but Lost Valley's Apprenticeship

Program seemed the perfect antidote to my Los Angeles malaise. There I could slake my thirst for meaning, which had come to a ridiculous, raging boil.

I fired off an impassioned application for the program, confessing that for years as an actor I had been little more than a pretty-faced pitch-man for pharmaceuticals, detergents, booze, and even the British beef industry (I was the last beef spokesman before the outbreak of mad cow disease in England). I needed redemption. I wanted to change my life. Please accept me into your heavenly hippie home, et cetera. By early June, I was shopping for supplies and packing my bags.

Somewhere around Fresno, my vehicle vomited oil all over the interstate and broke down at a gas station. I broke down myself, blubbering and wondering just what the hell I had done with my life. Somehow I managed to sleep, right there in that buzzing parking lot, my first night ever in my brand new (30-year-old) VW camper.

Brian Love of the Gateway Field project, whom the author worked with during his stay at Earthaven Ecovillage in North Carolina.

Leaving my shitty life in L.A. was going to be even lonelier and more terrifying than I'd imagined.

Somehow I made it to Lost Valley, and the land's loveliness unraveled itself: sunny fields, gardens, meadows, streams, fir and cedar forests, cabin clusters, yurts, teepees, a solar shower, sheep, chickens, and children. The residents greeted me quietly, sweetly, but I could tell they were excited about the

(He would prove a lasting influence on me, a role model even to this day.) I was disoriented and ambivalent, but decided to join the pile in one of the cars. We got to Eugene a half-hour later and I dissolved into the crowd, still in some culture shock. Two hours later I was drenched and loopy from do-si-do-ing with the locals. Spirits fairly soared on the ride home, and I found comfort and relief in the easy camaraderie.

It didn't last. Within a week I was hermetically sealing myself into my camper. I was struggling hard with something I could only identify as "spiritual correctness," a somewhat stifling community rectitude—and I took the only refuge I knew, solitude. The apprenticeship program called for extraordinary immersion in personal-growth practices of all kinds, and that alone would have tested me. But then, even the everyday protocols in the community, like greetings in passing, seemed suffused with an odd, reflective hyper-awareness, a heaviness I could hardly pinpoint, much less address.

Was it my lack of reverence? Should I have more respect, be more spiritual? Was it all in my head? Or was everyone just stilted and morose? I could not know, and it left a relatively hardened city boy like me questioning his marbles. In meetings, for example, custom called for avoidance of the word "but" for its negative energy, in favor of the word "and." I

I went straight to the dictionary to confirm that she was indeed calling me an indolent, decadent, grape-eating faux-aristocrat.

---

arrival of this new batch of summer apprentices. Julie, a tall, gentle, lovely woman maybe a little older than me, looked into my eyes and furrowed her brow.

"You're very different from how I imagined." I guess she'd formed some ideas from the L.A. actor's essay.

"Maybe it's the shaved head," I replied, smiling. Right now I looked more like Shel Silverstein than George Clooney. I wasn't exactly sure what she'd expected, but I liked Julie already. She was real.

I heard talk of a folk dance that night at a school gymnasium in town. I think the idea came from Chris, master gardener, talented editor of *Talking Leaves*, and regional music aficionado.

tried to flow with it, but I was clearly a square peg (I mean, "and" I was a square peg) in a round hole. I was craving an ease, a lightness of being, maybe even a dirty joke to make things feel more grounded, more real. And the more I struggled, the worse it got.

My frustration, of course, aimed directly outward. In the morning sharing circle, I shifted and huffed while the other apprentices, who were roughly college-age and nearly all female, seemed only to want to process feelings—from last night's dramas to early childhood traumas. I was 30, male, and garden time was wasting. When my turn came it was always "Pass." In return for my hissing, judgmental bile, the women outvoted me nightly on the choice of kitchen-duty music (Ani Difranco—All-Ani, All-The-Time).

And so the tension mounted. At the weekly Well-Being meeting, I first encountered the process of "milling." Milling was where you drifted around a room from one person to the next, in a room full of people doing the same, stopping long enough to express aloud the single thought or feeling you would never otherwise want that person to hear. Then the other person got a turn, and then you moved on to the next one, and so on. The idea was, of course, noble: to foster deep honesty in a safe environment, to face difficult feelings from within and without, to grow and build a spiritual relationship with self, with other—with life!

have worn them out. But one day Dianne, a Lost Valley founder and elder, turned her infinite eyes on me during a meeting. She had the face (and spirit) of a shaman. She held both my hands and declared "I hope you stay." Not "good riddance" or "stop acting like an ass," but "I hope you stay." My momentum to escape broke then and there, and I finished the summer. She remains my dear friend.

By summer's end, the mood had lightened to the point where Larry and Karin, an important couple in the community, shocked a group of us at lunch with the hilarious, sexy, scandalous story of how they'd first met. I'd always liked them, but now I was getting the realness, the ease—the dirty joke—that I'd craved all summer. Only a couple of weeks earlier Larry and I had locked horns in a public, symbolic battle—a

I came up with a real humdinger of heartfelt communication: "You have a muscular back."

I wanted no part of it. I thought I did at first. But my virgin Well-Being had been torture, plain and simple. Conflicted and constipated, I faced one after another and croaked out some inanities that, mercifully, I don't remember. I finally got to one young woman, a fellow apprentice, and came up with a real humdinger of heartfelt communication: "You have a muscular back." I don't remember her reply, but it was downhill from there. Soon I was making myself scarce, same time every week.

Don't get me wrong. All told, the apprenticeship was a great success, in fact a dilettante's delight. I soaked up gardening wisdom at the foot of the master, Chris Roth; I learned (failed) to build a fire with sticks; I studied herbs and made candles; I stuffed myself giggly on roadside blackberries; I participated in powerful self-help seminars—taking my turn before 30 others to expand with loving, cosmic compassion one moment and to shudder in wracking

The field at Green Gulch Zen Center near Muir Woods, California.

grief the next; I swam naked in rivers and dodged rattlesnakes in the desert while fasting, alone, for three days—the mighty Vision Quest. And, ultimately, I was offered at least a provisional home at Lost Valley, if I so chose.

But between the high points, the doldrums always returned. I was always "almost-leaving." That poor community, I must

climax of tension between me and the community. Now as we laughed together I realized I could not blame "them" for my somber, often suffocating summer. I'd been the creator.

Lost Valley shaped my reveries so deeply that for years I wondered whether I should return there for the longer term. But the final analysis was clear: the Dilettante's adventures would continue.

Maplewood Farms

After Lost Valley, I learned not to be quite so dramatic with my search. A dilettante doesn't pull up all his roots and "change his life," sight unseen. To start with, he opts for smaller samples, and in that spirit, I arranged a night's stay with Maplewood Farms (not its real name), many hundreds of miles east of Lost Valley.

I love driving cross-country about once a year to visit my folks in Atlanta, so Maplewood was reasonably on the route. Also, I loved to read about Maplewood, more than about any other place. It just seemed too damned good to be true. They shared their income. They were stewards to hundreds of acres of wild forestland. They were numerous and, from the photographs, clearly happy. They played music in the woods and jumped off rocks into the river and ate together and worked harmoniously in any of a handful of bustling, impressive businesses. And this part of the country was stunningly beautiful. As the camper putt-putted over low, green, rolling hills, I could not wait to get there.

I hated it. I felt unwelcome from the first five minutes. They plugged me in immediately with the dinner crew, but for hours I chopped onions alone, failing to connect positively with anyone (I guess the newbie always gets onion duty). Some of the people were particularly ragged and, if not actually drunk, then two steps away. A woman brought a 12-pack of Budweiser to dinner and dropped it loudly on the front porch. The men vaguely glowered in my direction.

The Dilettante was not accustomed to such treatment. The next morning I managed to gain the favorable attention of one lone angel, Mary Beth (not her real name), who introduced herself at breakfast and offered to give me a tour of the land. I almost wept in appreciation and relief. We walked and talked, around the pottery shed and through the cow pasture and down near the river. I was full of questions and she was ready to confide some inside scoops, certainly feeling some frustrations of her own.

It seemed Maplewood had been having a hard time keeping some residents in line—and keeping newcomers at all. They had a music and rec room, which I think they renamed the "wreck"

Aboard the SSCS vessel Farley Mowat.

Sea Shepherd Conservation Society

After a couple of years volunteering for environmental and political causes, I took a position as office manager with what I considered the purest, most bad-ass organization in the world: Sea Shepherd Conservation Society. Its founder Captain Paul Watson, at a mere 50, was a legend already. He has called Greenpeace (which he helped found but then disowned) "the Avon Ladies of the environmental movement," and he rams fishing and whaling ships at sea and sinks them in port, though without a single human injury and only if those poachers persist in violating international conservation law.

Watson is a controversial figure, as one might expect. I came to the organization admiring him but otherwise without any personal investment. The Dilettante, however, chafed in his job duties. Set up payroll? How on Earth does one do that? After six months of office managing I quit. I disliked the work, yes, but I positively loathed my direct supervisor (who was fired just two weeks after I quit). Nevertheless, in this role I had helped select about half the ship's current crew of volunteers, and I'd always wished to be one of them. So now, since I was unemployed anyway, I took the opportunity to sail aboard the *Farley Mowat* from San Diego up to Seattle as a Sea Shepherd volunteer.

I hated it. I felt unwelcome from the first five minutes.

room, since the evenings unfailingly ended in drunken brawling. In a vicious cycle, Maplewood became gun-shy from hosting a series of uninterested visitors—thus the cold reception for anyone not bubbling over to join the community, and thus more uninterested visitors. Mary Beth herself was struggling to extract herself from a troubled relationship with a young punk I certainly didn't like on sight. The feeling, I noticed, was mutual as we passed him on our walk.

I have no idea how Maplewood is doing now, a handful of years later. I never again visited their website or read their materials. I wish them well and take simple solace in knowing that I and, eventually, Mary Beth, both made our escapes.

I saw no combat on the voyage. I did wage one battle, though, against seasickness. I swooned and burped for days but never puked. (So did I win?) Anyway, even the salty crew admitted these were the worst seas they had seen all summer, and a few of them took to their beds for a spell. At night it was like trying to sleep on a giant roller coaster. I lay in my bunk for three nights, listening to the ship pop and crack and groan like a person, and wondered how the hell the thing stayed together. I considered a watery death and felt surprising serenity.

The crew could not have embraced me more warmly than they did, from the first night when they handed me a beer to the last waves good-bye as they putted and blared their way out of San Francisco Harbor. And they formed a perfectly harmonious, if unlikely, community. They had their strict assignments and carried them out as if in the military. Some had come on board only a few weeks ago and others hadn't left in years. The head mechanic was a crusty Brit in his early sixties. His assistant was a woman in her forties, soon to be the mother of an Iraq war veteran. A young woman from Germany, a conservatory-level musician, was 19. One gentle

I am not sure if anyone ever really gets used to the impossibly loud, stabbing clang of a monk's hand-bell at 4 a.m. I can tell you that the Dilettante did not. However, for the first time in my life, I meditated in deep peace and comfort for two virtually uninterrupted hours, almost every morning. The Zendo at Green Gulch was the most serene and beautiful sanctuary I have ever seen. Giant globes hung low from the high vaulted ceiling, turned only to the dimmest setting in the

For the first time in my life, I meditated in deep peace and comfort for two virtually uninterrupted hours, almost every morning.

Canadian in his early 30s was a Disney animator. He drew hilarious, uncanny caricatures of the whole crew.

I disembarked in San Francisco, by the way, only because of the heavy seas. Seattle was another five days away, and I ain't stupid. But it saddened me to leave the Farley Mowat, and I could tell that a few crewmembers genuinely hoped I would change my mind. So to this day, the Dilettante will occasionally rub his chin and consider future whale-saving voyages with the Sea Shepherd "community."

Green Gulch Zen Center

Green Gulch is just too beautiful and good to be true. But there it sits anyway, successful for decades now as a Zen retreat center and sprawling seaside organic farm in Marin County, California. A stone's throw from the Golden Gate Bridge, towering eucalyptus trees line the steep hills surrounding their northern California land, which also neighbors Muir Woods, a jewel of the state's redwood preserves.

I, the Dilettante, am a spiritual seeker without a practice and an organic farmer without

SSCS crew member Joost Engelbert shows author Frank Beauty (right) the view from the crow's nest.

a farm. So, three springs ago, Green Gulch's six-month farm apprenticeship program was calling out to me. Apprentices participate fully in the community's formal Zen practice, as well as in the curriculum of the farm program. But before I could establish my candidacy, I had to complete a two-week trial run of meditation and work.

pre-dawn. The quiet had substance, blanketing us and keeping us warm, and as the sun slowly took over and lit the windows high above the birds lifted the blanket, one chirp at a time.

This practice actually felt right. I could almost imagine a life here. But alas, I am a you-know-what, and so this two-week trial—a dilettante-detection device of sorts—discovered me and gently rooted me out. While other work-students at bedtime were reading Zen Mind, Beginner's Mind, I had hooked into The Party's Over—Oil, War and the Fate of Industrial Societies, and was freaking myself out but good. Also, I was chatting a lot with the farm apprentices and filling my notebook with names of nearby farms and farmers, stars from the world of sustainable agriculture. I started to chomp a bit at the bit.

I didn't leave Green Gulch because I was drowning in spiritual torpor. No, in fact I was delighted by the easy and down-to-earth, time-for-the-dishes kind of geist around the place. And I actually enjoyed the rigor. Green Gulch would emerge a clear and formidable contender for the Dilettante's affections, but I had only two weeks' vacation and suddenly much else to see. So after only half my scheduled stay, I set out on a one-week, whirlwind, seat-of-the-pants northern California sustainable-farm communities tour.

To be continued in the Winter '06 issue.

Frank Beaty works as a medical editor, volunteers in progressive politics, and is helping start both a community garden and an alternative fuel co-operative. As of this writing, he still lives in Los Angeles.

Author Frank Beaty, left, at Teaching Drum Outdoor School in Wisconsin.

THE Dilettante's JOURNEY, PART II

How do you pick a community to join if you're interested in . . . EVERYTHING?

BY FRANK BEATY

*A*uthor Frank Beaty considers himself a dilettante because he's "something of a dabbler, a sampler of life." In Part One he described his brief visits to Earthaven Ecovillage in North Carolina, Lost Valley Educational Center in Oregon, Maplewood Farms (not its real name), Green Gulch Zen Center in California, and his voyage aboard a shipboard community, the Farley Mowat, as a volunteer for the Sea Shepherd Conservation Society. Never staying in one community long, the Dilettante next visited sustainable education centers in northern California.

Occidental Arts and Ecology Center (OAEC)

I knew very little about Occidental Arts and Ecology Center (OAEC) except that reportedly the land was beautiful. It was the first stop on my spontaneous whirlwind northern California eco-community tour.

Redwoods, blue skies, the ocean just a few miles over the golden hills to the west, and crisp, technicolor brilliance form my lasting impressions of the area. OAEC's entire rural property seemed to rest on one hillside, so that its tilt was strangely uniform, and pockets of steeper slopes above hid clusters of yurts and cottages, barely visible behind lush foliage. As I started along the path, I felt a tingle. This place was enchanted.

The man who greeted me quietly in a French accent, Harold, offered to guide me to the gardens. We passed through a leafy archway of vines. Upon first glimpse of the first garden, I quite actually choked up. The Dilettante had sampled beauty in his day, but this field surpassed much of it.

Next I met Doug, head gardener and botanist, and his apprentices. As we worked and talked, my respect for Doug, for other residents I met at OAEC, and for the organization, took hold and deepened. The intentional community is called Sowing Circle; OAEC is its research and teaching foundation. Its last job posting, for example, called for someone to manage a water quality monitoring project for the region. Many of the OAEC staff are scientists as well as activists and communitarians, working in their region and nationwide to fight for environmental and related issues. On site, they teach courses in ecology, sustainable building, community, and art. Adam Wolport, a professional painter, directs OAEC's Arts Program and co-leads its course on starting new intentional communities.

Friday evening I attended the 2nd Annual Chautauqua show at OAEC's new outdoor amphitheater. This is a program based on the spirit of the Chautauqua movement that spread over the United States a century ago, which combined lecture, debate, entertainment, and practical education to benefit rural areas.

The audience of area locals murmured and filled the rich, polished hardwood benches. Community craftspeople had only recently built these benches into the earth, forming a permanent amphitheater under a twinkling grove of huge

OCCIDENTAL ARTS AND ECOLOGY CENTER

Community members, including Doug, the head gardener, at OAEC in California made quite a good impression on the author.

performances and engaging Native American bands. During a side-splitting piano revue that lampooned members of the community, I turned and found Doug in the audience when his name came up. I hardly recognized him; his quiet composure had dissolved into beet-red uncontrollable laughter. A woman brought a stool to the stage and delivered an eloquent update on the successful local fight against genetically modified foods.

As I started along the path, I felt a tingle. This place was enchanted.

oaks. A beautiful stage, also of hardwood, completed the circle and a stone-pit fire marked its center. Faerie lights strung in the trees filled the area with a glow. Before the show had even begun, I sat and basked in the feeling that this was my kind of place and these were my kind of people.

A fair young man opened the show playing a lullaby on tall, weird instrument made from an African gourd, which he had learned to play during his time in the Peace Corps in West Africa. He plucked the two dozen strings and sang perhaps the most heartbreaking song I have ever heard. After a moment of resistance I let the tears flow. No use fighting it.

After him, and separated by lively musical interludes, came mimes and hilarious skits and historical lectures re-enacted with poignancy and passion. I watched wild spoken-word

Every act was professional-grade, and the talent was all local. Afterwards, people visited friends they saw there or formed small groups at the fire for more singing and laughter.

The magic of the Chautauqua fulfilled every promise of the tingle I'd felt when I first came to OAEC, and it remains among my most cherished memories. I left reluctantly that night. And I still wonder how I might breach their ranks someday and return there, to fill a role and make a home. But theirs is a serious operation, and the Dilettante would have to raise his game a few notches before hoping to play with the big kids.

Ecology Action

Next I visited John Jeavons, the legendary gardener, author, and teacher of French-intensive, bio-intensive-style gardening at his farm, Ecology Action, near Willits, California. Jeavons shows you how to grow more vegetables than you ever thought possible, and on less land than you could ever imagine (and in fact wrote a book with a similar title). He started his tour with a classroom slideshow covering the history of human population growth, which took a slight dip during the Black Plague on its way to today's explosion. He told our group of visitors that the end of cheap hydrocarbon energy is upon us and that, at our present rate of soil erosion, thanks to today's methods of commercial agriculture, we have at best 40 years of topsoil left worldwide. At best.

In short, he scared the bejeezus out of us. His burly, grizzled presence added *gravitas* to his dire message. But he also soothed us with assurances that, with the proper techniques, we could grow enough food to feed a family of four, all in a small garden plot.

Next he led us down the terraced gardens of his farm. The flat land that holds Ecology Action's buildings abruptly ends at a cliff-side slope of 45 degrees. This steep hill is actually the growing area, and it looks out over the valley town of Willits, surely thousands of feet below. As you stand on the upper edge of this field, the effect is positively vertiginous,

and I have never seen any farm so majestically severe. Cold springtime mist-clouds whip up this slope from the nearby Pacific, and dry August sun bakes the rocky soil. Often this farm endures these weather extremes in one day.

Most farmers would probably not buy this property, but here it is, flourishing. Jeavons has deep, sure knowledge of what works, knowledge borrowed from Middle-Ages Europe and gained from his own years of personal and staff research. You name the obstacle; he can overcome it. Hardship is his game.

Theirs is a serious operation. The Dilettante would have to raise his game a few notches.

He showed us the best way to compost, a method radically different from anything I'd learned elsewhere. He defined double-digging and demonstrated the most energy-efficient physical movements needed to do it. He urged the examination of exact calories burned growing a crop, versus calories yielded in that crop. He showed us cheap and easy ways to grow cash crops like lavender and prepare them for market. All his helpful hints rang with the knowing that tough times lie ahead for us all. But I didn't mind. I found his tone hopeful and his practical wisdom hugely valuable.

Ecology Action hosts a handful of well-educated, sincere interns from around the world, and my own tradition required that I consider, at least briefly, joining their ranks. But the cost of the internship was more than I could afford, and despite my deep respect for Jeavons and my keen interest in his approach, upon honest reckoning it became pretty clear that this weren't no place for no Dilettante.

Teaching Drum Outdoor School

In the summer of 2005 I was off again to visit intentional communities. I also set out to learn some basics of wilderness skills, of living on the land, Native-American style. I didn't necessarily want to live like that forever, but I hoped to find a viable community around such values and practices, and see where it might lead. Did such a place exist?

Teaching Drum Outdoor School hides deep in the North Woods of Wisconsin. The school offers a longer-term, more authentically Native American approach than your average Tom Brown-type primitive skills weekend course. Students at Teaching Drum, called "seekers," commit to a year-long course, living around a big national forest lake through all four seasons. In the warm months they learn tanning, fire-building, for-

The Dilettante was also mighty impressed with the show-stopping Chautauqua performance held in OAEC's outdoor amphitheater.

At Teaching Drum Outdoor School the author got introduced to the art of traveling by canoe.

aging for wild edibles, and Native purification ceremonies. In winter they learn to make snow-cave homes and then live in them. According to the founder, Tamarack Song, none of these skills will really live in you until you've learned to connect deeply with the land. That process takes time.

Tamarack had a huge gray beard and round specs, and he spoke softly, unblinking, as he greeted me. One of Tamarack's assistants, Glen, drove me from the school's cabins out to the lake where the students lived. We hiked through a rolling forest of birch and pine until we came to a primitive shelter in a clearing. We met a few students, then Glen canoed me across

red when raw, brownish-gray when cooked, lung generally had to be fried to a crisp or else it was too chewy and spongy. It tasted like liver.) During dinner conversations flowed. People ranged in age from roughly 19 to 45, and even included a 12-year-old boy and his parents.

The instructors called meetings daily, all 25 or so gathering in a big circle under the birches. Here the casual conversations would meander from where best to harvest burdock to some deep personal or spiritual matter, long silences between topics and even between words. I spent the first half hour wondering "so when are we going to get down to the busi-

The casual conversations would meander from where best to harvest burdock to some deep personal or spiritual matter.

a wide, beautiful lake to meet my host camp, where we met more people, clad mostly in forest-green khaki. I bade Glen farewell and collapsed in my tent.

That evening another camp crossed the lake in canoes to join us for dinner. They brought eggs, wild greens, fruit, and some mystery meat, and combined it with our stashes to make a feast for a dozen. (The meat, I learned, was deer lung. Bright

ness at hand?" Eventually I realized this *was* the business at hand. The practical and the personal, instruction and inspiration, met and merged without transition. I began to see these meetings pulse and flow with the spirit of this, a very real community.

This crowd had personality and a keen wit. A student from Latvia, Alex, officially and repeatedly requested a class on eating bugs. He was maybe the skinniest guy I've ever met,

A Teaching Drum student prepares deer lung for the evening supper.

and was soulful and hilarious. The bug-eating class, despite his earnest consternation, had become a running community joke. I met young people, evolved and thoughtful, each of

Working feverishly and face-first in searing heat, I ran out of drinking water.

them on a quiet, profound quest for meaning. Some were anarchists, some poets. A few wore their depth (or damage) on their sleeves, while some had the light, urbane demeanor that I am more accustomed to on the "outside."

Another student, Matt, had appeared at the first meeting in a full buckskin suit he'd made himself, talking slowly through a toothpick about a fallen tree he'd found, in case anyone wanted to join him in a birch-bark harvest. Giving much credit to Teaching Drum, he told me later that he'd transformed himself from a belligerent, alcoholic, right-wing Navy sailor into the person I saw now: a man with clear eyes and a calm, even heroic competence. He liked to look far away into the forest, listening to things I could not hear, and then come back to me quickly with a twinkle and a teasing question.

Another student, Katy, single-handedly saved my ass on at least three occasions. When I'd first arrived and was searching forever and in vain for a tent site, Katy went searching herself, unnoticed. She returned presently, tugging at my sleeve, and led me to a perfect, level clearing. Late another afternoon, watching the skies, she suggested that we put a tarp over my tent, against my strong urge to stay near the fire and continue eating cashews. She worked like a mule on that tarp, with my feeble help, and got devoured by mosquitoes in the process. Throughout that night a vicious thunderstorm raged, but my tent stayed dry. I would have been a sopping, suicidal mess without her.

Days later I accepted the honor of serving as fire-tender for the sacred sweat-lodge ceremony. An insulated earthen dome became an oven as Tamarack led 20 naked students and teachers inside for a Native purification ceremony. That was their test; mine was to keep the huge fire outside blazing, while hauling massive, red-hot boulders from fire to lodge, one after another. Working feverishly and face-first in searing heat, I ran out of drinking water. But I was alone and couldn't abandon my post during the most serious ritual of the year. Just as my vision faded and I started to expire, Katy loped out from the forest like some mute angel, gallons of water in each hand. She'd served me and saved me repeatedly, automatically, with perfect timing, and without being asked. And not just for me—for everyone. It was simply her role: how she served, loved, and belonged.

During my short stay I learned some of the art and science of the canoe; I picked wild edibles for dinner; I learned to poop in nature and wipe with damp bog moss (the most difficult challenge of the week). I learned that mosquitoes will kill you if you let them—they'll just keep sucking, and call a thou-

Teaching Drum students found their deer lung dinner delicious.

sand friends over to suck, until you disappear in a terrible cloud and you have no blood left and you are dead.

I watched four young women take apart a road-killed deer with small knives, quietly and without complaint or hesitation. Over time they filled a box with neatly wrapped bundles of meat. The smell of guts hit me, and I watched the black-green flies swarm and bite. I found a leafy branch and shooed vicious flies from the women's exposed arms and faces. Allison sang a lovely song and conversations rose and fell, but this was difficult work, physically and emotionally. At least two of the women were vegan. One woman, Chelsea, went to bed before sundown, exhausted, and dreamed all night about the deer.

For three days the seekers fasted in preparation for the dreaded Mosquito Course. Tamarack declares mosquitoes the greatest teacher of his life. Naturally, he takes his students through the same kind of hell he's suffered. This course begins with a purifying sweat ceremony and culminates with the students venturing out to their own private forest spot, naked and still, and letting the satanic swarms have their way unhindered. Until I knew for sure whether I would participate, I fasted with the rest. Even after Tamarack and I decided that I would sit out the course (I ain't that stupid), I found very little

Alex, a student from Latvia, officially and repeatedly requested a class on eating bugs.

> # *I watched four young women take apart a road-killed deer with small knives, quietly and without complaint or hesitation.*

food. I ate three apples and a handful of Brazil nuts over my last two days.

I decided to leave after day five, and the goodbyes were sweet and true all around. But I confess I giggled like an idiot as I drove off, my heart already set on the first fried-chicken buffet I could find.

My time at Teaching Drum humbled me some. And no matter how madly the Dilettante dashed away from the place, I positively glowed with the discovery of yet another diamond out there, another priceless and precious community of people. For those people I hold nothing but love and gratitude.

Earthaven Ecovillage

Which brings me back to the remainder of my visit to Earthaven Ecovillage in North Carolina, in the spring of 2006. As evening came after a day of plucking roots from the Gateway Field agricultural project, I made my way to the Trading Post cafe for a snack and some wireless emails, courtesy of stream-

fed hydro-power. Chris Farmer (called "Farmer"), the project's co-founder, came in, as he'd promised, to buy me a beer. His gratitude for my handful of volunteer hours at Gateway Field, I assured him, was excessive. But I accepted his kindness and raised my bottle in excited praise for the barn, the field, the whole damn thing.

Farmer's brother Derek had donated a full day out there too, and apparently he did so fairly often despite having plenty of work in Asheville. I had grown quite fond of his honesty and genuine kindness. As we wrapped up work earlier, Farmer had approached Derek and thanked him sweetly, adding that without his help they could never have finished the roof today. They hugged each other tight.

"You don't even know," Farmer told me over his beer. "My entire life, Derek has never raised his voice to me in anger. Not once. And growing up, even though he's four years older, every time I wanted to go with him and his friends somewhere, he always let me. Every time." All day I'd resonated with Farmer, with his co-founder Brian Love, with their commitment and vision to their Gateway agricultural project. And earlier, seeing Earthaven's land, learning about its projects, and meeting its people had excited and moved me just as much. But not until that moment, as I swigged my beer and looked around on the porch of the Trading Post, did I know I could make a life here.

But first things first.

I've scheduled a little talk with the Dilettante.

Frank Beaty works as a medical editor, volunteers in progressive politics, and is helping start both a community garden and an alternative fuel co-operative. As of this writing, he still lives in Los Angeles.

Interns and work exchangers learn a wide variety of sustainability and community living skills, like Volunteers For Peace volunteer Audrey Lothe, who learned to build with cob at O.U.R. Ecovillage in British Columbia.

What Interns and Work Exchangers Say
About Us...

I absolutely loved my stay at Lost Valley, recalls Polly Robinson, who served as an intern and later a live-in course participant at Lost Valley Educational Center in Oregon. "I loved being surrounded by people of all ages who genuinely cared for me, and the generally relaxed atmosphere of the place, I felt like I was a community member the whole time I was there."

Communities magazine asked a handful of temporary communitarians—work exchangers, interns, and live-in course participants—to share their experiences of temporary community. These women and men reported that their lessons were often planting and building; their teachers, the gardens, animals, and children.

Nathaniel Nordin-Tuininga, who also lived at Lost Valley, first as a work trader, then an intern, and lastly as a residential student, is equally enthusiastic about his time there.

"Interacting with Lost Valley and participating in both their permaculture and personal growth workshops taught me so much about myself, my relationship to the surrounding environment, and my connection

> *"I went through a full-on transformation."*

with others. I learned a great deal about my own capacity to grow and develop into the person I most want to be, while cultivating a harmonious relationship to the rest of the natural world. I was introduced to new ways of interacting with plants and animals in order to meet my basic needs. I received personal instruction and hands-on training in land and garden projects. I participated in yoga, dance, mediation, saunas, hot tubs, stargazing, sports, games, group outings and other events—and always had an amazing group of people to share these experiences with. And emotional well-being was better attended to at Lost Valley than in any other community I have visited or been involved with."

Similarly, work exchanger Ron Laverdiere found true utopia at La'akea Community in Hawai'i, not because it was perfect—but because it was real.

"At La'akea I was able to be fully honest with myself in all aspects," he reports. "This came from being transparent in relationships, offering support whenever it

---

"I learned to stretch myself."

---

was needed and feeling supported at all times, plus the willingness of community members to connect in speech or dance or music."

Even the simple joy of eating food on the same day he helped harvest it amounted to a life-changing experience for him.

"Everything in my life was up for question and I resolved many issues with the help of the community," he adds. "I went through a full-on transformation during my time there."

Surprising perhaps is the amount of time such a transformation required. In Ron's case—just a month.

As enthusiastic as many folks are about their time in community, some had concerns as well.

Nathaniel notes that finding enough personal space at Lost Valley was challenging at times.

Michael "Mojohito" Tchudi, an apprentice and then a work trader at Emerald Earth community in northern California, found that the community's policies regarding interpersonal interactions only served to become chal-

lenges themselves. "A disadvantage of maintaining a practice of nonconfrontational communication is that it was difficult and awkward to address issues of disrespectful or passive-aggressive behavior with permanent members of the community," he says.

Sometimes the short-term nature of the experience hindered the social acceptance of people who don't have an outgoing nature.

"As an introvert who doesn't make friends very quickly, I did sometimes miss the close relationships that long-term living situations have provided me in the past," recalls Carrie Dickerson, who lived at Twin Oaks Community in Virginia for three months as a conference intern. "This was also my first experience living away from the city."

What's in a Name?

Work Exchanger, Work Trader. The community exchanges room and board for labor. Usually it's a straight-up trade, but sometimes the work exchanger pays a small fee; often just to cover the cost of their food.

Intern, Apprentice. The community offers a more formally organized educational experience with onsite courses and workshops as well as room and board, in exchange for labor and a substantial fee. An internship or apprenticeship is often in a specific area, such as garden intern, natural building apprentice, and so on.

Residential Student, Course Participant. The community (or one of its members) offers a formal educational program such as a class, weekend workshop, or longer-term course, and room and board, for a fee (and sometimes for work in the community as well). Community-based courses can include yoga, meditation, permaculture, natural building, herbal medicine, and so on.

—Editor

THEME ✦ WHAT THEY SAY

Polly Robinson

Michael "Mojohito" Tchudi

Molly Morgan

RICK BEACH

Mostly, however, the people we talked with found that their growth experiences in community far outweighed any challenges.

"Most notably I discovered that my capacity for physical work and exertion is far greater than I had thought, and that I am capable of working in rather extreme heat," observes Mojohito. "Maintaining a lifestyle of living close to the land and contributing in projects that directly benefitted both the community and myself was so satisfying."

Work trader Molly Morgan turned 50 during her three-month stay at Emerald Earth, a milestone that she says was accidental in timing but rich with its rewards.

"I learned to stretch myself while there," says Molly, whose interests were building and gardening. "I was learning so many new things, and I was really clumsy and slow at them, but the community members were unfailingly supportive and patient with me. I learned that even at mid-life I could feel awk-

What Community Hosts Should Know

"Be as transparent and up-front about expectations and opportunities as possible, such as, for example, different housing options available, and possibility for longer-term participation in the community," advises Michael "Mojohito" Tchudi, who served as an apprentice and work trader at Emerald Earth in California. "Also, permanent members need to be highly proactive in addressing internal issues and personality conflicts to minimize the negative effects these can cause on short-term residents," he cautions.

"Thoughtful planning, organization, and setting realistic expectations are key," advises Jodie Emmett, who has a background in nonprofit management and program development, and recently completed a 10-week natural building course in a rural ecovillage. "Expressing a realistic picture of the program will allow potential course participants to determine if it will be a good fit for them. Telling people the community is one thing but providing another underestimates the participants. This kind of dynamic requires the community to go above and beyond the students' expectations in order to succeed, but it usually just sets up the community for failure."

"The Emerald Earth people needed to interview me and also work with me to be sure they all thought I would fit in," recalls Molly Morgan, who was a work trader at Emerald Earth. "You can do a lot of interviewing, but there's always a vibe that's important to check out in person before you both commit to serious time together."

"Having a personal liaison or 'go-to' person from the community is helpful," suggests Travis Fowler, who was a work exchanger at La'akea in Hawaii. "Also, having an up-front agreement to how long a visit is going to last and/or how to deal with situations that aren't working out is very important. There shouldn't be any surprises surrounding this."

Ron Laverdiere, also a work exchanger at La'akea, found morning check-ins especially helpful. "Morning check-ins were a really good way of connecting community residents to each other," he recalls. "It also helped me to feel that I was important to the community. I had everyone's attention at least once every day."

—D.F.

ward and untalented and still be okay with learning new skills and processes. It was humbling and encouraging."

For many temporary residents it seems that the most amazing experience a community offered them was the simple gift of caring, a social blessing many reported to be far too rare in their regular lives in fast-paced, money-obsessed mainstream society.

"I loved the fact that the well-being of the people of the community was just as important as the work," says Polly Robinson about Lost Valley. "I loved that there was such a diversity of thought and ways of life, yet we all accepted each other, and for the most part, lived together in peace."

"I learned a great deal about my own capacity to grow and develop into the person I most want to be, while cultivating a harmonious relationship to the rest of the natural world," notes Nathaniel about Lost Valley.

Although the level of participation for temporary workers obviously varies from community to community, Molly recalls that Emerald Earth welcomed her into a role far more substantial than that of visitor or observer. She was made to feel just as welcome at the meeting places or around the kitchen table as any of the full-time residents.

"The community members were very open about their lives and inclusive of the work traders," she says. "There were very few meetings to which we were not invited. I asked a lot of ques-

---

The problem occurs when participants see the gap between the founders' vision and what's actually on the ground.

She stressed that she'd never felt so well cared for her in life. "It was the first time I had ever had all my needs met—physical, emotional, social, spiritual. I had so much love and support that I felt like I was able to truly flourish."

Travis Fowler, another La'akea work exchanger, explained how living in such a radically nurturing environment truly proved to be the social garden he needed for growing into the person he desired to be in life. "I realized how emotionally closed I was in the 'real world,' how I could not express my true feelings or ask for what I wanted or needed for fear of being judged. The community was supportive and was a safe place to express myself. In the community, I felt more free to give the love I was keeping inside—and wow, that felt good!"

tions and I was never once told it was inappropriate to ask that nor received any other bad vibe. This was especially important to me because the community was dealing with some very serious personnel issues while I was there and not knowing what was going on would have been very uncomfortable."

The communities in our small sample seemed to do a pretty good job making their short-term residents comfortable, too. Although rustic accommodations can often be a visitor's complaint, many of these visiting workers stressed that the drastic and unique change in housing and food only amounted to an even better experience for them.

"I felt particularly grateful to stay in a beautiful, hand-built natural straw bale and cob house," Mojohito says.

Travis Fowler

Guillermo Maciel.

Jodie Emmett

"I was always well fed, and always had a warm dry place to sleep, so my physical comfort along with everything else was well taken care of," says Polly about Lost Valley. (Yet Nathaniel must not have thought so, since he recommends "improved housing options during the rainy season" for the same community.)

Although Molly disliked her stint living in a tent at Emerald Earth, she raved about the meals. "The food—it was sensational! I ate a lot and still lost 15 pounds. It was great!"

"What I really enjoyed was the intense focus of learning natural building techniques, the opportunity to share our experience in the natural building trade, and the variety of people and experiences in the program," recalls Guillermo.

Yet the couple was surprised to find differences between their expectations of a course and the reality they found once they got there. For example, they expected to be living in an intentional community, but soon realized that only the program

Sometimes they didn't know what was expected of them in terms of work hours, community participation, financial arrangements, or how long they could stay.

Two short-term residents both liked and felt some disappointment in their community stay. Guillermo A. Maciel and Jodie Emmett were participants a ten-week natural building course at a rural ecovillage. "I liked the natural building teachers immensely," Jodie reports. "Two instructors in particular were incredible people; each was an inspiration to me. I also enjoyed the natural building projects we worked on in other locations, as well as the optional weekend workshops on specialized topics. Plus, we were living in a gorgeous setting."

Ted Sterling

director/founder and his partner lived on the property on a permanent basis; the other founders either lived elsewhere or were no longer involved. "It would have been a lot easier for all of us if we were told in advance that there was no 'community' currently," Jodie observes. "And that the founding group was going through a transition and wanted natural buildings for what they would be doing sometime in the future."

Guillermo and Jodie also expected that they and the other students would have much more say in how they'd live their daily lives in a place which was billed as "your community." But they were often told that they couldn't do or make use of certain materials, go to certain locations or use certain buildings on the property, or employ certain kinds of communication styles. "It was difficult to tell when appropriate regulation of behavior was for the common good of our 'community' of students, and when it was just micro-managing us to fit the program director's vision of community," recalls Guillermo. It gradually became clear that there were three distinct parties on the property with different rights and responsibilities: the program director and his partner (resident owners who had final say on everything), the program staff (who reported to the program director), and the course participants, who didn't in fact have much decision-making voice. "There was a genuine intention to create an inclusive environment and avoid an 'us versus them' mentality," he adds, "but unfortunately, towards the end of the program, we failed in this intention." The process was exacerbated when the program director would change the rules about what was expected of participants, or what was or was not allowed on the property. It would have helped, Jodie points out, if there had been complete transparency about the role the students were to play in the evolution of the ecovillage.

Yet the couple respects the program director and admires what he's trying to accomplish in the project. They don't believe he misled the group consciously. "I think the idea that the community belonged to everyone is part of his vision about what a community could and should be, and he was trying to tell this to *himself*—like having his own personal mantra," Jodie speculates. "I don't think he could be honest with himself about the real situation, because visionaries can live inside their visions—the problem occurs when participants see the gap between the founders' vision and what's actually on the ground."

In fact, the most common concern of the people *Communities* interviewed was "structure." Many of these temporary residents, while insisting on the magic of their stay, admitted that the lack of a more formal structure ended up cheating their experiences out of some of the potential worth. They gave examples of not knowing what was expected of them in terms of work hours or community participation, a lack of communication regarding financial arrangements or how long they could stay, and sometimes a general lack of any kind of direction for the work they were expected to do.

Several suggested that communities who host short-term workers designate a go-between who could meet with them not just as the beginning of their stay, but several times throughout the visit to check their progress.

One suggested that communities also work to get a commitment from long-term residents in terms of their treatment and involvement with visitors. "Make sure there is a solid commitment on the part of as many community members as possible for including temporary members and rolling them into the fabric of daily life," advises Ted Sterling, who served as a three-month intern at Dancing Rabbit Ecovillage in Missouri.

But Ted certainly liked what he saw at Dancing Rabbit, so much so that a year and a half later he moved back and remains as a full-time resident today.

"I met my partner here. We now live here in a home we built and have had a child together, Aurelia, who is not quite six months old," he says. "Talk about life changing! I consider myself a changed person."✿

Darin Fenger works as a newspaper reporter in southern Arizona.

Planning Your Own Community Adventure?
Field-Tested Advice from Interns and Work Exchangers

If you're planning your own short-term stay in community, consider the advice of these experienced community visitors.

• Get comfortable with the community members. I was hesitant to open up at the beginning, but when I saw community members speaking from their hearts, it made me comfortable enough to follow suit. Do your research. I read about La'akea first, and went there with some confidence that I would fit in. It's important to know what you're getting into. —*Ron Laverdiere*

• Don't be shy or embarrassed to ask questions or ask for what you need. Strive to be emotionally honest—even if what you have to say is not the 'easy' or 'pretty' answer. Don't be afraid to share affection or appreciation. Be confident that you can handle anything that comes your way. —*Travis Fowler*

• If you have a good sense of what you want to learn and experience while at a community, make sure you communicate what you want clearly and have an agreement about how this is going to happen. Go into the situation with an open mind and heart to see if you can learn and experience things you'd never have imagined. —*Molly Morgan*

• Discover and establish boundaries between your personal time and community time. If you don't take the time for personal space, it may become difficult to engage fully with the community. Keep an open mind, actively seek out projects that engage you, and cultivate kindness. —*Michael "Mojohito" Tchudi*

• Live it fully. Plunge in with abandon and trust those around you to respond to your zeal. Act as a community member to the extent that you can, contributing to making the community one that you would like to live in. —*Ted Sterling*

• Ask yourself ahead of time how participating in the community's program is part of your own vision and values, and how it will further your own goals. —*Guillermo A. Maciel*

• Even if you already know a lot about community or the subject of focus in its course or program, really learn to be a student; stay in a proactive observer space. Take what you need from the experience. And if things aren't quite what you expected, know that you can change your experience; it's only temporary! — *Jodie Emmett*

—*D.F.*

Francine Hughes

Adventures in Temporary Community:
An Interview with Liat Silverman

By Kim Scheidt

On a breezy last day of September, I had the pleasure of meeting with Liat Silverman. She trekked
the three-quarter-mile walk to my cabin at Red
Earth Farms from her home at Dancing Rabbit Ecovillage (outside Rutledge, Missouri), where she has lived for
a year and a half. A lively woman in her 20s, Liat values living in community, and she enjoys participating in festivals
and gatherings of many kinds—a form of temporary community. I was excited to meet up with Liat and hear about
the experiences she's had with the gatherings she's taken part

in recently: the Superhero ride, Burning Man, and the
Rainbow Gathering.

Superheroes

Kim: You participated in the Superhero Haul of Justice ride
across Missouri this month. Can you tell me about the Superheroes and how their group functions as a community?

Liat: The Superheroes are a temporary intentional community that never stays in one place for long. They are a group of

Group shot of the Superheroes with Patch-Co (Liat) at far left.

192

Liat outside of her home at Dancing Rabbit—a converted school bus.

Every participant comes from a unique background. Riders range from toddlers to retired folks. Some have graduated college, hold professional jobs, and have kids, while others perhaps were unschooled, hop trains, and live very alternatively. Some Superheroes have biked across the United States while others may have never biked in their life! I think the diversity of participants adds greatly to what the group becomes.

I was impressed with how organized and prepared the group is. Riders come together for one month out of the year, yet are strongly united as a group. One thing that builds the togetherness is the emphasis placed on ritual. The rituals vary; some are lighthearted and silly, while others are deep and thought-provoking. I found that taking part in these rituals helped us bond quickly. It was a way to learn more about the other Superheroes and to share in their daily experiences. Also, jobs (such as cooking, navigating, and giving massages) are given out to small groups of people and rotated daily. This helps ensure that everything we need gets done and everyone pulls equal weight.

Kim: How does someone become a Superhero?

Liat: Every Superhero creates their own identity; this usually involves a fun name and a costume. For example, I chose the identity Patch-Co* because I enjoy sewing, patching, and reusing things. As Patch-Co, I go around doing what I can to "patch the problems of the world." My costume was fairly simple: I had

people united in the common goals of biking and doing service. The group operates by consensus, and the decisions on where to go and what to do are made as a group. There is no established hierarchy, and anyone who has been a Superhero in the past can plan a ride. Every ride is different because they each take place in different locations, are composed of different people, hit different roadblocks, and have different amazing adventures.

many patches on my clothes and a cape trailing behind me.

You can either start at the beginning of the ride, or join up along the way. Every rider needs a bike, a way of carrying their own gear, a good attitude, a desire to help others, and a willingness to be open to whatever comes along.

Burning Man

Kim: You were at Burning Man this year. What was memorable for you about that event?

Liat: Tens of thousands of people from all different backgrounds come together for one week each year to congregate in the dry, desolate desert and create a huge, temporary community full of life and activity. Some people have their own private camps while others set up large camps that function like subcommunities where people live together, share meals, hold workshops, and party.

Most people were very friendly. If I needed a place to take shelter from a sandstorm, I would duck into the nearest tent, bus, or geodesic dome and was always welcomed with a smile.

The thing I was most impressed with about Burning Man is that almost everything there is initiated and led by the participants. Anyone can present a workshop, lead a dance or yoga class, or perform in front of a crowd. People are very giving with their time, energy, and resources.

Kim: Were there any negatives for you?

Liat: I didn't feel the festival was good ecologically, and since I make ecological living an important part of my existence, that was hard for me. I saw an abundance of waste, and this bummed me out much of the week. I was also put off by the entrance fee, which I feel selects for people who are financially well-off and discriminates against the economic backgrounds of the majority of people in this world.

I like to travel and meet lots of people, but I don't like cities or suburbs. Taking part in these events is a great outlet for me to get away from home temporarily and still fulfill my desire to be living in community.

Rainbow Gathering

Kim: You have also attended a Rainbow Gathering that was held in your home state of Florida. How does that experience compare or contrast with your time at Burning Man?

Liat: As with Burning Man, you see a great diversity of backgrounds among the attendees of Rainbow Gatherings—although I would have to say that the Rainbow Gathering is more accessible to people who earn lower wages. I saw a lot of the freegan**, dumpster-diving culture evident there. It also seemed more eco-friendly to me.

Similar to other festivals, there were lots of different things

going on simultaneously, so what you choose to be involved with will determine your time there. There were many repeat attendees. And really, it is the mix of people which makes each gathering into what it is.

Festivals and Community

Kim: Why do you enjoy attending festivals and gatherings?

Liat: I enjoy attending these types of festivities for the experience of it all. I like to travel and meet lots of people, but I don't like cities or suburbs. Taking part in these events is a great outlet for me to get away from home temporarily and still fulfill my desire to be living in community. A big part of the attraction for me is attending workshops and learning new skills. I also enjoy the social networking aspect of these gatherings, and I typically come away with new friendships and good contacts.

Kim: What is it that you value most about living in community, whether as your regular home or as a temporary community?

Liat: Living, sharing, and working together with others is what I seek in life. There are challenges to living in community, but there are so many benefits. I value the ability to borrow tools from neighbors, share resources and living space with community members, work on projects with friends, eat meals with other people, and vent my frustrations and emotions with friends who understand where I am coming from. I also really like that I live close enough to people to simply walk outside my door and meet up with someone. I don't ever have to think about getting in a motorized vehicle in order to be social.

Kim: What advice would you give to someone who is planning to take part in one of these festivals or gatherings?

Liat: Go into the experience without expectations, and be open to whatever might happen. ❀

Kim Scheidt is a founding member of Red Earth Farms in Rutledge, Missouri. She earns money doing accounting work for the Fellowship for Intentional Community in addition to her full-time job as mommy to a toddler. She enjoys reading, cooking fabulous dinners with wood heat, and planting things in the dirt.

*The term "co" is a gender-neutral noun or pronoun that can take the place of the words woman, man, she, he, etc. It is common jargon among members of many intentional communities.
**Wikipedia defines freeganism as "an anti-consumerist lifestyle whereby people employ alternative living strategies based on limited participation in the conventional economy and minimal consumption of resources."

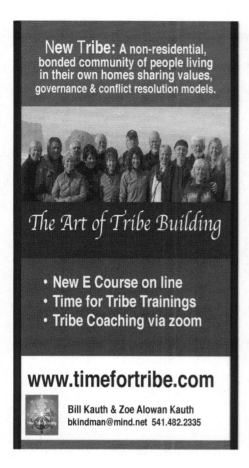

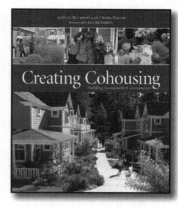
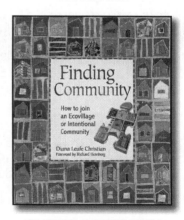

Burning Man:
Experiencing the *Playa* Community

By Kayla Wexelberg

The first community I came across during my recent studies of intentional communities happened to be a temporary community. Burning Man is the largest art festival in the world and has become widely known as a week-long intentional artist community.

Burning Man History

Burning Man began in 1986 on the evening of the Summer Solstice. Larry Harvey and Jerry James decided to build a wooden structure in the shape of a human. The wooden art piece, approximately eight feet tall, was meant to be an effigy of a lost love from Larry's past. They set the figure up on Baker Beach in San Francisco and lit a flame. As the figure burned, it drew a crowd of intrigued onlookers. This was the most remarkable event that had occurred on that small beach. That evening a woman stepped forth and held the unlit hand of the figure; the wind had forced the flame down and off the left hand of the structure, so the woman held it as the rest of the woman burned away. This gesture was the first of many spontaneous art performances throughout Burning Man's history. About 20 people came that night. The following year, when the event repeated itself, the crowd quadrupled in size. This time the man was 20 feet high, with 80 onlookers in awe of its blazing glory.

Over the next four years, the Burning of the Man remained in San Francisco at Baker Beach. The man grew in size and so did the crowds. By 1990 the Man had reached its now consistent height of 40 feet, and around 800 participants gathered to admire the spectacle. However, the crowds had swelled to

From the left: Temple at sunset. On the Playa during the day and at night. (Burning Man Festival 2008.)

All photos by Kayla Wexelberg

an overwhelming size for the quaint Baker Beach community and soon the police came to stop the burning. Larry Harvey and Jerry James convinced the police to allow them to simply erect the figure on the beach and not burn it. It was then when the proposal to move the burning to a different, more remote location was introduced. Black Rock Desert in Nevada quickly became the home for the annual Burning Man event, and along with the change in location the date also switched from Summer Solstice to Labor Day weekend. Larry called the empty lake bed (wet during the winter months) in which the festival now occurs the *Playa*, because in late summer it is composed entirely of dry mud that has the tendency to crack and crumble into dust, similar to the composition of sand. The change in location allowed the event to lengthen to a week and provide room for larger attendance.

Festival Infrastructure and Logistics

Burning Man prides itself on having the most sustainable festival infrastructure that has ever been created—part of the "intention" that binds together this community. In terms of environmental consciousness, Larry Harvey and his large crew also pride themselves on practicing LNT (Leave No Trace). At the end of each festival the Burning Man clean-up crew stays an extra month to make sure that all remnants of the festival are erased. All "Burners" (participants) are expected to clean up

their own MOOP (Matter Out Of Place). One of the requirements printed on the Burning Man ticket is two hours of volunteer cleaning of the Playa. The cost of the ticket starts at $295, and rises as the time of the event approaches. The ticket does not include food, water, or camp fees. Revenues from ticket sales directly fund the infrastructure of the city. This includes the setup of the post office, airport, medical services, art installation moving devices, clean up crew, and a year-long office headquarters, mostly to organize the large number of Burning Man volunteers. Volunteers are widely known as the "makers" of the Burning Man community. They contribute so much love and energy into ensuring everyone's Burning Man experience goes safely and smoothly.

Rhythm Wave Camp

I was fortunate to be a "Burner" in Black Rock City in 2008, and to take part in the colossal event, Burning Man's 23rd year of existence. Before I traveled from Berkeley to Black Rock City, I signed up to be a member of the Rhythm Wave Camp. This dance camp specializes in the meditative movement of the five rhythms: Flowing, Staccato, Chaos, Lyrical, and Stillness. The dance lasts an hour or two as a DJ smoothes the transitions between the waves of rhythm. Each camp gives a gift to the Black Rock City Community and ours was a large bamboo dance floor.

Being part of a community is very important. There is normally a set fee, which includes camp area, water, kitchen, shower setup area, a shade structure, and the camp gift. There is also a food option, in which you pay a bit and the camp provides you with food. Being part of a camp helps one to create a smaller sub-community within Black Rock City, a place to return to after a day out on the Playa. I found this camp experience to be extremely rewarding. The connections and family I formed contributed greatly to my comfort and acceptance in Black Rock City. Camp is not a hired service; everyone takes part in creating the camp area, which for us included the bamboo dance floor, the shade structure, the kitchen, water containers, etc. Everything is erected by the members of the camp. Essentially, the camp acts as a small town, with each individual assuming a specific role and contributing what he/she can. I volunteered to be part of the meal plan committee to do my service to the camp.

These communities stretch beyond the participants involved, and I believe they help broaden the minds of others and cause a shift in our ever-globalizing world.

Journey and Arrival

Before leaving for Black Rock City, I knew little of the exciting camp I was about to encounter. The community that was built made all the stress of preparing for the event worth it. The process of arriving at the festival was rather tedious. I set off with my boyfriend Gabriel en route to destination Black Rock Desert on the long straight shot to Nevada. It took only six hours to arrive at the entryway to the festival. However, we ended up waiting another six hours until we were actually able to enter Black Rock City. The dust storms that evening were so chaotic and unresisting that the gateway to Burning Man was closed for several hours until it let up. At 1:30 a.m., we finally arrived at our destination. Unable to find our camp, we slept in

the car that night, and in the morning awoke to a fantasyland displayed on the desert floor before us.

Finding our camp was like coming home. It was such a warm and exhilarating experience meeting new people and sharing the excitement and energy of the festival with them. Being able to share my love of cooking and contributing to my newfound community, I felt fulfilled, and that I was playing my part and truly becoming a member of my community. Everything came together smoothly as I quickly became comfortable in my new world. Contribution seems to be an intrinsic part of the Burning Man experience. Every Burner feels a need and desire to give back to the community that gives them so much. After participants leave Black Rock City and return to the "real world," many still feel a desire to give to one another in the form of loving-kindness. Unfortunately, many begin to feel disheartened by the lack of reciprocation. There needs to be a give and take for it to flow naturally without any remorse, and this is how Burning Man succeeds.

Life on the Playa

Each day, Gabriel and I would set off out onto the Playa with our beat-up "Playa" bikes. I felt a certain amount of warmth and comfort biking around Burning Man. Each participant was here for the same basic reason. There was no need to fight, steal, or exclude one another. In fact, it was quite the opposite; everywhere I turned I met a new friend. We were all just humans thriving in the same world, with the same intentions; to be present and enjoy the society created around us. Every day I would meet new people and welcome them into my life. I would often return to camp bearing gifts from people I had encountered during my adventures around town. Each morning I would set

From the left: Biking the Promanade. Rythm Wave.
Sunset at the Festival. (Burning Man Festival 2008.)

day. Who knows what will happen and it doesn't matter: it's just life. When I remember to take each moment as is, I appreciate life, and become more innately grateful for being in this world. Because of this exercise I am less stressed and find myself more giving and inclusive towards others. The energy and presence I have now give off a more permanent and positive light to the individuals around me. My actions in the "real world" in turn affect others who begin to trust and be open to their surroundings, including new individuals like me.

In my opinion, the Burning Man community has done an excellent job in helping to shift the world towards a brighter light. The welcoming atmosphere it creates within its borders stretches far beyond the limits of its seven-day installation. During my time in Burning Man I was able to conduct several surveys of various "Burners" and I discovered that many participants held the same opinion. When I asked Vytas Sunspiral, a friend of mine, if there were any aspects of Burning Man that he would want to bring back and incorporate in his daily life at home, he answered:

"Certainly. I had a moment a while ago where I had challenges with some of my colleagues in the workplace. And then I thought, 'Wait...I do have good social skills, just in a different context.' I just needed to bring that skill to a different setting. I realized the lessons I learned here, in Burning Man, I could also apply elsewhere."

Vytas and many other participants have taken the lessons learned in Burning Man and applied them to the real world, stretching the energy of the festival far beyond its limits of a temporary intentional community. These communities stretch beyond the participants involved, and I believe they help broaden the minds of others and cause a shift in our ever-globalizing and capitalist world. Vytas' colleagues would agree that there was a shift in Vytas' thinking and acting, which resulted in a shift in themselves. Moreover, the lessons he learned in Burning Man helped him to adjust the way he interacts with those around him in the "real world." He brought a more personal, welcoming atmosphere to the workplace, helping others to feel comfortable and accepted, much as I and many others have done with the Burning Man experience. ❋

off with no knowledge of what to expect that day. I had no set plans but to ride the wave of life and to be comfortable with taking any turns that came my way. I truly lived in the present as a naked human facing the world—as a newborn baby seeing everything for the first time.

By the end of Burning Man, I had fallen in love with Black Rock City and my Rhythm Wave community. I learned that being part of a community involved constant work for all participants. There was always clearing or setting up to be done around camp. But along with work, there was always play. Towards the end of the festival I found myself fully entertained by just staying in my camp and enjoying everyone's company. Each person taught me something new, and I in turn gave what I could to him or her. We all banded together during the trying dust storms, which often rose up quite rapidly and could last for hours. The weather played a key role in my experience, helping to develop the warrior within in order to push through and take the whiteouts.

Returning to the "Real World"

Returning from Burning Man was rather shocking to my system. I went through a week of pure exhaustion and minor depression trying to recover from my experience. Burning Man was so intense and different from the "real world" that I found it hard to reintegrate myself when I arrived back home in Berkeley. I had become accustomed to my life out on the Playa, and then all of a sudden Black Rock City had turned into a distant dream world. It had all gone by so quickly. However, after the culture shock wore off, the feelings and lessons I had learned in Burning Man slowly crept back to me, this time in a much more desired fashion. I found myself approaching the "real world" in ways that I had approached Burning Man. Every day I would open my eyes and all the errands and work I had to get done quickly formed a stressful list in my mind. Then I slowly took a deep breath and reminded myself that it is just another

Kayla Wexelberg is an ethnographer and a photojournalist who is completing her senior thesis research on intentional communities. She spent four months in 2008 traveling around the United States experiencing and participating in different intentional communities including Burning Man, Still Meadow, and Dancing Rabbit. Kayla is from Berkeley, California and will graduate from Global College of Long Island University in May 2009 with a degree in Global Studies.

Comin' Home to the Rainbow

By Scott Shuker

"Welcome home, brothers and sisters! Lovin' you!" is usually the first greeting I receive upon arriving at the Rainbow Gathering, an appreciated one after a very long drive and long hike down the main trail with full camping gear. Newcomers are surprised, even shocked, by such openness from strangers, but soon come to express the same openness to others. Sleep deprivation actually adds to the sense of elation I feel, and I am anxious to get to my campsite. Upon first arrival I am greeted at "the Gate" by dedicated folks who have kept the campfire going all night to welcome people home. After getting oriented, I look for a parking spot, then go to the "Welcome Home" kitchen for a bite to eat and say "Howdy folks." I ask where things are and after some uplifting conversation, head down the trail to "Main Meadow"—the center of the Gathering—to find my mates and camp. Off in the distance I can hear a rousing "We LOOOOOOOOVE You!"

I'm home.

The Rainbow Family Gatherings are free, non-commercial festivals which occur throughout the year worldwide (always on public land in North America, usually on private land on other continents), to heal Mother Earth and each other. The Gatherings grew out of the 1960s counterculture, originating from two festivals known as Vortex which took place in Oregon in 1970 and Washington state in '71, attracting tens of thousands of people. The first known Rainbow Gathering happened in the Rocky Mountain National Park in northern Colorado July 1-7, 1972. That year, the White House called out the National Guard to stop it, causing the Family to move to another site. Thus began an antagonistic relationship with the federal government which unfortunately continues today.

Why the metaphor "rainbow"? Many say it is because the rainbow in nature has many colors which remain separate and autonomous while creating a beautiful phenomenon of light. In that spirit we gather as free individuals working together to create an alternative to the consumer- and fear-based culture. Gatherings are not just festivals. We are an international intentional community, void of borders, who see ourselves as a human family, making anyone with a belly button a member (though this consensus was amended to include those who don't, like test-tube babies and extra-terrestrials—ha ha). We even have nicknames to describe our...uh...diversity: "High Holies" (parental and/or authority figures), "Drainbows" (adults who do little while "draining" others' energy), "A-Camper/ Roaddogs"(alcoholic hobos), "Tourists" (high-tech gear, spiffy-clean weekenders with lots of money), "Dog Warriors" (black-clad, pierced, and anarchistic), and "Wingnuts" (crazies).

We have many traditions that make a gathering Rainbow. We firmly assert and maintain our First Amendment right to gather peacefully on public lands. It must

All photos by Garrick Beck

Left: Thousands gathered in large meadow for dinner circle at Colorado '06 national gathering. Top and left on this page: The latest Granola Funk Theater designs. Bottom right: People having a bite outside of Kid Village.

be totally free (no fees are charged). All money is given by donation, usually to the "Magic Hat" which is focalized (facilitated) by a Banking Council who distributes it as equitably as possible to meet Family needs. All work is done voluntarily. We camp in ways respectful and sensitive to nature and leave no trace after we leave, even reseeding and restoring where necessary. Sanitation is an important priority, difficult yet manageable in a primitive situation. In North America, a gathering must always happen on public land to avoid any ownership authority. We have no legal status, no leaders, and make all Family decisions by consensus. "Ignore all rumors of cancellation and organization" is one of our mottos. There is a silent meditation for world peace every July 4th morning until noon, broken by a colorful children's parade.

We strive to solve all conflicts non-violently and maintain a health and safety squad known as "Shanti Sena" (peacekeepers). Weapons, especially firearms, are prohibited (though law enforcement agents refuse to respect this). We move to a different state for the 7/1-7/7 National every year. Alcohol consumption is discouraged and kept at the parking lot or "A-Camp" (A stands for alcohol). We publish a yearly listing of names, addresses, and phone numbers, given voluntarily, in the "Rainbow Guide," as well as a yearly newsletter known as the "All Ways Free." All the music is homegrown and acoustic, electronic music being kept to the parking lot.

And the food! It's to "die for," served with love and care. We feed ourselves through a system of temporary kitchens which all serve whenever a group of people feel like cooking and serving, as well as dinner at Main Circle every evening at "Rainbow Time." Small gatherings might have only one kitchen. Large internationals may have up to 100. I have always loved "kitchen-hopping" in the evenings for a wide array of delectables and "zu-zus"(sweets) and might even

run into a drum circle, music jam, or story-telling. The names of the specialty camps and kitchens are as diverse as the sub-tribes who attend: Lovin' Ovens, C.A.L.M. (The Center for Alternative Living Medicine), Warriors of the Light, Phat Kids, Jesus Camp, Bread of Life, Kid Village, Tea Time, Popcorn Palace, Montana Camp, Safe Swingers, Brew-Ha-Ha, and the Granola Funk Theater. My favorite is Info, a.k.a. Information and Rumor Control, which receives and disseminates information about the gathering for anyone who needs it, including maps, guides, newsletters, and legal info. "Rumors stopped...and started here," we like to say.

A Forest Service supervisor once described the gathering as a "cosmic accident." But it is anything but an accident. The process of creating the gathering is very intentional, organic, and voluntary. It begins at least a year before when the region is chosen by consensus at "Vision Council." Scouts volunteer to look at maps, camp on potential sites with lots of meadows, campsites, firewood, and clean water, and meet the locals. Later they rendezvous at "Spring Council" to agree on a site. Shortly thereafter the word gets out on the "Rainbow Grapevine," then inevitably to the internet. Soon after, folks show up to begin "Seed Camp," spending weeks building an infrastructure of water taps and pipelines, digging slit-trench latrines known as "shitters," clearing trails, and developing fire pits. The first kitchens are developed, sensitive areas are identified and protected, parking determined, food supplies coordinated, Banking Council focalized, and Main Meadow chosen.

During the main part of the gathering one can attend a multitude of events emphasizing creativity and sharing. The "circle" is the most common way of doing that in Rainbowland. There are drums, heartsongs, singing, meals, meditation,

(continued on p. 73)

COMIN' HOME TO THE RAINBOW (continued from p. 33)

ceremonies, spontaneous music jams, theater performances, dancing, councils, and even roving "hug patrols." The population and energy continue to grow until the peak days, after which clean-up begins and everything is removed and disappeared. The last of the skeleton crew might leave a full month after the last "official" day.

Yet every rainbow has its darkness lurking somewhere behind. Though we love each other, we don't always like each other. And we must deal with many conflicts, dramas, and dysfunctions like any other family—like too many dogs, drugs, litter, booze, violence, and legal hassles—yet see the gathering as a place of healing and do our best to deal with these matters in the most loving way possible. The most difficult aspect for me is the ever-increasing police presence and their militaristic use of force to discourage, intimidate, and often physically assault gathering attendees due to a long-standing conflict between the Family and the federal government through the US Forest Service (USFS), which generally regards Rainbows as dirty, pot-smoking criminals, not citizens with rights. After many years of coordinated yet failed efforts with state and local authorities and the courts to stop it, the USFS made a bureaucratic, not democratic, decision in 1994 to require any group of 75 or more to apply for a special-use permit requiring multiple fees, millions in insurance, and leaders to be responsible for the entire gathering. There is evidence that this regulation was created specifically to stop the gatherings, and we see it as a blatant violation of the First Amendment.

We have always worked well with the rangers, and though the Family has made mistakes, we almost always receive a glowing clean-up report. It has been the law enforcement arm of the USFS (known as LEOs) that has consistently targeted attendees for petty traffic violations, illicit drug-use offenses, and identifying "leaders" to sign a permit as a means of making money from the Family. Some Rainbows have done time in jail, many others have been ticketed just for being at the gathering. The US Drug Enforcement Agency, Central Intelligence Agency, and Department of Homeland Security have all infiltrated US gatherings and likely many foreign gatherings as well. At the 2008 National Gathering in Wyoming, mustard pellets—non-lethal bullets filled with tear gas—were fired by LEOs at Kid Village during an arrest of a brother for suspected marijuana possession (this can be viewed on YouTube.com). The USFS office in Washington later issued a national press release stating they were "defending themselves" after being attacked by "400 Rainbows with sticks and rocks"—a total fabrication, as I was an eye-witness. We have always sought to resolve and heal this ongoing conflict through dialog and in the courts, but have usually lost on the permit issue. Regardless of the LEOs' violent and malicious tactics, we have always kept the peace and have never violently retaliated in any way.

Regardless of the dramas, gatherings are sooooo worth it—a place to heal what ails you. They can really make you feel good. So if you're looking for a Rainbow Gathering, it's only a click away at either WelcomeHome.org or WelcomeHere.org to find out the where's, when's, how's, and why's. We look forward to welcoming you home too! ✳

Scott Shuker has been a Rainbow Family enthusiast since 1990 and a contributor to COMMUNITIES *since 1997 on behalf of the Lama Foundation, where he still maintains a Continuing Membership. He currently lives in the mainstream of Santa Fe, New Mexico while working on his college degree.*

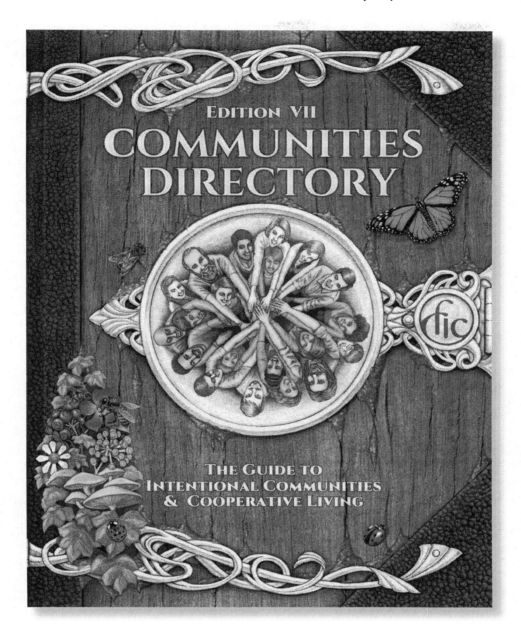

Communities Directory book!

In addition to profiling more than 1,000 communities, this new book includes full-page maps showing where communities are located, charts that compare communities by more than 30 qualities, and an easy index to find communities interested in specific pursuits. Also included are articles on how to start or join a community, the basics of group dynamics and decision-making, and countless additional resources and links to help your community thrive!

Order your book today: www.ic.org/New-Directory

Top left: Big Top Goes Up. Miaya helps raise the circus tent used as a dining hall. (Summer Camp West 2004.) Top right: Dome Construction. Sixteen feet in the air, Thia assists as Francesca stretches to place the next strut in the 40-foot diameter geodesic dome used as a meeting space. (Summer Camp East 2008.) Bottom: Creek Lunch. A rock in the creek makes an intimate spot for lunch-time conversation. (Summer Camp East 2008.)

Network for a New Culture Camps

By Pati Diehl, Melanie Rios, Michael Rios, and Sarah Taub

Melanie: *During my first day or two at Network for a New Culture Summer Camp in 1999, I felt uncomfortable, and labeled the experience "false intimacy." Here I was, gazing into the eyes of a stranger for far longer than seemed proper, laying my hand over a stranger's heart, and listening to our group leader ask us to imagine sending love to this person. Whoa! I feared for what might come next, since normal boundaries had been set aside. But the funny thing was, by the end of camp, after sharing this and many other experiences with a hundred other campers, this same type of exercise created in me a feeling of authentic and safe intimacy, a deep feeling of love for these particular people and for humanity in general. I wondered what had happened in these ten days to bring about this transformation. Would this sense of overflowing connection persist after camp was over?*

At Network for a New Culture (NFNC) camps, currently located in Oregon, West Virginia, and Hawaii, adults come together to learn about and practice ways of living together different from the norms of mainstream culture, experimenting with new ways of relating to themselves, to their work, to others, and to the world. Workshops and other activities encourage participants to explore intimacy, freedom, and radical personal responsibility, with the goal of fostering the personal empowerment and emotional resilience that would allow a cooperative, nonviolent culture to emerge. The strong relationships that form at camp create the basis for a vibrant community all year long.

> *At NFNC camps, intimacy isn't just another word for sex; it's about "transparency," being truly open about who we are and what we want.*

Intimacy and Transparency

At NFNC camps, intimacy isn't just another word for sex; it's about "transparency," being truly open about who we are and what we want. This begins with honest self-reflection, asking ourselves about what we are really feeling and thinking, even if the answers embarrass us. At one opening session, a couple told us what their spoken dialog might have been when they first met each other, along with their internal dialog. "Hello," said the man; then to himself he said "Wow, I love her outfit, and her smile. I wonder if she's single? Does she notice the zit that popped out on my face this morning?" It was an amusing skit that encouraged us to look at our own internal dialogs as we met each other.

Charla: *I found it relaxing to live in a community where you didn't have to pretend you were feeling great all the time. At first,*

*Top: Cuddle Pile. Campers bliss out and con-
nect in a small section of a very large cuddle pile.
(Summer Camp West 2004.)
Bottom left: Orientation Crowd. The entire camp
gathers in the dome for orientation. (Summer
Camp West 2004.) Bottom right: Lounge.
The outdoor lounge at Summer Camp West.
(Summer Camp West 2007.)*

I thought I'd be expected to hug everyone all the time. Not so. The hugs I gave were from the heart, not the mind. They started deep in the body and I felt I was "at choice" all the time. I could live the rainbow of my emotions without embarrassment or shame. I could reach out or withdraw according to my own rhythm. I learned to give myself empathy, and to feel respected by others.

The norm at camp is to share freely with others what we are thinking and feeling—while always being "at choice." One way that this transparency is practiced is the ZEGG Forum (not related to Landmark Forum). It is a listening circle to which we can bring problems, achievements, and issues, or just show ourselves to the community. People take turns walking around in the center while talking about what's true for them in that moment. A "Forum leader" sometimes walks alongside this person to deepen the sharing, or to encourage them to more dramatically express themselves. While the goal of the forum is simply to share rather than to solve problems, often shifts occur simply as a result of understanding each other.

Sarah: *When W. arrived at camp, he was angry about the work shifts he had been assigned. As work coordinator, I had a poor first impression of him; he was socially awkward and did not make eye contact. A few days later, he got up in Forum. He shared with the group his longing to connect with others in a loving way, and his lifelong inability to do so. He had been angry about his assignments because they conflicted with a workshop that he desperately hoped would be able to help him. Because of this sharing, I was able to see him as a loving spirit with a difficulty in perceiving and responding to social cues. During camp clean-up, I had the privilege of having him as my work partner; it was one of the most harmonious shared work experiences I've ever had.*

Camp organizers, who are all volunteers, try to model this transparency, openly sharing issues that come up between them. At the second NFNC camp, held in 1996, conflict broke out among the organizers:

Miaya: *I was mortified that our dirty laundry was being aired so publicly. Things heated up so high that, in one Forum, my brother offered an "old culture" invitation to my partner to step outside and slug it out. Surprisingly, the feedback that we heard from the campers was mainly appreciation for our openness to share so much of our discord and angst, and willingness to look like fools. There were many hurt feelings among the organizers during that second summer camp, but, in the end, we all knew we had just had a beautiful trial by fire.*

A "Fishbowl" structure provides another opportunity for participants to practice transparency. The campers are divided into two groups, such as parents and childfree adults, men and women, or straight and queer. One group sits in the center and speaks among themselves while the other group listens in silence.

Melanie: *I remember one time listening to men talk about their experiences with impotence. It was like being a fly on the wall of a men's group, and I felt my heart expanding with compassion.*

"Seven-Minute Dates" are another format that fosters people getting to know each other at camp. People partner with someone for a short time to discuss a topic offered by the group leader, such as "Was it easy for you to make and keep friends when you were younger?"

Bodhi: *Cuddled face-to-face with a new friend, I shared my past struggles with being socially acceptable—the enormous effort of pretending to be "normal" when inside I felt very much the stranger in an increasingly strange land.*

There's playfulness as well—the kids at camp aren't the only ones who get to have fun. Campers keep on the lookout for pretentious or spoofable moments, and there are plenty!

Camper: *I know that it's not the time for lost-and-found announcements—but could someone help me? I can't find my chakras!*

Freedom of Choice and Personal Responsibility

One mainstream norm that is challenged is monogamy as the only option for responsible sexual relationships. At camp, all loving relationship styles are honored, including celibacy, monogamy, and open relationships such as polyamory. Workshops offer guidance on creating fulfilling romantic relationships. In one workshop, participants practice asking for what they want while respecting each other's boundaries. A camp aphorism is that "It's okay to ask if it's okay to hear 'no.'" We find that "no" is the most intimate thing you can hear from another human being—because if you can receive their "no," you can trust their "yes."

Sometimes campers have strong feelings, such as embarrassment, or anger, or jealousy; they are encouraged to feel their feelings fully, while letting go of demands and expectations they have for others. As always, each one is "at choice."

Living in a culture that is truly "at choice," while practicing radical personal responsibility, can be startling when someone first arrives. At a workshop, one person may come a half hour late; another is lying on the floor, apparently asleep, just a few feet from the presenter; another gets up to leave halfway through. Since none of these activities directly interferes with others' participation, no notice or offense is taken.

Likewise, camp is clothing-optional; and this reflects the real meaning of "at choice" as well. People are free to wear whatever they choose—or not. The usual result is that a few campers are

> *I was mortified that our dirty laundry was being aired so publicly. Things heated up so high that, in one Forum, my brother offered an "old culture" invitation to my partner to step outside and slug it out. Surprisingly, the feedback that we heard from the campers was mainly appreciation.*

Top: Goodbyes At Morning Circle. Four campers who are departing early say goodbye at Morning Circle. (Summer Camp East 2007.) Middle: Massage Chain. Shared work leads to shared support and intimacy, as campers build a 40-foot geodesic dome for a meeting space. (Summer Camp East 2008.) Bottom: River Gang. Campers relax by the river. (Summer Camp West 2004.)

actually nude, about a quarter are not "street legal" in some way, and the rest are covered to a more-or-less conventional degree. Clothes are for costume or comfort, not emotional protection.

First-year camper: *It felt like I had a gym membership with a special focus on the muscle group of "choice" and "choosing."*

Experimenting with New Ways of Being

Experimentation is at the heart of camp. Rather than offering a set of "solutions" for personal and social problems, the emphasis is on developing the skills and the willingness to try new things, and sharing the results with other campers. People often try out new identities or behaviors that might feel unsafe in the mainstream world.

One person who attended camp for several years seemed painfully shy. One day, some campers asked if he'd be willing to try an experiment. They brought him to the camp costume closet, and dressed him up by pinning red hearts on his white shirt and giving him a red cape and white leotards to wear. They coached him on how to stand up tall and smile with confidence. Then they introduced him to everyone at the morning circle as "Passion Man," and requested that he warmly hug everyone he met for the remainder of that day who was willing to play this game. He enthusiastically hugged people that day and for the rest of camp, even after returning to his normal clothing.

During the past few years, one new way of being that many men have explored is becoming more comfortable expressing physical affection with each other. The women from the early years were good at cuddling and hugging people of all genders, and all campers understood that cuddling with another person didn't necessarily mean sex was available, or even of interest. But the men in the early years of camp seemed to be afraid of touching each other.

Michael: *By 2002, another man and I decided it was time to change things. In a men's meeting, we stood up, moved to the center, and cuddled each other—and invited the others to do the same. One by one, each man moved toward the center, touching, then later cuddling with each other. In 2003, my friend and I got together ahead of time to figure out how to make the same point that year. We got to the men's group slightly late, and found the entire group was already one giant cuddle pile!*

Owning Our Sexuality

Sexuality is dealt with openly at each camp. There are workshops on erotic energy, safer sex, sexual healing, and more. Over the years, because of an atmosphere of openness, much of the charge on this topic has dissipated, and many campers discuss their sexual concerns and delights much the way they would talk about any other part of their lives.

Camper: *I was raped when I was a teenager. Since then, I have had relationships only with women. I felt safer at camp than I had ever felt before, so I asked a man to help me be sexual with men again; he agreed to proceed slowly and gently, with time to feel all my feelings and to stop completely if I said so. Afterwards, I shared this with the women's circle, who celebrated with me in reclaiming this long-lost area of my sexual power.*

Presenters and Workshops—Learning Together

Each year, camp has presenters on topics meant to educate or inspire the community. Campers aren't expected to agree with the presenters; they take what works for them, and leave the rest—or challenge the presenter. When things go "wrong," we get to practice what we are learning at our workshops. People at our events are encouraged to use upsets and painful reactions as gateways to personal growth and deeper intimacy.

Sarah: *During a playful exercise, pretending to be animals on all fours, a man nipped my heel. In a panic, I slapped his back and yelled "Don't do that!" He apologized immediately. The workshop leader asked us to share what happened; but in the process, he told me that slapping the man's back was a violent act, and asked me to apologize. I refused. There was intense reaction among the group; some felt that violence is never appropriate, and others were horrified that a woman was being told that she was wrong to counter a physical assault. The leader continued to loudly defend his position. People gathered in informal small groups to provide support for each other, and to explore what had happened.*

The next morning, after talking with many campers, the workshop leader told me that he had learned a lot from all the ensuing discussion, and apologized. He then went before the whole group, and shared his own process and new understandings; that he had reacted from his own triggers around violence, and especially being in the position of the workshop leader, had unfairly used his position of authority in front of the group. The leader and I wound up with a warmer and deeper connection, sensing a mutual commitment to communicating from the heart.

First-year camper: *The dialog that followed that event was the moment I knew this community was different. It was committed to dealing with things as they came to us and not sweeping things under the rug.*

Going Home—What Now?

Even after camp is over, many participants find that what they learned at camp carries over into their "real world" life. Some of the organizers have joked that the success of camp should be measured by the number of people who go home and quit their soul-destroying jobs.

Jade: *I came to Summer Camp East for the first time this year,*

mostly on a lark. My response to the experience was so intense that I took another two weeks off work to attend Summer Camp West— just to see if it was all real. When I returned, I walked into my manager's office and told her that I cannot continue to spend 45 hours a week in a building where windows do not open. I related my Summer Camp experience and thoughts in detail and she told me to consider the path of a healer or a teacher. Since then, my company has agreed to make my job part-time and telecommute, and I have moved to a New Culture intentional community 250 miles away.

Several land-based intentional communities have been inspired by the Summer Camp experience, including Heart-On Farm in Oregon, La'akea in Hawaii, and Chrysalis in Virginia.

Melanie: *The communication skills and life attitudes I learned at camp have increased my ability to connect with my family and friends at home in an honest, loving manner. Inspired by what I found at camp, I moved to Oregon and co-created an ecovillage in Eugene using those principles and insights. Many former campers live in Eugene, and I've deepened those friendships as well. Even though the romantic connections among these folks may come and go, the friendships mostly remain steady, creating a tribe of people who love and support each other.*

Besides the tribe in Eugene, there are several others that have grown out of camp; people who connect with each other frequently, even daily, who consider themselves part of an intentional community, even though they don't share the same address.

The Authors: *We're excited to be part of an intimate community that explores personal growth, intimate relationships, sexuality, communication, community, social change, and global consciousness, all while trying to find practical ways to "bring it all home." What we have learned is that personal growth is not enough; the change needed for human survival cannot happen piecemeal. Our new understandings can be most effectively implemented in the larger society by changing our culture, our customary ways of thinking and acting. The core insight of New Culture is that powerful change comes first to our daily lives.* ❀

> *There was intense reaction among the group; some felt that violence is never appropriate, and others were horrified that a woman was being told that she was wrong to counter a physical assault.*

Pati Diehl has been active in NFNC since its beginning in 1995, and served as co-organizer of NFNC Summer Camp West (2000-2004). Melanie Rios is a long-time resident of Maitreya Ecovillage in Eugene, Oregon. Michael Rios co-organized NFNC Summer Camp East (2004-2008) and NFNC Summer Camp West (2004) and co-founded Chrysalis Community in Arlington, Virginia (www.chrysalis-va.org). Sarah Taub co-organized NFNC Summer Camp East (2004-2008) and co-founded Chrysalis Community. For more information on Network for a New Culture, visit www.nfnc.org.

 **REVIEWS**

Visions of Utopia, Part Two
Experiments in Sustainable Culture
A Documentary by Geoph Kozeny
**Available from store.ic.org or 1-800-995-8342.
($30 plus shipping; or $50 plus shipping for
Parts One and Two together; additional discount
available to FIC Members.)**

Reviewed by Tim Miller

Geoph Kozeny lived in community for more than a decade and then created a new life for himself—one of community networker extraordinaire. He lived mainly out of his pickup truck for many years, traveling around the country and visiting hundreds of intentional communities. Along the way he devoted a great deal of energy to supporting the work of the Fellowship for Intentional Community. It's a fair statement that no one in recent memory has done more to promote communal living and to strengthen ties among America's thousands of communities than Geoph Kozeny did.

I remember berating Geoph for keeping a vast library of information in his head but not recording it permanently. He said I shouldn't worry about it. And he was right. The cream of Geoph's info-trove has surfaced as his inspiring two-part video, *Visions of Utopia*. Part One came out in 2002, but Part Two needed to be issued posthumously, alas, because he died after completing the filming but not the editing of that portion of the project. Many of his friends then joined together to see that his project reached fruition.

Part One featured an overview of the long history of cooperative living and then provided video snapshots of seven communities founded since 1961. The new Part Two provides portraits of 10 more communities, all founded since 1970. One real strength of the video (both videos, really) is the diversity of the communities featured. In Part Two we visit Catholic Worker houses, which provide front-line service (food, housing) to persons in deep need. We take an excursion to The Farm, a classic hip commune that has evolved into an ecovillage that has changed its economic structure but kept its ideals largely intact. We drop in on Remote Village, a pseudonymously-named enclave in northern California so remote that its residents are snowed in four months of the

I remember berating Geoph for keeping a vast library of information in his head but not recording it permanently. He said I shouldn't worry about it. And he was right.

year. We take a look at N Street Cohousing in Davis, California, whose residents have crafted a cohousing village from existing neighborhood homes. The other groups in Part Two are the Community Alternatives Society (with two locations in British Columbia, one urban and one rural); Ganas, of Staten Island, New York; the Goodenough Community of Seattle; Hearthaven, in Kansas City; the Miccosukee Land Cooperative, near Tallahassee, Florida; and Sandhill Farm, near Rutledge, Missouri.

I found it all both enjoyable and informative, and came away with a greater appreciation than ever for the real diversity that exists in today's intentional communities. Indeed, diversity exists not only among communities, but within them. Ganas is especially intriguing in that regard; as one member says in the video, you can choose a level from total involvement, including income sharing, to not much involvement beyond sharing space with others. Several other featured communities, including Goodenough, Miccosukee, The Farm, and N Street Cohousing, are sufficiently decentralized to allow members to make their own choices about levels of involvement, even if they do not have income-sharing core groups. On the other hand, several communities retain tighter structures. The income-sharing Sandhill Farm, for example, really resembles nothing so much as a loving family.

I was also struck by the continuities American communities have with those of the past. The Catholic Worker houses remind us that intentional communities have long served the needs of the down-and-out of society. Sandhill Farm is still agriculture-based, something that has characterized communal life as far back as we can see. One particular historical reenactment is apparent in the Community Alternatives Society, with its two locations, including a rural one that lets the urban members spend time on the land. The intentional community that is usually reckoned the first of that genre in what became the United States, Plockhoy's Commonwealth, or Swanendael, in Lewes, Delaware, had just that same dual-arrangement, with one base for the community's urban merchants and another for the farm workers. (Or at least that was the community's plan; it was wiped out by an invading army a year after its founding in 1663, a fate that most contemporary communities, happily, are not likely to face.)

At the end of the video I sat transfixed as the long list of credits scrolled across the screen. Again the power of the communitarian ideal was evident: all kinds of people pitched in to make *(continued on p. 79)*

(continued from p. 80)

this video happen. Yes, it's Geoph's idea, and his project, but its creation was truly a community effort. He could not have a more fitting memorial than this testimony to the power and vision of those who work toward a positive future for the human race by joining others to create a cooperative society.

Keep watching until the credits have finished. The video closes with a touching final scene. Geoph is on-camera to make a final statement. But he flubs his lines and kind of dissolves, laughing at himself. A very human being has made a visual document that testifies to the life commitment that he and thousands of others share. By all means get the video and pass it around. Get Part One as well, if you don't have it yet. The world of competition and strife is too much with us; it's high time that as many people as possible were introduced to other possible ways to live. There's no better place to begin than right here.

Tim Miller teaches in the Department of Religious Studies at the University of Kansas and is a historian of American intentional communities. Among his books are The Quest for Utopia in Twentieth-Century America *and* The 60s Communes: Hippies and Beyond, *both published by Syracuse University Press.*

Sunset over our home in the parking lot.

Emergency Community

By Jesika Feather

Aeriel view of the Made With Love Cafe.

There is still beauty amid the destruction.

Our community fell together in Waveland, Mississippi, post-Katrina. We all found our separate ways to the New Waveland Café, a relief kitchen started by the Rainbow Family days after the Hurricane ravaged the Gulf Coast. When Rainbow gathering meets disaster zone, over-stimulation is an understatement. The hum of the refrigerator trucks eternally cloud the background. Oddly costumed kitchen volunteers stride here and there with boxes of zucchini, chicken legs, mayonnaise, and tomato sauce.

The parking lot where our kitchen was stationed was shared with a distribution center staffed by a church group. Their counters carried everything from evaporated milk and Vienna sausages to fall-themed centerpieces at Thanksgiving. A bird's eye view would show dreadlocks, mini-skirts, and baggy overalls amiably mingled with gray crew cuts and lime green t-shirts reading, "The Church Has Left the Building."

We washed dishes, chopped cantaloupe, smoked meat, and sanitized surfaces until the city of Waveland could stand on its own, at least as far as pancakes and pulled pork were concerned.

From there we moved on to St. Bernard Parish, Louisiana, where we started a non-profit, Emergency Communities. Our new relief kitchen, The Made with Love Café and Grill, served an average of 1000 meals a day from December 2005 until June 2006.

We came to know one another over the span of months. Our facility housed thousands of volunteers. Each day was a blur of names and faces. Most volunteers were available for short periods of time (one week to one month). Those of us who couldn't bring ourselves to leave, developed a ragtag family.

The parking lot of a destroyed horse betting establishment, Off Track Betting, became our home. A geodesic dome, borrowed from a Burning Man camp, became our dining room. Two long rows of port-a-potties actually started to feel normal. Our pantry consisted of a series of refrigerator and freezer trucks along with a large army tent we named Hot Lips. All this was connected by paths made of pallets—to keep our feet from touching the Katrina-poisoned earth.

For the first time in our lives, cement was clean. Grass was dirty. In the disaster zone, all laws are changed. At least cement can be bleached. It's a quick fix, but it will take years for the earth to heal herself.

None of us are from Louisiana. Like all good hippies, we've eaten our fair share of beans and rice, but apparently we were naïve to the subtle intricacies of Red Beans and Rice, the way "mama" makes it. For one thing, it's supposed to be served on Mondays. The locals pushed their way into the kitchen, determined to teach us about Gumbo, Jambalaya, Bread Pudding, and even fried alligator. We swallowed our pride, handed over our spatulas, and took notes.

Though the action at Made with Love centered around the kitchen, many of my current housemates fell into responsibilities that had little to do with food.

Valisa and Benjah took on the job of reigning in the ruckus that occurs when hundreds of homeless locals, rebellious volunteers, and passionate eccentrics reside in tight quarters. Their work was complicated by the ubiquitous presence of "flood liquor." In essence, Katrina gathered up every liquor bottle in New Orleans and tossed her bounty to the masses. Unopened bottles could be found in trees, streets, and abandoned buildings. Benjah, Valisa, and the other volunteers on security never suffered a boring moment.

When we arrived in Eugene, we were a crew of traveling volunteers. Now we have a mortgage payment, a baby, full-time jobs, a Subaru wagon, and bags of shorn dreadlocks in the garage.

Lali, aside from facilitating at least two meals a day, initiated the ritual of "singing the menu." As the residents of St. Bernard Parish waited for the serving line to open, Lali, followed by a convoy of volunteers, wound her way around the dining room. The dancing procession improvised a rhythmic rendition of the menu. The dome echoed with jubilant calls about ham, potato salad, rolls, and peas.

Brian was our rock. As the months wore us down, our already zany idiosyncrasies became increasingly pronounced. Brian stayed solid through it all. He was generally indispensable in every area. Primarily he headed up the First Aid tent but he also washed dishes, provided technical support, worked security and, most importantly, made sure we all wore sunscreen.

I specialized in breakfast. And, because I have an internal alarm clock, I was also the self-appointed wake-up fairy. I crawled from my tent at 5:30 in the morning, still in my pajamas. I pulled on my muck boots and traipsed from tent to tent, rousing volunteers to begin cracking eggs, lighting the griddle, mixing pancake batter, and chopping apples. I picked out a CD—the soundtrack that would define our morning.

By 6 a.m., the kitchen was a hodgepodge of personalities. No one ever had to wake up, but somebody always did. The volunteers were different every day. Sometimes they were hungover, sometimes they hadn't gone to bed yet. Sometimes they were grandmas who effortlessly threw down pancake batter for the masses like it was your average Sunday brunch. Sometimes they were 19-year-old college girls who, when confronted with the prospect of fruit salad for 400, displayed such performance anxiety you'd think they'd never peeled an orange in their lives. Frequently it was gutter punks, conspiring over corned beef hash in a wok—demanding an uncustomary array of spices, swearing "this is how the locals like it!"

Now, when I try to remember us three-and-a-half years ago, it's as if I'm remembering a dream. Those people—pretending they know how to cook green bean casserole with onion crisp-

Top left: Benjah takes a moment during the St. Bernard Mardi Gras parade to pose in front of the flood-damaged oil refinery. Top right: Inside Hot Lips. Middle left: Alice and Valisa in front of the domes. Middle right: Hamburgers for dinner at The Made With Love Cafe. Above: Lali, Uncle Van, Heather, Eric, Arjay, Cynthia, Danno, and Kiki enjoy Thanksgiving dinner in the new house. Opposite page: Members of the Heart and Spoon Community after a house meeting. Back row left to right: Evan, Lali, Brian, Valisa, Johnny, Jesika, Lisa, Nathan. Front: Ash and Benjah.

ies, and then serving it to 700 mouths... those people rushing around at 2 a.m., their tents crushed by the weight of the rain, tarping 300 bags of ginger snaps, wondering if the ovens would work in time to cook the frittata. Those people, with filmy June-in-Louisiana skin. Was that really us?

At the end of June, The Made with Love Café and Grill closed down and Emergency Communities founded three new relief kitchens. Our haphazard group of 10 tired, financially pressed disaster relief volunteers crawled into a VW van, a Toyota truck, a Mercedes with no reverse, and pointed ourselves west.

I still can't define what held that tentative caravan intact over the year and a month it took before we sat in an office with a notary and a realtor, signing piles of home ownership papers with a Turkey feather quill.

The year that transpired between starting the ignition on our caravan, and hanging Mardi Gras beads in the window of our new home, was a huge transition for all of us. Whether it was conscious or not, that year led to drastic changes for both our communal and individual identities.

Co-owning a house is a huge financial and social commitment. All decisions affecting our home are made by consensus. This ties us to a considerable financial obligation and a lengthy amount of time invested in communication and conflict resolution with our co-owners.

These choices were not made carelessly. We spent eight months meeting weekly to create the legal document that bound us. During this time, several people realized that this was not a decision they were ready to make. Some backed out entirely, others lowered their level of commitment by choosing to be renters rather than owners. By the time we were ready for signatures, there were five of us still committed to owning.

The eight months we spent creating our legal documents could never be defined as a honeymoon. As far as understanding the personality types we were venturing to work with, we bore no false pretenses. However, there is a certain "reality" surrounding our financial commitment that could only set in over time.

When we arrived in Eugene, we were a crew of traveling volunteers. Now we have a mortgage payment, a baby, full-time jobs, a Subaru wagon, and bags of shorn dreadlocks in the garage. You could say our glamor has been a little...tarnished. Truthfully, if something akin to Katrina struck our country now, we'd be hard pressed to donate our time so freely.

We all have different ways of reconciling with our new identities. I beg someone to play with my son so that I can sit in a coffee shop, eat huevos rancheros, and organize my life into paragraphs. Lali bought a second-hand clothing store and assuages her fears of "normalcy" by wearing and designing the most conspicuously striking outfits in Eugene. Benjah smokes cigarettes with homeless men and swaps theories of impending disaster. Valisa slides recklessly after Frisbees and takes lengthy excursions to other countries. Brian…well, to be honest, I'm not really sure if anything ever fazes Brian. But he, as always, nurtures plants and people.

Our financial commitments have had both positive and negative effects on our community. On one hand, we have a contract that gently nudges us back together when we feel inclined to stray. If there were any glaring issues, we could ultimately end it all, but the added complications keep us from making spontaneous or flighty decisions.

It is imperative that we work through any conflicts that arise. We can't push anything under the rug. We plod our way through agitation about too much dog poop in the yard. We acknowledge fears that some folks get more respect than others, and we hold discussions about whether or not a gun is allowed in the house.

After three years of bi-monthly house meetings and spontaneous breakdowns over sinks full of dishes, confrontation is not nearly the graceless, self-conscious scene it used to be. Now we have a common vocabulary and experiences to draw from. The communication skills we've honed while living together have also pulled us through difficult scenarios in our jobs and personal relationships outside this community.

Our financial commitments have also worked *against* our communal bond. Most of us make the majority of our money by working social services while holding side jobs that involve our other passions. In this way, we manage to serve our larger community while keeping our creative spirits alive. This also means that we work more than 40 hours a week. Af-

Sean Peterson

I know we can maintain this community through a disaster, but I still wonder if we can stick together through the mundane.

ter prioritizing the nine-to-five job, the art work, the management of art sales, and miscellaneous personal situations, it can be hard to make it home for dinner, much less to attend a house meeting.

It is realistic that after dedicating one year to disaster relief and another year to founding this community, people have to nurture their personal ambitions. If individuals aren't fulfilled, the community cannot thrive.

It is also clear to me that working through intense experiences to achieve common goals is what gave this community its sticking power. Maybe that's why, after we'd signed our names, haggled over rooms, and hefted in the piano, I started to get nervous. What would we do with nothing left to work towards? In my mind, the sweet feeling of success was muted by the fear that we'd reached a dead end. I know we can maintain this

community through a disaster, but I still wonder if we can stick together through the mundane.

Within days of signing our home-ownership contract, we discovered that I was pregnant. Mostly, I would call this a coincidence. However, I can't deny that with the end of our home-search in sight, I was zealous for a new community project. The idea of a baby, at least temporarily, absolved those fears. As we all know, it takes a village to raise a child…right? Nine months later, reality set in.

Ash, our baby boy, is currently 13 months old, and we are 13 months wiser. My husband and I learned that the ol' "it takes a village" routine doesn't actually apply to the first year of life. Unless the village is so hell-bent on child rearing that they invest in an industrial breast pump and start inducing lactation, the first year

(continued on p. 77)

EMERGENCY COMMUNITY

(continued from p. 27)

Sunset over our home in the parking lot.

is going to belong to the mama. The infant dwells in a very small neighborhood consisting of the left boob and the right boob. He'll broaden his horizons later.

Only in the last few months has Ash begun to belong to our village as a whole. While every member of this household is undoubtedly invested in his upbringing, a community mission statement this child is not. In fact, for my husband and me, he has been another individual project, diverting our attention from the community.

However, when he pushed his five pound, four ounce body into this world, every member of this community was present to cheer him on, and he knew, from his very first breath, that his support system extends far beyond his father and myself.

Now there are days when my life consists of nothing more world-changing than five loads of laundry folded in increments between playing with my son and baking a pie. Each member of our household wakes up to an individual alarm clock, gazes into a day planner blotchy with appointments, and rushes off to nurture the world, individually. I can't help but wonder if we aren't wasting our group potential. While I clean a sink full of eight people's dishes before making myself a bowl of oatmeal, I can't help but wonder...what exactly is the point?

On other days I rush to my job, secure in the knowledge that my son is giggling at home with Valisa. Someone else scours my egg pan, and I glide expertly through quibbles with co-workers. Maybe I am

getting something out of this.

I have to remind myself that learning to live together does make the world a better place. That raising my child in a household that faces conflict, but hugs afterwards, is a form of disaster relief. That cooking 10 different dishes, simultaneously, in a very small kitchen, and enjoying it, is a community bonding ritual.

In answer to the question, "what does your community do?" I would have to say, we are growing up together. We are inspiring one another to live to our full potential, and we are squeezing every ounce of passion from the mundane. At least, while I fold the 489th diaper, I can giggle at Lali, in the background, clomping her cowboy boots and singing "Hey, mama rock me."

As I look into the changing faces of my housemates, I remind myself that this is only one of many cycles on our life path. The rich history that binds us is truly a blessing. I should be equally grateful that we've been given this time to focus on our individual needs. Hopefully, in the near future, we'll find a way to combine our service skills to create a new phenomenon of beauty. Let's pray that it won't be prompted by disaster. ❀

For information about current rebuilding projects in New Orleans and St. Bernard Parish: www.stbernardproject.org/ v158, lowernine.org.

Jesika Feather is a teacher, mother, and writer. Currently she is a member of the Heart and Spoon community in Eugene, Oregon.

A Community Newcomer Finds Her Rhythm

by Melanie Ravensong Martin

A s the full moon balances on the cusp of the horizon, at the merging of heaven and earth, I see shades of gray transforming into subtly glowing shapes radiating with auras of ethereal light. This world and the dream time reveal themselves as one. In this land, we revere and revel in the moon cycles, and the changes happening throughout nature at every moment—the coming of the bluebirds, the ripening of blackberries, the sudden appearance of mushrooms. With each swift or gradual change we become renewed, taking on new hues and intensities as surely as the forests, the deer, and the meadows.

When I arrived in Eugene, Oregon after a long nature retreat in the rainy forests of British Columbia, I felt my anticipation turn to terror. There I was, in a new town nearly a continent away from my former home in western Pennsylvania, guided by nothing more than the belief that I would find community here. I'd grown up in a neighborhood where no one really knew each other, in a town where I didn't seem to fit in. In college, things were somewhat better, but I still hadn't experienced a strong spiritual network of family and friends. My own spirituality was very different from that of many of the people I lived amongst, and though I believe in accepting one another despite those differences, I yearned for what I hadn't yet experienced.

Wandering the streets of this new town, I felt daunted by the idea of searching for housemates. I wanted to find a cave somewhere and hide from all these strange people and this town filled with new parks, new coffee shops, new libraries, new streets. I hadn't expected that everything would feel quite so foreign. I decided to look for a small cabin where I could begin to ground myself.

I found an ad for a one-bedroom cabin at a community house, but though the cabin sounded great to me, I wondered how I would adapt to living communally. As much as I wanted to find a new circle of friends, finding a secluded little cave was sounding more and more appealing.

I dialed. The voice on the other end said they were on their way home from the Saturday Market, and I could meet them at their home now. Ten minutes later, I was pulling up to a beautiful house surrounded by a lush evergreen forest, a house that looked like a cross between a castle and a spaceship. "Welcome to the Mothership," the owners greeted me warmly.

They were David and Omni, a middle-aged couple with a playful spirit that made them seem almost like kids at times. They had just acquired a sizable quantity of strawberries at the market, and as I helped them wash and slice some for freezing, they began reliving their own story of how they had found this place, still clearly feeling amazed that they lived in such a palace. Omni swept me through the house, telling stories of how they had made it into their own space, watching the land and their little community evolve. Along the way, I took in the vibrant beauty of her many feltings and weavings that decked the walls, turning the house into a colorful art gallery. The main communal space consisted of a large round room with a kitchen, music area, and cozy places to sit, with

The Mothership.

Tona Appletree

Sunheart's main band members, Omni, David, and Eostar.

Pamela Wible

Do they think I'm weird for just showing up and expecting everything to work out for the best?

glass doors leading out to a spacious deck overlooking a breathtaking view of Spencer Butte and the surrounding forest. Above, a huge skylight flooded the space with sunshine. Seven or eight people usually lived in this house, a large double yurt (triple on one side). I would have my own little cabin just a short walk from the main house, in its own little clearing. When they said I could move in that day, I was thrilled.

I had never lived communally before, though, and I usually needed a lot of time to myself. The same spaces that looked cozy and inviting at first glance seemed intimidating when I realized I'd been ingratiated into a house of musicians, who tend to attract other musicians, filling the house with people and sound. Could I get used to this? I wondered. And do they think I'm weird for just showing up and expecting everything to work out for the best?

Many of them, I learned, had been through similar experiences. Omni told how David had shown up at her door in the rain 25 years ago, saying he'd come to Eugene to find his family. And they did their best to make me feel welcome—in my first week there, as their band, Sunheart, practiced for an upcoming gig, they invited me to join them, and I happily played tambourine, a buffalo drum, and maracas. That weekend, I joined them for their performance at the Essene Garden of Peace in nearby Triangle Lake.

Something about music can transform people from a bunch of individuals to a cohesive group. Feeding off the ecstatic energy of the crowd, I felt pure joy at being part of a creative force larger than myself. The energy of the music transported us all to a higher realm, where we remembered that we are one soul with all other beings: with all the people dancing, with the animals, forests, and stars of that

August night.

Soon I began playing keyboards with the band, and performed with them at a house party held at the Mothership. Guests brought a plethora of organic vegan food, and I almost couldn't believe that as a vegetarian of 10 years, I was finally in the majority.

Later, I would begin playing harmonium during kirtans with Fearless Love, led by the amazingly talented singer and songwriter Eostar Kamala. At these kirtans and at their concerts, the soul-stirring music and lyrics built a vibration so high that people could sense it in the air and left revitalized. Through music, I felt my sense of connection to others deepening profoundly. I still needed plenty of solitude, but an attitude of *carpe diem* had helped me to find my new community, and it was helping me to feel more at home in it as well. Finding a balance was difficult at times, and I had to step back often to replenish my energy. But through music, I felt the spirit that flows through all uniting me with others, reminding me that we are all sacred beings filled with the same divine essence that pervades the forests and meadows where I'd usually seek tranquility.

Within our circle of friends, most of us seemed to take this holistic approach, connecting with other living beings and the place where we lived on a spiritual level. By eating healthful foods produced humanely and locally, we celebrated our interdependence with nature, as well as the health of our community. We celebrated seasonal changes with the understanding that they reflect changes in our own selves. Days like the equinox or Beltane, which had been just another day where I'd grown up, became a chance to join together in celebration of the divine within all creation. On the spring equinox, I found myself torn between going to a poetry reading at a local nature preserve, a celebration at a spiritual center in town, and a party at a friend's in the country. I opted for all three. After a quiet, relaxed reading session with other poets, I found myself joining hands with a multitude of new and old friends, singing to Gaia as we spiraled around with hands joined. Then, I went to the party, where everyone sat deep in meditation while Eostar played the sonorous undertones of her didgeridoo. I quietly stepped in and joined the group, feeling surrounded by joy and awareness of the rhythm of life, reinforced by the steady vibration of the music that united us all.

At the same time, though, I sometimes felt myself falling out of alignment with my own inner rhythms. It was all too easy to forget my own needs for solitude until I started to feel drained. There's a fine line, I realized, between embracing community and expecting too much of myself. I wasn't going to develop into a bubbly, extroverted person, and I didn't really want to, even though many people seem to perceive that as the epitome of happiness and inner alignment. I liked my meditative, reflective tendencies; they form a large part of my identity. I still have to remind myself every day that my own feelings are valid and healthy, after growing up in a world that says they are not.

Living in community, with so much going on around me, I have to continually check in with myself to learn whether I should spend more time alone, or take a break during a gathering. Sometimes a part of me craves being involved in whatever happens to be going on at the moment, but I feel a stronger need to step aside. When people congregate together in the evening, I'm often starting to feel tired and in need of space, though I'd like to catch up with them about their day. It's a difficult balancing act, compounded by the fact that I'm a writer who needs plenty of quiet time to pursue projects. Because the dynamics of community continually shift, with some months (and members) quieter and some busier, my own balancing act continually shifts. I'm still adapting, and to some extent I probably always will be, but it keeps life interesting and dynamic.

In May, when the full moon came around, rumors began spreading about a musical gathering on top of Spencer Butte. Several bands and other musicians would be up there playing bluegrass music all day long, in this jamboree honoring the full moon. When I hiked up the butte with friends, we found dozens of people dancing and picnicking high above the busy town and countryside. As the sun set over the reservoir in the distance, everyone cheered and gave it a standing ovation. When the sky darkened and the moon rose over a distant mountaintop like a great orange pumpkin, people howled ecstatically.

I stepped back, closed my eyes, and listened. I allowed myself to simply watch, reminding myself that was all right. I sat on the side of the hilltop and looked out over the lights of the town, then over the darkened countryside stretching toward the horizon. In stillness I listened to the lively music and chatter, as if in meditation. After a long while, I stepped back into the circle, feeling more grounded.

I thought of how, to a distant observer, it might have seemed like just a party, but as locals well knew, these parties were a form of ceremony, a way of celebrating spirit. And as long as I nurtured my needs for solitude and tranquility, I could allow my own energy to merge with that of others to create something that transforms us all.

Going to the hot springs in the nearby mountains was, and continues to be, another very sacred type of ceremony—a ritual done with small groups of friends under the cover of dark. In the crisp chill of night, we hike down the woodland path and then step into the healing waters, their steam rising toward the spires of Douglas firs. We sometimes sing, or just sit in silence. The land nourishes us here as it did the indigenous people for thousands of years, and we radiate thankfulness in the blissful stillness of a starry night.

In these ways, we baptize one another in earth and water, love and light. And in these ways, we become family, for in remembering our rootedness in the cycles of nature, we remember who we are. ✳

Melanie Ravensong Martin is a freelance writer and editor with a master of arts degree in English who especially enjoys writing about nature and human cultures. She is also a storyteller who especially loves stories that emphasize our place in the larger community of nature. Find her blog at storygrove.blogspot.com.

From left to right, it's lead singer and guitarist David Sunheart, singer and guitarist Don St. Clair, drummer Glenn Falkenberg, drummer Nanda Dulal Das, lead singer Omni Mountainskyrainbow, and keyboardist Melanie Ravensong Martin. Barely visible behind David is bass player Troy Keys.

Rukmini Russell

Second Family

By Arizona Nashoba

The dreaded day in every mother's life finally arrived for me. All my children were out on their own, scattered around the world. It quickly became apparent that living in the family home, quietly waiting for the kids to have time to come visit me, was not a lifestyle I could adjust to. So, I sold my house and started moving around the country trying to find a place that would feel like home. Inevitably, everywhere I went included four empty walls that were devoid of the laughter, conversations, and shared work that I had become accustomed to while raising my children. Working, cleaning, and cooking for myself alone was just not worth the effort. I was stuck and I was going crazy. Empty-nest syndrome left me feeling lonely and without a purpose.

Author's housemates and second family, "The Nashobites." From left to right: Mr. Tom, Shakaya, Steve, Gwyn (a regular primary child of Madge), Madge, Jayel, Eve, Diane, Arizona, Marione, and Piper.

Four years later, in total desperation, I took my search to the internet looking for unique community living experiences. I thought that I could find a neighborhood that shared occasional potluck meals and truly interacted with each other. What I found instead was the Federation of Egalitarian Communities. The more I read about these intentional communities, the more excited I became. Could I have found my answer?

After days of carefully reading about each community, I decided to write a request to visit Twin Oaks. That single decision has led to a series of life-changing events.

The three-week visitor period provided me with ample opportunity to see how the community functioned. I worked alongside community members, ate with them, socialized with them, and quickly fell in love with the community lifestyle. My decision was made. I was applying for membership. The 10-day wait for 100 people to decide the fate of my choice was one of the longest periods in my life, but finally the wait was over—I had been accepted for provisional membership.

The move and subsequent adjustments to life at Twin Oaks were not quite as easy as my visitor's period had led me to think they would be. The labor scene was difficult to balance. Most days ended with me feeling totally exhausted and just wanting to climb into my bed and escape into dreamland. The social scene was also not as I had anticipated after my visitor's period. Now that I was a member and not a visitor, it was up to me to make the effort to reach out to other community members. They had their lives and routines and I had to attempt to become a part of that.

The days passed by quickly and each day I wondered if I had made the right decision. Perhaps I had made the choice too quickly. I wondered if lack of former community experience meant that I was not going to adjust or be accepted. And still I plodded through each day, reaching out to people when I had the opportunity, fulfilling my responsibilities, and trying to grow.

Around my three-month mark, halfway through my provisional period, I was walking to the writing group that I co-facilitate. One of the topics I had chosen for the group to write on—"Home"—was leading me to serious contemplation about my life here at Twin Oaks. It certainly isn't a perfect utopia.

Personal and community dramas are on display for everyone

(continued on p. 77)

SECOND FAMILY

(continued from p. 40)

to see and comment on. Everyone has their own beliefs about how the community should operate, which many times cause lively discussions about community intentions, finances, and businesses. Members have different viewpoints on just about every part of life, from work ethics to what should be served at dinner. Living here has provided me with daily challenges regarding personal interactions.

I continued walking and contemplating the lifestyle I have here at Twin Oaks. Tonight I have the writers' group, tomorrow is art therapy, and Wednesday night is cards with my housemates. On other evenings I may go to a dance party or make a walking date with another Twin Oaker. Sunday mornings bring a pancake breakfast with my housemates, at which we share Steve's delicious pancakes heavily seasoned with lots of good conversation and laughter. My work scene has begun to balance out; I know every day what tasks I am going to perform. Somehow or other, I too have quietly fallen into the nice comfortable routine filled with the laughter, conversations, and shared work that I was looking for. I have a new family, friends, and a purpose for this second part of my life.

As I walked along the forest path enjoying the acceptance of my new lifestyle, I heard the voice of one of the community's children call out. "Arizona! Arizona, I love you." I took a deep breath and smiled. I was home. ❀

Before joining Twin Oaks, Arizona worked as a software engineer. The fall of WorldCom/ MCI soured her perspective on the modern corporate world and led her to work completely for herself while researching the problems with businesses in today's world and our impacts on that world. Her findings left her searching for a better way of life.

Illustrations by Ethan Hughes

Power and Disempowerment on the Ecobus

By Chris Roth

I arrived for my first day on the Conservation Society Ecobus (not its actual name) wearing my Conservation Society t-shirt. I was happy and proud to finally be part of a tribe—to join something larger than myself that I could actually believe in. To me, the t-shirt symbolized this new beginning in my life, and the larger movement to which I was now dedicating myself.

Imagine my surprise when I was told to turn my t-shirt inside out.

The guides explained that by wearing t-shirts with writing on them, I and other students were serving as advertising placards, presenting images to other people in an effort to create impressions-by-association, rather than presenting our true, unbranded selves. T-shirts with writing showed inner insecurity, and furthermore, they were offensive and tiresome to look

at during hikes. By turning our t-shirts inside out, we would be reclaiming our power and our integrity, instead of giving them away to societal forces by buying into something that wasn't really us.

Not everyone agreed. While many of us had never considered this issue before, some had already sworn off corporate t-shirts but felt good about wearing environmental ones. A few people said they liked to wear t-shirts representing groups and causes they cared about, because it helped promote those causes and also was an excellent conversation-starter with others who had similar interests. But the guides and second-year students immediately became more emphatic, and the dissenting voices soon piped down. We apparently needed to agree on this. No one wanted to get off on the wrong foot. We all agreed to reverse our t-shirts, or wear plain ones.

Thus began a two-year journey during which I simultaneously gave away power and empowered myself with an expanded perspective on the world—lost my voice and aspects of my self while also discovering both. I've heard similar tales from others who've joined intensely focused, insular groups (what some label "cults," though that is not a term that the Fellowship for Intentional Community considers useful or fair, as it's an oversimplified, judgmental term in every case).

The questions that arise are similar among many of us, whether our experiences were in separatist Christian communities, ideologically-driven social experiments, radical environmentalist enclaves, groups guided by charismatic leaders (a category that can overlap with others), or any similarly focused community endeavors:

Were we being controlled, or had we found a new freedom in our adopted tribe? Had we lost our individuality, or gained a new sense of self? Were we simply conforming to new standards, or were we gaining the courage to resist conformity to the larger society's norms? Were these the best times of our lives, or the worst?

The answer was often: both. But I'm getting ahead of myself. So far, I'd only flipped my t-shirt inside out.

* * *

At 20, feeling isolated, alienated, and out of harmony with the world around me, I had left my traditional liberal arts college and set off on an entirely different course. The Ecobus' parent organization, the Conservation Society, had been a cornerstone of American environmentalism for decades, and had taken this traveling, consensus-run experiential education school, and its nine-month-long experiments in community living and outdoor learning, under its wing.

The Ecobus aimed to help its guides and students rediscover the awareness and practices needed to live in balance with ourselves, each other, and the natural world—to restore healthy individual, social, and ecological relationships. I stepped onto the bus brimming with idealism and enthusiasm (as well as some understandable fear at the newness of it all), and met the 22 people who'd be my fellow students and community-mates for most of the next year. The first lesson, about t-shirts, while unexpected, felt strangely liberating. The nuances of the issue seemed less important

than the opportunity to be "in this together." Something about the black-and-white framing of it, the radical shake-up of the default mode of being in the modern world (in which advertising was so pervasive that few questioned putting it on their bodies), comforted, even exhilarated me. The t-shirt decision solidified us as a tribe. Many more such decisions followed.

When applying to join the bus program, all of us had already consented to certain norms. We'd agreed to eat whatever was served, rather than following different diets. (Catering to individual dietary needs, we were told, would be too complicated and would also divide the group.) Dedicated meat-eaters, the guides made it clear that meat would be a regular element in the group diet. Although I'd been vegetarian for three years, I had agreed to this change in diet because I'd felt desperate for an actual group experience that would bring me back into harmony with the world and myself. There would be no alcohol, drugs, or tobacco, restrictions which were fine by me. Quite significant for many students, we had also agreed to refrain from "exclusive relationships" while on the bus—meaning not only sexual relationships, but "best friend" and confidant-type relationships. Our primary relationship was to be to the group as a whole—nothing could be said to any individual that was not OK to share with the entire group. (As those who tested this territory discovered, anything said to anyone that might raise any "issues" or indicate any personal or interpersonal tension ultimately would be aired in the whole group, by that person or by the person who caught wind of it.)

The men on the bus had also agreed to cut their hair so that the tops of the ears were visible, and to remove facial hair, because we didn't want to offend some of the "resource people" we'd meet on our travels by appearing to be hippies. We'd received a list of suggested clothing to bring, and partly as a result, we ended up not only cutting our hair similarly, but dressing similarly (though the patterns on our flannel shirts showed a bit of variety).

Much of the uniformity in our living habits was dictated by our situation. Each student's belongings needed to fit in a small cubby on the bus and a backpack on the roof. Living outdoors and camping, essential parts of the educational experience, were the only options

available to us. Some of us tended to sleep in tents, others under tarps, others under the stars, but we all slept outside except in the direst weather emergencies (which occurred on perhaps two nights during my two years with the program).

* * *

I found the new experience of sleeping outside deeply satisfying. I'd grown up in a suburb of New York City, and had been camping only a few times in my life. The Ecobus took us to beautiful natural places all over the country, exposed us to environments more varied and awe-inspiring than I could ever have imagined, and put us in direct, tactile contact with the earth every night. Not every camping experience occurred in the wilderness—in fact, wilderness hikes comprised just a fraction of our time together—but whether camping in a town, on a Native American reservation, in a developed state park, at a KOA campground, or in the backcountry, we were opening ourselves up to the outdoors, becoming comfortable with the earth (rather than a building) as our home. Given the previous trajectory of my life, I probably never would have done this on my own.

Camping felt quite empowering. Not only was I less dependent on "civilization," and able to take care of my own (minimal) shelter needs (with a little help from modern tent and tarp materials), but I shared my bedroom with the natural world, which I realized held more beauty and endurance than anything we humans can construct.

Sleeping outside together in a group of 23 people every night also offered a unique experience of community. Even when we spread out (as we often did), I felt a sense of solidarity with others that I have rarely felt in my life. For years afterward I would periodically miss that feeling—especially when I was

continuing to sleep outside, as all good Ecobus students did, but no one around me was. Where were my Ecobus mates? At those times, I would miss the tribal togetherness that had us all sleeping out together, whether the weather was balmy or extreme (as it sometimes was).

Dedicating ourselves to this practice, especially when it wasn't easy, challenged us and brought us together. If any of us had slept inside (in those rare situations where that might have been possible), it would have felt like a betrayal. In fact, sleeping outside was not only a practical matter—it was a moral statement and essential sign of our alignment. It embodied our commitment and loyalty to the group and to the earth. It was a nonnegotiable part of being an Ecobus participant. It was part of the same reassuring, black-and-white package of lifestyle choices that had us flipping our t-shirts inside out, eating whatever the group as a whole ate, refraining from couple relationships, and grooming and dressing ourselves nearly identically. It unified us as Ecobus students. It brought power to the group.

* * *

And at least once, it brought unexpected discord. On a night fairly early during my first year on the bus, we had set up camp in a state park, and many of us had chosen to sleep without tent or tarp, under the clear, star-filled sky. Part way through the night, an unanticipated rainstorm wakened us. Those without weather protection faced a choice: take their tent or tarp down from the roof of the bus and set it up in the pouring rain, or crawl under the large, roofed picnic shelter that was next to our campground. Most of the unprotected campers chose the latter course, and woke up in the morning relatively dry, grateful for the fortuitous location of that shelter.

But not everyone was so happy at this good fortune. At our

morning meeting (we met, always as a whole group, for several hours on most days), one of the guides uttered the "magic words" (words that were repeated, by various people, quite frequently—and that almost always resulted in a stoppage of all other activity and a devotion of the entire group's attention to the issue, for as long as it took to deal with it): "I have something to bring up."

He described what had happened the previous night, and asked if the people who'd chosen to sleep under the pre-constructed shelter had anything to say for themselves: What had they been thinking? How did their choice reflect our desire to be self-reliant, to set up our own shelters? Hadn't it been an example of taking the easy way out? Didn't it contradict what we stood for as a group? Wasn't this the first step on a slippery slope that would have us sleeping inside shelters built by others elsewhere as well? Had they honestly believed that this was the best choice to make? How serious were they about this program, anyway?

The students offered some explanations and apologies, but by this time most people knew that genuine debate was not wanted, that acquiescence was the only safe route, the course of least damage. They promised never to do it again. Had someone felt empowered enough to challenge the guide's assertions, they might have said:

That park shelter was built much more sustainably, using more local and durable materials, than our nylon tents and tarps made in China. The more we set up and take down those tarps and tents, especially in inclement conditions, the sooner they will wear out. The environmentally responsible choice is

to make use of an existing resource rather than, for arbitrary ideological reasons, using an alternative with larger negative impacts.

The guide might well have responded that sometimes the best choices *do* exact environmental costs, and that in this case the purity of our camping experience, our direct contact with the earth, held more importance than the negligible wear and tear on our equipment. But that conversation never happened, and none of us actually got to make that choice. Or rather we *did* make it—we ran by "consensus," after all (in unfacilitated meetings dominated by the loudest voices and without any training or formal consensus process)—but we made it under great duress. We had already given our power of choice away to those who ran the Ecobus. We already understood that we were there not to learn by making choices and seeing the results of those choices—we were there to learn by following the leaders' choices and adopting their worldview, or at least trying to.

* * *

In the first week or two, actual multi-sided conversations, exchanges of ideas held independently by individuals on the bus, had still attempted to occur. But the pattern established by our initial t-shirt discussion asserted itself quickly: if given a chance, people might start to share their own perspectives, but the guides and second-year students quickly moved in with the "Ecobus" interpretation of whatever we were discussing. Most problems were the result of "Prejudice Against Nature." "White-smockers" (soulless reductionist scientists, obsessed with measurements and logical arguments and cut off from the living, breathing earth) shared the blame for the plight of the planet with greedy corporations and clueless consumers. Most educational institutions (except the Ecobus) deliberately separated us from the earth in order to mold us into cogs in the machine of western civilization, which was destroying the planet and the native peoples who once lived in harmony with it. Our feelings were the voice of nature speaking through us, and they connected us with the rest of the living earth. By returning to actual, experiential connections with "Culture, Nature, and Self"—by recreating our understandings of and relationships to those, as we formed a subculture more attuned to them—we could help heal the damage the dominant culture had done.

The worldview was compelling in many ways, and I still believe that much of it has validity. I also now see other aspects of it as oversimplified, black-and-white interpretations of a nuanced, "gray" world. But during the Reagan years, that world seemed to have gone mad, as ecological concerns had been pushed to the margins (and often off the edge) of the national discourse. Corporations had seized power in Washington. The agencies responsible for our parks and wildlands had been deprived of enforcement power and taken over by corporate lackeys, and even most environmental groups had been forced to compromise until there was nothing left to give away. Our Secretary of Interior believed that the end of the world was near, and that if humans failed to use up all additional natural "resources" by that time, we would have sinned by failing to utilize the gifts that God had given us. He gleefully urged mining, drilling, and resource extraction everywhere—the more the better. In this atmosphere, the radical, often antagonistic response exemplified by the Ecobus seemed not only understandable, but justified.

Conversations would not end until all seemed to have "agreed" or at least acquiesced to the guides' point of view—until all dissenting voices were silent. The processes of forming consensus in our day-to-day decisions and of figuring out the meanings and reasons behind the issues we discussed relied on attrition, on wearing down the will of those who may have seen things a bit differently but got tired of arguing. Ultimately, resistance to the dominant view seemed futile—an ironic twist, in that our group prided itself on resisting the worldview of the dominant culture. Perhaps, in holding strong to that resistance,

we needed an unusual degree of unity—one that, if it didn't come naturally, had to be forced or constructed.

By a month into the program each year, most students wouldn't even bother stating an obviously alternative viewpoint—in fact, they seemed in competition with one another to articulate the "Ecobus" viewpoint first. How did we feel about the stripmine? As student after student reiterated (reinforced by the guides' approval), it was a rape of the earth. I had also noticed how colorful and awe-inspiring the rock exposed by the mining was—I had actually enjoyed seeing it—but I didn't dare say so. I kept quiet.

* * *

I noticed that I kept quiet a lot. Long discussions would go by and I wouldn't say a word. Some other students wouldn't either. Near the end of each discussion, a guide or one of the more voluble students, usually a second-year, would say, "I wonder why so-and-so [often 'Chris' during the first year, until I learned to prevent it by saying at least *something* before being called out] hasn't said anything? What is s/he thinking? Where is s/he at with this?"

In a group that discouraged alternative or more complex viewpoints, that pressured its participants into ideological conformity, it seems little wonder that some of us clammed up rather than giving our power away by saying things we didn't wholeheartedly believe, or that didn't express the full picture as we saw it. Instead, we chose to give our power away by *not* talking. I remember a period when I had difficulty articulating anything, even in normal conversation. I felt almost as if I'd lost my voice entirely; when I did manage to squeeze something out of my voicebox, it seemed to me strained, feeble, full of tension. People often asked me to repeat it, to speak up so they could hear me. I would, but I didn't really feel like talking. In retrospect, I'm sure my physical voice faded away because I didn't feel safe speaking about what was really going on inside, of which I was often in denial.

And yet, in a sense, I did also find my voice during those two years. I had been trained to be polite, socialized to not "rock the boat." I had often censored myself rather than raising difficult questions or offering potentially critical perspectives. The Ecobus turned this formula on its head. The guides encour-

aged us to criticize ourselves and each other, to "bring things up" whenever we saw a hypocrisy or inconsistency, to hold each other accountable to our group covenants and ecological principles. Experienced Ecobusers made it a habit of *not* saying "good morning" or "hi" or even, it seemed, smiling—those would distract, apparently, from the weighty business of focusing on how we each were failing to live up to our ideals. Displays of affection, casual touch, and hugging were absent from our culture, and actively discouraged by the guides; in fact, predictably, one of them blocked a proposed group hug at the beginning of my second year on the bus (such a thing had never even been proposed the first year), ensuring that the suggestion would never be repeated. A community we certainly were—but one committed to mutual challenge and confrontation rather than mutual support. The guides saw this as excellent training for challenging and confronting the people in agencies and companies who were ruining the planet—and we even got some practice with that, as we visited government offices and power plants and asked questions that made our hosts squirm.

Interestingly, the higher-ups seemed relatively immune to confrontation and challenge. Having figured out the "Ecobus way," they were responsible for embodying and articulating it. When our bus got together with the two sister buses in the program, I noticed that the guides and students on those buses seemed to act in the same ways, have the same discussions, hold the same worldviews and opinions as our bus. In fact, all the guides seemed to hold the same philosophy and even use the same jargon as the original founder of the Ecobus program, who guided one of the buses. It turns out that all five of the non-founder guides had been proteges of the founder on the original Ecobus, and were now doing their best to spread his understandings, which had become their own.

And during the course of those two years, many of those understandings became my own as well. I found that a lot of them did make sense to me; they helped me understand and interpret the world in ways I hadn't before. Especially in my second year, I became more outspoken on the bus. I felt that I agreed with most of the philosophy but didn't always agree with how we were attempting to embody it.

Increasingly, I felt able to "rock the boat" when I thought it needed rocking. I challenged the meat-eating dictum on environmental grounds, and almost succeeded in converting my bus to vegetarianism on a trial basis (stopped only by a couple holdouts who were unwilling to even attempt it). I remember questioning how much time we spent driving around instead of staying in one place. I found myself able to express my perceptions of other people and their personal challenges (as well as my own), and I rediscovered my ability to write. I was no scientist, just a beginning student of ecology, and a very poor naturalist at that point in my life, but in the areas of "psychology" and "English" I got high marks from fellow Ecobusers (both figuratively, and literally, in our very awkward mutual-grading ritual at the end of each semester). I also discovered a passion for Native American culture, which led me, upon graduation, to move to a reservation I'd first visited with the Ecobus. For the next four years, I continued to follow the "Ecobus code" by sleeping outside in all but the very most inclement weather, including all through the winter. And to this day, I have continued to be influenced by the ecological and cultural perspectives I gained on the bus, although I see that they were infected by varying degrees of fundamentalism, intolerance, decidedly *un*compassionate communication, pseudo-consensus, dysfunctional power dynamics, self-righteousness, hypocrisy, and naivete.

* * *

When I tell people about my times on the bus, they have one of two reactions: "That sounds *amazing*!" "That sounds *awful*!" Often the same person says both things during the course of the conversation; the order of the statements depends only on which parts of the story I happen to tell first.

Our group had experiences in natural ecosystems, on Native American reservations, in other land-based subcultures (from communities of Mennonite farmers to Appalachian mountain dwellers to remote Sierra Nevada homesteaders) that affected many of us profoundly, and permanently expanded our ideas about the world and its possibilities. We also witnessed power plants, mines, chicken factories, and environmental devastation; we spent time with policy makers and wild food foragers, folklorists and archaeologists, activists and conservationists. We all picked up musical instruments, sang together (learning songs particular to each region of the country we visited), and held our own contra-dances. We eschewed consumerism, mass media, and electronic entertainment of all sorts (although laptop computers and cell phones didn't yet exist, we would likely have boycotted those too). In their absence, we created, however awkwardly, our own culture and lives together during those years.

We talked and formed community. Were we always speaking our full truth, and was it a community of equals? No, and no. We each gained some inner power, and lost some inner power, by joining this tribe. Fortunately, most of us still had many decades ahead of us to continue to figure out how best to speak about our feelings (which we'd been told were the most important things, nature's way of expressing itself through us); how to relate most effectively with others (by being more compassionate, and less judgmental, than we'd been on the bus); how to connect most fully with the earth (for me, it wasn't riding around in a bus and camping, but rather gardening and immersing myself in local ecosystems in place-based intentional communities); how to distinguish between choices that were truly ours and choices that we made under pressure; and how to integrate everything we'd experienced on the bus in ways that empowered rather than disempowered us.

* * *

An intense, 24-hour-a-day, seven-day-a-week world unto itself, the Ecobus asked for total commitment from its participants. Was it a "cult"? In the sense that most people mean it, maybe it was. But the ease with which that label can apply to many aspects of it proves to me the uselessness of that label. I learned and grew through my time on the Ecobus in ways that I value to this day. My experience on the bus made unique contributions to my life, both through its "positive" and "negative" lessons, influencing everything I've done since. And it left

me with many memories (most more comical than troubling in retrospect, and many of them beautiful) that continue to inspire me, or at least provide good fodder for conversation. You haven't heard the half of them.

But here are a few more: there was the night we were drenched by the municipal sprinklers set on "automatic" in the town park; the frigid winter evenings sitting in a circle around a non-campfire talking about how cold we were, but how the act of enduring extreme low temperatures was more aligned with nature than building a fire; the hike along Baxter State Park's narrow Knife Edge, during which several of us had uncontrollable bowel ailments...and the welcome we felt at southwestern pueblo dances; the quiet of a backcountry canoe trip; the transcendent beauty of the song of the canyon wren; the glimpses we offered each other into our own complex, tender inner worlds, in which the answers were seldom quite as easy as those offered by any single worldview, no matter how comprehensive. And there were the many times when we got past the words and I felt, on a much deeper, more tactile level, that we were indeed part of the earth, living in community with one another in ways that were *not* forced, finding our power from sources more fundamental and enduring than the relatively insignificant human power dynamics of the day.

About the t-shirts: I now wear them right-side out...except when I choose not to. ❧

Postscript: In the decades following my two years on the Ecobus, the program evolved considerably. A new generation of leaders replaced the original guides, introducing new ideas, a much greater emphasis on diversity (in everything from thought to diet), increased bioregional focus, and more compassionate communication. Yet there were also tradeoffs; latter-year students, who could enroll on a single bus for only a semester at a time (a shortened and more-expensive one at that), by most reports experienced less intensity, less unity, less commitment, fewer contra-dances danced, and fewer folk songs learned. Regrettably, financial and organizational challenges eventually forced the cessation of the Ecobus program. It is sorely missed and still mourned by many of its alumni, from every era.

Chris Roth edits Communities *and currently calls Rutledge, Missouri's tri-communities area home.*

> *The Ecobus asked for total commitment from its participants. Was it a "cult"? In the sense that most people mean it, maybe it was. But the ease with which that label can apply to many aspects of it proves to me the uselessness of that label.*

Subscribe to COMMUNITIES Magazine

BRIDGING SOCIAL AND CULTURAL DIVIDES

COMMUNITIES
Life in Cooperative Culture
Spring 2018 • Issue #178

CLASS, RACE, and PRIVILEGE

Barriers to Diversity
White Bias, Black Lives
Class-Harmony Community
Confronting Cultural Appropriation
Combating Racism, One Community at a Time

Your source for the latest information, issues, and ideas about intentional communities and cooperative living today!

Each issue is focused around a theme:
• Ecovillages around the World • Finding or Starting a Community
• Community and the Law • Food and Community • Community for
Baby Boomers • Technology: Friend or Foe? • Business Ventures in
Community • Gender Issues • Renewable Energy • Youth in Community
• Diversity • Spirituality • Permaculture • Right Livelihood ...

• Reach listings—helping communities looking for people and
people looking for communities find each other.

What Readers say about COMMUNITIES

I love COMMUNITIES magazine. Deciding to be communal is the best decision I've ever made in my life. Communities has been there from the beginning.
—**Patch Adams, M.D.**, author and founder of the Gesundheit Institute

COMMUNITIES has become one of our go-to sources for thought-provoking pieces about people opting out of the rat race and living life on their own terms.
—**Christian Williams**, Editor, Utne Reader

Each issue is a refreshing antidote to the mainstream media's "me, me, me" culture. COMMUNITIES overflows with inspiring narratives from people who are making "we" central to their lives instead.
—**Murphy Robinson**, Founder of Mountainsong Expeditions

Community has to be the future if we are to survive. COMMUNITIES plays such a critical role in moving this bit of necessary culture change along.
—**Chuck Durrett**, The Cohousing Company, McCamant & Durrett Architects

For more than 40 years COMMUNITIES has done an outstanding job of promoting the communitarian spirit as well as serving intentional communities and other groups coming together for the common good.
—**Timothy Miller**, Professor of Religious Studies, University of Kansas

For many years we've been associated with and have strongly supported COMMUNITIES because we're convinced of its unique contribution to the communities movement in the United States and the world.
—**Lisa and Belden Paulson, Ph.D.**, cofounders of High Wind community

COMMUNITIES has been important to me ever since I began researching intentional communities back in 1980.... The Editors have always been willing to include critical articles which challenge accepted norms.
—**Dr. Bill Metcalf**, Griffith University, Brisbane, Australia

COMMUNITIES mentors me with real human stories and practical tools: networking, research, and decades of archives that nourish, support, and encourage evolving wholesome collaborations.
—**Shen Pauley**, reader and author, Barre, Massachusetts

COMMUNITIES is an invaluable resource for information on the many forms of intentional communities. I have received every issue since the magazine's very beginning in 1972.
—**Professor Emeritus Yaacov Oved**, Tel-Aviv University, Yad Tabenkin Institute

I feel as though I have traveled around the world and experienced a wide range of community perspectives each time I finish an issue. It's an uplifting gift each season!
—**Devon Bonady**, Founder, Fern Hill Nursery, Cottage Grove, Oregon

Subscription rates (print plus digital unless you specify): 1-year $25 US ($35 international), 2-year $45 US ($65 international), 3-year $60 US ($90 international), lifetime $500 US. Sample of current issue: $7 US ($9 international). Prepurchase of 10 copies of single issue: $50 US. Please specify if digital-only (in which case US rates apply regardless of location).

To subscribe or order copies by mail, please send us your name (of individual or contact person), phone, email address, group name or affiliation (if applicable), street, city/town, state/province, and zip/postal code, with the total amount paid by check or by Visa/MC/Discovery, with card number and expiration date. For gift subscriptions, please send addresses of gift recipients. Also, please let us know if you do not want your name shared with like-minded organizations.

Please mail to FIC, 23 Dancing Rabbit Lane, Rutledge, MO 63563, call 1-800-462-8240, or subscribe online at ic.org/subscribe.

Now including digital subscriptions and digital-only options! ic.org/subscribe

Ad Astra per Aspera: Through Adversity to the Stars — A Community Member's Passage to India and Back

How must a student cooperative member readjust her sense of community and mindfulness in order to live in an ecovillage in India? Perhaps a better question is how she must deal with reentry into the United States and her original living situation once her stint in India has ended. These are two questions I faced this winter as I embarked on a journey to the state of Tamil Nadu to work on a reforestation project connected to the Auroville Community, just miles from the town of Pondicherry.

Although the Auroville community was founded in 1968 by the Mother, protégé of the philosopher and spiritual leader Sri Aurobindo, the community in which I lived and worked, called Sadhana Forest, was founded only six years ago in December of 2003 by an Israeli couple and their daughter. Founders Yorit and Aviram invested their life savings into the land on which the community now sits, and in doing so they began a bold reforestation project with the help of volunteers from around the world. In exchange for work in the now-lively dry evergreen forest, as well as work around the community of self-made thatched huts, volunteers receive free room and board for a stay of one month or more. The main goal of Sadhana Forest is to reforest a plot of land made arid by the Indian government in times past. However, further goals include an experimental lifestyle seeking a vastly reduced carbon footprint combined with community oneness among a large group of volunteers.

Upon joining the Living Routes study abroad program founded by the University of Massachusetts, I agreed to a host of guidelines including mandatory sobriety, a vegan diet, and forest work each weekday. However, it was not until I entered the forest that the reality of these criteria hit me. Forest work began just after dawn, once the community members were awakened by the music of one or another volunteer with a drum or a guitar, whose job it was to enter each of the huts and gently rouse the volunteers from sleep. Sleep itself was an issue for me at times. It took longer than I would have liked to adjust to both my jetlag and the hot, humid climate, not to mention the beds which were woven from local, indigenous fibers and which seemed

to bow in the middle after a few nights of tossing and turning. Furthermore, we were lucky enough to be in Tamil Nadu during the New Year, a time during which temples open at four in the morning, blasting music to prepare Hindus for the auspicious change from the darker phase of the year into the lighter season.

But I was determined to make the adjustment, and adjust I did. I began paying attention to the more minute details of this very intriguing community. The community hosts anywhere from 50 to 200 volunteers, depending on the season. During our stay this winter, there were upwards of 150 volunteers, winter being the most popular time to visit southern India to avoid the stifling heat of the summer months. Of the community's population, about 15 were members of families, including Aviram, Yorit, and their two young daughters. There were also families from Russia and South America.

I discussed the dynamics of raising a family in this setting with the other students in my group. The children were brought up using a method called

Photos by Chelsea Cooley

"unschooling," in which they weren't prompted to learn any specific skills or information, but were rather taught only those things which they first discovered themselves. Only when asked by the child did a parent shed light on any particular topic or skill. This method of childrearing was certainly hotly debated, not only among the group of students but also among other members of the community. It wasn't rare for an "unschooled" child to pee on someone's yoga mat during a workshop or wipe his rear-end with a spoon before passing it out for a group meal. Honestly, I sometimes felt envious of these children, who rarely wore clothes and seemed so uninhibited and free, but I was also often aggravated by them. Oftentimes children would play too roughly with the small puppies in the community, and younger children would scream and shout throughout every group meeting or event, even while others were talking. "Should I not tell these children to be quiet?" I thought, frustrated. "Shouldn't 11-year-old so-and-so know how to read by now?" I asked myself when I noticed one child was still illiterate.

Nonetheless, the level of unity among this hodge-podge of volunteers from around the world, some (like us) staying no more than a month, was remarkable. I believe that we were able to bond so quickly because we shared a common goal that was higher than each of us as individuals. We were each there as a steward of the earth and indeed of all living creatures. Through our commitment to sustainability and non-harming, we naturally adopted a gentle attitude toward one another—nothing else would make sense in such a community. The practices of veganism and environmentalism combined with the prohibition of competitive games made peacefulness the obvious mode of behavior.

In this community focused on saving the land and appreciating life, a multitude of sustainable living practices flourish. Sadhana permits the use of only biodegradable soaps and detergents, and since there is no running water but rather the use of a hand-pump, water is much more readily conserved than might otherwise be the case. Various composting methods were also in the works—including a vermiculture system introduced by a couple of students in my group—and dishes are cleaned with potash and vinegar.

I was both impressed and concerned by Sadhana's cashless economy. Unlike my community in the US, where there is no hierarchy and no singular leader or landlord, Sadhana has definite leaders in Aviram and Yorit. At each meeting, the volunteers are told to be thankful to them and their children for letting us stay at their home. It follows that Sadhana Forest is their investment, and since Sadhana engages in no cash enterprise, they depend on donations to make necessary purchases. They don't require rent, only charging a small amount to cover expenses for food and biodegradable toiletries (an amount made even smaller, when compared to US dollars, by the small value of an Indian rupee).

Given this situation, I found myself scrutinizing the financial situation in my own student co-op household, in which we each pay rent that goes into a general fund used for maintenance, bulk food, supplies, etc. After living in Sadhana, I feel lucky, time and again, to have luxuries like running water and electricity. With Sadhana as a comparison, rather than wish my household didn't waste these things, I more often find myself thanking my lucky stars that I have them at all. As a student in Sadhana, a place that *maybe* has electricity for an hour a day, obtained through solar panels or human-powered stationary bikes if at all, I found it difficult to complete any school-related assignments or even to contact my parents back home. This was not made easier by the fact that there is very little privacy in the community, unless one ventures into the forest alone. Each room in the dorm-style huts is separated from the next by only a sheet or a mosquito net.

After so much new input and experience, one of the greatest questions in my mind as I flew home from India was how in the world I would reintegrate into my old lifestyle. How could I employ such drastic lifestyle changes in my own life in the US and my laid-back student cooperative? I spoke with my roommates at the Ad Astra House in Lawrence, Kansas about Sadhana in our first house meeting after my return, but I felt I was

(continued on p. 77)

Opposite page left: The huts in Sadhana and nearby Auroville are thatched by hand from indigenous fibers. Opposite page middle: Student Amanda Staton sits in front of the Main Hut in Sadhana Forest. Opposite page right: An organic rice farmer in Auroville tells students about the sustainable use of water.
This page starting left: Ad Astra House in winter. Sign out front. Roomies in the kitchen. Laundry line.

AD ASTRA PER ASPERA: THROUGH ADVERSITY TO THE STARS

(continued from p. 61)

only rambling, only scratching the surface of what this vastly multidimensional experience taught me.

So I decided to be, as Gandhi said, the change I wished to see in the world. Although I was vegan before going to Sadhana, I began paying closer attention to all the food I buy and ingest. I started buying more local, organic food, as is the practice in the forest. I'm also more shamelessly vegan now than I was before, when I acted almost apologetic for my dietary choices, not realizing the scope of environmental and physical degradation caused by the meat and dairy industry. I started using only biodegradable soaps and detergents and encouraged my roommates to do the same—a practice which has had positive effects on my skin and hair as well as my community's ground water.

Luckily, as the "buyer" for my house, the person who purchases supplies and bulk food, I was able to put these ideas into practice on a grander scale that affects my whole household rather than just me alone. Most importantly, I was able to incorporate the maturity and philosophy of humility I learned at Sadhana, as well as the necessary work ethic, into my life at home. The world no longer revolves around me as it did before. Rather, I am only one aspect of a unified whole. I am responsible for a certain amount of waste and suffering in this world,

and I can make the conscious decision to minimize them both.

My only continued concern after reentering my household is our lack of group unity as compared to the community at Sadhana. As a student, each member of my household has a different, busy schedule. We eat group meals only once every couple of weeks rather than three times a day, and chores often go undone, perhaps because we don't have group work sessions as they do in Sadhana. I'm concerned by this lack of unity, but I also feel as though different circumstances call for different measures. Since we each do work outside the community, less energy is focused on the house itself. I wonder, for a busy college student, could life be any different?

And of course, I'm concerned that my house is in no way capable of matching Sadhana in its ability to practice the three R's: reduce, reuse, and recycle. This is true despite the fact that my house consumes much less and recycles much more than the average household. Sadhana represents a studied and conscious approach to sustainability, where conservation is itself the main goal of the community. At my cooperative, sustainability is *a* goal, but not the main one. I am the only vegan, and there is still a trashcan full of waste at the end of each week—to which I contribute my fair share. I wonder, is there time or desire for sustainability to be the main focus of my community? Given the state of the world and the environment, *should* sustainability be the main goal?

I believe successfully forming a community like Sadhana in the US requires taking into account certain material considerations, and I wasn't the only visitor to think so. In all practicality, in order for a society accustomed to capitalism, consumerism, and creature comforts to accept sustainable living practices, those practices must be made attractive somehow. I doubt the majority of Americans will adopt hand-powered water pumps over running water or open-air thatched huts over enclosed living spaces—even if a small group of people might enjoy such things for a time. Water conservation must become a way of life instilled in American children from the youngest age, and permaculture must be both attractive and comfortable to take root on a vast scale. I believe these things are possible, and I appreciate Sadhana for employing them in their extreme, raw forms. It's now up to students like us to bring such ideas back to the US and shape them in such a way that they are applicable to our society at home. ❧

Chelsea Cooley is a radio DJ and student at the University of Kansas, where she studies world religions and history. She lives in the Ad Astra student cooperative in Lawrence.

It Takes a Community to Grow an Elder

By Rebecca Dale

Growing up and growing "elder" together. Right: The author celebrates her 70th birthday with her community, and gets a birthday hug from one of the community kids, Jade, who turned seven on the same day.

Growing older was not sitting well with me. At 65, I was having an identity crisis worthy of adolescence, moodiness and all. Who was I now that I was retired, no longer able to answer the question "What do you do?" with a job title? Who was this person in the mirror with gray hair and wrinkles, with aches and pains and other intimations of mortality? When people my age got their names in the paper, they were usually labeled as "elderly," a term that sounds like "has-been" to my ears. Although we sometimes refer to older people who have great influence and responsibility as "elder statesmen" or "elders" in our churches, we don't seem to have a respected role for "elders" in everyday life, so I didn't know how to be one. All the messages I had received up to that point told me there was no honor in growing older, only a gradual shuffling out of the category of adulthood into a separate world of retirement communities, senior centers, and the patronizing smiles or thinly veiled impatience of people who think you no longer have a brain. No wonder I was depressed.

I had been widowed for a decade. My children and grandchildren lived at opposite ends of the continent. I tried to fill the identity gap with volunteer work: nature education, garden writing, agitating for a farmers market. But these things held little value in a place where shopping malls and suburban sprawl were bulldozing their way across the family farms and small towns I had once known, and which now seemed as obsolete as I felt. My old way of life was gone, my sense of place, my human connections. Then I learned about intentional communities through the internet, which led me not only to a new home but a new life partner as well.

Currents is a small community in rural southeastern Ohio, founded nearly 30 years ago, along with several other small communities, in the beautiful foothills of the Appalachians. Five original members remained at Currents, all 60-ish and beyond, all community elders with much community wisdom to share. I would be joining them as an elder in community with much to learn. Since my joining, two mid-life couples

with young families have become members also, and so I've become something of a bridge. Like the younger ones, I'm a newcomer to community life, but I'm also an older person growing into a new role of...elder? What can this mean?

That summer of 65, the summer of my discontent, I went to a week-long study gathering with Joanna Macy called "The Great Turning." I was sharing some of my feelings about aging with another woman of my generation, when she smiled brightly and said, "Why, don't you know? We're the hope of the future!" Surprised, I answered, "I always thought children were the hope of the future." "Oh no," she replied, "Children ARE the future. But we're the HOPE of the future because we hold the wisdom."

We hold the wisdom. That sounded so right, yet the more I turned that statement around in my mind, the more it seemed as if I had been handed a gift that needed to be unwrapped. And each layer of wrapping was like a provocative question, and my search for answers became like a little treasure hunt through my own life.

Is it wisdom, then, that makes one an elder rather than merely old? What is this wisdom? And where does it come from? Obviously age alone doesn't automatically make one wise. No more than simply reaching 18 or 21 automatically makes one an adult! One can be childish and self-involved at any age, but I've noticed that those we call elders are those who have done their inner growth work, who have successfully navigated the developmental stages of life.

I looked again at the human development theories of Abraham Maslow, Erik Erikson, Jane Loevinger, and others, and was struck by how much our society functions like an adolescent, competitive and concerned with appearance and social conformity, things that I stopped caring about long ago. I'm much more inner-directed now, while probably more idealistic and outwardly focused than ever. Mainstream society looks at me and says I'm past my prime; developmental theories suggest I'm just now getting there. This is definitely good news! Aging doesn't have to mean drying up. On the contrary, it appears that when people open to inner growth, including its ethical dimensions, "they still bring forth fruit in old age, they are ever full of sap and green." (Psalms 92:14 RSV)

OK, so we're flexible (green), draw on juicy, nourishing resources (sappy!), and continue to be fruitful. But what is the shape of this new fruit? And how is it to be shared? In traditional societies, the elders assimilated and passed on their culture's skills and values. But in our adolescent culture, educational institutions and mass media assume that role, teaching the values of wealth and the skills of competition. Such "conventional wisdom" tends to drown out the voices of our true elders who could call us to a saner way of being human. We have a culture that marginalizes our elders, so many of us have no models for elderhood. Who will show us how to access our own wisdom and share it?

Recently I read about some studies reported in the New York Times indicating that our brains actually learn a new trick as they age.[1] They are better able to take in seemingly irrelevant bits of information often overlooked by younger brains. And in spite of occasional memory glitches, our older brains, while a bit slower, actually get more creative in drawing on our storehouse of these many bits of knowledge and experience and integrating them into helpful forms. What this suggests to me is that if wisdom is experience grounded in maturity, I actually have an inner elder ready to kick in and put together some wisdom when I need it. And so do my mature and ripened friends, who have different knowledge and experiences. What if we let our inner elders out to play more often, maybe in circles of elders, maybe together with others of all ages? Could we conjure up some wisdom magic? How cool would that be?

Actually, I've just described what I've seen happen on those occasions when community works well, especially multi-generational communities like mine. Younger people can develop nurturing, non-parental relationships with older ones; our presence can help to anchor their lives in a deeper historical context. I think this is part of what "holding" the wisdom means. Older people get to see the world anew through younger eyes. This keeps us on our toes, gives our wisdom-generating apparatus material to work on.

But there is a particular form of wisdom that our community elders are in a unique position to share: the values and the skills of creating and maintaining community. This is not my personal wisdom because I came to community late in life. It is something that I am learning from those who have been here for many years, who know something (however imperfect our actual practice may be) about organizing, resolving conflicts, cooperation and communication, and just plain thinking well about what community really means—and what it can mean for a world that sorely needs more of it.

What is MY wisdom? What can I pass on to a generation that is inheriting a dramatically changing world?

What is MY wisdom? What can I pass on to a generation that is inheriting a dramatically changing world? Knowledge of ecology and restoring the land, yes. Knowledge for re-skilling in food growing and processing, of course...but knowledge isn't wisdom.

I used to think that my ability to navigate change was my particular gift. I once lost a farm and a way of life that I loved. I moved on and found other good ways to live and love. But "moving on" is not the same as thriving unless one becomes anchored again in a place and with a people. Just changing careers is not enough. People who have lost their way of life as so many did in the wake of Katrina, and now in the Gulf disaster, cannot simply be re-trained and "move on." One needs a sense of place, and connection to a people and a way of life that matters, and that continues. The many young people and families who are finding their way to Currents (and other communities) these days to experience these things are longing for them.

This kind of placemaking is the wisdom that our community elders hold. I trust they know how very valuable and wise this way of life is, this way that they have struggled for, this way into a future with hope. This is the wisdom that I am learning, the wisdom that is turning me into an elder, instead of merely elderly. ✍

Rebecca Dale is a late-blooming communitarian living in Currents Community in southeastern Ohio. She has been a farmer, worked as a nurse, librarian, and occasional free-lance writer, and used the freedom of retirement to complete graduate work in Earth Literacy and earn a certificate in permaculture design. Digging in the dirt and hanging out in the woods are high on her list of favorite things.

1. www.drweil.com/u/QAA400422/My-Aging-Brain-Whats-Your-Name-Again.html

And I Listen

Staying connected and building trust when adult children choose the "alternative" lifestyle of living in community

By Victoria Albright

My first experience of living in an intentional community was at age 53, and the first four days there were among the most challenging of my life.

It was 2001, and I had come to Lost Valley Educational Center near Eugene, Oregon, at the invitation of my then 25-year-old daughter Sarah who was there for an organic gardening internship. She was enjoying her time there and wanted to share the experience, *plus* the community needed someone to head up food preservation activities, something I knew about from growing up in an Iowa farm family and from preserving the fruits of my avid gardening. She wanted me to share my skills and teach the young adults there how to "put up" food.

I jumped at the opportunity for the two-month work-trade position. My friends in Houston thought I was crazy: "A visit, yes, but two months? What are you thinking?" Sarah and another community member met me at the train station, gave me a warm welcome, and settled me into my room at the guest house. She introduced me to a few people, including one of my "supervisors" for the food preservation project—an intense young man with scary tattoos and lots of piercings (even in his nipples...I had never seen THAT before!). The next day, my daughter left for the weekend. Her new boyfriend (who eventu-

> *Had I been in possession of a car, I would have written a "Dear Sarah…what have you gotten me into?" letter and been out of there.*

ally became her husband) was leaving town for a month and wanted to celebrate her birthday. So off she went, bidding me to settle in and enjoy myself.

Although I'm not a shy person, it was a long and lonely weekend for me. Many of the community members were gone for a few days and the others were running a four-day personal growth workshop (Naka-Ima) so they were totally focused on those responsibilities. Throughout the weekend I would hear shouting, howling, and cries of despair coming from the classroom area. Hmmm. I was invited to share meals, but the intensity of the dinner-table conversation related to the workshop drove me to eat alone in my room, partly to honor the process of the workshop participants but also because I didn't have a clue what anyone was talking about!

Had I been in possession of a car, I would have written a "Dear Sarah…what have you gotten me into?" letter and been out of there. But I had no car, so I retreated completely to my room. When Sarah returned on Monday, she found me curled in a fetal position on my bed contemplating my navel and trying to comprehend the situation.

She encouraged me to tell her what was wrong, so I really let her know EVERY-THING that was wrong…in MY opinion. She listened…and then listened some more. She apologized for "leaving me stranded in this alien land," as I had put it. It turns out that the community members had thought that Sarah was going to give me an orientation and spend the first few days with me, while she had assumed that they, probably the Pierced One, would take care of those things…and I simply fell through the cracks.

As I berated her for "throwing me to the wolves" and insisted that she arrange transportation to a rental car location or the train station, she gently encouraged me to calm down and work through this so that we could carry on with our original plans. But I was beyond mad and in panic mode and would have none of it…*especially* when she said that she would find a third person to "sit" with us (which I soon learned is community-speak for a mediator). I believe my response was something like "Absolutely not. This is nobody's business but ours!"

That's when I saw her love for me, her trust in the members of the community, and her strength as a woman living her heart's passion come together in a way that would eventually transform our relationship and my life. She stood up, took hold of my shoulders and looked me in the eyes. "If you won't do it for yourself, Mama, *do it for me.*" That's the day I fully realized that the "elder" in a situation is not necessarily the "older." Those words of wisdom coming from my daughter pierced through my fear and my anger and opened the door to the adventure of a lifetime.

A few hours later, we "sat" with one of the elders of the community, who was at least 10 years younger than me, and I once again experienced the profound beauty and healing of deep listening and compassionate communication. Dee was a loving and compassionate woman who had spent years developing these skills. She helped me cut through my anger to the core of the pain I was feeling, encouraging me to reconnect with the special bond that Sarah and I had as mother and child, and leading me to a place in my heart where I could see and respect my daughter as the beautiful and confident young woman she was becoming.

Before we started, we sat together in silence and slowed down our breathing, gathering our awareness into the present moment and relaxing into each other's presence. When she looked at Sarah and me, I could see that she was genuinely interested in us and wanted to support us. There was no sense of urgency or impatience and, to my

amazement and relief, no apparent judgment on her part that I was some clueless mainstream mama from Texas.

As Sarah had done earlier, Dee listened…and then listened some more. She asked, "What about this situation threatens you?" and "What is your greatest fear related to Sarah?," all the while encouraging me to go deeper with each question, never judging but sometimes reflecting back what I had said to make sure that she had understood me correctly. She turned to Sarah and asked, "What are your needs related to your mother's visit and to your relationship in general?" On it went for almost two hours…asking, listening, openly sharing, reflecting, going deeper, and, in the process, transforming.

So I stayed for the two months, immersed myself in community life, made new friends (including a deep appreciation and love for the Pierced One), and happily fulfilled my work-trade duties—picking blackberries and apples, making jam and apple butter, and teaching canning techniques to dozens of young people. I also did things which, though unplanned, turned out to be some of the most valuable and transformational activities of my life, such as participating in the Naka-Ima workshop which had alarmed me that first weekend. I learned a lot about myself, all the while thoroughly enjoying my new relationship with my daughter.

During that summer, I realized that many of my fellow communitarians were working through struggles with their parents regarding their own decisions to live in community. I heard their stories and found myself, unexpectedly, growing into the role of elder as I began "sitting" with some of their parents who had come for a visit. This role culminated the weekend that I finally participated as a student in Naka-Ima, along with three other mothers, while our daughters assisted at the workshop. Everyone at Lost Valley lovingly dubbed that weekend "Mama-Ima." [A description of this experience is online at lostvalley.org/talkingleaves/node/133.]

In preparation for writing this article, I asked my friend, Devon, to recollect her conflict with her parents around her decision to join Lost Valley. She recounted:

I am not sure when I communicated with my parents about choosing to join the community as a "member." I just remember how difficult it was and some of the fear-based responses that I heard from them. "You can't do this to us." "It's a cult and we are worried about you." "It's not fair to us." "Join the real world." Etc. I felt upset that they were not owning their feelings but instead putting them on me, telling me that my decisions caused them pain and fear and, therefore, I was being "selfish."

The tension in their dialog eased the weekend Devon's mother participated in "Mama-Ima."

At the workshop, she had plenty of time to talk with the other mothers. They shared their experiences, fears, worries, and concerns. I think it was a great relief for my mom. They also created a ritual to release their daughters as children and connect with them as young women. It was powerful and transforming. I know some things shifted for my mom that weekend.

While participating in community life with my daughter, first in Oregon and later in communities in France, Iowa, and Missouri, I have met dozens of young communitarians who are truly devastated by the conflict they are experiencing with their parents over their decision to pull away from a mainstream lifestyle. I think it is pretty safe to say that most parents want what is "best" for their children and for their children to be happy. But the rub is that parents can usually offer only what they know, which may include a steady job, benefits and health insurance, a traditional family lifestyle, and modern conveniences (cars/planes, computers, appliances) that all translate to them as a safe, secure life. Living in a community rarely fits into that picture.

Intergenerational conflict is nothing new, but we are living in transformative and chaotic times. Whether those of us who are parents like it, or not, our lives are different in ways we never dreamed or expected, including our children's lifestyle choices. To reduce the parent-child relationship to a debate about the merits or costs of these lifestyle choices or other issues is to jeopardize some of the most wonderful things about

Victoria and her daughter, Sarah, alternate playing role of "elder" in their relationship.

Victoria and Sarah's first breakthrough in communication came from "sitting" with another community member who helps facilitate the process of compassionate communication and deep listening. They have continued this practice for 10 years, this time with Keren at The Possibility Alliance.

being human—our heart connection, our capacity for love and acceptance, and our joy.

Parents have a choice…to open up and stay connected with their children by truly seeing them as adults who have the God-given right to choose their life's path OR to forfeit that connection by resisting and attacking the life their children have thoughtfully chosen. Devon wrote:

I feel grateful that my parents have been willing to accept me no matter what, and I know it has not been easy for any of us. While living in community, I met many people who had severed all ties with their families.

Sarah called from England to excitedly share the "wonderful news" (I thought she was going to tell me that she was pregnant!) that she had decided to be car-free! THUD. I told Sarah that it felt like she had just spit in my face!

Their parents did not even know where they were living. At times, I actually envied them. I had so many struggles, and still do, communicating with my parents! Even so, I am extremely grateful for their acceptance and love.

Just like their parents, adult children also have a choice… to show respect and express their appreciation and gratitude to their parents for the values they share in a compassionate and loving way OR to focus only on the disagreements and create a permanent barrier to a loving connection.

Sometimes in community, it felt easier to just adopt the other friends and residents as my family rather than work on loving and accepting my own family. But by making that effort and doing the

work, I have come to really appreciate my parents and I am so glad that I have.

Most of us go to great lengths to avoid emotional struggle and pain, but the truth is that by doing so we inevitably cause more of it. Based on my experiences, and those of so many others that I have witnessed, mustering up the courage and making the time to communicate and discuss these sensitive issues pays off a hundred-fold.

It is worth noting that the need for this work never stops. Several years ago, Sarah called from England to excitedly share the "wonderful news" (I thought she was going to tell me that she was pregnant!) that she had decided to be car-free! THUD. Memories flooded in…joyful road trips together, the freedom to travel at will, the promise that "Even though Ethan is carfree, I will *always* ride in the car with *you*, Mama." I felt like I was in one of those movies where you can time-travel to the past in a spinning vortex…. right back to 2001 in that lonely room in the guest house filled with anxiety that I had lost all connection with my daughter. The hurt was no different. I told Sarah that it felt like she had just spit in my face! All of my pain and fears rushed out at her over the phone. We were both surprised and devastated for our own reasons.

But this time, at least, I knew there was work to be done and how to do it. This time, I *listened*…to my own pain and aspirations and to those of my daughter. As she crossed the Atlantic to come home, I wrote her a long letter sharing what I had learned. This "conflict" became another opportunity to grow closer. And we did.

If the community of Lost Valley had not made the decision to offer workshops that teach the skills of nonviolent (compassionate) communication and deep listening, my relationship with Sarah may never have achieved such positive transformation. I thank them for this gift from the bottom of my heart. It is my fervent hope that other communities will see personal growth and loving interpersonal communication as priorities, and make them available to their members and visitors as well.

My daughter, Sarah, and her husband, Ethan, went on to found a new community in northeast Missouri called The Possibility Alliance. Our paths continue to align, so my husband and I purchased a home where I can live close-by during half the year. For the past three years, new community members, interns, and visitors have arrived at The Possibility Alliance in Missouri who are struggling with family conflict over their lifestyle choices. As the gray-haired mother/grandmother/elder figure (let's be honest, that's how they see me, at least until they

get to know ME), I encourage them to invite their parents for a visit and, whenever I can, I host the older generation at my nearby home (affectionately called "The Annex") so that we can have a talk.

When the time is right, I share my story, this story…and I listen. ❧

Thirteen years ago Victoria Albright left a 25-year career as a medical writer and wellness educator in Houston, Texas, to explore holistic healing practices and environmental education. Her search led her to an earth-centered spirituality and a passion for simplicity, sustainability, service, and nonviolence. Victoria's work as a community event consultant has included ecology conferences, sustainability fairs, feminine spirituality retreats and croning ceremonies, peace festivals, nonviolence workshops, and eco-education events for all ages. She is currently writing a facilitator guide for a 10-week series exploring The Wheel of Nonviolence, a personal and social transformation model based on the teachings of Gandhi. Her vision is to work with other cultural creatives to bring about a culture of peace.

Victoria wishes to thank Devon Bonady, Dee Kehoe, Sarah Wilcox-Hughes, Ethan Hughes, Ann Sieber, and Trish Haas for their inspiration and collaboration in writing this article.

Victoria's "Farewell Circle" before departing for her winter home in Houston, Texas. The "Farewell Circle," part of the ongoing compassionate communication and deep listening work practiced at The Possibility Alliance, is an opportunity for community members to express their observations and heart connection with the person who is leaving (who opens their heart and receives what is said without responding). Quite an experience!

A Mental Health Patient Seeks (But Does Not Find) Religious Community

By John Wachter

As a mental health patient seeking an alternative to mainstream treatment, I've looked to various religious intentional communities for better solutions. Over a number of years, I have spent at least a couple weeks apiece at over a dozen different residential religious centers, from varying traditions (Buddhist mostly, but also yoga and Catholic).

I first became seriously interested in religion because I developed a serious mental illness. In addition to being severely depressed about the fact that I had been having auditory hallucinations for the past two years (although they had nearly ceased by then), I was very paranoid when I first came to an intentional community. I had also developed an unhealthy preoccupation or obsession with psychic and paranormal phenomena and a substance abuse issue as well. I did not feel comfortable talking about being crazy and I didn't feel I had to, although I regretted that decision later. I spent five months at a lay religious center and it helped me feel much better, although I never formed any close relationships and left without any real answers to my questions about reality. I had come to the conclusion that the correct path for me to follow would be a religious life, so my next stop was at a monastery, where I spent a month, which caused me to rethink my path again.

Over the next three years I visited many religious communities, contacted many more, and struggled with my mental health issues. I had no friends other than my family during this time. I never found a place that seemed to support me. They told me what they wanted me to do, but not *how* I should deal with the things that prevented me from doing it. Failure was met not with understanding and encouragement to do better, but with impatience and anger. When I left the community no one ever referred me to someplace else that might be a better fit for me or followed up to check on how I was. (At best, I'd be put on a mailing list, but the communication was never personal.)

I understand that every community has leadership or authority of some kind and I accept that. It was always the methods that were difficult for me to accept. My first complaint is that I didn't feel cooperation was wanted, but only obedience. It was their way or the highway. Discussions rarely happened, but preaching was consistent. And when they were talking about or trying to instruct their way, it never seemed to be honest and frank, but instead cryptic hints and no accountability.

I obeyed all the rules, but I still felt very unworthy, unwanted, and unwelcome.

Many times there was also a quantity of hypocrisy. A lot of lip service was given to ideals that seemed to be absent. People in these communities didn't seem to be any wiser or happier than people in the secular world. If these communities are supposed to be places of healing, the people need to work on their bedside manner. One last thing: I always felt guilty because I couldn't afford to give much money to the community, I had (still do) a difficult time holding a job. Most of the programs are rather expensive.

I got very angry at the end of these three years and finally was hospitalized and entered the mental health system, which, in retrospect, I should have done much earlier. During the next six years I stayed away from the communities, although I would stop in with local centers on occasion. Unfortunately, I failed to build a life for myself in society, so I once again turned my attention back to the community scene. I revisited the first of the communities I had stayed at because they had been helpful, and some new ones, once again got turned down by many more, including the monastery I had spent a month at, but found living in community even more difficult than when I was younger. Despite the fact that I was obeying all the rules and informed them of my mental health past and present, I still felt very unworthy, unwanted, and unwelcome. I never stayed for more than a few days because I'd get too angry and depressed. Fight/Flight response perhaps. I thought it would be better to leave than stay and say or do something that I'd regret, since I found the intensity of these emotions overwhelming.

I have always been stubborn, and slow to understand implied wishes, I prefer people to be direct and frank with me. So, I guess I should've given up earlier. I had just studied so much of the literature and wanted so much to do what was best, that I couldn't give up, even when it was obvious the advice in the books wasn't working. Not to mention that I've never been successful at much of anything in mainstream society, anyhow.

Finally, I wish to express gratitude to the Abbey of the Genesee for so clearly and definitively informing me that someone who has had such a history of emotional and mental issues would find living in their community too difficult. The unambiguous answer was welcome. I just wish I had heard it three years ago when I started looking at religious communities again, instead of rejections without explanations, or a group allowing me to visit but not caring whether the visit was a good one or not. I'm considering looking for a non-religious intentional community, but not sure that it will be much different. ❧

John Wachter is a 33-year-old American who lives in Arizona. He has been on mental health disability for many years.

REVIEW BY CHRIS ROTH

Damanhur Schloss Glarisegg Sieben Linden La Borie Noble Tamera
Valle de Sensaciones Matavenero Schloss Tonndorf Krishna Valley Finca Tierra

A NEW WE

*Ecological communities
and ecovillages in Europe*

L.O.V.E.
Productions

www.NewWe.info

Hopeful New Stories from the Old World

A New We
Ecological communities and ecovillages in Europe
DVD, 120 minutes, L.O.V.E. Productions, 2010
www.NewWe.info; fic.ic.org/a-new-we.php
Available from store.ic.org/a-new-we

Two hours does not seem like a lot of time to visit even one community, let alone nearly a dozen. Yet Austrian filmmaker Stefan Wolf has managed to accomplish something amazing: he has created a feature-length film that gives viewers a sense of real familiarity with 10 diverse ecological communities and eco-villages throughout Europe. Even more important, by profiling such a wide variety of communities, all of them mold-breaking experiments in ecological living and cooperation, *A New We* leaves one with the feeling that the possibilities for such projects are endless. Stefan reminds us that these 10 are just a small subset of thousands of like-spirited experiments worldwide (a glance at the Communities Directory or visit to www.ic.org backs up his assertion), but his film also makes clear that nothing is "cookie-cutter" about these groups—quite the opposite.

Against a backdrop of beautiful videography, each community segment starts with a concise textual profile of the group (including number of residents, land area, organizational structure, percentage of diet produced on site, energy and water sources, etc.) and ends with contact information. In between, we visit each place and hear from some of its residents. The pace is never rushed, and yet each segment covers a wide range of topics, including some of the personal challenges that community members face.

The video tour includes: Damanhur, an Italian network of 1000 people living in 20- to 30-person eco-communities; Schloss Glarisegg, a 34-member Swiss holistic seminar center; La Borie Noble, a 13-member community in France inspired by Gandhian ideals of non-violence; Krishna Valley, a 150-member Hungarian community with 95 percent food self-sufficiency; Matavenero, whose 70 residents inhabit a formerly abandoned Spanish mountain village rebuilt through the Rainbow movement; Schloss Tonndorf, a 60-resident, especially child-friendly German ecovillage encompassing an old castle; Finca Tierra, a small, nature-based community in the Canary Islands; Sieben Linden, a growing 120-member German ecovillage with a radically reduced ecological footprint and innovative decision-making model; Valle de Sensaciones, a remote Spanish

(continued on p. 79)

HOPEFUL NEW STORIES FROM THE OLD WORLD

(continued from p. 80)

eco-community emphasizing direct experience in nature; and Tamera, a peace education and research center in south Portugal inhabited by 200 people.

While Stefan obviously chose interviewees who believed in each project (rather than seeking out, for example, disillusioned ex-members, of which I would guess there are some), the candid nature of the interviews here make each video portrait both believable and ultimately inspiring. I never felt as if I were being "sold" anything, only given a window into each way of life—one that effectively conveys how hopeful and game-changing these kinds of life choices could be as humanity faces an uncertain future.

Of course, in reality, a 10- to 20-minute video portrait can only scratch the surface of what there is to learn about each group. I sensed that there were many more stories to tell about each place, which a video of this length could never hope to include. Based on my own community experiences, I could sense (or project) unspoken dynamics and issues into several of the settings. I never found myself rolling my eyes, but I did raise my eyebrows at the opening of one segment, in which the female cofounder is peddling away on a human-powered washing machine while her male partner lounges in a hot-tub and philosophizes about luxuriating in the senses. (Later, though, this comically unbalanced first impression is corrected when he introduces us to an intriguing mandala game he designed to distribute household tasks in a fair and fun way.) In another segment, I couldn't help but wonder about the power dynamics in a small community created by a single visionary individual; and in another, about whether members might eventually backtrack on their current degree of buy-in to a shared spiritual philosophy, and whether there were any "doubters" that we didn't meet.

But none of these questions derailed the experience of watching the video; instead, they just provoked more curiosity. I found myself interested in learning more about every situation.

This English-language edition of the original foreign-language film includes overdubs and, where more appropriate, subtitles—done, mostly, with skill, and always understandable.

A New We could not have come at a better time. It can benefit both current communitarians/ecovillagers and those who don't yet even know that eco-communities exist. It opens our eyes to the amazing diversity of approaches to eco-community that are possible—and even more important, to the fact that those dreams are being put into practice by real people, in real life, at various places all over the globe. ❧

Chris Roth (editor@ic.org) edits COMMUNITIES.

Illustration by Yulia Z.

My Search for Community and Intimacy: Is Cohousing the Answer?

By Robin A. Alexander

I was born yearning for community and connection. Well, if not born so, I was soon aware of an emptiness, loneliness, and sadness that of course as a young child I had no name for but it was as palpable as a stomach ache. I was lonely and isolated as a child but as I grew older and my family settled down to a relatively stable life in Princeton, New Jersey, I began to acquire some good friends and by the end of high school was much improved over my early years. Yet the sense of something lacking was always lurking in the background.

The Path toward "True" Community

Then I "left the nest" and headed off to the University of Wisconsin at Madison.

Homesick, yes, but new experiences, freedom, friends, and youthful romances (as well as intellectual stimulation) made this a very exciting time with lots of ups and downs.

During my years in undergraduate and then graduate school I lived in student rooming houses and was lucky in having good apartment mates and friends. Yet there was a limit to the sharing and still something missing.

Then came the crisis that led me to find what I'd been looking for my whole life. I was discouraged at the progress (or lack thereof) on my Ph.D. dissertation in Math, and this led to a full-scale depression accompanied by a few other symptoms thrown in free of extra charge such as agoraphobia. This was definitely the low point of my life and I had no idea what I was going to do.

Salvation came through an amazingly improbable set of coincidences. I had gone to UW Health about some symptoms and was seen by a Dr. Chosey who practiced psychosomatic medicine. He did not mince words: "You look terrible," he said. I told him a bit about my situation. His response: "Why don't you do something about it?" He meant therapy and I expressed my negative opinion about that. Then he did something that transformed my life. He handed me a set of pamphlets written by Dr. Maxie Maultsby, who had been a psychiatric resident there before moving to the University of Kentucky. Dr. Maultsby had developed a therapy based on Albert Ellis' Rational Emotive Therapy that could also be used as a self-help method or in peer groups. Dr. Maultsby called his version Rational Emotive Behavior Therapy (REBT) and the handouts Dr. Chosey gave me explained the foundations and practice of REBT.

Rational Emotive Behavior Therapy

In order to understand how this led to community, I have to explain briefly how REBT works. If you want to learn more, see www.transthought.org/rsc/rsc.html or pick up a copy of any of Dr. Maultsby's books.

REBT relies on the assertion that it's not people, things, or situations that upset us. Rather it's our thoughts, beliefs, and attitudes we have about those things. If you think and believe depressive thoughts about a situation and you have a healthy functioning brain, you will feel appropriately depressed. The second key insight is that not all thinking

is equally "rational" and for now we can think of rational as realistic, though there's much more to it than that. To apply REBT the "client" (as we'll refer to the person with the problem) identifies and analyzes his/her thinking that caused the upset. By then substituting more rational thinking, the client usually feels better and deals with the situation more effectively. Over time, with practice, assistance, and support from the group, the unnecessary upset may disappear or be greatly diminished.

I read the handouts with growing excitement. The idea that not only was I causing my problems with my thinking but that there was a systematic way to examine and change that troublesome thinking was very encouraging. Immediately I felt about 50 percent better and my agoraphobia essentially vanished. I even attended a crowded Joan Baez concert with my girlfriend that evening with no phobic symptoms.

Group Work

Then began my journey into community. The peer groups that Dr. Maultsby had started continued meeting after he left. The group met for two hours once a week and periodically Dr. Maultsby returned to conduct a weekend-long workshop. My timing was excellent; soon after I joined, a weekend workshop was scheduled featuring not only Dr. Maultsby but also Dr. Ellis—a double dose of high power REBT. Though I was not used to identifying, yet alone admitting my irrational thinking, I persevered.

And that is the key to community/intimacy-building in the REBT groups. In order to get help, one had to take the risk of exposing one's real, unvarnished, possibly irrational thinking to this group of people. Maintaining one's usual facade would get one nowhere. The group was supportive, critical perhaps of the thought but not the thinker, and the members were encouraged to relate their own similar issues once the client was finished. Unsolicited advice was discouraged. Not only did I get assistance but I learned that others had problems similar to mine, which countered my sense of being uniquely flawed. Through this process I got to know the group members at an entirely new level and a degree of intimacy built up in the group.

Some of the group members started a commune near campus. Sensing that this was the kind of group I had always wanted to be a part of, and though they were full, I got in by being willing to inhabit a small room in the basement. It felt like coming home for the first time. I was so happy to be there I didn't even mind the various illnesses that swept our tight quarters during the first winter I was there. Almost everyone attended REBT groups, providing some immediate cohesiveness to our community. We ate together nightly and I remember lots of laughter and a great sense of belonging and camaraderie. Eventually a couple moved out and I graduated from the basement to the first floor front room and life was complete! I remember sitting in my room one afternoon and thinking to myself, "I'll never be depressed again!" That was how good it was, though unfortunately after I left Madison I did manage to re-experience depression.

Community Lost

Doing REBT groups did not pay the bills. Unfortunately my solution to this problem was to leave Madison for a Ph.D. in Accounting at Northwestern University—with the intention of returning to Madison, but that didn't happen. I somehow thought I had the secret now and could generate a similar community elsewhere, but I was wrong about that. The Madison community had been very special, and recreating it was not going to be easy or even possible.

Scott Peck and the Foundation for Community Encouragement (FCE)

So, no more community for me until some years later when someone introduced me to Scott Peck's best selling book, *The Road Less Traveled*. That led to *The Different Drum*, with the subtitle: *Community Making and Peace*. By then I had some idea that my experience in Madison had something to do with community, so I read how Dr. Peck had inadvertently stumbled on a model for community-building. One day he showed up unprepared for a workshop he was giving. Not knowing what else to do, he had the participants form small groups and encouraged them to talk about what was on their minds. Expecting little from this, he was surprised when people began to share deeply. The experience was so powerful that he used it to design a workshop process with the purpose of giving people a taste of community.

In order to spread the word on community more efficiently, Dr. Peck and some associates created The Foundation for Community Encouragement (FCE) with the mission of bringing the experience of community to as many people as possible, mostly through his workshop model. FCE sounded exciting to me so I took the first opportunity to fly to FCE headquarters in Knoxville, Tennessee for a weekend workshop.

The FCE Workshop Process

It may be helpful to describe briefly the workshop process. A group of from 20 to 50 people gather in a comfortable space arranged in a circle. Two facilitators give a brief introduction and state that the goal is for the group to *lead itself* into community. The facilitators will assist by making occasional observations about group process, but their job is not to lead the group. One of the facilitators then reads the story of the Rabbi's Gift (see *The Different Drum* or search for this moving parable online). There is a short period of silence and then the process begins. The idea is for the group to experience and work through the four stages of community formation

---

As the weeks went by, participants felt safer and began to speak their minds.

---

that Dr. Peck identified: pseudo-community, chaos, emptiness, and true community. I found that groups differed considerably in all respects including the degree of community attained.

The workshop experience was sufficiently encouraging that I returned to Knoxville in August of 1988 for FCE's annual three-day Community Continuity Conference. I visited FCE headquarters in Knoxville's west side and even attended a search committee meeting with Dr. Peck as they searched for a new Director. I was most impressed with the openness of the organization and how they were trying to use their community-building principles in the search process.

I wanted more contact with the organization and a fortuitously timed sabbatical the following year allowed me to spend the fall semester at FCE as a consultant. I was treated like any staff person and attended meetings and retreats, which allowed me to observe and participate fully in their community-building process.

Admirably, the FCE staff was determined to walk the talk and attempt to work "in community." Compared to a weekend workshop this was a much more challenging process. Early in my stay we held a one-day staff retreat using the Peck community-building model. The fear and discomfort in the room were palpable. But as autumn progressed and the staff got used to working together and we continued our community-building efforts, the improvement was obvious and by the time I left at the end of December, the staff was much more at ease talking about important personal and business matters.

Two key factors in the staff's success were 1) their willingness to back their commitment with process time and 2) their method of incorporating community-building into their weekly staff meetings. Following Dr. Peck's lead, every group activity at FCE began with a period of community-building, which consisted of making time for people who were "moved to speak" to do so. Each staff meeting began with a couple of minutes of silence after which anyone who was "moved to speak" could do so. At first nobody seemed so moved, but as the weeks went by, gradually they began to feel safer and began to speak their minds.

Working at FCE became more fun as the community process improved, and by the time I left in December, we had made good progress towards working in community. But I was to re-experience an almost Madison-quality depth of community the following summer when I returned as a paid consultant to work on their budgeting system. When I arrived in June I was amazed at the progress they had made as a community. It felt like coming home and that summer was one of the best experiences I have ever had. They still had their weekly staff meetings with the community-building component at the beginning, but now working smoothly with little fear of sharing. They had become a smooth and effective team.

I was ready to quit my job at the University and work at FCE when I learned again that all good things come to an end. The Knoxville office was closed in 1991 due to financial problems stemming from the recession. So, disappointed, I returned to my University job but kept looking for opportunities for community.

Cohousing—the Last Hope?

In 2002 I quit my job at the University, planning to go into nonprofit work to do something more "meaningful." But so hungry was I to re-experience community that when my wife and I became aware of a cohousing group in North Carolina that had an opening, I went down to visit and look it over. I was there on a "good week." They had an excellent business meeting, a nice common meal, and a social outing to see the town's minor league baseball team play. So we jumped in, though it meant a long difficult move and not ideal climate for me and my border collie (arctic version).

We liked the house, the layout of houses along a central pedway, the area for dogs and kids to romp in, and the helpfulness of some of the members in showing us the ropes. A few people went far out of their way to help when my wife had emergency surgery a few months after we arrived. People enjoyed the common meals and other social events and meetings usually went quite well. But after a few weeks I became increasingly aware that something was missing. It was so different from what I had expected. Most people were helpful and friendly but somewhat distant. For me the difference between community and pseudo community (using Scott Peck's term for a group that has not taken the risky step into intimacy) is its feel or spirit. In the REBT and FCE communities I felt a sense of aliveness, energy, creativity, connection, family, and excitement. At the cohousing community most of those feelings were either absent or only weakly present.

Then a highly involved member of the group shocked me, but also confirmed what I'd been feeling, when she said that if I wanted community I'd better look elsewhere. I already knew that on a feeling level but it was still discouraging to have it so strongly confirmed. There was enough good that we probably would have stayed, but a change in the Wisconsin State health system made living out of state unaffordable and we returned to Wisconsin.

Reflections and Lessons from These Three Experiences

It seems important to try to understand the problem this and perhaps other cohousing groups have with community, because I am convinced that community is a very desirable condition. The popularity of cohousing indicates that many people hunger for greater community and intimacy, and the cohousing experience shows that it is not always easy to achieve.

What characteristics might have

encouraged the almost automatic creation of community in the first two experiences?
1. There was a shared purpose that was both internally and externally focused and considered valuable by the members of the groups. That shared purpose also was intentionally or unintentionally supportive of community.
2. Being vulnerable and sharing deeply important aspects of self (including feelings, concerns, strengths, and weaknesses) was encouraged and supported in a safe environment.
3. Community-encouraging participation was ongoing, consistent, and involved a reasonably stable set of people.
4. Both groups benefited from unusually skillful facilitators/teachers.

In contrast, what might some of the barriers be to community in cohousing?
1. Most people don't know what community is (as I'm using the term) and have not experienced it. When I returned from FCE I gave a number of talks on community. My assertion that most have not experienced community comes from direct statements by the participants to that effect. Without having experienced deep community, some cohousing members might think that having common meals, reasonably civil meetings, and other group events means they have community. They do, but they may not be aware of how much better it can get.
2. People join a cohousing group for a wide variety of reasons. Not all want deeper intimacy. There would need to be a critical mass that does.
3. The critical mass would need to both know that vulnerability and risk-taking are

---

Many cohousers hunger for greater community and intimacy, but it is not always easy to achieve.

---

required and be willing to begin to take those risks. Since this process can be uncomfortable at first, they have to have some idea that it's worth it, which they might not have because of not having experienced it, and so on—a vicious circle.
4. Practices that inadvertently inhibit community may be used. For instance, I've seen many group facilitators begin meetings with a directed exercise. This can have the opposite effect of the "moved to speak" model and stifle a member's vulnerable sharing.

How might community come to cohousing?
1. If the group hangs together long enough, community can gradually develop "by accident," though there are many ways in which it can get derailed if it is not done with intention.
2. There are facilitators skilled at community-building that the group could hire to speed the process.
3. Enough participants need to be both aware that greater community is possible and willing to do what it takes to get there.

Having experienced deeply satisfying and enjoyable instances of community, I will probably keep searching, but it is unfortunate that it is so rare. Perhaps cohousing will eventually provide a more consistent path to community. ❧

Born in Berkamstead, England, Robin A. Alexander moved with his family in 1950 to the US, where he's lived in New Jersey, Wisconsin, Minnesota, and North Carolina. He now lives in Madison, Wisconsin with his therapy dog Teddy, doing writing and learning web design.

SPIRITUAL COMMUNITY BY KARINA SABOT

Buddha Being...Buddha Doing

Bone deep. Literally. That was the impact on my body after 10 days of personal retreat at Deer Park Monastery.

There were 5 a.m. mornings when I told myself, half asleep, warm and comfortable camping in a pickup truck, "Nope, today I will NOT respond to that gong. I will NOT walk up that hill in cold darkness; I will NOT sit in that chilly meditation hall, NO, Nada, it *ain't* happenin'!"

Then my 12-step recovery would kick in, "If you want what we have, you have to do what we do...this is an action program. You take the action, you get the result."

UGH!

Quickly out of the warmth, splashing sleepy face with cold water, pulling brush through hair, wrapping a scarf around and around, then "trudging the road of happy destiny" up to the meditation hall, with certainty that by now, with all that internal dialogue, I was late.

And behold, every friggin' day I was early!!! This meant I had to sit LONGER than the shadowy figures quietly arranging themselves on cushions for the next 15 minutes. Karma, karma, karma, karma.

It served me well. Diligence, not discipline, "Progress not perfection."

What actually happened there?

I lived with Zen Buddhist nuns who all seemed bilingual in English and Vietnamese. I ate warm (important adjective), nourishing, healthy vegan food. I walked when they walked, worked when they worked, sat when they sat, bowed when they bowed, and would sing when they were singing, even when their preferred language was foreign to my ear consciousness.

What did not happen?

I did not drive any vehicle or machinery for 10 days. I did not speak on the phone, although I did text a few times while being mindful of doing so, and took a few

photos as well. I did not read novels, or watch dramatic films, read newspapers, use a computer, listen to music, dance, or write except to journal at night occasionally. Always striving to be mindful, always watching what was arising within my mind.

"Practice, practice, practice," a sister said to the small group of lay women visitors. "Use *all* your time here, *everything*

you do, as an opportunity for mindfulness practice."

Observing what arose in my mind and emotions, while living and practicing in a monastic community committed to transforming suffering into loving kindness, was profoundly beneficial.

The TMJ, jaw pain that the dentist said could not be cured, disappeared. Gone. Outta here friends, vamos!

I relaxed to my bones. This was a unique sensation. Something deep within had slipped away and something equally profound had grown in its place. All very subtly, while I was resisting, acquiescing, working, resenting, feeling confused, etc. I kept practicing mindful breathing, mindful walking, mindful eating, mindful thinking, mindful resting, etc. Even mindful turtle-raft-building, for the two

Photos courtesy of Karina Sabot

It was the application of the teachings that produced the result.

cold reptiles seeking sun refuge in the nuns' pool.

It wasn't the philosophically induced, intellectual realization of dharma teachings. It was the application of the teachings, the actual gardening to get vegetables, "watering the seeds" of loving kindness to manifest loving kindness, that produced the result. The ripening of conditions manifested in myriad ways.

Prior to 12-step recovery, before exposure to Thich Nhat Hanhs's books and monasteries, I visited many intentional communities in North America. This included hippie communes, land trusts, organic farms, Radical Faeries, Michigan Wimmins Festival, tribal reservations, et. al. You name it, I was probably there searching for a "true home," where people lived and worked cooperatively.

In lieu of finding Utopia, exhausted and road weary, I slithered into a stone and mud underground hole in the sizzling Sonora Desert. I also designed my

Left photo: Deer Park Entrance.
This photo: Deer Park main Meditation Hall, guitarist visiting on Day of Mindfulness.
Right photo: Deer Park, climb from Clarity Hamlet to the main Meditation Hall.

suicide by freezing to death in the Northern Territories of Canada, which was six months away, and in the meantime tearfully entered a 12-step recovery program. That was 2002, Amerikana time.

Working the 12-steps of spiritual recovery for nine years, in areas of my life prone to clinging kleishas, mental obscurations, and attachments to all dualistic formations possible, put a pause into my untidy life of action/reaction. "We pause when agitated or doubtful and ask for the next right thought or action," says the Big Book of Alcoholics Anonymous. Hmmm? Ommmm. Ahhhhhhh!

Years ago I discovered Green Mountain Monastery and stayed there unexpectedly while visiting Vermont for a lesbian wedding. I recall crying a lot over the deaths of my two closest friends, cleaning the nuns' house with obsessive zeal, and being told by a Sister that it would be best if I didn't fly back to Tucson so soon.

"But I have a job interview," I whined.

"You won't do well in the interview," she stated honestly.

I called a friend with long-time 12-step recovery.

"Dorothy, the nuns think I should stay. What do you think?" I asked tearfully.

"I left a place once after being advised to stay. I drove around lost for eight hours. It wasn't fun," she replied.

The Sisters got on their computer and re-arranged my flights, I returned the rental car, and allowed myself to be held in the fine golden threads of compassion.

THANK YOU SISTERS!!!! Many blessings to you all, even though you told me I was too OLD to be a nun…

In Arizona I continued visiting the Garchen Buddhist Institute, sitting with Singing Bird Sangha, led by an OI member in Tucson, listening to the Dalai Lama whenever, and reading dharma texts.

I was able to attend Thay's teaching in Deer Park, and later "One Buddha is Not Enough" in Estes Park, where I posted a sign for a 12-step meeting, and had a great time sharing with other folks in recovery from around the globe!

My latest visit to Deer Park held a small wish that I might be able to escape from being a weary RN and unfulfilled

This photo: Deer Park Solidity Hamlet, Monks' Dormitories.
Top photo: Deer Park Clarity Hamlet, Sisters' Meditation Hall.
Opposite page top: Deer Park Meditation Hall.
Opposite page bottom: Deer Park, large bell rung at 5 a.m. by monk or nun, with chanting, bringing in the dawn.

writer/filmmaker, and from a bunch of muddled aspirations to do "the next right thing," with skillful means.

What happened was miraculous. The Buddha said there are 84,000 paths available, just hop on one and get going. I have so much gratitude to Thich Nhat Hanh, and Sister Chan Khong, for designing places where monastics and lay folks can live and grow together in their dharma practice! It is vitally important for me to be able to read and practice the dharma in the footsteps of Thay.

Thank you again Sisters and Brothers, and lay friends. May all beings benefit. 🐌

Deer Park Monastery is a community in Escondido, California, in the tradition of Thich Nhat Hanh. For more information, visit plumvillage.org.

Karina Sabot welcomes your correspondence at kasabot@gmail.com.

Growing a Culture of Gratitude in Argentine Patagonia
A WWOOFer Experiences Community Living

By James Collector

Top to bottom:
1. Located in the Lakes District of Argentina, El Bolsón is host to many rainbows, such as this brilliant vignette over one of Wunjo's greenhouses.
2. From left to right, Juliane, Gabriela, Camila, and Eric help dread Asa's hair while she sips maté in the community kitchen.
3. Author James Collector.

The blanket was crowded with little squares of cloth. Each held a handful of corn, quinoa, wheat, vegetables, herbs, fruit, nuts, or honey. Wild lupines, roses, and other flowers formed a vignette around the colorful spread. One by one, we began to throw it all in the fire.

I had traveled to South America to learn the basics of organic farming through a program called World Wide Opportunities on Organic Farms (WWOOF). Now, in Argentine Patagonia, I had immersed myself in a culture of growing. As the smoke from our offerings drifted up into the canopy of coihue trees, the other volunteers and I exchanged confused looks. Our farm hosts, a young couple seated in the circle beside us, continued the summer solstice ceremony by passing around a seashell filled with smoldering incense. They asked us to voice our gratitude. Supermarkets were not among the things for which I said thanks.

WWOOF is a program for which anyone interested in an affordable cultural experience can be thankful. The format is simple: volunteers work in exchange for meals and a place to stay. In 1971, the program was started in England to provide access to the countryside. Today almost 100 nations accept WWOOF volunteers in North America, Latin America, Africa, Europe, the Middle East, and throughout Asia. At the WWOOF website, one can buy an inexpensive membership (I paid $45) which includes a current list of all the farms accepting volunteers in the chosen country. I picked Argentina.

In early December, I hopped off a bus outside of El Bolsón, a small town in the Rio Negro province of Argentina, with my long-time friend, Asa. We stood with our backpacks in the cloud of dust from the departing bus and stared at the wooden sign. Wunjo, the farm was called. We had sent volunteer requests to over 20 farms and Wunjo was the only one that responded. From a few email correspondences with a woman named Gabriela, we knew that the people here needed help gardening and building a house, that we would sleep in tents and eat a vegetarian diet for the next month.

Inside the gate, a cat was dozing in the grass just outside the perimeter of a sprinkler. A few minutes passed until a shirtless man walked up and introduced himself in *Castellano*—Castilian Spanish—as Luigi. He led us down a dirt path and through a grove of cherry and plum trees to a small adobe building. There we met Gabriela and the handful of other permanent residents of the farm. They were placing the last tiles into the mosaic floor of the newly constructed community kitchen. Wunjo had only begun accepting volunteers one year before, in 2009. Except for one German girl, we were the earliest volunteers to arrive that summer.

Anxious to demonstrate our work ethic, Asa and I offered to help, but Gabriela handed us plates of potato salad and, in broken English, suggested we relax. Sitting beneath racks of drying herbs, we ate in silence, acutely conscious of the language barrier. After we finished, Luigi showed us where we could pitch our tent, and how to use the bathroom, a dry outhouse designed to turn human feces into fertilizer by mixing it with wood shavings.

The learning curve was steep. But within a week, our *Castellano* had improved and we settled into a routine. Each morning, the 8 AM breakfast was announced with the blowing of a conch shell. We ate meals together in the community kitchen—a hubbub of playing children, begging dogs, the grandmother's dream interpretations, unexpected guests, and maté-fueled discussions about the daily agenda. Then, we worked. Our efforts were split halfway between gardening and building a house of almost entirely natural materials.

More volunteers arrived to help, among them Eric Ferrer, 29, from Bordeaux, France.

Ferrer had previous experience working on WWOOF farms in Europe and India before he traveled to Argentina.

"As a carpenter, I wanted to learn about natural construction more than anything else," Ferrer wrote via email after staying an extra month at Wunjo. "I feel like I learned some good things. I realized that we can build our houses with a lot of energy and just a little knowledge—more or less—and that everything doesn't have to be square and straight to have a good-looking little house."

Though it has not received much press outside of Argentina, El Bolsón is the setting for a natural construction movement. The house we helped build reflected the—for lack of a better word—hippie ethos of the Wunjo. The house blueprints were chalk sketches by its soon-to-be inhabitants, a single mother, Brisa, and her two young sons. The support and crossbeams were all roughly hewn tree branches and trunks. As a result, there was hardly a right angle in the whole house. Following Brisa's vague directions, we used wire and nails to install glass panes and wine bottles as windows. For insulation, we poured a mixture of water and clay over piles of straw, then stuffed it by the handful into networks of baling wire in the walls. Once it was dry, we added a smooth layer of grey adobe. By lunchtime at 2 PM. each day, we were invariably smeared with clay from head to foot. Moreover, the disorganized work would aggravate our Western sense of efficiency.

Not until everyone at the farm sat down together to talk one day, did I begin to understand what I was learning. A few of the other volunteers, including Ferrer, expressed a sense of urgency to accomplish more in the garden and the construction of the house. Luigi, Wunjo's head carpenter, listened until they had finished. Then, he put our lesson into words. He said the garden and the house should come second to personal work. I was stunned. As an American, no "boss" had ever said something like that to me.

In the following weeks, I started unlearning to worry. I began to enjoy

work and, as a result, accomplish more. The strawberry patches were soon completely weeded. In less than a week, we insulated all the remaining walls in the house.

In addition, I began to understand the people and how their views on modern culture had compelled them to start a sustainable community. I was progressing in a different kind of education.

Other volunteers also experienced unexpected growth. Juliane Damm, 22, from Chemnitz in Saxony, Germany encountered a culture at Wunjo that made her rethink how people live in Western society.

"The respect between people at Wunjo was good to see," Damm wrote via email. "I always wanted that to be the ideal way for people to interact, but at the same time thought that it wasn't possible. After some weeks at Wunjo, I got a kind of quietness within me that told me that it could be possible."

Granted, we did exchange modern worries for more rustic ones. The earthworms that occasionally flopped out of the faucet in the kitchen sink still disturbed me. When

> ## Not only was my "common sense" continually challenged, but a part of my heart, like the oven door, had unexpectedly fallen open.

Brisa's four-year-old son would bring us maté during work, I found it difficult to trust that he would make it up the rickety wooden ladder barefoot holding a thermos of hot water. The oven door, it seemed, needed hinges. Not only was my "common sense" continually challenged, but a part of my heart, like the oven door, had unexpectedly fallen open.

The greatest challenge snuck up on me in my last week at Wunjo: I realized I was in love with this place and I didn't want to leave. I had never before lived in such an intimate community. My childhood neighborhood was a suburban maze of strangers. Sadness washed over me to think of returning to the default world. I found myself unable to explain these melancholy feelings even to myself, much less other people.

I went into the forest to meditate. The afternoon tree shadows had drifted into zigzag shapes when suddenly I remembered that Gabriela had taught me that the word "Wunjo" comes from the Old English rune for "Joy." Joy! I had tasted it and it would forever live inside me. Leaving Wunjo was not back-tracking into the default world. Rather, I would be venturing out to share the joy of community culture that I had experienced here. Now, I knew.

I returned from the forest determined to give back to these people who had given me so much. I volunteered to cook dinner. Cooking a vegetarian meal for 12 people using a wood fire and river water, all the while communicating in rapid-fire *Castellano*, is the kind of challenge I had traveled to Argentina to encounter. The dinner table is where culture and agriculture truly converge. Before we ate, it was a custom at Wunjo to say a prayer of thanks. That night, and every night since, I've felt grateful just to have been there. ❧

For more information, see the Wunjo blog at www.elespaciodemagos.blogspot.com and the WWOOF website at www.wwoof.org.

Born in Boulder, Colorado, James Collector, 24, graduated from the University of Colorado with a degree in journalism. His quest is to answer the question: "How to be?" But he's not dying for answers; the search is the life lesson.

Spirituality and Community Living

By Clistine Morningstar

I didn't know what I was getting into when I joined the intentional spiritual community of Global Community Communications Alliance. Yes, I was a spiritual seeker—I always had been since my early childhood when my concept of heaven was a superb flower garden where God (in a dark blue Robin Hood outfit) and Jesus (in a light blue one) went around endlessly watering the plants from little tin watering cans. Later, I realized that I was one of the plants that needed watering, and I sought sustenance from many spiritual avenues.

Shunning orthodoxy, I made my way through teachings of the Theosophical Society, a wonderful Indian Sikh Guru who taught me the Yoga of Inner Sound and Light, Rudolph Steiner, Krishnamurti, and certain angles of the New Age. I gleaned from everywhere but in the end was satisfied with nowhere. At 60 years old and seeking still, my leading wish was to one day "become enlightened." But I didn't know that I still had a long way to go to understand the underpinnings of true spirituality.

It was at this point that I encountered community—a style of life I had never sought or wanted, but nevertheless was drawn into—and fairly soon I committed myself to becoming a member of Global Community Communications Alliance. It was not a rational decision. It was just that deep down I knew the doors of spiritual destiny were opening for me and I was "meant" to go through them in this way. Shakespeare said, "There is a tide in the affairs of men, which, taken at the flood, leads on to fortune." In this case "fortune" for me meant rare spiritual opportunity—so that was that!

What was being taught in this spiritually-based community deeply resonated with me and further expanded my spiritual horizons. And the people were very special. They had a good sense of humor and seemed honorable and kind. They too were seekers but more grounded than many seekers I had encountered. And they somehow seemed to thrive in the hierarchical system that with grace and direction held the community together. To be under authority in this manner however was not initially appealing to me. I had to shelve my prejudice until I realized that those who held the helm were exceptional souls who were totally worthy.

While I was letting time solve this dilemma, I explored my new way of life. Now, here's the wild card! While I was still seeking spirituality in my "Somewhere over the rainbow, way up high" frame of mind, an entirely new aspect of spirituality crept up on me, and it was one that provided a nucleus for all my previous aspirations. It slowly dawned on me that solitary pursuit of enlightenment is like trying to bake a loaf of bread without the yeast. The factor I had been missing was relationship, not just with God, not just with special friends or biological family, but with many other diverse

One has to face one's lower self that constantly has its own agenda.

I'm weaving my individual God-given pattern in a dance of colored threads with many others. Springtime Maypole Dance at Avalon Organic Gardens & EcoVillage.

Perspective has shifted from "get off the wheel of karma" to "seek to serve others."

We all act as catalysts for one another to grow spiritually.

human beings of all ages in close day-to-day contact.

How could I have been so blind! One simply cannot be virtuous in a vacuum. When challenged with the need to be increasingly real and transparent from moment to moment with a hundred other people in pursuit of the common good, one has to face one's lower self that constantly has its own agenda. Oh yes, it means facing down one's own limitations and imperfections, often referred to as our "darkness," in order to come closer to the light—the darkness that can be so neatly hidden from oneself most of the time, and only significantly erupts in the occasional volcano! In the attempt to integrate my life more with that of others and work a common plan, I've discovered many obtuse angles in myself that I wasn't previously aware of. Yes, I've definitely been opinionated, impatient, and too self-absorbed.

My discovery of these shortcomings is due to the fact that at this community we all act as catalysts for one another to grow spiritually in a way we simply couldn't do alone. Our shared goal to genuinely overcome our hidden faults isn't easy to implement, but it's infinitely worthwhile. We come to see that there's nothing we do, think, or feel that can't be raised to growing levels of spirituality. We learn how to give and receive honest (but loving) admonishment more effectively. We see that what holds us back is almost always pride in one guise or another. We make progress, fall down, and pick ourselves up again. We benefit from the wise counsel of our Elders. And we laugh a lot!

So, I've found myself in the "Spiritual Olympics" for the past 17 years. And this has meant constant training sessions in spiritual house-cleaning and sore spiritual muscles! But it's also given me the opportunity to try to "live" all those noble ideals that I'd been giving lip-service to. And through the alchemy of community I've started to convert my dross into small nuggets of gold! Having moved from the world of "me" to the world of "us," I see the web of life as no longer a theory but a living loom—a loom on which I'm weaving my individual God-given pattern in a dance of colored threads with many others. From this place, perspective has shifted from "get off the wheel of karma" to "seek to serve others."

Through community living I'm learning better how to walk my talk while embracing a cosmic perspective that includes the fundamentals of all world religions. It's a relief to be able to laugh, weep, grow, and serve together; to aspire to work towards "enlightenment" for the whole world in whatever ways we can bring our gifts to bear.

And so we find ourselves daily committed to outreach to the general public as well as to inreach to the God within us.

It's still that inreach, that personal relationship with God, that is the leading factor in my life, but how much more challenging and rich it's become! I believe that this is one of the great potential benefits of belonging to a community, so long as that community is effectively and benevolently run, and is committed to spiritual growth.

"As above, so below," has become much clearer to me. God isn't just wandering around up there in His garden watering the flowers in a blue outfit, after all. For if we look deeply enough, He's there behind the eyes of our fellow travelers, looking out at us. As the great Persian poet Hafiz has said: "Everyone is God speaking. Why not be polite and listen to Him?" ❧

Clistine Morningstar is a graduate of the Royal Academy of Dramatic Art, London, and for 20 years she researched into movement as a catalyst for personal growth, while teaching dance, movement, and fitness. Her acclaimed book Growing with Dance *arose from her Early Childhood teaching at the University of British Columbia. Clistine is now the school coordinator of Early Childhood programs at Global Community Communications Alliance, and is also Music Director of the 50-voice Gabriel of Urantia's Bright and Morning Star Choir there. She is 77 years young!*

The Lighter Side of Community: A Communitarian Appreciates *Wanderlust*

By Chris Roth

Disclaimer: *the following article about the film* Wanderlust *contains multiple "plot spoilers." We don't think it will spoil the experience of watching the movie, since the plot is hardly its most important aspect—but you are forewarned.*

M y former community had a ritual we called "The Lighter Side." Usually done as part of a personal-growth workshop, it consisted of a series of skits we created—planned in advance, improvised on the spot, or a combination thereof—to make fun of ourselves and the dynam-

ics of either the workshop or of our lives in community. Often in response to particular incidents, we exaggerated what had happened for comic effect, relieving tensions that might still linger (embarrassment, disappointment, the awkwardness of miscommunication, etc.) and allowing us to laugh at ourselves. The Lighter Side helped us take ourselves less seriously, while also letting us share insights and uniting us in loving self-parody and laughter. Occasionally, a skit would "go south," resulting in hard feelings that would then need resolution—but when done in its intended spirit of self-parody rather than mockery, The Lighter Side eased far more tensions than it created.

When I heard about a Hollywood movie depicting the adventures of a couple from New York in a fictional intentional community in Georgia, I was wondering what the ratio of loving parody to mockery would be. I'm happy to report that the filmmakers have made a movie in the true spirit of "The Lighter Side," fond rather than cruel in its send-up of community life. I am trusting that moviegoers who do *not* have experience in intentional community will also appreciate the spirit in which it is made, rather than taking its contents literally.

For a movie containing well more than its share of crude sexual humor (parents and the very sensitive, beware), and some obligatory stereotypes, *Wanderlust* also contains some of the most nuanced, savvy humor about intentional community living I've seen. What *I Heart Huckabees* did for both grassroots environmental activism and New Age psychology/science/mysticism, *Wanderlust* does for at least some segments of the intentional communities movement. It is *not* a fair representation of intentional community living; it has little in common with the wave of informative documentaries that started with *Visions of Utopia* and continues with *A New We*, *Seeking the Good Life in America*, and the forthcoming *Within Reach*—other than the fact that, increasingly, that genre is also becoming entertaining, provoking laughter as well as expanded worldviews. But *Wanderlust* **is** an elaborate parody full of what are almost "inside jokes" (though accessible to anyone with experience in the movement), at least some of whose creators appear to have a deep sympathy for community living.

Dueling Realities

The movie traces the journey of a couple, Linda and George, between two worlds—mainstream America and an intentional community called Elysium. Facing hard economic times in New York and with both of their careers in disarray, they enjoy a transformative stay at Elysium's "bed-and-breakfast" on their way to a disastrous visit with George's brother Rick, who has offered George a job in his "construction supply" business. When the contents of Rick's character prove distressingly similar to that of the Porta-Potties he rents to contractors, Linda and George hightail it back to Elysium, and the real fun begins.

These two worlds could hardly be more different. Like his coworkers, George hates his job with a firm in New York—from which they're all liberated when federal agents investigating financial crimes shut it down. Linda tries to sell her documentary about penguins with testicular cancer ("it's *An Inconvenient Truth* meets *March of the Penguins*") to HBO executives who reject it because, although they like to feature violence and heartache, her picture isn't "sexy" enough. The real estate agent who sells them their "micro-loft" changes her tune about its merits as an investment as soon as they try to sell it back. Once they arrive in Georgia, they find Rick even more insufferable in person than he is via Skype—not only offensive but abusive, flaunting his business success through conspicuous consumption while cheating on his wife and humiliating his employees. Rick's wife Marisa has a "little bit of a SkyMall problem" and watches multiple TVs all day while on a steady diet of Wellbutrin and margaritas. Rick's son Tanner is even more rude than Rick is.

In contrast, the colorful cast of characters Linda and George meet at Elysium seem, for the most part, truly happy. They live close to the land and in apparent harmony with one another. They're eccentric, to be sure: a nudist winemaker/novelist, a guesthouse operator with "verbal diarrhea" prone to gluing sticks to orange peels; a founder who insists on repeating all his co-founder's names at every opportunity—and they host eccentric guests, including an entire conference of nudist winemakers. While the ex-porn star is sometimes off-putting, for the most part these are friendly, very likeable, happy, healthy people, not only tolerating but appreciating one another's eccentricities, and appearing much more alive and interesting than the deadened people in Linda's and George's former lives.

Culture Creation

Like Linda and George, Eva is a refugee from New York (as are a surprising number of communitarians I've met). She doesn't miss "the stress, the Blackberries, the sleeping pills, the triple latte"—nor do her companions, who spend their days enjoying rural life. George gets initiated into shoveling manure as part of Elysium's abundant gardening operation, while Linda has the new-to-her, revelatory experience of picking an apple, bagging it, and selling it at the community's fruit stand. Children (much happier than Rick and Marissa's hostile son) play with one another and with adults, easily mingling in this

multi-generational community. Yoga, tai-chi, frisbee, meditation, music-making, dancing, and skinny-dipping co-exist with building sheds, hauling haybales, digging garden beds, harvesting and cooking for the group, and tending the fruit stand.

Cooperation is the currency of choice. One of the group's first acts after Linda and George arrive is to right their car (upended when George attempts to escape in reverse gear from the sight of the eager-to-be-helpful winemaker's genitalia). The group also unites to oppose plans to construct a casino on their land—the result of backroom corporate-political deals, initially promoted by a clueless media until Linda becomes the group's hero by "exposing" the truth (and more) to the bulldozers and the TV cameras. Their group activism ("the people will be heard!") inspires the founder to declare, "the revolution has begun!"

Elysium members create their own culture. They're proud to be free of the electronic communication devices and computers that occupy most people's lives (in fact, they're so behind the times that some of the technologies they describe themselves as escaping from have been obsolete for years). The scenes of community life make it clear that they have plenty of entertainment and communication among themselves every day without needing to "plug in" to the mass forms of either of those. While actual intentional communities span a huge range of approaches to this question, a significant portion resemble at least aspects of Elysium in its emphasis on homegrown culture—and some take it even further.

Commune? Boo, Hiss, Chuckle...

The response of one member to Linda and George's description of Elysium as a "commune"—"*Commune?* Boo, hiss. We prefer the term *Intentional Community*"—is triply humorous. First, it is a fairly accurate paraphrase (with attitude) of what many communitarians tell those with preconceived notions about communities, and of what the Fellowship for Intentional Community itself states in every issue of Communities magazine. Second, while most intentional communities are *not* communes, Elysium most decidedly *is*. Members hold all land and property in common and share income—it's "all for one, one for all." The third, least subtle reason for laughing is that the stereotype of a commune as "a bunch of hippies smoking pot and playing guitar" (the reason Elysium members say they object to that designation) *can* seem to apply to them, especially to the party scenes, though in reality their lives are filled with much more than that.

Elysium's communal economy—like every communal economy—has both benefits and drawbacks. Rodney immediately gives George his shirt when George says he likes it—the natural thing to do since "we share everything here." In contrast to other characters in the movie, Elysium members don't let money (or the lack of it) consume their lives, and appear to have found a comfortable way to support themselves in harmony with the land and one another. Their ideology aligns with their practices: Wayne's novel is a political parable about "the flaws of capitalistic society," and Carvin, the founder, insists repeatedly that "money buys nothing—literally nothing."

> # George never quite gets used to "doing his business" while others casually talk with him in the bathroom.

But one of the communal economy's downsides comes to light when George's car, full of most of the couple's belongings, ends up at the bottom of a lake because Rodney needed to borrow it. The link between non-ownership and lack of responsibility—the failure to take care of others' or the group's things—is a challenge not unique to Elysium, though the unplanned but somehow taken-in-stride car-sinking ("I know, crazy, right?" is Rodney's assessment) offers an extreme example of the phenomenon. The community's sometimes appealing but simultaneously naïve attitude toward money is also reflected later on, when one member considers $11,000 fair payment for something worth $10 million (I can't spoil every aspect of the plot).

Most modern intentional communities are far more sophisticated in their approach to money than is Elysium, but the mixture of idealism, vision, and accompanying liabilities of their approach will also strike chords of familiarity for many in the communities movement.

Values, Curds. Turds, and More

Elysium's commitments to nonviolence and to ecological sensitivity, which compare favorably with the aggression and insensitivity displayed in the wider culture (notably at Rick's house), also echo common themes in the movement. Needless to say, *Wanderlust* lampoons them: swatting a fly means George has a "fetish for violence." Clapping is "too aggressive," so Elysium's members rub their fingers together instead when they want to cheer or express approval. (While I haven't seen this particular variation in real life, I have spent time in communities where "twinkling"—moving the upraised fingers rapidly—had replaced clapping.) And in a scene probably familiar to anyone who's lived in a vegetarian or vegan community, new member Linda sneaks off to town for a meat fix, only to find the founder in the same diner, unapologetically scarfing down a wide array of meat products because "you can't live off macrobiotic bean curd shit all your life." Meanwhile, most members are truly devoted to their veganism and to their homegrown food—celebrating their first victory against the casino developers by breaking out the tomato chutney.

Again like many communitarians, Elysium members are not only more at ease living close to the earth than most mainstream Americans are, but also more comfortable with their own bodies and bodily functions. No one bats an eye at their resident nudist or at the conference-load of his fellow nudist winemakers, nor is skinny-dipping a big deal for anyone. Linda soon gets comfortable peeing outside, but George never quite gets used to "doing his business" while others casually talk with him in the bathroom. (No community I know of assumes that people will be eager to converse while defecating, or will be comfortable doing that within plain sight of others—but neither of those are unheard of in the world of community either.)

We even witness a natural childbirth, whose radiant mother again compares favorably with the testy, pregnant HBO executive lamenting her "swollen belly, hemorrhoids, and second thoughts." The parents keep the placenta attached, carrying it around in a bowl with them and the baby as they wait for it to fall off naturally. (This is not something I've seen personally in community, and definitely not the most common approach, but I'm sure it happens.)

Underneath the "Herb'n'" Legend

Wanderlust plays on the stereotype of the "drug-filled commune," which is where its satire is perhaps least subtle and also least accurate. Cannabis (the best George has ever smoked) is freely available, and at one community ceremony ayahuasca tea is passed around. But notably absent from Elysium are evidence of any alcohol problems, tobacco, "heavier" drugs, or synthetic drugs of any kind (whether illicit, prescription, or over-the-counter). The members seem savvy about drugs and their consequences—one of them blames the founder's mental confusion and repetitiveness on an earlier, less cautious era ("Thank you, acid," Rodney says in exasperation as he leaves the table at the launch of yet another recitation of the co-founders' names).

Although *Wanderlust's* characterization of pot-friendly Elysium inaccurately represents the majority of intentional communities, the broader picture it paints does hint at the truth: that communities in general may be places not to escape *into* drugs but to escape *from* a drug-addled culture, to liberate oneself from both pharmaceuticals and from the destructive drugs of choice of many non-communitarians. (Rick's house and even Linda's and George's former medicine cabinet undoubtedly contain a far larger array of drugs, most of them much less natural, than does Elysium.) In my own experience in community, I've lived with many more people committed to physical, spiritual, and emotional health and well-being through substance-free living (and also through *mostly* substance-free living) than I suspect is typical in the wider culture.

"Doors Are Bullshit"

The movie also exaggerates, to comic effect, the amount of privacy sacrificed when joining a community. Elysium has removed all doors between inside rooms, because "doors close us off from one another." Flush with the excitement of joining the community, George agrees that "Doors are bullshit." Later, he has second thoughts, telling Linda that "I can't have 15 people involved every time we have an argument." (Again, anyone who has spent any amount of time in

community is likely to have heard similar words from those adjusting to sharing their lives more closely with others.)

In reality, most intentional communities in the 21st century honor members' needs for privacy, and I've never lived in or visited a community that had removed all its doors, but this doesn't negate the underlying truth that community living involves letting down or removing some boundaries and sometimes being "visible" when one does not want to be. The thought of community living often inspires exaggerated fears of loss of privacy—a phenomenon mirrored by the exaggerated loss of *actual* privacy in *Wanderlust*.

Trust, Communication, Respect...and Sex

Related to the loss of privacy and boundaries is Elyssium's attitude toward sexual relationships. When one member approaches George to suggest a sexual liaison, he and Linda learn that they've joined a polyamorous community, in which "open sexual boundaries lead to a deeper honesty." In positive contrast to Rick, who has been surreptitiously having affairs for years, the members of Elysium are absolutely honest about whom they are desiring or having as sexual partners. Hesitancy about "free love" is the final impediment to the couple's deciding to stay past their initial two weeks, until Linda relents and agrees that she will embrace that practice too. "As long as there is trust, communication, and respect," she earnestly tells the amazed George, "we can all enjoy each other intimately." (Which raises the question: was the script transcribed directly from recordings made during its writers' visit to a polyamory-friendly intentional community?)

Soon thereafter, George is equally stunned to hear these words from another community-mate: "I just made love to your wife in the next room." But while Elyssium members seem to have relaxed into their polyamorous lives with little drama or nervousness—an apparently natural choice, given that "monogamy is sexual slavery"—the new couple seem to believe that they are obliged to participate in order to fit in, and George's over-the-top attempts to psyche himself up for polyamorous sex end up backfiring. Nevertheless, the problems caused by polyamory at Elysium seem to reside mainly within Linda and (mostly) George, not in other community members, and the idea that "when you pick a fight with your body's sexual chi, you

drive it inward, creating disease" ends up seeming plausible.

By depicting a community that has open sexual boundaries, *Wanderlust* may create the mistaken impression that most intentional communities are that way, or that groups that include any poly-amory at all are universally polyamorous (whereas in reality, in groups open to this choice, most often monogamists and the celibate coexist with polyamor-ists). At the same time, *Wanderlust* paints polyamory (at least among established Elysium residents) as more drama-free than it may be in real life.

"Hit Her with Your Truth!"

And at Elysium—as in many intentional communities—intimacy doesn't just mean sex; in fact, it often doesn't mean sex at all. In one memorable scene, a member calls a "truth circle," in which participants are encouraged to "share something true"—reveal something that will help others know them better, or that will help heal or build relationships. So far so good—I have been part of hundreds of such circles over my years in community, and while not every intentional community incorporates this kind of practice, many do, especially those in which members work and live closely together. Such forums often prove extremely helpful in supporting both individual and group well-being and effectiveness.

But immediately, the circle goes comically awry. Linda hasn't yet spoken when she is accused of telling lies and being "full of shit." She wisely defers to another member to start the truth-sharing, but when the attention returns to her and George, the accusations return as well, amped up even more. Circle members interrupt all attempts to speak and prove exceedingly unhelpful with their intrusions: "hit her with your truth!," "this is when the breakthroughs happen!," "don't edit yourself!" Linda and George can barely get a word in edgewise, but when they do speak, they end up bringing out deep issues in their relationship that might not have surfaced otherwise, which finally calms the eager "assistants" to their process. Linda does gain genuine insight into herself, leading one participant to declare, "Linda, you just met Linda."

If you have not lived through personal-growth workshops that have occasionally gone awry in similar ways, you may not find this scene nearly as funny as I did. But many communitarians will recognize an exaggerated but hilariously evocative depiction of apparently inappropriate (yet paradoxically often breakthrough-inducing) "truth circle" behavior, on steroids.

The free flow of feelings and words at Elyssium also includes such practices as "primal gesticulating," in which the individual goes to the woods to shout out things they don't like (war, clearcuts, pollution, climate change, etc.) in order to release "anxieties, tensions, and fears." While some communitarians (particularly those in urban settings or cohousing groups) may never have witnessed or practiced anything like this—nor heard initially unidentifiable shouting or wailing from the far end of the property, which turns out to be therapeutic self-expression—a good number of us have. Again, this way of dealing with tensions seems orders of magnitude healthier than, for example, how George's sister-in-law Marisa attempts to cope with her troubles. And while Elysium members are blunt in their speech, they are also generally loving—a stark contrast to George's brother Rick's verbal cruelty.

The Elephant in the Room

No discussion of *Wanderlust* would be complete without mentioning the "elephant in the room"—the flawed charismatic leader, Seth. The group's "teacher, guide, guru, coach, shaman," he himself denies being the leader, professing that "Mother Earth is the only leader we need." But his central role and status as "alpha male" are obvious, as are some of the methods he uses to enforce his authority—including a voice which fluctuates between natural, relaxed speaking

and an assumed accent with deepened tones (sounding as if it may have come from the British Isles via treks through the Amazon), with which he seems to assert his position and spout quasi-profundities.

Like many leaders (both within communities and in the larger world), Seth is full of contradictions, intensified by his highly visible role. In this supposedly cooperative setting, he turns a spontaneous guitar-playing session into a competition, leaving George and his strummed chords in the dust by launching into virtuosic fingerpicked solos and demanding that George respond in kind. With George sufficiently humiliated, Seth then improvises a sensual love song on a topic ("The Wind") suggested by Linda, causing most of the women in the group to swoon and edging himself closer to adding one more (guess who?) to his list of sexual partners. He eventually shows the

---

Circle members interrupt all attempts to speak: "this is when the breakthroughs happen!," "don't edit yourself!"

---

duplicity he's capable of by planning to abandon his "brothers and sisters" in Georgia in order to start a new life in Miami with the woman he's decided is his soul mate, aided by a certain $11,000. "I love you," he tells the others, "but I love me more." To their credit, they all abandon him.

Needless to say, human history is replete with examples of flawed or corrupt leaders at every level and in every type of social organization, intentional communities included. Some leaders of both religious and secular communities have abused their power many orders of magnitude more egregiously than Seth does in *Wanderlust*. In the end, Seth actually seems more foolish, self-involved, insecure, and naïve about the world's realities than actively malevolent.

But Seth does crystallize several dynamics that communitarians may have run into: a charismatic leader claiming that a group is leaderless (or more broadly, a group failing to acknowledge power differentials); an alpha male meeting his sexual needs and desires by asserting dominance within a group; an articulate, visionary person who is in some respects also a fraud; a seemingly wise person who is also unrealistic and misguided; a proponent of cooperation who is actually highly competitive.

Most communities don't experience the kind of serious power abuses that make some people wary of joining any kind of organized group (Kool Aid, anyone?). But many do go through a variation of the "Seth phase" before maturing, as Elysium does, into a group more equally sharing power.

From Honeymoon to Transformation

While the movie's depiction of its subject intentional community is necessarily specific—and therefore couldn't be universal even if it were literally accurate—its tale of its protagonist couple's journey may strike near-universal chords of recognition among communitarians of all stripes.

Like many newly-arrived community visitors, Linda and George quickly get over their shock and fall in love with Elysium. "Who *are* these people?" George asks Linda in wonder. The promise of lives consciously filled with "nature, laughter, friendship, love" soon draws them back, and, welcomed "with open arms and open hearts" as resident members of Elysium, they feel as if they can "breathe for the first time in years."

(continued on p. 75)

THE LIGHTER SIDE OF COMMUNITY:
A COMMUNITARIAN APPRECIATES *WANDERLUST*

(continued from p. 63)

(The one slight letdown in this initial honeymoon period occurs when they discover that their accommodations as new members will be significantly less luxurious than they were as guests—another pattern that may ring bells in several communities.)

Then another common pattern emerges. Linda grows into life in the community—feeling "alive every day," playing with the children, and eventually becoming the hero of the group with her inspired protest at the casino ground-breaking—but George has more and more doubts. Linda proclaims, "I really feel like this is my home...for the first time in my life, I feel like I have a purpose." George, on the other hand, misses "meat, air conditioning, and being able to close the bathroom door."

In real-life communities, too, equal levels of enthusiasm for community living between partners can sometimes seem like the exception rather than the rule—with possible outcomes being separation, both partners staying, or both leaving (often, with one having serious regrets). In *Wanderlust*, George and Linda finally do see eye to eye about their priorities, and, true to their philosophy and general good nature, the community members cheer the couple's commitment to each other even though it doesn't include staying at Elysium.

Community as Catalyst

Linda and George start their adventure as a frazzled New York couple with little sense of control over their lives and with little time or opportunity for non-harried communication, self-expression, or self-examination. Elysium catalyzes their personal growth and transforms their lives in ways they could never have imagined—and they return the favor not only by helping precipitate positive changes at Elysium but by empowering former community-mates and themselves through the new business they establish when they return to New York. By the end of *Wanderlust*, far from melting down, Elysium has emerged from its casino land-deal trials stronger than ever, more egalitarian, and with a more positive "media image" to boot.

This kind of story may seem like the stuff of Hollywood movies—but I've personally witnessed similar transformations both within intentional communities and within those who spend time in them. Even years later, communities often receive letters of appreciation from those who see their lives forever changed for the better by experiences there.

This doesn't mean that intentional community—or any one style of community—is for everyone, indefinitely. *Wanderlust* highlights some of the reasons why a place like Elysium will not work, long-term, for people like George. But it also affirms community living as a legitimate choice—one that may be a lot more fun (and full of more material for loving parody) than the disconnected, unhappy lives of many modern people. At the very least, it asks its viewers to shake up their assumptions, and maybe explore a little—even if only to find that the community best for each of us is whatever we can create in our own lives, once we've learned what we need to learn in order to create it. ☙

Chris Roth edits COMMUNITIES, *currently lives at Meadowsong Ecovillage outside Dexter, Oregon, and has spent most of his adult life in community of one form or another. Contact him at editor@ic.org.*

CREATING THE IDEAL INTENTIONAL COMMUNITY
(OR REVITALIZING AN EXISTING ONE)

I, Sahmat, grew up in intentional communities and have lived in 10 of them. I have been so dedicated to Community with both humans and Nature that I've been called "The Community Guy". The communities I grew up in shared a fairly strong "sense of community". I call this deep and sustained sense of community "Common-unity" because it's a state of unity we share in common, with the unique individuality of each human and each species still honored. It's this state of Common-unity that I've found most valuable in life and to me it's the main reason for living in an intentional community. When a group is deep in Common-unity together, there's a shared sense of love, joy, and peace that tops any other group experience.

However, I've found that in all the communities I've lived in, the sense of community is not nearly as deep and sustained as it could be. It's precisely this lack of Common-unity that is the root cause of the catastrophic global suffering of racism, wars, child abuse, abuse of women, environmental and species destruction, etc. So the ultimate goal is ending global suffering through "Global Common-unity": the spreading of Common-unity throughout the world by forming a global network of Common-unity-dedicated Communities.

So I've spent my life learning how to create Common-unity-dedicated communities that share true Common-unity: a deeper and more sustained sense of community. There are two keys to starting a Common-unity community (or moving an existing community into deeper Common-unity):

1. The first key to Common-unity is for everyone to be "Common-unity-dedicated" as their top common priority. This doesn't seem to be the case in any existing community, which results in focus and energies being bled off into other priorities. So maintenance of Common-unity doesn't get enough time and energy.

2. The second key to Common-unity is to learn "Common-unity Skills", skills that must be practiced to maintain Common-unity: Speaking from the Heart, Empathetic Listening, Emptying of Ego-attachments, Conflict Resolution, Consensus, Heart Wound Healing, Cooperative Housing, and Cooperative Economics. Modern culture does not teach us these skills.

We at the Alliance for Global Community have developed free workshops that train you in these Common-unity Skills. The workshops contain the Sharing Circle process developed by M. Scott Peck, a Nature connection exercise developed by John Seed and Joanna Macy, healing exercises developed by Byron Katie and Richard Moss, and exercises in creating Cooperative Housing and Cooperative Economics. We've tested various versions of these Common-unity Skill Building workshops over the past 25 years, and we've found them to be quite effective in teaching Common-unity skills that can help maintain Common-unity. If you'd like to start a Common-unity-dedicated community, or if you'd like to bring more Common-unity into an existing community (perhaps through a Common-unity sub-community or "pod"), you need to learn or improve these Common-unity skills as soon as possible.

To find out how to sign up for a free public Common-unity Skills workshop or schedule a free workshop for an existing group or community, please go to my website thecommunityguy.org There you can also find out how to get a free copy of the book "Skill Building for Global Common-unity". You can contact Sahmat directly at info@thecommunityguy.org or at 434-305-4770.

COMMON-UNITY WITH HUMANITY AND NATURE

Journeying on the Ark:
One Woman's Experience at L'Arche

By Janna Payne

Pilgrim,
when your ship,
long moored in harbour,
gives you the illusion
of being a house;
when your ship
begins to put down roots
in the stagnant water by the quay:
put out to sea!
Save your boat's journeying soul
and your own pilgrim soul,
cost what it may.
—Dom Helder Camara

Boarding the Ark

I have been serving as a live-in assistant at L'Arche Daybreak (Richmond Hill, Ontario) for the past year and a half, which means I have been creating home with assistants from around the world and core members (individuals with intellectual disabilities). In my home there are four core members and four assistants. L'Arche is an organization that seeks to provide safe, nurturing homes for individuals with intellectual disabilities, honouring their unique value and vocation. The word *L'Arche* means *the ark* in French, which has been described as a place of refuge and of safety from the flood in various L'Arche documents.

Moving into L'Arche, I brought openness to intentional community life and to learning in and through relationship with core members and assistants alike.

I came excited to be a part of a community of difference. I saw responding to the needs of core members as an important part of building community, and was eager to live out Jean Vanier's invitation to sacrifice my own freedom while building relationships based on mutuality, handing over power, claiming (significantly) less space, making peace with difference, and honouring/ celebrating the core members.

Kim Lageer

Artwork by a core member at L'Arche Daybreak.

LAGEER

KIM

Courtesy of Janna Payne

(L to R) Lorenzo Sforza Cesarini, Janna Payne, Carl MacMillan, and John Bloss perform in a L'Arche Daybreak Gala Event featuring artists with and without intellectual disabilities.

Mooring in the Harbour

While I started off with a lot of momentum, it wasn't long before I realized supporting the value and vocation of the core members was serious business. As a live-in assistant, I was trained to provide extensive physical, emotional, social, behavioural, and spiritual support for approximately 60 hours a week. Assistants in my home were encouraged to be physically present to the needs of the core members throughout the day, and advised to listen, learn, observe, and respond to their offers if we wanted to build trust. Assistants were also encouraged to see the core members as the true artists and visionaries while sacrificing their own freedom and practicing self-control. This meant core members had individual support from 7 a.m. to 10 p.m. with assistants on hand to interject at the first sign of a core member becoming sad or angry. Assistants were directed to counsel, comfort, console, or offer to pray with a core member to de-escalate a situation or prevent a core member from having a verbal outburst. Looking around the house, there seemed to be correlation between supporting the core members and stroking their hair, sitting directly beside them, and responding to their every comment, tear, yawn, sneeze, question, or complaint along the way!

Living in a gentle, conflict-free space proved tiring. I questioned how the philosophy of L'Arche was being played out, and was skeptical of whether or not it was in the best interest of the core members. I started to think the philosophy of care fostered dependency, stifling the growth and expression of the core members. I recognized many of the core members had complex needs and would benefit from having assistants trained in more than befriending. I didn't think it was healthy for assistants to be meeting the relational and emotional needs of the core members (without establishing healthy boundaries or facilitating opportunities for connection outside of the home). I started to believe it is possible and crucial for all people—with or without intellectual disabilities—to confront parts of themselves, manage their own emotions, meet their own needs, and listen to their inner voices without always having an assistant—albeit a needy one—to thank. I was uncomfortable shielding the core members from pain, and uncomfortable living in a fantasy land.

As someone who values independence and individuality, I should also fess up I found myself burnt out from continually providing excessive care and continually being in relation with others. I felt like a being-for-others, which, quite frankly, blends well with Freire's definition of oppressed (see *Pedagogy of the Oppressed*, Paulo Freire, 1968, 1970). I felt small, silenced, and stifled.

I hated living in a dream land, and became bored dwelling in peace, safety, and security. I resented heralding the voices of the core members, and resented a community ideal that saw assistants refusing to insert their identities into the space, and withholding their "I believe" and "I think" assertions in the presence of those with disabilities. I was saddened that those with disabilities were not having the opportunity to encounter real people—the wrath of authentic, fully alive, fierce, creative, beautiful people. I hated being in a space where self-control trumped self-expression, and where the stories of assistants centered almost exclusively on what they had learned from L'Arche or the core members. I found the philosophy disempowering.

I yearned to tell my own story, and to open myself up to the stories of others. As Jeanette Winterson wrote, "I was not being myself, but I didn't know how to be myself there. I hid the self that I was and had no persona to put in its place." *(Why Be Happy When You Could Be Normal?)*

Putting Out to Sea

Serving at L'Arche was a painful process that saw me doubting my own capacity to care, feigning diplomacy, and struggling to remain open to the community and to

Performers take the stage in a L'Arche Daybreak Gala Event featuring artists with and without intellectual disabilities.

(R to L) L'Arche Daybreak assistant Janna Payne takes in a view of Lake Ontario with core member Heather Goodchild.

Courtesy of Janna Payne

Courtesy of Janna Payne

those telling me to "die to self." It was a delicate dance, but with much frustration and even more reflection, I gradually came to some pretty great revelations about myself, about caregiving, and about community-building.

Being thrust into the position of caregiver at L'Arche challenged my self-understanding. I found myself yearning for space to collaborate, insert my identity, and share my true self. I found myself becoming empathetic toward others in caregiving roles, and more attuned to fellow assistants who were disconnected from the work and scrambling to form their own identities (in their limited time away from caregiving). I now believe assistants, like myself, could provide better care if we had outlets for telling our own stories, making our own meaning, developing our own talents, having power, having intimacy, taking ownership, and working toward mutual liberation. Being whole means giving the gift of the self—not emptying the self.

While L'Arche promises spiritual becoming in exchange for labour, I would argue caregiving has little to do with spiritual becoming. I think spiritual becoming means exchanging the self, which happens in moments of mutuality along the way. It can be a part of caregiving, but I think seeing caregiving as a compassionate act or as something others deserve undermines the services being provided. I believe working toward a balance that is mutually liberating and life-giving for assistants would better support the core members.

When it comes to responding to the needs of core members, I also think assistants could benefit from learning more about the importance of emotional and creative expression in their own lives and in the lives of core members. Self-advocacy hinges on core members developing their capacities to lead, tell their own stories, enter into dialogue, honour their emotions, and demand justice. Prophets were known for angrily demanding justice, and anger is an important emotion that can be cultivated for good.

Maintaining a gentle web doesn't necessarily support the growth, expression, and independence of anyone and often leads to dependency. Encouraging emotional and creative expression is essential for engaging in life, building/restoring relationships, linking one's life with others, and journeying against, toward, and with others.

Being at L'Arche has strengthened my philosophy of community. I initially came to L'Arche thinking that if I wanted to build community, I had to enter the world of the core members and respond to their needs. While some people are helpers at heart, I now think community happens when people turn toward one another, share space, and remain true to the self. I've seen this happen at an art show featuring work of artists with and without disabilities, when people

L'Arche Daybreak assistant Janna Payne visits Lake Ontario with core member Heather Goodchild.

with and without disabilities share the stage, and when people with and without disabilities show openness to the perspectives, stories, and beauty of others.

Community is about vulnerability, and I see vulnerability as having the courage to express the self, the courage to declare "this is who I am," and the courage to be open to truly meeting with others. Vulnerability happens when we enter our true selves into relationship with others. Building community means telling the truth, sharing the self, and moving forward in and through relationship. Community is raw, honest, vulnerable, and sometimes awkward.

Journeying Forward

Irving Zola writes that disability demands "a continuing effort to reclaim what we have lost: the right to act sexy, get angry, be vulnerable, and have possibilities." My hope is that as I weave my way in and out of community I can co-create spaces of difference where people with and without disabilities can fully embrace the self, inviting sex appeal, anger, vulnerability, and possibility into the conversation. I believe in honouring the voices and identities of myself and others. I also hope to connect with others who are navigating issues of identity, process, and power while telling their own stories and engaging their social imaginations. Recognizing I'm called to become an individual in community, to stand up for justice, and to assert my true self into the world might just help me to move forward, grow in self-understanding, care for myself and others, and build community while offering something authentic into the world. ❧

Janna Payne is a Canadian storyteller, master of divinity candidate, and live-in assistant at L'Arche Cork (Ireland). She wrote this reflection while serving as a live-in assistant at L'Arche Daybreak (Canada). She strives to tell her own story while honouring the stories of the individuals with intellectual disabilities she supports. She can be reached at paynejanna@gmail.com.

Courtesy of Janna Payne

Transitioning into the Heart of Community

By Tara Pettit

I lie in my bunk, thoughts of the day's events swirling around in my mind. I replay the morning's group devotional, the day-long campus visit, and the wonderful Slovenian specialty stuffed pepper dinner—daily events that were made even more special in the company of my community members and which were emphasized by the laughs, stories, and moments of truth dispersed throughout. I mindfully meander back through the past two months I have spent with my brothers and sisters in community. My brain cannot even wrap itself around all that I have experienced, felt, communicated, seen—the intense emotions that have surged through my body, the skin I have touched, the warmth I have felt from having slept so close to my sisters, the uplifting encouragement and support I have received from my brothers.

And yet, amidst the comfort that my now-familiar bunk bed provides while reminiscing this summer's stay in foreign lands, an even more familiar feeling of sadness begins creeping up on me. It's a feeling that envelops me at about the same time in all my international community projects, when life together is drawing to a close and the reality of going home alone hits me like a brick. Although it's an emotion that is strongly rooted in the separation anxiety I experience, time and time again, after leaving my "summer family," never failing to remind me that the time for saying our goodbyes is drawing near, it has also become an elemental factor in the functioning of the temporary communities I devote my time to and in the larger vision of my life's work.

You see, for me, living in community has always been a transitory experience, in which beginnings and endings are just a part of the dance. Being a part of summer project spiritual work teams requires one to adopt a lifestyle that is transient in nature and which allows for adaptability with regards to not only the changing of community teams and bunk mates, but also the shifting of cultures with various beliefs, ideals, and social norms. Living and working with these changing community teams over an entire summer—groups that are introduced, meshed, entwined, and split up within a few months' span—becomes somewhat of a whirlwind journey of immediate and intense relationship, emotion, and shared experiences.

My first adventure overseas with the summer work teams was to Ljubljana, Slovenia, a small European country that had never been visited by any summer project team under the parent organization. I was only 19 years old, but bright-eyed, idealistic, and ready to take on the world with my passion for cultural integration and spiritual conversation. I was also excited by the idea of collaborating with other college students in a project based on long-term goals and purposes and that gained lasting, meaningful results. Our

View of Drežnica (Kobarid), Slovenia.

Slovenian national costumes.

mission was to integrate ourselves into the Slovenian lifestyle, survey the cultural and spiritual climate, and engage citizens (particularly college-aged individuals) in spiritual conversation that sought to educate us, as Americans, about the country's religious views in contrast to westernized Christianity. In turn, we also sought to share our spiritual experiences with Slovenian natives in hopes of establishing common cultural ground. Our team self-identified as Christians, but we longed to create bridges with other cultures rather than burn them.

To this day, five years later, I can still recall such vivid detail from my time spent in that beautiful, homey European city, from the smell of my bed sheets to the way I felt walking the town square every morning—deeply content, with peace residing in every bone of my body. Our days were busy, filled with team meetings, appointments with locals, shared meals, training, and community events. We were focused in mission and set our sights on uncovering the mystery that was Slovenian culture and spirituality.

We dedicated ourselves to meeting people through random conversation and building friendships in love and interest. Our purposes unfolded in very organic ways, relational in nature, as we assimilated into the culture, spending our days in busy cafés and engaging locals in deep, thought-provoking conversation about

life, God, and how they seek happiness. However, no matter how much hard work and purposefulness went into pursuing our cultural outreach goals, it was quite obvious how important tending to our own little community became in relation to each member's overall experience and pursuit of higher, more conscious living.

Our summer work was built upon the community we cultivated within our own group as we strengthened our ties with each other, not only to become more effective in our area outreach, but also to learn how to exist peacefully and intentionally, albeit humanly, as children of God. We found more than friendship in our relationships with one another—something more akin to life partners, as we shared our rooms, laughs, and tears for the summer, creating soul-satisfying memories and substantial principles that would stay with us for a lifetime.

Let's just say that within these short-term summer project communities, life vibrates at a much higher frequency and human experiences are elevated to much greater heights. The temporary and transitional nature of our communities undoubtedly contributed to the speed and intensity with which we dove right into life together; we knew our time was short, but dramatically impacting. There was no holding back for us from the start. While other, more permanent, communities had the time to test the waters of group dynamics, our purposes as a group required us to collide into one another's lives like crashing waves. From our shy hellos to tearful goodbyes, pretty much everything was shared: European hostel rooms and dinner at the local Thai joint, but especially the exhilarating highs and crushing lows that come with the hard work of pursuing the spirituality of other cultures through building relationships and establishing ourselves as a spiritual resource in the area.

As a whole, we all bore the disappointment one team member experienced from being rejected or ignored, or the heartbreak another experienced from having been attacked. We also communally celebrated the joy of having made a new friend, the excitement from making spiritual connections with others, and the fulfillment of breathing life into another by sharing our life purposes and happiness. As a group we collaboratively experienced inner growth and witnessed the transformation that took place within each of our souls as we grew into a more diverse, more loving, stronger, better people. We fell in love fast and hard, quickly realizing that our shared experiences would bond us and mark us as members of our summer community project for life.

Recognizably, under any circumstance, human relationships are complicated, but they become even messier when all of life's events are amplified in group living. Even in our temporary community, it was obvious that members would have to deal with the inevitable squabbles and disagreements that are simply a product of conflicting human personalities and the occasional claustrophobic feeling after living on top of one another for several weeks. The conflicts are bound to happen with any random mix of people; however, what helped us achieve our equilibrium was our dedication to common goals and values and the realization that regardless of differences, we were embodying the unifying love of Christ. We sought to love what each person brought to the group because it's what makes up the community that we built and are vitally a part of—the community that is distinctly ours. Our capacity for love began with the love we cultivated for each other, which overflowed into our love for the local area we were living in.

Days were not always easy. Sometimes it took special effort just to feel somewhat amiable towards my team members, which made it that much harder to muster the energy for city outreach. While our work was not overly "hard," it could be energy-zapping and time consuming, requiring dedication and emotional availability in extending oneself to the needs of others. It was a daily practice that we failed in, succeeded in, but nonetheless continued in. Loving is not easy and every single day presented challenges, whether it was the choice to neglect the member who hurt you, lash out at the friend who has been annoying you, or to just drop all preconceived notions and rash assumptions while choosing the path of acceptance and forgiveness. Embarking on a journey in community will present all types of messes and I learned that I could rely on the very people my mental, emotional, and egotistical persona battled against to find my way through the muddiness, to find peace in all the ways we are humanly beautiful.

Our life as a community was short, but the wealth of knowledge and experience gained from each moment spent in those summers followed each of us back to our hometowns and persisted, growing with every subsequent community endeavor. Each summer transformed us for life. Before the experience of living every waking moment in close quarters and with such a diverse group of people, it's easy to succumb to the mindset that people are far too opinionated and different, full of their own quirks and set in their own ways to mesh into a viable community—that it takes a special breed of people to make intentional community work. But our short-term communities proved that conclusion wrong, after continuously creating and recreating new communities, adapting to new people and new experiences and just when comfort sets in, saying goodbye and doing it all over again with a new group of people.

Slovenian specialty stuffed peppers.

After having lived out community, intentionally, with a group of people you've had to learn to trust with your vulnerability, you see how it serves this deep craving for belonging, sharing, and acceptance present to some degree in every human being. This is not to say that everyone is designed to live in as close a community environment as I have experienced for extended periods of time, but that on some level, every person experiences some degree of inner satisfaction, fulfillment, and growth from sharing everyday life with human beings, who, for the most part, are made of the same emotions and desires that we see in ourselves.

You cannot experience community and remain the same. You cannot experience community and not in some way connect to the same vulnerability and longing you witness in others as you feel yourself.

Snowy scene in Slovenia.

Community helps you to see just how different we can be in terms of personality, communication styles, and personal expression, but just how similar we all are when you strip back the layers, the protective shields we have learned to hide behind. Stripped down, we are the same flesh and bone, have the same root flaws and tendencies, and are created to enjoy the same sensations, feelings, and experiences.

Communities are far from perfect. Our community was far from perfect. In fact, communities may include some of the messiest, most lost, erratic individuals on earth. That's what makes community necessary. We need each other, more than we ever know, and collaboration towards greater intentional purposes requires a diversity of thoughts, opinions, personalities, and experiences. Reentering the "real world" several times after periods of living in the community bubble has always been an adjustment for me as I confronted feelings of withdrawal and loneliness and had to reacquaint myself with the silences in eating alone, sleeping alone, and occupying my time by myself.

Before community, I sort of suppressed those deep-down feelings—longings for the diversity and excitement that a close group of people brings to life. I was okay with doing things alone and just went about my way, harboring thoughts, feelings, and opinions to myself. But oh, after community, it's as if the world became Technicolor. My sociality blossomed and I opened myself up to people in such personal, vulnerable ways. I learned how people can help you to cherish each moment, to make each moment fun, fulfilling, and worth living. People's quirks and habits met with my own, blending into my personality and behaviors. We morphed into one unit and pursued life together full-force.

For the time being, I have transitioned out of community to pursue my career. It's hard living alone these days. Waking up alone just isn't as fun as waking up to a room full of girls singing and carrying on. Ice cream runs by myself just aren't as fulfilling as strolling around the town square with gelato in hand and friends at my side. It's these moments, with my family, that I will always look to as a cure for loneliness. I will always carry that communal spirit in my heart. Although somewhat displacing, those times in my life were remarkably transforming, and I will always look to them to re-center myself within creation's larger design, our deeply human purpose of celebrating life as a body of believers, a community. ❧

A graduate of Ohio University's Scripps School of Journalism in Athens, Tara considers herself a sort of "ramblin' woman" who dabbles in a lot of different activities and projects which lead her to her next literary idea. Currently, she is a writing partner with the United Nations and has been devoting many of her freelance writing projects to her interests in Ayurveda, nature, and social justice.

CREATING COOPERATIVE CULTURE REVIEW BY CHRIS ROTH

Cycling toward Sustainable Community

Within Reach
By Mandy Creighton, Ryan Mlynarczyk, and friends
Into the Fire/Reach Within/Doctrine Productions, 2012, 1:38 run time
DVD available from withinreachmovie.com

Nearly five years in the making, *Within Reach* is a major new documentary about the promise of intentional community and cooperative living. Its creators suggest that the dream of "sustainable community" is within reach of all of us, and, through their personal story, offer many possible paths to that hopeful future.

Mandy and Ryan left their mainstream jobs and lifestyles to cycle 6,500 miles across the United States over a period of two years, visiting 100 communities of many different flavors and talking to people everywhere they went about ways of living more sustainably. Accompanied at times by fellow videographers and additional cyclists, they documented their journey, assisted by a crowdfunding campaign. The monumental task of wading through, excerpting, and editing together portions of their countless hours of footage into a coherent film took another couple years.

Happily, the result is a broadly-appealing mixture of "road trip" movie, community documentary, and exploration into practical approaches to social and ecological sustainability. Entertaining and understandable enough for a mainstream audience, it also delves deep into the "sustainable community" movement to offer fresh material to even the most experienced communitarians and eco-living activists.

Its central conclusion is perhaps best summed up by cohousing pioneer Jim Leach: "Community is the secret ingredient in sustainability." In scene after scene, we see vibrant pockets of community, and witness firsthand all the ways in which cooperation allows and encourages people to live more lightly on the earth while creating resilient webs of mutual support.

Eight years after doing service work together in Central America, where they first experienced "small communities living simply, in harmony with nature," Mandy and Ryan (who

fell into much more conventional, increasingly unsatisfying lives in the interim) find each other again and decide they want to recapture the magic they felt there. They embark on an epic "quest for utopia," hoping eventually to find a new home aligned with their ideals.

The film documenting their journey ingeniously overlaps several thematic progressions. Its structure is not entirely linear, but rather a set of overlaid patterns. While most of the visits are presented in chronological order, this is not a rigid guideline; when it serves the purpose of the movie to jump ahead or back to a setting or interviewee with something important to say about a theme, it does.

One progression (indicated by three dimensional letters embedded in the landscape at the start of each new section) attempts to answer the initial question, *what is sustainable community?* The answers, in order, are that community is sharing; community is family; community is a legacy; community is food; community is education; community is service; and community is economical. The film then poses and attempts to answer another question—*what does it take to live in sustainable community?*—and concludes with suggestions about creating community wherever you are.

Another progression concerns type of community. We start with cooperative houses, then visit cohousing groups, transition towns, ecovillages, spiritual communities, extended communities growing "beyond the community border," working

(continued on p. 78)

WITHIN REACH DVD REVIEW

(continued from p. 80)

farm communities, groups focused on education and self-education, service-oriented communities, and a green town.

While we see relatively short clips of dozens of different communities, certain groups get significant segments of at least several minutes each; these include Earthaven, The Farm, Cobb Hill, Ecovillage at Ithaca, The Possibility Alliance, Dancing Rabbit, Joyful Path, Hummingbird, and the "green town" of Greensburg, Kansas.

The film also catalogs a broad range of sustainable-community-related practices and technologies (often highlighted with on-screen text), including consensus process, solar cookers, suburban farm animals, community kitchens, skillshare workshops, gardening and permaculture, natural building, community potlucks, eating local diets, "unschooling," homemade entertainment, neighborly collaboration, and eco-retrofitting.

Our view alternates between the small picture—one couple's trip around the country—and the big picture—national and global social and environmental trends that make a change of direction toward "sustainable community" paramount for our survival. Richard Heinberg, Bill McKibben, Rob Hopkins, Aron Heinz, and others offer valuable insights, interlaced throughout the film, on everything from the end of cheap fossil fuel, the urgency of addressing climate change, and the increasing dissatisfaction and social isolation in America over the last 50 years, to the importance of localization, of deep listening, and of self-examination. Just as valuable are the reflections of community members on what life in community is like for them. While they tout its many benefits, they also discuss some of the challenges: decision-making can be an ordeal, and compromising can be difficult. As one Cobb Hill resident observes, our culture doesn't teach most of us how to live in community, so we have a steep learning curve when we decide to.

Fortunately, community can also be an ideal place to safely engage in the emotional and inner work that helps us become better community members. That work is necessary to create the "social sustainability" that, many in this film observe, is the backbone of ecological sustainability. "The way we treat the planet is really connected to how we treat [each other and] ourselves," says one student visiting Ecovillage at Ithaca.

Yet the magic of community is felt most directly not through words, but through the many scenes in which community members are fully engaged in creating "sustainable culture" themselves—through sharing music, food, play, practical projects, helping one another live not only more ecologically but more joyfully. The spirit of community is palpable, leaving viewers with the (correct) impression that there is a whole world of cultural and ecological-living innovation awaiting them, if they move beyond the constraints of mainstream America.

An engaging soundtrack—comprised of homespun music reinforcing the grassroots perspective of the film, alternating with interviews, the bikers' reflections, and community scenes—helps the movie stay stimulating and dynamic. The videography, surprisingly professional given the sometimes challenging traveling and shooting conditions, conveys the experience of the journey well. Titles and captions are also used to excellent effect.

My favorite single segment depicts the Superhero Alliance in La Plata, Missouri—probably the most radical experiment included here, a service-oriented group operating on the gift economy and dedicated to simple living not dependent on modern technology. In this section, the power of engaging in "emotional inner work" is per-haps most clearly described: speaking in candlelight in this electricity-free community, with flashes of lightning visible through the windows behind her, Keren Ram describes how healing it is for people to "see my dark areas and still love me" in an environment that is so supportive and embracing of each person's humanness. She also conveys clearly the power of shared dedication to being present and spiritually centered, of which the "bell of mindfulness" is a common reminder at the Superhero Alliance Sanctuary.

(I must admit that my personal acquaintance and several longstanding friendships

> # The magic of community is felt most directly through the many scenes in which community members are creating "sustainable culture" themselves.

with those we meet in this segment help make it my favorite. In fact, the movie is full of people I know and/or have at least met, part of the extended community network of friends and colleagues that helps this feel like a "movement" rather than just a set of of isolated cultural aberrations.)

Every in-depth segment has its memorable moments and revelations, from the interviews with the children participating in Ecovillage at Ithaca's Primitive Pursuits program (best line, from an extremely imaginative child: "It's not imagination!") to the reflections from ex-suburbanites learning rural skills at Cobb Hill and from ecovillagers learning how to create homes for themselves at Dancing Rabbit.

For someone already familiar with much of the intentional community landscape—and perhaps for any viewer—the most inspiring, hopeful segment may be the depiction of Greensburg, Kansas. Following a 2007 tornado that destroyed 95 percent of the town, townspeople banded together to rebuild using green principles, doing community planning as a group. They decided not to re-erect their backyard fences, but instead to encourage neighborly inter-action wherever they could, while adhering to an ecological approach that, rather than being dogmatic, meets each person "where they are" and helps them move organically toward more sustainable practices.

Greensburg's mayor, Bob Dixon, is one of the most eloquent voices for community in this film. Describing the social isolation that has overtaken our society in recent decades, he says it's time to change from being "back porch, back patio people," walled off from one another, into once again being "front porch people," who get to know our neigh-bors and thus are able to deal much better with the issues we'll inevitably face together. Perhaps because they've learned the lessons of the tornado, the town's residents all seem up to the challenge of working together. The fact that such a radical movement toward sustainability and community can happen in a "regular" middle American town inspires real hope that it can happen anywhere.

Each town, city, or rural area may need to confront its own form of "disaster" in order to make such a transition. Since current trends suggest that we will have no shortage of those in coming years and decades, the best we can hope for is that we start making these changes before the full force of disaster strikes. In an age of resource depletion and climate change, such an approach can mitigate both local and global suffering.

At one hour and 38 minutes, this film cannot be exhaustive in addressing the issues it raises, or in depicting all dimensions of the intentional community world. One funda-mental question that it does not answer is: are any of these "sustainable communities" truly sustainable? They are all clearly moving in the direction of, or working towards, a way of being that is regenerative rather than self-destructive—but in the modern world, true "sustainability" is hard to ascertain and may be impossible to achieve with-out larger-scale, more fundamental changes. Even Mandy and Ryan's human-powered trip around the country was fueled by many "unsustainable" elements. The idea that simply by moving to (or creating) a place calling itself a "sustainable community" we've achieved sustainability strikes me as an illusion. Instead, all any of us can do is take steps toward what that kind of world could be; it seems unlikely that any of us will arrive there in this lifetime.

The movie does a good job of depicting both the joys and challenges of Mandy and Ryan's bike journey, including mechanical, breakdowns, injuries, difficult weather, dwindling finances, hostile authorities, and personal and relationship challenges (at one point, we learn, Ryan has smashed his computer and quit the project in frustration—he later apologizes, relents, and rejoins Mandy). But it doesn't maintain the same balance in its depiction of the communities the couple visits.

True, as already mentioned, multiple interviewees talk about some of the difficulties they've experienced; especially in the areas of collective decision-making and compro-mising our personal desires, they remind us that our culture hasn't taught us how to live in community. But we viewers don't see these difficulties first-hand. We don't experience any of the pain and disappointment, the frustrations and breakdowns of various sorts, that happen in community just as they happen on bike trips. In effect, with each com-munity, we—like the short-term visitors we're accompanying—are in a "honeymoon phase." We get to see how appealing each place can be; we don't get to feel how challeng-ing it can be. And ironically, when interviewees talk about the challenges, their honesty makes their communities seem even more appealing.

The most common criticism of this film is likely to be that, while it opens viewers' eyes (including mainstream viewers' eyes) to many new horizons related to sustainability and community, it does so through rose-colored biking glasses.

However, one movie cannot be all things to all people. This one is a surprisingly in-depth introduction to the wide-ranging world of forward-looking community-building. It demonstrates that it is possible to leave a mainstream lifestyle and enter into a world that most people only dream about. It also shows that one can make changes in one's own life and community to move much closer to a future that is healthy and friendly to both people and the planet. The film doesn't hit us—at least not viscerally—with the potentially discouraging news that life in community can be just as challenging as life outside of it, fraught with potential pitfalls. How-ever, if we are making conscious choices, these pitfalls occur in the context of a real-ity we feel more aligned with, and that has more staying power than the lives we've left behind.

The movie concludes with Mandy and Ryan's arrival at Hummingbird, the com-munity they have chosen as their new home—"but," an on-screen caption tells us, "their journey toward a sustainable life never ends." In the years since their bike trip ended, they have in fact moved on from Hummingbird. Mandy now lives at Dancing Rabbit, and Ryan, having tried Dancing Rabbit as well, now lives outside of intentional community, in Hawaii. In other words, for each of them (as for any-one who commits to an extended explo-ration of community), the "honeymoon phase" has passed.

Yet the lessons of their film remain just as valuable, and the journey they share is a compelling one. This docu-mentary deserves to be seen not only by those in the "sustainable commu-nity" movement, but by a much larger mainstream audience as well. It has the capacity to change lives—and, whether creating ripples or waves, it can make a real contribution to the more regenera-tive, community-based future that, we hope, is still "within reach." ∿

Chris Roth (editor@ic.org) edits Communities.

Seeking Community
A Conversation to Shape Our Future

By Paul Born

As a reader of COMMUNITIES I am pretty sure you would have no problem agreeing with the statement, "Whatever the problem, community is the answer." For those of us who are intentional about community, it is hard to imagine how there might ever be another solution than to involve those we care about to share our concerns and needs.

When I was first married, my wife Marlene and I lived for five years on the ninth floor of a relatively new apartment building in Waterloo, Ontario. I am having trouble remembering even one significant conversation with a neighbor in that building. I do not recall ever having a meal with one of our neighbors.

We came and we went. There was little or no connection between us and the others who lived there. There was no green space near us, no common room within which to gather, no building association—and, even though many children lived in the building, no playground for them to enjoy. If there had been a fire at night and we were huddled outside in the dark and someone asked me, "Are the people on your floor here?" I am not sure I could have identified them.

This is a terribly sad story. I had no sense of ownership or belonging in this community. No one there cared for me, and I did not take care of them. My story has of course changed and now my neighbors and extended community fill my life. But as I travel the country speaking about community and hearing others' stories, my experience living for those five years in an apartment building is far too common a story.

Chaotic Times

We are living in chaotic times, and I believe things are going to get worse. This from a guy whose wife introduces him as seeing the glass not as half empty or half full but as overflowing (though she quickly adds this gets annoying some days). Why does this eternal optimist have a growing sense that things are going to get a lot worse? Because the systems we have come to rely on are broken. They no longer serve us well. The environment is a mess, the economy is unstable to the point of being wonky, and people are angry and scared. They're rising up all over the place, both against injustice and in fearful reaction.

Some may think my outlook is unwarranted. We live in a time of rapid and massive change, fueled by the hope of technology. We forge ahead, boldly believing that innovations are near that will help us address any challenge we might face. Science, we are told, is en route to curing every major disease, and solving every possible disaster. When this belief is challenged, the reply is confident: All we need is more time and more money and we will overcome this. We are asked to believe that we are a people of possibility, a people without limits.

Community, as experienced by generations before us, has broken down. Years of embracing individualism and consumerism and relying on government intervention to meet our needs have left us with few resources for building community. We live more densely than ever, but many of us do not know our neighbors, and most families are spread far and wide.

Traditional observances and religious practice are on the decline. Television and other individual pursuits have stripped us of the skills to play together and share our stories. The frenetic pace at which we conduct our daily lives carries—no, hurls—us forward.

Let's Talk

I believe that people want to talk about the future of community in their lives and the growing need for community in these chaotic times. More people want to be able to rely on their neighbours and families and feel the assurance that when times are tough they can reach out to others.

I do believe that this need for a good heart-to-heart between us is about more than just fear. There is an awakening arising within humanity. There is a growing belief that relationships can trump most problems. If we are going to build a better world, enjoying each other, learning to care for each other, and working together to build our future, community is the solution.

To facilitate these conversations the Tamarack Institute (www.tamarackcommunity.ca) has launched a campaign to help people to talk and learn together about the possibilities of community. The campaign is called *Seeking Community*.

Seeking Community

The Seeking Community is organizing around three themes: enjoy each other, care for one another, and work together for a better world.

To enjoy each other is build the social capital and resilience between us. The work of Robert Putnam, a professor at Harvard, has influenced our thinking here. The premise of social capital is that resilient relationships are the glue that binds us. If we know each other well enough and enjoy each other's company, we will be more likely to look out for one another and care about their well-being.

When mutual acts of caring happen, you will most often find a deep sense of belonging. There seems to be a connection between giving and receiving, caring and feeling cared for. Jeremy Rifkin's book *The Empathic Civilization* has inspired us greatly. As humans, our ability to share in another's plight connects us. Empathy is innate and natural.

To combat our fear, we can simply gather with others to first make sense of the worry and secondly, to work together to improve the condition. However, we do not want to organize against others and to allow our fear to drive our response. Instead, we want to unite our altruistic intentions, a process we call *collective altruism* to better the conditions around us. The joy of working together for a better world in this way opens us not only to others but to each other. My experience in building a Habitat for Humanity home is that those who build the house together receive as much or more from working with others as the eventual homeowner does in getting a new home. Altruism, when shared, builds community like nothing else.

In order to create spaces for and to inspire conversation, Tamarack is launching the programs described at www.seekingcommunity.ca.

Seeking community.ca is a learning community where you can share your stories and engage with other community seekers. On this site you can build your profile, blog, engage in groups, and attend online events and small group conversations. There is an amazing library of resources and papers to fuel your curiosity and build your knowledge about community. Once you join this learning community you receive a free e-magazine called the *Seekers Journal* that connects members to each other on a monthly basis. This learning community is open to anyone and is led by a group of 10 thought leaders and a community animator.

A Book

I have recently completed a book with a working title of *Much Joy—seeking, finding, and building community*. With this book we have produced a free Learning Guide that can be downloaded at seekingcommunity.ca and used by people to both become inspired and learn together about community and how to deepen their experience. A central theme in the book is that we all have many communities in our lives and that we have a choice about how deep or shallow our experiences of community are. Living in a neighbourhood means you live in a community. Waving to your neighbour as you drive into your garage may be all the community you want—this is a shallow experience. On the other hand, inviting your neighbours to join together with you and each other in friendship is a deeper experience. Community, I say, is not an option, but the experience you choose is. This book is available on amazon and other leading distributors.

Neighbours

There is a growing interest in neighbours. Communities are hosting neighbour days all around the world: encouraging people to get out and meet each other. We want to help fuel this movement and so we have started in our own community. We are sponsoring the Uptown West Neighbourhood Association, a dynamic community in Waterloo, Ontario. We are also supporting a group of young people (see Eli Winterfeld's story in this magazine) who call themselves the Stone Soup Collective. They are in the midst of engaging in their neighbourhood more deliberately and documenting these experiences on our learning community. As all of this unfolds, we are starting a larger conversation to discuss how policy can be written and adopted at a city level to support neighbourhood solutions to local issues.

1000 Conversations

Our short-term goal is to inspire 1000 conversations about community and have these recorded at seekingcommunity.ca. To this end, we have hired a conversation animator who is working with communities to host conversations and record them. We plan to group themes that arise from these conversations and produce learning guides and policy statements to strengthen community and investment in community. Ultimately we want to prove the statement, "Whatever the problem, community is the answer." To support this campaign, please host a conversation and then simply join the learning community at seekingcommunity.ca to post it.

In working with COMMUNITIES to sponsor this issue, it is our hope that you, who are already intentional about community, will help us grow our reach to help many thousands more to also become more intentional about the community in their lives.

Much joy. ❧

Paul Born is a best-selling author and activist who grew up with Mennonites—a people who taught him the value of the statement, "Whatever the problem, community is the answer." He is the cofounder and president of the Tamarack Institute, a Canadian think tank and lab with a mandate to advance collaborative leadership, citizen engagement, and community innovation. Tamarack sponsors Vibrant Communities—Canada's largest network of cities reducing poverty. Their goal is to reduce poverty for one million people. They are a quarter of the way there.

REVIEW BY NANCY ROTH

Christianity in Community

The Intentional Christian Community Handbook: For Idealists, Hypocrites, and Wannabe Disciples of Jesus
By David Janzen
Paraclete Press (www.paracletepress.com),
Brewster, MA, 2012, 352 pages

It happened one afternoon several years ago, in a small conference room. I had arranged to meet there with individuals who wished to discuss aspects of their ministry that had arisen during a clergy wellness program in which I was a faculty member. A young priest named Ted came in and sat down. After a period of silence, he began to speak. Rather than the usual questions about prayer disciplines, difficulties in the parish, or the challenges of scheduling family time while being a faithful pastor, he surprised me with "I believe that I have a call to found an intentional Christian community."

If only *The Intentional Christian Community Handbook* had been in existence then! Although I tried to advise him (and certainly recommended a subscription to COMMUNITIES!), I did not yet have access to this book, which is engagingly described on its back cover as being "for young seekers and for old radicals. Like a farmer's almanac or a good cookbook, it's a guide that doesn't tell you what to do, but rather gives you the resources you need to find your way together with friends in the place where you are."

I began to read my copy because I had promised to write a book review, but soon read it because it was so interesting. While designed for the specific purpose of guiding those who are taking part in what is sometimes called "the new monasticism" (seeking or participating in residential religious communities), it shed light also on "the place where I am": my own experience of parish, neighborhood, and family.

The author begins with identifying the yearning for community as part of the human condition. The three chapters that comprise Part I remind us that we are creatures who by nature want to be together.

We are given first-person examples of people who give life to that theory: it is obvious that this book is grounded in many conversations all over the United States, for Janzen travels from community to community to do his research.

People also seek community because of disaffection with the culture they live in and the desire to live according to other values. This can be true not only of religious communities but those based on environmental sustainability, justice, or serving the poor. In the case of Christian communities, the impetus is often following what the earliest followers of Jesus called "the Way," and Jesus called "spreading the kingdom of God": the way of service to the outcast of society, of forgiveness, respect for all human beings, healing, and peace.

The Iona community, for example, began life in the slums of Glasgow, although people most often associate it with its beautiful setting on the island of that name in the Inner Hebrides. The Taizé community, near the border between Germany and France, began as a witness to peace, after a war that devastated Europe. L'Arche communities were formed to serve the mentally and physically challenged among us. Koinonia in

Georgia was a witness against racism before the civil rights movement, and created Habitat for Humanity, which is now a worldwide initiative.

Part Two helps those who feel a "call" (as Ted did) discern whether it is bona fide, and, if so, to what incarnation of community one is best suited.

The next four sections might be labeled "pregnancy," "birth," "youth," and "maturity." Communities, like the human beings within them, go through stages of life, each with its gifts and challenges, and understanding that fact helps communards avoid undue expectations and fears. It is not easy, even in a Christian context (or, one might argue, sometimes *especially* in a Christian context!), to move from an individualistic worldview toward one that includes others. Janzen comments that so-called "contemporary" Christian music reveals the extent to which the "Good News" of Jesus can be "straitjacketed" by the culture: "so many songs are about 'me' rather than about 'us' as the objects of God's love. 'Mine, mine, mine; Jesus is mine.'" A wise warning to the institutional church and its liturgists and musicians!

Janzen sees this journey of growing from an "I" framework to a "we" framework to be the prime work of a lifetime—not a grim duty but a joyful task. Dorothy Day sums it up in the final paragraph of this excellent book by quoting Catherine of Siena: "All the way to heaven is heaven." ❧

The Rev. Nancy Roth, an Episcopal priest and writer, worked for several years as program coordinator at Holy Cross Monastery in New York's Hudson Valley, and is an Associate of the Order of St. Helena, an Episcopal women's community based in Georgia. She has visited members of the Taizé Community in Manhattan and the Iona Community in Scotland. As a communitarian's parent and avid reader of COMMUNITIES, she also has become familiar with several other intentional communities in the United States.

REVIEW BY CHRIS ROTH

Encyclopedic

The Encyclopedic Guide to American Intentional Communities
By *Timothy Miller*
Richard W. Couper Press, Hamilton College Library, Clinton, NY, 2013, 608 pages

This massive volume collects in one place information about as many American intentional communities as the author's research could identify, from early European colonization of what are now the United States down to the present. To keep the subject matter manageable, certain categories (such as Christian canonical communities) are not included that otherwise fit the definition of an intentional community—and nevertheless the book documents approximately 3000 communities, giving brief descriptions of each along with up to three references to sources for further research.

A longtime Professor of Religious Studies at the University of Kansas and author of several previous volumes about communal living, Tim Miller includes groups here that have, or had, "a sense of purpose and distinctiveness, with deliberate intent to be a community; some kind of shared living space; some shared resources; and critical mass [defined as a membership of at least five, not-all-related adults]." A few active groups I am familiar with are missing from the descriptive section (the Possibility Alliance, featured several times in COMMUNITIES, was too small in population at the time of Tim's research; another group I know never bothered to list themselves online until recently). However, most qualifying communities that are or were ever open to being known publicly (like those listed in the FIC's *Communities Directory*) are included in this book. What makes this book's coverage broader than the *Directory* (which lists about 1000 American groups) is its inclusion of historical communities—very useful if one is attempting to get an overview of the communities movement throughout American history, or find information about a specific group that once existed but no longer does.

The downside of attempting to be so comprehensive is the brevity of each description: one paragraph for each group, anywhere from two to 10 sentences (with about 4 or 5 being most common). Moreover, the number of groups listed precluded getting up-to-date information on all the current ones (as evidence, the population data on my own home community is 8 years old). Creating a truly comprehensive, up-to-date resource of this type would require more than one person's efforts, even if that person is as meticulous a communities scholar as Tim Miller. Including current, accurate information in any communities reference resource depends on active participation of the many communities listed—which is why the FIC's *Communities Directory* has always needed to be a broadly collaborative effort. Today, the online Directory at directory.ic.org is so useful only because the groups included help keep it current.

So don't expect to get a full or entirely updated picture of any group here; Tim's purpose is only to provide a starting point for further exploration or research. And if you've had personal experience with any of these groups, you may even find yourself with suggestions for improvements or changes in emphasis in their listings. In most cases, a book or multiple books could be written about each of these groups and still oversimplify the community's experience; to reduce that richness to a paragraph is necessarily to sacrifice depth for the breadth of a one-volume reference.

On the other hand (and it'd better be a strong one—the *Guide* can double as a door-stop), this resource will be extremely helpful to anyone who's longed for that kind of one-volume reference—including both formal and informal students of intentional community and its history in the US and colonies. Communal Studies professors and departments, members of the Communal Studies Association, and other intentional community buffs will surely welcome this tome into their libraries.

At $70 per copy, it is unlikely to find itself onto the bookshelves of most current communitarians or communities. And by itself, it says very little about what life in community is actually like; Tim himself warns that it cannot capture the "spirit" or "vibrancy" of any of these groups. It's more an enhanced "index" than anything else, but for those whose interest extends beyond present-day communities (covered more thoroughly in the FIC's own *Communities Directory*), it fills an important gap. From its thoughtful introduction through its painstakingly-assembled (if necessarily incomplete) listings, it's a major contribution to the field of communal studies. 🐦

Chris Roth edits COMMUNITIES.

REVIEW BY CHRIS ROTH

Community Rhythms

The Rhythm of Rutledge
By the Last Volunteer
DVD, 28 minutes, 2012
postcarbonfuture.org;
therhythmofrutledge.com

The Rhythm of Rutledge is a beautiful, radically original film. Depicting life at northeast Missouri's tri-communities—Sandhill Farm, Dancing Rabbit Ecovillage, and Red Earth Farms—it contains almost none of the standard information community documentaries usually attempt to convey. Instead, it immerses the viewer in essential experiences to be had in this rural hub of cooperative living, along with a few simple conversations about what life is like there for a few of the residents.

The majority of the footage comes from Sandhill Farm, where long shots of beekeeping activities, grain processing, meal preparation/sharing, and natural scenes are interspersed with personal conversations with Micah, Stan, and Laird, each sharing their experience in community and on the land. At Red Earth Farms, Alyson hangs

---

The simple rural and cooperative skills shown here have been passed down through generations.

---

laundry and pushes her daughter on a swing while reflecting on the reasons she has chosen this lifestyle and way of parenting. Dancing Rabbit has the shortest segment, with Tony describing why the founding group chose to start their ecovillage on "average" rundown farmland. The movie both opens and closes with train scenes, in which first cows and then communitarians find ways to relax and/or entertain themselves in a land where almost everything happens much more slowly and deliberately than it does among the hustle, bustle, and overstimulation of typical modern life.

The cinematography is striking. We often get an unexpected view—whether perched on a tractor next to a spinning duct-taped steering wheel, watching from behind a beehive smoker, sitting at butcher-block level in the Sandhill kitchen, or being eye-level with Micah's feet in the solar shower. Though expressing lots of appreciation for their lives in community, the interviewees don't sugar-coat them—Stan mentions the many weeds that slow down harvesting, Micah mourns the lack of wilderness in northeast Missouri as she recalls the pure fun she used to have outdoors before she took up farming, and Laird talks about the trickiness of navigating a marriage while living in a separate community from his wife. For each person, though, the benefits far outweigh the drawbacks, and this film helps us feel why.

I found a particular resonance with this film because I have lived in the tri-communities—for a total of about two years at Sandhill Farm (in 1989-90 and in

2010), for several months at Dancing Rabbit in 2010-11, and as a friendly neighbor with Red Earth throughout my 2010-11 stint. The "rhythm" that this film portrays is very much the rhythm that attracted me there and that drew me back when I was seeking again to live "at nature's pace." Even the soundtrack (in which I noticed, among others, the distinctive songs of the wood thrush and Carolina wren, not present where I live now) evoked memories of being there. It's a magical place on the planet, and the simple rural and cooperative skills shown here have been passed down through generations. I believe the film captures the rhythm of Sandhill and Red Earth much more accurately than it does the rhythm of Dancing Rabbit, which is more densely-settled and therefore typically busier on the human level—but because it spends almost no time there anyway, this is a minor complaint.

I've shown this film to a few dozen people now, none of whom have lived in these places, and the universal reaction is the same as mine: this is beautiful, extremely well made, a pleasure to watch, a work of art, inspiring. Unlike many documentaries, this is one I could watch with pleasure many times. As already mentioned, this movie is not information-rich; it's not a way to find out about governance and ownership structures, budgeting, community documents, how to set up visitor programs, etc. Instead, it shows what it could be like to live in one of these places—which very few other community documentaries more than hint at. I hope it inspires more such efforts. ❧

For the filmmakers' perspectives, see the article, "Finding Community, Producing Durability," p. 80.

Chris Roth edits COMMUNITIES.

Finding Community, Producing Durability
Learning from the rhythms of Rutledge

We don't know what we'll find when going out to film. This has come to define our approach to filmmaking: going out to explore and learn instead of searching for something specific already in mind. When first starting work on *Finding Community* we were searching—searching for a counterculture fighting in the United States. When we got to Rutledge, Missouri, however, we didn't find any fights. Instead we found something more creative than antagonistic. We learned about a different movement—something more like a music, resonating underground.

In fall 2011 at Dancing Rabbit we screened a rough cut of *The Rhythm of Rutledge*, the second film of the *Finding Community* collection, which focuses on the tri-communities of northeast Missouri: Sandhill Farm, Dancing Rabbit Ecovillage, and Red Earth Farms. Two of us braved a brutal Q&A session afterwards. "I don't mean to be rude, but what's the point?" was one question that particularly stuck out. "I found it agonizingly slow," was another concerned comment. Despite the challenges it posed, this was the most important part of the process for us. Without the collaboration of the community, there is no *Finding Community* project.

As a rule, we didn't film during our first 10 days at Sandhill. Part of our approach to documentary is being aware of our status as outsiders when entering a new community. Knowing that this status is exaggerated by the presence of a camera, we kept the equipment in bags and out of sight. We hoped to connect with

community members first as friends, not as cinematographers. During the first community meeting we attended at Sandhill, there was a great appreciation for this process. Not only does it foster a trust, but it also allows us to construct a deeper and more honest representation through our film. If we were to start filming on arrival, we would look at stereotypes and latch on to anything that resembled our presumptions about life in the Rutledge community. Instead, we got to know folks more intimately and began to participate in their culture.

A few voices from Dancing Rabbit's crowded common house felt the pace of the film did not accurately represent the pace of the community. Although the final version of the film is perhaps more "pointed" than the first rough cut we screened (and a subsequent screening at Dancing Rabbit suggested that the community agreed), the critique of having made a "slow" film is a fair one. A community aspiring towards a village of 500 to 1000 residents does indeed keep a busy schedule. But to communicate what we found most inspiring about these three com-

(continued on p. 79)

FINDING COMMUNITY, PRODUCING DURABILITY
LEARNING FROM THE RHYTHMS OF RUTLEDGE

(continued from p. 80)

munities, we sought to represent our perceptions of living within them—not simply their numbers or mission statements. We realized what we wanted to communicate only after immersing ourselves in the rhythms of Rutledge.

Learning a new culture means learning how another experiences their world. It goes to the fundamental level of perception: how their daily existences give shape to their world, how they experience time and space. We could not have learned this by working from stereotypes. Yes, we found windmills and solar panels; but more importantly, we found a new way of perceiving.

Laird Schaub offers some of the relatively few words spoken in the film: "I can tell within 24 hours when the spring peepers will emerge from the mud and start singing because I can feel it, after living here through 37 springs." Reflecting on how he has "stumbled into rootedness," into a sense of place by slowing down enough to learn its rhythms, he suggests that "it's something [that] is a deep human connection most people had, because most people lived in one place...even the nomadic tribes had their circuits. We don't have it—as a contemporary Western civilization—and I think that's why we've lost our way as a culture; we're rootless." A long shot in the film doesn't precisely signify the pace of the community. Rather, it represents the possibility of immersing oneself in a place by slowing down to look. The audience can then begin to feel the rhythms of a place and imagine the possibilities of participating in its vernacular culture.

Amongst thousands of acres of corn and soy, the Rutledge community is part of a great movement, but not because they are growing organic. Sure, they have constructed impressive agricultural and energy systems towards self-sufficiency. But when considering *what is possible*, we've learned that there is much more. When talking to people about intentional communities, we are often confronted with accusations that they are examples of escapism and idleness. We understand how it might be difficult to see from the outside the ways the movement can create social change. After all, it was only by immersing ourselves that we were able to learn about these forms of activism thriving in intentional communities. Their approaches teach us that we don't need a radical overthrow overnight when revolutionary action and thought is embedded in the culture and created through daily existence. This process of producing durability is a slow and deep movement.

Perhaps a great shift will come not through confrontation but through resonance, through learning the unique music of place. And when we learn to resonate with our place, and when these places begin to resonate together, the song will last forever. ❧

The authors write: "the Last Volunteer (tLV) is a self-organized community of producers. Our work is a life project and a project of life. As a group we seek to collaborate with the people we encounter through our work and share the ideas we come to embody. We are baking, crafting, farming, loving, learning, sharing, dreaming, walking while questioning: what is possible? We are currently working on a third film, Saving the Past, *about Southern Exposure Seed Exchange, a cooperatively owned seed business based at Acorn Community, and writing a book titled* Producing Durability."

For upcoming screenings, see postcarbonfuture.org/events.html. See also therhythmofrutledge.com; the review on page 78; and Community Bookshelf at store.ic.org for possible future availability of this DVD..

Wilderness Journeys Meet Cooperative Culture:
Teens in Community on the Trail

By Mary Murphy

"I think we should decide this by consensus," Albert declares, running a hand through his wild uncombed curls. Eight teens and two adult guides are circled up on a flat spot on this steep mountain trail in New Hampshire. Our bulky backpacks are lined up on the side of the trail, and everyone is sipping water from their colorful Nalgene bottles.

"Okay, who's going to facilitate?" Eric asks.

"I will! Let me get out some paper to keep stack," Rita volunteers. "What is the question again?" she asks, swatting at a mosquito that buzzes around her head.

"We need to decide whether we are stopping for the night at the campsite that's closer, or pushing on to the one that's still four miles away," I remind her. "Our decision needs to fit with the Leave No Trace guidelines we have learned, so we have to stay at an established campsite."

The group settles down on the ground and dives into the consensus process.

Albert, ever the organized thinker, points out that the longer we hike today, the less distance we'll have to cover tomorrow when we traverse the Presidential Ridge. Bobby grimaces at his words, rubs his sore calves, and reminds the group how nice it would be to stop early today and make a really nice dinner and play some games. Rita scribbles notes and stack lists on her writing pad, biting her tongue with concentration as she tries to keep up with the lively discussion.

This group knows each other well: we have just finished a nine-day canoe trip in Maine and this is our first day on the backpacking section of this wilderness trip. As in any community, there is a wide diversity of strengths, weaknesses, and personal styles among these teenagers. Some are very fit and eager for a challenge, others are out of shape and want to drag their feet. Some think of the group first, others feel a need to prioritize their own needs. I'm lucky to work as an expedition guide for Farm & Wilderness Summer Camp, a Quaker-based camp that already embraces many of the principles of consensus in its daily routine and culture. On this trip my co-leader (who was trained in Formal Consensus in the student co-ops at Oberlin College) has taught a simple consensus decision-making process to our trip group. She and I have facilitated it for them twice before, but this is the first time the campers have done

A musical canoe journey on the St. Croix River in Maine.

Settling down for Silent Meeting on the trail in New Hampshire.

Working as a team to portage canoes and gear around a dam on the Androscoggin River in Maine.

Shallow waters on the St. Croix River in Maine.

the whole thing on their own.

The discussion grows and weaves in the dappled shade of the mountain birches. Finally Rita announces a series of proposals and the campers all vote. Three pass, and a new discussion blooms about how to best combine them into one decision. The end result is a complex and nuanced negotiated agreement that involves dinner recipes, the time we get up in the morning, who has to retrieve the bear-hang food stash for breakfast the next day, and promises to play a round of the game Mafia on top of Mount Washington when we get there. I never would have guessed all these things were pertinent to a decision about where to camp for the night, but the glow on the teens' faces show me that they were. They are all relieved to have navigated the consensus process successfully, and they shoulder their backpacks with an enthusiasm and determination that never would have surfaced if I'd made the decision for them.

I've been leading wilderness trips professionally for eight years, and following the intentional communities movement for 12 years. While I find that many wilderness guides I've worked with don't know what an intentional community is, the culture of the outdoor education industry embraces many of the same guiding principles as communitarians do. A wilderness trip group is its own community, albeit a temporary one. Each trip has a different synthesis of individual personalities, so wilderness guides have to learn to set up community structures and norms that will accommodate whoever shows up. Unlike most residential communities, we can't screen out members of our trip community based on emotional maturity or willingness to compromise. Whoever pays the trip fee will come on the trip. Therefore, most wilderness guides who last more than a year or two in the profession are those who learn to nurture harmony and cooperation amidst the many kinds of diversity they find on their trips. We use many of the same strategies residential communities do: creating shared agreements, rotation of leadership, fostering trust, sharing emotions honestly, and mediating conflict.

I have found that many kids take to this like a fish to water. After they are taught the skills and see them modeled a few times, they start initiating these techniques themselves. In the opening scene of this article, the teens themselves decided they could use consensus to make the decision. Having seen it work well twice before, they suggested it immediately when the conversation about campsites began to feel tense. Kids instinctively recognize healthy cultural norms when they experience them, and they naturally gravitate toward them. While many adults come to this work with emotional scars and triggers from the past trauma of living in a hierarchical power-over culture, kids have less emotional armor and an incredible willingness to try new things. The level of functional community that a group of teens from diverse backgrounds can create on a 15-day wilderness trip rivals that of any intentional community I've visited. The number of lifetime friendships that are forged on my trips attests to the staying power of positive group culture.

So, let's learn from the youth! Below is a list of some of the group-building activities and conflict management strategies I use on my wilderness trips. All of these are teen-approved and have worked well to foster a community culture among the youth I work with. Most of them are common activities that are used widely across the outdoor education industry.

• **The Group Agreement:** The night before the trip starts, the group gathers together and brainstorms guidelines, behaviors, attitudes, and norms that they would like the group to strive for on the trip (always phrased in the positive). The agreements typically include respectful communication, positive attitude, following safety guidelines, using forest-friendly Leave No Trace practices, etc. We talk about what these statements mean to each person, discuss and clarify any controversial ones, and, once everyone can agree, we all sign the agreement. We carry this agreement with us on the trip and refer to it whenever conflict arises. In essence, this is a simplified version of the agreements and bylaws most intentional communities create for themselves.

• **Fears in a Hat:** On the first night of the trip, we sit in a circle. Each person writes down three fears they have about the trip and we put all the anonymous slips of paper in a hat. We each draw out someone else's fears and read them aloud. Typically many people share common fears, so hearing that others have the same worries eases their minds. This also helps group members take actions to prevent triggering other group members' fears: if three people said they are afraid they won't be able to keep up, the speed demons in the group may be inspired to self-regulate their pace (and the guide can remind them of the fears when addressing impatience).

• **Truth Circle:** In the evening we sit in a circle, speak a self-reflective question or prompt, and then pass a talking stick. Each person may talk for as long as they

Teens celebrating their new confidence on the Presidential Ridge in New Hampshire.

Portaging a canoe in the backwoods of Maine.

like with no interruption. The talking stick goes around the circle again and again until no one has anything else they'd like to say. In this way we learn how others think about themselves and have a space to speak vulnerably in a safe and predictable environment.

• **Evaluation Circles:** Every few days we circle up and each person answers two questions: What do you think the group is doing well? What do you think could be improved? We speak our answers and promptly move on to the next activity. This activity fosters awareness of group dynamics and how behaviors are affecting others, while also asking each person to think about what is working for the group, not just what is working for themselves. The evaluation circle acts as a self-correction mechanism for the group: usually everyone takes action to improve dysfunctional dynamics that have been spoken in the circle, without any discussion or nagging.

• **Leader of the Day:** Every day a different camper leads the group. They carry the map and compass, they decide when we have rest breaks and where we have lunch. This mirrors the systems of non-hierarchical leadership that inspire many intentional communities to rotate their leadership roles.

• **Silent Meeting:** When working for Farm & Wilderness, a Quaker-based camp, we have a daily 20 minute gathering to sit in silence together in a beautiful spot. This shared reflection time allows our spiritual selves to be honored in the same place without any layers of dogma. I find that the shared silence brings the spirits of all the trip participants into a quiet harmony once a day, gives us a break from any conflict that may be present, and fosters an attitude of gratitude. Many spiritual New Age communities open their meetings with a period of shared silence for the same reason.

I hope these activities will inspire readers to try some new strategies for keeping their own communities cooperative and dynamic, and offer kids who don't live in community a way to learn about cooperative culture: go take a hike with a wilderness guide! ◆

Mary Murphy is a community-minded wilderness guide. After eight years of guiding for teens, she has recently started her own wilderness trip company (www.mountainsongexpeditions.com) focusing on spiritually grounded backpacking and canoeing trips for adults and families. She lives in Worcester, Vermont, on a cooperative homestead she shares with four adults, two kids, and various goats, chickens, and llamas.

A hazy mountain view in the White Mountains of New Hampshire.

Canoeing Lake Umbagog in Maine.

REVIEW BY PAM DAWLING

Communes Britannica: A History of Communal Living in Britain 1939-2000
(The Second Volume of Utopia Britannica, 2000)
By Chris Coates
Diggers and Dreamers Publications, 2012, £25
www.utopia-britannica.org.uk,
www.diggersanddreamers.org.uk

This big book, over 500 pages, is fascinating, intriguing, fun, and well-written. Some of the stories I know from my years of communal living and networking in the UK (1972-1991). Others were a complete surprise for me. I am grateful to Chris for preserving so much of the history of our movement.

The last hundred pages comprise a directory of communal groups 1939-2000, including those that have folded, and two pages of fictional ones invented for literary or spoofing purposes. I remember our surprise at Lifespan community when monthly articles about "The Lodge" started to appear in the national *Guardian* newspaper, clearly written by an "insider," later identified as Bob Fromer from Birchwood Hall.

The author, Chris Coates, is a long-time friend of mine and we collaborated (with others) in editing and publishing the first two *Diggers and Dreamers* directories of communal living in the UK. I know he knows his stuff! Chris lived communally for 20 years at People in Common in Burnley, Lancashire. He is now a member of Forgebank Cohousing in Lancaster.

The book is easy-to-read. For instance, the first chapter, about pacifist groups during the Second World War, includes the story of the Bruderhof moving to the UK in 1936 to escape the National Socialist regime in Germany. All went well until 1940, when British forces suffered under the German army in France. Some British people were no longer happy with German nationals owning land in Britain, suspicion grew, and under duress, the community decided to emigrate to the Americas (across the U-boat patrolled Atlantic). The continuing story of the Bruderhof is found in the second chapter, with a note telling readers this, so those wanting to follow the story know where to find it.

I was unaware of the rich history of pacifist communities and conscientious objectors banding together to provide agricultural and forestry services during WWII (1939-45). In 1945, Leonard Cheshire set up Cheshire Homes for disabled ex-servicemen, where the "patients" were expected to join in the chores. The shared sense of purpose helped many rebuild their lives. In the '40s and '50s, a new Bruderhof community formed in Shropshire; Braziers Park Community was set up; small communities around London were founded by professionals—some purpose-built cohousing type developments, others rented existing property; others squatted ex-military facilities.

In 1961, a mainstream women's magazine ran an article by Isabel Cole, one of eight adults with one child living communally. I know community members now in their 20s and 30s are often surprised to realize we in our 50s and older experienced much the same challenges, desires, and ideals as they now do. I look at the photo from *Woman's Mirror* in 1961, the men in suits and ties, the women in twin sets and pearls, and realize, yes, they probably too dealt with issues of sexual jealousy, ideals about socialism, gender politics, and alternatives to monogamy and nuclear families.

After the war, residential schools for children with disabilities were set up by the Camphill movement. In 1955 the much-respected Botton Village was established as a permanent home for adults with special needs ("villagers") living in family groups with coworkers to help them.

The concept of community as therapy grew as the Anti-Psychiatry movement and People Not Psychiatry (PNP) expanded in the '70s. They provided sanctuaries for people facing a breakdown who didn't want medications or psychosurgery, and people who wanted to support them. Jenny James founded the Atlantis Commune in 1974, after several years running a PNP house offering free encounter groups and primal scream therapy. Atlantis was a center of dramatic, noisy, frequent emotional release. In 1987 the community moved to Colombia.

Probably the British spiritual community best known in the US is Findhorn, in Scotland. Nowadays, Findhorn combines spiritual and personal growth courses, ecological buildings, retreats, and various other businesses, under the umbrella of The New Findhorn Association, which has over 350 individual members and about 32 organizations as members.

I found it hard to read about many of the spiritual groups. So many "celibate" gurus weren't; so many gullible people lost their savings, their homes, years of their lives, and in some cases, their children. Scientologists, Gurdjieffians, Rajneeshees, Divine Light Missionaries, Children of God, Jesus Freaks—all had some bad surprises.

The Transcendental Meditation Movement of Maharishi Mahesh Yogi attracted celebrities including the Beatles. Later the TM movement shed its hippie image and targeted business people, academics, and government workers. They set up several more centers, and then started a political party (the Natural Law party) and a Golden Dome in Skelmersdale, Lancashire, where Yogic Flying and Transcendental Meditation are taught.

(continued on p. 74)

COMMUNES BRITANNICA

(continued from p. 73)

Moving on from TM, George Harrison bought Bhaktivedanta Manor for the International Society for Krishna Consciousness (ISKCON), aka Hare Krishnas, to be an ashram, in 1973. At that time, I lived in a community in nearby Radlett, and commuted daily into London. I well remember the Hare Krishnas walking the commuter train tinkling bells and chanting, and meeting some women in the laundromat, folding many yards of saffron saris.

For many Buddhist monasteries, communal living was incidental to the spiritual path. An expelled teacher from the Vihara Centre set up a new non-sectarian monastic center. From this grew the Friends of the Western Buddhist Order, who ran summer retreats for up to 80 people at a time, introducing Buddhism to many Brits, who then wanted to practice in their everyday lives. In the early '70s, the FWBO expanded rapidly, set up Right Livelihood businesses, and networked with other Buddhist groups and other communal groups. They were accessible, open, low drama, single gender households. In the late '90s, a crisis hit when the guru was accused of pressuring young men into having sex with him. This was while he was claiming to be celibate. The FWBO did come to terms with what had happened, after soul-searching internal debate. In 2010 the movement changed its name to Triratna Buddhist Community.

In the '70s, the New Creation Christian Community, later known as the Community of Celebration, had a well-known musical outreach group called the Fisherfolk. After amalgamating with another Christian community, Post Green, they developed more communal homes, becoming known as the Jesus Fellowship. The anti-cult movement was very suspicious of them, and the group was expelled from the official Church. In response, they exercised their freedom and formed the Jesus Army, seeking converts among drug addicts and alcoholics.

A Christian Community Congress in 1980 attracted 42 established religious communities and 50 lay residential communities. They established the National Association of Christian Communities and Networks (NACCAN), with a quarterly newsletter. They helped set up new Christian communities. Little Gidding and the Pilsden Community (with residents supporting visitors in need of respite, drug addicts, homeless people, ex-prisoners, runaway teens etc.) were the forerunners of a wave of similar communities such as Kingsway and Bystock Court.

"Big House" communes were the stereotype of a '60s or '70s commune: a faded country house with a bunch of long-haired hippies on the lawn, surrounded by a gang of exuberant kids. Crow Hall in Norfolk, established in 1965, survived until 1997. Eel Pie Island Free Commune started in 1969 in an old hotel on an island in the Thames. The group grew to 100-130 residents, after it became famous as a crash pad. It was a chaotic community with fairly high drug use and very little money. After their utilities were cut off for nonpayment, they started to heat the house by burning the less-necessary woodwork. During a mass arrest of most of the members at a local pub, a perhaps-connected fire occurred at the house. The owner threatened to evict them, and the group disbanded.

During the '60s, about 40 communities formed and joined the 10 or so surviving communes from the post-war period and earlier. In 1963, a vegan group, the Agriculture and Hand Industries Mutual Support Association (AHIMSA), aimed to help other communes start up. Unfortunately, disagreements led to a splitting off of a Vegan Communities Movement (VCM), later the Communes Movement. A magazine called *New Life* (a revival of *The Broadsheet*, which had published info about communities), came out. In 1969, the members of the New Life Movement who were interested in communes merged with the Communes Movement. A period of growth occurred, the magazine came out regularly, and a fund was set up to help finance other communities. The London alternative information service BIT helped connect people. The Communes Movement published their magazine bi-monthly, and drew up a manifesto for *A Federal Society Based on the Free Commune.* Gatherings were an assortment of organizers and partiers. In 1970, Joan Harvey in Cambridge formed the Commune Services Agency to help groups form communes, with weekly Communes Seminars. She started Parsonage Farm community outside Cambridge with others, including Sarah Eno and Patrick Boase, who in 1975 became two of the founders of Crabapple Community. Crabapple, of which I was the fifth founding member, was modeled on Twin Oaks. I lived there for the first six years. We quickly bankrupted our labor credit system because we couldn't bear to set quota higher than 50 hours a week, and yet it was impossible to pioneer a new community on as little as that. We couldn't afford for anyone to "cash in" their labor balance and take the amount of vacation we'd earned. So we scrapped the system and kept on building community.

Other "Big House" communities were established in the '70s. The annual directory for 1972 listed 30 groups. Squatters groups, free schools, alternative technology centers, and books about communities were all thriving. Communes Movement was not—it was dysfunctional, tied up in disputes. Communes Network was formed in 1975 to bypass the problems. In 1976, the book *Communes, Sociology and Society* by Phillip Abrams and Andrew McCulloch surveyed communes in Britain. The authors showed awareness of the gap between the "myth of communes" as described by other authors, and the commune-on-the-ground, and noted that "The special quality of their lives has to be found in their efforts to shift the implicit values of their experiences step by step towards their ideals through such simple, difficult things as forcing themselves to face up to the meaning of quarrels, of demands for privacy or of the failure of some to contribute what others consider their share. What distinguishes them from families is not the absence of such episodes but the effort that is made to treat them as occasions for serious self-questioning and collective change."

In the late '70s a rival organization, the Alternative Communities Movement, was started by a community called the Teachers. They prided themselves on extreme rationality, on following their leader, and a fairly severe set of rules. They ran gatherings and published directories, which received mixed reviews. At the end of the '80s they faded from view amid accusations of right-wing ideologies and child sexual abuse.

Another attention-grabbing effort (more beneficial) was Cartwheel, a group who pushed a giant cartwheel around the country to gather recruits and resources for a large-scale alternative community. They gathered many people, but were divided on how to proceed—whether to start "seed sites" in order to have something on the ground, or to keep working for the big vision. Jan Bang wrote, "This debate was never effectively resolved, and the consensus nature of the decision-making process effectively blocked a great deal of progress. In effect, it was possible for one person, or a small group, to veto any suggestions, and this happened time and time again over the next two years. The question of membership was discussed at great length, but no formal structure was ever set up. This had the effect of giving newcomers as much voice as everyone else immediately, even though they were not familiar with previous discussions and decisions on issues."

Another large, brave effort that came to nothing was Fair Ground, an attempt to help new communities set up by giving them loans raised on the strength of the equity of properties owned by existing communities. Members of 15 communities met quarterly for three years to set up Fair Ground. I often attended. Efficient meetings they were not. We had no fixed starting or ending times for the meetings, weren't good at facilitating, and attempted to reach unanimity of whoever showed up. Some delegates were more focused on the social side of the weekends. It's a testa-

ment to the persistence of a few that Fair Ground did see the light of day, although by the time of registration with the Registrar of Friendly Societies, the original 15 members were reduced to seven. Unfortunately only two were then actually willing to put ownership of their homes into Fair Ground. The magnificent vision had got bogged down under the discussion of legal structures—a male-dominated discussion as I remember it—and the ordinary communards no longer saw the value of giving up autonomy in decisions about their own property.

Rapid Transformations was a cross-community collection of members with building skills who would travel in a green bus once a year to a community to work on some big, skilled project, usually roofing. They included training newbies, and worked just for board and lodging, and a party provided by the host community.

The Communes Network Infopack was another cross-community effort, which was intended to be the precursor to a video, but in fact led to *Diggers and Dreamers*, the biennial directory of UK communities.

As Chris draws towards the end of his book, he points out that doing his research

Anyone who has lived communally will find some episodes here to resonate with. I found many.

into late 20th century communities showed up the influence of the Second World War communal groups. Specifically, he mentions the connections between communal living, peace, and non-violence; the development of therapeutic communities; the vein of apocalyptic thinking after the war leading to back-to-the-land communes and environmentalism. Perhaps the counterculture has led us to the green movement, sustainability, organic farming, appropriate technology, the many kinds of equal rights, the Transition Network, the Occupy Movement. At the same time communities persist, providing a viable way for a wide variety of people to organize living arrangements more consistent with their values and preferences.

Chris's "Author's Tale" is a delight to read: honest, sweet, amusing, inspiring. I felt empathic with Chris describing his decision to leave People in Common (PiC): a long time living a simple life led to "a poverty trap of our own making—the longer you stayed, the harder it was to get out, as you had no collateral to feed into the housing market." Secondly, he became frustrated "over the lack of progress on any expansion of the community—or any real opportunity for growth. Despite repeated times when we looked to become a bigger group—it never happened. Why? Perhaps because the people who joined were attracted by what we were, not what we might be... Our visions were just too big for our resources and all the things we had dreamed of were never going to happen if left to such a small bunch of people." This second part precisely mirrors my own reason for leaving Lifespan for Twin Oaks in 1991. Anyone who has lived communally will find some episodes to resonate with. I found many. ❧

Pam Dawling lives at Twin Oaks Community in central Virginia, where her main work is as the manager of the vegetable garden. Her book Sustainable Market Farming: Intensive Vegetable Production on a Few Acres *is available at www.sustainablemarketfarming.com, or by mail order from Twin Oaks. Pam's blog is also on facebook.com/SustainableMarketFarming.*

REVIEW BY NANCY ROTH

Spiritual and Visionary Communities: Out to Save the World
Edited by Timothy Miller
Ashgate Publishing, 2013, 248 pages

I had a fascinating time "armchair traveling" recently while I was reading the collection of essays in *Spiritual and Visionary Communities: Out to Save the World*. Each chapter, written by a member of the community I "visited" in the pages of this book, not only provided information about the community, but gave me a feel of what it was like to live there. Writers were lively, articulate, and honest.

Timothy Miller, the editor of the volume, acts as travel agent, preparing us for the journey with an introduction entitled "Persistence Over Millennia: the Perennial Presence of Intentional Communities." He gives us an overview of the history of the human beings who chose community living through the centuries, beginning with the Buddhist Sangha (still going strong after 2,500 years); Qumran, of Dead Sea Scrolls fame; and the early Christians, reported in the book of Acts to have "all things in common," distributing their possessions and goods "to all, as any had need."

We learn that the movement is flourishing in our own day, as well. In subsequent chapters, our itinerary takes us all over the Western world, with each writer serving as a tour guide, sharing frankly their experiences and those of others in their community and focusing on various themes.

At our first stop, Damanhur, located in the Piedmont region of Italy, we learn about dealing with change, as we watch its members adjust to some of the unsettling shifts that happen in any human institution.

When we head north to France, we visit Mandarom, the "holy city" of Aumism, a blend of *advaita* Hinduism and Western esotericism, and hear about persecution by outsiders. Its leader, Hamsah Manarah, was considered by his followers to be a "cosmoplanetary Messiah" destined to usher in a Golden Age, but the French public and hostile media decided he was *fou*—crazy—and possibly dangerous, and proceeded to generate false rumors about the activities there.

A chapter entitled "Henpecked to Heaven?" tells the story of a man living at a matriarchal retreat center in Oxford, England, where the power struggles involved, in his words, "tough, pint-sized sisters facing down brawny brothers," usually with the tough prevailing over the brawny.

A disturbing chapter follows, about a young woman under the spell of an autocratic Tibetan guru in the British Isles.

It is a relief to encounter a healthier environment at Tamera, a "model for the future" in Portugal, where a Solar Village has created a water landscape in an arid land and developed an international peace education program. The words of the founder, Dieter Duhm, would resonate with all who work for a better world: "The crisis inside of us and the crisis in the environment are two parts of the same whole and can only be solved from that perspective."

Those two crises are addressed in practical ways in the Camphill villages, found all over the world. Inspired by the teachings of Rudolf Steiner, the residents serve children with special needs, tending the spiritual and emotional development of the children along with tending their gardens biodynamically: parallel ways to respect the integrity of life.

I will not give away the further adventures that await the reader, other than to tell you where they will be: The Farm, an eclectic religious community in Tennessee; the Twelve Tribes Community, zealous for the "simple beginnings" of Christianity; The Family International, a fundamentalist Christian, world-rejecting movement, mostly comprised of "converted hippies"; and "Arks" founded to provide refuge from impending doom during the war-torn 20th century.

In the final chapter, for those who would like to embark on more local travel in our own country, Timothy Miller provides an overview of those groups who came from elsewhere and still flourish, most already familiar to the reader: Shakers, Mennonites, Mormons, Theosophists, Krishna devotees, and Harmonists (see my article in COMMUNITIES #149 about Jane Owen, the late matriarch of New Harmony in Indiana.)

The last paragraph helps us understand why this literary journey has had so many destinations: the universal human longing to live with others and work together for something worthwhile. For that reason, I would suggest that almost every intentional community can be described by the title of this book: *Spiritual and Visionary Communities*. I have not heard of one yet, or visited one yet, or read about one in COMMUNITIES yet, that does not fully deserve those adjectives! ❧

Nancy Roth is a writer, an Episcopal priest, and the parent of a communitarian. She has worked at a monastery in the Hudson River valley and visited New Harmony in Indiana, a branch of the Taizé community in New York City, and the Iona community in Scotland. She is ready to travel to more and is happy there is a magazine that enables her to do so through the written word.

VISION, MONEY, AND SUSTAINABILITY
Bringing in Renters while Building the Dream

By Jane Moran

A sunny spring morning means muddy puppies tussling gleefully around the kitchen table—on duty, sort of, keeping the free-range goats and chickens out of the kitchen and off the table and counters. The outdoor kitchen takes some getting used to, especially on cold, rainy, winter nights, but in nice weather it's one of the great joys in our little village. Guests love it. Hardly a positive review goes by that doesn't mention the puppy-dog-goat-and-chicken-show and their mealtime entertainment.

The puppies yap loudly in play and a twinge of frustration arises—nervously I hope they are not waking those sleeping roadtrippers in the A-frame cabin, that nice couple from Virginia who're here renting some of our peace and quiet for a few days. The rising buzz of the generator or power tools feeds, too, a niggling conflict—we're building a greenhouse so we can grow more of our own food, year-round, but what about the quiet retreat our guests are paying for? And what about the real vision: a sustainable village with space for more cabins and families who want to live this idealistic lifestyle, complete with work, noise, and long-term commitment?

Our remote village/intentional community in northern California, nestled on a large private parcel way out in the National Forest, was originally built around the ideas of sustainability and community. We're totally off-grid: composting toilets, gravity-fed spring water, woodstoves fueled from the dense forest around us, and a few acres of land cleared for extensive kitchen gardens and a bit of solar power. The three smaller cabins and the massive-feeling Community Center were—and still are—intended to house those intrepid souls ready to make this land their home and this their life.

Over the nearly six years since the first of the land was cleared, there have been at least several dozen of these intrepid idealists, including several families, who have lived and worked on the land for anywhere from a few days to a few years. Five years' worth of WWOOFers, commune-hoppers, past and future zen monks, and prospective community members of all stripes have helped build this place into what it is now, and for the last year or so, hundreds of short-term renters have flooded in to enjoy the fruits of their labor.

Last April, less than a year ago, a small nomadic family contacted us and let us know they were ready to move in and commit to residency—our village was everything they dreamed of and they couldn't wait to live the sustainable life, they said. Within days, they were happily housed in the Community Center and getting dirty in the gardens, learning what young broccoli plants look like and how to manage a composting toilet system. Since they had no money and no income, we took the two parents, small child, and tiny dog on as WWOOFers. We offered two months of this arrangement, time for them to figure things out and establish their own income stream, whether from work in town, online, or otherwise.

Around the same time, on a lark, we had posted one of our cabins on a popular online vacation-rental sight—never imagining the booming popularity we would find for our remote, off-grid accommodations. The family eventually moved on, and for this April, we've been contacted by an art-rock band from Canada who wants to rent the Community Center for two months to record an album—paying us $7000. With that kind of competition, we no longer feel so free to offer up the Community Center to those idealistic "potential community members" who may or may not end up working out long-term and who, short-term, have "only" their energy and

enthusiasm to contribute. How sad that energy, enthusiasm, and idealism lose out to $7000. And yet—running a community on enthusiasm alone is somewhere between impossible and unsustainable.

Renters have turned out to be great contributors of energy, enthusiasm, and idealism as well. They may stay for only a night or two, but the great majority seem to be nearly awestruck with what they find out here in the forest. Escaping city-dwellers, many express their dreams of living in tiny cabins in the woods surrounded by goats, chickens, and gardens. They are inspired by what we're doing and are expressively appreciative of the chance to experience this lifestyle, even if it's just en route between the city where they live and the city that they're visiting.

With short-term renters taking up most of the available real estate, we are faced with the challenge of growing a more permanent community while so many of our resources are dedicated to the business of rentals. Is this the sell-out end of our idealistic community visions? Or is there a way to balance long-term community with short-term financial enrichment?

In my better moments, I see the current process as an evolution of this community, in step with the larger evolution of our socio-economic environment. Just as we mix and blend species and systems in our permaculture designs, so too would an ideal human community integrate all types of participation and roles. Short-term renters can provide an infusion of energy and cash, which is used to support residents who take care of guests' needs while also caring for the land and the shared village resources. Housing can be delegated appropriately—reserving the high-dollar digs for those who choose to contribute to the community with their high dollars.

Building the roof on a sunny day.

Greenhouse under construction overlooking one of the small cabins.

I spent a blissfully happy season at the Lama Foundation in New Mexico as a "summer steward," paying towards a community food fund, living in my own tent, and working 20-30 hours per week running the retreat center activities, which in turn funded the whole community. I never felt like an employee, though; I chose my hours and my chores and mostly remember taking part in the bountiful offerings of the community in the form of beautiful gardens and hiking trails, classes, meals, events, drum circles, meditations, music, visiting teachers, and a rich network of "Lama Beans" from current residents to visitors to founding members. Lama maintains a vastly complicated "blended ecosystem" of community members—from summer stewards who contribute a modest amount of cash and labor, to residents who work long hours and are paid a tiny annual stipend, to guests and visitors who pay more for fancier digs and less work.

Envisioning that kind of future feels so overwhelmingly *big* as I sit here in the garden watching the sprinkler wave deliberately back and forth over the first spring seeds. It's just little ol' *us*—three of us living here now, including two permanent residents and one woman on a personal healing journey, who's set up camp down by the river and mostly keeps to herself other than the one day per week that she trades for rent. On Monday a new WWOOFer arrives—bursting with enthusiasm and rarin' to spend two weeks experiencing whatever it is he imagines we are doing out here. The weekend is crowded with Spring Break renters; a journalist and a playwright brewed us up a phenomenal ginger-turmeric-vanilla-hemp-milk-latte this morning and are now out exploring with their dog on the forestry roads. Two couples from San Francisco will spend the weekend in the Community Center; their visit pays for the polycarbonate roofing we just installed on the new greenhouse.

Last spring was my first experience with growing food. Sure, I had helped weed or harvest a couple gardens in my life, but I honestly could not really

In-demand rustic cabin in the woods.

One of seven puppies vying for guests' attention.

Photos courtesy of Jane Moran

believe that planting seeds would actually lead to food coming out of the ground. I tried to plan and record everything I did in the garden, but the organic chaos of life soon took over and, by summer, only God knew what seeds were planted where. We watered and weeded faithfully, and eventually, to my astonishment, food appeared. Some seeds seemed to have disappeared, while others magically transformed into enormous plants full of delicious food.

Part of the project here—"living in tune with nature"—means allowing space in our lives for the active, unpredictable participation of sun, rain, ice, animals, birth, death, and unplanned growth and change. As a still-beginner gardener, I don't *really* know which seeds will come up, or when, or what they'll look like. Every intentional community I've ever witnessed has been in some state of flux, with active questions about the future: how to support growth, which seedlings to thin, which limbs to prune, how to integrate all the beings that arrive on the proverbial doorstep with their gifts and needs in tow.

Especially given the remote location of our village, building financial self-sufficiency through cottage industry and renting would be the best possible situation for current and prospective residents. Our community may not *need* this business to survive, but it sure fertilizes our soil—sometimes literally. So, today I will plant seeds in the garden and change the sheets in the cabins, not *really* knowing what plants will come or how our business and community will grow together. But apparently, our merely-human efforts will combine with the somewhat unpredictable forces of sun, rain, fate, chance, etc. to produce some bountiful yield of unnameable challenge and delight. ❧

Jane Moran grows potatoes, herds goats, and hosts visitors on an experimental mountaintop commune-of-sorts in northern California, and co-runs a holistic health center "in town" in her spare time. She can be reached at jane.v.moran@gmail.com.

The Dirty Business of Growing a Cohousing Community Farm

By Sandy Thomson

The idea of creating Heartwood Farms came about during a visioning retreat in 2007. You know the type, an all-day, community-wide retreat hosted in the common house with lots of positive energy, good food, and everyone in a good mood? Picture five or six smaller groups gathered around, on the floor, sitting on couches, hanging out around the kitchen island, all trying to come up with the perfect vision of what our community would look and feel like in 10 years!

We live on roughly 250 acres in rural southwestern Colorado. Seventy of those acres are irrigated and we as a community have agreed to steward them in the best way possible. Now we are basically a bunch of city kids wanting to experience the rural lifestyle...environmentally friendly with strawbale houses, kids collecting eggs as one of their chores, that sort of thing. So when the idea of growing our own food came up in numerous subgroups within the retreat, a group of us decided that of course we need to grow our own food. Let's do it! We produced collages, word boards, and pictures in our heads of beautiful vegetables and fruits grown organically on our land by people we love. We pictured days sitting in the grass while the children played with the baby goats and chased good-natured chickens around the pasture.

Simple, right? We had land and we had water, now all we needed were some seeds. We even had a whole community that eats organic and supports local food sources AND an experienced grower to grow that food living right here in the community. We have a word for this kind of idea at Heartwood; it is called a "no brainer." Only a "no brainer" at Heartwood is not what you think. A "no brainer" here means an idea that you think could not possibly have any opposition, that everyone will agree with, as in "duh, that's a no brainer," but in reality there are a thousand questions and almost as many concerns. This is a difficult dynamic ever-present in community; there is always a group raring to go and another group wanting to consider every possible thing that can go wrong. But what it ultimately comes down to is power and trust.

Our core identity statement *(see sidebar)* reads: "We cultivate a fertile ground in which members bring forth their gifts, talents, and passions to manifest a marvelous diversity of creations. We embrace, celebrate, and support those diverse manifestations that are consistent with our stated values."

Sounds wonderful, doesn't it? But many questions can come up when a business venture is proposed that operates within a community setting, especially if the members are creating the business primarily to meet the needs or desires of the community. Be forewarned it is not an easy process no matter how well your community functions. There are so many things to consider when resources are shared and

293

relationships are complicated and interdependent.

Community members might want to know:
• Who owns the business?
• What are the liability ramifications for the community?
• Should the community be compensated for the use of community resources? If so, how much? (This is a big one.)
• What kind of oversight is needed for the business entity? (We're all members here after all.)

Not to mention the complexities associated with hiring interns *(see sidebar)* to work on the business. Interns were an essential part of the farming operation and our goal of making the world a better place.
• Do they pay HOA dues?
• Where do they live?
• Who is responsible for their behavior or their use of community resources?

Well, we have a pretty amazing community. They were willing to jump right in and say go for it even though there were still so many unknowns.

The first few years were exciting and fun. We built thousands of dollars worth of infrastructure with seed money from individual community members, fund raisers, and veggie sales—not to mentions thousands of volunteer hours from interns and community members. As the farm grew and prospered, changing, growing organi-

First harvest out of the high tunnel. This is in April in southwest Colorado at 7000 feet.

Heartwood interns Claire, Rachel, Miguel, Sammy, Gina, Steve, Tony, Cameron, and Heartwood kids Gabe and Zander.

Kids, interns, and farm manager plant squash on a beautiful spring day.

Photos courtesy of Sandy Thomson

Interns: The Spice of Life

Interns are the spice of life in a cohousing community. You take the soup of families with kids of all ages, older single people, retired couples, dogs, cats, and you add the secret ingredient: that 18-25 age group that is notoriously missing from cohousing. They are upbeat, idealistic, friendly, hard working, and fun. They aren't afraid to get dirty and they dive right in. The kids and dogs love them because they are willing to look silly and come down to their level. The older set love them because they can hire them to do some of the backbreaking labor around their homes. The 40-50-year-olds love them because they wake up that often dormant feeling of hope and idealism that is so important at that time of life when we are questioning if it can be done and is it worth fighting for or not?

Our interns have added so much to the experience of living in cohousing that when members are asked, "What is the best part about the farm?," it is not the food, or the land stewardship, but the presence of interns that is often the answer. They answer it with a slight smile on their face as if they are remembering that time in their own lives—the time in their lives when anything was possible.

Intern energy! I wish I could bottle that and sell it. I bet I could get a lot more for it than the dollar a pound we get for potatoes.

Intern energy is like a litter of golden retrievers with powerful brains that are working all the time.

Some things that can be heard when eavesdropping on the interns at common meals:

"Hey let's try to do without money the rest of the season."

"I finally got the recipe for shampoo right—look, my hair actually looks clean. Now I don't have to buy into all those chemical corporations."

"Maybe we can just all live in trees and live off the land, wouldn't that be great?"

"Yeah and we can play music and make art and be happy."

"I want to learn how to be totally self-sufficient. I want to learn how to grow my own food, build my own house, and make anything that I might need."

You just don't get that kind of energy from the meat and potatoes of cohousing!

—S.T.

cally, some members of the community were getting uncomfortable with the still unanswered questions. But a business like a farm is hard to pin down. A farm is not a clod of dirt; it is more like mud that slips through your hands, gets on your boots, and is tracked all through the community. We wanted this to be an integrated farm and it was—deeply integrated with the community. Now a few members were asking for it to be separated out, put in a box, and defined. Some members didn't trust the farm because the members on the farm board couldn't answer all these complex questions.

Bad feelings developed on both sides. Some of the energy on the farm turned sour. The member who was the primary grower left for greener pastures or ones less bogged down in the manure of community process. This trying to define and pin down the farm has gone on now for the last two years. We have had meetings and more meetings. We formed a task force that did great work on trust, hurt feelings, and misunderstandings. We recently consensed on a new structure for the governance of the farm, but questions still persist. Our next retreat will be with a skilled outside facilitator who will help us see where the process went wrong. He will help us further untangle issues of power and trust that have been brought to light by this experience.

For those of us who have been part of the farm since the beginning it has been an exhausting two years—much more exhausting than all the physical labor that we put in during the first two years making the farm great. I am not sure where the farm will

Sweet Ally Baba loving fresh-picked Heartwood Beets.

Summer bounty from Heartwood Farms sold on the terrace of the common house.

Jessica, one of our interns last year, was passionate about bees. She helped us get our honey production up.

Community Vision and Values

These are Heartwood Cohousing's community vision and values:

Vision

To create and live in a community which fosters harmony with each other, the larger community, and Nature.

Values

Honesty and Trust: We act with openness and honesty because of the trust we have in each other. We have the courage and trust to speak up when we see contradictions or inconsistencies between our behavior and our stated values and goals.

Cooperation: Through tolerance, generosity, sharing, and compassion, we live cooperatively with one another. When appropriate, we place the interests of the community ahead of our own self-interests.

Interconnectedness: We recognize our interdependence with all life. To all that came before us, we offer our respect and remembrance. To all with whom we share this world, we seek mutual understanding and respect. And to all who will come after us, we strive to leave for you a better world.

Commitment: Though we know that the path may be rough at times, we are committed to our Vision for the long haul.

Participation: Knowing that our community is fueled by the energy we give it, we all actively participate in community life and work at Heartwood. Each of us chooses how to give his or her energy.

Support: Our community supports friendship and an extended family environment, thereby creating a sense of belonging. We support the growth of each other individually and the relationships amongst us. Each of us is willing to work on our own personal growth so that we can improve those relationships.

Respect: We respect the freedom of each person to live as he/she chooses, so long as that doesn't interfere with the freedom of others in the community to do the same. We respect personal privacy. We respect diversity in ideology, spirituality, interests, talents, beliefs, opinions, race, age, income, and so on. And we welcome expressions of that diversity.

Equality and Fairness: We value every member, including children, equally and treat them with fairness.

Stewardship: We live gently on the Earth. We are thankful for Nature's resources, being conscious to take good care of them and use them efficiently.

Safety: Our community is a safe place—emotionally, physically, and spiritually.

Balance: We maintain balance in our community life: between group and individual; between building for tomorrow and enjoyment of today; between heart, mind, and soul; etc.

Responsibility: Each of us, as well as all of us as a community, takes responsibility for our actions.

Education: We seek the exchange of knowledge, skills, and resources with each other and the larger community.

Flexibility: Creating community is an ongoing process. We remain flexible to change.

—S.T.

go from here. The constraints from the community and from the county have us bogged down. It feels heavy, like walking through the heavy clay soil we have to work with. Some see it as a new beginning, a chance to create something new with full community buy-in. I am worried that trying to do something like this in the confines of community is too exhausting and time-consuming to deal with. But I have hope. I have to.

What have I learned from this process?

• It is very difficult to run a business within a community setting.

• It is important for people to know how to follow as well as lead.

• Nothing polarizes a community faster than talking behind each other's backs.

• There is nothing cut and dried about farming.

• Sometimes a squeaky wheel is just a squeaky wheel.

• Being in community is about letting go but not giving up.

Really when it comes down to it, it has to do with trust. Trust in each other. Trust in the process. Trust that everything will turn out all right.

If I had it all to do over again, would I do it?

Yes. It is in alignment with my values and those of the community. *(See sidebar.)*

What would I do different?

I would follow our interpersonal agreements and insist that others do the same. *(See sidebar.)*

It seems easy when you look at it this way. Just follow your vision and values and every one of your interpersonal agreements. Anyone who lives in community knows these are ideals and hard to live up to all the time. It is the 20-somethings, those goofy interns, who continually remind us to keep striving for those ideals. It takes work and sometimes it's messy but in the end it is worth it.

If you want to start a business inside a community structure put your hat on, pull up your boot straps, and hang on. You are in for a wild ride. ✒

Sandy Thomson is one of the founding members of Heartwood Cohousing in Bayfield, Colorado: www.heartwoodcohousing.com. She and her husband Mac have raised three children in their community. Sandy created and ran a homeschool co-op when her kids were little; now that they are in high school she has turned her attention to creating Heartwood Farms, a nonprofit foundation to support local agriculture and the education of our future farmers (www.heartwoodfarms.org).

Sandy Thomson helping out on the farm...such a peaceful place in the morning.

Interpersonal Agreements

These are Heartwood's interpersonal agreements:

To Communicate with Integrity: I agree to tell my truth, with compassion for myself and others, and to trust that others are doing the same.

To Listen with My Heart: I agree to listen respectfully to the communications of others and attune to their deepest meaning.

To Own My Feelings: I agree to take responsibility for my feelings and how I react to the words and actions of others. And I agree to express those feelings in a spirit of openness and compassion.

To Honor Each Person's Process: I agree to acknowledge that everyone, including myself, is making the best possible choice or decision we are capable of at that moment.

To Express Appreciation: I agree to appreciate others and myself.

To Cooperate with Others: I agree to maintain a sense of cooperation and caring in my interactions with others.

To Honor Our Differences: I understand that goals are often the same even though methods for achieving them may differ.

To Be Aware of Conflict: I agree to look for the unresolved issues within me that create a disproportionate adverse reaction to another's behavior.

To Resolve Conflicts Constructively: I agree to take problems and complaints to the person(s) with whom I can resolve them, at the earliest opportunity. I agree not to criticize or complain to someone who cannot do something about my complaint, and I will redirect others to do the same. I will not say behind someone's back what I am not willing to say to their face.

To Maintain Harmony: I agree to take the time to establish rapport with others and then to reconnect with anyone with whom I feel out of harmony as soon as it is appropriate.

To Freely Participate: I agree to freely choose and re-choose to participate in the Heartwood Cohousing Community. It is my choice.

To Lighten Up!: I agree to allow fun and joy in my relationships, my work, and my life.

(Note: These Interpersonal Agreements are based in large part on those of Geneva Community.)

—S.T.

Core Identity

What makes the Heartwood community distinctive?

• We are a close-knit, multigenerational, rural cohousing neighborhood.

• We are committed to deeply knowing, supporting, respecting, and caring for each other and ourselves as distinctive individuals; as a result, deep interpersonal relationships are possible here.

• We share with each other the value of sustainable interactions with the planet, though our individual efforts and choices may vary. We steward our land to maintain or improve its viability and vitality over the long haul.

• We are interconnected with all of humanity. We welcome new ideas and interactions with the larger community and are open to associations and the sharing of resources with those who share our values.

• We cultivate a fertile ground in which members bring forth their gifts, talents, and passions to manifest a marvelous diversity of creations. We embrace, celebrate, and support those diverse manifestations that are consistent with our stated values.

All of these distinctive qualities are part of our enduring core identity, which does not change. What does change are the various manifestations themselves. These dynamic expressions that come and go over time add a rich flavor to our community culture.

—S.T.

The Community We Built

By Carly Fraser

W*e are on our way home from an impromptu day at the farm. The back of the van is filled with sleepy children, half of them wearing their dress-up princess dresses. As we turn the corner onto the street, a small group of people waits on the road between the apartment complex and the big stone house. There are parents waiting for their children, other children ready to play, and new tenants with familiar faces. All of them are friends and community members. As soon as the van door opens, the children scatter, pulling adults into their world of play and storytelling. Later, around a crowded dinner table, this simple story is retold and described as being a magical moment.*

This story captures the beauty and spirit of the community that is continuously forming, growing, and evolving in our neighbourhood in Guelph, Ontario. We are a group of engaged people going about the building of an intentional and environmentally conscious community.

Our community is different from a lot of the communities that are typically written about in COMMUNITIES. We live on suburban streets that are like so many others in urban centres. The physical presence of our unique community might be landmarked by the chickens on the roadside hill, or the stone house with the giant park-like backyard that people tend to congregate around and its network of adjoining backyards, but the community spreads down the streets and through the backyards of so many others. Some of us own houses in the area. Some of us rent houses or rooms within houses. Some of us rent apartments, or rooms of apartments, or even beds of apartments! And some of us are WWOOFing, travelling through and trading our time and work to stay in this community.

There is a place for everyone, no matter the stage of life or financial circumstance they are in. We have found this to be a great strength in the creation of a unique dynamic in the community and for building resiliency. Over time the community expands and contracts as people move in and out, but it does not collapse because it is not dependent on a single space or specific people to keep it going.

A contributing success factor to the community is that it has been built over time in an existing neighbourhood. Slowly the landscape is beginning to change and capture the unique set of characters and personalities that make up the social fabric. Although the physical structure of the neighbourhood existed, the building of community has been sought out intentionally. Community members seek out and find shared experience, connection, and recharge in their neighbourhood.

To do this in a sustainable and successful way, communication is first priority. There are meetings to discuss larger happenings, for voicing concerns and sharing visions. This is the broad-scale communication that occurs. To improve one-on-one communication many members have taken or are currently engaging in a training course that is more personal. Having open lines of communication and a shared language and awareness around the unique needs of others helps this community thrive. Communication ensures clarity and builds trust.

One strength of our community that is continuously brought up is the fact that everyone has some space that they can call their own and define the rules within. Common issues in communal houses include tension over welcoming children or pets into the space, and having to come to consensus over household

Photos courtesy of Derek Alton

298

rules. Since everyone owns or rents their own space, there is enough separation to allow rules to be set to meet personal needs. For example, in certain spaces children are permitted to run freely from home to home. In others it is expected that children would ask permission before entering. The children understand this and the boundaries are respected. It is possible to have community with personal boundaries that meet individual needs; it is important to remember that these boundaries can still allow for connection.

There are spaces and times created specifically to bring the community together. For example last year we started a weekly potluck. Typical attendance ranged between 80 and 100 people! With so many people biking in and children running loose, the street was closed to traffic, essentially making the potlucks a weekly street party. The potlucks also created a pick-up spot for community supported agriculture (CSA) farm boxes and acted as a networking event for all the amazingly skilled people that live in the area. The potlucks will continue this summer.

With so many people to reach, in wintertime it is a challenge to maintain the same level of connection that seems to happen naturally on the streets and in backyards come summertime. But still the intention of maintaining community keeps the spirit alive as people seek opportunities for getting together.

Another thing that unites us is our children. It is very easy to see how it "takes a village to raise a child" living in this community. All of the regular challenges of parenthood still exist—finding childcare for the kids, getting the kids to bed, coordinating the comings and goings of daily activities, balancing work and family time—but working together makes it all doable. Parenting is hard work, no matter what, but parenting together makes it possible to still be energized at the end of the day and to always be present and giving when you are with the kids. The children learn so much from all of the different adult role-models in their lives and it is such a privilege to watch them grow and explore together.

We are creating a functional model for people to live in suburban community wherever we are, in a way that meets and challenges a variety of social, economic, and ecological values. To learn more about

us check out our blog at junctionng.wordpress.com or email us at thejunctionng@ gmail.com. ✑

Carly Fraser was introduced to the benefits of community while living with four wonderful roommates in her undergraduate years at the University of Guelph. She is now giving intentional community a try as a "WWOOFer" at Two Sisters River Urban Farm in Guelph, Ontario (and loving it!). Carly likes to spend her days outdoors learning to garden, playing with children, sorting and thinking about garbage, playing ultimate frisbee, and chasing after escaped chickens. She is very excited to begin studying food waste this fall as a master's student in the Department of Geography at the University of Guelph. You can reach Carly at carlyelizabethfraser@gmail.com.

A Baby Boomer Rediscovers Community

By Jeffrey Mabee

Community was important to me as a child. My mother's parents came to the United States from Austria-Hungary. They were devout Russian Orthodox and founded and built a church around which a sizable community grew up. I spent many happy hours in that community, running free and yet knowing there were watchful eyes in most windows. All of my grandparents' peers had suffered persecution and they knew hunger and poverty. The US was their hope and their freedom to worship was their salvation. They were very grateful for the place they had found for themselves. They tithed. Their legacy is one of great generosity and gratitude.

Generations of families lived, worked, and played in this community. I was the second generation and enjoyed all the fruits of my family's labors. I had little idea of how hard won all this was, although my parents would remind me, when I did not want to eat something, that there were "starving people in Africa." I sometimes have thought of this as shaming, but it was an important lesson. Waste is an issue for me, and yet my parents made sure we were wanting for nothing. My mother labored her childhood away in her father's various industries. Her mother died when she was 13. She did not want me to suffer and she tried to protect me from her own suffering. She gave generously of herself and to her church also. She was both frugal and generous.

My father's legacy to me was more complicated. He protected me from the horrors of war that he experienced. He wanted to make sure that I would never have to experience the heartbreak that he, as a combat physician, had endured. He talked about it not at all except for two funny stories. I never saw my father get very upset about anything. It was as if there was nothing that important to fight for in the day-to-day living of 1950s small town life.

I do not know if my father had learned to create peace in his heart or if he just wanted to avoid conflict. But I do know that he never would have allowed me to go to Vietnam. He did not have to show his cards on that one because I pulled a high number in the first draft lottery. I believe my father was a peacemaker and felt heartbroken that we were at it again.

I decided at a very young age that I wanted to create a community to live in. I believe that this idea must have been born during my time spent in my mother's family's community. I saw a place where everyone lived in peace, where there were no arguments and everyone loved one another. Steve, the man who came once a week to do our landscaping, was a member of the Russian Orthodox community and I used to talk to him about my vision. He would often greet me with "How is your utopia going?"

I left home for college and moved into a dorm with 550 other freshman boys (and I do mean boys). I loved it and thrived in this thrown-together community of burgeoning testosterone and newfound freedom. It is a miracle I survived it. My thirst for creating community increased and then I attended the festival of music at Woodstock and it was here that I came to truly believe that we could live together in peace. I returned to the university and fought against the war, helped shut down the university, and marched on Washington DC. A community came together in unity against the war. I moved into a

> **I took my broken heart home and my vision blurred. I started on the same journey that so many of my peers were on.**

men's coop of 25 men.

And then my world fell apart when my father died. I took my broken heart home and my vision blurred. I started on the same journey that it seemed so many of my peers were on—wanting to continue living in the manner to which we had become accustomed. And so I did: a wonderful wife, two amazing stepchildren, an oceanfront home, good work, and two cars in the garage. My wife and I helped found a church, just like my grandfather.

But I was so disappointed in the first baby boomer president who I had so much hope for. Then came the second one who perpetrated war and told us all to go shopping. It seemed as though we boomers had lost our way. Where was the outcry against war? Why did we have to fight so hard to protect our environment? What was I doing living in an enormous house using 800 gallons of fuel/year for me and my wife? I felt I had lost my way in the pursuit of happiness.

Belfast Cohousing and Ecovillage has given me the opportunity to redeem myself in so many ways. Here I live in an energy efficient home that, last year, was net zero. What a good feeling to conserve in this way. I also love that I no longer need one of everything. One notice on the community website or a few phone calls gets me anything I might need in, literally, minutes. This is frugality of the highest order. I love that my trash men are eight-year-old boys who also will collect my recyclables because we develop only a small plastic grocery bag of trash per week. That they understand the difference is a joy as well.

Living here also gives me the opportunity to correct some of the legacies that were not so useful. Here I am learning to speak my truth out loud, even if it is anger or pain or fear. I am learning how to accept the many different ways people have of encountering their world, which in the case of living in community might also be mine. It is one thing to witness people from a distance and another entirely to have to make decisions with them. There is, I would venture to guess, no more challenging place for me to learn how to create peace in my heart—no more challenging place for me to create deep compassion. It is incumbent upon me here, like no other place I have lived, to take responsibility for how I create my reality.

I think many parents of baby boomers would find this way of life fascinating. I wish my parents and grandparents were around so I could show it to them. And Steve, I've found my utopia, it just isn't quite as utopian as I had fantasized! ✒

Jeffrey Mabee has lived in Belfast, Maine for 33 years and is a founding member of the UU Church of Belfast and Belfast Cohousing and Ecovillage (mainecohousing.org). He is a seaman, plantsman, photographer, horologist, grandfather, kite flyer, and bubble master. He has a psychotherapy practice with his wife of 25 years. Now that he has downsized by 75 percent he spends his time trying to figure out what to do with all his stuff!

Photos courtesy of Jeffrey Mabee

Short-Term Vacation Cohousing: A Great Way to Learn

By Deborah Carey with Ray Shockey

We are two retirees whose horizons have expanded through new opportunities offered in the intentional communities world. We hope other groups and individuals may be inspired to pursue similar options, which can benefit all parties while facilitating the transition to community living. This is our story...

A Turning Point

We are at another turning point in our lives together. After several decades of relative stability in our living situation, it is time once again to make changes. There are many reasons for this.

First, our only child, Carey, is now a grown man, graduated from college, and in the Coast Guard. He is stationed in Gloucester, Massachusetts, due to be discharged in June of 2015 and preparing to enter graduate school when he is no longer on active duty. He has also has passed the Massachusetts Firefighters' tests. With a great boxer mix dog, and a lovely girlfriend, he has made his choices known for the next few years, at least. He will be in Boston.

I grew up in the milder climate of Long Island, New York, and Ray in Seattle, Washington. We met when I went West to graduate school. After I graduated, Ray found employment in California, which took us away from his brothers and best friend in Seattle. Soon we found jobs in Connecticut and ultimately our present location in Massachusetts. While living on the East Coast allowed us to be physically close for a rewarding reconnection with my parents Allene and Dick, and my brothers and their families, the passage of time brought with it my parents' struggles with mortality and finally their deaths. Our "temporary" stint back East has lasted 24 years and counting!

Now we are both "retired." However, because of our 11-year age difference, planning for the future has been more difficult than anticipated. Ray left his career in the public power industry 10 years ago. I left my architecture job to join him at 60, three years ago. The first year of my employment freedom (my Panamanian friend calls it jubilation) was a whirlwind of travel and obvious overcommitment to regional volunteer work. Now I find I need a more focused effort. However, Ray is happy reading, puttering, cooking, and serving on a few city boards.

Although we live in a highly functional town, we find ourselves becoming more isolated from much of it. When we bought our house, we knew it was within walking distance

View FrogSong's common house and children's playground and play structure.

Photos courtesy of Deborah Carey

to a grocery, the library, and town hall, and Carey walked to elementary, middle, and high school. There was also great energy in our neighborhood, with children learning to bike on our dead-end street, potlucks, and so forth. Our village has many social support networks. When a house burns or someone has an illness, there are instant fundraisers and other efforts to help. There are many activities in which we can participate and have done so, from the library book club to serving on a city committee. What isolates us is the harsh winter weather, the need to drive to attend most events, and the fact that because our son is grown, and we have left the work force, we have removed ourselves from the daily social and business life around us. We feel this separation deeply.

We are also living "lighter" on the planet. We have fully insulated our 1920s bungalow, put in energy efficient windows, and built a deck constructed with recycled plastic and certified sustainable lumber. We converted to a highly efficient gas furnace, refrigerator, and even a 2001 Prius. We garden, purchase winter and summer consumer supported agriculture shares, and such. We recycle and share our skills and resources.

The Move toward Cohousing

As a permaculture and Transition Town advocate, I find that shared housing is also a cultural fit for me. However, I wasn't sure that Ray would be interested in this approach.

To downsize and move seemed a good idea, while we both have healthy lives and are young enough to have the energy to make new connections and friends. When we agreed that we wanted to move "back" to the West Coast, the next decision was what did we want to move to? Would it be a yurt on a small farm, or a modest house in a neighborhood, or some other traditional retirement solution? Were these the only options?

I knew about cohousing, having learned about it in architecture school. I mentioned the idea to my husband. His reaction was less than enthusiastic! Ray was worried that living with consensus decision-making would be tedious and intrusive, and that his privacy would be circumscribed. I too worried about endless meetings. We had attended meetings for a start-up cohousing in our area. If cohousers ran their meetings like this group of well-meaning folks, then maybe this option was not for us.

I decided to spend more time learning about cohousing, because I recognized that living in this manner would provide us with functional community from the start. We would also be able to share resources and meals. My 80-year-old parents had missed the opportunity to move to a supportive community, and I saw the result in the way that they became separated and alone.

First I did more online research. Exploring the Cohousing Association's website, I learned that many groups took a long time in forming, and that some never got built. In addition, I learned a bit about active listening, and continued to take the opportunity to visit cohousing communities. In the summer of 2011 I stayed overnight at Loch Lyme Lodge in Lyme, New Hampshire, not far from Hanover and Dartmouth College, where Pinnacle Cohousing is being built. There we had a visit from the Ecovillage at Ithaca designers, and I listened closely. I was energized by the possibility but unsure of how to proceed.

On February 15, 2012, Liz Ryan Cole, my contact at Pinnacle, sent out an email. "Unique opportunity to experience cohousing life in beautiful Sonoma County, California, during one of the best times of the year... AVAILABILITY: March 26-April 28, 2012. $1300 for the nearly five weeks includes wi-fi, water, gas, electricity, garbage, laundry, community facilities, hot tub, etc. Owners pay HOA dues. No smoking...contact Kate."

Fate had dropped in and given us a chance to try out cohousing for a month, in one of the most beautiful parts of the country. How could we lose? I remember yelling upstairs to my husband, here's a great opportunity and his reaction was "Why not? If we don't like it we can always visit the city, and if we do, that's fine too." With no apparent effort while on vacation, we could live in cohousing for a month, sampling community meals, meetings, and events. I immediately contacted Kate, who with Marcin owned the unit. Once assured we would be selected, we worked out the arrangements online. I credit our landlords with being completely open to this approach; their generosity and kindness speaks legions about what cohousing can offer.

Testing the Waters at FrogSong

We arrived at FrogSong sight unseen, and were introduced to the community (www.cotaticohousing.org). First, Kate and Marcin picked us up at the Park and Ride. Once we were checked into the guest room they gave us an orientation. Kate had made a map of all the owners with their names and animals. Marcin took me to his yoga class in Sebastopol. They gave us access to the listserv, so we could sign up for community meals and join committees if we wanted to. They gave us a tour of the facilities (the laundry room was a highlight because of the system for letting others know what to do with clothes in the machines), connected us to community "mentors," and introduced us at the community meal. We signed a contract, gave them a damage deposit, and then off they went on THEIR vacation!

Living in the cohousing was different. Some rules were overt and some were not. Learning how to live there meant taking social relationships baby steps at the beginning. For example, loving gardening, I was happy to see the community garden needed help, and there was an Earth Day plant and mulch. So I joined the landscape committee to assist them, went plant and mulch shopping with members, and Ray and I pitched in to help that day.

But initially we weren't so sure we wanted to participate in every community meal, and we wanted to investigate the town, so we ate out and cooked at home often. The FrogSong community email listserv was very helpful, for arranging rides, finding out about group events like trips to concerts and speakers, and team decision-making. But some of the activities were informal, not listed, like the three-time-a-week walks, some celebrations, once-a-week group yoga instruction, and group meditation. To learn about them, we talked to our "mentors" and met the rest of the group at community meals. We participated as much as we could.

To learn more about consensus decision-making was very important to me, so I attended the monthly business meeting. Here I saw the five-card consensus system in action for the Homeowners Association voting portion, and for the cohousing discussion. I was impressed that this group had asked everyone to take facilitator training and then to use it in meetings. Along with respect for the rewards and difficulty of the process, we saw evidence of deep community in their interaction and mutual support. Apparently cohousing folks had developed a system for consensus decision-making which was both relatively expedient and inclusive. That was very encouraging and inspiring.

A Sea of Opportunities

During the time of our first of four month-long visits to FrogSong, we traveled to cohousing communities in Portland, Oregon and stayed overnight at one in Corvallis. We wanted to see if our California experience was unique to this cohousing, or shared. What we found was that although each cohousing community is made up of different people, with somewhat different visions, most had very similar values, facilities, and activities.

Because of this rental opportunity, we have learned about the value of conscious

(continued on p. 73)

Informal walking group.

SHORT-TERM VACATION COHOUSING: A GREAT WAY TO LEARN

(continued from p. 45)

community for us, as well. In *Creating Community Anywhere: Finding Support and Connection in a Fragmented World,* authors Carolyn R. Shaffer and Kristin Anundsen describe the difference between a functional community and a conscious one. "In a conscious community, members not only help each other take care of business together—the external task—but they also reflect together on their common purpose, internal processes, and group dynamics... (It) honors the individual as well as the group, knowing that the well-being of one cannot be bought at the expense of the other... Such a community renews itself regularly, celebrating individual and group passages and revising and recommitting to its vision and mission. In doing so it challenges its members and itself to move beyond roles to wholeness...like a living body..." (CCC Press, CA, 1993/2005, page 11).

Since our first visit in 2012, we have been back three times. We visited other built cohousing communities and settled on becoming full members at Oakleigh Meadow Cohousing in Eugene, Oregon, with the same architect, and similar shared values (www. oakleighmeadow.org). We have learned how the character of cohousing intersects with our own character, because we have had the rare opportunity to rent for a short term. Indeed, we recommend this approach to others who want to explore what cohousing means to them, both as a way of housing and as a way of living. Short-term vacation cohousing: what a great way to learn! ∿

Deborah Carey discovered cohousing while getting her architecture degree at the University of Washington. She didn't get serious about living there until she retired from the Commonwealth of Massachusetts in 2011. Her husband Ray Shockey didn't consider living in cohousing until they rented a unit for a month. Now she and her husband are involved in Oakleigh Meadow Cohousing in Eugene, and in explaining the value of short-term "vacation" cohousing rentals to others. Email her at boiester@gmail.com if this appeals to you as a way to "try on" cohousing.

Diana Leafe Christian
Consultations & Workshops

"The most rewarding workshop I've ever experienced."
—Mark Lakeman, City Repair, Portland, OR

"Your workshop was fantastic! You are a master at taking complex material and making it simple."
—Gaya Erlandson, Lotus Lodge, Asheville, North Carolina

"You're a sparking trainer and a joy to work with. LA Eco-Village was energized for a year following your workshop."
—Lois Arkin, Los Angeles Eco-Village

"I was riveted! You hit the fundamental, untold truths about cohousing and decision-making."
—Mark Westcombe, Forge Bank Cohousing, Lancaster, UK

"Quite simply the finest workshop I've ever attended. You quickly cut to the chase, providing hours of practical answers."
— Denis Gay, Champlain Valley Cohousing, VT

"I don't think I ever learned so much in such a short time."
—Susanna Michaelis, Pacific Gardens Cohousing, British Colombia

www.DianaLeafeChristian.org

ELDERBERRY

An Adult Cohousing Community and Creative Alternative to Urban Living

Elderberry is situated on lovely rural land in Rougemont, 30 minutes north of Durham, NC. We provide a unique, self-maintained lifestyle for simple living, supporting one another as we age, growing food, and enjoying activities we love with close neighbors and friends.

a creative community for life

www.elderberrycohousing.com
Go to "Elderberry Cohousing" on Facebook.

Building an Affordable URBAN COLLECTIVE
Sustainable Vegetarian **HOME**
Vegan Permaculture Solidarity
Kids **FOR** Community Rights
Radical Art Social Justice
Ecology **ACTIVISTS**
Peace
Consensus Bikes Food not Bombs
2 Houses Gardens **SYRACUSE ⋜**

BreadAndRosesCollective.org

The Communities Directory VII is on sale now!

**Find your community
Build your dream
Explore communities across the globe**

www.ic.org/ New-Directory

Immigrating to a
COHOUSING PROJECT

By Katharina Jones

I come from Berlin, Germany. Berlin is currently a very popular town. Whoever I talk to who has visited it has been impressed by its liveliness and its history and attractions. Berlin, however, is also the town where you can sometimes see stickers in the underground trains: "be friendly," "be considerate." The senate spends a lot of money to introduce some basic rules of decency in a town that all over Germany enjoys a reputation of being pretty gruff and gritty. Being greeted by a Berlin public bus driver or receiving a smile from a stranger: be aware, tourist, that such events are rare enough to be marked in your calendar.

Last year I moved to Oregon with my then partner, now husband. He wanted to go back to his country after five years in Germany, and I was ready for a big change in my life. We were looking for some place where English is spoken that would still remind us of Berlin: a little kinky, more original than beautiful, alive, insubordinate, cheeky, and creative. We ended up in Eugene.

In this place where we knew nobody else, it was a necessity to find ourselves a community. And so we did: it was love at first sight. The lot was a meadow by the river, right next to a bicycle path—15 minutes to downtown. On the meadow a dozen or so people welcomed us with friendly openness.

Many people in Europe know that Americans in general are very nice. They are so nice that Europeans get irritated: this can't be genuine. They are so superficial, those Americans.

Not true. I didn't see any more false friendliness here than I had seen in Europe. And wherever it comes from, in comparison to Europeans Americans are a lot more accessible to the stranger. They smile more, and they approach others and just start talking to them. In a few weeks I had more conversations here with complete strangers than in an average year in Berlin.

Most Americans would meet a stranger with a friendliness and openness that is as big and wide as their country. As a stranger you can arrive here amazingly fast.

Unless you have to deal with the US Customs and Immigration Service.

First, we had to apply for a fiancée visa in Germany. It took seven months, cost about 1000 bucks, and included correspondence with the USCIS and the embassy, visits to doctors, and a trip to Frank-

furt/Main to finalize the visa application. I got the visa. I don't know what would have happened if I had been diagnosed tuberculosis or AIDS—although, wait a minute, HIV was not checked. I think the whole test frame still comes from the days of Ellis Island.

I have worked for many years with immigrants to Germany. Like the rest of Europe, our country has a discriminatory immigration system. If you come from a rich country and have either a lot of money in your pocket or a job offer, you are fine. If you come from Northern Africa with no money, the immigration system will do its best to get you out of the country asap. However, none of the immigrants, no matter where they are from, is ever being asked for a health check in order to get a visa. It's not very flattering when the country of your dreams is sending you to a doctor on first encounter. The results of the blood and X-ray tests are delivered to the applicant in a sealed envelope. If you open it to

find out what it looks like, you can forget the whole visa application.

After all this, and after we had gotten properly married in Eugene, I thought the rest of it—getting the Green card—would be an easy walk. Yes, I had to send in another application with a lot of papers. But after all, what should happen now?

Well, *nothing* happened, basically, for the entire six months ever since I applied. I was invited to leave my fingerprints at USCIS in Portland. And the system has been telling me since late December that my husband and I will be scheduled for an interview. Other than that, nothing. Nada. Nichts.

Consequently, I don't have a Social Security number. I can't get a credit card, and can't build up a credit history in the US. My income would be important for us to get a mortgage for our unit in the cohousing project—luckily I have been able to continue to work remotely for my German employer—but without my credit history my income doesn't count. My driver's license is a temporary one and won't be extended any more this summer—unless I come up with a Green card. It took me about 10 calls to get a health insurance plan without a Social security number. I am not allowed to work for a US employer.

But the worst part for me is: I am not allowed to leave the country as long as I haven't received the Green card. I can apply for permission if I can deliver a good reason why I need to leave. This reminds me of the country I grew up in. I wasn't allowed to leave it either, and there was a wall around it. However, that was a whole other society, and which one, I won't mention, because it would be a godless comparison. But I will stick to the rule. A friend of mine in the very same situation, years ago—before 9/11—had not read the fine print and left the US for a visit in Germany. When re-entering she found herself being arrested and handcuffed, and sent back on the very next plane to Germany.

I learned later that I should have applied for a work permit and permission to leave the country when I applied for the Green card. Somehow I missed that. I thought why apply for this all, when I get it with the Green card anyway? Now I know. The Green card takes so long, that it pays to apply for parts of it before, because these parts take only about three months. I don't know if it still pays for me to do that. For sure it would cost me, and I still wouldn't have a Social security number.

A visit to the future site of Katharina's cohousing community.

Cohousing project cohort.

Author Katharina Jones.

Photos courtesy of Katharina Jones

I know that my experience is nothing in comparison to what people from other countries and those who are not married to a US citizen go through. I think of the immigrants from the South more often since I have applied. How must it be for them, if this is what I have to put up with? I feel uprooted and the long path to becoming a legal alien is uncomfortable, but there are millions who don't even see a chance to ever be legal, or it takes them many years.

I like to be here. I wait, and in many other aspects I am arriving here pretty well. I feel welcome. I love the width of this country. I believe I even smile more often. And when I don't feel like smiling, it's also ok. Because it's just not true, that they are so superficial, these Americans. ◆

Born 1970 in East Berlin, Katharina Jones grew up with four siblings and a constant flow of visitors in her parents' house—her first taste of community. She worked as a nurse, telegram messenger, surveying assistant, waitress, foreign language secretary, trainer, caregiver, social worker, consultant, teacher, translator, and writer while living singly and in flat-sharing communities, mostly in the city, before moving from the Berlin area to the US in 2014 to join a cohousing community. Nearly a month and a half after writing this article, she received her Green card!

FINDING COMMUNITY
Outside of "Community"

By Sam Makita

In intentional community circles we use the phrase "in community." Like, "This is how we handle conflict in community," "Life is so much better in community," and "How long have you been living in community?" It's a matter of convenience, I guess, to leave out the word "intentional" but the truth is, even those of us who don't live in intentional communities live "in community" with other people and organisms. Our non-intentional communities are colorful and complicated and not always unintentional.

I left Dancing Rabbit (near Rutledge, Missouri) about a year ago. Since then, I've slowly been acclimating to life on the outside (I moved to Bakerton, West Virginia). The rules are different out here, and "community" means something different. Out here, a community is a more fluid thing. In some cases the communities I've found in my post-community life have been intentional, even if they're not "intentional communities" in the vernacular of folks in community. In other cases, community pops up quite unintentionally. Here are some examples.

Communities I Took with Me

What's the one community that communitarians and non-communitarians participate in with equal vigor? What community has become vitally important to the "communities" movement over the last couple decades, even though many people in this community have never heard of COMMUNITIES? The internet, of course. There are online communities of embroiderers, gamblers, recovering gamblers, teachers, students, every sexuality you can think of, church goers, scuba divers, science fiction writers, and book makers.

Each interest, or sub-community, has its own forums, blogs, and Facebook pages. People get to know each other, share ideas and information, have relationships, and conduct business. On the internet we can find people with whom we want to share certain aspects of ourselves and share exactly what we want. It's like intentional community with protection. You've heard of the power of two feet; Facebook and other online communities afford us the power of the unsubscribe button.

I make my living from home, and until recently my son was home schooled, too. In the winter we can go a week at a time without stepping foot outside the door. Our primary community is each other.

Photo courtesy of Sam Makita

We have agreements and responsibilities, and we rely on each other in the most basic ways. We're governed by a system of informed and compassionate dictatorship. I can't really say our relationship began intentionally, but we hold the health of our tiny community—one adult, one child, one cat, and five fish—purposefully.

The Bus Stop

Just a few days ago, the child started back in public school, in part to offer him more opportunities for relationships with peers, mentors, and those who might learn from him. I have more quiet time to work uninterrupted and I feel the ease that comes with something very important (my kid's education) being taken up by someone besides myself. Plus he finally learned to tie his own shoes, in order to avoid embarrassment in front of the other kids at school. The unexpected benefit has been getting to know our neighbors better, and getting to be known by them.

Waiting for the bus to arrive the first day I found out that there are a lot more kids within walking distance of us than I ever knew. Kids I'd never met came out of houses I can see from my bedroom window. There's a little girl named Sam (like me!), and a two other boys in my son's grade. Unlike families at Dancing Rabbit, and other intentional communities, we can live out here almost on top of each other and never have a reason to interact.

The really valuable thing for me happens on the other end of the day. Around four o'clock the grown-ups start drifting toward the bus stop and hanging around. There are younger kids to entertain and be entertained by. Cigarettes are smoked. Shit is shot, judgments passed, and vetting accomplished. Now the other parents in the neighborhood know what I do for a living, my marital status, and what I smell like. And I know those things about them. We make eye contact, and share the experience of the bus being late, of missing our kids, and of being glad to see them again. We share a thunderstorm, a newspaper, and space.

Little Things

There are little micro-communities that form among just a few people, or just for a few moments, all over the place, if I'm looking for them. The four people standing at the gas pumps on a cold day, for example. We're all cold. We're all watching the dollars roll away on the pump dial. We have four different lives, we're going four different directions, but for now, we're all here, doing this thing together. There's the funny little dance two people do when they encounter a door that could be held, that one person goes through first and the other second. The laugh, the thanks, and the parting.

These were the encounters that comforted me on the long drive from DR to our new home. They showed me that people are connected, though lightly, even in the briefest encounters.

Taxpayers

When we first arrived in our new area, we didn't have a place to stay. The weather was warm enough, and we were prepared enough, that we could stay in a campground until we found a place to rent. That campground wouldn't have been there if it weren't for the community that is the county deciding that money and land should be used for public parks. The same goes for the Community Center and its gymnastics and dance classes, the public library with its free internet, roads, and all the other things that taxpayers and donors pay for at least in part.

Even without the public funding, those examples of common infrastructure represent the decisions of a community about what's important to make available to everyone, and what ways they want to share and interact with each other. We went to see the fireworks at the Community Center and it felt like the whole county was there. It's not the kind of community that we get "in community" with consensus models and big financial or ideological buy-in, but it is an aspect of community that exists everywhere in the US, and most of the world.

One of the major differences between my life in community and my life finding community in the wider culture is that if I don't want to be involved in decision making, I don't have to. It's still an element of community, but it's not something I feel obliged to participate in directly. From what I read in the local paper, it's just as full of listening and not listening, speaking and not speaking, good and bad choices, and vociferous Monday morning quarterbacking as governance in community, and I think I'll steer clear. That's just me, though, and I count myself fortunate that I live in a community (the United States, my new home state, my new home county and town) where other people are willing to step up and do the governance.

The Co-op

One of the first things I sought out when we landed here was the local UNFI co-op. I found it. I can order UNFI once a month and pick up some "extras" that my regular grocery store doesn't carry. I thought finding and joining the co-op would be a major part of building my new life here, but it hasn't really worked out that way. I see my work shift co-workers once every few months,

and we haven't really clicked. Despite having in common that we are somewhat particular about our food and toothpaste choices, we haven't become best friends in the eight hours we've spent together, bored and resentful of spending our Saturday mornings sorting other people's food orders.

Bulk food purchases in low-overhead business models are an element of community that I appreciate, though. It's not the most efficient food distro I've ever seen, but I feel grateful I found one at all.

The Neighborhood

Besides the library, the co-op, and public school, I also appreciate the run-of-the-mill suburban grocery store and our neighborhood general store. The grocery store is part of a system of sharing labor and resources that means I don't have to grow all the food my family eats. I have to write stuff and do other services for people all over the world, in exchange for funds I can spend on some truly luxurious food stuffs. It's all part of the global economic community.

The general store is even better. It's a lot like a suburban American version of Dancing Rabbit's Milkweed Mercantile and The Grocery Store combined. The entry way even acts kind of like the neighborhood "all" list. There are several bulletin boards and a business card rack where folks can post available goods and services, lost items, and other kinds of requests. I successfully scored bottles for my wine- and beer-making, and unsuccessfully tried to get people to sign up for RelayRides.com so I could sell my truck and still count on having a vehicle available when I need one.

The store owners must go out and get one of every essential—cereal, aluminum foil, butter, cake mix, even soy milk—and replace it when someone buys it. It's super handy for those "oh crap, we're out of x" moments and an easy walk for everyone in our little neighborhood. Those who can walk, anyway.

It was before we moved here, but the story goes that the house next door to ours used to belong to an elder who had trouble getting to the store. Neighbors would stop by to bring him necessities and visit with him. Community.

It's the kind of community politicians want to evoke when they say things like "in our communities" and it shares a lot of the good elements with our lives at Dancing Rabbit. We're surrounded by people who know our names, and watch out for us. It's a slower process out here than in a group like DR that makes helping newcomers get settled and feel welcome a very intentional part of the responsibility of individuals in the group, but it is happening.

Our neighbors on the other side have helped us feel welcomed, too. They bring over flowers, and corn, and other little gifts for us. They let us pick from their cherry trees, and we brought back jam and sourdough bread for them. There are friends for my kid in the houses on our block, and they can ride bikes and skateboards back

(continued on p. 74)

> We're all cold, and watching the dollars roll away on the gas pump dial. We have different lives, are going different directions, but for now, we're all here, doing this thing together.

FINDING COMMUNITY OUTSIDE OF "COMMUNITY"

(continued from p. 17)

and forth. Their parents and grandparents look out for him and let me know when there's trouble. The folks down the street watched our cat when we went back to Dancing Rabbit for a visit.

Missing DR

Friendly neighbors and well-established economic systems are great and all, but there are aspects of intentional community I haven't found out here in the big wide world. I miss feeling more comfortable letting people see my pit hair, and stopping for friendly chats on my mid-afternoon walks. I miss having people to talk to when something funny happens, or something sad or frustrating.

We don't have a car co-op out here, which is the one thing I thought was most important about what Dancing Rabbit was doing. It drives me crazy to see multiple cars in each driveway, every single day. There are houses with more cars than people, for crying out loud, but I don't feel like I can use any of them. Even trying to get people to use RelayRides.com didn't work. (That makes sense; their service is expensive and geared more toward urban people with newer cars.)

Speaking of driveways, trash day is a little weird, too. When I was looking for bottles for wine- and beer-making, I knew that there were plenty of bottles in the recycle bins, but I didn't feel like I could go get them. Also, it seems like there must be a more efficient system than the garbage truck stopping twice at each single-family dwelling. Coming up with ways to bring car sharing and other efficiencies of intentional community to extant neighborhood communities has become kind of a hobby of mine.

The pond and the 100-plus acres of protected wildlife habitat were possible only because of the intentional nature of the community of Dancing Rabbit. I miss them. Also not possible without a high degree of buy-in and sameness of intention are the decision-making structure and level of involvement in decisions usually left to individuals in the wider culture. My new neighborhood definitely doesn't get together to decide by consensus whether it's okay for me to cut a couple of young trees that shade my solar panels, and I don't need anyone's permission to adopt a dog or something. Those kinds of things help move a community toward its commonly-held intentions. I don't really miss them.

Then there's the community I've always had. My parents, my siblings and their spouses and children, aunts, uncles, and other elders, coworkers from previous jobs, and of course my friends out at Dancing Rabbit form a sort of "cloud community" that's always there, even when I don't talk to them for long spells, even when we're not on the best of terms. Family and old friends, I guess, are the most unintentional of communities, so they'll always be there, even though my intentions may change. ⚘

Sam and son lived at Dancing Rabbit from November 2009 through August 2014. Now she's a freelance writer, blogger (www.makingrabbittracks.com), and web developer. They're living outside the communities circuit but with all the same values and quirks they had "in community."

THE UNEXPECTED JOURNEY

By Elizabeth Matson

Elizabeth at Findhorn.

Elizabeth at Sirius.

Once upon a time, long ago and far away, like maybe 30 years ago, when I was in my 20s, I went on an Unexpected Journey.

I had just dropped out of a graduate social work program and written a children's book. I dreamed of a different sort of life, one filled with art-making and community. But, in fact, I was very alone and had no idea what I was going to do with my life. Somewhere I read about this Three-Month Living/Learning Seminar in Alternative Communities, offered for graduate credit through the University of Wisconsin-Milwaukee. Participants would live one month each in three different intentional communities, High Wind in Wisconsin, Sirius in Massachusetts, and—the only community I'd heard of, the Shangri-la of alternative communities—Findhorn in Scotland. I signed up.

Then I moved back home since my lease had run out and I was no longer going to school. Squeezed back into the family home, my dreams contracted as well. It was hard to imagine being able to just go off to live in community for three months and imagine a better world. It seemed unrealistic somehow. And it occurred to me that I would have to tell my parents. I canceled my registration.

And Belden Paulson called me. The professor behind this three-month seminar and founder of High Wind Community with his wife, Lisa, called to persuade me to give the seminar a chance. Like a herald, his call sounded a clarion, reawakening my dreams and desires to build a bright new world. I told my parents about this seminar I had signed up for. To my great surprise they offered no objections. I emphasized the green building and organic gardening. The fact that the seminar offered graduate course credits probably didn't hurt either.

I arrived at High Wind with 12 other seekers. I was not the only one who had temporarily backed out at the last minute. We came together as a group of explorers, reveling in morning talks with David Spangler and others, working on community projects in the gardens, kitchen, and bioshelter in the afternoons, creating rituals and art-making. We explored community through labor, art, and spirituality within an intentional community but, more than that, we became a community. The 13 of us became our own traveling community.

> ## As we explored labor, art, and spirituality within each intentional community, we became a community ourselves.

I wrote a story within a story, a mythological representation of our coming together as a community. Borrowing from a recent *Star Trek* movie with only slight adaptation, just because I liked the sound of it, I named the 13 of us together the Koboshi Maru and each of us separately the Warrior, the Prophet, the Seer, the Shepherdess, the Scholar, the Healer, the Harpist, the Mystic, the Bard, the Jester, the Builder, the Sage, and the Spinner. Our last night at High Wind, I read aloud the tale and found my voice as the Spinner of Tales.

I continued the story as we traveled to Sirius, reading the latest installment aloud before we headed to Findhorn, but I never finished it. This unintentional intentional community we had become, the Koboshi Maru, gave me my most direct lessons in community. As we left High Wind to join Sirius and then Findhorn, we were now something more than just a random gathering of individuals. We were a community trying to fit inside another community. Our boundaries clashed, contracted, and expanded. The shifting dynamics of community,

the difficulties of consensus, the challenges of personalities, changing allegiances, and individuals leaving and joining were all experienced personally, not theoretically or by objective observation.

> ## We experienced the challenges of community directly and personally, not theoretically or by objective observation.

I had no final installment to read before we left Findhorn. Instead, I badly sprained my ankle trying to return a bag of treasured rocks to the beach. This was my sign to stay, a nomadic wanderer, three more months in Great Britain in order to return to Findhorn for a three-week Sacred Dance Workshop, another dream I had

High Wind kitchen.

Universal Hall, Findhorn Community.

Photos courtesy of Elizabeth Matson

Tribe of Thirteen.

thought impossible until I did it. For many years, the story hung over my head in its incompleteness. Maybe because I knew how it went. The Koboshi Maru, the 13 who were no longer 13, scaled the Glass Mountain, found the treasure and variously weighed themselves down with it or gave it back to the beach, and then returned home, going their separate ways. It was a tale of There and Back Again.

It was over.

Except it wasn't.

The Three-Month Seminar remains a touchstone experience in my life. I often feel I have not lived up to its expectations. I have not lived the life I dreamed of living. I have not changed the world. I have not created an artists' community or even created a living as an artist. I am not the writer I had hoped to be (though I have not entirely given up hope either). I could go on but do we ever entirely live up to our youthful dreams and expectations?

Life takes us on a journey and it is rarely the journey we had expected or planned. My three-month travels into and part of intentional communities gave me the tools to make sense of the journey. To know when it is time to enter the darkness and wait for the seed to germinate; when to nourish the seedling; when to relish the beauty of full bloom; when to harvest, give thanks, and let go.

When I remember the lessons rather than the dreams of community, I know I am who I am because I once was and always will be one small pearl on the string of the ever-expanding Koboshi Maru. I am a storyteller because of the three-month seminar. I found my voice as a shaper and teller of tales at High Wind. I moved to Wisconsin because of the ties I formed to the land and people there. And I have traveled from there to live and work in various other parts of the country because I learned it was possible to make community wherever I went. I may have never lived in intentional communities beyond those long-term visits but I have carried the desire to create community with me. The pull of community has led me to facilitating a neighborhood Eco-Team; to becoming a folklorist, a librarian, a yoga teacher; to starting story circles and dream groups; to choosing to travel by foot and public transportation when I can; to meeting my neighbors as I walk the dog; to finding myself ahead of the curve when it comes to organic produce, green living, sustainable economy.

It is the small things from this Unexpected Journey that have shaped my life. Motherpeace and Angel cards. The Game of Life. Art-making as a process rather than a product. Ritual. The power of imagination. The friendships and connections. Rutabagas. Listening for that small still voice within. But those small things add up. They become part of the daily choices that I make. Bilbo may have used his ring only to make magical appearances and disappearances from Shire gatherings after he came home from his Unexpected Journey but he was changed, nonetheless, in a deeply profound way. When you go There and Back Again, you never come back the same, even if the life you slip back into is a profoundly small and ordinary one. Once upon a time, I went on an Unexpected Journey. Though I left and came back home again a long time ago, the Journey itself has never ended. ✒

Elizabeth Matson participated in the three-month Living/Learning Seminar in 1984. She is a storyteller, writer, and yoga teacher, currently making her living as a youth/teen librarian in Arizona.

Community

By Barbara B. Prendergast

we bonded at High Wind
settled at Findhorn
on the North Sea
our little community
within a larger one
then to an island
off an island
off an island
among the caretakers of Erraid
an isle in the Inner Hebrides
later we journeyed to Eourres
a community
become a village
in the French alps

we loved and lost
broke promises
forgave ourselves
walked the woods
with a friend
we did not know
listened to lies
kept the secret
pretended not to
notice nakedness

slammed cows in the dark
on the way to the loo
plied our tormenters
who made us work
with *American* whiskey
shoveled manure
planted the gardens

work is love in action

we played 'The Game'
transformed a bit
drank tea and meditated
repaired their windows
fed their cows
gathered mussels
made noodles
drank their beer
sang their songs
danced our hellos
danced our goodbyes

work is love in action

French mud between our toes
French ants in our beds
off to work we go
through the mountains
to plant squash plants
just before the freeze

lost one another
found one another

refused help
gave thanks for help
fell off the path
sank in the mud of Iona
looking for fairies

*if what you are doing
doesn't work don't
keep doing it*

we left our rings
and our tears
in a cloister walk
sacrificed ourselves and others
felt bad kissed and made up
left others out
got left out

*if what you are doing
doesn't work don't
keep doing it*

we held hands
promised to be faithful
lost our tickets
lost ourselves
gave the ancient
dying trees water
from a sacred well
healed each other
healed ourselves
with chocolate
and lavender

we ate nettle soup
and flowers on cake
under the Bougainvillea
learned French
from the cook
stirred the pots
washed the dishes
chanted ancient songs
in ancient places
painted walls
rebuilt houses
herded goats
who slimed us
if we sat down to rest
we made cheese
and lay in the sun

work is love in action

we came home changed
and started again

thank you

so glad you noticed ✒

Barbara B. Prendergast is a long-time member of the board of High Wind. She participated in and led the Three-Community Seminar which often transformed the lives of those who attended. She is a workshop presenter and a trained guide for The Game of Transformation. Barbara lives in Milwaukee with her husband Thomas.

THREE KINDS OF COMMUNITY—
Three Kinds of Experience and Learning

By Belden Paulson

When I went overseas just after college I never imagined I'd end up working there with a movie actor in a high-stakes community project, or later become immersed in an inner city community about to explode, or help to organize an intentional community committed to sustainable living.

In my 20 years of schooling I learned a lot. But I soon found that the learning outside of the classroom and campus went way beyond even what my best teachers had to offer.

I. Community for Refugees

It began in the early 1950s. World War II had ended and Europe was just beginning to dig out from the rubble of massive destruction. After biking across the Swiss Alps with three classmates, and carrying rocks up a steep mountain in northern Italy to help build a youth center, I happened to meet Dr. Teofilo Santi.

An Italian medical doctor from south Italy, he was volunteering his skills and giving out food and clothing to thousands of people living in caves and ruins in Naples. Naples was one of Europe's most heavily bombed cities, and Santi's work centered in the slums where most of the homeless existed on the margin of life. He invited me to join him and his dedicated staff if I agreed to stay for at least six months. My subsistence would be covered.

I soon saw that simple relief work wouldn't solve the problem. Together, then, Santi and I organized *Casa Mia* (My Home), a social assistance center in the heart of the rubble. Every day we served hundreds of the homeless with meals, clothes for entire families, a kindergarten, literacy classes, vocational training, and a medical clinic, as well as helping to find jobs and new housing. We recognized that only comprehensive help, becoming involved with whole families over a long period, could lift these

Actor Don Murray and Beldon Paulson at the Refugee project in Sardinia, Italy, 1957.

desperate war victims out of hopelessness.

In 1953 I finally left Naples with my future wife, Lisa, whom I'd met at *Casa Mia*. My plan was to enter grad school back home. First, though, I spent a couple of days orienting my successor, Don Murray, a conscientious objector who was putting in his two years of alternative service.

Three years later, Don called me. Back in America, he had just finished his first film, *Bus Stop*, playing opposite Marilyn Monroe. I hadn't known he'd been an off-Broadway actor; now he was up for an Oscar and was in the Midwest on a promotional tour. Lisa and I had since married and now lived in the "rabbit patch," a warren of prefab huts for student couples at the University of Chicago.

Don stopped by, and the three of us sat up most of the night reminiscing about Italy. Don said, "I have a few dollars in my pocket now, but I'm not ready yet to go to Hollywood to be one more movie star. There are thousands of refugees still stagnating in those barbed wire camps in Italy and I want to go back to help. I need you."

While working with homeless Neapolitans, another of our assignments with Dr. Santi had been to provide welfare for refugees in five camps ringing the city. These were Iron Curtain escapees from communist East Europe, as well as leftover "D.P. s" (displaced persons) still in camps after the war. They were all "hard-core"—they'd been rejected for emigration and all other solutions. The United Nations and Italian Government authorities had given up on them.

I told Don I had a new wife and a two-week-old baby to consider, and had to finish my Ph.D. Don pleaded: "At least go back to Italy with me to make a study." I did, and we ended up buying 135 acres of virgin land on Sardinia, the island off the west coast of

> **Only comprehensive help, becoming involved with whole families over a long period, could lift these war victims out of hopelessness.**

Italy. I postponed my degree, and Lisa, young Eric, and I moved there in 1957 for the next two years. Our project with Don gradually transferred 15 families, a few at a time, to Sardinia. We created a small community based in farming and small industries, such as poultry and manufacturing concrete blocks for refugee homes and the local market.

In the course of our two-year stay on Sardinia, and then two more with the United Nations High Commissioner for Refugees office in Rome, with a job to help clear the camps, there were valuable lessons:

1. Never Say Impossible. We were told again and again by top authorities: "The project you propose to resettle hard-core refugees on Sardinia won't work. These refugees have lived in the camps for years and are completely dependent. Having been rejected by everyone, they have no faith or trust in anything. They will never become self-sufficient. We appreciate your youthful idealism, but you'd be wasting your time and our resources. Your project is impossible." Don and I could only reply: "You're probably right, but we'll give it one last shot."

The first Christmas, we invited the refugees in Sardinia to visit the camps again in order to take a break from their more rigorous life in our project. Obviously, their work had been hard compared to their former idle life. In the early months with us, even though they didn't trust each other, they united as one bloc to voice their complaints against us, the Americans. I wrote Don in Hollywood: "Much as they hate the camps, they may not come back to us. We may have to accept that the authorities were right." But every refugee did return to our community, and they brought several new ones. Their small industries began to flourish, they gained confidence, and integrated into the neighboring vil- lage. Later on, I asked the U.N. mental health consultant from Geneva who visited us: "How do you explain our success when others far more experienced failed?" He said: "You created a community where trust was built. This restored their faith

in themselves and in life. You showed them that when you plant a seed, it will grow. Also, you never read the details in their thick dossiers; since you didn't know all their problems, you assumed they could make it."

2. Equal Opportunity Doesn't Assure the Same Outcomes. We made sure that the minute the refugees left the camps they would be treated with maximum equality. This would be one way to build trust. But we soon found that this policy didn't work. For instance, there was Mario from Yugoslavia. His resume included harrowing escapes from the Nazis and later the Tito communists. In the camps he'd lost one lung to T.B. and subsequently was rejected by 13 emigration commissions. It turned out that he was quite a brilliant entrepreneur. We helped him to manage and eventually own the block industry, employing others. Or there was Nyc, a Czech, who had been in camp for years with unknown problems. Smart and independent, he worked his piece of land on his own; he hired no one and wouldn't work for anyone. Or Tony, a Spaniard who'd been moved from camp to camp since the Spanish Civil War. He preferred to hire out for a daily wage so that he wouldn't have to take personal responsibility. Each refugee was absolutely unique. The dogma of "equal opportunity" really made little sense because each one related to opportunity differently and required different solutions to his needs.

II. Inner City Community

After the refugee work in Europe, Lisa and I returned home. I was soon dealing with a very different kind of community. I completed the Ph.D., and with two small sons now, we moved to Wisconsin in 1962 where I joined the University of Wisconsin faculty. Working out of Milwaukee and Madison, in due course I helped the university organize a new department dedicated to "doing something" about poverty and racism. This was not just an intellectual exercise; the city of Milwaukee's inner core—the heart of one of America's most

Beldon Paulson and Don Murray taking a break with the volunteer staff in Sardinia, Italy, 1957.

The caves of Naples, Italy where hundreds of the homeless from World War II found refuge, 1950.

Photos courtesy of Belden Paulson

racially segregated ghettos—was ready to explode.

A several-square-mile area north of downtown, it had all the economic, social, political, and educational liabilities of disadvantaged central cities. People were not actually starving as they were in Naples, but they were more ready to challenge the system—violently if necessary. The university realized that it had to get involved.

The residents themselves referred to the area as "the community," but their interpretation of community was quite different from that usually discussed in this magazine. Many people didn't know or couldn't personally relate to one another, yet their lives fit into an array of experiences, needs, and complaints they all shared. Their "community" was as well defined as any intentional community.

One of the early construction projects in Sardinia, Italy, 1957.

A brilliant local black activist, Reuben Harpole, took me under his wing. We sat in inner city bars, met pastors in the churches, spent hours in the schools and just meeting folks. Some local leaders thought an important need was to find out what was happening with the young people. My department helped to organize a house-to-house, random-sample survey covering 60 central city blocks. We trained 30 volunteers from the area and they administered 300 one-hour questionnaires.

We found not only shockingly deficient reading skills, but by the time the kids reached sixth and seventh grade, a cluster of related problems followed: school tardiness and absenteeism, then all the usual behavioral problems. We organized a summer demonstration reading project in one school located in the middle of the area. At first the kids wouldn't

Hundreds of Italians often had only one meal a day provided at Casa Mia in Naples, 1951.

show up, so our teachers had to go and actually drag them out of bed. But the project worked, and eventually it led to expanded cooperation with a sizable number of schools in the area.

Since these were local institutions, they needed empowering

support from the neighborhood. A nucleus of residents worked with us to create the Harambee Revitalization Project (Harambee is Swahili for "Let's Pull Together). HRP is a community organization initially based in 12 square blocks. Later it expanded to encompass 30,000 people. Given the multiple needs, along with the school projects we organized major initiatives dealing with housing and economic development, health, human services, and also the Ombudsman Project. This latter was an amazingly effective network of 200 block leaders trained to respond to the individual questions and problems of everyone on their block.

From this experience of serving an inner city community, here is what became clear:

1. Defining "Need" Is Far More Complicated than Assumed.
I'm convinced that this is one reason so many well-intended programs don't work. Needs are often an interrelated collection of problems, not just a single variable. It's also easier to focus on overt symptoms rather than the underlying causes, and we tend to invest *most* resources to measure results that may have the least *real* significance. Take, for example, a "reading problem" facing a central city youth. Start with how the school system works: Can the teacher and administrator reach the student? Is the curriculum relevant to the child's background and interests? What about the home environment—is there at least one interested parent or guardian present to help with studying? Is there space to do homework? Is there nutritious food and attention to health? Or look at the economic system: Must the child work to help support the family? Is there money for books and reading matter, not to mention clothes? Or the political system: Does the family accept the legitimacy of the school authority? In other words, giving the child a real chance takes more than

analysis of reading test scores.

2. Dealing with Racism Requires Personal Immersion. As I moved around in the inner city and its largely black population, I quickly recognized the gap between the people I was working closely with and the many other folks I dealt with in the larger environs of Milwaukee and the state. I developed respect and admiration for the energy, resourcefulness, and effectiveness of Reuben and my other minority colleagues on our university staff. I was amazed as I viewed the results of the 200 block leaders in the Ombudsman Project. On each block, folks volunteered their time, participating in training to become mediators/facilitators between their neighbors and authorities in the larger political system—whether it was contacting services in the bureaucracy or getting garbage picked up. When I met the teachers we worked with, I became aware of their sensitivity and desire to serve their community. Yet when I talked with employers in the corporate world, or officials in the maze of agencies, or with some school administrators and many folks in the larger (white) public, there was often a jaundiced perception of the black population. Since no one, of course, would admit to racism, this was a bias conveyed in many subtle or bureaucratic ways. However, the people I ran into who actually knew Reuben and many others I could mention felt as I did: that by far the surest and best strategy was through both races working shoulder-to-shoulder to counter one of our most fundamentally intractable cultural issues.

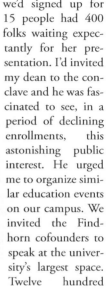

Belden Paulson with Reube Harpole, a colleague in inner city development in Milwaukee, Wisconsin.

While residential communities, important as they are, will remain limited in number, the expansion of consciousness is unlimited.

III. Findhorn and High Wind

While I was still deeply involved with inner city issues, in October 1976, my wife Lisa visited the legendary Findhorn community in Scotland. This may have been its spiritual heyday, with people attracted from around the globe. The some 200 residents were not only designing a model of "the good life"; they were trying to live it every day.

Lisa brought back bundles of notes from talks presented there, including those of David Spangler, a mystic and teacher who, early on, articulated the vision of Findhorn as a seed point for a coming "New Age." He said there would be a "fundamental change of consciousness from one of isolation and separation to one of communion and wholeness, to build a future different from what we already know or expect."

After more than 20 years of marriage, I'd never seen Lisa so fired up. She obviously didn't want to be dragged back from the heights of the New Age into Wisconsin's mainstream culture.

I arranged for her to report on Findhorn at a big conference in Chicago. The room we'd signed up for 15 people had 400 folks waiting expectantly for her presentation. I'd invited my dean to the conclave and he was fascinated to see, in a period of declining enrollments, this astonishing public interest. He urged me to organize similar education events on our campus. We invited the Findhorn cofounders to speak at the university's largest space. Twelve hundred people showed up from all walks of life—folks I had not imagined would be interested.

In 1978 I figured it was time for me to visit Scotland, and I did become convinced of the significance of this model for rethinking the future of our culture—both from a philosophical standpoint and also considering the looming, worldwide crisis of natural resource depletion. Over the next years I got approvals from university officials to line up a series of seminars that drew not only traditional students and academics, but people from across Wisconsin.

Some 50 people, of all backgrounds and ages, attended virtually every class we offered, and bonded as a group. Many of them traveled to Findhorn on study trips we organized. At a certain point, there was a small rebellion: "We love these classes, but now it's time to stop talking and *do* something that will be a practical, real-world demonstration." This led to the creation of High Wind, an intentional ecological community on rural land 50 miles north of Milwaukee.

Since the High Wind story has been written about in this magazine (most recently, in "High Wind: A Retrospective," issue #145), and detailed in several books, I'll simply focus on a few of my own observations.

With a full-time university job, I often valued my periodic distance from the details of community life and relationships because I could weigh what was happening at High Wind against my larger world. When the community was cohesive and members felt clear and excited about creating an alternative model, this truly pointed up the dysfunctional culture I experienced in the mainstream. But also, relationships sometimes soured, and now and then members would leave, disgruntled. At times, meetings were endlessly unproductive because our consensus process paralyzed decision-making.

Most members were working their hearts out—with little monetary compensation. We held regular "community building" meetings and internal conferences where everyone was encouraged to express needs and wishes and gripes. Sometimes when feelings ran high over an ongoing dilemma, we brought in an outside resource person.

When I didn't get upset if things weren't working out, or when the interpersonal "stuff" boiled up, I was criticized for being "insensitive." My own postwar overseas experience, when I was dealing daily with people in dire life and death situations, forced me to develop a thick skin—not always advantageous in intentional communities!

One of High Wind's impacts had to do with education. We sponsored courses and major conferences, often with the university. Our Three-Community Seminars brought a small group to live for a month each at High Wind, Findhorn, and a third community. People from all over descended on High Wind for tours and workshops. We contracted the public schools for inner city kids to spend time at the community. On the national level, we cooperated with various groups to begin designing a holistic think tank to recast national policy. The common underlying element was to rethink our culture, pushing for a change in consciousness, which in turn could begin transforming institutions to build a sustainable world.

Among the significant insights of these years with High Wind, I cite two:

1. Ordinary People with an Extraordinary Mission. What

made us think we had something to offer about birthing cultural change? How could we stand up to the sometimes hostile status quo environment? How could we—ordinary, flawed human beings, often disagreeing as to how to proceed, and also finding it difficult to fit our diverse personalities into close living quarters—possibly offer a credible alternative to the larger world? I, for one, sensed that there must be mysterious forces at work—the unexplainable insights that popped out from some depth within us, faith that defied logic, belief in the potential of ourselves and others beyond all reason, the impulse to drop everything else to serve—all these I'd call spirit. Some call this "Factor X," that added intangible dimension that makes things work. And ultimately we did achieve successes, and the number of those attracted to what we represented multiplied.

2. Alternative Community Redefined. A few years ago the High Wind board conducted a survey of some 200 people who had had close contact with High Wind. In analyzing results, the board was impressed with the significant impact on many lives. I learned from my years at High Wind and from all the folks associated with us—residents, event participants, outside supporters—that we needed to redefine the meaning of "community." My concept now is that it might be a place, a residential enclave, but it also represents a paradigm or set of values delineating how one sees the world and the commitments one is prepared to make. This dramatically opens up the potential for historic change because while residential communities, important as they are, will remain limited in number, the expansion of consciousness is unlimited. ❧

After graduating from Oberlin College in the early 1950s, Belden Paulson created innovative projects overseas, was a faculty member at the University of Wisconsin for 35 years, and with his wife Lisa, cofounded the High Wind Community near Plymouth, Wisconsin. His varied adventures are detailed in Odyssey of a Practical Visionary, *and in* Notes from the Field: Strategies toward Cultural Transformation. *He and Lisa still live in their solar home in the now "relaxed" eco-neighborhood.*

Bel and Lisa and their solar home at High Wind.

From left to right: Bel Paulson, Lisa Paulson, Bob Pavlik, David Lagerman, Barbara Prendergast, Maureen Gallagher.

THE LONG TRAIL HOME:
Discovering My Own Community

By Clistine Morningstar

Community is like a big wheel with many spokes. I am reminded of the Medicine Wheels, or Sacred Hoops, of Native American spirituality that have been constructed by laying stones in a particular pattern on the ground. Most of them have a center cairn of stones from which lines of stones radiate in spokes to an outer ring of stones forming the periphery. These wheels are considered to be a major symbol of peaceful interaction among all living beings on Earth.

Ideally, a community would embrace this golden rule of honoring "All My Relations." To the extent that each person in a particular community is included (or not) in a web of cooperation, understanding, and purpose, then that community seems to flourish (or to wither). Wellness of the individual is inseparable from the harmony, or the unity (but not the uniformity) of the group. So the spokes of the wheel can become the different elements that contribute to its well-being.

I now look back over 81 years to remember my various community experiences. The earliest one took place in a big school in the north of England. Having experienced an isolated early childhood in which I had spent much time alone in my big, green backyard, I didn't know how to interrelate with the other children. So I was a shy watcher for quite a long time and always felt rather overwhelmed by the numbers and the noise. But eventually I did very well there as a student, and particularly enjoyed morning assembly where we all sang a beautiful hymn together. Some of those hymns have haunted me all my life! I would say the major spokes in the wheel that sustained the well-being of this school were respect for the teachers, appreciation for what we learned, and a predominating sense of goodwill. When I had to leave at the age of 11 in order to move to a London suburb, I felt wrenched from my growing roots. Some of the spirit of this community has stayed in my heart and it still helps to guide me when I teach young children in the community where I now live.

In due course I was sent away to a girls' boarding-school in Sussex, and starting then, school was a nightmare! This school at times resembled a Dickens' novel in its strict and narrow ways, and we never had a solitary moment. I felt as if I were living in a world without sunlight, and became depressed just as those people who suffer from lack of winter sunlight can become depressed until the spring comes around. Only spring did not come around and I dropped out in heart, mind, and spirit! Some essential spokes that would have contributed to our well-being were definitely missing in the wheel of this community—its stern creed of ethics needed to be complemented by a measure of encouragement and understanding, and its dry pattern of repetition fossilized what could have been the living spirit of the place. From this I learned how crippling the letter of the law without the spirit of the law can be.

Many years later, with my second husband, I discovered another type of community on an island close to Vancouver Island in British Columbia. We had moved there in order to abandon the rush, push, and jostle of city life and we found ourselves part of a loose-knit population of like-minded folks. There we joined an excellent choir, went to a free-wheeling church on Sundays that discussed spirituality but rarely dared to mention the word "God," hosted poetry readings, went for backpacking trips with nearby neighbors, built a cabin, and became part of it all. The spokes in this island community wheel were built on neighborliness, recreational and hobby interests, growing small gardens, and fighting the forest industry who were threatening to log the remaining wild areas on the island and desecrate the wildlife there. Such a wheel can sustain one's interest but not one's soul! I was seeking something deeper but didn't yet realize the kind of setting this would require.

During this same time period I worked as a life-skills coach, becoming part of a close-knit working group in a Job Project that helped young people find and keep jobs after a rocky start in their lives. We had nine staff members and we blended well; but although we achieved good results with our clients, the work was repeatedly challenging. There were some life-giving spokes in this work-based community wheel that were new to me—the goal of serving others; dealing with continuous challenge for a positive purpose; and deriving mutual support from working closely with colleagues under good leadership.

Perhaps it would seem that this purposeful work-based community, when added to my more open-ended island-based commu-

A Cosmic Wheel of Destiny ceremony conducted by Spirit Steps Tours.

Photos courtesy of Global Change Media

nity, would provide enough balance between them for a meaningful life, particularly when supplemented by frequent fun visits from my now grown-up children and their families. But I continued to long for deeper meaning and fulfilment—a spiritual element that my own personal truth-search and efforts at meditation did not sufficiently mitigate. When we are ready, it seems our destiny can come to meet us, as I did not plan for the next set of surprising circumstances.

My husband decided to finish the degree necessary to be able to teach in our local school system, and so we took what we thought was a vacation down through the western US in order to look first-hand at two or three universities that required only a year more of study. On the way we stopped at a bookstore where I found a booklet on the vortexes at Sedona. It described them as gateways of spiritual energy, and I immediately developed a strong desire to visit them. Because we followed this urge, the next anticipated chapter in our lives that we had so carefully planned never took place. Instead, we experienced the beginning of another story....

Walking along the banks of Oak Creek in Sedona on the day before we were due to return to Canada, I met a woman who began to talk to me about the intentional spiritual community she lived in. She told me they studied *The Urantia Book*—which I was already reading—and that they were receiving continuing revelation as well. In an extraordinary moment of realization that transcended my sense of logic, I knew that destiny was calling me! Despite my dour memories of boarding school, my husband and I both decided to find out more. We did not go back to Canada the next day, but stayed to investigate. Within a few weeks we joined this community that is now based in Tumacácori, Arizona and is

known as Global Community Communications Alliance.

I've now lived at this community for 20 years. At the hub of its life-affirming wheel is the pursuit of personal, group, and planetary transformation, and its many spokes support this ideal. Does this sound like a kind of nirvana? On the contrary it's a tough school, and even though we experience much joy of fellowship it will only really work out for those who fully desire to follow this path of spiritual commitment.

My past experiences in the job community where I was a life-skills coach gave me a grounding in how to deal with continuous challenge. However, my present community doesn't repeat the mistakes of my strict boarding school by embracing a static philosophy. Instead it upholds positive change, and we are all requested to shed our old snake-skins of erroneous habits just as quickly as we can. We obviously can't effect meaningful change in the world if we don't start with ourselves, and this deliberate process of shedding our lower selves is what makes it tough as well as highly rewarding.

In my past community experiences I was able to observe varying degrees of leadership, ranging from good to poor. I'm personally suspicious of leadership until the leader or leaders earn my respect because so often leaders can pursue the goal of personal power. When I first came to Global Community Communications Alliance I learned that there was a hierarchy of leadership consisting first of the cofounders, next the rest of the eldership, and then those who had mandated positions as assistants at various levels. Below that were the broad category of "students," although in a sense everyone here is a student. I wasn't sure what to make of it so I adopted a wait and see policy. In a fairly short time I came to realize that everyone who had leadership authority had fully earned it. I saw that our two well-loved founders, Gabriel of Urantia and Niann Emerson Chase, as well as our dedicated Elders, were able to offer us the wisdom, balance, counsel, and understanding that comes with spiritual ascension.

Over time, this impression has deepened. I see that this pyramid of leadership is very necessary for the well-being of everyone here and that without it we couldn't possibly have sustained our growth and vision. One balancing factor is that we are all are trained and encouraged to become leaders ourselves.

Another spoke in the wheel of this community is the implementation of procedures. These are intended to create commonsense ways of doing things for the general good, rather than

Author Clistine Morningstar.

Clistine conducting the children's choir during a Christmas performance at an assisted living home in Tucson.

Author Clistine and students of Global Community Communications Schools for Teens and Children enjoying A Day in the 1885 Schoolhouse program at the Tubac Presidio State Historic Park.

Sharing concepts and experiences of ecovillage living with a group of international students visiting Global Community Communications Alliance in Tumacácori, Arizona.

having individuals just do their own thing—which, with 120 people, would make for quite a degree of chaos. At first I often found following procedures irksome, but as I moved gradually from a focus of "me" to "we," I came to see the wisdom and the logic behind the protocol we were asked to follow.

There is a large quota of goodwill within our community, but at times conflicts do arise as they always will when numerous human beings are gathered together. Our methods of conflict resolution represent another helpful spoke in our community wheel. The type of "care-fronting" and counseling we have developed provide a realistic training in human relationships in which we gradually acquire greater humility and the art of being more transparent.

The kind of counseling we can also seek for personal problems encourages us to improve our relationship with the living spiritual forces in order to align with right action. It sounds Spartan, but it really works when we choose to follow it—because we then move out of victim mode and are capable of being partners with God in our own healing.

All of this requires a degree of what is commonly known as "sacrifice," but what we're actually sacrificing are the patterns of our lower-driven selves. In return we experience an increasing sense of who we were created to be, plus a more loving group awareness that I wouldn't have dreamed possible in my younger years. We also become more suitable vessels to incorporate change in our dark, troubled world. And that is what we came here for.

We seek to create a Sacred Hoop that is life-sustaining in its many aspects. This has meant building our own ecovillage, supporting ourselves from our organic farm produce, and sharing what we learn in these processes with all who seek to know. It's also meant developing various other outreaches including a hospice that gives comfort to many, and a legal department that supports those who are in the immigration process.

Another life-affirming spoke of our Medicine Wheel is our dedication to the arts. We are all encouraged to develop our artistic talents in order to express and share beauty, truth, and goodness. We thus reach out to the general public through our own talented musicians, visual artists, and writers, and we have our own arts center in Tucson.

Through these many aspects of our life together I've at last found a community that matches my soul-longings. With all the challenges, fellowship, vision, laughter, sweat,

(continued on p. 77)

THE LONG TRAIL HOME: DISCOVERING MY OWN COMMUNITY

(continued from p. 55)

and tears, I realize that I have indeed found my own "tribe" within The Sacred Hoop.

My own contribution to Global Community Communications Alliance—where I've chosen to live for the rest of my life—consists of refining what and who I am, and in giving back in various forms of service. I've always loved teaching, writing, and making up songs, and now I do all three as part of this service. I teach and train other teachers at our own children's school; I write in various genres for different readers when time is available; and I make up songs for the children's choir which I also direct. I'm a leader, a follower, a change-agent, and a student of revelation all at the same time! This is fortuitous as it creates a rounded, unwritten curriculum of personal development for me! I can feel the yeast of goodness working within our community of diverse people who have united in their spiritual goals. Although expansion through the dynamics of change and growth is often uncomfortable it's also wonderfully recharging for my heart and mind.

Perhaps I've always longed at some unrecognized level to be with others in this way. I'm reminded of the words of Cecil Spring-Rice in one of those hymns that I used to enjoy singing at my first school. These words speak of the vision of light and life for the greater community of the whole world. It's the vision of The Sacred Hoop fulfilled:

And there's another country, I've heard of long ago,

Most dear to them that love her, most great to them that know;

We may not count her armies, we may not see her King;

Her fortress is a faithful heart, her pride is suffering;

And soul by soul and silently her shining bounds increase,

And her ways are ways of gentleness and all her paths are peace. ❧

Clistine Morningstar is a graduate of the Royal Academy of Dramatic Art, London, and a poet. She wrote her acclaimed book Growing with Dance *after years of research and teaching in that field. She is now teacher trainer and choir director at Global Community Communication Schools for Teens and Children.*

Offerings to the Land

By Mary Murphy

I can't remember a time when I didn't feel as though the trees, rocks, rivers, hills, lakes, and mountains were my trusted friends and confidants. I have heard of studies that show a long walk in nature to be as effective as antidepressant medication, and other studies measuring how the number of close friends one has increases one's mental resiliency and lifespan. To me these two assets, green places and friends, are at least somewhat interchangeable. I've had many a good long cry by a sympathetic river or a favorite tree that leaves me feeling lighter and clearer about what I must do than any visit to a therapist ever has. I also tend my green places like one might care for a friend, heading out into the woods with my ax and saw to trim back the trails, chop a path through fallen trunks, and open up new views. When I return to my family's home, a walk down the trail to the rocky Maine shore is just as important as paying a visit to Grandma.

I have been a wanderer most of my adult life, a nomadic wilderness guide who moves with the seasons and goes where the next job leads her. Most of my jobs involve a strong sense of community, and on the occasions when I've needed a place to live that is not a tent, I usually rent a room in a large house share to enjoy another layer of camaraderie. Human community has been abundant in my life and it is important to me, and yet wherever I go, I find that my deepest sense of connection is with the land itself, not the human beings.

I know a few other people who are this passionate about the land itself as a friend, but not a huge number. People often chuckle at me when I get excited about introducing them to a tree I know. There is a spectrum of relationship to the land: some exploit it only as an industrial or agricultural resource, some value it vaguely for "ecological services" like carbon sequestration, others are appreciative or even passionate about the beauty of a landscape, as if it were a fine painting. What I'm talking about is having an actual relationship with the land, a friendship, a flirtation, and a sense of community. This happens when you come to know a specific place so deeply that it ceases to be interchangeable. When you visit a place often enough and pay close attention, you no longer think that *this* pine tree is the same as all the others. You come to know its exact shape and its relationship to everything around it. It becomes *your* pine tree, not in the sense of you owning it, but in the sense that someone is *your* friend: you are in particular and specific relationship with it.

Once trees and trails and hills become specific and non-interchangeable to you, it becomes possible to care enough to put some effort into the relationship. You might take the time to prune the tree when a limb becomes diseased, or build a little shrine of stones and flowers at its base, or show up at a planning commission meeting when someone proposes a new building where your tree-friend now stands. Intimate relationship with your surroundings gives the land a face and a story for you. Once this happens, you understand how the land in a far away place also has a face and a story for someone else. You can't help but care.

While your friendship with the land may inspire you to give, you will also receive much from it. The land gives us beauty, health, and a renewal of spirit. The land is also a very steady friend. While some of its moods are more inviting than others, it is always present for you and has much wisdom to teach. I often get my best ideas when walking down a trail. The gifts of the land are freely given to anyone, but you have to take the time to build a connection to receive the full bounty. The land reserves its best gifts for the people it trusts.

Here are some suggestions for nurturing your sense of friendship with the land. You can do these alone or as group activities with your community. Some of these ideas are easier to implement in a rural area, but many can be done even in small green spaces in the city.

1. Learn to identify the species of the trees and plants you can see out of the windows of your home or office. Learn the names of any hills or bodies of water you can see. Tree

Learning to Track: Students track forest creatures through the snow at a Mountainsong Expeditions class.

identification guides and local topographical maps are usually available at your public library.

2. If you have a meditation practice, find a place you can practice it outside.

3. Pick a specific "sit spot" to return to once a day or once a week. Visit it throughout the seasons and at different times of day. Just observe.

4. Walk or run on trails near where you live. Learn them so well that you don't need a map.

5. Sing to a tree or a rock. Try different songs and see if you can sense which ones it likes the most.

6. Read books which describe a mystical connection with the land and its intelligence. Try *The Wood Wife* by Terry Windling, *The Magic of Findhorn* by Paul Hawkin, or *The Enchanted* by Elizabeth Coatsworth.

7. Make offerings to the land. In old European cultures in places like Ireland and Sweden, it was considered reckless not to leave a few offerings for the land spirits on a regular basis, in order to stay in their good graces. Try a little milk poured on the ground, a few shiny pennies, or some birdseed.

8. Create a shrine somewhere on the land you are befriending. This can be anything from a few stones or twigs arranged subtly at the base of a tree to raising some standing stones using local rocks. Be thoughtful about introducing manmade materials into your shrine, and don't use anything that could harm an animal or pollute the soil.

9. Climb trees.

10. Return your hair trimmings and nail clippings to the earth in a thoughtful way, conscious of the ways the earth feeds you and you can feed it.

11. Learn to identify the birdsongs of common species where you live.

12. Learn to identify wildlife tracks in the snow, mud, or sand.

13. Walk your land with a hunter and ask her to describe how she sees the landscape from the perspective of her quarry. You'll likely be shown details you never noticed before.

14. Hold meetings outside.

15. Go skinny dipping.

16. Take your problems and questions to the land. Hold a question in your heart while you wander through a natural area and notice what you encounter. Can you read a message in it?

(continued on p. 75)

April 6, 2015: Writing with the Land

The snowflakes twirled down today, out of a cotton-ball sky, dancing as if they don't know they'll melt when they hit the ground. They enjoy themselves while they are distinct. Perhaps they enjoy melting into the ground too, creeping up into the rootlets of a young fern and doing the Chlorophyll Waltz with the sunlight in the citron green leaves of spring. Winter has been my bedfellow for many long nights, wind howling down the valley to rock my little house like a ship at sea. I have curled into winter, soothed by the long dark nights. Who might I be when the spring comes? How will I melt into a new thing? How will the alchemy of sunlight work upon me? Where is the vein of sugar-sweet sap for me to tap, boiling away everything but what will fuel me, what will pleasure me, what will carry me forward? I want to turn over all the rocks, plumb the deep pools in the stream, climb the trees to see a wide view, and lie for days beside a little fawn, delicate and still, waiting for the moment when it will venture forth on uncertain legs and taste the green fern fronds made of snowflakes and sunlight.

—M.M.

Caring for the Land: Mountainsong Expeditions instructor Jesse Scarlato helps to keep the trails clear on our Archery Biathlon course.

Interdependence: Heating my tiny house with wood reminds me how much I depend on the local forest.

Photos by Mary Murphy

OFFERINGS TO THE LAND

(continued from p. 19)

17. Take a young child to the land you are building a relationship with. Notice what they notice.

18. If you pray, try praying outside.

19. Learn about edible plants in your area and try eating something that you wildcraft from your land.

20. Sleep outside on a clear night with no tent.

21. Learn to make an herbal remedy from something growing on your land.

22. Paint or draw a beautiful spot on your land.

23. If you have a private spot where you will be safe and not disturb anyone, have sex outside. You can involve another human if you like, but doing this solo might allow you to focus more on the energy of the land around you.

24. Bring beautiful pieces of nature into your home where you will see them often: a sprig of pine, an autumn leaf, a few wildflowers, a beautiful shell.

25. Where it is safe to do so, walk barefoot on the earth.

26. Go outside to acknowledge the solstices and equinoxes in whatever way feels right to you. Notice how your land changes with the seasons.

27. Write a poem to or about the land.

These ideas are just a start. Anything that will help you come to know *this* piece of land in a specific and distinct way is a promising practice. Engage your creativity and try new ways of breaking down the barriers we place between ourselves and the out-of-doors. These ideas apply whether you have lived on the same piece of land for 60 years or you are spending three weeks on a farm for a sustainability course: befriend the land where you are and you'll never be lonely. ❧

Mary Murphy is a wilderness guide and hunting instructor. When her wandering years came to an end she founded Mountainsong Expeditions in the wild forests of Vermont, where she helps people learn to be in deeper relationship with the land and each other. Your can learn about her work or send her a message at www.mountainsongexpeditions.com.

Find more resources at
ic.org/communities

Statement of Ownership, Management, and Circulation.

Communities, publication #0199-9346, is published 4 times per year with annual subscription of $25. Contact Kim Scheidt 660-883-5545. Publisher's address, office of publication, and publisher's headquarters is Fellowship for Intentional Community (FIC), 23 Dancing Rabbit Lane, Rutledge, MO 63563. Chris Roth is Editor. Owner is FIC, a nonprofit, nonstock corporation. No security holders. Tax status unchanged in preceding 12 months.

Extent & Nature of Circulation	Avg. No. Copies Each Issue During Previous 12 Month	No. Copies of Single Issue Published Nearest to Filing Date
A. Total number of copies (net press run)	2,070	2,040
B. Outside county paid subs	945	951
1. In-county paid subs	7	7
2. Sales through dealers and other non-USPS paid distributions	880	866
3. Other classes through USPS	11	10
C. Total paid distribution	1,843	1,834
D. Free/Nominal Distribution		
1. Outside Country	0	0
2. In Country	0	0
3. Other classes through USPS	0	0
4. Outside the Mail	0	0
E. Total distribution	1,843	1,843
F. Copies not distributed	227	206
H. Total	2,070	2,040
I. Percent paid	100%	100%
J. Paid electronic copies	28	32
K. Total paid copies	1,871	1,866
L. Total distribution	1,871	1,866
M. Percent paid	100%	100%

Finding Home

By Eridani Baker

Editor's Note: *the author sent us this story in late September 2015; its timeline reflects that date.*

He aha te mea nui?
He tangata.
He tangata.
He tangata.

What is the most important thing? It is people, it is people, it is people.

—Maori Proverb

In the past year and a half I have called a lot of places home. Last year I left London, my home of two years, and traveled to Greece. I stayed a month, made new family, then traveled to Eugene, Oregon and called Lost Valley community my place for three months. I left America for India and lived at the Ananda Ashram near Pondicherry; it was home for over half a year. Then I went back to Greece, an unsettling place to be at this point in time. I stayed for three more months before hopping a plane back to London en route to my final destination, New Zealand, where I was born.

The history of words teaches us that together we are stronger. Community, from the Latin *com* meaning "with, together, in conjunction, joint" and *munire*, meaning "to fortify, strengthen, or defend," reminds us that it is in unification with the other that we are truly heartened. To live in a group requires an amount of dissolution of Ego. To share space with another implies a level of support. To a degree you are saying to your fellows: I am committed to your safety and security; fear not for we are in this together.

Living in intentional community offers insight into a fuller spectrum of earthly experience than one could ever hope to glimpse living in a city of great population. At Lost Valley I was able to discover what it really means to be connected, not only to the other residents but also to the environment. I loved watching the beans grow up the corn stalks while the summer squash crawled around on the ground; we watched it actively but without judgment. It's the same for people in community: the people you live with bear witness as you falter, they see that you go down when you ought to go up, they see signs of decay before a normal life cycle would suppose it, and so they provide a stake. Without becoming responsible for another person, and without letting one rotten apple spoil the barrel, for the most part the overall effect of community is that it creates a structure, it offers scaffolding as well as something to graft to. In the natural flow, eventually you will be picked up and moved forward.

Community living takes time to settle into and my time at Lost Valley marked the beginning of a new chapter. I'd left the media industry in London and was on the long way home to New Zealand to work somewhere in the field of yoga. My plans were vague. My experience of being at Lost Valley was one of primordial support.

It afforded me time to compost, to turn the soil and create a rich base to grow out of. For me, to see the world existing in miniature, to see a community operating as a whole whist still being within a wider local structure, gave me pause to reflect on who I have been, who I am, and the version of me I want to be in the future. It offered me space to share stories and personal histories with other people; sharing, and living with the people with whom I had communed, was an accelerant to the digestive process that has to come before moving on. Composting is hard and dirty work.

At first, community living didn't seem much different from sleep-away camp or a holiday at a campground. I didn't immediately feel like I was part of something, but when I went to leave I realized that I had glued these people to my heart and now they were being ripped away. Let me tell you just one story that made me realize that I was becoming part of something. I spent one sunny day shoveling duck and chicken poop, filling wheelbarrow after wheelbarrow and moving the stuff to a different part of the property to make potting mix. I did this with a guy I'd instantly recognized as my opposite. Unlike me, he preferred to be nude, he always used soft words, and he is the kind of hippie that will crawl up in your lap and sing himself to sleep. We swapped stories and shared our ideas, no Nonviolent Communication techniques required, just talking and listening, both of us just sincerely striving to understand the other's experience of being alive.

That story doesn't have a profound conclusion; it's just something that I think would only happen in community, and I feel richer for having shared time with someone so different from me. I feel personally invested in him; I want life to be good for him. The night before I left Lost Valley everyone came out to the basketball court to have a big family photo. It wasn't a very well-planned photo-shoot; we weren't all there at the same time and it was getting dark. But I love that I have those photos and I know that everyone came out because they had, in whatever small way, tried to understand me; however mildly, those people feel personally invested in me. Community living helps you to understand "other" and that's the kind of thing that will change the world.

In yoga circles, when a bunch of people hang out together it is called Satsang. "Sat" means truth and "sanga" means company, so to be in Satsang is to be in the company of other truth seekers. Delete the religious connotations this brings up for you: yoga is not a "religion" in the modern sense of the word. It's more like being on a scavenger hunt with a bunch of people who have different skills than your own. Together you are just jamming it out, trying to figure out which pieces of each other's knowledge help you towards your goal. You are doing this with an open mind, letting go of things you've previously held as valuable. That can be a really hard thing to do. I have a ring with a red stone in it. I used to think the stone was a ruby; now I know it's not, but since I've seen the ring as hugely valuable monetarily for years, it's hard to make my brain understand that really, it's not. What I'm saying here is that sometimes someone else's knowledge is more valuable than your own.

Living in India will make you rethink all your previous irritations really quickly. I flew out of Eugene, Oregon bound for Chennai. The last coffee place I visited in the States had run out of nondairy creamer; I was pissed because, like, I'm a vegan so I do no harm. *Shut up*, I now tell that past "me": most of the village people you meet in India have literally never experienced the feeling of "full"; they have never loosened a belt or popped the button on their jeans as a symptom of overeating. The size of your large popcorn bucket is utterly incomprehensible to them. Milk comes in a vacuum-sealed pouch in India; if villagers can afford it they have most likely worked harder than you; and coffee is a luxury.

I lived at the Ananda Ashram near Pondicherry while completing their intensive residential six-month Yoga Teacher training. Ashram living is not for the wanderlust traveler. MC Yogi is not here, not everyone wants a hug, and if you are wearing a bindi you are wearing only one and it is with sincerity, to remind other people that we should be residing here, at the ajna chakra, the center

for deep contemplation. Living in an Ashram is like living in an intentional community only that the person you'll spend most time with exists only in your mind. That little demon in your head that has been telling you that you are ugly and stupid for years will be given a microphone. With nothing else to do you will sit down and listen, but with no place to escape to and a routine you can't get out of, you will start to notice that the demon is not you, you're the one listening, and you don't have to. Ashram life runs like clockwork; the same things happen at the same time every day, and it can feel like you are going around in circles, but when you look back you see that you are actually spiraling upward. In India I learned about consolidating the community in my own head.

When I left India I just sort of floated around Greece and Cyprus for a few months, with no fixed group of people and no real plan. It was the opposite of community and it was alarmingly destructive. I left India feeling like I was Captain of my own vessel and arrived in New Zealand having forgotten how to swim. Unless you are a monk or a nun, people need people. I think even monks and nuns need people.

The moral of the story is: find a passion, have goals, surround yourself with other people with clear passions and goals, and then talk to each other. Hopefully you will come to understand some truths that are different from your own, and those moments of understanding will propel you forward in a direction that will be good for everyone. 🐦

Eridani Baker is a yoga teacher living in Auckland, New Zealand. She has spent time living in Melbourne, Greece, Cyprus, Oregon, London, and India. Her dream is to start a yoga studio that doubles as a permaculture education centre.

REDISCOVERING COMMUNITY:
A family's journey back to appreciating Home

By Devon Bonady

This fall, my family received an unexpected gift, in the form of an unsolicited offer to buy our homestead. When I agreed to write an article for this issue of COMMUNITIES, I had no idea that this gift was coming to my family. I was planning to write about my family's journey towards finding our true vision of community. Before I got too far into writing, we were blindsided with the unexpected offer and my daily life became an emotional roller coaster. One day I was excited and ready to pass our home along to a wonderful family and find our new community—one that would be larger and more "intentional" than we have at our single-family homestead. The next day I was in tears imagining the effort it would take to explore and find a new home with a toddler and newborn in tow, not to mention a not-very-mobile family business. (We run an edible, medicinal, and native plant nursery.) At one point in the process, I even drafted this article as if I had sold my "home," because that is what I thought we were going to do! We had an opportunity to really delve into the emotions and issues on both sides of our choice.

The happy ending of the story could be that we accepted the offer with gratitude and grace, appreciating the way in which it allowed us to pursue finding community in a new place, something that we have been envisioning. But that's not the happy ending we are living now. The gift for us was the chance to very seriously examine the reality of leaving our home, which until this point was just a "pipe dream" or visionary idea. After much examination and many long nights, the gift allowed us to really see how much community does exist in our lives and to appreciate all that we have instead of longing for that ideal place with "more."

Here are some of the issues we have been dealing with in the past few years around creating and finding (or re-finding) community where we are and elsewhere:

Community is not static. How can we stay in one place, continue to get our community needs met, and adapt to change?

I have lived in the same small western Oregon town for over 15 years, with a few short breaks, and have lived on the same land for over 11 years. While I have stayed, so much has changed! When I look around at the friends I have in my neighborhood, only a handful have been here even half of the time that I have. My neighbors have changed drastically and, because of that, my friends and local community too. Quite a lot of people have come and gone here on our property as well. In some ways, that is the nature of community, especially among 20- and early 30-year-olds.

Community is not static. Even if I stay in one place, community changes around me. This has positive and negative impacts. I appreciate change and, I, too, am always changing, as my vision for community also changes. When I first moved to this small town, I was excited to have like-minded 20-somethings around me, doing service work and environmental work and spending a lot of time getting to know each other. Many of my wonderful friends from that time have moved on, and as a parent, I am now seeking other people with small children focused on alternative education. Committed to staying here, I try to adjust and create new avenues for community. Sometimes I get frustrated and sad and miss "the old days." Then I wonder, "Could I find more of what I need now somewhere else?"

The paradox of wanting to grow roots in one place, but participating in the ever changing community that grows out of our modern "moving" culture.

I have lived here longer than any other place in my life. When I moved here in 2000, as a young college graduate, I was excited to move across the country. I was also excited to grow roots and make a serious commitment to place: land and community. To me, the idea of "home" is meant to be for the long haul. Fifteen years later, I am a mother and overwhelmed and apprehensive about moving at all, especially if it means moving away from my first-ever "home." Now, as before, I seek a stable long-term committed community.

Having children and creating a family has helped me see how important extended family is for our overall health and well-being. Traditionally, in early "American" culture, before suburbia and the push to move for a career, most people grew up and grew old in the same place, surrounded by family. Whether or not they got along exceptionally well, family members helped each other when needed; grandparents and aunts and uncles watched young children so their parents could work. In many cases, children had instant playmates. I experienced much of this, growing up in Wisconsin within an hour of where my parents grew up and where all of my family lived. As an only child, I still had frequent playtime with my cousins and lots of social time with many aunts and uncles. Now, I am very far from that family in physical distance and in lifestyle choices and values. When I think about what community lifestyle I envision for my family, I see how it is very close to what the extended family role has been. Basically, what my husband and I, as well as many of the intentional community and cohousing seekers out there are looking for, is to **create a new extended family**.

One of the main challenges I see is that people are still moving. At this point, if I want to stay in one place, the place where my "new" extended family also lives, I need to either accept that members of this family will come and go, or make some kind of pact with family members that we all agree to stay together or move together. The latter seems quite unrealistic, even for true relatives. For now, I see that accepting the fluidity of community and "family" will allow me to accept and appreciate what I have.

As a new parent, my needs for community are changing. My family's needs for community are changing and our vision for community is changing. Do we adapt to what we have, find ways to create what we want, or find a new "home?"

A year after I moved to this town, I was very excited to be part of a dynamic community of inspiring people. My previous plans to travel fell away as I made the choice to delve into community and place. I attended a 10-day course at an intentional community less than an hour drive from my current home. During my stay, I met some amazing people and learned about the personal growth work that the community was focused on at that time. Recognizing my need to do similar work, I participated in several courses over the next five months and then made a decision to move to the intentional community. I felt sad to leave the place I first landed and yet knew I needed to make the move.

One of my friends responded to my choice by saying, "So, the grass is always greener, huh?" At the time this statement truly hurt me because I felt fear that I was letting down the people I had committed to work with that year. It also shook up the part of me that always feels uncertain and ungrounded about large decision-making experiences. Is there really something better or am I just projecting my vision onto a different place instead of trying to create what I want where I am?

Reflecting on that experience, moving was just what I needed. And soon I came back to this community where I first landed, to reconnect with friends like the person I mentioned above, who remains an essential part of my community to this day. This reflection reminds me to follow my instinct and heart, and trust that the right path will unfold.

If we want to find a new "home," where and how do we start our search?

Visioning is always the first step for me. I like to do visioning every year for my personal needs and goals, my work and business goals, and my family. As new and busy parents, our visioning took a back seat after our

Devon Bonady.

Rachel Foster

Lindsay Howells, a friend and community member who lived and worked with us this past year, mixing earth straw and sand to install a beautiful earthen floor in our home.

Brian Basor

Our seasonal intern Claire helped us with growing and harvesting food.

Brian Basor

son was born. As we talked casually about finding ways to better meet our needs for community, we kept "meaning" to find time for more visioning. The reality of making a serious legally-binding decision to move forced us to put visioning back at the top of the list. As I looked through our old vision writing, it was interesting to note two things. Our vision that we worked hard to write out clearly has changed very little. Much of our current home and community is aligned with our vision, except for a few key things. The key things are what we grapple with and what urged me on to considering a move.

With our vision in hand, including general geographic areas of preference, it was time to start searching. I felt daunted, and still do, about the idea of finding the community we envision, knowing that we might not find a place that fits all of our criteria. I want to be hopeful and trust that we will find what we need, yet also must keep my feet grounded in reality so that we can be successful. That is why we must include in our vision the following questions: **What do we need? What can we give up? Can we make it work where we are?**

Our initial search included searching the ic.org site for communities that might fit our specific vision of living rurally with other families interested in home-schooling and creating community around children while also allowing us to make at least some of our living off the land. We found some great questions posted by some communities to help us clarify our needs and how we might fit best in one or another intentional community or cohousing setting. I particularly appreciated the following questions, from Champlain Valley Cohousing:

> **What about you (and your family) makes cohousing a good choice for you?**
> **What is the one thing—yes, an actual thing—that you could never live without in your next home?**
> **In fifteen words or less, what's most important for your happiness?**
> **What do you need that you don't have right now? (There's no wrong answer!)**

During our search, we found a few options that looked good "on paper" at least. It was easy for me to get very excited about the possibilities, then have a reality check reminder that we really have no idea what a community is like until we visit and get to know the people. For me and my family, community is all about people. At that point, and the place we are today, we feel like we need to visit places and stay a while to really get a sense of if that place might be worth considering our future home. That said, traveling across the country with a toddler and newborn is not easy. Not to mention that we have a homestead and nursery to care for at home, although luckily we have great neighbors willing to help out a little. And those great neighbors are the people who keep bringing me back to focus on staying where we are.

The lesson I learn when I get the chance to spend time with my "real" extended family is to focus on shared values to create connection. I believe that is also one way to discover and rediscover commu-

nity in my current home. Instead of seeing the differences between me and others in my existing community, if I focus on the similarities such as shared values, shared needs, and shared vision, I will see the possibilities!

In recent years, I have worked hard to create opportunities to feel surrounded by the community that I want. When my first son was born, I began to see clearly that I needed a network of moms. I started a weekly play group at my home with a handful of mothers and young children in my town. Whether the children played together or not, it was a great chance for us mothers and fathers to connect and share resources and support. I also started a child-care trade with a good friend and neighbor which has continued consistently for over a year. We each watch our two boys for one morning a week, which means we each get one morning free. We also have time to connect and chat before and after. I find that regular scheduled meet-ups are the key to consistency and continuation of relationship. Some of these same families and others from a nearby larger city have joined us in celebrating seasonal festivals; this is very nourishing for me.

Our business and homestead have also provided opportunities for creating community. We have two smaller structures on our land where we can house guests or young people excited to learn by helping us. This past year we hosted two people who helped us grow food and plants for our nursery business. We also hosted someone who helped us install an earthen floor, do home remodeling and a variety of maintenance and building projects. We shared meals and other opportunities to connect as these people became enfolded in our family life.

Our nursery and botanical sanctuary hosts workshops for local people to learn about plants and gardening. My husband and I both get the chance to teach on- and off-site. We enjoy the connections made through teaching with other institutions, communities, and individuals. Our business thrives on word of mouth and personal connection. We also hold open houses for people to come and see what we do. We have strengthened our community ties through our business as well as personal endeavors.

During the time in which we were grappling with our timely decision to sell our land and start again, we attended and hosted events for our nursery business. Each day that we spent connecting with people about our passion for plants and food and healing I could see how lucky we are to be part of this community. While I struggled to remain grounded in choosing to go or stay, I felt an upswelling of appreciation for my friends and community as I called on them to listen and give advice about this big decision. It was the biggest decision I have ever made in my life. And it was so amazing to have so many people to call and talk with, most of whom live nearby. Imagining that we might choose to move across the country, away from such a strong support network, helped me to appreciate my community and home so much more. ❧

I struggled to remain grounded in choosing to go or stay.

Devon Bonady is a gardener, mother, and teacher living in the Oregon forest. She is excited about creating and participating in community around family, nature-based homeschooling, and seasonal festivals. She can be reached at devon@fernhillsanctuary.com.

Finding a Healthy, Happy Cohousing Community that Fits Your Values

By Cynthia Dettman

How does one go about locating a cohousing community that is a good personal fit? Here are my suggestions on how to go about finding a healthy, vibrant, and happy community.

For lots of background information, join and follow the national cohousing listserv (www.cohousing.org/cohousing-l) to read current conversations that are taking place. Watch videos about cohousing (www.cohousing.org/videos) and read the *Best of* COMMUNITIES Cohousing Compilation (www.ic.org/community-bookstore/product/cohousing-compilation). Use a variety of ways to do your research (www.cohousing.org/node/1717) and follow Diana Leafe Christian's tips for making the most of your cohousing visits (www.cohousing.org/node/1538). Go to meetings, eat meals, and interview people. Don't be afraid to ask the hard questions, and don't rely on what just a handful of people tell you.

If you really are adventuresome and willing to relocate, travel the country and visit a wide variety of communities, as did Keith Carlson (maryandkeith.blogspot.com) and Two Chicks and a Guppie (twochicksandaguppy.wordpress.com). Or find a housesitting or short-term rental opportunity (www.ic.org/short-term-vacation-cohousing-a-great-way-to-learn) in a community. Better yet, rent or share a rental with someone in a community for a longer period, as I did, before making a commitment.

What Will Your Questions Be?

Identify first your own high priority needs and values. Are you mostly looking for a sense of community? Or is sustainability an equal passion, with specific ideas you want to see implemented? Do you most value support for aging in place? Living with many generations, including children? Support for children and families? A high level of shared resources and activities? A farm or ecovillage with lots of land and gardens, or an urban, bicycle community? Intense focus on sustainability and climate change activism, or not so much? A spiritual focus and strong commitment to consensus, or more focus on efficiency with some hierarchy involved? A community with a lot of meetings and teams, or one with less to do and more fun? Shared meals that cater to your food preferences, or are you an omnivore?

Communal Life

Most folks are drawn to cohousing communities primarily for their social, collab-

orative, and communal cultures. Here are the questions you might ask:

• How do people get along at such close quarters and how well do they communicate?

• What is the community's culture in regard to decision-making and conflicts?

• Generally, how do people treat each other?

• Are children's and families' needs addressed?

• Are people helpful and caring in times of crisis?

• Does the community use a traditional consensus model of decision-making and how successful is it?

• Has sociocracy (www.cohousing.org/node/2610) been considered?

• How much time is spent in meetings?

• Is the community in transition and why?

• How high is the participation rate in the ongoing work of maintaining the community?

• How well does the meals program function and how important is it to the community's sense of family?

• How does the community handle "difficult" people who are not as skilled in expressing and resolving concerns in a positive, collaborative, compassionate, and solution-focused manner?

• Are renters treated as equal participants, including in decision-making?

My recent visits to three cohousing communities in Santa Fe confirmed my sense that communities do go through stages, and that strong meals programs, regularly used shared spaces, and a culture of respectful communication are three keys to creat-ing a happy environment.

According to Ellen Kemper, one of the founding members at The Commons (santaf-ecohousing.org) who seemed to have her finger on the pulse, her well-established community's social fabric is strong. "We truly love and respect each other here—it runs deep." The community has an active meals program and monthly work parties. Many have attended communication trainings and have actively worked to promote collaboration and peaceful conflict resolution.

At Sand River (www.sandriver.org), a seniors-only community, a consensus-based culture was established during formation by a spiritually inclined group of folks from Buddhist and Quaker backgrounds who already had experience with peaceful collaboration. "That really made a difference," says Pam Gilchrist, one of the founding members.

Another community was in a period of transition. At the small community of Tres Placitas (tresplacitas.blogspot.com), founding members chose to save for rather than immediately build a common building for shared activities. Later the plan was modified and the building was never built. They have also struggled with the consensus model of decision-making. But communities do evolve. The current residents are working hard to increase their connections, with more shared meals in their homes and more focus on collaboration.

What about a community's relationship to its neighbors and larger social environment? Here are more questions about external relations:

• If the community is or was a part of a larger-scale gentrification of the area, what is happening to support people and businesses of color in the area to prevent economic flight?

• What efforts did the community make at its inception to address racial diversity and affordability? What efforts are being made now?

• If the community is located in a low-income and racially diverse setting, does it welcome its neighbors and support "off campus" neighborhood events?

• Are there activists in the community who are working on social justice issues in the larger area?

Although Columbia Ecovillage, my community, appears to be primarily focused on sustainability, food production, and climate change issues, I've been pleased to see a fairly high degree of involvement in neighborhood issues. People don't want to put up a gate. CEV members are active in various area efforts to clean up, show up, and support the community. But we have not made much progress on making our units more affordable or accessible to lower-income folks. People of color seem a long way off, except for the African American and Latino neighbors living in large apartment complexes all around our four-acre property! More could be done. This is probably true of many communities.

Cynthia Dettman

A recent weekly community dinner with 50 family and friends at The Commons on the Alameda, Santa Fe.

Sustainability

Cohousers are also drawn to cohousing because of its focus on sustainability. People want to live a smaller, simpler life with less impact on the environment. In my case, I was primarily drawn to one aspect of sustainability: gardening and farming and producing healthy food. What I didn't know was that in this "ecovillage," the largest source of conflicts appear to be related to land and plantings. I didn't know that we had sustainability factions with hot disagreements between ornamental gardening, native plant, and permaculture factions. We disagree about planting and taking down trees, about moving plants, about maintaining the landscaping, about how we will continue to do the hard manual work as people age. And we have eco-activists like Marilee Dea (atu.com/news/local/City-Council-approves-anti-oil-train-resolution-considering-another) and permaculture advocates in our village who may be disappointed that most other members of the community are not so interested or engaged. Find out what exactly your prospective community is focused on in its efforts to be sustainable and decide if the type of focus is a good fit for you.

Take Responsibility!

There is no perfect cohousing community. As you interview residents, you will probably hear a wide range of opinions about how healthy or happy their community is. One resident will tell you there are lots of problems and conflicts. Another will tell you that the community is harmonious and that folks are content. A third may be moving out because cohousing didn't fit them, and a fourth may tell you it's the best thing they ever did.

Once you choose a community that seems the best bet, take responsibility to create an experience that is fulfilling, peaceful, and satisfying to you. In the final analysis, much of your satisfaction will depend on where you place your focus, with whom you spend time, and with which areas of the community's work you want to be engaged. If you are actively involved in governance, you may experience significant conflicts and need to become skilled at compassionate assertiveness. If you contribute service hours only to activities you truly enjoy, such as gardening or cooking where policies are not being debated, you may be happy as a clam. If you hang out with folks who are unhappy, you may become more unhappy yourself. If you have trouble adjusting to the relative lack of privacy and autonomy in a community, you may rebel. And if you have fixed opinions about how things should be done, you may make yourself miserable.

I moved into my community in stages; first a three-month rental, then a 12-month

> Much of your satisfaction will depend on where you place your focus: which people and work areas you invest your time in.

rental, then finally a purchase. When I first moved in, I threw myself into multiple work groups and projects. I learned with time to better balance my community involvement with my life outside the community. I found I was not sufficiently motivated or skilled to participate in teams where I experienced a lot of conflict or domination by individuals. I became clearer about what aspects of community life I really enjoyed. I learned that governance leadership roles, after all, were not right for me. I also learned that I was most able to contribute to happiness and health through food production, cooking, and meals program support. It was up to me to create my own joy within a group of equally imperfect people and processes. My main aim was to be part of a "family," to share, to grow spiritually, and to develop greater patience and serenity. I contribute to larger policy issues but try to do it in a respectful and constructive manner. My aims have been more than met. I hope yours will be as well. ❧

Cynthia Dettman recently toured the Southwest in her camper van and visited four cohousing communities, delighting in their variety. For more details on cohousing in Salt Lake City, Utah and Santa Fe, New Mexico, check out her blog posts on cohousing at Voyage to the Present (voyagetothepresent.wordpress.com). Cynthia has been a member of her community's conflict resolution team and is working on developing her NVC (nonviolent communication) skills. At Columbia Ecovillage (columbiaecovillage.org) in Portland, Oregon, she leads the meals team and tries to inspire cooks to prepare delicious and affordable food for meals and celebratory events.

Queer, Person of Color, or Low-Income; IS COHOUSING POSSIBLE FOR ME?

By Cynthia Dettman

The predominant demographics of American cohousing communities are pretty clear: white, middle or upper middle class income and background, educated, liberal, with a strong tilt towards older folks and older women. There is a small sprinkling of non-white people, but very few are African American, Latino, Native American, or Asian. What are the realistic options for people who are interested in cohousing but don't fit the typical profile?

My experience has been positive, but I have only one mild strike against me, and in a liberal pool, it's barely a strike. I'm a lesbian.

Birds of a feather flock together. LGBT folks have created their own intentional communities for decades with need for safety and support (see www.ic.org/wiki/queer-community). In North Carolina, Village Hearth Cohousing (www.villagehearthcohousing.com) is forming for LGBT folks and allies. The current planning group is an all-lesbian group of older women. As the US has become more gay-positive, most cohousing communities pride themselves on LGBT acceptance.

My only complaint at Columbia Ecovillage (columbiaecovillage.org), where I live, is that I feel invisible. There are so few of us queer folk and our rich history as a minority subculture is lost in the homogeneity of our largely heterosexual community. Most of us LGBT folks are older, which means we grew up in a more closeted, conservative era and are not on the cutting edge of queer culture.

Aitch Muirhead (theadventuresofaitchalexandar.com), a young transitioning man who lives with his wife at Wasatch Commons (content.csbs.utah.edu/~ehrbar/coho) in Salt Lake City, has felt accepted during his transition from woman to man and the couple are happy to be living in a supportive community. If we queer folk were half our communities, however, and if more of us openly challenged traditional gender and sexuality norms by refusing gender pronouns or practicing polyamory, there would likely be negative reactions or concern. In general, though, cohousing culture seems to be a safe place for those of us queer folk who can afford to join!

I do otherwise fit the cohousing profile: middle class, educated, liberal, and 64 years old. I am not a person of color nor am I poor. If I were, I would face almost insurmountable barriers to living in cohousing today.

Cohousing communities are increasingly concerned about their homogeneity, but seem pretty much stumped on what to do, particularly when it comes to race and ethnicity. Why do people of color not typically join cohousing planning groups nor purchase or rent in cohousing? When Diane Leafe Christian, a leader in the cohousing movement, queried how communities are responding to this challenge in a National Cohousing Association blog post (www.cohousing.org/node/1672), it looks she didn't get any replies. She was of the opinion, however, that cohousing communities are "welcoming" to people of color.

Tavi Baker, who works for the Boys and Girls Club of San Francisco and is one of several organizers of the The People of Color Sustainable Housing Network (www.meetup.com/People-of-Color-Sustainable-Housing-Network), would likely disagree. Baker has experience living in cooperative housing and attended meetings of the East Bay Cohousing network to consider cohousing, which is predominantly white. She left, she says, to join other people of color to set up the POC Network and to plan their own communities. "I was tired of being the only one in the room," Baker says.

Mainstream cohousing organizations tend to reproduce the same unequal power relationships that exist in society, says fellow organizer Deseree Fontenot, who is in the process of getting a masters degree in Social Transformation. POC Network organizers agree that cohousing and other communities must engage and provide a "point of entry" for people of color from their beginnings and must focus not only on sustainability and community, but also on activism and social change—including being willing to share power.

And, they say, people of color will not be drawn when they are a tiny minority in a white cohousing community. Without a critical mass of racial and ethnic minority representation, many interested people of color will not feel truly welcomed, no matter how friendly cohousing planners might be.

We liberal white folks are often unaware of our own attitudes and subtle behaviors when it comes to race and class. We typically lack personal connections to and within minority communities. We are often blind to our privileges and are not able to put ourselves in the shoes of someone who is racially or ethnically different, surrounded by white people. And we easily forget that people of color continue to be economically disadvantaged and targeted.

Some cohousers like Zev Paiss, a former Executive Director of the Cohousing Network, have theorized that people of color may not have the same need for intentional community as white folks do (www.ic.org/wiki/desire-diversity-cohousing-perspective). The POC Network organizers disagree. "There is a rich history of intentional communities developed by people of color," says POC Network organizer Lina Buffington, an organizational consultant and activist with a Ph.D. in Philosophy. African American farmers were the first to use land trusts in the South. The Black Panthers created a variety of communal housing groups. The MOVE activist community in Philadelphia lived communally. Most of these efforts, she says, were systematically destroyed by the white establishment, but all were en-

> ## We liberal white folks are often unaware of our own attitudes and subtle behaviors when it comes to race and class.

gaged in social justice work.

In the Bay Area there is clearly a high interest and demand among people of color for intentional community. The need is especially critical in Oakland and the Bay Area in general due to gentrification and extreme increases in housing costs. The POC Network, launched in February 2015 as a Meetup group, already has 140 members with 450 friends on Facebook. The Network's aim is to create and support the development of POC-centered sustainable communities, with an eclectic, connected network of alternative housing and organizing communities in the area. Options could include cohousing, land trusts, bedroom rentals, large shared houses, accessory dwelling units, and more rural communities with existing or new construction.

Cohousing communities today are typically not focused on issues of poverty, racism, sexism, immigration, LGBT or other community justice issues. In contrast, the POC Network's projects will emphasize social change activism by and among residents, with organizing centers and mutual networking and support. The leaders are themselves activists, and say that without this focus, people of color are unlikely to be attracted to cohousing communities.

The POC Network organizers report that they have drawn a racially diverse group of folks, including a significant number of LGBT people. Although the majority are in their 20s to 40s, the network hopes to draw an intergenerational community of participants. Currently their focus is to build infrastructure by raising funds for staff. Current projects include helping to develop two three-acre communities in East Oakland and El Sobrante using a land trust model. This model would allow communal land use that is affordable for low-income families in perpetuity, protecting residents from the vagaries of the housing market and economy.

Although the busy volunteers who have spearheaded this movement are focused on the Bay Area, they are in communication with a variety of similar efforts throughout the country. They are willing to provide support and consultation to other networks of color. "We are in the infancy stage," says Buffington, who was preparing to speak to a group in Atlanta who wanted to discuss ideas for a joint communal land purchase. "And we want to connect people to each other whenever we can."

I trust that this Network will be a catalyst for communities of color, at least in urban areas with high diversity and activism. I have doubts, however, that the current mainstream cohousing world will begin to attract more people of color without a significant shift to social justice aims and activities, and without better addressing issues of privilege and affordability.

The good news is that affordability is a hot topic within the cohousing world. Communities are very focused on environmental sustainability, and build or remodel housing units using green, high-cost technologies. Large properties with significant communal structures require higher prices. Many cohousing communities have various limits on the number of rentals permitted. Cohousing tends to be concentrated in urban areas with high housing costs in general. And because of the concentration of older residents, there is sometimes conservative resistance to non-traditional housing arrangements which may cost less.

Creative solutions are beginning to emerge, with some good results. Within the constraints of local housing regulations and available affordable housing programs, communities are expanding affordable options, including government-subsidized units, shared housing, and construction and rental of small accessory buildings.

At The Commons (santafecohousing.org) in Santa Fe, 11 casitas (little attached homes) were constructed next to their larger, more expensive homes to provide lower-cost rentals. At Sand River (www.sandriver.org) in Santa Fe, a seniors-only cohousing community, a partnership with a local affordable housing program permitted the construction and sale of several lower-cost homes. Troy Land and Gardens (www.communitygroundworks.org/what-we-do/troy-land-gardens) in Madison, Wisconsin uses a land trust model to create a majority of income-restricted homes. And the nonprofit Partnerships for Affordable Housing (www.affordablecohousing.org/home/mission) is working nationally to support the development of affordable cohousing options for low- and moderate-income residents, with a mission that includes empowerment of tenants and greater involvement in local community social justice goals.

As a person who has worked in social and empowerment services my whole life, I continue to feel ambivalent about the concentration of whiteness and relative wealth in cohousing. But if I were still living alone in a single family home, would I somehow have more integrity? Not really. I have to be honest that I am flocking with birds of my feather, and that I prefer communal living to solitude, no matter what social justice values I may find missing from my community. It's my own responsibility to promote these values within and without the fences of my ecovillage, and to help create the kind of community I want to see.

Cynthia Dettman is a lesbian and retired community college counselor who moved in to Columbia Ecovillage in 2014 and has not looked back. She worked as a legal aid attorney and later coordinated empowerment services for low-income women at Mt. Hood Community College. In retirement, she is writing about social justice issues, working on a novel set in South India where she grew up, teaching college success classes, and cooking gourmet meals for her cohousing community.

Aitch Muirhead and Shira Frank, a trans man and his spouse, who live at Wasatch Commons in Salt Lake City.

Photo courtesy of Cynthia Dettman

LEAVING EDEN:
One man's quest for community in a divided land

By David Leach

In the summer of 2010, the International Communal Studies Association gathered at a college near Afula, in Israel's Jezreel Valley. The symposium coincided with the centenary of the legendary kibbutz movement, but the event held an oddly mournful air. Some American and European members had balked at visiting the country in the aftermath of the Israeli Defense Force's Operation Cast Lead and the Gaza Flotilla deaths. The heyday of the kibbutz had passed, even attached to the iron lung of tenured attention. Over the previous decade, most of Israel's socialist communes had undergone "privatization" that stripped away the radical equality on which they'd been founded.

By the end of the conference, the scholars were hungry for inspirational words about our common future rather than bemoaning our tainted present or fixating on a nostalgic past. A panel of experts discussed the communal impulse and why it matters even more today, with the dogmatists of global capitalism waving victory flags. A feel-good aura descended on the auditorium.

Then a tall delegate with a shaved head raised a hand. He was in his mid-30s but dressed younger and had been video-recording talks and tweeting highlights on a smartphone. "Hi, I'm David," he said, in a North American accent. The moderator asked him to speak up. He talked about the growing divide between the ideals of the kibbutz and the global environmental and social-justice movements. He described how "Zionism" was becoming a dirty word for a generation of international activists and progressive Jews in the Diaspora.

"I've been surprised that 100 years after Zionism, 62 years after the founding of the State, 43 years into the Occupation of the West Bank and Gaza, there wasn't discussion whatsoever of an Arab-Palestinian narrative. Of how some kibbutzim were built on them. Of how Arabs who tried to join kibbutzim were refused membership. Of how the plan to create an Arab model for a kibbutz was not allowed. All this talk about how we're equal and we want to live together as equals just completely ignores the fact that...."

The room ignited. People clamoured to be heard. Several demanded the microphone. "This will tear the association apart!" shouted one Israeli academic. The moderator tried to regain control. "Stop right there!" he demanded. "I think that's a big area. We could spend a whole session on how the kibbutz has responded to the Occupation. But I would like to bring us back to this room. We are all experts in community...."

Clustered in the foyer, several attendees told David he had raised a vital question that still tainted the kibbutz: How can an intentional community of equals exist in a larger society of oppression? How long can the kibbutz—and Israel—ignore the aspirations of the Palestinian people before cognitive dissonance eroded their higher ideals? And how can an uncompromising seeker of utopia find a home in our broken world?

• • •

David Sheen seems an unlikely shit-disturber, a gentle giant with a restless heart and a buoyant optimism we can build a better world. That we *should*. A few days after the conference, we arranged to meet on the beachfront promenade of Tel Aviv. Even in a crowd, David stands out. He towers six inches above the average Israeli and eschews beach-wear for the radical chic of the urban anarchist. An Arab *keffiyeh* hung around his neck, a Mao cap perched on his bald dome.

Our rendezvous was next to the boarded-up shell of the Dolphinarium, a once-thriving nightclub. I asked what happened to it. David told me it was the site of a suicide bombing, in June 2001, at the start of the Second Intifada. A Palestinian bomber had walked into a queue of young Russian immigrants and detonated a belt of explosives. Twenty-one bystanders died; another 120 were injured by shrapnel. In 2003, Israel began to erect its Security Fence, ostensibly to prevent similar attacks. Nine years after the blast, Tel Aviv had sunk back into its days of languor, its nights of forgetting. And yet the Dolphinarium remained a derelict monument to the past.

David suggested we meet his journalist friends at a cafe on Ben Yehuda Street, so we dodged strollers and talked about his personal quest for the Holy Grail of community. He used the C-word with solemnity, as though "community" were as solid as the gold standard, the only thing of true value in a society that reduced every relationship to a commodity. And yet finding community, for David, had proven as elusive as tracking down El Dorado in the rain forests of the New World.

Talking to David felt like stepping back in time and meeting a kibbutz pioneer. He had the same intellectual intensity, I imagined, as the young Jewish *chalutzim* from Eastern Europe who had founded Degania, the original kibbutz, and built a new society from scratch. Like many of these pioneers, David grew up in a conservative, middle class Jewish family that ate kosher and went to synagogue on *shabbat*—in Toronto, in David's case, rather than Tsarist Russia or Poland. He was a bookish child with an artsy bent and a future guided by his bourgeois upbringing: a professional job in the city, big family, bigger house.

His father had been born in Israel; David had visited many times and spoke Hebrew, so he moved to Tel Aviv at age 25 to escape Canada's harsh winters and start a career as a graphic designer. But the art of advertising felt barren, and Tel Aviv's relentless entrepreneurialism lost its lustre, too. He longed to be an artist. Instead he found himself shilling for weapons-makers, pornography stores, and—even worse for a vegan—producers of *foie gras*. "How do I get out of this system?" he wondered. "How do I live a life that doesn't involve these moral quandaries?" His instinct was to get his hands dirty to cleanse his soul. "I had a romantic idea of going back to the land," he recalled. "I wanted to work in agriculture or horticulture, something to do with nature."

David was a creature of the city, however, and knew little about farming. He hadn't even joined the Scouts or Jewish youth groups as a kid. In Israel, he approached the Kibbutz Movement, where officials gauged his suitability for joining a community with a battery of psychological tests. "They weren't able to discover my inherent axe-murdering tendencies!" he joked. He was a young, healthy, well-educated, highly skilled, ideologically motivated immigrant from North America. He toured a different kibbutz every other weekend. Communities with open doors, however, tended to be in demographic decline or economic crisis and desperate for young blood. David had no interest in a kibbutz that had abandoned its socialist ideals. "I was looking for a place that had not gone through a privatization process—and wasn't planning on it."

He moved to his first kibbutz and marveled at desert scenery straight out of *Lawrence of Arabia*. There, David learned about permaculture and fell under the spell of a new religion:

David Sheen speaking at a church in Atlanta, Georgia in November 2015.

Photo courtesy of David Sheen

ecological architecture. "It really moved me," he recalled. "I ended up spending the next decade being obsessed with it."

He lived on the kibbutz for nearly six months. One weekend, he caught a bus to Tel Aviv for a wedding. In his absence, the

"I wanted there to be a community that was ecological and *really* socialist—not just socialist for the Jews."

kibbutz secretary posted a notice, called a meeting, and oversaw a vote in favour of an issue that troubled David: foreign labour. The original kibbutz movement had been built on the philosophy of "self-labour": neither exploiter nor exploited. However, over the years, many kibbutzes had outsourced farm labour to Arab hired hands, new Jewish immigrants, foreign volunteers and, more recently, Thai guest workers, who were often housed—and sometimes treated—like second-class citizens. Guest workers were a major issue on kibbutzes in this area. Many members felt the agricultural branches couldn't stay profitable without cheap labour. At the kibbutz, David had argued against the idea. In a kibbutz democracy, any important decision was usually advertised a week in advance, so members could mull the consequences before the vote in the general assembly. But this time, the decision happened in mere days. David felt betrayed.

"Many people's commitment to human rights and against racism ranked lower than economic concerns," he said. "And the way of getting that decision approved was antidemocratic. What depressed me was that even in a community of 150 people there was still political manipulation. I realize that in a system of millions there will be a lot of abuse. That's why I want to live in community, so that we can have human-level interactions with each other and honest dialogue, not bureaucratic interactions. But that wasn't the case here."

After the decision to allow guest workers, he couldn't live on the kibbutz in good conscience. He wrote a long, emotional letter and left copies in every member's mailbox. Then he walked out of the desert Eden.

"At first, I didn't know what the solution was," he admitted. "I wanted there to be a

community that was ecological and *really* socialist—not just socialist for the Jews."

Before leaving the kibbutz, David had articulated his evolving political philosophy to his boss, who gave him a copy of *The Dispossessed* by the science-fiction author Ursula K. Le Guin. In her novel, a tribe of austere anarchists live as colonists on a moon that circles a planet ruled, in stark contrast, by a decadent capitalist society. David felt inspired again. He read everything he could about anarchism and discovered a philosophical tradition deeper than the stereotypes of bomb-tossers and punk-rock anthems. "These are the principles that are important to me," he realized. "This is an accurate description of how the world should be." The self-sufficient cooperative society of equals mirrored ideas in Peter Kropotkin's classic manifesto *Mutual Aid*, the blueprint for the early kibbutz movement. In Israel, a hundred years of compromises had eroded these ideals. David realized he was frustrated living in a society that wasn't—and didn't want to be—as good as it could be. He wanted utopia in *his* lifetime, not his grandchildren's.

David returned to North America and apprenticed with reclusive eco-building gurus in mud-walled, straw-baled, solar-paneled, compost-toileted off-the-grid lairs. He learned how to hand-craft "cob" houses. He studied "biomimicry," the design philosophy that mirrors, rather than dominates, its natural surroundings. A friend donated a video camera, so David recorded interviews as he travelled around the world to the meccas of natural building: the cob mansions of Dorset, England; the millennium-old rock-hewn cities in Ethiopia; the straw-roofed villages and mud mosques of Ghana; the adobe counterculture "earthships" in New Mexico. He edited the footage into a documentary extolling what he called "uncompromising ecological architecture." He had seen the future. And it was made of mud.

In 2006, he returned to Tel Aviv and organized a collective of eco-communards to start an off-the-grid settlement. For a hundred years, Zionist organizations had helped young Jews colonize the Promised Land. But a band of anarchists who rejected corporate capitalism? No thanks—not any more. David's collective of Israeli eco-anarchists faced a dilemma. "We were too politically radical to get funds from the state, nor would some of us have wanted to," he said. "But there wasn't a critical mass of us to start from scratch."

Then David remembered visiting Kibbutz Samar, in the Arava Desert. He returned to give a talk there about ecological building, stayed for 10 days, and asked if he could remain longer. Samar had been founded in 1976 as a rejection of authority and bureaucracy—of the state, of the family, of the old kibbutz hierarchy. Its members were true anarchists. The kibbutz's economy was built on organic date plantations and members had rejected the "need" to recruit cheap Thai labour for the harvesting. It was perhaps the last kibbutz in Israel to hold to the original Zionist ideal of self-labour: *Do the work yourself or not at all.*

• • •

Other communities had embraced a libertarian philosophy of almost total freedom, both in Israel and abroad, but few lasted more than a year or two. "Samar deserves its place in the communal equivalent of the *Guinness Book of World Records*," observed Daniel Gavron, in 2000, after a visit. Not everyone was impressed by Samar's woolly ways. In Tel Aviv, I asked a kibbutz leader and former member of the Israeli Parliament about the anarchists in the Arava Valley. "Samar is not a kibbutz!" he exclaimed. "They're like Bedouins in the desert!"

Just the idea of Samar divided people. The kibbutz had been founded by young members from traditional kibbutzes disillusioned with the ideological drift of their homes. Samar's founders declined an offer to settle in the occupied Golan Heights and travelled instead to the desert on a quest for wisdom. Here, away from prying eyes, they could discard their parents' mistakes. Here, communal living would give people more freedom, not less. What they wanted was a blank slate—both freedom *to* and freedom *from*, in the famous distinction by philosopher Isaiah Berlin. Freedom to express their better selves. Freedom from bureaucratic rules. After retiring from public life to Kibbutz Sde Boker in the Negev Desert, David

Ben-Gurion, Israel's founding prime minister, had written: "For those who make the desert bloom there is room for hundreds, thousands, and even millions." The pioneers of Samar took him at his word.

It's hard to separate fact from legend in the story of Samar. On the kibbutz, no single authority, no guru set the rules or even said there were no rules. Such *laissez faire* anarchism had been tried in communes and hippie outposts throughout North America and Europe. It usually imploded after a few years, when finances ran low and emotional tensions ran high. Love might be free; not much else was. Somehow the members of Samar made it work. They did away with the weekly work schedule and job rotation. Members decided when and where they laboured; if a kibbutznik needed help on a job, to milk the cows or pick the dates or scrub the kitchen, he or she made a request, stated the case, and took whomever would come. Usually, the work got done. Samar's financial philosophy was equally radical. In the traditional kibbutz system, every member received a tiny allowance while the kibbutz paid for living expenses. To buy anything extra, a member had to plead to the finance committee; the result of the vote was final. The tense, political, and often humiliating experience made adult members feel like pre-teens asking their parents for a raise in allowance.

Samar said to hell with that. If members couldn't trust each other, their community was doomed, so they agreed to keep an open cash box. If someone needed to take a trip to Tel Aviv or Jerusalem, they could go into the dining room, flip open the lid, and—if enough money was there—remove the bus fare and maybe a few shekels for a falafel. The box was refilled with profits from the date orchards or other enterprises. If the cash box was bare, everyone made do.

The common purse was a giant middle-finger to the Tragedy of the Commons—the thought experiment that assumes when a resource can be accessed collectively, people will devour more than their fair share until the resource has been squandered. Conservatives believe the Tragedy proves our genes really are selfish and we should accept capitalism as natural law; some environmental activists use the Tragedy's outcome to argue for state intervention before we consume all our natural resources. Samar's experiment in radical trust cast doubt on the theory.

• • •

On Samar, David Sheen found an outlet for his restless energies amid the social, cultural, and political life of the desert commune. He held slideshows and films, talks and concerts. Inspired by his experiences at the Burning Man Festival in Nevada's Black Rock Desert, he tried to organize a similar event on Samar. He made an immediate impression on the kibbutz—and not always a welcome one.

David understood his communal faux pas. "What I did was the equivalent of walking up to your face and screaming. In the city, you have to be loud for anyone to hear you—there are so many competing messages. In a community, they don't have huge billboards, you don't have the same level of intense dialogue and debate. It's quiet. It's the desert. You have to be more measured in your discourse. Some people felt that I had come to the community and started preaching. Some people felt that I was talking too loud. Other people felt I had no right to do it at all. They said, 'Only after living here for seven years do you have a right to start talking about your opinions.'" Even an anarchist utopia has rules, apparently. "Obviously, I can't abide that," said David. "That's stymieing voices. That's not cool. It's imperial to say, 'We'll take your labour but not your personal opinions.'"

When David applied for full membership, residents of Samar debated his suitability, whether his personality felt simpatico with the kibbutz. His friends could not sway the skeptics. The vote failed. David could remain living there as a non-member. But he didn't want to live in a village where he felt the majority of his neighbours didn't value his voice and might not even want him around. It was a painful discovery. After a decade of searching, David

found his personal utopia, an organic Eden in the desert of Israel that was more than a mirage. Samar had only one problem: the kibbutz didn't want David.

• • •

David still lives in Israel. He copy-edited for the left-wing newspaper *Ha'aretz* and produced documentaries and YouTube exposés. He fights the rightward political tilt in Israel and gives presentations around the world about his experiences. During the "J14" economic protests in the summer of 2010, when young activists camped out in Tel Aviv and 500,000 people marched the city's streets, David chronicled how even this mass revival of progressive ideals avoided any mention of the Occupation. His country continued to frustrate his ideals.

"Why do you keep being drawn back to Israel?" I asked. He seemed locked in a love-hate relationship that bordered on the codependent. "Do you consider yourself a Zionist? An eco-Zionist?"

"That's a loaded question," he replied. "Today, there is a new parlance. Yes, there is Zionist. There is also anti-Zionist. There is also non-Zionist. There is also post-Zionist."

David professed to be an "ambi-Zionist"—a Jew who has not firmly committed to Zionism, non-Zionism, or anti-Zionism. "Someone who is still on the fence," he explained, "because they feel there are some positive elements to the word and some negative elements to it."

David still felt the tug of family and cultural history in Israel. It fueled his extended

> ## He had found his personal utopia, an organic Eden in the desert. Its only problem: the kibbutz didn't want David.

argument with the divided nation. "I do feel a connection to the land." He laughed. "Call it education, call it brainwashing."

A year and a half after I first met David Sheen, I was back in Israel and curious if he had made any progress in his quest for community. He and his now-wife had moved from Tel Aviv into a rental unit in Jaffa, so I reunited with him under the clock tower at *(continued on p. 74)*

LEAVING EDEN:
ONE MAN'S QUEST FOR COMMUNITY IN A DIVIDED LAND

(continued from p. 27)

the entrance to the Old City. David was shooting activist videos about racist incidents against Ethiopian immigrants and the internment of Sudanese refugees. His wife was Jamaican-Canadian and often felt uncomfortable walking the streets of Tel Aviv. "She thinks that people here look at her like she is ugly," said David. "Over time, that wears you down."

The couple was planning to move to Dimona, a town of 33,000 in the Negev Desert. Dimona was also home to Israel's nuclear facilities and a community of so-called "Black Hebrews." In 1969, the 40 original Black Hebrews followed their charismatic leader from Chicago to Israel. They were African Americans who believed they belonged to the lost tribe of Judah and lobbied for citizenship under Israel's Law of Return. More followed and stayed illegally in the country. They forged a syncretic religion from Torah laws, African traditions, and their own unique holidays. Orthodox rabbis never recognized their claims of ancestry; only a handful of the 3,000 residents ever received citizenship. In 1984, the Speaker of the Israeli Parliament threatened to evict them with force; two years later, a standoff with the Israeli Army nearly ended in bloodshed. And yet the Black Hebrews remained in Dimona until they became an accepted, if eccentric, facet of the nation's multicultural mosaic. "Your community is beloved in Israel," said President Shimon Peres on a visit in 2008. "Your destiny is our destiny." Their gospel choir tours Israel and overseas, while the locally grown, organic, vegan diet of the Black Hebrews has become so fashionable that they opened restaurants in Jerusalem and Tel Aviv. A banner above their gate announces to new arrivals: *Welcome to the Village of Peace.*

"If you're talking utopian communities," David told me, "at least in Israel, I can think of few that are so exemplary."

Well, except for one hitch, according to David: the Black Hebrews remain a patriarchal cult of personality that treats women as second-class citizens. "They're old school," he said. "There are things that we can't accept." He and his wife were considering how to enjoy their company without joining the settlement. "If we move next to them, we could have the advantage of having them as a community—without living by their rules."

The injustices he witnessed on a daily basis in Tel Aviv and Jaffa, his own financial insecurity and awareness of getting older made David philosophical about the receding possibilities of utopia. Can we ever reframe how we live as a society to be more fair and less damaging to our planet?

"I used to think we could change *everywhere*—that we could create a small fractal to change everything. Then I thought, at least we could create something that could be a refuge from all the shit. Now, I'm at the point where I don't think I'm capable of doing that. Not for a community and not even for myself. So I'm willing to accept less shitty. Less cesspool in my life—that's my goal right now."

"That's not exactly a good bumper sticker," I suggested. *"A Life Less Shitty."*

He laughed. "I shouldn't be a motivational speaker!"

The road from ideal to compromise, from utopia to suburbia, is a well-worn path. I'd seen it repeated on every kibbutz I'd visited; it pulls at every alternative community that dreams of a creating a perfect society in an imperfect world. Building community will always be ad-hoc and messy. David Sheen's frustrated quest for a flawless city upon the hill to call home was hardly unique. It reflected the century-long plot arc of an entire movement.

He nodded at the suggestion. "It really is the evolution of the kibbutz." ≈

David Leach is the Chair of the Department of Writing at the University of Victoria and the author of Chasing Utopia: The Kibbutz in a Divided Israel *(ECW Press, Fall 2016).*

The Dog that Brought Us a Community

By Jim Daly

The Fates can be capricious. Three years ago I was hale and hearty, financially sound, and my novel had just been published. The doctors caught my wife's breast cancer in its earliest stage and had successfully removed the affected tissue. Though she still faced a program of radiation, we felt optimistic.

The sun shone on my two grandchildren, me, and our terrier as we played in the backyard with a weakly inflated volleyball. My wife smiled upon us through the kitchen window while she peeled apples for a pie. I kicked the ball into the air and we all ran, yelling, to retrieve it. The Fates have their fun. I reached the ball as my dog grabbed for it. Her tooth grazed my finger, breaking the skin on the order of a paper cut. So minor that I didn't stop playing. Nothing serious, right?

The next evening I didn't feel well and went to bed early. In the morning, my wife could not awaken me. At the hospital, I was diagnosed with septic shock and was helicoptered to a bigger hospital in Seattle. I was in a coma for a week and kept in the hospital and rehab facility for two months. When I was able to come off dialysis, I returned home 40 pounds lighter, balance problems, no fingers and nubs of thumbs on both hands. The Fates lost interest in me.

Eventually, I regained my strength and health but could no longer count on my fingers. I was confronted with a series of challenges. Putting on my socks for the first time was a great victory. Even though everyone around me seemed amazed at all the things I was able to accomplish, some challenges flummoxed me. I could no longer mow our large lawn or clean the gutters on our two-story house. My wife became cancer-free and assumed many of my duties. I felt less of a man and slipped into a dark hole.

My doctor prescribed Zoloft and counseling, and I climbed slowly out of my "melancholy," a.k.a. depression. We decided that we needed less yard and a smaller house closer to town. We also had a taste of the care and love, that came during our period of need, from our congregation and from acquaintances we knew only slightly.

Because I had experienced how life can change in a moment, I had a new feeling of vulnerability. Our neighborhood seemed sterile. The houses were far apart, with many vacant lots in between. The neighbors nodded and waved politely, but withdrew into their houses, garages, cars without much contact.

I had left my slowly accrued friends in southern California, and had not made any close ones in the 10 years we had lived in the small town of Port Townsend, Washington. We wanted to become part of an involved community. We wanted more friends.

One evening, we ran into a couple we knew, Pat and David, at Sweet Laurette's, a restaurant in town. They too had some physical limitations and were pondering how they could take charge of their future. They had heard of a concept that was both intriguing and quite foreign to my wife and me, the idea of being in what our friends described as a committed community, among like-minded people committed to being supportive, cooperative, friendly, and helpful. But because it seemed like an overwhelming undertaking, a pie in the sky idea, I left it on the table along with the remains of my pasta dinner.

Then our church's education classes offered a course in *Aging Successfully*. My wife and I got in on the last session, and found our friend Pat from the restaurant leading the class. Different ideas were being discussed for a senior population on how to take charge over the course of their aging. One of the speakers, a handsome man in baggy pants named Chuck Durrett, along with his pretty wife Katie, turned out to be the gurus of cohousing in the US and Canada.

His imaginative ideas grabbed us. The idea of a group of like-minded people buying a site, hiring an architect, and constructing their own community sounded inviting but scary. We talked more to Pat and David. As it turned out, the project was already in progress. They had gathered a small group, hired McCamant & Durrett, Architects, and were in the process of moving forward.

Being curious but cautious as we always have been, we took a half-way step and became associate members of Quimper Village. We attended meetings, joined one of the teams, and went to the social gatherings. The caliber of the members, their congeniality, and

(continued on p. 78)

Photos courtesy of Jim Daly

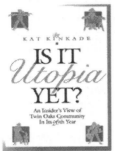
THE DOG THAT BROUGHT US A COMMUNITY

(continued from p. 55)

their ability to move their ideas along impressed us.

They accepted us readily and we soon felt a part, and we became full members. This meant more commitment, which included paying up to the cash calls that had been required to that point. I awoke some nights asking myself: *What have we gotten ourselves into? What happened to our cautious selves?*

But every contact with members of the group set my mind at ease. We held workshops with Chuck Durrett and conferred with his wife Katie. We participated in deciding what the common house would include and how it would look. We joined the marketing team and learned quickly that we could market only to Washington residents. Soon we found ourselves as co-chairs of the policy team, which automatically put us on the coordinating team. No backing out now; we were in!

A few people wavered and some dropped out, but the aggregate number grew.

We participated in designing the 28 individual units. Our team wrote several policies, including the unit selection policy, the pet policy, and the smoking policy (No smoking).

We created innovative ways to get the word out, through a web site, speaking engagements, Google, bumper stickers, and other means, and now we have sold most of the units and hope to have the remaining ones sold by spring when we expect to get our building loan and begin construction.

We are excited to take charge of our future and happy to be a part of a talented and friendly community.

I know that my lack of fingers means I will need to work hard to fulfill my contribution, and I am willing to do so. It is worthwhile to have a community that will help if the Fates turn their attention on me again. ❧

Jim Daly is a 78-year-old retiree who lives in Port Townsend, Washington with his wonderful wife, faithful dog, and ho-hum cat. He is a member of Quimper Village, an adult cohousing community for Washington residents only.

COMMUNITY IS THE BEST MEDICINE
A guide to cooperative living on a disability income

By Lily Silver

Your disability income will be the same almost anywhere you go. In community, you may find it can go a lot farther and take you to a lot more interesting places.

There are groovy, interesting, creative communities out there of every imaginable size, shape, and flavor. Many people find that intentional communities are a way to be less isolated, have a higher quality of life, and live in a more meaningful way.

In the quest for your new home, here are a few things to watch for, and a few things to watch out for:

The Quest for Community

Living in community can bring a great deal more friendship, warmth, and purposefulness into your life. The Fellowship for Intentional Community website includes a list of over 1,000 intentional communities: communes, ecovillages, community farms, land trusts, artist communities, cooperative houses, spiritual communities, cohousing, and bunches more.

There is also a Communities Classifieds section with a list of dreamers and seekers looking to start their own communities or find their "people." You can post your own dreams here or read through to see what others have posted.

Many people find that living in community can mean a much higher quality of life on much less income. However, if you're simply looking for cheap housing, intentional communities will not be a good match for you. Most communities are seeking people who are like-minded and genuinely wish to be part of their community life.

Finding Your People

When you contact a new community, you may discover that no one else living there right now is on disability. You may also discover that no one else who has ever lived there since the beginning of time has ever been on disability. Someone has to be the groundbreaker. You can pave the way for others.

Even able-bodied people don't find the perfect match right out of the gate. Be persistent. Contact as many communities as you can. And be patient. Folks may need a little time to get to know you and your situation. With time, you will find somewhere that is a good match.

Most people visit more than one community before finding one they click with. For a person with disabilities, this is easier said than done. If you are able, though, it's nice to be able to explore.

When you arrive at a new community, don't be shocked if it seems very different than what you read on the website. Some people are "aspirational" when writing these descriptions. The person who wrote that website may have had big dreams. They also may be long gone by now.

Work Contributions

Some communities ask for work contributions and others do not. If you are too ill to work, it is still possible to find a community that may be a great match for you.

In some places, the work contribution is small—for example, one day per month. If you cannot build buildings or dig ditches, there are usually some gentler, more sedentary ways in which you can contribute.

If you have physical disabilities, some newly-forming communities may not be the best match. These communities are often looking for people who can construct buildings and cultivate the land. Keep an eye out for more established communities where the buildings are already built.

Don't be scared off if you feel you don't have enough to contribute. If you are a nice person, and you get along well with the people living there, and you have a stable income from your disability check, and you wish to be part of the community life, there are many communities that may be happy to have you.

Financial Contributions

Some communities are quite pricey and others are dirt cheap. In my experience, cohousing communities in particular tend to be on the pricey, middle class side. If you are poor, this may not be a good match. Then again, if you see somewhere you just love, it does not hurt to contact them and ask. Someone in the community may have a room or space available for rent.

Some communities require a buy-in, join fee, or land purchase. For a new or forming community, it may be hard to join if you don't have the financial means.

Please don't be scared off by all join fees. In an older, more established community, you may find the join-in fees to be a bit more flexible. If the community is large and located in an isolated area, there are more than likely a few houses or rooms sitting empty by now. Someone might be quite pleased to rent you one of these places, and you might be quite pleased with the amount of rent they charge.

Some years back, I visited a land trust community. The website mentioned nothing about being able to rent, but when I got there, there were several empty rooms and houses, and plenty of options.

Income-Sharing Communities

In some communities, all finances are separate and each person has their own largely independent life. Other communities are "income-sharing" or "egalitarian" and resources and/or money are shared. Income-sharing is a very different lifestyle than most of us are used to. Some people find they really love it.

I was initially under the mistaken impression that all income-sharing communities would be looking for full-time work contributions to the community. Apparently, not so!

The nice folks from the Fellowship for Intentional Community were kind enough to set me straight: "Some income-sharing communities may have a full-time work week, but others have a more flexible approach. Some may actually be ideal for people with disabilities."

Community and Disability Benefits

If you are on Social Security, Medicaid, or other benefits, there are a few special considerations you may wish to think about before moving to community (or before moving anywhere, really). For that matter, you might want to think about some of these things even if you are just staying still.

It is especially helpful to learn a little more about how your benefits may be affected before joining in a community business, shared income, shared property, shared cars, shared food, or a community that gives you a place to live but does not charge "rent." All of these things are possible, but if you know the disability regulations, it will make your life a whole lot easier.

It is also worth noting that there are different home care and Medicaid programs in different states. (If you are going to move anyway, you might as well move somewhere with good services!) You can read about all this and much more in this Guide to Disability Benefits and Intentional Community: howtogeton.wordpress.com/community.

Caregiving and Caretaking

If you are unable to care for yourself and need assistance, you may find it difficult or impossible to find a community that can accommodate this.

You may wish to look into state homecare programs that can provide you with a caregiver. This can give you more options for communities to join. Most people with disabilities do not know that all 50 states offer caregiving programs to help low-income people with disabilities in their homes. The type of care, ways to qualify, and hours available vary wildly from state to state. See www.howtogeton.wordpress.com for more information on finding homecare in your area.

The way you approach a community may have a big impact on the kind of response you get. It is wonderful if you can let people know who you are and why you are interested in their community. If you feel you will need special assistance, you might see if it is possible to bring a friend or caregiver with you when you visit.

Not all who wander are lost. Keep wandering and keep questing. You may not find your perfect community overnight, but if you keep an open mind and an open heart, there is a new life out there waiting for you. I hope you find your people, and the community of your dreams. ❧

Lily Silver is disabled and primarily homebound with CFS/ME. Luckily, she lives in an informal community of like-minded, kind-hearted friends and familiars who brighten her days. Lily is assembling a free online guide to Disability, Medicaid, and Home Care. Come by and visit at www.howtogeton.wordpress.com.

Artwork by Elizabeth D'Angelo

Elizabeth D'Angelo—artist, spreader of love and hope, illness warrior, and force of nature—often paints with her arms pinned to her sides due to severe weakness and muscle spasms from advanced ME/CFS. In the midst of an illness that keeps her confined to her 12 × 12 ft. bedroom, she makes vibrant work that has captivated a loyal following. Painting is her meditation, her grounding rod, and her calling, but it is the connection with others through her art that inspires her the most. To see more of her artwork, visit www.elizabethdangelo.com.

Problem: In the face of rampant greed and short-sighted self-interest, it's so easy to lose connection to the extraordinary creativity displayed around this planet.

Response: Establish a centralized access point to sources of social and environmental inspiration — enabling activists and organizers, students and citizens to identify and amplify what might help our own acts of creation.

EXEMPLARS!

a free, searchable, living library of what is hopeful,

fascinating, and sustainable.

Visit **www.exemplars.world**

your portal to designing a sustainable future

<u>Browse</u> the 4 domains of **www.exemplars.world** For each Exemplar, the initial insight, the organizing strategy, tools, outcomes, and a link to websites.

<u>View</u> relevant essays and videos.

<u>Submit</u> Exemplars you have created or know of, as we expand the data base.

1. Cities, towns & communities

2. Businesses and organizations

3. Systemic interventions

4. Cultural sustainability

Curated by Paul Freundlich, pfreundlich@comcast.net

Founder, Green America

345

An Invitation to Single Men: Consider Cohousing

By Carolyn Schlam

Before I get into my topic and put forth my arguments, I want you to qualify me for the task. I am a member of a cohousing community in Taos, New Mexico, Valverde Commons, and have been interested in cohousing for a good decade. Though I now practice as a full-time artist and writer, I have worked many years in the real estate field as a broker and professional branding/marketing expert.

Because of my background and experience in selling real estate, Valverde Commons enlisted my aid in selling our community. Our model is a bit out of the ordinary. We are a subdivision, and sell lots; members then build a house to suit their requirements and budget. In the scheme of things, my task in selling VC was a relatively easy one. We have a really beautiful location just outside the historic district of arty Taos. You can walk to the library and our town plaza, and though so centrally located, we are surrounded by open land with horses and cows grazing. Idyllic, truly.

Selling cohousing is the essence of targeted marketing. There's a dedicated database of folks who desire to live in community and they turn to the Intentional Communities website for news and information. IC.org constituted the only advertising I undertook, aside from our website, www.valverdecommons.com. I restructured the latter to point out our community's great assets: the weather and pastoral environment, an art-focused town with many creative people already members of the community, and the opportunity to build a house, daunting to some but an exciting prospect to many.

The calls and emails began almost immediately after I took on my assignment. I had long phone discussions with people from all over the US, and persuaded many of them to plan a visit to our relatively remote town. I worked on the project for a year and a half, during which time I sold all 13 remaining lots, three of which I sold twice, for a total of 16 contracts.

Now to the topic at hand. I have talked with and met with literally hundreds of people, some with a particular interest in our community, and many just exploring the possibility of cohousing somewhere.

I haven't kept count, not thinking at the time that I would write about the job eventually, but in a year and a half, 18 months, I would say that I spoke to an average of eight individuals or couples a month and approximately 140 total. This is a very rough estimate, but feels about right.

Not a huge sampling, but enough, I think, to suggest a trend. Here are the rough stats. Out of

Commoners doing zumba.

Valverde Commons.

the 140 odd couples and singles, I would say about 60 percent were couples and about 40 percent single women. Notice I don't have a category for single men—either single, divorced, or widowed. Why? Because I think there were three in total, one a never-married Texan who liked the town, one a friend of a member who, yes, actually did buy a lot and build a house, and one caller who was rather disenchanted with my pitch.

Of my 16 sales, the breakdown is as follows: nine couples, two of which were same-sex, six single females and one single man. I've not done a comparative study of other cohousing communities, but I would guess the breakdowns are similar. Most of the inquiries I get from people starting communities are from couples or single women. I have never been contacted by a single man interested in initiating a community.

Why? Single women seem particularly disposed to the cohousing model. They love the idea that they can enjoy the privacy of their own homes, and yet have friends just a short walk away. They love the camaraderie, the chance to plan meals and dine together, the classes, meetings, and other get-togethers.

The married women and the married men also enjoy the group activities. We have a full roster of men at our zumba classes, and they are whooping it up with their wives and the single women.

It just doesn't seem to occur to single men to proactively look for and join a cohousing community. Is it, I have wondered, that they don't expect to be single for long? That they are accustomed to women making social arrangements and proposing living arrangements and choices?

It has always seemed to me that single men actually would have the most to gain from joining a community. First and not insignificantly, the plethora of single females to hang with. The availability of ready company, dinners, group activities of all types. Wouldn't this be swell, I ponder.

I would ask if I could, but since only three single men have inquired, I haven't had the chance exactly. But I would like to very much. I would point out all the fun they might have being the center of attention of their single female cohousers, and how much more fulfilling their lives might actually be. Then there's zumba and all the other possibilities of community life they have never previously entertained.

As I am currently working on perhaps a new community in our town (I'm still getting calls and VC is sold out), I am reaching out to single men and asking them to consider our enviable lifestyle. It won't hurt a bit, I promise, and it might open up a new world.

Here's my pitch, men. We want you and we need you. It's a new paradigm. We are not strictly hunters or gatherers anymore. We can do both, and we can do it together. Help make our cohousing communities a haven for all of us, young and old, male and female, gay and straight, and yes, single men and single women. A good life for all, together. Please consider it. 🐦

Carolyn Schlam is a painter, sculptor and author. Her book, The Creative Path: Process and Practice, *will be out in 2017 and she regularly writes for many publications on art, real estate, and lifestyle. She is a member of Valverde Commons Cohousing. Her websites include: www.carolynschlam.com, for art; www. realestatewriterpro.com, for writing; and www.valverdecommons.com, for her cohousing community.*

Valverde Commons.

Photos courtesy of Carolyn Schlam

The Value of Community: WHAT DEFINES SUCCESS?

By Deborah Altus

Fruitlands community farmhouse, now part of Fruitlands Museum, as it appeared in the 1990s. Fruitlands, founded in 1843, was a Transcendentalist community that lasted less than a year, but its influence continues through the museum and various writings. Professor Tim Miller suggests that Fruitlands might be viewed as the first ecovillage due to its focus on sustainability, health, ethical principles, and simple living.

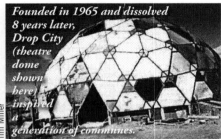

Founded in 1965 and dissolved 8 years later, Drop City (theatre dome shown here) inspired a generation of communes.

The cemetery in Amana, Iowa.

When Rosabeth Moss Kanter conducted her research on commitment mechanisms in 19th century utopian societies for her book *Commitment and Community* (1972), she classified groups as "successful" and "unsuccessful" based on their length of existence. For Kanter, a group had to last for at least 25 years to be labeled successful.

Certainly, long-lived communal groups have a great deal of useful information to share. They can teach us how a community maintains its vision for the long term, remains economically viable, retains members, outlives the founders, and sustains relationships. But should longevity, alone, be the defining measure of success? Conversely, should short-lived intentional communities be viewed as failures?

In the mid-1990s, I traveled from Florida to Alaska for Professor Tim Miller's 1960s Communes Project. My job was to interview people who lived communally in the '60s and '70s and to visit intentional communities still in existence from that period. I quickly learned that the length of time my interviewees lived in intentional communities wasn't correlated with their sense of identification with, and feelings of fondness toward, these communities. Often the people who were the most eager to speak with me were those whose communal experiences were the shortest. One interviewee traveled many miles to talk at length about a group that, nearly 30 years earlier, he had belonged to for a few weeks. Another had written a book-length manuscript about a group that had lasted for a couple of months.

What became clear to me was that the experiences of my interviewees were deeply meaningful and life-changing, regardless of their length. These experiences often impacted their life trajectories in profound ways—the careers they chose, the people they lived with, the groups they joined, the political and social issues they fought for, the way they spent their money and their leisure time, the way they raised their children. They continued to seek involvement in cooperative ventures—food co-ops, buying clubs, alternative schools, barter systems, and more—and deliberately chose occupations that aligned with values related to cooperation and sharing. And many of them expressed the desire to live communally again in retirement.

These feelings rang true to me. Over 30 years ago, I spent over a decade living in a series of cooperative living arrangements. While each group was interesting and memorable, one stands out as particularly formative. We pooled our money to pay the rent and buy our food—cooking and eating together each night at a rickety picnic table in the dining room of our run-down farmhouse. We hung out together—listening to music, talking about current events, walking the dog, bicycling, watching movies, gardening, laughing, crying, and sharing the ups and downs of our lives. Then, after a couple of years, we gradually went our separate ways. There was no big breakup. We simply had opportunities and interests that took us in different directions.

Despite our short time together, this experience taught me how much I loved sharing life with others in deep and intimate ways. From there, I sought experiences that strengthened relationships with the people in my life and that allowed me to practice my cooperative values. Although I went on to live in a nuclear family, I became a board member of my food co-op, started a dinner co-op, joined a credit union, joined a parent participation preschool co-op, continued my involvement in the FIC and the Communal Studies Association, and incorporated information about intentional communities in the courses that I taught. Without having lived cooperatively, albeit for a relatively short time, I don't know that I would have sought out these experiences—at least not with the same level of passion and commitment.

I also learned practical life skills in my co-op years—cooking, home maintenance, bookkeeping, group decision making, meeting facilitation—skills that have served me well throughout my life. My experience with cooking for a large group helped me land one of my all-time favorite jobs as a cook at a biological field station. My experience with co-op meeting facilitation helps me run meetings in my paid and volunteer work. My experience with co-op labor-sharing systems helps me promote equitable distribution of work in the groups to which I belong. The list goes on.

My experiences and those of my interviewees are not unique. When examining the history of communal living, it is easy to find examples of short-lived communities that had lasting impacts on their members and the larger society. Robert Owen's New Harmony is a striking example. New Harmony lasted only a couple of years (1825-1827), yet it is arguably one of the best-known historic utopian communities in America. Countless scholarly publications have been written on New Harmony and its impact on the natural

Century (2013), Pitzer describes how experiments by 19th century utopian communities in universal education, democratic governance, and equal rights helped to bring about reforms in these areas in the 20th century—though the communities often did not last. Similarly, Pitzer points out that the communes of the 1960s have shaped "major features of world culture in the twenty-first century." Many of these communities, of course, were short-lived, but Pitzer notes that "they pioneered changes in eating habits and health care and made commitments to tolerance and spirituality, equality and justice, peace and love that have helped move the world toward multiculturalism, gender equality, interfaith dialogue, and peace initiatives."

In a recent book, *We Are As Gods* (2016), on the 1970s back-to-the-land movement, author Kate Daloz describes how intentional communities from the '70s, even when short-lived, continue to influence practices and products of today. As examples, she points out the popularity of natural food stores and organic products, along with the now-mainstream brands of Celestial Seasonings, Cascadian Farm, Stonyfield Yogurt, and Tom's of Maine. In her words: "Every last leaf and crumb of today's $39 billion organic food industry owes its existence in part to the inexperienced, idealistic, exurbanite farmers of the 1970s, many of whom hung on through the '80s and '90s, refining their practices, organizing themselves, and developing the distribution systems that have fed today's seemingly insatiable demand for organic products.... Every mixed greens salad; every supermarket

It is easy to find examples of short-lived communities that had lasting impacts on their members and the larger society.

sciences, public education, public libraries, workers' rights, women's rights, the abolitionist movement, architecture, and more. Robert Dale Owen, Robert Owen's son, and Frances Wright, abolitionist and founder of the Nashoba community, spent years working for social reforms that were influenced, at least in part, by their experiences at New Harmony.

Donald Pitzer, professor emeritus and former director of the Center for Communal Studies at University of Southern Indiana, developed the theory of developmental communalism to explain how an organization or movement does not necessarily end even when its communal period dissolves. Rather, Pitzer noted that communal groups may evolve into new forms of association or otherwise continue to impact society beyond the end of their communalism. The Amana Colonies, for example, ended their communal phase in 1932. However, they have carried forward some aspects of the communal era to the present day, such as the distinctive Amana Church and land that is collectively owned by the Amana Society. As scholar Jonathan Andelson has noted, burial in Amana cemeteries still proceeds in rows by order of death, not in family plots, continuing to emphasize long-held values of simplicity and equality.

In a chapter on developmental communalism in the book, *The Communal Idea in the 21st*

carton of soy milk; every diverse, stinky plate of domestic cheese; every farm-to-table restaurant, locavore food blog and artisanal microbrew has a direct ancestry in the 1970s' countercuisine."

Daloz allows us to see that the back-to-the-landers and the intentional communities they built, even if they didn't survive for long, offered something valuable to their members and to society. She emphasizes this point through the words of a 1970s communitarian: "Just because we didn't end up with what we thought we were going to end up with doesn't mean we ended up with nothing. We ended up with something else. Which is beautiful."

In 2013, three women in Pittsburgh published a book, *My House, Our House*, about their experience with cooperative householding. In the book, they chronicled the joys and struggles of living together and offered a plethora of how-to information to help those wanting to do the same. Their home-sharing experience ended two years after the book was published and 11 years after they moved in together. But the women do not view the experience as a failure. On the contrary, they view it as a successful venture that met their goals. The experience also allowed them to teach others about how to make a cooperative household work—not only through their book but through their website, blog, numerous presentations, and even an interview on the Today Show with Jane Pauley.

When they started their household, they made an explicit agreement to stick together for five to 10 years—and they made it one year past the long end of that agreement. Not only do they remain friends and look back fondly on their time together, but two of them went on to live together in a different city. In a blog post, they wrote, "We can confidently tell you that it is possible to disband a shared living arrangement in an equitable way that preserves the friendships—no, more accurately, the LOVE—that grew in our home for 11 wonderful years."

In her book, *Commitment and Community*, Kanter described commune seekers of the hippie era as "children of the affluent who dislike school and feel that they have no place else to go. It may be only a temporary episode for these people, a year out of their lives." A year, perhaps. But a year can be pivotal. A year can be life-changing. The value of an intentional community to its members and to society cannot be determined by the mere passage of time. ❧

Deborah Altus lives in Lawrence, Kansas. She is a professor at Washburn University, a board member of the International Communal Studies Association, and former member of the editorial review board for the FIC.

REFERENCES

Andelson, J. G. (2017). Amana cemeteries as embodiments of religious and social beliefs. *Plains Anthropologist*. dx.doi.org/10.1080/00320447.2017.1291393

Bush, K. M., Machinist, L. S., & McQuillin, J. (2013). *My House, Our House: Living Far Better for Far Less in a Cooperative Household*. Pittsburgh: St. Lynn's Press.

Daloz, K. (2016). *We Are As Gods: Back to the Land in the 1970s on the Quest for a New America*. New York: Public Affairs.

Kanter, R. M. (1972). *Commitment and Community: Communes and Utopias in Sociological Perspective*. Cambridge, MA: Harvard University.

Miller, T. (1999). *The 60s Communes: Hippies and Beyond*. Syracuse, NY: Syracuse University.

Pitzer, D. E. (1997). The new moral world of Robert Owen and New Harmony. In D. E. Pitzer (Ed)., *America's Communal Utopias* (pp. 88-134). Chapel Hill: University of North Carolina.

Pitzer, D. E. (2013). Developmental communalism into the 21st century. In E. Ben-Rafael, Y. Oved, & M. Topel (Eds.), *The Communal Idea in the 21st Century* (pp. 33-52). Leiden and Boston: Brill.

INTENTIONAL COMMUNITY IN A NICARAGUAN JUNGLE:
Honoring my duality through community practices

By Elizabeth Arnott

Sunset overlooking Ometepe's volcano.

Elizabeth Arnott

I have always been two things at once...literally marked on my body through a pair of confused eyes—one blue, one brown, and reiterated through my visit with a Shaman in the highlands of India, as he stared into these tangled eyes and uttered the words "you are this, and you are that, and you forever will be both." It took many years to understand what he meant, but as I entered an intentional community in the Nicaraguan jungle, I began to understand.

I was studying international law at the time, and with this came a bureaucratic world full of elitist language and moot court competitions and a long, complex thesis. I loved this part of myself; I loved dressing up and drinking expensive wine and talking political jargon at exclusive events. For many years, however, this came at the expensive of the mystical goddess inside of me—the woman who longed to be jumping barefoot through the jungle with knotted hair and a hammock for a bed. I struggled with this duality inside, not quite understanding how I could be both of these things at once and consequently ignoring, arguably, the more important part of me. Others would struggle with it too—and such black-and-white judgments took a toll on the way I viewed myself. I spent a lot of time pushing this goddess away, trying to hide and ignore her for fear of criticism. But, just as placing a band-aide on a wound only hides but does not heal, this goddess eventually bled out.

In the company of my academic friends, I was often able to receive a type of intellectual stimulation that I will forever thrive on. I would spend my evenings partaking in heated political debates and sharing legal insights, always learning and growing from each other's knowledge. But when it came to my desire to feel more spiritually connected to the earth, to spend time in nature, and to investigate alternate states of consciousness, many of my academic friends thought I was a little out of my mind. By the same token, when I would spend time with many of my friends who embarked on a less conventional and more spiritual path, I also faced judgment for being "too far into the matrix." For years, I felt torn between one group of friends who judged me for dancing around fires, and another who judged me for throwing on mascara and kickin' it at the office. But as the Indian Shaman had cautioned me so many years before, I am this, and I am that, and I forever will be both. I owe my Nicaraguan experience to embracing this beautiful symmetry in my life.

My stay at an intentional community in Nicaragua taught me that not only is it okay to move in between these two worlds, but that anybody else's judgment about this has never actually been about me. Furthermore, it taught me how to harness the moral foundation of intentional community and use it as a tool which I am free to pick up and put down throughout my life, as I see fit.

Here are three lifelong lessons that my stay at an intentional community taught me:

Unplug

First, and perhaps quite obviously, the benefits of unplugging from technology are indescribable. It is evident that as a society, we are over-attached to technology. In community, we had access to Wi-Fi only during certain hours and in a common space far from the rooms where we would eat, meditate, and sleep. We were encouraged to lock our technology away and to call upon it only when deemed necessary.

Ironic as it may seem, living in a community setting can largely be about finding solitude and creating a safe space for self-reflection. Of course, solitude is hard to find when you are constantly plugged into the outside world, so it is important to turn off and remove these harmful distractions. It is hard to do at first out of your own sheer will power, but after easing into this transition with the help of my community, it is a practice I will forever draw up in order to re-balance.

Unplugging from technology creates the shift into the next lesson learned:

Experience genuine connection without expectation

Staying in an intentional community allowed me to practice honest love and connection with my fellow human beings, without judgment or expectations. As a group, we often created and participated in workshops that, to someone outside looking in, probably seemed a little strange. We mimicked animals, we danced topless, we expressed ourselves however we felt fit—all without a wince of judgment. Through participating in a space free of judgment, I was able to let go of judgments about others and myself.

When we release these expectations about how people should behave, or how they should treat us—when we let go of that energy we've been taught that sees a black-and-white world in which people are either wrong or right—we leave room for something magical to happen: authentic connection. We create freedom.

The people I spent time with in the community were from all over the world, coming and

(continued on p. 74)

INTENTIONAL COMMUNITY IN A NICARAGUAN JUNGLE: HONORING MY DUALITY THROUGH COMMUNITY PRACTICES

(continued from p. 47)

going, with different kinds of goals and ambitions. But none of that mattered, because we were there to sit with each other in the moment, to see each other as we truly are, and then to let go. I will forever strive to bring genuine connection without expectation into all of my relationships.

Strive to create a lifestyle in line with your morals

The intentional community helped to remind me of the very basics: put your money where your mouth is. If you don't support animal cruelty, don't eat factory meat. If you are worried about the state of the environment, be conscious about the amount of water you are using, about leaving your lights on, etc. Respect your body—think of food as fuel; you wouldn't pour tar into your car engine and expect it to run properly, so don't put it into your body and expect different results.

In our kitchen, we did not allow meat or dairy. We ran on a diet of organic fruits, vegetables, and grains. Apart from the kitchen, other sources of water were located far down a hill. This meant that every time I wanted water, I actively had to work for it. Moreover, my cabin had no electricity, which reminded me that a bedroom is an intentional space used to rest and recharge, not to sit up and text late at night.

Although many of the things listed above may seem obvious, they can be very tough to actually implement into everyday life. These are the simple lessons that support me in my symmetry—that I continue to draw upon whenever I am, at times, feeling a little overwhelmed by a bureaucratic world. I will forever come back to community-based living whenever I feel a disconnect between this symmetry.

Regardless of your lot in life, I truly believe spending some time in a community-based setting has something magical to offer everyone.

Through spending time within this community, and living freely without judgment, I began to understand that the duality within me is something to be honored, not judged.

I am this, and I am that, and I forever will be both.

Elizabeth Arnott is from London, Ontario, Canada. She has spent the past three years traveling for work, academia, and her own personal growth. A cultural alchemist, she has traveled through Haitian highlands to Indian jungles, experiencing the meaning of community in many different ways. Elizabeth works in human rights law and has most recently been living in a small Mayan community on Lake Atitlan, Guatemala. Contact Elizabeth at earnott8@gmail.com.

A Community Journey

By Brittny Love

I had never put much thought into changing my lifestyle, or embarking on establishing a community, until I spent the nine months of my pregnancy living remotely in the National Forests of Arizona. It was then that I realized our old world was falling in on itself, and there's nothing more motivating to make change than when you're about to bring life into this world. This precious time in nature showed me that it's crucial to learn how to work with the land and strengthen community.

After my son was born, I discovered the Intentional Communities website and decided it was time to travel the country and explore the variety of ecovillages and alternative lifestyles on the planet. Over the course of six months, my son and I traveled from Washington state, down through the Southwest, and up the East Coast to New York City, stopping at multiple well-known communities along the way.

The first thing that stood out, with each community we visited, was the incredible architecture, unique homes, and the shared intention of building with minimal impact. The Lama Foundation, in New Mexico, had the most breathtaking views from their mountain oasis, and I admired their pristine craftmanship. Almost all the communities had structures that were designed from sustainable materials, such as cob, as well as minimizing the need for fossil fuels and implementing solar and hydropower for electricity. "It's highly likely that in my lifetime, there will be a collapse and we are going to need an ecological way to live and coexist. There are so many things in our culture that we think are necessities, but are really luxuries. We need to learn not only how to grow food, but how to work together on a social level," said a member from Earthaven, located in North Carolina. Freedom of artistic expression was also a shared theme at the ecovillages, which was a joy to see, especially since it's such a rare find our modern world.

All the communities had their own organic gardens, most of which were grown in a permaculture setting. I wouldn't say they were completely self-sufficient, but most were close when it came to growing their own food. Community meals became a favorite ritual of ours at each stop, as we were provided some of the most delicious and nourishing meals I'd ever experienced, and I enjoyed being with everyone. As a single mother, I also found the childcare programs to be so helpful and the children truly loved being together. Avalon Gardens, near Tucson, Arizona, had one of the best academic programs, where the students not only learned general studies, but also had quality time for arts and crafts, creating music, and spending time in nature. "I wouldn't want to go to a regular school because they teach you to think in a limited box," said a seven-year-old boy. "I love all my friends here and how much time we get to be outside. My favorite subject is math."

Each community had various work-hour requirements and structured meetings. It did appear that the communities with daily check-ins and weekly quotas had members that were less stressed and were getting a lot more accomplished. Another key factor I found influencing the success of the various communities was the drug and alcohol policies. The places where the use of alcohol was more prevalent seemed to also have a lot more drama and members coming and going. Open and clear communication was another big challenge, but the communities where meetings were held on a more regular basis did not struggle as much with this issue. "Community living comes with its own set of challenges. We have to practice being able to deal with people that you may not like, or agree with, but you still need to be able to sit down and have coffee with that person," said a member from Acorn, in Virginia.

"I've been a part of several communities throughout my life, and I think the reason I was called to them was because I was searching for family. I see community living as an imperfect avenue where people don't have to live in a hypnotized way and don't have to contribute to building an empire. You have food that you know is good quality and you learn how to be self-reliant. The other thing is, we live in a society that isolates us as human beings. But to live in a place where the intention is to break down the walls of emotion and reclaim your vulnerability—to share in your joy and your tears, it's a profound and beautiful thing. Living in community is a way to take back your humanity and everything that's been taken from us," said Mick, from Heathcote, in Baltimore, Maryland.

Since returning to Arizona, I have begun working with a beautiful, young, and inspired group of friends who are making a big difference in this area. We currently have a community house in the suburbs, but we've transformed the lawn into an organic garden and host neighborhood block parties, so we can share information on growing food, composting, and being there for our fellow humanity. We've adopted the weekly meeting check-in, which has been a powerful tool to get to the root of an issue and to address emotional needs. Our next step will be acquiring land, which now we are extensively researching.

My journey across the country was so humbling and gave me a strong renewed sense of faith. Coming together to work for the betterment of life and each other is happening and it's working! The success of coexisting comes with the remembrance of why we chose to come together in the first place, and not losing sight of that. Challenges and setbacks are a part of life, but we can never give up. We need to look out for one another, do our part on this Earth, and not expect everything to be handed to us. There are some things in life that take work and effort, but it's worth it! I hope you never feel you're too small to make a difference... ❧

Brittny Love is the author of the inspiring travel series, Diary of a Starseed. *Her books and videos are available at StarseedStory.com.*

DREAMING of a Different Way

By Amanda Crowell

My parents wanted the American Dream. Both college dropouts with blue collar jobs, they valued education and the trappings of middle-class living. By the time we were in high school, we had transitioned from a rented city house to a post-war ranch house in the growing suburban town where my mother had gone to high school. No matter the financial strain, we always had our school supplies, church clothes, and family photos. I knew funds got tight pretty frequently, although my parents would never talk to us about the realities of family finances and they continued to run the air conditioning and buy new furniture as though they did not have any worries. My mother in particular enjoyed being a modern woman, with a television in her bedroom and boxed and canned food ready to eat. My own predilections towards the outdoors and hand-crafting encouraged by my dog-eared copies of *Little House* and *My Side of the Mountain* were indulged as cute, until high school when I spent a messy afternoon baking bread with my high school boyfriend and got banned from the kitchen.

Going to college was never a question for bookworm me, though I understood that I would have to pay for it myself. I earned a few scholarships, not enough to pay room and board as well as tuition, so I took out loans. I naively picked biology as a major based on what I thought would be most "right" for a career, and ignored my own inclinations primarily because I had no idea about careers or aptitudes. I went into a major I had no talent for. Two years in I switched to English because I loved to read and could do that better than the math-intensive classes I was failing. I still had no direction, but at least the courses were more interesting and I had the knack for them. I was able to take some classes that sang to me, but still did not inform any plan for my future—Amish History and Culture, Missouri Fish and Wildlife, and, oddly, Macroeconomics. At the same time I moved from work-study jobs into more professional jobs, including substitute teaching, which I did not care for. I was struggling with intense loneliness; living in the dorms had been fun, but moving off-campus left me isolated. I invited people over all the time, often to the detriment of my school work and my own integrity. Spending leftover loan funds filled the space with hardcover copies of classic novels and matching kitchen sets, but I was still lost.

At the end of my junior year, a friend introduced me to Sandhill Farm community. I had no idea intentional communities existed, and to spend time at Sandhill and learn about Dancing Rabbit, Twin Oaks, and others excited me about the future. May Day celebrations! Outdoor work! Environmental justice! Family living! After some discussion with a resident at Sandhill, though, I was told that I could not live there until I had paid off my student loans, as there was no mechanism in that income- and expense-sharing community for dealing with resident debt. Before it had even begun, my future seemed over. To a 21-year-old English major, $15,000 of debt seemed insurmountable.

With the goal of paying off the loans, I approached a professor for advice. Knowing little about me besides my aptitude for books, he suggested graduate school was my only option. Looking back, I realize that I could have gone to career services, just as I could have questioned the financial aid office's blindly giving out maximum student loan dollars to someone whose Bachelor's in English might not make for good risk. At the time, I had only the example of my parents, who got loans for houses and cars, who put everything on credit card, and who seemed to be doing well. I applied for graduate school, and of course, more loans.

At some point after I started graduate school, I gave up my goal. Perhaps it was the mounting debt—I took out the maximum every year, whether I needed it or not, and spent it on trips and furniture and constantly moving from apartment to apartment, trying to find a "home." It might

The author's husband tuning the banjo for a Friday Firepit.

Front yard farm on the Fourth of July.

A community garden in St. Louis.

Potluck!

The author and her son on an errands walk, Pine Bush: the Alien Capital of New York.

First New York pumpkin, 2010.

have been seeing my friends from undergrad go on to get jobs and start families. It may just have been accepting what I felt was inevitable: I would become a teacher and get better furniture and maybe someday I could retire and travel. Whatever the reason, giving up for me meant self-destruction. I spent more money, blew through credit cards, had frequent and mostly awful relationships in my fight against loneliness, and stopped most of my green habits. Luckily I had made some good friends who held me through depression and nasty break-ups, but I was still searching.

Finally I decided, mostly subconsciously, that I needed stability. I found a willing partner on short notice, got married (ignoring all the signs that it was the wrong decision), and almost immediately got pregnant.

And gradually found my center. How could I have my son and justify destroying the world he was going to live in? At this point, I had over $100,000 in student loans. The year I had my son, my parents' house was foreclosed on after bankruptcy. I saw the future, and I knew I didn't want it. I turned into a different person, or rather, I rediscovered who I wanted to be. My stunned husband agreed to recycling, a ban on processed foods and soda, and joining materials-sharing sites such as Freecycle.

A near-suicidal bout with postpartum depression after a move to an isolated suburban ranch house catalyzed us to buy a big old house in the center of St. Louis. I reveled in the public transportation, shopping at the farmers' market on Saturdays with my son, planting flowers in my yard, and getting to know our neighbors. When my brother died just before my son turned two, I channeled my grief into two abandoned city lots on my block, turning them into flourishing community gardens. My family and friends all came out to help, drawn together by creation after loss. The day over a dozen people, including my father, my two best friends, my husband, half a dozen neighbors, and some students helped me build the final beds in the second garden was the day I realized that I was not limited to a "fantasy someday" move to an intentional community. Cobbling together part-time teaching jobs was not going to make me debt-free, and my time priority was my son. But I had wonderful people surrounding me, all of whom seemed to crave the same connectivity.

The community gardens provided a solid link to my community. I'd get up on a Sunday morning at 5 a.m. before the sun got too hot. My son and I would slip out of the house to the gardens, him digging in the piles of compost the city delivered for free, me weeding. By 6:30, neighborhood kids were out and would stop by to dig, see worms, and stare in bemused disgust as I nibbled mint leaves straight off the plants. I would crack the hydrant with the tools given to us by the water department so we could water the garden, and I'd set up a sprinkler to water the kids and the garden. When churchgoers stopped their cars to compliment the gardens and tell me about the gardens their grandmas had, I would press zucchini or cucumbers on them. I always offered my students extra credit for community service, and every semester I would have a handful working with me in the gardens. Some kept coming after classes ended. The local nursery donated fruit trees; Gateway Greening donated seeds. I got to know neighbors, my alderman, my state rep, the city foresters, and all the local greeners. While it wasn't perfect—there was occasional vandalism and always lots of squash vine borers—nothing was better than coming into the house with my filthy but smiling son after a long day in the community gardens.

Monthly potlucks at my house provided

resident policies. I was hoping that we could work something out where I would work my job as a teacher to pay my debt, but my family could still live there and dedicate ourselves otherwise to the work of the community. Yet again my loans were an impediment—residents were not allowed to work outside of the community businesses, and personal debt burdens were unwelcome within the group's shared purse.

The next few years were difficult. Working full-time at a job that had 80-hour weeks or 10-hour weeks depending on the time of the semester took adjustment. My husband and I, long rocky, divorced. My father was diagnosed with terminal lung cancer, necessitating many trips back to Missouri. Financially, living in New York is much more expensive. While many in New York are friendly, communication is different. "We'll have you over for dinner sometime soon," does not actually mean a dinner date; it is a standard farewell. Distance in New York is different, too. In St. Louis, distance never seemed a social challenge, with potluck attendees sometimes driving an hour to join us. In New York, distances of a half hour or more are often a real barrier to gathering, although probably the weather and the mountain roads are to blame. Other than trains or buses to the city, there isn't public transportation, so having a car is crucial, despite our efforts otherwise. There are also more limited schooling options for my son, who has very high anxiety that does not mesh well with standard public school formats.

Luckily, we were adopted by a farming family who had lived in the same place since 1775. The seventh generation of Westtown Lains took us in as renters and as family. They plowed a garden for us, taught us the different planting cycles of the Northeast, and invited us to their family reunion. Even after I had to move because of the divorce, they remained friends. They gave my son an extended family when he was truly longing for all the relatives left behind. Otherwise, creating a community here has been harder; my "welcoming to all" attitude has sometimes left me open to those who were not supportive and who did not understand my more direct, Midwestern commu-

> I've learned over the last 20 years that community, no matter where, is the people who show up, whether to work or to eat or to toast marshmallows.

more community. All those stories of barn raisings and church socials inspired me to find a giant table secondhand; every month we'd invite everyone whose email address we had. Coworkers, grad school friends, high school friends, family, neighbors—they all came at various points and in various configurations. We pulled our mismatched chairs up and talked about politics, music, movies, books, dreams, and, of course, gardening. We shared food, tried new recipes, and laughed as the children in attendance ran in circles around the table. In good weather we ate outside and sometimes toured the gardens; in bad weather someone might bring a game or crafts. It was what I had wanted all along: a full house of people, relaxing, living, and working together (we always cleaned up before dessert!). The fewest guests I ever had was three during an ice storm; the most was 42, which was the last potluck before I moved to New York.

Moving to New York was hard. Finally having found my community, I had to leave it, again because of the student loans. My husband had heart failure at 28 and could no longer realistically work the desk job that was killing his spirit and his body. I had to get a full-time position doing something I was still not sure I wanted to do as a career. We found a tiny apartment (even upstate New York is pretty pricey) and left the gardens, the friends, the family, the neighbors, and the potlucks.

My husband discovered a local intentional community while we were scrambling to find our place, and when we toured I asked about

nication. Having personal upheavals also prevented me from really meshing into a community, although I'm very lucky that my son's father has remained close as a great co-parent. One of the blessings of working full-time is that after failed attempts at public school, I can send my son to The Birch School, an experiential school that shares similar values and is small and active enough to alleviate his anxiety.

Seven years into my life in New York, I am finally finding the community sweet spot again. I'm now married to a man who has also longed for a deeper community connection; we've got a little house in a Mayberry-meets-Norman Rockwell kind of town where we can—and do—walk to the grocery store, the hardware store, the nursery, and the farmers' market. We know our neighbors' names and have enjoyed lending them a hand as well as appreciated their help (Thank you, Gary, for snowblowing the last 26-inch snowfall off our driveway!). We have made a point of being involved in street festivals, road cleanup, and pancake breakfast fundraisers. What we cannot grow in our yard, we buy from nearby farmers. Our students honk at us as they pass us walking our dog; the UPS driver finds us with the note, "That family whose front lawn is a farm," and our mail carrier's dog plays with ours at the dog park. Last summer we tried out the concept of a "crop mob," where several families put in one rotating work day every month at each other's houses. It was barn raising, 2016 style! Potlucks haven't really worked out here, but we built a firepit in our tiny back yard, and in summer we have monthly Friday nights when we invite all to bring snacks and sit around the fire. Talented musician friends bring their instruments. It's a house full of family again.

I have not given up on intentional communities. One change I made after my son was born was to live within my means. Now that I'm full-time, the exchange for all the work hours is that I'm slowly paying down my student loans. By the time my son is out of school, I should be able to pick up and go; the thought of finally being able to live in an intentional community still holds attraction. Whatever happens, I will not be discouraged if I cannot live in an intentional community. I've learned over the last 20 years that community, no matter where, is the people who show up, whether to work or to eat or to toast marshmallows. My parents wanted the American Dream; I found out how joyful it is to wake up from that dream and meet reality. If I had not been turned away from Sandhill and the other community because of my indebtedness to that dream, I would not have met the people I share my life with now; I would not have discovered the community I needed was there all along. 🍃

Amanda Crowell is an English professor at Orange County Community College. She lives with her husband and son in Pine Bush, New York, although her heart will always belong to the Cardinals. She recommends avoiding student loans to anyone who will listen.

FORTY YEARS IN COMMUNITY: Has It Made a Difference?

By Linda Moore

When I was in my 20s, living in community became a lifestyle that pollinated my soul. I was living in a tenement-style building in what is now known as Mile End in Canada's largest bilingual city, Montreal. Prior to that, I had grown up in a nuclear family on the west coast, in Victoria, aptly named after one of England's monarchs. As we sat together over coffee, one of my new roommates asked, "Aren't there a lot of WASPS in Victoria?" *WASPS*? Like the ones that sting?? I was confused! My friends laughed openly. "Uh, no, White Anglo Saxon Protestants!!" Thus struck the first crack in my cultural conditioning. I came from a place where almost everyone was a WASP, which explains why I didn't understand the acronym. I was now living in a cosmopolitan city, and there was a lot to learn about culture.

A year later, in 1977, I returned to complete my final year at the University of Victoria. I was excited about alternative lifestyles, and wrote an essay for a sociology course that included references from COMMUNITIES magazine. I got involved in cooperative housing, a Canadian publicly funded housing experiment that had taken hold in that period. I attended weekly planning meetings that would result in extending the original cluster of four duplexes to include two new buildings that could house another 20 families.

Over the years, I have lived in two communities that have included several households, homes for 20 to 40 people. The first was a rural experiment on Quadra Island based on spiritual principles that encouraged one to work on one's self in the context of sharing daily life in a group. Through collective efforts, we ran a successful grocery business that introduced organic food to the islanders, started a Waldorf School, ran a fruit stand, grew food in two large gardens, celebrated through shared meals, song, and dance, and nurtured the young lives of at least 12 children. The interpersonal relationships that developed at that time were the most deep and meaningful I've had in my life. In my youthful idealism and based

on my studies, I believed that was normal. This is how life works! Sharing endeavors with others, developing ongoing meaningful relationships, knowing where your food comes from, it seemed like the only way to live.

Our dream was to build a community that would last for 200 years. Alas, we fell short of that goal; it lasted only four. Imagine my shock when the group decided to disband and move to the city. This idyllic life came to a rather abrupt end when the major shareholders decided to put the property up for sale. It didn't take me long to realize that I could not caretake the property without the community, and I reluctantly followed some of the others to take up an urban lifestyle.

It was 1986. The food store concept we had been working with metamorphosed into an urban version that included artful displays of organic and gourmet food, fresh baked goods, bulk foods, and an amazingly popular café, an awesome menu, and genuine service. People loved it.

That same year the Chernobyl nuclear power plant exploded. The news of the devastating effects of nuclear energy resounded around the globe. The thinning of the ozone layer hit home quickly; my own sister was diagnosed with basal cell carcinoma. I no longer wanted to bask in the sun. On the positive side, the Montreal Protocol was an astounding breakthrough where nations of the world came together to take action against the beginnings of climate change for the first time ever. I remember feeling that all my life decisions would have long-lasting consequences. What should I do? How could I bridge my interests in community, the environment, growing food, and education? The answers to those questions emerged slowly, and led through a series of shared living arrangements, until in 1997, I became an active member involved in developing Vancouver's second cohousing project, Quayside Village.

I have lived at Quayside Village in North Vancouver, British Columbia since the beginning; our 20th anniversary is on the horizon. During the planning phase, we decided that the name should reflect the experience of

Quayside Village Cohousing is home to 19 families and a corner store, all under one roof: an architecturally designed, colourful building completed in 1998.

Graham Meltzer

days gone by when people lived closer together. Quayside Village is actually a four-story building that includes two- and three-story townhouses as well as several one- and two-bedroom homes, 19 in total, and our local corner store. It is home to (give or take) 35 people, ranging in age from five to 81.

While Quayside no longer lives up to my ideals around environmental sustainability, it certainly provides a village-like atmosphere. Currently in Vancouver, there is a surge in interest in building more cohousing projects, including ones that incorporate greater ecological sustainability for the longer term. People are seeking affordable alternatives, and while the actual building costs in the city are not what many consider to be affordable, it is the other social qualities of cohousing that make the pursuit attractive to a cross-section of people. Trading off smaller-than-average living spaces for shared common areas is a formula that increases social interaction, and increases the richness of those who choose to live this way.

Today, a typical Sunday in spring, it's 10 a.m. and the yoga class is getting going in the common house. Tables and chairs are moved aside, and 10 regulars roll out their mats and go through the *asanas* under the guidance of a certified instructor. At noon there is a work-party planned to finish the fence repair around the building. Meanwhile one of the residents will be preparing food in the common house kitchen for tomorrow's dinner for the 20 of us who have signed up to attend.

Living in close proximity with others is transformative, never dull. But it's not all peace and happiness either. A recent example: I had spearheaded a small committee to deal with the fact that for the past two summers, our food, herb, flower, and fruit gardens were not getting enough attention. Increasingly hot, dry summers meant that more frequent watering was needed, and the help had not been forthcoming. The committee proposed to install an automated irrigation system that would minimize human effort. In the larger group, there were differences of opinion as to whether or not we needed such a system. A series of dynamic communications ensued. Community values were explored in face-to-face meetings. Questions were asked on a wide range of issues. From there, several people expressed a willingness to participate in a "do it ourselves" system. With a remarkable combination of several people's skills, we now have an elaborate manual system designed to ensure that the food and flower gardens get the water they need in dry summers. And we have volunteers to carry through on the watering of the various areas that sustain plant life around the entire building. How great is that?

From my first year in the city, I found ways of growing food in small spaces. Although I started simply with peas and lettuce in a container on my balcony, each time I moved to a new place, I would ensure that I could grow more food than in the previous one. Following that trajectory over the 30 years I've been in the city, I can honestly say that our evening meals today almost always include something I have grown and harvested, either fresh, stored, or preserved.

Being able to grow food in an urban environment is one of my greatest passions. It has been exciting to see my neighbors jump in with both feet to allow more plant life on our street-facing landscape. Passersby comment on what they see: children creating flower mandalas, blossoming apple and plum trees, lettuce and kale plants peeking out between colorful patches of tulips, architecturally designed raised vegetable beds growing greens year-'round. I can't think of another townhouse or apartment landscape on our long street that comes anywhere close to the display we have here.

I look forward to seeing this year's food-growing results at Quayside. We will find out how well the irrigation system works in the longer term. Regardless of the results, I do know that working together has been a "win" for the community this year. It is a living example of what happens when people are deeply committed to the village lifestyle; there is a synergy that can overcome apparent obstacles.

I feel encouraged being with others who value community. I love that people of all ages live under our big roof, that all generations are represented. Our diverse group includes writers, educators, artists, musicians, a midwife, consultants, zero-wasters, carpenters, students, business people, and more. These are real people on their own personal journeys, putting their energies into making the world a better place.

In community, we can take on projects that fulfill long-held dreams. We can work through differences when they arise. We can celebrate simple and special occasions. We come to know and understand ourselves better. While we hope to make a better world one step at a time, there are times when I ask myself, "Is this enough? Am I fulfilling my purpose? Have we made a difference? Can we avert a climate disaster?" These are tough questions! We can live our lives embracing these questions. Who can tell us the answer? I have hope in the "30-plus" generation, those who are having their own families now and those who understand the environmental challenges we all face. I feel that they are the generation that can move us forward. Our great grandchildren will live with the results of all our efforts. And I will continue to ask myself, "What have you done with the garden entrusted to you?" ❧

With one foot in the corporate world, Linda's other foot is firmly planted in the garden to keep her life in balance. Starting at her grandfather's knee, growing food in small spaces, in a time of climate change, has become a thrill unto itself. Whether in containers, raised beds, or the greater expanse that a community garden provides, there is a daily attuning to what is going on with the seeds, the young sprouts, the strong plants, the pests and diseases, the harvests, and the joy of sharing these with others. See joyfulgreenlife.com, cohousing.ca.

---

1. Antonio Machado's poem "The Wind One Brilliant Day," translated by Robert Bly.

Relaxing around the table in the common house after Thanksgiving dinner, always a popular and well-attended event. The stained glass windows were salvaged from one of the three buildings circa 1912 that stood on the property when the land was bought, carefully refitted into the dining room.

Marylee Stephenson

Last year's plum harvest: the tree was so laden with fruit that the branch broke! Heather and her grandchildren pick a crop of Italian prune plums to be shared with all.

Marylee Stephenson

GANAS:
Finding Home in an Urban Community

By Aviva Derenowski

I grew up in Kibbutz Kinneret, one of the oldest kibbutzim in Israel, but my home and my heart are in Ganas, a multigenerational community in Staten Island, New York.

In my 40s, I moved from Israel to a rural community in Missouri. There I first learned of Ganas, a sister community to the one I lived in. "Ganas" means "desire to act" in Spanish. I stayed in this urban community for a few days during a visit to my cousins in New Jersey.

Eight years later, anxious to be married, I decided to move from my rural community to an urban community where I could increase my chances of finding a mate. I opened the *Communities Directory* and started to email communities who might be willing to accept me as a member.

I was determined to continue living in intentional community. I believed it was my calling. It was a privilege to live in the United States, away from the political turmoil in Israel, but I couldn't tolerate the thought of living on my own.

I emailed about 15 communities. Ganas was the first one to respond. The contact person asked me some clarifying questions. I told them all they wanted to know. A week later I received a new email, very short. It said: "When are you coming?" With those few words they stole my heart.

Once I arrived, I became involved in the process of deciding on delicate issues such as membership. As a rule of thumb, if we have an empty room, a new member can step in. But it's always "case by case." This is one of the most fundamental guidelines of my community. We have only four rules: No violence, No exploitation, Nothing illegal, and No non-negotiable negativity. The first three rules are pretty sensible; the last one may need some explanation. The people in Ganas realized that negativity, if not taken care of, can harm the community and the individual. This is why members are required to bring their concerns to the morning meeting, or to someone who can do something about it.

It doesn't always happen. Someone may vent on how messy the counter in their kitchen is, and decide to take no action. Unfortunately, when it happens, if nobody else cares about that kitchen, the issue will remain unsolved until somebody else is motivated by the same situation to come to the meeting and see what can be done about it.

Ganas is a diverse community. Some people work in the city in their profession; we say "they work outside." Others work in the community, either in one of its businesses or helping maintain our life by working in maintenance, housekeeping, or administration. There are those who have a fixed income, and others who combine these options.

In addition, we offer a place to stay for those who visit New York from a few days to a few years. Some of our friends come to stay with us regularly once or twice a year. We are always happy to see them, and exchange news from the last time they passed by.

We have a meeting five days a week for 90 minutes each morning, that each member is welcome to attend. They're called "planning," the main forum of discussion in Ganas. It's not perfect. Some people feel that others control the floor. Others don't like to come because 7:45 is too early for them. Sometimes what we discuss is so upsetting to me that it carries over for a few hours later. Last week someone who moved in wanted to keep their dog, and was devastated that no exception was going to be made for them. I was sad because I liked them, but we could accommodate only so much. They had to find a home for their dog somewhere else.

This year our expenses are going up, and as a consequence we struggle to increase our revenue. One idea, lately, was to sell new dressers in the secondhand furniture store. It was a complicated discussion. Some of us value the green business of selling used furniture, reusing valuable possessions instead of dealing with fast and cheap appliances. Others remind us that the demand for dressers is beyond our capacity at the moment. They said "If we are in business to make money, we must get cheap dressers and sell them a bit more expensive." The discussion is still open.

Feedback is one of the tools we use to solve problems. The theory behind this process is that others see angles about your problem that you don't. You may be surprised by what your friends come up with. When I am in conflict with a friend, I am initially convinced that I'm right and they're wrong. Through exposing the different aspect of the disagreement, I have a larger frame to deal with the situation. I can even see how this particular issue has happened before with other people. By focusing on solving the problem, I heal some of my past relationships. I have a dynamic with a coworker that reflects one I had with my younger brother. Through being the protagonist in many feedback sessions, I've become a more thoughtful person.

On my own, I'd never have followed paths that were suggested to me by my friends. When I came to Ganas, I was overly sensitive to the word "crazy." I regarded the person who said it in passing as if they related to a deep truth about me. Through my life here I learned to be conscious about having bipolar disorder, be religious about taking my medication, and rely on my friends to tell me if I'm unconsciously acting out.

Early this month I got an email from NAMI (National Alliance on Mental Illness). They asked for applicants to work with New York Police Department. This opportunity could happen only in an urban setting. The selected people would be trained to educate the police force how to deal with mentally ill people. I responded immediately. I hoped they selected me, but even if they didn't, I was glad that training took part in my city.

Some people find this lifestyle too intense. They don't want to share their bathroom with others, find dishes in the sink, and a full load of them in the dishwasher. They are disturbed when somebody is watching a show they don't like in their living room. It's not easy to share your house with others who feel as strongly about everything from the mundane to their housemates.

There are many reasons to be unhappy in community. Some of the people leave, others disconnect from public activity and concentrate on their work and their friends. They make it work for them, and they stay.

I, on the other hand, feel grateful each day that I live in community. I always find someone to share my joys and my sorrows. I can share a meal with others every day if I want to. People care about me, and I know each person I interact with. I work in Ganas in housekeeping. I usually clean or prepare the food for the cook. Sometimes I work in the clothing store and every Saturday I work in the Book Cafe for half a day. My life is full, and very rich. I love the people I work with, and when I have disagreements I can work them out directly or through my manager.

When I came, 13 years ago, I didn't date because I thought I was not good enough for the men I found attractive. I was loud, opinionated, and had a short fuse. As I talked to my friends (and listened to them), I started to date online. I followed my buddies' advice and said "yes" to anyone who said "yes" to me. I never ran out of dates. To date in New York City can be great fun, because you meet new people and and get to know the city at the same time. My goal was to meet a man I'd marry, and three years later I got married to Alex. I met him on OkCupid, a dating site, but found out immediately that he lived 10 minutes' walk from Ganas. When we met, Alex liked me but was not interested to live here. A few years later he could not resist the homey feeling. He was so well liked and appreciated. So he moved in. A year later we married.

It's amazing that my life led me to combine community living with the complexity of New York. There are so many opportunities here to develop and grow. Alex and I are into meditation. On Sundays we go to Zendo Village and meditate with others. Other times we meditate with friends in Ganas. It's all a matter of initiative. In the summer, the city teems with free art opportunities, music, and dance. I especially like The Theater of the New City that presents high quality plays. We walk to the ferry, take it to Manhattan, and join the venue.

There are quite a few artists in Ganas. Twice a year we put on a talent show, and I'm amazed by the amount of talent we have among our 75 members. We have comedians, musicians, poets, and story tellers, to name only a few. You may see one of our artists' pictures on the walls of the Book Cafe. Others participate in the open mic.

Our other businesses are a secondhand furniture store, and a secondhand and vintage clothing store. These businesses provide a great way to interact with the larger community. They contribute to a culture of conserving what we have, and making use of items others didn't want to keep.

We keep in touch with several communities, especially Twin Oaks in Virginia. They are our cousin in the country. We exchange visits and keep track of how each of us is doing.

Staten Island is the greenest borough of New York City, and it is a delight to hear the birds in the morning, see the lush greenery around us, and be close to the beach for a swim...all while living in this urban community. 🐌

Aviva has lived in Ganas community for 13 years, and previous to that in East Wind community in Missouri. She loves to meditate with her husband Alex, and to collect vignettes when she Skypes with her mother, who lives in Israel, for her coming book, As I Was Talking to My Mother. *She sells vintage clothing online as an experiment to see if it can be a new business for her community. You can check it out on Etsy at www.etsy.com/your/shops/VintageAtAviva/tools/listings?ref=seller-platform-mcnav and Postmark at poshmark.com/closet/avivanextobest. For more information about living in Ganas, email susan@ganas.org.*

Photos by Aviva Derenowski

Chris, David, and Laura work digging holes on the berms for the raspberry plants at Lake City.

THE RADICAL SABBATICAL:
Discerning an Urban-to-Rural Move

By Laura Lasuertmer

I've long harbored dreams of living in a farming community, all the while relishing the convenience of town life and the "farming" we do in our urban community. At the Bloomington Catholic Worker[1], we've turned our lawns into garden beds, planted fruit trees in the back yard, tended chickens, and warded off rats. We store rainwater for gardening—and for the kids to use in their mulch-and-mud culinary creations. On spring days, when the sun is warm but the air is cool, Leo, my two-year-old, stops his play to point and shout, "A woodpecker, Mama!" I often feel like this is the only life I should live.

Perhaps it is. But what of those farm dreams? My husband, David, completed a permaculture design course last summer and now feeds our two children onion grass, creeping charlie, and even the occasional grub from the compost. He salvages downed locust trees by the railroad tracks to build garden beds. He's channeling his anxiety about climate change into acquiring skills and getting intimate with the natural world. He's willing to make the move, but I can't imagine leaving our community and the conveniences of town life.

So the question arises: What do we do with our daydreams? How do we decide which life we should live?

The Radical Sabbatical: A Tool for Discernment

Over the last three years, our community has embraced sabbaticals and other routinized breaks from our shared life. We now have staycations: two weeks each year (one in the spring, one in the fall) in which we cease all communal activity. We have also instituted annual six-week breaks from our shared work of housing people experiencing homelessness. But the crown jewel of routinized breaks is our radical sabbatical. Every seven years, each family (there are currently four) is required to leave the community for two months and set out on an adventure. At the beginning of June, David and I and our children, Alice and Leo, took leave of the community to try out the farming life at three Catholic Worker farms.

The original Catholic Worker farm was founded in 1935, two years after Dorothy Day and Peter Maurin began publishing *The Catholic Worker* newspaper. However, the farms did not flourish and spread the way the urban houses of hospitality did. It is only in the last 10 years that the Catholic Worker farm movement has grown significantly: there are currently 19 farms across the United States. Over our years in the movement, we've become friends with some of the farmers.

We knew that a radical sabbatical at Catholic Worker farms would not only root us in work on the land and with community, it would also allow us to engage in questions of social justice and faith. For me, discerning whether to start a Catholic Worker farm is not simply about the farming. It's about studying the ways in which the farming life addresses injustice and inequality, issues that are at the heart of the Catholic Worker movement.

---

1. The modern Catholic Worker movement includes people from diverse religious backgrounds and some non-religious members as well. It is not officially affiliated with the Roman Catholic Church.

A New Philosophy of Labor
Lake City Catholic Worker Farm,
Lake City, Minnesota, June 2–June 19

"Manual labor is not something to avoid. Manual labor, in and of itself, is what we are striving for.... The payoff is to live off the fruit of your own labor, which is the only just way to live," Paul explained. We were sitting by the fire pit behind the barn, eating beef roast from a neighbor's farm, drinking hard cider from Door County. It was an evening of celebration and discussion, a time for the venerable Catholic Worker practice of clarification of thought. It was also a moment of rest at the end of two weeks of hard work. Paul continued, "There's this idea, that we resoundingly reject, that life should just be smooth. And that smooth life is because we are able to let someone else grow our food."

The Freids were living at the Winona Catholic Worker house in 2005 when they began to reject the idea of the easy life. They knew that their life-long vocation was to the Catholic Worker, but they no longer wanted to live on donations that the house of hospitality received. They dreamed of making and selling communion wine. After working in a vineyard in Winona, they began to look for land with a south-facing slope and found 51 acres near Sara's parents in Lake City. For two years, and with a three-year-old daughter, they camped on the land as they built their strawbale house. When they finished the house, they built a barn, and a chicken coop, and winter housing for their pigs and piglets. Aside from constructing buildings, Paul noted that manual labor has also built relationships, especially between the Lake City Catholic Workers and people in need: "Chris [a former guest] would not be out here if we did not work together. Nor would Sean [a 17-year-old neighbor]. If we said, just come out here and hang out, we wouldn't be as integrated in our relationships."

We built our relationships at Lake City planting 1,000 raspberry bushes into berms that traversed 30 acres of pasture. The first task was to cut down the shoulder-high grass. One afternoon, I strapped on the weed whacker and pushed through the grass to find the berm. With headphones and goggles in place, I found myself immersed in a muted whir. It was not peaceful work—and I was grateful. When I had imagined farm life from the comfort of my living room, I had imagined the picturesque bits. I couldn't hear the incessant squeals of 30 pigs

waiting on me to get their feed ready in the morning. I didn't know to imagine myself pushing a wheel-hoe through dry dirt, bending down to inspect the ground for miniscule carrots. Here I was learning that I could enjoy weed whacking, not because it was fun, but because it needed to be done and I could do it.

Sometimes, though, it was overwhelming to walk through the farm and imagine myself as the farmer. At home, I tend two children, a small house, and a small garden. It often feels like more than I can manage. So how do you tend acres of plants and 40 pigs and three children and 20 chickens and a large house and a guest experiencing homelessness, all the while singing in the church choir and taking your kids to tennis camp and working part-time off the farm? Or rather, how do you do all that and remain as joyful as the Freids? The answer is that you have to love the work. Did I love the work? I had begun to relish the exhaustion and satisfaction I felt after digging holes all day. But was I bored as I weeded the carrots? Or was it good for my soul to tend the vegetables? I left Lake City uncertain about my relationship with manual labor.

Founded in 2007, **Lake City Catholic Worker Farm** is Sara and Paul Freid, their daughters Clare (12), Louise (6), and Millie (5), Shay O'Toole, and Jake Olzen. At Lake City Catholic Worker, the long-term vision is to bring about a new philosophy of labor by creating a farm that employs the community, guests, and the under-employed in the area. They aspire to start a just business based on perennial and humanely raised animal agriculture. In all things they do, they desire to bring a spirit of joy.

Clockwise from bottom left at Lake City Catholic Worker: Clare Freid, Sean (neighbor), Brian, Shay, Paul Freid, Chris (friend), Louise Freid, Sara Freid, Millie Freid.

Lake City: One of 1,000 raspberry plants enjoying the sunset from its new home on the berm.

Shay O'Toole mixes milk with corn to feed the sows, at least one of which is pregnant. Lake City Catholic Worker Farm.

The Lake City strawbale house.

Alice and Leo stand at the pen of 56 chickens about to be butchered at Anathoth Farm.

Mike and Barb at Anathoth Farm still farm with a used 1960s tractor.

The steers at Anathoth Farm enjoy a fresh patch of wildflowers and grass every day.

The entrance to Mike and Barb's home at Anathoth Farm.

Photos courtesy of Laura Lasuertmer

Sacramental Agriculture
Anathoth Community Farm, Luck, Wisconsin, June 19–July 4

They call it sacramental agriculture. It looks like big, gorgeous steers eating wildflowers in lush pasture surrounded by fragrant pines. It looks like laying hens wandering through tall grass. It is a four-year rotation in their two acres of garden: vegetables, pigs, cover crop, potatoes. The rest of the world calls it regenerative agriculture and rotational grazing. For Mike Miles and Barb Kass at Anathoth Farm, it is sacramental agriculture because it mimics the invisible grace of the natural systems that restore health and fertility to plants, animals, and our earth.

Mike and Barb founded Anathoth Farm 30 years ago, but it did not begin as a farm. "We were looking for a place to stage resistance: nonviolent, gospel resistance," Mike said. They had moved, pregnant with their third child, to northern Wisconsin in 1983, after spending three years as part of the Jonah House activist community in Baltimore. They immediately joined local groups who were protesting ELF, a nuclear submarine communication system. Over the years they were involved in significant activism work, including 10 years organizing the Wheels of Justice bus that brought stories from Iraq and Palestine to folks across the United States.

While they always grew food for themselves, it wasn't until 10 years ago that they started raising animals. Mike read *The Omnivore's Dilemma* by Michael Pollan, which introduced him to Joel Salatin. "I began looking at the amount of petroleum on my life and wanted to remove more and more of it. [I] started asking if I can't make an impact on the world within three hours of where I live, then what's the point?"

They started looking at the topography of the farm. They were taking hay off the hayfields and they realized they could turn that hay into protein—raising meat and sequestering carbon at the same time. This year they are raising seven steers, four pigs, and four batches of 60 chickens. They move the animals once or twice a day to ensure that the pasture is tended by the animals rather than destroyed.

Ethical living has been foundational to life at Anathoth. Mike and Barb's reconstructed 1892 log cabin sits on a basement greenhouse that filters the greywater from the kitchen and bathroom sinks. The composting toilet has a urine diverter that funnels pee to a 55-gallon drum, from which comes the most wonderful of fertilizers: pee-tea. The only shower in the house is a wood-fired stand-alone tub in the greenhouse, used only in the winter. Solar showers are used in the summer. Newly installed solar panels supply electricity.

"We earn next to nothing. But we're living like kings," Mike said, sitting down to a dinner of their own grilled steak and asparagus. They have created systems that eliminate waste and produce abundance, without costing much more than their own labor. Observing their lives, I saw that land was essential to their pursuit of a just and ethical life. It allowed them to opt out of the exploitative food and energy systems we are dependent upon in the city. At Anathoth, I started to understand the connection between justice, labor, and life on the land.

The night before we left, I asked Mike and Barb if they had any advice for us.

"Be realistic about your skill sets," Mike said.

"That doesn't mean [you have to know] everything," Barb countered. "How do you castrate a steer? Look on YouTube."

Mike laughed remembering their first attempt. "When you look at the YouTube video and the cowboy says, 'Do this' and you've got a little calf on its back outside with a rope around its neck...and you cut the end of the scrotum and you're digging down in there with your fingers, you're kind of committed. So yeah, think about your skill set." He paused. "The other thing is to realize that grace happens.... You just have to be open to it."

I felt open out there among the towering pines, with the eagles overhead and the wildflowers swaying in the pasture. I felt open to imagining a different life for myself. When a neighbor remarked, "Learning to farm is not the hard part. The hard part is finding the courage to do it," I knew he was right. At Anathoth, courage sprouted, small and fragile but with the potential to bear fruit.

> Founded in 1987, **Anathoth Community Farm** is Barb Kass and Mike Miles. They practice regenerative agriculture, rotational grazing, vegetable gardening, and hospitality to all who come their way.

The Agronomic University
St. Isidore Catholic Worker Farm, Cuba City, Wisconsin, July 4–July 28

Our first full day at St. Isidore, we spread fabric below the mulberry tree, climbed into the branches, and shook. "It's raining mulberries," I said to my kids, Alice and Leo, who gathered fruit in their mouths instead of the bowls. Raquel, an intern at the farm, was walking the roadside in search of black raspberries. Brenna, a community member, was canning bourbon cherries on the outdoor wood-fired cook stove. Two chickens we'd butchered at Anathoth Farm were baking in the oven. Mary Kay, a community member, was up on a ladder harvesting more cherries. Eric, Brenna's husband, was behind the barn splitting firewood. Peter, Mary Kay's husband, was out in the pasture putting up new fencing for Violet, the milk cow. When the mulberries were harvested, David transformed them into a mulberry crisp and that too went in the cookstove oven. That night we feasted entirely on Catholic Worker farm food. "If we're not eating well," Mary Kay said, "then I don't know what we're doing out here." Good food and regenerative farming are parts of St. Isidore's mission, but there's also the Agronomic University.

Peter Maurin's vision for the Catholic Worker farm was a place where workers would be scholars and scholars would be workers. "His vision," Eric said, "was to create communities on the land that were basically centers for training people to engage and transform society." At St. Isidore that means that prayer, study, and labor are crucial parts of each day. St. Isidore also hosts workshops, college groups, and Growing Roots sessions, which are four-day radical education retreats for up to 20 participants. These programs always include time to labor on the farm, with the belief that good education feeds not just the mind, but also the body and spirit. "Our Growing Roots are ways to think critically about society, but it's also a time to just be human, fully human together, and engaging on all levels of our personhood," Eric said.

At Growing Roots, which coincided with the last week of our Radical Sabbatical, I was surprised by the singing. Songs flew around the farm—from the fields where we harvested garlic to the barn where they broke the silence of morning prayer. Growing Roots discussion sessions took us through the conquest and colonization of Native Americans, placing blame not only on European settlers but also the Christian Church. We needed songs—of sorrow, of repentance, of hope. One night I

The centerpiece of the outdoor kitchen at St. Isidore is the wood-fired cook stove. All of the meals for Growing Roots were prepared outside. It is also used in food preservation.

The entrance to St. Isidore Catholic Worker Farm, a mosaic that was created by the author's community mate, Chris Elam.

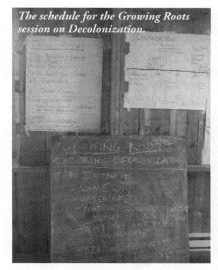

The schedule for the Growing Roots session on Decolonization.

The restored barn at St. Isidore is a superb space for hosting discussions and singing songs.

The farm house at St. Isidore.

Violet is moved daily, sometimes to the front lawn to help keep the grass short. David and Leo watch her graze. St. Isidore Catholic Worker Farm.

sat in a circle of 15 women with Liz Rog, a song leader from Iowa, teaching us parts of simple, layered a cappella songs. All levels of my being were engaged. Song somehow synthesized the labor of our hands, the work of our minds, and the ache of our hearts, bringing an emotional center to Growing Roots. When we departed St. Isidore on the last morning, we left thoroughly changed in body, mind, and spirit.

> St. Isidore Catholic Worker Farm was founded in 2016 by Brenna Cussen Anglada and Eric Anglada, and Mary Kay McDermott and Peter Yoches, and their children, Micah (6) and Clare (1). St. Isidore's mission is to live in such a way that all creation may flourish.

The Return:
Imagining an Urban-Rural Relationship

Our sunflowers are taller than the house. Ripe tomatoes dangle from sprawling plants like a string of red lights. We are home. Before I left, I imagined I would return home still uncertain about the farming life. I find instead that two months of examining this question has confirmed a deep desire to live in community on the land.

We have begun to dream of a Catholic Worker farm just outside of Bloomington. I see the families from our community there, sometimes for days or weeks at a time. The kids run in the woods looking for morels and wild blackberries. I dream that guests who need respite from the city come to soak their feet in the creek and catch fish in the pond. I dream that our work there is to tend the land, to detach ourselves from unjust systems, and create a community where reverence and gratitude for creation are integral to daily life. I dream that we have hundreds of blueberry bushes, their branches adorned with deep purple globes. Together we harvest and eat.

This is a dream of the evolution of the Bloomington Catholic Worker, not a severance of ties but a transformation. When I dream this dream, I see it all in the golden light of the sunrise, as if all the seeds will sprout and rain will fall exactly when we need it and there will never be conflict in community. The gift of our sabbatical is this energizing vision and the stories of other dreamers who made the move from the city to the farm. They have given us the courage to dream. It is our work now to pull that dream down from the clouds and root it in the ground, tending it and giving it life. ❧

Laura Lasuertmer is a member of the Bloomington Catholic Worker (BCW) community in Bloomington, Indiana. With her husband's help, she is finding new ways to balance motherhood and writing. She is grateful to Lake City, Anathoth, and St. Isidore for their generous welcome, revelatory conversations, and good ol'-fashioned hard work. For a taste of the Catholic Worker movement, all are welcome to join our annual Midwest gathering, held every September near Preston, Iowa. Email lertmer@gmail.com for more information.

TERRA FIRMA:
A Single Mother Discovers Community

By Shoshana Magnet

My story of intentional communities is partly the story of having a child on my own. When I was 34, the relationship that I'd been in since I was 20 broke up, and all of a sudden I was the loneliest I had ever been in my adult life. I knew that I wanted to have a baby, and although I was lucky to have incredibly loving and supportive family in town, I also knew that I needed to develop more of a community around me—in part because I wanted lots of connections for the child I hoped to have.

Although I owned a lovely house in a child-friendly, urban neighbourhood in my hometown of Ottawa, I found myself walking my dog every day without running into a single person I knew, circling my block, longing to have someone with whom to have a few minutes of conversation. Although I am a dogged and eager community builder, I had struggled for years to make the communities of which I was a part cohere and thrive. People moved away, people were busy with work or with children. Sometimes, the thought of coming home to my lonely house on Friday evening, with a long weekend ahead of me, made me want to fall to my knees and howl. I actively dreaded the weekend, when others would disappear into the routines of family life. I liked my neighbours in my old neighbourhood, and enjoyed talking to them on the street, but I felt shy about keeping them talking on the street too long when the expectation was that they were headed in the door.

In the midst of this period, I took a lot of long walks and listened to a lot of podcasts, including one on intentional communities. I had never heard of this term, but the emphasis on geographic proximity and being connected to your neighbours immediately felt like a thrilling possibility. Intrepid researcher that I am, on one long evening alone in my single family home, I plugged the term "intentional community" into Google along with my city's name, and up came a single search result. For weeks, my to-do list had at the top "call intentional community," but I felt too shy or too disheartened to do so. Finally, I summoned up my courage and called directly. The lovely member who was the contact for Terra Firma immediately invited me to dine with Terra Firma members.

Terra Firma is a small cohousing community centrally located in the neighbourhood called Old Ottawa East. Organized as a condo, in which there are condo owners, Terra Firma originally consisted of two triplexes that share a common and enormous backyard. The group started meeting in 1992, bought the properties in 1997, and has since joined the two triplexes together with two more condo living spaces as well as a common house, including shared kitchen, guest room, and bathroom. We are small; there are 12 member families of Terra Firma. Seven families live in the condos that have a common backyard; my family and four other families also are members but live on the same block or close by. Terra Firma has organized dinners in the common house twice a week, on Wednesdays and Sundays, although some families come less often.

What one of my neighbours calls the "hard" advantages of Terra Firma are numerous. There is a beautiful shared backyard and facilities include a hot tub, a sauna, a beautiful and enormous garden, a set of swings, a tiny little pond, and a tree house. What we like to think of as the "soft" advantages of Terra Firma have to do with both practicality and connection. It is easy to find someone to collect your mail or put out your recycling. We have a listserv where we ask each for everything from a ride to the airport to the name of a good plumber. I love living in an intergenerational community where I can talk about music and math with neighbours in their 70s or how to best kick a soccer ball with a neighbour under 10.

Having used a clinic with an anonymous donor to become pregnant, I joined Terra Firma when I was four months pregnant. I rented out my big house, found an apartment to rent down the street from the condos, and (having received a huge amount of moving help from my family and chosen family) took a deep breath and left my single-family home of 10 years. The change for me was instantaneous. While pregnant and on my own, sometimes a challenging or isolated venture, I could walk my dog around the block and have my neighbours ask me how I was feeling, or if I had felt the baby move. I received spontaneous dinner invitations or just had nice daily conversations that made me feel more connected. And I also had other people to nurture—to me one of the life experiences that makes me feel connected and happy. I had people to shuttle to or from the airport. I had plants to water or people for whom to hem curtains. After I'd had my baby, Terra Firma members collected and got me a generous gift certificate, and most importantly, they were eager to meet my baby. I love that members greet my son by name and are interested in his growth.

After a year in the community, I knew that I wanted to stay, and I was lucky enough to be able to buy a house which my best friend and I share across the street from Terra Firma. We love our chosen family home, although it's important to note that this purchase results in part from my class privilege. I had enormous help from my family. The only house that was available needed tons of renovations, which would have been impossible to manage as a single mother of an infant without my family meeting contractors and helping me to make it possible.

Terra Firma members helped as well. Still amazing to me is that, when I needed to move out of my new house due to the extensive renovations required, I wrote to Terra Firma members and asked if they knew of anything coming up for rent. My neighbours Keith and Diane were going to visit their son out West, and they offered their condo to me and my infant son free of charge for the two months that I needed to move out of my house. It still brings tears to my eyes to think of the email I got telling me that they would love to have us stay there—they even refused to let me pay for utilities despite all the laundry I did with my infant. Terra Firma helped to make the world feel like a warmer and more welcoming place to me as a single mother.

Our community has challenges. We sometimes have conflicts that are difficult to resolve. Terra Firma has tried a number of different strategies for conflict resolution. These have included using outside mediation as well as practicing resolving the conflict ourselves. Some strategies are drawn from the Quaker tradition. For example, if community members are in conflict, each one might be appointed a support group of a couple of members of their choosing from the community. Each side of the conflict can then vent and debrief with their support people privately. After allowing for this support period, both sides and their support teams meet to try to work out the conflict.

I myself greatly benefited from a related technique when I had conflict with a member of the community about money. When we met to talk, following Quaker tradition, she suggested that we begin with a moment of silence, and that we have a person from her Quaker community to hold a supportive space. I'm Jewish, and this ritual was unfamiliar and a little bit frightening to me at first. When we had our meeting, I could not believe how helpful it was to begin with a moment of silence. It allowed me a quiet moment to think about all the things for which I am grateful—that I was part of a community where people were committed to working through conflict. It gave me a moment to just give thanks for all the wonderful and challenging parts of my life. And I was also grateful to have an outside person there to silently be with us in our conflict because it encouraged me to speak using my best self. I felt I learned a lot from this method of conflict resolution, and I felt closer and more connected to the person with whom I had the conflict. One of the things we have learned, and that we would encourage, is that other communities develop a process right away for how they will be engaging in decision-making and how they will resolve conflicts when they arise.

Our community continues to have ongoing conflicts, as do all people who are in relationships with one another. Some of them have been helpfully resolved and some have not. We are still struggling to figure out how to grow as a community when we have different needs and different desires as to what we want our community to look like. Although these relational processes are a challenge, the opportunity to be connected to one another is, for me, incredible. I feel so lucky to have all these adults and kids saying hi to me and my son. Sometimes parenting is a lonely venture. Often in these moments, a quick chat with a neighbour, the offer of a shared glass of wine on a neighbour's porch, or a trip together to the park can be completely uplifting. Or one of my intentional community members might just hold my baby while I put on his snow suit, and the extra pair of hands and friendly smile make all the difference. I met one of my new closest friends because she was friends with one of the Terra Firma members, and this friendship with a woman on my block who has a baby of the same age has been an incredible gift. Had I not joined Terra Firma, I would never have spoken to my best friend about moving in together, and our shared house has been the most wonderful living situation of my adult life.

I'm so grateful to be part of Terra Firma. Just this morning, I was feeling a bit blue. While we were all putting out our recycling in our pajamas, a number of my neighbours stopped by to chat. I had the chance to have a two-minute vent session and a hug from one of my neighbours, and being seen, however briefly, in my sadness, was a profound and mood-changing experience. These "soft" forms of connection made possible by my intentional community make life a so much more pleasurable and connected place for me and my son. ❧

Shoshana Magnet is Associate Professor at the Institute of Feminist and Gender Studies at the University of Ottawa.

Photos courtesy of Shoshana Magnet

Review BY SARAH M. PIKE

living sustainably

———— What Intentional Communities ————
Can Teach Us about Democracy, Simplicity,
and Nonviolence

A. WHITNEY SANFORD

Being the Change

Living Sustainably: What Intentional Communities Can Teach Us about Democracy, Simplicity, and Nonviolence
By A. Whitney Sanford
The University Press of Kentucky, Lexington, 2017, 298 pages

A. Whitney Sanford's new book introduces readers to the worlds of both urban and rural intentional community dwellers across the United States. Her cases include Catholic Worker houses in several American cities, Dancing Rabbit Ecovillage and the Possibility Alliance in rural Missouri, Cobb Hill Cohousing in Vermont, Twin Oaks Community in Virginia, and many others. Some of these communities have completely separated themselves from the fossil fuel economy, while others practice car-sharing; some emphasize regional sustainability, and others self-sufficiency.

Sanford's study of the ways in which democracy, simplicity, and nonviolence are practiced in these communities offers many thought-provoking models for a different kind of life in contemporary America. Her book is an engaging overview of the quirks and challenges that these communities face, as well as their many achievements. Sanford is a trustworthy guide, whose sensitive and nuanced portraits are based on many hours of participant observation and interviews. The men and women she speaks with and the communities she visits practice a wide variety of ways of living sustainably, yet they all share the desire to "be the change they wish to see in the world" (240).

In some ways these communities are as different from one another as they are from the outside society, and they are both separate from, and living in continuity with "the world." Here is where Sanford's study has broad appeal. Readers will come away with an understanding that these communities are not outliers, that their agendas have relevance for many Americans.

For instance, "deciding what to eat" plays a significant role in the book, reflecting Sanford's interest in food and gardening. These communities overlap with the larger DIY (Do It Yourself) movement and the proliferation of farms, CSAs (Community Supported Agriculture), and restaurants catering to the many Americans who want to eat locally and sustainably. Interest in "reskilling," which is central to these communities—canning, grafting, animal husbandry, construction—is also of wider interest. Although many of these communities have chosen a spatial isolation that more easily allows for experimentation with new ideas and practices, they also share with many people outside intentional communities an emphasis on what Sanford call "the three legs of sustainability—equity, ecology, and economy."

Yet what marks these communities as separate from the concerns of most Americans are the constraints of living in community with other people. Negotiating the tension between the needs for privacy and for community, "finding a balance between personal autonomy and community life" (77), is a central preoccupation of Sanford's interlocutors. While her book gestures at the paths people take to these communities and the problems that arise when they join them, I would have liked to see fuller stories about individuals' journeys to and struggles within specific communities. The disadvantage of a study that is so broad and includes so many different kinds of communities (which is also a strength of the book) is that readers do not get a full sense of the intimate processes of dealing with conflicts and tensions. For example, nonviolent communication is a central concern of the book, but we do not get a real sense of how it takes place at ground level in interpersonal relationships and community meetings.

Another facet of community life that Sanford glosses over is the practice of spirituality, religion, and ritual. Many ritualized activities are mentioned, but not analyzed or discussed in much detail. How do community rituals around food, one of the most contested areas of community life, create cohesion; resolve or increase tensions? How do personal religious or spiritual commitments shape participants' experiences of these communities? Reading *Living Sustainably* on the heels of a recent trip I took to the Shaker Village at Pleasant Hill, Kentucky, I was struck by the absence of ritual and spirituality in Sanford's study.

Last summer I visited the Shaker Village, not far from where I grew up in Louisville, Kentucky, and I could not help thinking about the Shakers and other 19th century communitarians as I read *Living Sustainably*. Recent restoration work at Pleasant Hill has focused on restoring native prairies, with breathtaking results: wildflowers, medicinal plants, butterflies, and birds were in abundance during my visit. The Shaker Village's restaurant sources many ingredients from its gardens and serves livestock raised on site. While this is no longer an active community, but more of a living museum and tourist site, I could not help but wonder how the history of the Shakers and their earlier version of DIY might provide an illuminating backdrop for the communities readers encounter in Sanford's book, especially the ways in which spiritual commitments infused every aspect of Shaker life and work. While *Living Sustainably* could be adopted in a variety of courses in disciplines such as environmental studies and peace studies, it does not provide much historical, religious, or cultural context of the rich history of intentional communities in the US. The focus is very much on the present and future, not the past.

Readers like Sanford and myself who have not chosen to live in intentional communities, but are interested in living more simply and sustainably by commuting on bicycle or growing our own food, will find this book just as valuable as those who live in these kinds of communities. And for those of us who have not departed from more individualistic lives and homes, this book may change our minds. It will certainly leave its readers with a richer understanding of both the tribulations and joys of living in intentional communities. ✒

Sarah M. Pike is Professor of Comparative Religion at California State University, Chico, and the author of Earthly Bodies, Magical Selves: Contemporary Pagans and the Search for Community *and* New Age and Neopagan Religions in America. *Her latest book,* For the Wild: Ritual and Commitment in Radical Eco-Activism *was published in September 2017.*

Review BY CHRIS ROTH

A Universal Story

Hippie Family Values
Video/DVD by Beverly Seckinger
64 minutes, 2017
Available to the educational market through New Day Films, newday.com/film/hippie-family-values; available for individual streaming and home DVD purchase through hippiefamilyvalues.com; also check film website for upcoming community/ public screenings or contact bsecking@ email.arizona.edu to arrange one

*H*ippie Family Values is a beautiful film, shot over a 10-year period at a 40-year-old communal ranch in southwest New Mexico, and also benefiting from archival videos and photos. We get to know members of four generations—including the hippie elders' own parents, children, and grandchildren—as residents explore what it's like to call a remote desert outpost home, building lives together based on countercultural principles, cooperation, and back-to-the-land ethics and practices.

We witness transitions—departures, returns, new children, deaths—as well as the birth and waning of various projects and dreams. Most of all, we get an intimate feel of this unconventional extended "family" and how it—like any family and any community—goes through inevitable changes.

The Ranch faces the same dilemmas any long-lived community does: how do we care for our elders? How do we bring in "new blood" and welcome innovation while not losing our core values and practices? How can we be home to both the old and the new? How do we cope with the gradual slide that often seems to happen from collectivism toward individualism—and how can we come back together when we seem to be drifting apart too much?

It also faces dilemmas particularly acute for rural, back-to-the-land communities: how do we keep people here when local economic opportunities are few? How do we balance the counterculture we have created with the prevailing cultural forces that surround us? How do we stay connected to the outside world—including friends and family who have not chosen to join us, and in fact may have very different aspirations—while at the same time staying true to the land, the community, and the vision that we've committed our lives to? And how do we follow our personal passions and paths when they seem to diverge from life on the ranch, or when a larger or different adventure calls, or when our remote rural community begins to feel like a dead-end rather than a paradise? And how do we deal with the emotions that come up when we separate from people who are, in effect, lifelong family, through community if not through blood?

Hippie Family Values is an intimate view of community members who, over the course of time, ask these questions of themselves and of each other, but who, throughout, also live very much in the present. I found myself growing fond of different Ranch members, then experiencing the pangs of their departures (or of the waning of their hopes as a particular plan became unworkable). I'm sure my vicarious emotions were just a taste of what the actual individuals involved felt at each transition or setback, but they were also a reminder of what any one of us who experiences such cycles personally goes through emotionally.

In her email introducing the film to me, filmmaker Beverly Seckinger described its nature well: "*Hippie Family Values* is not really an issue-oriented film, nor does it have a strong narrative plot. Rather, I see it as more of an ethnographic film—an intimate slice of life, filmed over many years, in the course of which we experience a bit of the texture of life in this back-to-the-land community, and ponder the phases of life, from birth through death, with an emphasis on aging. What did it mean to commit to this community, and live for decades there, raise children there, and now face aging and death, wondering if the community will survive into the next generation?"

Far from being a "downer," though, this honest meditation on change, loss, and transition—as well as connection, fulfillment, caring, and fun—within a loving community felt liberating to me. Every moment it depicts comes across as alive and palpable in the present, and also, in the end, proves evanescent—a realization that sometimes comes as a rude shock. But if communitarians and communities can recognize these transitions as inevitable—signs of having lived, rather than of failure—then I think we'll have a lot more acceptance and joy, and more ability to embrace or at least appreciate every stage of the multiple overlapping journeys that we experience as community members and simply as human beings. In fact, this is a film that I believe anyone—hippie or not, communard or social conservative—has the capacity to relate to in some way, and to learn from.

Chris Roth edits COMMUNITIES *and is not getting any younger himself.*

Made in the USA
Columbia, SC
11 November 2021